THE LONGMAN
DICTIONARY
OF
POETIC TERMS

Longman English and Humanities Series
Series Editor: Lee Jacobus, University of Connecticut, Storrs

THE LONGMAN
DICTIONARY
OF
POETIC TERMS

Jack Myers
Michael Simms
Southern Methodist University

Longman
New York & London

The Longman Dictionary of Poetic Terms

Longman Inc., 95 Church Street, White Plains, N.Y. 10601
Associated companies, branches, and representatives
throughout the world.

Copyright © 1989 by Longman Inc.

"Self Portrait at Twelve" by Allison L. Hunter. © 1985
by Allison L. Hunter.
"Checking Myself" by John Ebert. © 1985 by John
Ebert.

Developmental Editor: Gordon T.R. Anderson
Editorial and Design Supervisor: Walter Glanze
Production Supervisor: Karen Lumley
Composition: Graphicraft Typesetters Limited
Printing and Binding: Malloy

Library of Congress Cataloging in Publication Data

Myers, Jack Elliott, 1941–
    The Longman dictionary of poetic terms/Jack Myers,
    Michael Simms.

        p.   cm.—(Longman English and humanities series)
        Bibliography: p.
        ISBN 0-8013-0344-3
        1. Poetics—Dictionaries.   I. Simms,
        Michael,   1954–   II. Title.   III. Series
    PN1042. M94 1988   88-29561
    808.1'03—dc 19   CIP

9 8 7 6 5 4 3 2 1   93 92 91 90 89 88

ACKNOWLEDGMENTS

A. Poulin, Jr., "The Widow's Taboo," from *The Widow's Taboo: Poems After The Catawba*. Copyright © 1977 by A. Poulin, Jr. Reprinted with the permission of A. Poulin, Jr.

"Lyrics" of *Permit Me Voyage* (three lines), from *The Collected Poems of James Agee*. Copyright © 1962, 1968 by the James Agee Trust. Reprinted by permission of the Houghton Mifflin Company.

"Traveling Through the Dark" (four lines) and "Vacation," Copyright © 1960 by William Stafford; "The Animal That Drank Up Sound," Copyright © 1964 by William Stafford from *Stories That Could Be True: New And Collected Poems By William Stafford*. Reprinted by permission of Harper & Row, Publishers, Inc.

"Teaching the Ape to Write Poems," from *Absences* by James Tate. Copyright © 1972 by James Tate. Reprinted by permission of Little, Brown and Company.

"When You Leave," by Kimiko Hahn from *Columbia: A Magazine of Poetry and Prose,* Issue #3, Fall 1978. Copyright © 1978 by *Columbia: A Magazine of Poetry and Prose*. Reprinted by permission of the editor.

"Good Morning, America" (six lines), from *Good Morning, America*. Copyright © 1956 by Carl Sandburg. Reprinted by permission of Harcourt Brace Jovanovich, Inc.

"The Conjurer," from *Snow on Snow* (six lines), by Maura Stanton. Copyright © 1975 Yale University Press. Reprinted by permission of the publisher.

"Anniversaries" (five lines). Copyright © 1960 by Donald Justice. Reprinted from *The Summer Anniversaries* by permission of the Wesleyan University Press.

"2433 Agnes, First Home, Last House in Missoula" (six lines), "Degrees of Gray in Phillipsburg" (twelve lines), "The Only Bar in Dixon" (three lines), "Indian Graves at Jocko" (two lines), from *The Lady in Kicking Horse Reservoir,* Poems by Richard Hugo, by permission of W.W. Norton & Company, Inc. Copyright © 1973 by Richard Hugo. "A Snapshot of the Auxiliary" (one line), from *What Thou Lovest Well, Remains American,* Poems by Richard Hugo, by permission of W.W. Norton & Company, Inc. Copyright © 1975 by Richard Hugo.

Marvin Bell, "An Introduction to My Anthology," from *Stars Which See, Stars Which Do Not See*. Copyright © 1977 by Marvin Bell. Reprinted with permission of Atheneum Publishing Company.

"Form Rejection Letter" (nineteen lines), by Philip Dacey reprinted from *Shenandoah: The Washington and Lee University Review,* Vol. 24, No. 2, Winter 1973. Copyright © 1973 by Washington and Lee University. Reprinted with permission of the editor.

"Dick and Jane," by Judith Kroll from *In the Temperate Zone* published by Charles Scribner's Sons, 1973. Copyright © 1973 by Judith Kroll. Reprinted by permission of the author.

"Ars Poetica" by Vicente Huidobro. Copyright © 1963 by Empresa Editora Zig'Zag, S.A. Reprinted by permission of New Directions, Inc.

"Lifting Belly" (six lines), from *Bee Time Vine & Other Pieces (1913–1927) The Yale Edition of Unpublished Writings Of Stein*, by Gertrude Stein. Copyright © 1953 Yale University Press. Reprinted by permission the publisher.

Excerpt from "Redwings," from *To a Blossoming Pear Tree* by James Wright. Copyright © 1973, 1974, 1975, 1976, 1977 by James Wright. Reprinted by permission of Farrar, Straus and Giroux, Inc.

"Boarding" (four lines), by Dennis Johnson from *The Incognito Lounge,* published by Random House, Inc. Copyright © 1982 by Dennis Johnson. Reprinted by permission of Random House, Inc.

"Torso of an Archaic Appollo," from *Selected Poems: Rilke,* by Rainer Marie Rilke, edited and translated by C.F. MacIntyre. Copyright © 1940, 1968 C.F. MacIntyre. Reprinted by permission of the University of California Press.

"Notes Sur la Poesie" (three lines), by Andre Breton and Paul Eluard translated and edited by J.H. Matthews from *Introduction To Surrealism* by J.H. Matthews. Copyright © 1965 Pennsylvania State University Press. Reprinted by permission of the publisher.

"American Poetry." Copyright © 1963 by Louis Simpson. Reprinted from *At the End of the Open Road: Poems,* by permission of the Wesleyan University Press.

"Daughters of the Earth" (two lines), from *The Typewriter Revolution* by D.J. Enright. Copyright © 1971 D.J. Enright. Reprinted by permission of The Open Court Publishing Company.

"Memories of My Deaf Mother," by Jack Driscoll from *The Ohio Review,* 11/25/80. Reprinted by permission of The Ohio Review.

"Family/Watch," from *Faith,* by Albert Goldbarth, New Rivers Press, 1981. Copyright © 1981 by Albert Goldbarth. Reprinted by permission of the author.

"On Frozen Fields" (seven lines), from *Flower Herding On Mount Monadock* by Galway Kinnell. Copyright © 1964 by Galway Kinnell. Reprinted by permission of Houghton Mifflin Company.

"Howl," by Allen Ginsberg (lines 1–2), from *Collected Poems 1947–1980* by Allen Ginsberg. Copyright © 1956 by Allen Ginsberg. Reprinted by permission of Harper & Row, Publishers, Inc.

"The Garden" (four lines). Copyright © 1980 by Louise Glück. From *Descending Figure* by Louise Glück, published by the Ecco Press in 1980. Reprinted by permission.

"Poem After Apollinaire" (four lines), from *Palm Reading In Winter,* by Ira Sadoff. Copyright © 1978 by Ira Sadoff. Reprinted by permission of Houghton Mifflin Company.

"The Birthday" (four lines), by Phillip Dacey from *How I Escaped from the Labyrinth and Other Poems.* Copyright © 1977 by Carnegie-Mellon University Press. Reprinted by permission of the publisher.

"Fixing the Foot: On Rhythm," by Philip Levine from *The Ohio Review,* Winter 1975. Reprinted by permission of The Ohio Review and Philip Levine.

"Poetry of Departures" (eight lines), by Phillip Larkin. Reprinted from *The Less Deceived* by Phillip Larkin. Copyright © 1955 by The Marvell Press. Reprinted by permission of the publisher.

Three line haiku by Basho, reprinted from *Western Wind: An Introduction To Poetry,* by J.F. Nims. Copyright © 1974 by Random House, Inc. Reprinted by permission of the publisher.

"no charge" (five lines), from *Burning In Water, Drowning In Flame: Poems 1955–1973,* by Charles Bukowski. Copyright © 1976 by Charles Bukowski. Reprinted by permission of Black Sparrow Press.

"Sailing to Byzantium" (two lines), from *Collected Poems Of W.B. Yeats.* Copyright 1928 by Macmillan Publishing Company, renewed 1956 by Georgie Yeats.

"Moles" (four lines), from *The New Yorker Book Of Poems,* by William Stafford. Reprinted by permission; © 1950, 1978 The New Yorker Magazine, Inc.

"Stopping by Woods on a Snowy Evening" (two lines), from *Complete Poems of Robert Frost* by Robert Frost, edited by Edward Connery Latham. Copyright 1923, © 1969 by Holt Rinehart and Winston, Inc. Copyright 1951 by Robert Frost. Reprinted by permission.

"Where Knock Is Open Wide" (two lines). Copyright 1950 by Theodore Roethke from the book *The Collected Poems Of Theodore Roethke.* Reprinted by permission of Doubleday & Company, Inc.

From "The Love Song of J. Alfred Prufrock" (two lines), in *Collected Poems 1909–1962,* by T.S. Eliot. Copyright 1936, by Harcourt Brace Jovanovich; Copyright © 1963, 1964 by T.S. Eliot. Reprinted by permission of the publisher.

"Keeping Things Whole" (seven lines), from *Reasons For Moving* by Mark Strand. Copyright © 1968 by Mark Strand. Reprinted with permission of Atheneum Publishing.

"What does not change/is the Will to change" (one line), from *Selected Writings* by Charles Olson. Copyright © 1966 by Charles Olson. Reprinted by permission of New Directions Inc.

Reprinted from *First Practice,* by Gary Gildner by permission of the University of Pittsburgh Press. Copyright © 1969 by the University of Pittsburgh Press.

"Take Yourself Back" (four lines), by Diane Wald from *The Iowa Review,* Vol. 8, Number 2, Spring 1977. Copyright © 1977 The Iowa Review. Reprinted by permission of the editor.

"Bantu Combinations" (twelve lines), from *Technicians of the Sacred: A Range Of Poetries From Africa, America, Asia, And Oceania,* by Jerome Rothenberg. Copyright © 1969 by Jerome Rothenberg. Reprinted by permission of The Sterling Lord Agency, Inc.

"Poem to be Read and Sung" (five lines), reprinted from *Neruda and Vallejo: Selected Poems,* translated by Robert Bly, John Knoepfle and James Wright, Beacon Press, 1971. Copyright © 1971 by Robert Bly, reprinted with his permission.

"The Ruined Street" (eleven lines), from *Residence on Earth* by Pablo Neruda, translated by Donald Walsh. Copyright © 1973 by Pablo Neruda and Donald Walsh. Reprinted by permission of New Directions Inc.

"My Photograph," from *Memory's Handgrenade,* by Thomas Lux, Pym-Randall Press, 1972. Copyright © 1972 by Thomas Lux. Reprinted by permission of the author.

"Musee de Beaux Arts" (four lines), from *The Collected Poems of W.H. Auden,* by W.H. Auden. Copyright © 1940 by W.H. Auden. Reprinted by permission of Random House, Inc.

"Watch" (seven lines), from *New and Selected Things Taking Place,* by May Swenson. Copyright © 1965 by May Swenson. Reprinted by permission of Little, Brown and Company.

"Rerun" (two lines), from *The Family War,* by Jack Myers, L'Epervier Press. Copyright © 1977 by Jack Myers. Reprinted by permission of the author.

"Rx:," by Jaime Sabines, published in *The Chariton Review,* Vol. 3, #1, Spring 1977. Reprinted with permission of The Chariton Review.

"Fire," from *The Voice Of Things* by Francis Ponge, translated by Beth Archer. Original edition: *Le Parti Pris de Choses.* Copyright © 1942 by Editions Gallimard Paris. Reprinted by permission of the publisher.

From *Poems* by Yehuda Amichai "My Child" (four lines). Translated from the Hebrew by Assia Gutmann. Copyright © 1968 by Yehuda Amichai. Copyright © 1968, 1969 by Assia Gutmann. Reprinted by permission of Harper & Row, Publishers, Inc.

Two lines from "Out, Out," from *Poetry of Robert Frost,* edited by Edward Connery Latham. Copyright 1916, © 1969 by Holt, Rinehart and Winston. Copyright © 1944 by Robert Frost. Reprinted by permission of the publisher.

"aaple," by Aram Saroyan. Copyright © 1969 by Aram Saroyan. Reprinted by permission of the author.

"Silent Poem," from *Like Ghosts of Eagles,* by Robert Francis. Copyright © 1970 by University of Massachusetts Press. Reprinted by permission of the publisher.

"Self in 1958" (ten lines), from *Live or Die,* by Anne Sexton. Copyright © 1966 by Anne Sexton. Reprinted by permission of Houghton Mifflin Company.

From *Poems* by Yehuda Amichai "King Saul and I" (eleven lines). Translated from the Hebrew by Assia Gutmann. Copyright © 1968 by Yehuda Amaichai. Copyright © 1968, 1969 by Assia Gutmann. Reprinted by permission of Harper & Row, Publishers, Inc.

"High Windows," from *High Windows* by Philip Larkin. Copyright © 1974 by Philip Larkin. Reprinted by permission of Farrar, Straus and Giroux, Inc.

"What were they like?," from *Poems: 1960–1961* by Denise Levertov. Copyright © 1966 by Denise Levertov Goodman. Reprinted by permission of New Directions, Inc.

"Atavism" (ten lines), from *Hard Labor,* by Cesare Pavese, translated by William Arrowsmith. Copyright © 1976 by William Arrowsmith. Reprinted by permission of Viking Penguin Inc.

"The Clam Theatre" (four lines), by Russell Edson. Copyright © 1973 by Russell Edson. Reprinted by permission of the author.

"The Reason Why the Closet-Man Is Never Sad" (one line), by Russell Edson. Copyright © 1977 by Russel Edson. Reprinted by permission of the Wesleyan University Press.

"The Battle Hymn of the Republic: Brought down to Date" (one line), from *A Pen Warmed Up in Hell,* by Mark Twain, published by Harper & Row, 1972. Permission granted by the estate of Mark Twain and International Publishing.

"a 340 dollar horse and a hundred dollar whore" (three lines), from *Burning In Water, Drowning in Flame: Poems 1955–1973,* by Charles Bukowski. Copyright © 1976 by Charles Bukowski. Reprinted by permission of Black Sparrow Press.

"If The Want Me to Be a Mystic, Fine, So I'm a Mystic," from *Selected Poems Of Fernando Pessoa* translated by Edwin Honig, Swallow Press, 1971. Reprinted with the permission of the Ohio University Press.

"Scale of English Vowel Sounds," from *Western Wind: An Introduction To Poetry* by J.F. Nims. Copyright © 1974 by Random House, Inc. Reprinted by permission of the publisher.

"The Blind Swimmer," (two lines), from *Threats Instead of Trees,* by Michael Ryan. Copyright © 1973 by Michael Ryan. Reprinted with permission of the Yale University Press.

"A Negro Woman" (thirteen lines), from *Pictures From Brueghel* by William Carlos Williams. Copyright © 1955 by William Carlos Williams. Reprinted by permission of New Directions Publishing Corporation.

"In the Winter of My Thirty-Eighth Year," from *The Lice.* Copyright © 1967 by W.S. Merwin. Reprinted with permission of Atheneum Publishing.

"Hallelujah: A sestina." Copyright © 1960 by Robert Francis. Reprinted from *The Orb Weaver* by permission of Wesleyan University Press.

"Si . . . Quand," by Andre Breton from *Introduction to Surrealism,* edited by J.H. Matthews. Copyright © 1965 by The Pennsylvania University State Press. Reprinted by permission of the publisher.

"Crickets," by Aram Saroyan from *Pages* published by Random House, Inc. Copyright © 1969 by Aram Saroyan. Reprinted by permission of the author.

"After the Funeral," from *Collected Poems of Dylan Thomas.* Copyright © 1935 by New Directions, Inc. Reprinted by permission.

"Night Signals," from *The Love & Death Boy,* by Roger Weingarten, W.D. Hoffstadt and Sons. Copyright © 1981 by Roger Weingarten. Reprinted by permission of the author.

CONTENTS

PREFACE

The authors of this book are poets and teachers. Our interest in compiling this dictionary began with questions that arose out of our own writing, our being moved by poems we had read, and our efforts to organize and articulate to our students the techniques, terms, and theories we have learned through these endeavors. Over the years, the countless times we were stalled at certain points in our own writing forced us to produce a repertoire of techniques or "moves" in order to transcend the problems. The stock of wonderful models of poetry we had memorized by loving them came to serve as standards of excellence. And the simplest question from a student—Is a title important?—forced us to confront and develop ideas about composition and the creative writing process itself that inevitably linked up ancient ideas with modern assumptions. We mention the background of the book in order to stress both the focus of our attention and our faith in the poet's essential job, learning the names of things.

So, this dictionary attempts to define a critical vocabulary for the poet and the student of poetry. The work is extensive, the most comprehensive list of poetic terms that has yet been compiled. Its domain includes (1) traditional, familiar terms that are often bandied about in lecture courses without knowledge of the terms' limitations and history (*persona, sonnet, allegory*), (2) contemporary workshop terms (*voice, deep image, leap*), (3) terms borrowed from other arts and disciplines (*crosscut, gestalt, archetechtonics*), and (4) archaic or specialized jargon (*bdelygmia, epanorthosis, periergia*). Perhaps even more important is the fact that this book contains original material on topics such as *line endings, titles, cinematic techniques, defects in control, rhythm, thematic structures, juxtapositions, clichés,* the *prose poem, myth,* and *translation,* as well as contemporary strategies of development (*cut-and-shuffle, fill-in-the-blanks, definition* and *list poem, sandwich construction*). While we make no claims that this book will directly create better poets, our contention is that it will help to educate and stimulate the poet so that he or she can better articulate critical opinions and can have at hand more technical options and aesthetic directions. In this spirit we begin to answer the charge that contemporary poetry lacks a coherent body of poetics, and (in a somewhat defensive posture of aesthetic patriotism) to think that, despite the annoying and sometimes petty busyness of the current poetry scene, the last quarter of the 20th century may just be that Golden Age that Ezra Pound prophesied would make the fertile 1920s seem like "a tempest in a teapot."

At first glance, the principles behind the selection of concepts in this dictionary may seem unclear. The book synthesizes many different disciplines—aesthetics, linguistics, lexicography, psychology, anthropology, history, and science, as well as the fields of theoretical and practical criticism. But the reader may find it helpful to think of the book as being three books between two covers: (1) a catalogue of definitions, (2) a companion-reader to traditional and contemporary poetry, and (3) a catalyst to the reader's own critical or creative writing. The reader will note that a major portion of the headwords in this dictionary were coined by Classical and Renaissance theorists to describe their understanding of the nature of language in reference to the imagination. We have intentionally restored these terms to modern usage because recent theorists (with the notable exceptions of I. A. Richards and Northrop Frye) have added little to poetics other than new understanding of old ideas. For example, the Chicago Critics' ideas are based almost entirely on the theories of Aristotle. Furthermore, American poets, on the whole, know less about the aesthetic and persuasive powers of language than did their counterparts in Renaissance Europe; and they, in turn, probably knew less than did their Classical counterparts. One of this book's aims, then, is to enlighten the contemporary poet by igniting his or her interest in ancient and modern ideas about poetry. As a companion-reader to poetry of the last 50 years, the book requires that we define some terms in an innovative way, and that we allow ourselves the freedom to expand these entries into analytical essays. In other instances, such as that of *organic composition,* we were surprised to find that a term that we thought was promulgated in the modern era actually has its roots in Romantic and pre-Romantic conceptions. In regard to the third and most elusive aim of this book, as a catalyst to writing, it is our hope that the reader will go beyond the facts presented here into the realm of memory and imagination and emerge with the treasure upon which this book is based, innovations in human expression.

The authors would like to thank Southern Methodist University and its staff, particularly Alice McCaulley for her tireless and diligent typing of the manuscript. In addition, thanks go to Gordon T. R. Anderson, executive editor of college and professional books at Longman, Inc., and to Walter D. Glanze, lexicographer, for their unswerving faith in this project. And, finally, Jack Myers would like to pay homage to the strength of the person who tolerated his obsessive myopia during the years it took to write this book: Willa Myers.

JACK MYERS
MICHAEL SIMMS

A NOTE ON THE ESSAYS AND APPENDIXES

Aside from being a comprehensive dictionary of poetry, this book also features essays, which collectively form a handbook. These entries consider ideas on contemporary technique, as well as traditional ideas on the theory, history, movements, and practice of poetry. The major essays include:

cinematic techniques	myth
cliché	rhythm
fractured narrative	sound system
juxtaposition	Surrealism
line ending	titles
metaphor	translation
meter	

Another feature worthy of mention is the inclusion of rhetorical and logical devices rescued from Renaissance texts. For a complete guide to these and other terms, see the appendixes.

PRONUNCIATION KEY

SYM-BOLS	KEY WORDS	SYM-BOLS	KEY WORDS	SYM-BOLS	KEY WORDS
/a/	hat	/oi/	boy	/ng/	sing, drink
/ä/	father	/o͝o/	book	/ngg/	finger
/ā/	fate	/o͞o/	move	/s/	sell
/e/	flesh	/ou/	sound	/sh/	shoe, lotion
/ē/	he	/u/	cup	/th/	thin
/er/	air	/ur/	fur	/th/	than
/i/	sit	/ə/	ago, focus	/v/	very
/ī/	eye	/ər/	murder	/w/	work
/o/	proper	/ch/	much	/y/	yes
/ô/	saw	/g/	good	/z/	zeal
/ō/	nose	/j/	gem	/zh/	azure, vision

No key words are needed for /b/, /d/, /f/, /h/, /k/, /l/, /m/, /n/, /p/, /r/, and /t/.

FOREIGN SOUNDS

/kh/

Scottish: **loch** /lokh'/; German: **doch** /dôkh'/, **Johann Sebastian Bach** /bäkh'/

/kh/

German: **ich** /ikh'/, **nichts** /nikhts'/

/œ/

French: **feu** /fœ'/, **peu** /pœ'/; German: **schön** /shœn'/, **Goethe** /gœt'ə/

/Y/

French: **tu** /tY'/, **déjà vu** /dāzhä vY'/; German: **grün** /grYn'/, **Walküre** /välkY'rə/

/N/

This symbol is not a sound but indicates that the preceding symbol is a nasal. French: /aN/ and /äN/ in **vin blanc** /vaN' bläN'/ and **ancien régime** /äNsyaN' räzhēm'/, /ôN/ in **bon** /bôN/ and **fait accompli** /fa'täkôNplē'/

A

abecedarius (from Medieval Latin for "alphabetical") a type of ACROSTIC in which each line or stanza begins with the letters of the alphabet in their normal order. For example, Chaucer's *An ABC* begins its first stanza with the word "Almighty," its second with "Bountee," and its third with "Comfort." A more difficult, line-by-line form, incorporating ALLITER-ATION, can be seen in Alaric Watts' lines:

> An Austrian army awfully array'd,
> Boldly by battery besieged Belgrade,
> Cossack Commanders cannonading come
> Dealing destruction's devastating doom.

Greek writers of the Alexandrian period, as well as Latin writers (e.g., Plautus), put the titles of their plays in the a.verses of the arguments. Ben Jonson imitated this device in *The Alchemist*. See *light verse* in APPENDIX 1.

absolutist criticism a type of criticism that interprets works according to an external, standard set of principles. See CRITICISM. See also *criticism* in APPENDIX 1.

abstract poetry a term originated by Dame Edith Sitwell to describe poetry that uses sound, rhyme, and rhythm to communicate a feeling, rather than depending, as most poetry does, on the denotative or connotative meanings of the words. This type of poetry is called "abstract" because it uses sound in much the same way that abstract painting uses color, texture, and shape. Sitwell's poem *Hornpipe* is an example of a.p. For related terms, see AMPHIGORY, NONSENSE VERSE, and TRANS-SENSE VERSE. See also *diction* in APPENDIX 1.

abstract terms and concrete terms *abstract terms*: terms that represent ideas or concepts and that are usually taken from *concrete terms*, which represent the sensuous and the particularity of things experienced or known. Abstract terms are usually broader and more general than concrete terms and tend to describe a domain of thought. For example:

abstract	general	concrete
beauty	woman	Helen of Troy

Abstract terms are informative and nonsensory, though they might carry strong connotations ("liberty, freedom, brotherhood"). Although abstract terms are most often found in the more abstract realms of literature, such as philosophy, it is generally thought that some of the greatest effects in poetry can be brought about by mixing a.t.a. c.t., as in this example from

1

Shakespeare's *King Lear*: "How light and portable my pain seems now, / When that which makes me bend makes the King bow . . . ."

Over the years, different ages have favored one or the other of these forms of word choice. The 18th century expressed many of its images as abstractions, intellectualizations of concrete phenomena (fish, a finny tribe), whereas the 16th century heard Sidney in his *Defense of Poetry* (1583) hold the power of the concrete above abstraction. Generally speaking, Romantics have touted the specificity and immediacy of the concrete to express emotions and experience, and poetic rhetoricians and philosophers have found the uses of abstraction germane to their efforts.

In the 20th century, according to Northrop Frye, it is very common to find the phrasal formula of "the adjective noun of noun," e.g., "the cold hand of death," in which the first noun is concrete and the second is abstract. See DICTION. See also *diction* in APPENDIX 1.

academic (derived from the olive grove of *Academe*, where Plato met with his students in the fourth century B.C., Athens) indicating a nonvocational school such as a university or college. As applied to poetry, the term is used pejoratively to refer to verse that is too formal, mannered, or tame. Modern academies (the Académie Française, the Royal Academy of Arts in England, the Real Academia Española in Spain, and the American Academy of Arts and Letters) propose to keep their respective languages accurate, to foster literature, and to recognize great writing. The famous "Platonic Academy" led by Marsilio Ficino in Florence, Italy, was modeled after Plato's and generated the neo-Platonism doctrines in the late 15th century which affected much Renaissance English literature. See WORKSHOP.

acatalectic /-lek'-/ (from negative form of Greek "leaving off") indicating a metrically complete line of verse. For example, an a. iambic tetrameter line is

The gírl whŏ brŏke mў heárt ĭn twó.

The noun *acatalexis* indicates the use of an a. line. When an excess of syllables is employed in a conventional metrical pattern, the line is hypermetric (commonly found in trochaic verse). If a line is metrically incomplete, it is called *catalectic* and is a form of TRUNCATION. See also CATALEXIS.

accent (from Greek for "song added to speech") the amount of emphasis placed on a syllable as it is pronounced. Although a. and STRESS are often used interchangeably, prosodists prefer to use a. to refer to language usage, and stress to refer to metrical qualities (see METER). In other words, a. refers to a combination of pitch, force, loudness, and duration, while stress refers solely to force.

Four levels of accent are usually distinguished. A heavily accented syllable is called a *primary a.* (ˊ); a lighter or medium-accented syllable is called a *secondary a.* (ˎ); a very lightly accented syllable is called a *tertiary a.*(ˌ); and an *unaccented syllable* is denoted by ˘. The word "ĕncýclòpédĭă" shows a combination of all four levels of accent. When two syllables are stressed equally, the occurrence is called *even a.* or *level stress*, as in the spondee "mánkínd."

In traditional Latin terminology, ICTUS is the name of the stress itself; *arsis* is the name of the unstressed syllable. In earlier Greek terminology, the terms were *thesis*, unstressed, and *arsis*, stressed.

Though there is disagreement among prosodists on the essential nature of a. (e.g., whether DURATION, or QUANTITY, is an element of a.), three basic types of a. are usually described: (1) *Etymological a.* (sometimes called *grammatical, lexical,* or *word a.*) is an emphasis given to a syllable or syllables in a word because of the word's traditional pronunciation, derivation, or relationship of prefix and suffix to root. (2) *Rhetorical a.* (sometimes called *logical* or *sense a.*) is an emphasis that occurs because of the relative importance of the word in the context of the line. A rhetorical a. may vary depending upon the intended meaning:

> Did you bríng the key?
>
> Did you bring the kéy?
>
> Did yóu bring the key?

(3) *Metrical a.* (sometimes called *stress*) is an element in an abstract pattern of recurring emphasis in a conventional line of verse. If the metrical a. forces itself over the etymological a., it is called a *wrenched a.*, a device often found in *folk ballads* and poems that imitate the style and manner of folk ballads, e.g., Coleridge's "He loves to take to marinéres / That come from a far countreé."

In general, metrical a. yields to rhetorical and etymological a. except in intentionally wrenched a. It should be noted, however, that some 18th- and 19th-century conservative prosodists held that rhetorical a. yields to metrical a. See PROSODY, RHYTHM, and SCANSION. See also ARSIS AND THESIS and FOLK BALLAD; also *meter* in APPENDIX 1.

accentual-syllabic verse (also called *"syllabic-stress meter"*) a type of poetry in which the metrical scansion takes into account both the number of stressed and the number of unstressed syllables in a line. It is the most commonly used system of measurement in English metrics. A.-s.v. groups syllables into units, each of which is called a FOOT. There can commonly be from one to eight feet in a typical line, though there are lines that contain up to twelve feet.

A.-s.v. tends to vary the patterns of the strict forms listed above. The process of adding or subtracting syllables is called SUBSTITUTION. See also ACCENT, ACCENTUAL VERSE, BLANK VERSE, METER, PROSODY, SCANSION, and STRESS.

accentual verse poetry in which the metrical scansion takes into account only the stressed syllables. A line of a.v. may have any number of syllables because only the stressed syllables are counted. There are usually four stresses and seven to nine syllables in a line, although Auden uses a three-stress line with six to eight syllables in *September 1, 1939*, and even in poems using a four-stress line there is much variation. Most Germanic and Anglo-Saxon poetry is a.v., and it remains one of the most widely used meters in English. The loose iambics of many modern poems, such as Yeats' *Why Should Not Old Men Be Mad?*, could be described as a.v. In addition, a.v. is the basis for Hopkins' SPRUNG RHYTHM. The system of using stresses to regulate a line is called *stress prosody*. See also ACCENTUAL-SYLLABIC VERSE, ANGLO-SAXON VERSE, METER, and STRONG-STRESS METER.

accidence (from Latin for "chance") grammatically, the morphological INFLECTION of a word; also, any book setting down the basic principles of grammar.

acephalous line /əsefʹ-/ (*acephalous*, Greek for "headless"; also known as "initial truncation") a line of verse in conventional meter, usually iambic, in which the first unstressed syllable of the line is left out. (The term TRUNCATION refers usually to the omission of the last syllable.)

Acmeism /akʹméʹ-/ (from Greek for "utmost, a pinnacle of") a school of modern Russian poetry which strove for clarity, precision, and texture. It opposed specifically the unworldliness and vagueness of Symbolism which was the dominant mode of writing in Russian poetry at the turn of the 20th century. The *Acmeists* included notable poets such as Akhmatova, Gorodetsky, Gummilyov, Kuzmin, and Mandelstam—all of whom were closely associated with the magazine *Apollon*. They were craftpersons who concentrated on the technical aspects of a poem rather than its prophetic vision. Their aesthetic aloofness from social problems, which earned them the enmity of both Soviet critics and the avant-garde, may have helped to make the movement short-lived.

acoustic scansion (see SCANSION) the use of a machine, such as the oscillo-graph or kymograph, to record voice patterns.

acronym a form of abbreviation in which the initial (or other) letters of words are pronounced as a word, such as "AWOL" (*a*bsent *w*ithout *l*eave). See ACROSTIC. See also *forms* in APPENDIX 1.

acrostic (from Greek for "topmost" plus "line of verse") a puzzle poem whose variations of initial, medial, and terminal letters in each line form a hidden word or phrase when read vertically and/or horizontally. The genre was derived from early Greek and Latin texts whose authors, it is thought, meant to devise verses that could easily be memorized and accurately passed on through the oral tradition. During the Middle Ages, the form was often used to spell out names or messages with religious significance. The common type of a. is the *true a.*, which employs a vertical reading of the initial letters of words:

Man
Is
Never
Dead

A *telestich* focuses on the terminal letters of words or lines, and a *mesostich* highlights the medial letters. A *cross a.* has an oblique ordering of the letters that uses the first letter of the first line, the second letter of the second line, etc., as exhibited in Poe's *A Valentine*. An ABECEDARIUS uses the alphabetical order of the letters, a form commonly found in the Hebrew Version of the Old Testament (see Psalm 119). Other forms include the ACRONYM. See *light verse* in APPENDIX 1.

acyron /as'ərən/ (from Greek for "incorrect in speech") a device of POETIC LICENSE, considered "tolerable" by Puttenham, that uses words whose meanings are opposite to those intended: "Sitting here is a waste of movement."

adaptation (from Latin for "to choose"; see TRANSLATION) the recasting of a work into a different medium. For instance, novels are frequently recast into plays. In poetry, the term usually refers to the process of changing the translation of a poem in order to make it a more successful poem in English. Ezra Pound's versions of Chinese poems are well known adaptations.

A. Poulin's a. of a Catawba poem indicates the power and precision that an a. can have, which, indeed, can be equal to an original poem. Poulin adapted this poem and others from Frank G. Speck's *Catawba Texts* (1934):

> *Widow's Taboo*
> Your husband's dead
> No one will talk to you
> for one year your tongue
> will be in his mouth

An a. retains the action, characters, and much of the language and tone of the original. In this way, the term differs from the reworking of a source. See IMITATION.

adjectival metaphor a METAPHOR in the grammatical form of an adjective, e.g., in the cliché "Something smells *fishy* here."

adonic /ədon'ik/ (from Greek name for Venus' lover; from Phoenician for "lord") a metrical unit consisting of a dactyl and a spondee (ˊ ˇ ˇ / ˊ ˊ) or a dactyl and a trochee (ˊ ˇ ˇ / ˊ ˇ). It took its name from the cry for the god Adonis, as in Sappho's "O Ton Adonin." Some Greek proverbs were in adonics. Also, the fourth line of the SAPPHIC stanza is usually printed as an a., although ENJAMBMENT may make the third and fourth lines one metrical unit. Adonics were widely used by a number of Latin writers including Seneca who used the a. in longer runs of "lesser Sapphics." See METER.

adverbial metaphor a METAPHOR in the grammatical form of an adverb, e.g., "He ran *blindly* after his desires."

adynaton /ədi'nətən/ (also called "*impossibilia*") a natural expression of exaggeration. There are two basic types of a.: The "sooner than expected" type says something will happen sooner than someone thinks it will; the "impossible count" type refers to the number of grains of sand on the shore, stars in the sky, etc. Although a popular device in Greek and Latin poetry, the a. virtually disappeared during the Middle Ages except for the Old French "fatrasies" which dealt with impossible or ridiculous accomplishments. During the RENAISSANCE, Petrarchists used the a. to recount the cruelty of their ladies, or to affirm their love for their ladies. The device has not been very popular since the Renaissance. See HYPERBOLE and PETRARCHAN CONCEIT.

aeolic /ē·ol′ik/ (also spelled "eolic") originally, the name of the Greek dialect in which Sappho and Alcaeus wrote. Now a. is a name for a class of meters in which dactyls and trochees are brought closely together so that a CHORIAMB (·--·) is formed. Prosodists disagree as to whether scansion of the a. is counted as choriambic or dactylic-trochaic and, alternately, iambic-anapestic. See ACCENTUAL-SYLLABIC VERSE and METER.

aesthetic distance (*aesthetic*, from Greek for "things pertaining to the senses"; sometimes called "*physical distance*" or "*psychic distance*") a term coined by E. Bullough in 1912 to describe the effect produced when an experience is objectified by a work of art independent from the personal experience of its creator. A.d. also refers to the degree of detachment and objectivity that a critical reader maintains in his evaluation and, in this way, keeps art separate from reality. A.d. is close to Keats' NEGATIVE CAPABILITY and Eliot's OBJECTIVE CORRELATIVE.

Critics agree that a certain degree of objectivity is a necessary prerequisite for artistic or critical contemplation, but they disagree on the amount of objectivity required. Bullough, for instance, felt comfortable with the "utmost decrease" in a.d., while Ortega y Gasset held out for the "utmost increase." At any rate, every reader and poet must find a balance between *overdistancing*, that is, being coldly withdrawn, and *underdistancing*, that is, being overly subjective.

The degree of a.d. in a poet's work is part of his or her STANCE. Certain poets, such as T.S. Eliot and Donald Justice, choose to have a high degree of a.d., while others, such as W.C. Williams or Sylvia Plath, choose to have a low degree. See also CONFESSIONAL POETRY, DISTANCE AND INVOLVEMENT, LOCATION, and OBJECTIVITY VS. SUBJECTIVITY.

Aestheticism a school of poetry in England in the second half of the 19th century; also, a view of poetics that maintains the autonomy of art regardless of moral, social, political, and other practical considerations. The roots of the aesthetic movement lie in Germany in Kant's theory that aesthetic contemplation should be "disinterested," in Schiller's emphasis on form and "revelation of the universal in the particular," and in the ideas of writers such as Goethe and Schelling. Oscar Wilde, the prophet of English A., promoted the creed "Art for art's sake" (ARS GRATIA ARTIS). English PARNASSIANS (Dobson, Lange, and Gosse) also took up the cause, though in a less vociferous fashion. Keats in his *Ode on a Grecian Urn* is said to have made the paradigmatic statement on A.:

> "Beauty is truth, truth beauty,—that is all
> Ye know on earth, and all ye need to know."

But the English VICTORIANS such as Tennyson attacked the tenets of A. Coleridge, Carlyle, and Emerson found an affinity with A., and Poe elevated it into "The Poetic Principle": "a poem written solely for the poem's sake" is the supreme work. The French SYMBOLISTS in their search for an Ideal Beauty and Ultimate Reality applied the poetics of A. not only to the work itself but also to its creator whom they considered to be a priest in "the religion of beauty." Pound and Eliot, interested in an objective and technical poetry, built their own form of aesthetics on those of the Symbolists and stressed the craft aspects of poetry writing. Ultimately, the most influential ideas arising out of A. are its emphasis on the autonomy of the artist in his endeavor, the independent existence of beauty as reflected in the form and content of a poem, and the importance of craft and technique in the writing of a poem. See FIN DE SIÈCLE. See also *criticism* in APPENDIX 1.

aesthetic surface the general effect that a poem's RHYTHM, PHRASING, SYNTAX, IMAGERY, LINEATION, TONE, and figures produce in combination. For example, the a.s. of Hopkins' *The Windhover* is rough, impacted, and clashing, while the a.s. of James Wright's *To a Blossoming Pear Tree* is smooth, clean, and clear. The a.s. of a poem takes into account the external appearance of the poem's inner theme, but the two could conceivably be in productive tension. See TEXTURE, TONE COLOR, and TYPOGRAPHICAL ARRANGEMENT. See also *melopoetics in* APPENDIX 1.

aetiologia: See ENTHYMEME.

affective fallacy a term originally used in a 1946 essay in *The Verbal Icon* by W.K. Wimsatt, Jr., and Monroe C. Beardsley in which a.f. is defined as an error in evaluating a poem by its effects—especially emotional effects—on the reader. Agreeing that the a.f. is an error of subjective judgment, the school of NEW CRITICISM warned that using this type of standard would lead one to subordinate the objective merits of a work to its emotional, psychological, and historical effects. But other critics, such as David Daiches (*Literary Essays*, 1965), maintain that there is much value in utilizing the a.f. since the response by the reader can be traced back to the techniques of the poem. Aristotle's theory of CATHARSIS, which calls for a vicarious emotional purge on the part of an empathetic audience, is a well known example of the a.f. See also CLASSICAL FALLACY, EXPRESSIVE FALLACY, IMITATIVE FALLACY, INTENTIONAL FALLACY, PATHETIC FALLACY and REDUCTIVE FALLACY.

Age of Sensibility an 18th- and early-19th-century movement within NEO-CLASSICISM that promoted pathos, instinct, and compassion (over the antithetical Rationalist values of the 17th century) as keys to understanding literature and human nature. In addition, this humanist philosophy called for a return to the rustic or pastoral life, as opposed to the more formal and refined urban sensibility, in order to restore the lost harmony between man and nature, among members of society, and between man and himself. See ROMANTICISM and SENSIBILITY.

alba (Provençal for "dawn", literally "white") a lyrical song or poem usually expressing the regret of lovers that dawn has come to separate them. There is no prescribed fixed metrical form, but conventionally the word "alba" ends each stanza. The term itself grew out of the watchman's cry that day had arrived. The earliest examples are from the Provençal and 12th-century French. Ovid inspired the TROUBADOURS who created the distinct literary genre. Chaucer's *Troilus and Chriseyde* and *The Reeve's Tale* contain albas. See AUBADE.

alcaics /alkā′iks/ a quantitative verse form of four quatrains with four long syllables in each line. The form was invented by Alcaeus in the sixth century B.C., and since it is based on QUANTITATIVE METER rather than accentual verse, there are no true English a., only imitations as in Tennyson's poem *Milton*:

> O mighty-mouthed inventor of harmonies,
> O skilled to sing of Time and Eternity,
> God-gifted organ-voice of England,
> Milton, a name to resound for ages.

The Roman poet Horace used a. some 37 times, and Swinburne also composed in the meter. Specifically, the first two lines of an alcaic are hendecasyllabic, line three is a nine-syllable line, and the fourth line is decasyllablic. See *forms* in APPENDIX 1.

alcmanic verse /-mā′nik/ quantitative metrical form featuring a dactylic-tetrameter catalectic line (‿‿/‿‿‿/‿‿‿/-). It is named after the seventh-century B.C. poet Alcman. Latin and Greek dramatic verse used the form in dactylo-epitrite or pure dactylic periods. Horace also used the meter. See QUANTITATIVE METER. See also *forms* in APPENDIX 1.

Alexandrine /-drin/ or /-drīn/ a six-foot, 12-syllable line form that became the dominant meter in France. The French version of the meter, perfected by Racine in the 17th century, usually contains four stresses, two main stresses falling on the sixth and last syllables, one or two lighter stresses with no fixed position, and a fixed medial CAESURA. The term originated either from Lambert le Tort's *Roman d'Alexandre*, a 12th-century romance based on Alexander the Great, or from the poetry of Alexandre Paris. Verlaine stretched the form toward FREE VERSE, and English examples of the meter are in iambic hexameters. Spenser used it as the concluding line of each stanza in *The Faerie Queene* (see SPENSERIAN STANZA). Pope humorously described the occasional sluggishness of the form by saying: "A needless alexandrine ends the song, / That, like a wounded snake, drags its slow length along." See *forms* in APPENDIX 1.

allegory /al′-/ (from Greek *allos*, for "other," and *agorevein*, for "to speak") a form of NARRATION that functions as a TROPE, lying somewhere between PERSONIFICATION and METAPHOR, in which persons, objects, settings, or actions are represented as physical entities referring to a second order of abstractions that lies outside of the text. For example, the character Despair in Bunyan's *Pilgrim's Progress* embodies and vivifies the notion of despair, and in Psalm 23 the Lord is represented as a shepherd and the speaker as one of his flock. As a form of metaphor, the a. implies its *tenor* and elaborates its *vehicle* for the purpose of moral instruction. The allegorical characters, objects, settings, and actions (Greed meets Generosity) tend to be literal, one-dimensional, sharply outlined, and rigid in the order of ideas they represent. On the other hand, a SYMBOL tends to be suggestive, containing multiple levels and a conglomeration of resonant qualities. A. differs from simple ALLUSION and AMBIGUITY in that it offers a running commentary rather than a single, static identity.

In some forms of a., the narrative is equal to or more important than the order of ideas outside the text; but in the *simple a.*, as in the FABLE, the abstract commentary has more importance. The *complex a.*, usually involving historical or political characters and events, places heavy emphasis on its external narrative and thus develops a strong tone of irony. Other forms of a. are the PARABLE, which is a story expressing a religious truth; the FABLE, in which animals reveal some truth about the foibles and follies of man; and the SATIRE, which, as in *Gulliver's Travels,* attempts to better the human condition through wit and humor. Spenser's *The Faerie Queene*, Dante's *Divine Comedy*, some of Milton's work, and many of the plays of Shakespeare are considered allegories, as well as many modern poems including Robert Frost's *The Road Not Taken* and Alan Dugan's *Love Song: I and Thou*. Twentieth-century critics have noted various unconscious types of a., such as psychological allegories and religious-myth allegories. See APOLOGUE, BEAST EPIC, and EXEMPLUM. See also *figurative expressions* in APPENDIX 1.

alliteration (from Latin for "to letter"; also called *"parimion"* ["the figure of like letter"]) repetition of consonants, vowels, and/or syllables in close proximity within a line. A. is deliberately used for the sake of melody (EUPHONY or CACOPHONY) and RHYTHM. The most common form of simple a. is BEGINNING RHYME or HEAD RHYME which occurs at the beginning of words and is usually consonantal, as in "Love laments loneliness," or as in James Agee's "Not met and marred with the year's whole turn of grief / But easily on the mercy of the morning / Fell this still folded leaf."

Less emphatic forms take place in the middle of words (see POLYPTOTON and at the end of words (see HOMOEOTELEUTON). Most commonly found in accentually based languages, and rare in quantitative ones, a. is a chief feature of Anglo-Saxon and Middle English verse. But in contemporary poetry, the device has atrophied into ornament and is often used as a vehicle for SATIRE in LIGHT VERSE.

More complex forms include *parallel* or *crossed a.* in which two different systems of a. are interwoven, as in Coleridge's "The *f*air *b*reeze *b*lew, the white *f*oam *f* lew"; and *suspended a.* in which a consonant-and-vowel-combination in one word is reversed in a succeeding word, as in Longfellow's "Herds of fallow *deer* were *feed*ing." Whenever the unstressed syllables of words are *alliterated*, it is called *submerged* or *thesis a.* Gerard Manley Hopkins, among modern poets, shows the most original and integral use of the device. See also ALLITERATIVE METER and ANGLO-SAXON VERSE; also *melopoetics* in APPENDIX 1.

alliterative meter /alit'-/ a structural feature of Old Germanic poetry, used to link and emphasize important words within the metrical units. Each line is divided into two half-lines (or HEMISTICH UNITS) of two stresses by a decisive pause or CAESURA. At least one and usually both of the two stressed words in the first half-line alliterate with the first stressed word of the second half-line; e.g., *Beowulf*, lines 205–209:

Háefde se góda	Gáeta leóda
cémpan gécorone	pára pe he cénoste
fíndan mihte;	fíftyna sum
súndwudu sóhte,	sećg wísade,
lágucroeftig món	landgemýrcu.

Each consonantal sound is considered to alliterate only with another occurrence of the same sound, but any vowel or diphthong is considered to alliterate with any other vowel or diphthong.

No one knows the origin of a.m., but one may assume that it arose as a MNEMONIC DEVICE to aid in oral recitation. In English, a.m. reached its most widespread use during the Anglo-Saxon period (see ANGLO-SAXON VERSE). During the Middle English period, the strict a.m. gave way to a less systematic verse which tolerated more freedom. Sometimes in 14th-century poetry such as *The Pearl* or *Sir Gawain and the Green Knight*, a.m. is loosely combined with intricate rhyme patterns. At the end of the Middle Ages, with the assimilation of French and classical syllabic meters into English poetry, a.m. disappeared for hundreds of years. In the modern age, English and American poets have rediscovered its primitive charm. Examples of modern poems that use a.m. include Ezra Pound's *The Seafarer*, C. Day Lewis' *As One Who Wanders into Old Workings*, Richard Eberhart's *Brotherhood of Men*, W.H. Auden's *The Age of Anxiety*, and Richard Wilbur's *Junk*. See also ALLITERATION.

alloestropha /ali·os'trofə/ (from Greek for "composed of irregular strophes") Milton's term describing verse composed in stanzas of variable lengths. His preface to *Samson Agonistes* explains that the form is in contrast to the fixed strophic forms of the ODE. See *forms* in APPENDIX 1.

allonym /al'-/ (from Greek for "other-named") a pen name of an author or a work published under a name that is not that of the author, as *"Publius"* marked the collaboration of Alexander Hamilton, John Jay, and James Madison in *The Federalist*, a series of papers that helped bring about the ratification of the U.S. Constitution. The term is related to the general term *pseudonym*. See NOM DE PLUME.

allusion (from Latin for "touching lightly upon a subject") in a literary work, a brief reference, implied or explicit, to a well known character, event, or place, or to another artistic work. Sometimes the reference may be to a little-known work or to highly specialized knowledge, as evident in the works of Ezra Pound and other Modernists such as Robert Lowell. The purpose of using the device is to share knowledge in an economical way and to enrich the work at hand.

Extended allusions can be divided into five basic types. The *topical a.* refers to recent events, such as Auden's *The Shield of Achilles* which uses a description of the results of the Trojan war to refer obliquely to the results of World War II. The *personal a.* refers to the author's own biography, such as Milton's *On His Blindness* and Robert Penn Warren's many poems about his boyhood in Kentucky. The *metaphorical a.* uses its reference as a *vehicle* for the poetic *tenor* it acquires in its new context; e.g., Robert Frost's *The Road Not Taken* acquires its symbolic meaning through the emphasis of the importance of the decision that has been made. The *imitative a.* parodies another work, as Donald Justice's *Counting the Mad* parodies *This Little Piggy*. The *structural a.* mirrors the structure of another work, as James Joyce's *Ulysses* mirrors *The Odyssey*.

altar poem (see CARMEN FIGURATUM) a shaped poem or *visual poem* in the form of an altar, as in George Herbert's *The Altar*. See CONCRETE POETRY. See also *forms* in APPENDIX 1.

ambience (from Latin for "to go about all sides"; see ATMOSPHERE) the quality of an environment or age. See also **mood**; also *dramatic terms* in APPENDIX 1.

ambiguity (from Latin for "to wander about, to waver") a word, phrase, or idea whose multiple meanings leave the reader in doubt as to the exact interpretation. The unintentional use of a. is seen as a stylistic defect characterized by imprecision and diffused reference. As an intentional device, a. has been used to impart chordal richness and largeness to language. Often it is achieved grammatically through the indefinite use of pronouns and abnormal word order; stylistically it is realized through the use of puns and compression of language. For example, Hotspur's speech in *Henry IV* mentions "crack'd crowns" which refers to (1) broken coins, (2) fractured heads, and (3) deposed royalty.

In 1930 William Empson collected and categorized the various interpretations critics had assigned to Shakespeare's work. He developed from these a controversial list of ambiguities in his book *Seven Types of Ambiguity*. They include: (1) "details of language that are effective in several ways at once"; (2) "alternative meanings that are ultimately resolved into the one meaning of the author"; (3) "two seemingly unconnected meanings that are given in one word"; (4) "alternative meanings that act together to clarify a complicated state of mind in the author"; (5) "a simile that refers imperfectly to two incompatible things and by this 'fortunate confusion' shows the author discovering his idea as he writes"; (6) "a statement that is so contradictory or irrelevant that the reader is made to invent his own interpretation"; and (7) "a statement so fundamentally contradictory that it reveals a basic division in the author's mind." Some critics have seen Empson's types of a. as being wrong or unhelpful. Another classification of a. was done in 1953 in France by J.D. Hubert, whose work is based on Baudelaire's *Flowers of Evil*.

Terms similar to a., but which don't convey a negative character, are AMPHIBOLOGIA, MULTIPLE MEANING, and PLURISIGNATION. See *figurative expressions* and *meaning* in APPENDIX 1.

ambition (from French for "going round or about") a poet's intended range, depth, and levels of meaning in a poem. See the related term RISK.

amoebean verses (*amoebean*, from Greek for "interchanging or responsive verses") alternating verses, couplets, or stanzas between two speakers, the first of whom introduces a theme and the second of whom enriches or elaborates it. The form was chiefly found in the pastoral poetry of Theocritus and Virgil. See *forms* in APPENDIX 1.

amphibologia (from Greek for "reasoning via ambiguity"; also known as "*amphiboly*") an AMBIGUITY in the sense or phrasing of words caused by either grammatical looseness or the multiple meanings of words, as in "I prayed for you frequently moping, / You wanted me barely coping." Also prophecies such as those told by the witches in *MacBeth* are a type of a. See *devices of poetic license* in APPENDIX 2, and *figurative expressions* in APPENDIX 1.

amphibrach /am'fibrak/ (from Greek for "short at both ends") a trisyllabic FOOT composed of a short syllable, a long syllable, and a short syllable (-˘-). A. was rarely used in classical poetry but is common in accentual verse. The phrase "*the old oak/en bucket*" contains two amphibrachs. See METER and SCANSION. See also AMPHIMACER.

amphigory /am'-/ (from Greek for "speech that circles about"; also known as "amphigouri") verse that contains little or no sense but which is melli-fluous, as in Swinburne's self-mocking "From the depth of the dreamy decline of the dawn / Through a notable nimbus of nebulous moonshine." See ABSTRACT POETRY, NONSENSE VERSE, and TRANS-SENSE VERSE. See also *devices of poetic license* in APPENDIX 2.

amphimacer /əmfim'-/ (from Greek for "long at both ends"; also known as "cretic") a Greek metrical FOOT composed of a long, a short, and a long syllable (-˘-) which is the opposite of the AMPHIBRACH. Tennyson's poem *The Oak* is a good example in accentual verse:

> Líve thy̆ lífe
> Yoúng ănd óld,
> Líke yŏn oák,
> Bríght ĭn Spríng,
> Lívĭng góld.

The form is thought to have been first used by the Cretan poet Thaletas (seventh century) and to have been a meter for the *hyporchema*, a song accompanied by dancing. A. is not very common in English verse. See METER and SCANSION.

amphilogia (from Greek for "speaking on both sides"; similarly used terms are AMBIGUITY and EQUIVOCATION) a word or expression whose meaning is ambiguous or in dispute. See *Devices of poetic license* in APPENDIX 2.

amphisbaenic rhyme /-bē'nik/ (amphisbaenic, from Greek for "to go both ways"; also called "backward rhyme") a term derived from the ancient

Greek fabled serpent with a head at each end of its body, appropriated to designate a pair of words whose rhymed consonants occur in reverse order, as in "belated" and "detail."

amplification (from Latin for "the action of enlarging") the elaboration or, sometimes, the contraction of a statement (as in MEIOSIS). Cicero considered this device of enlargement and ornament "one of the highest distinctions of eloquence." Quintilian listed four types of a.: (1) by augmentation (*incrementum*), (2) by comparison, (3) by reasoning, and (4) by accumulation (congeries). The device is prominent in epic and tragic poetry. See *figures of argumentation* in APPENDIX 2.

anacoenosis /anəsinō'sis/ (from Greek for "to communicate back, to reply") a figure of argumentation that seems to ask advice of one's judge or opponent: "Do you really want war? / Do you want your state divided?" See RHETORICAL QUESTION. See also *figures of argumentation* in APPENDIX 2.

anacoluthon /-loo'-/ (from Greek for "wanting sequence") a grammatical device that leaves a part of a sentence incomplete, or a part of a passage incomplete. The incoherence can be effective when used intentionally, but confusing (as in the dangling-participle construction) when unintentional. See *grammatical constructions* in APPENDIX 2.

anacreontic poetry /-rē·on'-/ poetry named after Anacreon of Teos (sixth century B.C.) whose liberated subject matter in some 60 lyrical poems praised beauty, eroticism, and the pleasure of inebriation. The verse form consists of trochaic quatrains, rhyming abab or aabb, in either tetrameter or trimeter. The three-foot type usually ends with an extra long or accented syllable (--/--/--/-) as in Blake's light and innocent *The Bard's Song*:

Píping down the válleys wíld

But the rhythm can be used for serious purposes too, as in Blake's awesome *The Tyger*. Originally, the meter of a.p. was --------, but a common variation in Classical Greek usage was derived by exchanging the final short syllable of the initial foot with the first long syllable of the second foot, so that we have ---- / ----. Notable poets to have used the form include the Latins Laevius and Seneca, and Longfellow in *Hiawatha*. See *forms* in APPENDIX 1.

anacrusis /-kroo'-/ (from Greek for "a striking up of a tune, an upbeat") the extrametrical or unaccented syllables that occur at the beginning of a line in order to introduce the regular metrical rhythm. These uncounted syllables, usually found at the initial position of a line, function as the opposite of TRUNCATION in which syllables in the last foot of a line are omitted. But sometimes a. can occur at the terminal position of a line, in which case it is called *end a.*: "Their shoulders held the sky suspended." A more accurate term for initial a. would be *procephalous*.

anadiplosis /-plō'-/ (from Greek for "doubling"; also known as "epanadiplosis") a figure of repetition that repeats the last word of a clause, line, or sentence in the first word of the next unit so that the two are united, as in: "What one loves, loves one back." Other figures of repetition include ANAPHORA, EPANALEPSIS, EPISTROPHE, PLOCE, and SYMPLOCE. See *figures of repetition* in APPENDIX 2.

anagnorsis /-nôr-/ (Greek for "to recognize, to discover") the moment when a character moves from ignorance to knowledge. In Greek tragedy, according to Aristotle's *Poetics*, the a. leads to the fall of the PROTAGONIST; in comedy, to his success. This dramatic moment leads to a reversal of the dramatic situation known as the PERIPETEIA, as in Sophocles' *Oedipus Rex* when Oedipus discovers that he himself is the slayer of Laius. See DRAMATIC STRUCTURE and EPIPHANY.

anagogical vision (*anagogical*, from Greek for "mystical") the quality of perception that increases and deepens the meaning of a work because its author was able to include multiple levels of reality in one image or situation. The term was adapted into literary criticism from theology by Flannery O'Connor. See ANAGOGE , LITERAL VISION AND A.V., and VISION.

anagoge /an'əgōjē/ or /anəgō'jē/ (from Greek for "mystical"; also called "anagogy" /an'-/) the spiritual or highest interpretation of meaning in a work as opposed to the literal, allegorical, and moral levels of interpretation; e.g., Jerusalem is literally a city in Palestine, allegorically the Church, morally the believing soul, and *anagogically* the heavenly City of God. According to Rilke, the function of the poet is to reveal a perspective of reality like that of an angel, containing all time and space, who is blind and looking into himself. According to Northrop Frye, a. is similar to Joyce's EPIPHANY, a point where all symbols unite into a single, infinite, and eternal symbol. In terms of form it is Hopkins' idea of INSCAPE. Similar views are implied in Valéry's conception of a total intelligence of the poem; in Yeats' "artifice of eternity,"·where man is the creator or all creation as well as both life and death; and in Dylan Thomas' hymns to a universal body. See ANAGOGICAL VISION and VISION. See also *meaning* in APPENDIX 1.

anagram /an'-/ (from Greek, eventually meaning "transposition of letters of a word") a rearranging of the letters of a word or phrase that results in a new word or phrase, as in "now" into "won," or "mead" into "made." While the device may serve to display one's own ingeniousness, it may also be used to convey a hidden name or meaning, as in Samuel Butler's novel *Erewhon*, which spelled backward is "nowhere," or the novel *Sumarongi*, which reads backward as "ignoramus." The PALINDROME is an a. that reads the same way backwards or forwards, as in "mom," "pop," and "wow." The whole sentence, "Madam I'm Adam," is a palindrome.

analects /an'-/ (from Greek for "things gathered or picked up"; also called "analecta") a compendium of short, selected passages from a single author or group of authors. It is often used as a generic title of books, such as *Analects from Confucius.* See ANTHOLOGY. See also *publishing formats* under *forms* in APPENDIX 1.

analogy (from Greek for "equality of proportion") a comparison in which something unknown is compared to something known so that an ARGUMENT may be made clear. The method is convenient but limited in its depth and accuracy since few things or ideas are ever equal beyond their surface appearance. The terms being compared are called *analogues,* as in the language correspondences of "mother," "madre," and "mama," or the literary analogues of *West Side Story* to *Romeo and Juliet.* See SIMILE. See also *figures of argumentation* in APPENDIX 2.

analysis (Greek for "unloosening, undoing") the breaking down of a poem so that its parts may be examined. Historically, Aristotle examined a work in relation to other works and categorized a work's parts into general or specific categories. Plato examined a work with the use of questions derived more from intuitive experience than objective observation. A poem may be analyzed according to (1) the structure and order of its language and grammar; (2) the meanings and relations of its ideas; (3) the hierarchy or structure of its ideas; (4) its textual interpretations either in the work under study or in relationship to interpretations found in other arts; (5) its social, political, and economic contexts; (6) the psychology of the writer or the characters within the DRAMATIC SITUATION of the work, and the examination of the creative and aesthetic experience of the work; and (7) the examination of the poem's GENRE, which is then related to a psychological typing. See CRITICISM.

analytical criticism a system of literary criticism that treats a poem as an independent work free from practical applications to its historical content. The poem is to be taken on its own terms and its parts are to be examined in context to the whole by various systems of scrutiny. The *New Critics* are said to have used the a.c. approach. See AESTHETICISM, ANALYSIS, and CRITICISM. See also *criticism* in APPENDIX 1.

analyzed rhyme (also known as "suspended rhyme") the shuffling of two or more rhyming words, usually of the assonantal and consonantal types, as in "run, hunt, fin, splint," or by use of consonantal and true rhymes: "clear, where, tear, air." When interlocked over a few lines, the device is effective in producing ECHO RHYMES. See RHYME.

anamnesis /-nē′sis/ (Greek for "a remembering, a recalling") a figure of PATHOS in which there is a sorrowful recalling of the past. The figure is often used in the DIRGE, the ELEGY, the EULOGY, and the LAMENT. Edgar Lee Master's *Spoon River Anthology* makes frequent use of the device. See *figures of pathos* in APPENDIX 2.

anapest /an′-/ (from Greek for "beaten back"; also spelled "anapaest") a trisyllabic FOOT consisting of two unaccented and one accented syllables (˘ ˘ ′). Often used to indicate excited motion, the foot was originally used as a march rhythm and later became known as the "galloping meter," as in Byron's

> Thē Ắssýr / iăn căme dówn / liǩe thē wólf / oñ thē foíd.

But it is also effectively used as a slow and mournful rhythm if it is mixed with variations. See ACCENTUAL-SYLLABIC VERSE and METER.

anaphora /ɔnf'-/ (Greek for "a carrying up or back"; also know as "epanaphora") a *figure of repetition* (see APPENDIX 2) that repeats the same word or phrase at the beginning of lines, clauses, or sentences, as in the Beatitudes of the Bible that make nine statements beginning with "Blessed are." The device is often used in oratory, sermons, and prophetic poetry. In *Richard II*, John of Gaunt uses the device effectively when he describes the England he loves. Also Walt Whitman depended on the device heavily, as did William Blake. See *figures of repetition* in APPENDIX 2.

anastrophe /ɔnas'trofē/ (Greek for "a turning upside down") a grammatical construction in which an INVERSION or reversal of normal word order takes place for the sake of emphasis in meaning, rhythm, melody, or tone. The syntactical shift can be a simple reversal of two words or their separation by an interposing word or set of words (called HYPERBATON). Milton uses a. in *Il Penseroso*: "These pleasures, Melancholy, give, / And I with thee will choose to live." A. can also refer to a switch within an order of ideas. Most poets from ancient to modern times have used the device. See *grammatical constructions* in APPENDIX 2.

angles (from Greek for "bend"; see CINEMATIC TECHNIQUES) a cinematic term that indicates the camera's or viewer's physical perspective of a scene. That view implies various psychological pieces of information about the characters, setting, and action being seen. The angle represents the height and tilt of the viewer's perspective. See BIRD'S EYE VIEW and LOW ANGLE SHOT. See also *cinematic terms* in APPENDIX 1.

Anglo-Saxon verse a body of ORAL POETRY composed by the Germanic tribes inhabiting England from the fifth to 11th centuries. The poetry is based on STRESS PROSODY and features the device of ALLITERATION. Each line is composed of two half lines (see HEMISTICH) separated by a CAESURA. Each half line contains two stressed syllables and a varying amount of unstressed syllables. The alliterated words number from two to four, and the accents fall on parts of speech normally accented in a particular grammatical construction. The system is said to have been devised to make the oral recitation easily remembered and rendered. *Piers Plowman* (14th century) illustrates the meter: "Went wyde in this world. Wonderes to here." See ACCENTUAL VERSE, ALLITERATIVE METER, and METER.

antagonist /ɔntag'-/ (from Greek for "opponent, rival") in Greek drama, the main character who directly opposes the PROTAGONIST or hero. Though the term has become pejorative in meaning because it is usually associated with the "villain" in a work, it was not originally meant to refer to qualities of good or bad, but to the character who acts as a foil to one on whom the plot's main attention is focused. Thus, if a hero of secondary importance opposes a villain who is the chief character, the hero is the a. and the villain is the protagonist. However, most dramas center their primary attention on the exploits of heroes and relegate the villain to a position of secondary importance. The character in this secondary position is specifically termed the DEUTERAGONIST. See *dramatic terms* in APPENDIX.

antanaclasis /-nak'-/ (Greek for "to reflect, to bend back") a word that obtains two or more meanings when repeated. The device calls attention to the word's origins or sound values, as in this example from *Henry V*: "To England will I steal, and there I'll steal." See PUN. See also *figures of repetition* in APPENDIX 2, and *figurative expressions* in APPENDIX 1.

antanagoge (from Greek for "a leading or bringing up") a figure of definition that works in contradiction by stating something negative and then balancing it with something of positive value, as in "The getting of money is tiresome and shallow, but once you get it, it's nice." See *figures of definition* in APPENDIX 2.

antecedent action (*antecedent*, from Greek for "that which goes before") the action or events that take place before the action that is represented in the work of literature. A.a. is offered to the reader to aid in his understanding of the work and is given by direct exposition, by FLASHBACK, or by means of DIALOGUE. If the action in the beginning of a work is already in progress, the work is said to begin IN MEDIAS RES. See *dramatic terms* in APPENDIX 1.

antepenult /-pē'-/ or /-pinult'/ (from Latin for "before the next-to-last") a word, syllable, line, stanza, or poem that stands in the third-to-last position. Thus the *antepenultimate* word in this sentence is "sentence."

anthimeria a grammatical construction in which a word used as one part of speech is exchanged for another. The device is common in traffic signs, e.g., "Drive careful" for "Drive carefully." Also, the common ungrammatical expression "I am feeling badly" for "I am feeling bad" is an example of a. See *grammatical figures of exchange* in APPENDIX 2, and *figurative expressions* in APPENDIX 1.

anthology (from Greek for "flower" plus "to gather") a collection of writings by various authors; sometimes in the form of a CHRESTOMATHY, a collection of passages usually by one author. Originally, an a. was a collection of poetic epigrams, usually in elegiac distichs. Collections were made as early as the fourth century B.C. Probably the best known is *The Greek Anthology*, some 4,500 short poems in Greek written between 490 B.C. and 1000 A.D., and compiled by numerous scholars through the centuries.

The earliest anthologies in English include *Tottel's Miscellany* (1557), *A Gorgious Gallery of Gallant Inventions* (1578), and *The Phoenix Nest* (1593).

In the 20th century, anthologies have become extremely popular, and some of them have had a great influence on poets, e.g., *The New Poetry*, by Harriet Monroe and Alice C. Henderson, published in 1917. In contemporary poetry, influential anthologies include Donald Allen's *The New American Poetry: 1945–1960*; Donald Hall's and Robert Pack's *New Poets of England and America*; A. Poulin's *Contemporary American Poetry*; and Daniel Halpern's *The American Poetry Anthology: Poets Under 40*. The purpose of these anthologies is to introduce contemporary authors to the public. See *publishing formats* under *forms* in APPENDIX 1.

anthypophora /ant·hipof'ərə/ (Greek for "against" plus "allegation") a figure of argumentation in which the speaker acts as his own foil by arguing with himself. Hamlet's famous SOLILOQUY, "To be or not to be," is an example of a. See *figures of argumentation* in APPENDIX 2.

antibacchius /antibəkī'əs/ (from Greek for "opposite of bacchius"; also known as "palimbacchius" [from *palin*, "back," and *bacchius*, from the Greek god "Bacchus"]) a rare trisyllabic FOOT in which the stress falls on the first two syllables (´ ´ ˘): "fíve dózĕn." A. is the opposite of ANAPEST (˘ ˘ ´), and the reverse of a *bacchius* (´ ˘ ˘).

anticipatory line ending (see LINE ENDING) a type of ENJAMBMENT in which information is purposely delayed in order to heighten the reader's expectations. The a.l.e. can be formed by any part of speech when a sentence, phrase, or syntactical unit is cut off from completion: "He went into/the store of/his/desires." The device can be overused, become annoying, or appear illogical if it occurs too soon or too consistently in a poem. See also *line endings* in APPENDIX 1.

anticlimax (from Greek for the "opposite of a ladder") first described by Samuel Johnson as "a sentence in which the last part expresses something lower than the first" (*Dictionary*, 1755). Today, the term commonly refers to an arrangement of descriptive or narrative details in an order where the lesser or the absurd is in the place where the reader expects the most serious or noble. Where a. is intentional, it is meant to show either an ineptly expressed idea meant to be lofty, or an ironic letdown. If the fall is sudden, the effect is comic or satiric, as in Byron's *Don Juan* (I,ix): "A better cavalier ne'er mounted horse, / Or, being mounted, e'er got down again." See BATHOS. See also *closure* in APPENDIX 1.

antihero a character who lacks the qualities needed for heroism—nobility of life or mind, high purpose, lofty ideals. *Hamlet*'s King Claudius is sometimes described as an a. See ANTAGONIST, DEUTERAGONIST, and HERO. See also *Dramatic terms* in APPENDIX 1.

antimasque (sometimes spelled "antimask") a light, bawdy dance, performed by professional actors and dancers, which was interspersed as a series of interludes among the more serious actions and dances of a MASQUE, performed by courtly amateurs. The development and origin of the a. are attributed to Ben Jonson. See *dramatic terms* in APPENDIX 1.

antimetabole /-tab'olē/ (Greek for "transposition") a *figure of repetition*, first described by Quintilian, that repeats the words of a preceding clause in reverse order: "Those who fear to love will never sacrifice. / Those who sacrifice for love will never fear." Usually two words in a phrase or line are repeated in reverse order in a succeeding phrase or line in an abba pattern, as in Shakespeare's

a   b   b   a
Love's fire heats water, water cools not love.

Oftentimes, as in the word "love" here, there is a morphological change in one or both of the repeated words. See CHIASMUS. See also *figures of repetition* in APPENDIX 2.

antiphon /an'-/ (from Greek for "musical accords" or "sounding back") a verse or song rendered responsively in separate parts. A. is usually found in church music.

antiphrasis /antif'-/ (Greek for "expression by the opposite") the ironic use of a word or phrase to signify the opposite of its lexical meaning: "Hitler was a real charmer." In Shakespeare's plays, characters use a. intentionally, as when Antony refers to Caesar's murderers as "honorable men," and, unintentionally, as when Othello refers to Iago as "honest." See IRONY, SARCASMUS, and SATIRE. See also *contraries and contradictories* in APPENDIX 2, and *figurative expressions* in APPENDIX 1.

antirrhesis a *figure of argumentation* that refutes and rejects authority because the authority is in error or is evil. A. forms the backbone of Thoreau's argument in his essay *Civil Disobedience*. See *figures of argumentation* in APPENDIX 2.

antisagoge a logical figure dealing with cause and effect, or antecedent and consequence. In a., the antecedent and consequence are linked together in a logical dimension: "Do as your father commands / and you will inherit his lands. / Do as your father asks not/and you will live by your hands." A. is often used in discursive as well as poetic PROSE. See *figures of cause and effect, antecedent and consequent* in APPENDIX 2.

antispast /an'-/ (from Greek for "drawn in the contrary direction") a metrical FOOT consisting of four syllables, two long or accented, flanked on either side by two short or unaccented (˘ ´ ´ ˘), or a combination of an iamb and a trochee:

thĕ húge mánsiŏn

Scholars are not certain whether this foot existed in Classical poetry. See METER and SCANSION.

antistrophe /antis'trofē/ (Greek for "a counter-turning") originally the name of the second stanza in Greek choral dance and poetry. The first is STROPHE and the third is EPODE. The chorus chanted an a. while returning from left to right stage as an answer to the previous strophe. In rhetoric, the term has come to mean a grammatical figure of repetition that reverses preceding phrases or clauses. It also refers to the repetition of a word or phrase at the end of successive clauses. See ANADIPLOSIS, ANTIMETABOLE, CHIASMUS, and ODE. See also *dramatic terms* and *forms* in APPENDIX 1.

antithesis /antith′-/ (Greek for "opposition") a rhetorical figure that juxtaposes opposite ideas (or conclusions) of similar grammatical constructions so that a balance of tensions is achieved. Pope, who often used the device, presents a clear example of a. in *The Rape of the Lock*: "The hungry judges soon the sentence sign, / And wretches hang that Jury-men may dine." Here, "wretches" is opposed by "Jury-men," and "hungry" is opposed by "dine." The clearest forms of a. are outright assertions or denials that imply what a writer is for or against in particular or general. It resembles a SYLLOGISM in its economy, clarity, and forcefulness. English and French writers used the device to display their wit; e.g., Samuel Johnson in "marriage has many pains, but celibacy has no pleasures." Today the device is chiefly used in LIGHT VERSE. See *grammatical devices of rhythm and balance* in APPENDIX 2.

antode /ant′ōd/ (from Greek for "opposite song") a metrical ode delivered during the intermission of a Greek Old Comedy by the chorus, expressing its author's views on religion or politics (PARECBASIS). The a. is an answer given by one-half of the chorus to a previous song given by the other half of the chorus during the intermission. It is similar to the ODE form.

antonomasia (Greek for "a naming instead") a rhetorical figure of speech under the category of "subject and adjunct" that defines by replacing a proper name with its most obvious quality or aspect, or by substituting a proper name with one whose name has risen to the level of a SYMBOL. The first type is seen in the phrase "She is the cat's meow," and the second is seen in Gray's *Elegy Written in a Country Churchyard*: "Some mute, inglorious Milton here may rest, / Some Cromwell guiltless of his country's blood." A variation of the device is the EPITHET ("wise Nestor"), in which the individual is actually named and characterized, but not referred to as a class of person. The device can be found abundantly today in popular expressions such as "He's a Don Juan" (signifying a lover), "She's a Jezebel" (meaning an evil woman), and "He's a Machiavelli" (meaning a man of clever intrigues). See *figures of subject and adjunct* in APPENDIX 2, and *figurative expressions* in APPENDIX 1.

aphaeresis /əfer′-/ (Greek for "a taking away") the deletion of a first syllable or vowel, as in "special" for "especial."

aphorism (from Greek for "distinction, definition") a short statement of truth or principle characterized by its depth of thought, as in Pope's "The proper study of mankind is man." The genre is similar to an APOTHEGM, maxim, PROVERB, saw, and adage. The term is attributed to Hippocrates, who wrote *Aphorisms*. See *clichés* in APPENDIX 1.

aphorismus a form of refutation that questions the use of some word or phrase, as in "How can you call yourself a teacher when it would be wrong to follow your example?" See *figures of argumentation* in APPENDIX 2.

apocarteresis a *figure of pathos* in which a speaker loses hope of gaining or maintaining something, so he turns toward something else: "I cannot help

those who have died here, so I must help the living cope with their loss."
See *figures of pathos* in APPENDIX 2.

apocopated rhyme /əpok'-/ (*apocopated,* from Greek for "cutting off") a
RHYME in which the accented syllables of two words make a true rhyme,
but in which one word has a masculine ending while the other has a
feminine ending, as in "find" and "blinder." The word *apocope* indicates
the loss or deletion of the last letter or syllable from a word, as in "curio"
from "curiosity."

apodioxis (Greek for "the action of driving away") a *figure of argumentation*
that rejects an opponent's argument as being ignorant, confused, false, or
absurd. See *figures of argumentation* in APPENDIX 2.

apodixis /-dik'sis/ (Greek for "the action of giving back") a type of
testimony in logical expressions that is based on common experience or
knowledge, as in "Hard work pays off." See *logical and figurative
expressions* in APPENDIX 2.

apologue /ap'əlog/ (from Greek for "account, story, or fable"; a similarly
used term is FABLE) an imaginative story with moral instruction employing animals or inanimate objects as characters. It is a form of ALLEGORY as
used in the Bible and some of *Aesop's Fables.* See also PARABLE.

apology (from Greek for "defense") a defense of a writer's reasoning or an
examination of a philosophical problem, as in Plato's *Apology,* in which
he defends Socrates, or in Sidney's *Apologie for Poetrie,* which discusses
POETICS. The term has come to be associated with guilt and can be used to
denote a work expressing sorrow or regret, as in Chaucer's retraction at
the end of *The Canterbury Tales.* See *forms* in APPENDIX 1.

apomnemonysis /apōnēmon'isis/ the use of an appropriate saying in the form
of a testimony designed to complement the speaker's purposes, as in the
following speech by a keynote speaker who is calling for unity at a
political convention: "Remember that no man is an island. There is
strength in numbers. A house divided against itself will fall."

apophasis /əpof'-/ (Greek for "denial") originally, a Classical rhetorical
figure of argumentation that works by dividing itself into reasons for some
purpose given but which holds back one main reason until the conclusion
and by that conclusion cancels preceding reasons. In modern rhetoric the
term has come to mean an ironic denial of one's admitted intention not to
speak of something while simultaneously speaking of that very thing.
Shakespeare used the device in Mark Antony's speech in *Julius Caesar.*
The controversial 1930s trial of Sacco and Vanzetti, in which Vanzetti
based most of his emotional appeal to the jury on a. before he was
sentenced to death, is remarkably similar to Mark Antony's approach.
Another kind of a., based on the senses, is found in Sylvia Plath's *A
Birthday Present* in which the speaker claims she will open her present
without the crackle of paper; but, of course, it is then that the reader hears
that sound. See *figures of argumentation* in APPENDIX 2.

apophthegm: See APOTHEGM.

apoplanesis a figure of argumentation that refutes an issue by evading it, as in this example from an imaginary court proceeding:

> JUDGE: Tell us where you were last night.
> DEFENSE: Sir, I will answer fully as a good citizen should. I have
>   always been a good citizen and have taken pains to do
>   the Commonwealth great good.

See *figures of argumentation* in APPENDIX 2.

aporia /əpō′rē·ə/ (Greek for "the state of being at a loss") a self-doubting argumentative SOLILOQUY, as in "To whom shall I turn? Who would listen to me?" or in Hamlet's famous "To be or not to be" speech. See *figures of argumentation* in APPENDIX 2.

aposiopesis /-sī·opēšis/ (Greek for "a becoming silent") a sudden breaking off in the middle of a sentence either from unwillingness or inability to continue speaking. A. is often used to hint at an awesome emotion or thought; other times, a. is used to leave out an obvious or sordid detail; still another use of a. is to make a transition between unrelated ideas. In any case, the term should not be confused with PARALIPSIS. See *figures of pathos* in APPENDIX 2.

apostrophe /əpos′-/ (Greek for "a turning away") a figure of speech in which the speaker addresses an absent quality, object, or person as if it were present and sentient. An a. is oftentimes an INVOCATION to the MUSES or an address to a famous person of the past, e.g., Wordsworth's *Milton! Thou Shouldst Be Living at This Hour.* Another well-known example is Tennyson's *Ring Out Your Bells.* Because a. is used as a deeply emotional expression, it is subject to PARODY and SATIRE. A. often uses EROTEMA, a questioning, and ECPHONESIS, a crying out. See *figurative expressions* in APPENDIX 1.

apothegm /ap′əthem/ (also spelled "apophthegm") a brief, famous saying, usually couched in FIGURATIVE LANGUAGE, that is ascribed to by most people, e.g., "Necessity is the mother of invention." A. differs from an APHORISM by being more pointed, focused, practical, and startling. Ben Franklin and Samuel Johnson are two of the most famous makers of apothegms in the English language. See also PROVERB; also *clichés* in APPENDIX 1.

approximate rhyme: See OFF-RHYME.

ara /ā′rə/ a *figure of pathos* that shows hatred for the evil in a person or the evil he carries with him. See *figures of pathos* in APPENDIX 2.

arbitrary figure an IMAGE or *figure of speech* used for convenience in one part of a poem but which does not fit with the rest of the poem. Arbitrariness is usually considered a defect in a poem, though many modern poets (particularly the writers of SURREALISM and DADA) have used disjunctive effects to their advantage. See *control* in APPENDIX 1.

Arcady /är'-/ (also called "Arcadia" /ärkā'-/) originally the name of a mountainous district in the Peloponnesus. The term came to stand for the PASTORAL verse of the Classical poets (especially Virgil) and the simplicity of an imagined Golden Age in which shepherds and shepherdesses devoted themselves entirely to their flocks and songs. A. is sometimes used synonymously with BUCOLIC poetry. See also ECLOGUE, IDYLL, and PASTORAL ELEGY.

archaism /är'kā·izm/ (from Greek for "old-fashioned") an obsolete word, phrase, or syntactical construction. Archaisms are used either to fit an old form or to evoke the atmosphere of a past era or culture. Words such as "thy," "thee," "quoth," "morn," and "e'er" are considered archaisms in modern poetry. If the device is used unintentionally, the result may seem contrived, stilted, or ridiculous. See DICTION. See also *clichés, control*, and *diction* in APPENDIX 1.

archetypal myth /är'kə-/ a narrative expressing an explanation of the origins, characteristics, rituals, or themes behind an elemental and universal image or experience of human existence (see ARCHETYPE).

archetype /är'kə-/ (from Greek for "original or primitive form") a SYMBOL, CHARACTER, IMAGE, event, or thematic pattern meant to evoke a profound response to and identification of a universal human experience. Common *symbols* include the sun, the ocean, darkness, and fire; *common characters* include the father, the mother, the snake, and the stone; common *themes* include birth, death, initiation, redemption, and love. C.G. Jung applied the term to "primordial images" which are the "psychic residue" of repeated types of experience in both our lives and those of our ancestors. He maintained that we possess a COLLECTIVE UNCONSCIOUS made up of image-symbols that might stem from man's early racial memory. As a literary device, a. is defined by Northrop Frye as an image-symbol that repeats itself with such frequency that readers are able to identify the a. as an "element of one's literary experience as a whole." Frye, dropping Jung's hypothesis of the archetype's origins, simply accepts its existence and develops an approach to CRITICISM stressing the underlying mythical patterns in literature using the a. as its basis (*Anatomy of Criticism*). J.G. Frazer's *The Golden Bough* (ca. 1900) was the first to trace elemental patterns of myth and ritual recurring in the legends of many cultures. The *New Critics* since the 1930s have used the archetypal critical approach to interpret literary works such as Coleridge's *The Rime of the Ancient Mariner* whose plot pattern is an a. of a spiritual journey that all men who offend God must take. See ARCHETYPAL MYTH and MYTH.

archilochian /ärkəlō'kē·ən/ a metric system attributed to Archilochus of Paros (eighth or seventh century B.C.) which was then termed *metra episyntheta* and consisted of verse written in an admixture of meters or metrical cola (see COLON). Horace used the form. The *versus Archilochius* is a dactylic tetrameter together with an ithyphallic, three trochees usually with a long syllable at the end which was used to end a long line. See *forms* in APPENDIX 1.

architechtonics /ärkitekton'iks/ (from Greek for "leading builder") an architectural term used in literary criticism to indicate the structural harmony of a well-organized, efficient piece of literature that combines form, content, and function into an organic whole. See FORM and ORGANIC COMPOSITION.

argument (from Latin for "re-fashioning, after this") a short thematic or plot summary of a work that may be explicit or implied within the work itself. Classic examples of an explicit a. are found in Milton's *Argument* at the beginning of each book of *Paradise Lost*, Coleridge's *Marginalia* in his *The Rime of the Ancient Mariner*, Dryden's translation of the *Aeneid*, and Spenser's eclogues. Nowadays the term usually refers to a paraphrase of the logical structure of a work. SYMBOLISTS such as Mallarmé and Modernists (see MODERN PERIOD) such as Dylan Thomas and Wallace Stevens have contended that the a. is unneccesary to a work. They substitute TEXTURE for LOGICAL STRUCTURE. See THEMATIC STRUCTURE. See also *figures of argumentation* in APPENDIX 2.

Aristotelian Criticism: See CRITICISM.

ars gratia artis /ärs' grä'tē-ä är'tis/ or /ärz' grä'shē-ə är'tis/ (Latin for "art for art's sake"; also called "art for art's sake" and "l'art pour l'art") a creed of certain writers in England and France during the late 1800s. It is a concept of aesthetics (see AESTHETICISM) that holds that art is independent of morality, politics, and sociohistorical conditions, a creed that many existential and realist writers still claim. See also AUTOTELIC and NEW CRITICISM.

arsis and thesis (*arsis*, Greek for "lifting up"; *thesis*, Greek for "setting down") originally Greek dance terms that indicated the upward and downward beats that occur while enunciating Greek verse. The gestures of a hand or foot accompanied the rhythm in which the unaccented syllable is the arsis and the accented syllable is the thesis. Romans used the arsis as the first part of a foot and the thesis as the second part; consequently, grammarians thought of this process as raising or lowering the voice, rather than an upward or downward beat. Thus the meanings became reversed so that arsis now indicates a long or accented syllable and thesis the short or unaccented syllable. See ACCENT, BREVE, ICTUS, and MACRON.

art ballad (also known as "literary ballad") a BALLAD of attributable authorship which has obvious literary merit, as opposed to the popular or FOLK BALLAD which is simpler in style and of unknown authorship. Well-known examples are Coleridge's *The Rime Of The Ancient Mariner*, Dylan Thomas' *Ballad Of The Long-Legged Bait*, Scott's *Rosabelle*, Rossetti's *Sister Helen*, Keats' *La Belle Dame sans Merci*, and Longfellow's *The Wreck of the Hesperus*, all of which are based on the form of the folk ballad. See ART EPIC.

arte mayor /är'ta mäyôr'/ (Spanish for "major art") a metrical form, common in medieval Spanish poetry, that consists of a line or group of lines of 12 stresses each and is divided into two hemistiches of six stresses each (see HEMISTICH). The stanzas were usually eight lines rhyming abbaacac, abbaacca, or ababbccb. Originally, the a.m. was a very loose form, but in the 12th century it became fixed as described here. Juan de Mena (1411–56) is often cited as the greatest practitioner of the form. See ARTE MENOR. See also *forms* in APPENDIX 1.

arte menor /är'ta menôr'/ (Spanish for "minor art") any verse that uses lines of eight syllables or less. This Spanish term is used in contrast to the term ARTE MAYOR, which, although since the 12th century it has denoted a specific metrical form, originally referred to any verse that uses lines of nine syllables or more. See also *forms* in APPENDIX 1.

art epic (also called "literary epic") a well-crafted, artistic long narrative by a single author that was meant for a literary audience and which is based on the more literal-minded FOLK EPIC. The term was created by the Romantic critics of the 18th century to indicate the art epic's exalted style. Virgil's *Aeneid* and Milton's *Paradise Lost* are good examples of the a.e., while the *Iliad*, the *Odyssey*, and *Beowulf* represent folk epics. In contemporary times, the distinction between the two seems to be breaking down. See ART BALLAD and EPIC.

art for art's sake: See ARS GRATIA ARTIS.

artificiality (from Greek for the quality of "a thing made of art") a quality of work that is self-consciously mannered, rigidly conventional, or deliberately studied. Although there is much debate among critics about which particular poets show signs of a., most would agree that EUPHUISM and GONGORISM display a high degree of it. See CONCEIT and PRECIOUSNESS. See also *diction* in APPENDIX 1.

art lyric a short, graceful lyric poem crafted with a skilled and delicate touch. Its subject matter considers the small and subtle manifestations of beauty—particularly women's beauty. Although it has been practiced since Classical times more as a style of writing than as a form, the 17th-century CAVALIER POETS, such as Carew, Lovelace, and Suckling, popularized the form and have become closely associated with it. In time, the a.l. became highly polished and refined in the hands of writers such as Herrick, Jonson, and Herbert; freighted with abstract ideas by Shelley and Keats; and widely elaborated by French poets into FIXED FORMS such as the TRIOLET, BALLADE, RONDEAU, and RONDEL (see *forms* in APPENDIX 1).

ascending rhythm (also called "rising rhythm") lines of verse composed of rising feet (see RISING FOOT), usually iambs or anapests. Although a.r. has been called the most common rhythm in English poetry, there is considerable debate about whether it can be distinguished from FALLING RHYTHM, usually composed of dactyls or trochees, since it is difficult to determine the position of stresses in an extended passage (see RUNNING RHYTHM). See also METER, RHYTHM, ROCKING RHYTHM, and SPRUNG RHYTHM.

aschematiston (Greek for "without scheme") a form of unpoetic utterance, under the category of "intolerable poetic devices" and POETIC LICENSE, that lacks vivid IMAGERY or original FIGURES OF SPEECH, or which is simply clichéd speech, e.g., "Nice weather we're having." See CLICHÉ and FLAT

STATEMENT for discussions of unpoetic utterances used for poetic effect. See also *devices of poetic license* in APPENDIX 2, and *diction* in APPENDIX 1.

asphalia a form of testimonial in logical argumentation in which the speaker offers to hold himself responsible or to give himself as hostage in order to secure the safety of his audience or that which his audience holds dear: "If I fail to set you free / Then I will trade with them / Your life for me." See *types of testimony* in APPENDIX 2.

associational logic the intuitive process of reasoning (as opposed to RAT-IOCINATION or formal types of logic) in which the mind associates one image, event, idea, or word with another. The process can take place through automatic, unconscious JUXTAPOSITION of things based on the conventions of a culture or universal archetypes (darkness associated with fear), the comparison or contrast of salient characteristics of things (red associated with hot, associated with danger), personal experience, or knowledge. Some linguists and psychologists believe that a.l. is the mind's natural way of processing thought and information, and is the basis for imaginative poetic devices such as the METAPHOR. See AUTOMATIC WRITING and LEAPING POETRY. See also *meaning* in APPENDIX 1.

associative cut a cinematic editing technique that develops an argument by splicing together shots that are thematically related to one another. It doesn't necessarily develop or further the plot or action. In poetry, the use of SIMILE, METAPHOR, and JUXTAPOSITION are devices that are similar to the use of a.c. in cinema. For further discussion and examples, see CINEMATIC TECHNIQUES. See also *cinematic terms* in APPENDIX 1.

assonance (from Latin for "to sound to"; also called "vocalic a.") the repetition of identical or similar vowel sounds—especially in stressed syllables—in a sequence of words close to one another. Thus, a. is often used as a substitute for end-rhyme in Dickinson and many later poets (see OFF-RHYME). Many poets, including Keats, Poe, Swinburne, Dylan Thomas, and Richard Hugo, have depended heavily on a. to create TONE COLOR. See MELOPOEIA, PITCH, and SOUND SYSTEM.

asteismus /astē·iz′məs/ (from Greek for "refined witty talk") a figure of definition that works through the witty use of the relation of words to reality and to each other. A. is a mocking reply that purposely misunder-stands a statement: "Do you want to be flogged with a rope? / No, with a noodle." In *Macbeth*, the porter uses a. as a form of EQUIVOCATION when he says that strong drink, having given one "the lie, leaves him." Here, at least three senses of "lie" are intended: (1) to call one a liar; (2) to lay one out flat; (3) to cause one to urinate "lie" = "lye," slang for urine). See EQUIVOQUE and PUN. See also *figures of definition* in APPENDIX 2.

astrophic (from Greek, for "without strophes") describing a poem that is not written in regular stanzas or other balancing structures. See STROPHE. See also *forms* in APPENDIX 1.

asyndeton /asin′-/ (Greek, for "unconnected") a device of balance and rhythm, similar to BRACHYLOGIA, in which words or phrases, usually joined by conjunctions, are presented in series, separated only by commas. Julius Caesar's famous "I came, I saw, I conquered" is an example of a. Many modern poets, for example Pound and Auden, use a. for its speed, economy, brevity, and force. See *grammatical devices of rhythm and balance* in APPENDIX 2.

atmosphere (from Greek for "vapor" and "sphere, ball") the tonality pervading a poem. Similarly used terms are MOOD and AMBIENCE. See TONE. See also *dramatic terms* in APPENDIX 1.

atonic (from Greek for "without tone") referring to the unaccented syllables of a word or FOOT. See ACCENT.

Attic (from the Greek region whose capitol was Athens) denoting an intricate and sophisticated literary style of writing, sometimes thought of as being artificial and at other times as being pure, extant in fifth-century Athens. The style is opposite to the DORIC, which features the rustic kind of simplicity as exemplifed in the PASTORAL.

aubade /ôbäd′/ (French for "dawn") a LYRIC about the dawn; a morning song. The a. may be a joyous celebration of morning, or it may be a lament that two lovers must part. The a. is usually considered synonymous with ALBA, though the former term is French in origin, and the latter is Provençal. There are many famous examples of aubades; probably the most striking is in *Romeo and Juliet* when the lovers must part after their wedding night. See *forms* in APPENDIX 1.

audience (from Latin for "to hear") the present or absent listeners of a work of literature. The speaker or author may be conscious of the a., or it may be an a. that can overhear the words.

audition colorée /ôdisyôN′ kôlôrä′/ (French for "colored hearing, hearing colors") one kind of SYNAESTHESIA in which sounds are perceived as colors. The most famous example is Rimbaud's sonnet *Voyelles*. The term is derived from Jules Millet's *Audition Colorée* (1892). See *imagery* in APPENDIX 1.

Augustan Age the period of the reign of the Roman Emperor Augustus (27 B.C. to 14 A.D.), during which Latin literature, led by the poets Virgil, Horace, and Ovid, reached great heights. The name A.A. was also adopted by English writers of the Neoclassical age (approximately 1700–45) because they admired and consciously imitated the Latin poets. Some of the better known writers of the English A.A. were Pope, Swift, Addison, and Steele. See DECORUM, NEO-CLASSICISM, and PERIODS OF ENGLISH LITERATURE.

aural (from Latin for "ear") pertaining to the sense of hearing. See PITCH, RHYTHM, and SOUND SYSTEM.

authority a quality or power in the voice of the poem that promotes the reader's belief in the experience it describes. A. is a contemporary term used to signify the poet's mastery of craft and authenticity of VISION.

autologue (from Greek for "self talk"): See SOLILOQUY.

automatic writing a compositional technique invented by the Surrealists that depends for content on the unreflected, spontaneous process of thought in the subconscious. A.w. differs from STREAM-OF-CONSCIOUSNESS in that the former is a way of discovering ideas while the latter is a stylistic device that is used for characterization; however, both techniques rely on ASSOCIATIONAL LOGIC. Also, in both, the writer continually pushes forward, linking thought with thought without the usual regard for structure and craft. By allowing the mind to go where and at what pace it will, a.w., according to André Breton, allows the possibility of watching the actual functioning of the mind by giving utterance to the illogical patterns of the unconscious. See SURREALISM.

autonomous line a line of poetry that makes sense by itself, whether end-stopped or enjambed, fragmented or whole. When the end of a line signifies the end of a complete thought, the line is autonomous, even if it is a sentence fragment and there is no punctuation at the end of the line. See END-STOPPED, ENJAMBMENT, and LINE ENDING.

autotelic (from Greek for "self end") describing a work of art that is free from practical applications and does not refer to any reality outside itself. Sometimes the term is used as a synonym for "nondidactic" (see DIDACTIC POETRY). A. is a frequently used term in the writings of NEW CRITICISM. See also AESTHETICISM and ARS GRATIA ARTIS. See also *forms* in APPENDIX 1.

auxesis (Greek for "amplification") a gradual increase in intensity of meaning. A. is a figure of argumentation that either replaces a word of smaller meaning for one of larger meaning, or indicates a CLIMAX of replacements from lesser to greater meaning. In the last line of *Love Song: I and Thou*, Alan Dugan uses a. For a related term, see AMPLIFICATION. See also *figures of argumentation* in APPENDIX 2, and *figurative expressions* in APPENDIX 1.

B

babble and doodle two processes within ASSOCIATIONAL LOGIC that take place subconsciously in the poet's mind. According to Northrop Frye, as the poet composes, his mind ranges freely over all the possibilities of the sound as well as the look of the poem.

In *babble*, RHYME, ASSONANCE, ALLITERATION, and PUN develop out of associations of sounds. The poet's sense of rhythm gives shape to the associations. Frye theorizes that babble is the extreme of *melos* or CHARM, hypnotic incantation that resembles a dance rhythm and has long been associated with magic and magic rituals. The works of Christopher Smart contain many examples of babble in its raw form.

Doodle is the process of playing with the visual patterns of words. The process is usually thought of as being subconscious, but some poets, for example Poe in his essay on writing *The Raven*, suggest that the process is deliberate. Although a lyric is meant to be heard, in modern poetry there is a tendency to address the ear through the eye.

Frye uses the term doodle to describe only the process of playing with the visual aspect of the poem on the page, but the term may be equally useful to describe the subconscious playing with the images of the poem. In the notebooks of Yeats, e.g., we can see how he often records disparate images that eventually find a harmonic pattern in his poems. See IMAGIN-ATION and INSPIRATION. See also AUTOMATIC WRITING, ORGANIC COMPOSI-TION, and STREAM-OF-CONSCIOUSNESS.

bacchic /bak'ik/ (from Bacchus, the Roman god of wine who is the counter-part to the Greeks' Dionysus) a trisyllabic FOOT composed of one short or unaccented syllable followed by two long or accented syllables, as in the phrase "ăboŭt faće." The foot, not common in English SCANSION, is frequently used in QUANTITATIVE METER.

backward rhyme: See AMPHISBAENIC RHYME.

balance (from Latin for "a pair of scales") in rhetorical terms, a structural and decorative device in which parts of a sentence or line are placed in parallel positions so that their contrasting or equal meanings are high-lighted. Although the units in balance do not necessarily have to be made up of the same syntactical or grammatical units, oftentimes they are, as in the following sentence from John Kennedy's *Inaugural Speech*, which displays similar syntactical and phrasal units with opposite meanings: "Ask not what your country can do for you; ask what you can do for your country." As a critical term, b. indicates a harmonious proportion among the basic elements in a work of literature in which no one element

dominates another element. See *devices of rhythm and balance* in AP-
PENDIX 2.

balancing image: See OPPOSING IMAGE OR B.I.

ballad /bal'əd/ (from Latin for "dance") a simple and highly MNENOMIC song
that tells a story in oral form through narrative and DIALOGUE. The *folk*
or *popular b.* is one of the earliest forms of literature and draws its material
from the early periods or rural sections of a culture. It is characterized by
simple DICTION, foreshortened action, REFRAIN, and an objective SPEAKER,
and themes of love, the supernatural, and physical courage. The story rises
toward a climactic and cathartic peak. Famous American ballads are *The
Streets of Laredo, Frankie and Johnny*, and *John Henry*. The folk b.
reached its height in 16th and 17th century England, and in the songs of
American contemporary singers such as Bob Dylan and Woody Guthrie.
James Child's *The English and Scottish Popular Ballads* is the standard
collection. The *literary b.* is a narrative poem written by a learned poet
in deliberate imitation of the form and spirit of the folk b. Some of the
greatest of these were written in the Romantic period, e.g., Coleridge's
Rime of the Ancient Mariner. See B. METER, B. STANZA, and COMMON METER
OR COMMON MEASURE. See also *forms* in APPENDIX 1.

ballade /bäläd'/ (French, from Latin for "dance") the most important of Old
French FIXED FORMS containing three eight-line stanzas (rhyming
ababbcbc) with a four-line ENVOY (rhyming bcbc). The meter is often
composed of iambic or anapestic tetrameter, although the syllable count
may vary. The last line of each stanza and of the envoy is usually
addressed to someone in power, and the entire form uses only three or
four rhymes. This demanding and sophisticated form flowered in 14th-
and 15th-century France. Chaucer's *Balade de bon Conseyl* is an early
example, while Rossetti's version of François Villon's grand *Ballade of
Dead Ladies*, whose refrain line is the famous "But where are the snows of
yester-year," is perhaps the best known modern example. The DOUBLE B.,
a variant form used mostly for light verse, contains six-, eight-, or ten-line
stanzas without an envoy. See STOCK. See also *forms* in APPENDIX 1.

ballad meter (also called "ballad stanza") the rhythm, rhyme, and stanzaic
pattern of the FOLK BALLAD. It is usually composed of four-line stanzas,
rhyming abcb, with the first and third lines metered in iambic tetrameter
and the second and fourth lines in iambic trimeter, as in:

> There lived a wife at Usher's Well
> And a wealthy wife was she;
> She had three stout and stalwart sons,
> And sent them o'er the sea.

The number of unaccented syllables in a line may vary, as in Robert
Herrick's sophisticated *The Passionate Shepherd to His Nymph*. An
example of an early Scottish ballad, *Edward*, uses tetrameter couplets with
a refrain:

> "Your hawk's blude was never sae red,
> Edward, Edward;

Your hawk's blude was never sae red,
My dear son, I tell thee, O."
"O I hae kille' my red-roan steed,
That erst was so fair and free, O."

See BALLAD and COMMON METER OR COMMON MEASURE.

barbarism (from Greek for "foreign mode of speech") in common usage, uneducated speech that misuses normal grammatical rules of case, gender, tense, etc., such as "Youse wasn't here when this guy socks myself in the mouth before he even speaked to me." SOLECISM is a similarly used term. Another use of the word b. refers to the mixing of two different languages to form a word, as in "cablegram" in which a Greek suffix is added to an English word. See *devices of poetic license* in APPENDIX 2.

bard (from Welsh *bardd*) a versifier of the ancient Celtic nation who was charged with celebrating the adventures, laws, and characters of his culture in verse which he composed and recited, often accompanying himself on a stringed instrument. In tenth-century Welsh, there were three kinds of bards, which fact denoted their standing in a hierarchy: the *pencerdd* (chief of songs), the *bardd teulu* (household bard), and the *cerdor* (minstrel), all of which were eventually grouped under the general term b. In Gaul these poets enjoyed special social status and passed on their rights and responsibilities to their heirs. From the 18th century to the present, the term has come to mean simply a *poet*. See *names for poets* in APPENDIX 1.

barzelleta /bärtselä′tä/ an Italian verse form originally characterized by a build-up of unconnected and sometimes senseless subject matter composed in similarly haphazard rhythms. See *forms* in APPENDIX 1.

base rhythm: See GROUND RHYTHM.

bathos (Greek for "depth, profundity") an unintended and excessive sinking from the lofty into the absurd and ridiculous just at the climactic point where true PATHOS and grandiloquence are called for. Strained, insincere, and overly sentimental writing are hallmarks of this negative effect. The term was originally used by Pope in his comic essay *On Bathos, or, of the Art of Sinking in Poetry* (1728) which was based on Longinus' *On the Sublime.* See ANTICLIMAX. See also *figures of pathos* in APPENDIX 2, and *control* in APPENDIX 1.

bdelygmia (from Greek for "a cutting") an emotional figure of speech that expresses ill wishes upon some person or thing. See FIGURES OF SPEECH. See also *figures of pathos* in APPENDIX 2.

beast epic a long allegorical tale based on a single episode that uses animals, such as the sly fox, the proud cock, the royal lion, for its main characters. The origins of the form are uncertain; some scholars point to folk origins, others to Latin scholastics. The oldest attributable example is that of Paulus Diaconus who was a clerk in the court of Charlemagne in 782–86. The Latin collection of fables by Phaedrus called *Aesop's Fables* (first century A.D.) and the 12th century *Le Roman de Renard* in France are the most famous examples of the genre. In the Middle Ages, the form was used as a vehicle for serious instruction. Other writers such as Chaucer (*The Nun's Priest's Tale*), Spenser (*Mother Hubberd Tale*), and Goethe also used the form. See ALLEGORY and BEAST FABLE. See also *forms* in APPENDIX 1.

beast fable   a short tale whose main characters are animals, as in *Aesop's Fables*. See BEAST EPIC. See also *forms* in APPENDIX 1.

beast language   a term used by the American Beat poet Michael McClure (see BEATS) for spontaneous poems written in a sort of phonetic English ("eers" for ears, "noze" for nose). Theoretically, it seems the language of the poem moves backward from conceptual words to an intelligence of pure sound utterance that calls attention to the form, meaning, and derivation of the word. The form is probably meant to be experienced more than intellectually understood, an experience that presumably links the reader with his own senses and the animal origins of language. See TRANS-SENSE VERSE. See also *diction* in APPENDIX 1.

Beats   (also known as "Beatniks"; perhaps from *beat* as in "defeated," and *nik*, Russian for "agent" or "concerned person") a 1950s movement of American writers (and nonwriters) who rebelled against the customs, values, and conventions of mid-twentieth-century America. They promulgated anti-intellectual and nihilistic behavior in a variety of expressive modes ranging from spontaneous jazz-poetry readings and *happenings* to experiments with drugs and writing. American writers such as Allen Ginsberg, Jack Kerouac, Gregory Corso, and Lawrence Ferlinghetti wrote in colloquial, loosely structured romantic styles which often focused on the absurdness of contemporary existence. *The Evergreen Review* in New York and the City Lights Press in San Francisco are two of the most famous outlets for their writing. The Second Culture in Russia and poets in England, Germany, Scandinavia, Italy, and other countries followed the example of the American B. in protesting social and political values in their respective countries. Historically, the B. have had a large impact on altering the lifestyle and writing styles in America. The B. share stylistic tendencies with the NEW YORK POETS.

beginning rhyme   (also known as "initial rhyme") a rarely used form of rhyme that occurs in the first syllable of a line. It has the mnemonic value and impact of INTERNAL RHYME rather than END-RHYME. Sidney Lanier's well-known poem *The Symphony* contains the device. See ALLITERATION and RHYME. See also HEAD RHYME.

belles-lettres   /bel letr'/ (French for "fine letters") originally, writing (in any genre) that displayed high aesthetic and imaginative qualities. Nowadays, the term has devolved in its connotations and has generally come to mean either light and frivolous writing or works whose task it is to appreciate and to extol the beauty to be found in literature in general. See PRECIOUSNESS. See also *forms* in APPENDIX 1.

bestiary   (from Latin for "cattle, beasts of the farm") a verse or prose collection describing the characteristics of both natural and mythical beasts, birds, and reptiles, such as the phoenix and the unicorn. The genre was developed to carry moral instruction by the Greek Physiologus in 150 A.D. and has continued to be used both for that purpose and as a rich repository of legendary and symbolic images for artists and writers around the world. Milton, Dryden, and Lyly, among others, adapted the material in the genre for their own work. See *forms* in APPENDIX 1.

billingsgate rough and abusive language meant as a harangue. The term, named after a London fish market, is derived from the notorious and colorful language of fishwives who delighted in abusing passersby. Shakespeare's rowdy Falstaff uses this type of language occasionally. See BDELYGMIA. See *figures of pathos* in APPENDIX 2, and *humor* in APPENDIX 1.

biographical criticism a form of *relativistic* and *historical criticism* (see CRITICISM) that reaches an evaluation or judgment of a work in relation to the author's personal history and the times in which he lived. See *criticism* in APPENDIX 1.

bird's-eye view (see CINEMATIC TECHNIQUES) a high-angle camera shot used in film-making that forces the viewer to "look down" on his subject in both literal and figurative senses. See also *cinematic terms* in APPENDIX 1.

blank verse (from equating blanks with prose) unrhymed lines of iambic pentameter often used in long poems and dramatic verse. The form is very flexible and adapts itself well to monologues and soliloquies in which richness and variation are key qualities. But it has also been a favorite and dependable form for a variety of moods and subjects over the past four hundred years. It is the most common form of stichic verse in the English language. Surrey's translation of *The Aeneid* (1540) was the first use of the meter, and it became the standard measure for Elizabethan and later drama. It reached its highest expression in the hands of Marlowe, Shakespeare, Milton, Wordsworth, Eliot, and Stevens. In recent times, critics tend to refer to any unrhymed metrical form as b.v., but the form is not used in CONTEMPORARY POETRY as much as it was in the past. See *forms* in APPENDIX 1.

blason (from Old High German for "shield"; also spelled "blazon") a short poem containing lines of eight to ten syllables, an epigrammatic conclusion, and a theme espousing praise or blame. Though it has at times been used as a form for satire, or the description of a single object, its most celebrated use is in describing a single aspect or part of a woman's body. *Blasons du Corps Feminin* (1550) is an anthology devoted to poems praising the female anatomy. The term originated in 1536 with Clément Marot's *Blason de Beau Tétin*. See *forms* in APPENDIX 1.

block poem a contemporary term indicating the typographical stichic form of a poem, usually of fifteen to forty lines in length, without stanzaic breaks. The space limitations of today's journals are said to have popularized this fashionable form, which is often characterized by economy and succinctness of expression. See STICH. See also *forms* in APPENDIX 1.

blues (from *blue devils*, agents of depression and melancholy) a melancholy song of loss or pain accompanied by guitar music and based on a repeating three-line set of lyrics. Although the songs were not known as "blues" until they were introduced into the mainstream of popular American music, they probably originated from the spontaneous "hollers" about hard times sung by Southern slaves and prisoners. Images of trains, prisons, and hard labor are common, and the themes usually concern oppression or loss of love. W.C. Handy, author of *The St. Louis Blues*, is the genre's most renowned composer, and Langston Hughes based much of his poetry on the form. See *forms* in APPENDIX 1.

boasting poem a poem whose speaker boasts of his prowess in battle as exemplified by the Old English epic *Beowulf*. The genre is very common throughout oral literature. See *forms* in APPENDIX 1.

bob and wheel (*bob*, from colloq. *to take up a bob*, to join in a refrain) the small REFRAIN that follows each stanza or verse of a song. The *bob* is the short first line of the whole refrain, which is called the *wheel*. The form was often used in Middle English romances. In *Sir Gawain and the Green Knight*, each unrhymed alliterative stanza ends with a bob of two syllables which rhymes with the second and fourth lines of the wheel, and the wheel is written in ballad form (8686, or 6666), rhymed alternately. The popular American folk poet Edgar Guest was fond of using the form. See *forms* in APPENDIX 1.

bombast (from the manners of the 16th-century alchemist Paracelsus, whose real name was Theophrastus Bombastus von Hohenheim; eventually from Medieval Latin *bombax*, for "cotton") a pejorative term for a type of DICTION that is verbose and inflated. Usually, b. is accompanied by extravagant IMAGERY and has the effect of making the speaker appear insincere and pretentious because his diction is disproportionate to his SUBJECT MATTER. B. is often found in the heroic drama of the late 17th and early 18th centuries, especially in Elizabethan tragedies. Marlowe's *Tamburlaine the Great* is often cited as a play that uses b. In general, most modern poets try to avoid b., though some, like the poets of SURREALISM and DADA, use it for comic or satiric effects. See *devices of poetic license* in APPENDIX 2, and *control* in APPENDIX 1.

bomphiologia speech or writing unintentionally pompous or bloated. Usually known as a "tolerable vice of language," it is a genre derived from a speaker's effort to seem more educated or elevated than he really is. See *defects in control* in APPENDIX 1, *devices of poetic license* in APPENDIX 2, and *diction* in APPENDIX 1.

bond density the thickness of sonic texture, based on a work's ASSONANCE, CONSONANCE, ALLITERATION, full and near RHYME, sound system, etc. B.d. may tend toward EUPHONY or CACOPHONY, depending upon the author's intention, but its function as part of the AESTHETIC SURFACE is structural. See SONIC STRUCTURE.

bonus (assumed to be derived from New York Stock Exchange slang)

William Stafford's term for the lucky and happy accidents of language and insight that sometimes occur to a poet while he is composing a poem.

bouts-rimés /bo͞orēmā'/ (French for "rhymed ends, end-rhymes") a set or sets of rhyming words conceived outside of lines of verse that were then fitted into an established form such as the SONNET. Originated and enjoyed in 17th-century Paris, the object of the game was to create a list of incongruous rhymes that would fit naturally and gracefully into a conventional form. The game declined in popularity around the 19th century. See *game forms* under *form* in APPENDIX 1. Also see RHYME.

brachycatalectic /braki-/ (from Greek for "short and incomplete") the specific kind of TRUNCATION of a line of verse in which two end syllables are deleted.

brachylogia /braki-/ (from Greek for "short of speech") a series of nouns that omits the conjunction between single words.

breve /brēv/ (from Old High German for "to point out") the mark (˘) that indicates a short syllable in the scansion of QUANTITATIVE VERSE. The symbol for a long syllable is called a MACRON, and the time it takes to pronounce a short syllable (duration) is called a MORA. See ACCENT and ICTUS. See also *grammatical constructions that are technically incorrect* in APPENDIX 2.

broadside (from *broadsheet*) originally, a BALLAD printed on one side of a large piece of paper called *folio sheet*. The ballad usually dealt with a current event or issue and was meant to be sung to a well-known air. B. ballads were very popular in Great Britain in the 16th century when they were hawked in the streets and at county fairs. Quite often they had a decorative woodcut and named the air they were to be sung to. Though the ballads were usually DOGGEREL verse, many were eventually made into folk songs.

In America, the b. ballad was very popular in the last part of the 19th century. Today, the term has come to mean a single poem published on high quality paper in a LIMITED EDITION of one or two hundred copies. The poet usually signs them, and they are framed and hung like a poster or painting. *See publishing formats* under *forms* in APPENDIX 1.

broken rhyme a word broken at the end of a line so as to highlight the rhyming syllable. Although the device has been employed at times for the sake of humor, serious poets such as Shakespeare, e.e. cummings, and Robert Lowell have used it. See RHYME.

bucolic /byo͞okol'ik/ (from Greek for "herdsman") originally, PASTORAL writing, especially about shepherds and the rural life, that is formal and imaginative in its conception. Virgil's ten pastoral poems are an early example of the genre, which is also known as an ECLOGUE. In recent times the term has been loosened to encompass any poetry that deals romantically with rustic life, but in modern criticism the term is often used pejoratively. See *forms* in APPENDIX 1.

burden (West Germanic for "extension") the last line of a verse or song that has the responsibility of carrying the main theme. See BOB AND WHEEL and REFRAIN. See also *forms* in APPENDIX 1.

buried theme thematic content or statements that are implied or obliquely put forth in a poem, as contrasted to the explicit thematic statements carried by poetic refrains and other such devices (see BURDEN and REFRAIN). As an intentional technique, it may be used to the writer's advantage to suggest rather than to state his theme so that the reader is more fully engaged in the work and, in a sense, recreates the poem. As an unintended device or result, the b.t. represents a defect. For other defects in writing, see *defects in control* in APPENDIX 1.

burlesque (from Italian for "ridicule, mockery") a humorous genre of writing that through its distance between subject matter and style creates a disparity ridiculing attitudes, characters, or conventions. The high forms of b. are the MOCK EPIC (Pope's *The Rape of the Lock*) and the PARODY. The low forms of the b. are represented by HUDIBRASTIC VERSE and the TRAVESTY. See SATIRE. See also *humor* in APPENDIX 1.

Burns stanza (also known as "Burns meter," "Scottish stanza," "habbie stanza," and "six-line stave") a stanza containing six lines rhyming aaabab, with the first, second, third, and fifth lines in tetrameter, and the fourth and sixth lines in dimeter, as in Burns' *To a Louse* and *Holy Willie's Prayer*. The B.s. is a variant of the TAIL-RHYME STANZA or RIME COUÉE because it features a series of lines succeeded by a shorter line, or tail line, which rhymes with a subsequent shorter line. Poets of English romances, Provençal poems of the 11th century, and writers of the Miracle Plays of the Middle Ages have used the form. See *forms* in APPENDIX 1.

C

cabal /kəbal'/ (from Hebrew for "received lore") a literary clique; also, a type of ACROSTIC whose letters spell out the initials of the five ministers of Charles II, *C*lifford, *A*rlington, *B*uckingham, *A*shley, and *L*auderdale. See ANAGRAM and PALINDROME.

caccia /kä'chä/ (Italian for "chase") an Italian verse form believed to have originated from the MADRIGAL. But it may have a different origin because the c. was known as early as in late-13th-century France. The c. has a final REFRAIN, and the main body is of a varying number of lines with or without RHYME. As its name indicates, the term was probably derived from the hunt, or possibly from its musical rhythm with two or more voices repeating lines reminiscent of a "hunt" between the voices. The form flourished in the 14th and 15th centuries in Italy. See *forms* in APPENDIX 1.

cacemphaton (Greek for "ill-sounding or equivocal") the use of foul speech or a combination of cacophonous sounds, often employed, as in this example, with an EPITHET: "You belly-aching, belligerent s.o.b.'s better brain-up fast." See BDELYGMIA, BILLINGSGATE, and BOMBAST. See also *devices of poetic license* in APPENDIX 2, and *diction* in APPENDIX 1.

cacophony /kəkof'-/ (from Greek for "ill-sounding") a harsh, unpleasant combination of discordant sounds, the opposite of EUPHONY. The use of c. may be intentional, as Browning and Eliot meant it to be, or it may be unintentional, thereby ruining the poem. Some examples of intentional c. include lines of Poe's *The Bells* and Browning's image of a flame being lit in his *Meeting at Night*. See SIBILANTS. See also *devices of poetic license* in APPENDIX 2.

cacosyntheton /-sin'-/ (Greek for "bad composition") a figure of POETIC LICENSE and a "tolerable poetic vice," similar to ANASTROPHE in that it marks a departure from normal word order by placing adjectives after nouns: "child innocent, youth unkempt, man remorseful." See *devices of poetic license* in APPENDIX 2.

cacozelia (Greek for "faulty imitation") a figure of POETIC LICENSE and a "tolerable poetic vice" that indicates the use of a classical language (especially Greek or Latin) to impress an audience: "As I have said, *passim*, the idea *tempus fugit* becomes *reducto ad absurdum* when *in terrorem*." See *devices of poetic license* in APPENDIX 2, and *diction* in APPENDIX 1.

cacozelon /kəkoz'-/ (Greek for "faulty imitation") a poetic device that employs a kind of misnomer in which one uses the wrong word in a botched attempt to appear learned: "My *conjuncture*, Sir, is that you are *fleckless*, and cannot even *puncture* a sentence properly." The character Archie Bunker, on the television show *All in the Family*, uses c. often. See MALAPROPISM and SPOONERISM. See also *devices of poetic license* in APPENDIX 2, and *diction* in APPENDIX 1.

Cadavre Exquis /kädä′vrekskĕ′/ (French for "exquisite corpse") a game of chance in poetry, invented by the Surrealists, which was meant to break through and transform clichéd language in order to discover new modes of perception. Each participant fills in a preassigned grammatical unit in a sentence without having seen the word or words that precede his or her own. The result is a series of unusually put-together phrases in correct grammatical order. C.E. is a phrase from one of these games. See *game forms* under *forms* in APPENDIX 1.

cadence (from Italian for "fall [of the voice]") a larger, looser unit of RHYTHM than the metrical FOOT (see METER). It relies on symmetry and balance between the phrasal units rather than a strict pattern of STRESS. The term c. is used to describe the rhythm of FREE VERSE, Biblical poetry, and poetic prose.

In the late 19th and early 20th centuries, many poets, including the Imagists, abandoned formal metrics for the c. which some, such as Pound, thought was closer to music and dance, as opposed to the mechanical rhythm of a metronome. W.C. Williams also called for a new measure based on speech, not metrics. Whitman is always referred to as the American originator of the c. rhythm. See also PROSE RHYTHM, PROSE, STYLE, and SCANSION.

caesura /sizoo′rə/ (Latin for "a cutting, a metrical pause") a PAUSE marked by (‖) in the RHYTHM or METER of a line. It can be caused by PUNCTUATION, SYNTAX, RHYME, or the sound and meaning of the preceding word. Usually, it occurs in the middle of a line (*medial c.*), but it can occur at the beginning (*initial c.*) or end (*terminal c.*) of a line. As a device, it can add variation to a regular rhythm or meter. In traditional terminlogy, c. indicates a pause within the metrical FOOT; and DIERESIS indicates a pause that coincides with the end of the foot. But usually, c. is a general term indicating any pause within a line.

The position of the c. was very regular in Classical prosody; however, with the development of the iambic pentameter line, the position became unpredictable. Alexander Pope claimed that in a ten-syllable line there is a natural break at the fourth, fifth, or sixth syllable.

Paradoxically, the c. is used either to emphasize the formality of poetic construction and its distance from conversation, or to loosen a strict meter and make it more natural and conversational. For example, Frost's *Out, Out* uses predictable c. placement for formal effect, while Eliot's *Journey of the Magi* varies the c. for a conversational effect.

A c. is said to be *masculine* if it follows an accented syllable, *feminine* if it follows an unaccented syllable. Sometimes the feminine c. is divided into (1) *lyric*, when the syllable before the pause is the normal unstressed element in the foot, and (2) *epic*, when an extra unstressed syllable occurs at the pause. See ACCENTUAL-SYLLABIC VERSE, ACCENTUAL VERSE, CADENCE, METER, RHYTHM, and SCANSION.

canción /känthyōn'/ (Spanish for "song") any Spanish poem made up of strophes in Italianate lines (11 and seven syllables) in which the first strophe stands as a model for all succeeding strophes. Many variations have been developed. See *forms* in APPENDIX 1.

canto (Italian for "song," from Latin *cantus*) originally, a section of a NARRATION long enough to be sung by a BARD or MINSTREL in one singing. Now it usually means a section of an EPIC or NARRATIVE POEM corresponding to chapters in a novel. Dante's *La Divina Comedia*, Spenser's *The Faerie Queene*, and Byron's *Childe Harold's Pilgrimage* are all divided into cantos. Ezra Pound used *The Cantos* as the title for his long poetic treatment of historic themes. See *forms* in APPENDIX 1.

canzo /kan'zō/ (from Provençal for "song"; also known as "canso," "chanso," or "chanson") a structurally diverse and subtly crafted genre of Provençal lyrical love poetry, refined by the trouvères of 12th- and 13th-century northern France. The lyric's themes predictably involve concepts of chivalric love developed with an ambition of perfecting original techniques in writing these poems. Early examples were composed of two-line stanzas of equal length with a concluding refrain after each stanza. Later, the five- or six-stanzaic structure proliferated into a variety of metrical and structural forms. Nowadays, c. generally indicates a poem, written in a simple style, which is intended to be sung. See *forms* in APPENDIX 1.

canzone /kanzō'nē/ or /käntsō'nä/ (Italian for "song") a French-Italian lyric poem, similar to a MADRIGAL, expressing praise of love, nature, or beauty, and which is meant to be accompanied by music. Although the form varies in structure, it is generally composed of five or six stanzas of seven to 20 lines apiece, and contains a shorter, concluding ENVOY. The *c. petrarchesa*, based on Petrarch's *canzoniere*, is the most sophisticated type; the Italian *ballata* and French-Italian *c. epico-lirica* are less refined variations. Dante, Leopardi, and Tasso were known to use the form.

caricature (from Italian for "to load, to exaggerate") a form of cartoon or exaggeration that depicts physical features or personalities via distortion. It is similar to PARODY and BURLESQUE but is more obvious. Etherege's *The Man of Mode; or Sir Fopling Flutter* depicts the humorous mien of the Restoration fop. See HYPERBOLE. See also *clichés* in APPENDIX 1, and *humor* and *light verse* in APPENDIX 1.

carmen /kär'men/ (Latin for "song, lyric") a term originally applied to oral poetry divinely inspired. The poet is the vehicle of an impulse to create hymns, spells, prophecies, and oracles. Horace, in his *Odes*, adopts this ancient role for himself. The term is used today to imply the spiritual and serious nature of a poetic work. See ANAGOGE.

carmen figuratum (Latin for "shaped song, poem") a poem whose TYPO-GRAPHICAL ARRANGEMENT depicts its subject matter. Herbert's *Easter*

Wings and Dylan Thomas' *Vision and Prayer* are well-known English examples. It was a common form in the RENAISSANCE. Herbert's *The Altar* is an obvious shape:

> A broken ALTAR, Lord, thy servant reares,
> Made of a heart, and cemented with teares,
> Whose parts are as thy hand did frame;
> No workman's tool hath touch'd the same.
> A HEART alone
> Is such a stone
> Thy power doth cut,
> Wherefore each part
> Of my hard heart
> Meets in this frame,
> To praise thy name.
> That if I chance to hold my peace
> These stones to praise thee may not cease.
> O let thy blessed SACRIFICE be mine,
> and sanctifie this ALTAR to be thine.

See also CONCRETE POETRY, and see *forms* in APPENDIX 1.

carpe diem /kär′pä dē′am/ or /kär′pē dī′əm/ (Latin for "seize the day") Horace's term for the theme of life's ephemerality. Generally speaking, the theme is used to persuade an audience to enjoy life's pleasures while there is still time, or to indicate the sad futility of that pursuit. The call is often used to dissuade virgins from their chaste state, to call attention to the appreciation of nature, and to rectify the fallen moral state of man. Flowers, particularly the rose, are often used as symbols for c.d. Milton, Blake, Shakespeare, Omar Khayyam, Spenser, and Herbert are only a few of the famous writers who have written on this theme. See "UBI SUNT" FORMULA.

catachresis /-krē′-/ (Greek for "misuse [of a word]") a figure of similarity and dissimilarity, which uses a word that belongs in one dimension of meaning in another dimension. For example, the phrase "I'm broke" denotes destruction or breaking but is normally applied to one's financial state. Another type of c. is sensually oriented: "Her hands sniffed into the bag of candy," in which hands act as if they were a nose. This type of surprising METAPHOR also lends itself to unexpected exchanges between the domains of the CONCRETE and the ABSTRACT, as in "Brightness falls from the air" (Thomas Nashe). See CATACHRETIC METAPHOR. See also *figures of similarity and dissimilarity* in APPENDIX 2, and *figurative expressions* in APPENDIX 1.

catachretic metaphor /-kret′ik/ a type of strained METAPHOR that may be figuratively effective but is logically misused, as in Shakespeare's "'Tis deepest winter in Lord Timon's purse." Only the staunchest literalist would look for ice and snow at the bottom of Lord Timon's purse. See also CATACHRESIS and PERIPHRASIS.

catacomesis a figure that compares and orders entities of greater, lesser, or equal characteristics, such as a series of words that progresses from the greatest to the least: "He is both a god and a man, of high passion and small deeds." In this order, c. is the opposite of CLIMAX in AUXESIS. See *figures comparing greater, lesser, or equal things* in APPENDIX 2.

catalexis /-lek'sis/ (Greek for "leaving off") a deletion of the first or last syllable in a regular metrical line of verse. The omission of the first syllable is specifically called *initial c.*, *initial truncation*, *acephalous line*, or *headless line*. A line that omits its final syllable is called *terminal c.* or *terminal truncation*. A line omitting two initial or terminal syllables is termed BRACHYCATALECTIC. Poets use various forms of c. to keep serious poems from sounding like light verse, and to add CONTRAPUNTAL music to relatively simple meters. See the opposite terms ACATALECTIC, HYPER-CATALECTIC, and ANACRUSIS.

catalogue verse (*catalogue*, from Greek for "list") a listing of entities used to show progression, generation, or commonality. The technique of c.v. is used, usually without transitional ideas or phrases, for the sake of compactness, dramatic effect, and economy. Early examples can be found in Genesis' genealogical list and the *Iliad's* recounting of the Trojan War heroes. Modern examples show up in the work of Whitman, Allen Ginsberg, and Philip Levine. See LIST POEM. See also *forms* in APPENDIX 1.

catalytic event (*catalytic*, from Greek for "able to dissolve"; also called "initiating action" or "initiating event") an action, idea, or setting that precipitates a dramatic turn in PLOT by transforming, defining, or accelerating conditions toward a moment of recognition or CLIMAX. The c.e. can be part of the DRAMATIC SITUATION of a poem and, therefore, can precede the actual contents of the poem, occur during the poem, or be implied after the closure of the poem. A recent variation of this plot element is the TRIGGERING TOWN, Richard Hugo's use of dramatic landscape as a metaphor for psychological conditions or tensions.

cataplexis (Greek for "striking down [by terror]") a figure of emotion (PATHOS) threatening a catastrophe upon some person or thing: "If you keep this up, you'll be sorry you ever lived!" See *figures of pathos* in APPENDIX 2.

catastrophe that part of DRAMATIC STRUCTURE in which the protagonist meets his demise and a resultant new or restored order is established. See *dramatic terms* in APPENDIX 1.

categoria (from Greek for "accusation, assertion") a figure of emotion or ethics in speech exposing some secret evil in an opponent: "You say you want peace / but you are planning war." See *figures of pathos* in APPEN-DIX 2.

catharsis /-thär'-/ (Greek for "a cleansing") generally, a purging of emotion. According to Aristotle's *Poetics*, "tragedy through pity and fear effects a purgation of such emotions." Plato's religious view of the term was a separation of the soul from the body's desires and demands so that the resultant balance would lead to purification. Although there is no one definitive literary interpretation, the term is generally meant to indicate a character's or audience's emotional or psychological release at living through or viewing the resolution of conflict in a DRAMATIC SITUATION. See CLIMAX and CRISIS. See also *dramatic terms* in APPENDIX 1.

cauda: See CODA.

caudate sonnet /kô′dā/ (*caudate*, from Latin for "tail") a form of TAILED SONNET that has fourteen lines followed by from one to six lines that summarize the themes or motifs, as in Milton's *On the New Forces of Conscience under the Long Parliament.* Usually the CODA is introduced by a half-line, which is followed by a COUPLET in pentameters. See *forms* in APPENDIX 1.

Cavalier Poets /kavəlēr′/ (*cavalier*, from Late Latin for "horseman") a 17th-century group of sophisticated English poets who wrote of love and patriotic affections. The most accomplished C.P., Lovelace, Suckling, Herrick, Carew, and Waller, considered their work influenced by Ben Jonson—indeed, called themselves "Sons of Ben." They eschewed the SONNET in favor of shorter lines and tight diction and structure, and they became known as melodious and gay stylists prone to Latin influences. Robert Browning, at a later time, was influenced by the C.P., and Theodore Roethke cited Waller as an important influence on his poetry.

cento (Latin for "patchwork") a pastiche verse made up of snatches from one or various authors, usually of Latin or Greek origin. Homer, Virgil, Petrarch, and Cicero provided rich and varied material for the c. See CHRESTOMATHY. See also *forms* in APPENDIX 1.

central image: See CONTROLLING IMAGE.

centrifugal interpretations and **centripetal interpretations** two forms of direction that a reader's attention must travel, according to Northrop Frye. The outward (*centrifugal*) *interpretation* of words is from the tautological unit of each word to its meaning, while the inward (*centripetal*) *interpretation* is a journey from the meanings of a word toward its association in the larger, surrounding text.

centrifugal structure /-trif′-/ (*centrifugal*, from Latin for "fleeing the center") the argumentative development of a poem that moves from its thesis outward to associate itself with various and disparate images and concepts that are related to one another through the author's TONE, THEME, and LOCATION. Robert Duncan uses this sort of thematic development of his argument in what has come to be called PROJECTIVE VERSE or OPEN FIELD COMPOSITION. The poem, or the field of the poem, has a large and loose structure and a widely focused thematic statement so that it can accommodate an almost unlimited amount of tangential content. Robert Duncan's *Food for Fire, Food for Thought* exemplifies the structure.

The c.s. can be schematically represented as:

See CENTRIPETAL-CENTRIFUGAL STRUCTURE, CENTRIPETAL STRUCTURE, CIRCULAR STRUCTURE, DEDUCTIVE-INDUCTIVE STRUCTURE, DEDUCTIVE STRUCTURE, INDUCTIVE-DEDUCTIVE STRUCTURE, INDUCTIVE STRUCTURE.

centripetal-centrifugal structure the combination of outward- and inward-moving thematic developments that, through association, refer inward to

the poem itself and outward to associatively related images and concepts. Michael Burkard's *Strange Meadowlark* exemplifies the structure. The c.-c.s. can be represented schematically as:
See also CENTRIFUGAL STRUCTURE, CENTRIPETAL STRUCTURE, CIRCULAR STRUCTURE, DEDUCTIVE-INDUCTIVE STRUCTURE, DEDUCTIVE STRUCTURE, INDUCTIVE-DEDUCTIVE STRUCTURE.

centripetal structure /-trip'-/ (*centripetal*, from Latin for "seeking the center") the argumentative development of a poem that moves from various levels and angles of thought inward toward its thesis, which may be stated or unstated, at the center of the poem's structure. Louis Simpson's *The Silent Piano* is an example.
The c.s. can be schematically represented as:
See also CENTRIFUGAL STRUCTURE, CENTRIPETAL-CENTRIFUGAL STRUC- TURE, CIRCULAR STRUCTURE, DEDUCTIVE-INDUCTIVE STRUCTURE, DEDUCTIVE STRUCTURE, INDUCTIVE-DEDUCTIVE STRUCTURE, INDUCTIVE STRUCTURE.

chain rhyme or chain verse a type of verse whose lines or stanzas are interlinked through RHYME or REPETITION, and whose last syllable in a line or stanza is repeated in new form or with new meaning in the succeeding line, as in Hopkins' "Despair, despair, despair, despair. / Spare!" The VILLANELLE can be considered a form of c.r. in which the repetition of variously ordered lines holds the poem together.

chance imagery a term, introduced by George Brecht in 1957, that refers to casual and incidental occurrences of images in nature, and images created by the artist with "a lack of conscious design . . . so that the images have their source in deeper-than-conscious areas of the mind." Brecht wanted a type of artistic imagery that was patterned after the randomness in nature, an endeavor that would bring the artist toward a more harmonious relationship with nature. See CHANCE POETRY and IMAGERY. See also *imagery* in APPENDIX 1.

chance poetry poetry that uses the element of chance as its ORGANIZING PRINCIPLE. Poets as diverse in style as John Cage and Donald Justice write c.p. The method of c.p. can range from the random selection of words to the placing of words in random order. See CHANCE IMAGERY.

chanso; chanson: See CANZO.

chanson baledée: See VIRELAY.

chanson de geste /shäNsôN'dəzhest'/ (French for "song of [great] deeds") an early French EPIC form recounting the deeds of fictitious, legendary, or historical heroic characters, such as Charlemagne and William of Orange. The early forms (*Chanson de Roland*, 1100 A.D.) are written in ten- or 12- line stanzas. By the 14th century, the form came to include supernatural characters, cycles in the life of a character, and lines numbering up to 1,000. The themes are usually of chivalric love and adventure. There are some 80 examples still in existence. See CANZO and TROUVÈRE. See also *forms* in APPENDIX 1.

chant royal /shäN'rô·äyäl'/ (French for "royal song") one of the most demanding French FIXED FORMS, composed in five 11-line stanzas that rhyme ababccdddedE. The c.r. concludes with an ENVOY of ddedE (an "E" indicates a refrain line). The form demands that no rhyming word appear twice, that the poem be addressed to a royal figure, that its theme be on a heroic subject, and that its diction suit the sophisticated speech of royal personages. The genre was originally used to couch a sensitive subject in allegorical terms. It is very rare in English. See *forms* in APPENDIX 1.

chapbook (literally, "cheapbook") originally, a pamphlet hawked on London streets by peddlars or "chapmen" in the 16th and 17th centuries. These pamphlets, invariably poorly printed and crudely illustrated, contained ballads, romances, biographies of notorious criminals, witchlore, or political essays. The pamphlets have been useful to modern scholars because they illuminate the trends and attitudes of that time. The term is now used to describe any small book (of about 20 pages) dealing with miscellaneous subjects. The c. has had a recent vogue among small presses, some of which produce fine books in LIMITED EDITION which are sometimes, ironically, quite expensive. See BROADSIDE. See also *publishing formats* under *forms* in APPENDIX 1.

character (from Greek for "a making distinctive") a person in a piece of literature whose identity is composed of easily recognizable (though at times complex) moral, intellectual, and ethical qualities. The *c. sketch* was a popular literary and dramatic genre in 17th- and 18th-century England and France. This form sketched out the obvious qualities and traits of a c. type such as the villainous "landlord" and the promiscuous "farmer's daughter." Its Greek origins reach back to Theophrastus' works in this genre. See CHARACTERIZATION. See also *dramatic terms* in APPENDIX 1.

characterismus a description concerning the body and/or mind of a character. C. is categorized under the rhetorical classification of "substance and quality." See the more general term HYPOTYPOSIS. See also *figures of subject and adjunct* in APPENDIX 2.

characterization the presentation in literature of fictitious people whose composite physical descriptions, attitudes, motives, and actions are lifelike enough for the reader to accept as representing real people. A *flat character* is one that remains undeveloped, while a *round character* is a fully fleshed-out portrait. If the character does not undergo change, its type is referred to as *static*; if the character is transformed somehow, it is termed *dynamic*. The proper selection and the particularization of detail make for characters that are specific but which contain universal significance. See CHARACTER and VERISIMILITUDE.

charientismus /kar-/ (from Greek for "gracefulness of style in unpleasant matters") the offering of pleasing, obsequious words, sometimes ironically, in order not to offend or to arouse displeasure. This figure of speech is listed under the rhetorical category of similarity and dissimilarity. For a related device, see EUPHEMISM. See also *figures comparing greater, lesser, or equal things* in APPENDIX 2.

charm (from Latin *carmen,* for "song, incantations") an oracular incantation, song, or verse meant to invoke or thwart the power of some deity or spirit. It was used to defeat threatening enemies or forces, instill luck and love, gain health, etc. Almost all preliterate communities practice charms as traditional and practical ceremonies. See *forms* in APPENDIX 1.

Chaucer stanza (also called "rhyme royal" and Troilus stanza) a seven-line STANZA in iambic pentameters, rhyming ababbcc. It is the only standard seven-line stanza in English, and is known as *rhyme royal* because King James I of Scotland used it. It is named after Chaucer who used it in the *Parliament of Fowls, The Clerk's Tale,* and *Troilus and Creseyde.* Wyatt, Shakespeare, and Masefield employed the form, which has such versatility that it can be used for narration, description, digression, and comment. As late as the 16th century, it was known as the standard English stanza to use for serious verse. See *forms* in APPENDIX 1.

chiasmus /kī·az′-/ (from Greek for "placing crosswise," or the Greek letter *x*) the semantic crisscrossing relationship between two pairs of independent and dependent clauses which, interchanged, would not distort the overall meaning of the construction (according to Hermogenes, a second-century rhetorician in Greece), as in Shakespeare's "Pardon me God, for I knew not what I did! / And pardon, father, for I know not thee!" More recently, c. has come to mean the placing together, with or without repetition, of sentence members that correspond in either syntax or meaning, or a rhetorical balance between two syntactically reversed parts of a sentence. See *grammatical devices of rhythm and balance* in APPENDIX 2.

Chicago Critics a group of authors associated with the University of Chicago who contributed to *Critics and Criticism: Ancient and Modern* (1952). They maintained that a particular critic's position will logically vary according to his experience of a piece of literature, his particular set of aesthetics and methodology for analyzing it, and the time in history during which the critic is living. Their second contribution was their Neo-Aristotelian aesthetic which rested on constructing principles and theories about a piece of literature only after experiencing it. In general, their criticism was more practical than theoretical. See CLASSICAL POETICS, CRITICISM, and NEW CRITICISM. See also *criticism* in APPENDIX 1.

choriamb /kō′ri·amb/ (from Greek for "choreus" plus "iambus"; also called "choriambus.") A combination of a "choree' (trochee) and an iamb, as in --˘˘--. It was often used by Sappho, Alcaeus, and Horace. See METER and SCANSION.

chrestomathy /-tom′-/ (from Greek for "useful learning") an anthology of selected passages in prose or verse by one author, such as *A Mencken Chrestomathy.* See ANALECTS, ANTHOLOGY, and CENTO. See also *publishing format* under *forms* in APPENDIX 1.

chria /krī'ə/ (Latin, from Greek) an expression of testimony in rhetorical logic that is a short summary of an action or saying and which names the quoted author: "Sir Isaac Newton spoke of gravity as an attracting force; Einstein said it was a physical corrugation of space." See *types of testimony* in APPENDIX 2.

Christabel meter /kris'-/ a four-stress line containing from seven to 12 syllables, usually part of iambic or anapestic couplets. C.m. derives its name from Coleridge's poem *Christabel*. The form is somewhat irregular since one of Coleridge's principles in this meter is to vary the line length according to dramatic passion. The accentual feature of the line had been previously used by the *Beowulf* author and Chaucer; Coleridge's contribution was to maintain a general pattern of four stresses in each line. See ACCENTUAL VERSE and METER. See *forms* in APPENDIX 1.

chronicle (from Greek for "time") a recorded history of events set in a temporal order. The c. functions more as a listing of events than an interpretation of them. The first outstanding book of an English prose c. is *The Anglo-Saxon Chronicle*, begun by King Alfred in the ninth century, which considers the history of that region from 60 B.C. to the 12th century. The c. was composed in prose or verse and contained both factual and legendary information. See *publishing format* under *forms* in APPENDIX 1.

chronographia (from Greek for "recording time") the creation of an era or milieu through words. The term is sometimes put into the rhetorical category of "substance and qualities." See HYPOTYPOSIS. See also *figures of subject and adjunct* in APPENDIX 2.

cinematic editing (*cinematic*, from Greek *kinema*, for "motion") the use of cuts and transitions as narrative and thematic devices in poetry. The terminology of filmmaking has been adopted by literary critics because both the filmmaker and the poet concern themselves with the expansion, compression, and simultaneity of time in narration, as well as elements of visual and verbal phrasing. For a fuller discussion of c.e., see CINEMATIC TECHNIQUES.

cinematic techniques devices of NARRATION and POINT OF VIEW that resemble the devices of filmmaking. Since the invention of cinema in the late 19th century, poets have seen the potential for using techniques borrowed from moving pictures, and filmmakers have seen the potential for using poetic techniques.Most of the c.t. applied to poetry have been borrowed from two basic areas in film: editing and camera positioning.

In the area of editing, techniques are concerned primarily with the creation of *cuts* and *transitions*. By these devices, an action is carried into the next action. The cutting and splicing of film segments has four basic purposes: (1) to expand or compress the actual time period of an event; (2) to show the simultaneity, emotional contrast, or equivalency of corresponding events (as in the use of ASSOCIATIONAL LOGIC, METAPHOR, and SYMBOL); (3) to insert a repeated visual (and sometimes aural) comment that anchors a series of shots to a motif or "idée fixe" (as in a

REFRAIN); and (4) to fill in or project pieces of PLOT by inserting scenes from the past or future.

In the area of camera positioning, techniques of placing and moving the camera create distinct fields of vision that evoke specific emotional responses in the viewer. Our point of view determines our role in the action (participant or observer), our attitude toward the action (sympathetic or antagonistic), and the intensity with which we undergo the drama.

Because c.t. have been widely adapted to poetry, and because the authors know of no comprehensive work on the cross fertilization of the two art forms, this essay will concern itself with an analysis of c.t. in poetry, discussed under four headings: *cuts, transitions, view,* and *movement.*

Cuts

A cut in film language is the joining together of separate shots so that the first shot is immediately replaced by the second. In poetry we call this immediate proximity of images, actions, or ideas a JUXTAPOSITION. There are four basic kinds of cuts: the *straight cut,* the *crosscut,* the *contrast cut,* and the *jump cut.*

The *straight cut* is linear in direction. It acts to further the plot or theme in a straightforward way, e.g., (cut 1) a girl goes to the store; (cut 2) she buys a loaf of bread. This type of cutting gives the film or poem a natural, easy sense of movement, and logical chronology. A good example of straight cutting is seen in William Stafford's poem *Traveling through the Dark.* The first stanza is:

>   (cut 1)   (cut 2)
> Traveling through the dark I found a deer
> dead on the edge of the Wilson River Road.
>   (cut 3)
> It is usually best to roll them into the canyon:
>   (cut 4)
> that road is narrow; to swerve might mean more dead.

The *crosscut* is used to show two different events happening at the same time. It is known in poetry jargon as the *cut and shuffle* (see CUT-AND-SHUFFLE POEM). D.W. Griffith was the first filmmaker to employ this technique; he used it to show actions taking place in separate locations: (cut 1) someone in distress; (cut 2) someone else trying to arrive on time for the rescue. Aside from this obvious kind of plot crosscutting, the crosscut can also be used to show ironic contrast or philosophical resignation: (cut 1) a man in the throes of a violent nightmare; (cut 2) the gentle fall of snow outside his house.

The *contrast cut* is similar to the crosscut. Both are used to heighten the tension in a situation, but the crosscut may use similar shots in juxtaposition, while a contrast cut always uses opposing shots. After establishing the character of an American soldier fighting in Vietnam, contrast cuts could be made to (1) the relative serenity of his wife's homelife back in the States; or (2) an act of infidelity on her part; or (3) the peaceful planting of a rice field which the soldier is about to shell. The possibilities are limited only by the imagination of the writer.

The *jump cut* is primarily used to shorten time. It is also known as *cutting to continuity*, a term that implies continuous but compressed action. The camera jumps from one action to another, showing only salient aspects of an action. In order to show a man entering a building it isn't necessary to record the full and actual span of time that the event takes in real life. The writer can merely show a shot of the building and the character entering it. In James Tate's humorous poem on the human ego, *Teaching the Ape To Write Poems*, the poet moves economically from one action to another in service of his message:

> They didn't have much trouble
> teaching the ape to write poems;
> first they strapped him into the chair,
> then tied the pencil around his hand
> (the paper had already been nailed down).
> Then Dr. Bluespire leaned over his shoulder
> and whispered into his ear:
> "You look like a god sitting there.
> Why don't you try writing something?"

Transitions

Transitions are editing devices that bridge separate images or actions. Transitions can be smooth, abrupt, expected, or unexpected. The two types of transitions that are most sophisticated and adaptable to poetry are the *metaphorical dissolve* and the *form dissolve*. In addition, there are the distinct but related devices of the *thematic montage*, the *flashback*, the *flashforward*, and the *substitute image* and the use of a *narrator*.

The *metaphorical dissolve* is a synthesis of two different actions or images that are united by their implied meanings. The first image is transformed into a second image that reinforces or changes the original image. For instance, a man who is about to have an automobile accident might be reading a "Dear John" letter behind the wheel of his moving car. The camera zooms in on the letter, which represents pain and loss, and then dissolves to the hospital sheet which covers the face of the man. The letter and the sheet then come to symbolize death. Similarly, in early gangster movies, it was common to see a man assaulted in a room that starts to spin; this image, in turn, dissolves into a spinning newspaper headlining the event.

The *form dissolve* links up two images with the same shape or color. A typical form dissolve might be one in which a man is pitting himself against torrential white water. As his boat capsizes, the camera focuses on the rushing water which is then dissolved into an image of water running down the bathroom sink where his wife is washing her hands. *Sound dissolves* are also common in films. A baby's wail might transform into a police siren. After a SYMBOL has been established in this way, it can be used as a LEITMOTIF in the film or poem. While film accommodates the form dissolve with a simple blurring or superimposition of images, poetry uses the SIMILE, METAPHOR, JUXTAPOSITION, and OFF-RHYME or PERFECT RHYME to effect a form dissolve.

The *thematic montage* intensifies the viewer's emotional reaction by putting together a series of metaphorically related images that collide around a theme. Section IV of Allen Ginsberg's poem *Kaddish* is an example of thematic montage in poetry.

The *flashback* is a segment of film that depicts action in the past. It can be used to heighten the drama of the present, to supply information not included in the surrounding text, or to connect the past with the present. It allows filmmakers and writers an economical and versatile use of chronology. Kimiko Hahn's poem *When You Leave* uses the flashback to explain the color of the sadness he feels. Actually, in this poem there are two past times, the near past in which his mother relates her story, and the distant past in which the events of the story took place. His flashback explains and dramatizes the present:

> This sadness could only be a color
> if we call it *momoiro*, Japanese
>
> for peach-color, as in the first story
> Mother told us: It is the color of the hero's skin
>
> when a barren woman discovered him
> inside a peach floating down the river.
>
> And of the banner and gloves she sewed
> when he left her to battle the horsemen, then found himself
>
> torn, like fruit off a tree. Even when he met a monkey,
> dog, and bird he could not release
>
> the color he saw when he closed his eyes. In his boat
> the lap of the waves against the hold
>
> was too intimate as he leaned back to sleep. He wanted
> to leave all thoughts of peach behind him—
>
> The fruit that brought him to her
> and she, the one who opened the color forever.

The *flashforward* is a segment of film that depicts action in the future. The device heightens present action by interesting the viewer in the process of discovering how the future event will come into being out of the present. The device has a prophetic quality and is often employed didactically as a moral lesson. W.S. Merwin uses the flashforward in his poem *For the Anniversary of My Death*, in which the speaker imagines the feelings he will have on the day he dies.

The *substitute image* is a cut in which a predictable image is replaced by an unexpected one. The second, substitute cut is usually metaphorically related to the first cut. The substitution may be used to increase drama, to make a statement about the action, to maintain decorum on subjects that are considered taboo, or to create a greater degree of anticipation by denying the satisfaction inherent in a linear structure. Sometimes the reader's imagination is able to supply the predictable, excised image (see STOCK RESPONSE). A common cinematic move is the scanning of a blank wall or ceiling while a murder is being committed off-camera. In the opening stanza of Dave Smith's poem *The Sex of Poetry*, the reader is graphically led through a scene of a woman undressing. Smith smoothly switches from images of her body to images of the natural world outside.

In this way, the natural landscape seems to comment on her sexuality. Part of the power of this stanza comes from the stock response of the reader who supplies the images of the substituted action.

The voice of a *narrator* is usually described as being in the first, second, or third person (I/we, you, he/she/they). Each of these persons has his own dramatic quality (see POINT OF VIEW). Sometimes in a story, poem, or film, characters within the omniscient narrator's voice speak about what they see. By using the eyes of the other characters, the narrator achieves a multiple viewpoint that lends the event a feeling of *synchronicity*, the simultaneous occurrence of separate events. The Japanese film *Rashmon* achieved this effect by having the same event recounted by several characters, each telling a different version of the story, according to his or her own prejudices. Norman Dubie uses similar narrator agents in his poem *1922*. As an old woman is dying, she looks out the window. The scene outside is depicted through her eyes, the eyes of a boy playing a tuba across the street, the eyes of passengers on a train, and the eyes of an elephant in a distant forest. All of these disparate characters are woven into the scene by switches in focus and point of view, and by metaphorical associations.

View

The view in film language corresponds roughly to the POINT OF VIEW in literary criticism. Both refer to the "eyes" through which we see the specific images and scenes that make up the work of art. Here we will be discussing two basic considerations of view: *range* and *angle*. (The related concept of *movement* will be discussed separately).

The *range* of the view refers to the distance of the camera from the scene. Scanning a battlefield from a distance makes the action smaller and lends an omniscient, impersonal quality to the scene; whereas looking up at the combatants through the eyes of a wounded soldier makes the action larger and more urgent. The view becomes more involving. In fact, the differences in range can determine the role of the viewer, whether he is a participant or observer.

The *establishing shot* is a long-range view of a scene. It is commonly used as an opening shot that allows the viewer a territorial framework in which to understand subsequent action. Films with exotic settings in which the characters are affected by the landscape are almost obligated to acquaint the viewer with the surrounding landscape, since it is a contributing factor to the plot and characters. *Lawrence of Arabia* opens with a long-distance shot of the desert over which a camel and rider move slowly against the rising sun. The vastness of the desert and the heat of the sun make an indelible statement about the harshness of survival in such a land. In the opening lines of Carl Sandburg's *Good Morning, America* he begins with an establishing shot of the megalithic urban setting:

> In the evening there is a sunset sonata comes to the cities.
> There is a march of little armies to the dwindling of drums.
> The skyscrapers throw their tall lengths of walls into black
>   bastions on the red west.
> The skyscrapers fasten their perpendicular alphabets far
>   across the changing silver triangles of stars and
>   streets.

Then the poem goes on to introduce man, the diminutive maker of these monolithic structures.

The *deep focus shot* enables the viewer to see background, middle-ground, and foreground clearly, a view that isn't normally possible with the naked eye or the unaltered camera. This shot was first used by Orson Welles in *Citizen Kane*. Ira Sadoff uses this perspective in his prose poem *Seurat*.

The *close-up shot* makes the viewer scrutinize details that might have otherwise been overlooked. In Maura Stanton's poem *The Conjurer* the speaker has cast a spell on the other characters, shrinking them to insect-sized complainers who infest her dreams:

> . . . those lovers crawled
> inside my left ear with candles,
> trying to find my brain in a fog.
> They moved deep among the stalactites
> searching for the magic spell they thought
> I'd lost in sleep . . .

The *angle* of the view refers to the elevation of the camera, as well as to the degree of variation from the horizontal position. The angle of a shot has an implied emotional message. For example, looking up at an accuser is more intimidating than looking straight at him. Of the many possible angles of the camera, only two have obvious parallels with poetic techniques: the *bird's-eye view* and the *low angle shot*.

The *bird's-eye view* is a high angle shot that makes the viewer look down on his subject in both a literal and figurative sense. The elevation of the camera implies attitudes such as condescension, omniscience, and accusation on the part of the viewer, and feelings of guilt, oppression, and insignificance on the part of the subject being viewed. At the beginning of the film *Twelve Angry Men* the boy on trial is shown from a bird's-eye view. The device implies that the boy is guilty. A similar shot occurs in the opening stanza of Alan Dugan's poem *For Masturbation*. The character in the poem is defiantly defending himself against feeling guilty for his desperate need. The reader sees the character crouched under a stoop.

The *low angle shot*, taken from ground level, gives a godlike stature to the subject and dwarfs the viewer's sense of himself. Cattle stampedes and onrushing trains are often depicted from this angle. In Donald Justice's poem *Anniversaries* the speaker remembers what it was like to be an infant:

> Many drew round me then,
> Admiring. Beside my bed
> The tall aunts prophesied,
> And cousins from afar,
> Predicting a great career.

Movement

A *pan* is the horizontal sweeping movement of a stationary camera. It is similar to the movement of our eyes when we are taking in a long, horizontal setting. Richard Hugo's opening lines in *2433 Agnes, First Home, Last House in Missoula* use the pan shot to establish familiarity with the setting:

It promises quiet here. A green Plymouth
has been a long time sitting across the street.
The lady in 2428 limps with a cane
and west of me fields open all the way
to the mountains, all the way I imagine
to the open sea.

A *moving shot* propels the viewer toward or away from the action. Poets often use it to recreate the excitement of a past experience. Reciting the landscape from a moving train, zooming toward a point of focus in a complex cityscape, or flying out at supersonic speed from the earth are a few of the various sets of compound images in which the viewer participates in a movement. James Dickey's poem *The Firebombing* reenacts a nighttime bombing mission over Japan. The reader experiences the topography of the land he's passing over as well as the excitement of the night flight.

Because no adequate terminology exists in literary criticism for the techniques described here, poets have freely borrowed and adapted the terminology of the cinema. See *cinematic terms* and *imagery* in APPENDIX 1.

cinquain /seNkeN'/ or /singkān'/ (French for "a collection of five") a five-line verse composed of lines of two, four, six, eight, and two syllables respectively. (It is somewhat near the American equivalent of a HAIKU or TANKA.)

In this specific sense, the term was first used by Adelaide Crapsey, but the five-line stanza form has medieval origins, and occurs in many forms. Many modern poets use a four-line ballad quatrain with an extra rhyming internal line to make it a c.; this stanza form is perhaps influenced by Coleridge's use of it in *The Rime of the Ancient Mariner*. Philip Larkin's *Home Is So Sad* is a contemporary example of the c.

The c. is often used for poetry of despair or solemnity because the inherent feeling of the form lends itself to imbalance and uncertainty. See *forms* in APPENDIX 1.

circular structure the argumentative development of a poem that thematically curves back upon itself, as opposed to a linear thematic development or developments that radiate outward or inward from a central thesis. Philip Larkin's poem *Poetry of Departures* demonstrates this structure.

The c.s. can be schematically represented as a line leading back to itself:

$$\circlearrowleft$$

A term that is related to the c.s. is the *circular ending*, signifying a reflexive CLOSURE of a poem. The circular ending is usually seen as a defect in composition since it simply restates an idea or posture and does not enrich the poem's depth or resonance, nor does it leap into a new domain of thought. Rather than acting to enlighten the reader, the circular ending reflects the poet's failure of ambition and imagination, as if the writer hit an insurmountable obstacle and had no recourse but to repeat himself. See

CENTRIFUGAL-CENTRIPETAL STRUCTURE, CENTRIFUGAL STRUCTURE, and CENTRIPETAL STRUCTURE.

Classical fallacy the misconceptions about language that were current among the Alexandrian scholars of the third century B.C. Alexandria had the greatest library in the world at the time, and since the language of the Classical texts (particularly Homer) differed from the language currently spoken in Alexandria and other Greek centers, the practice grew up of publishing commentaries on the texts as well as grammatical treatises elucidating the various difficulties that might trouble the reader of the earlier Greek poets. Misconceptions arose in two areas: (1) concerning the relation between written and spoken language; (2) concerning the manner in which languages develop.

(1) From the beginning, Greek linguistic scholarship was concerned primarily with the written language (the term "grammar" is derived from the word for "the art of writing"). Little or no distinction was drawn between sounds and the letters used to represent them. The spoken language was thought to be derived from the written language. The Alexandrian concern with literature reinforced the tendency.

(2) The Alexandrians thought that the language of fifth-century ATTIC writers was more "correct" than the colloquial speech of their own time. They also thought that the "purity" of a language is maintained by the usage of the educated people, and "corrupted" by the illiterate. This prejudice reigned unchallenged for 2,000 years. Modern linguists recognize that such terms as "purity" and "correctness," in this context, are meaningless.

Both of these misconceptions result from the traditional grammarian's assumption that the spoken language is inferior to and in some sense dependent upon the standard written language. The modern linguist, on the other hand, maintains that the spoken language is primary and that writing is essentially a means of representing speech in another medium. See AFFECTIVE FALLACY, EXPRESSIVE FALLACY, IMITATIVE FALLACY, INTENTIONAL FALLACY, PATHETIC FALLACY, and REDUCTIVE FALLACY.

Classical poetics a general term that refers either to poetic theory and dogma from 750 B.C. to 200 A.D. in Rome and Greece, or to the ideas found in Aristotle's *Poetics* and Horace's *Ars Poetica*. Briefly sketched, the main divisions, according to *The Princeton Encyclopedia of Poetry and Poetics*, are: (1) Preplatonic poetics (seventh century B.C.), which is characterized by moral and philosophical criticism; (2) Platonic poetics (427–347 B.C.), which deals with inspired sources of truth; (3) Aristotelian poetics (384–322 B.C.), which idealizes man's character and action; (4) Hellenistic poetics (third to first centuries B.C.), which defines various genres of poetry according to style; (5) Horatian poetics (65–8 B.C.), which refines Greek poetics; and (6) Greek and Latin rhetorical criticism (approximately first century and forward), which treats poetry as indistinguishable from prose and analyzes styles into high, middle, or low levels. Renaissance writers like Puttenham systemized the various devices in poetic composition as well as the various views of poetics. Although, in general, C.p.

views are on the wane, some of Aristotle's ideas have been revived directly through the theories of the CHICAGO CRITICS. See also CLASSICAL PROSODY, CRITICISM, and NEO-CLASSICISM.

Classical prosody the study of syllablic accentuation in Latin and Greek QUANTITATIVE METER, a system of scansion that eventually came to include not only musical pitch but also the duration of syllables. For instance, in Latin prosody the long syllable falls on the first part of a dissyllabic word, and on the last syllable of a polysyllabic word. In this system, two short syllables were considered equal to one long syllable. See METER.

clerihew /klerʹihyo͞o/ light verse that is similar to a LIMERICK in that it satirizes a well-known person by stating the ridiculous as biographical fact. The form usually contains two unevenly matched rhyming couplets and concentrates on illogical relationships between supposedly true events. The term takes its name from Edmund Clerihew Bentley (1875–1956) who invented the form and wrote the following example while listening to a chemistry lecture in school: "Sir Humphrey Davy / Abominated gravy. / He lived in the odium / Of having discovered sodium." See LIGHT VERSE. See also *forms* in APPENDIX 1.

cliché /klishäʹ/ (the name of a French stereotype plate used in printing) a hackneyed phrase or expression whose origins and freshness of appeal have been lost through overuse. For example, "hard as a nail," "sharp as a tack," "dead on my feet" are a few of the thousands of clichés that abound in the American language.

One of the first lessons every writing student learns is to avoid the use of clichés. "Blue sky," "green grass," "white snow" are other examples of the kind of driftwood that washes up in our speech when we don't take care to censor it in favor of more specific and original imagery. However, if clichés are used in a way that directs our attention to a new meaning or renews the cliché's origins, then they can become meaningful expressions.

Stanley Kunitz, speaking of certain elements of language that are available to be mined, could have been speaking of the use of clichés when he said:

> Language comes to you with certain pre-ordained conditions—
> it has for example, syntax; it has vocabulary; it has symbolic
> meaning. Nobody owns it. When you touch language, you touch
> the evolution of consciousness and the history of the tribe.
> You reach for a tool, a common tool, and you find to your
> surprise that it has a cuneiform inscription on the handle.

Here are some of the ways in which clichés have been exploited by contemporary poets:

Direct Use of the Cliché
Marvin Bell's bold offering of clichés concerning specific flowers and the rituals that accompany them comes through as touching and freshly perceived. Behind his guileless and exuberant tone, behind the metaphor of a bouquet as an anthology of poems, is the message that these flowers of emotion truly do speak for human innocence and vulnerability:

An Introduction to My Anthology
Such a book must contain—
it always does!—a disclaimer.
I make no such. For here
I have collected all the best—
the lily of the field among them,
forget-me-nots and mint weed,
a rose for whoever expected it,
and a buttercup for the children
to make their noses yellow.

Here is clover for the lucky
to roll in, and milkweed to clatter,
a daisy for one judgment,
and a violet for when he loves you
or if he loves you not and why not.
Those who sniff and say no,
these are the wrong ones (and
there are always such people!)—
let them go elsewhere and quickly!

For you and I, who have made it this far,
are made happy by occasions
requiring orchids, or queenly arrangements
and even a bird of paradise,
but happier still by the flowers of
circumstance, cattails of our youth,
field grass and bulrush. I have included
the devil's paint-brush
but only as a peacock among barn fowl.

The Unstated Cliché

Sometimes a poem will have a c. as its unstated theme. In the following poem by Thomas James, there lurks in the background the aphorism "Silence is golden," but the way in which James expresses this clichéd statement is utterly new and beautiful:

Letter to a Mute
If I could reach you now, in any way
At all, I would say this to you:
This afternoon I walked into a thicket

Of gold flowers that had no idea
What they were after. They couldn't hear a thing.
I walked among a million, small, deaf ears.

Breaking their gold into the afternoon.
I think they were like you, golden, golden,
Unable to express a single thing.

I walked among them, thinking of you,
Thinking of what it would be like
To be completely solitary. Once I was alone like that.

All the field was humming, brimming
With some brazen kind of song, and I
Thought that somehow I could disappear

Into the empty hall of your right ear,
Wandering through the slender bones of you.
But I know that I could never let you know

That it is late summer here, that I

Can hear the crickets every evening
Hollowing out the darkness at my window

That you have vanished into a dark tunnel
Where I have tried to reach you with my mouth
Till my mouth ran gold, spilling over everything.

Tonight I looked into your face, tenderly,
Tenderly, but I can never find you there.
I can only touch your quiet lips.

If I could stick my pen into your tongue,
Making it run with gold, making
It speak entirely to me, letting the truth

Slide out of it, I could not be alone.
I wouldn't even touch you, for I know
How you are locked away from me forever.

Tonight I go out looking for you everywhere
As the moon slips out, a slender petal
Offering all its gold to me for nothing.

Twisting the Cliché

There is a form of joke that twists aphorisms into new forms mostly for the fun of demonstrating how the original aphorism has come to be twisted, but the form could conceivably be used in a poem. The following story uses the saying "People in glass houses shouldn't throw stones" and cleverly invents a new aphorism based upon the wording of the old one. Watch how the plot develops the aphorism:

> Once upon a time there was an African king who was rumored to have a huge gold throne encrusted with gems which he had hidden somewhere in his village. Hunters who had heard about this treasure often found themselves setting out to find the tribe and steal the throne. One day a messenger arrived who told the king that a hunter only one day's journey from the village was approaching. The king instructed his people to build rafters in his hut, set the throne on top of them, and then to cover the ceiling with grass. That done, the king sat in a bamboo chair and awaited his greedy guest. When the hunter came and saw that the king was obviously poor, he questioned the king about the throne. The king laughed at the thought that such a priceless treasure could belong to so simple a people, and through his innocent manner convinced the hunter that the rumor was unfounded. As the hunter began to take his leave, there was a terrible sound of cracking timbers. The king looked up just in time to see the weighty throne come crashing down on him. With his last dying breath, the king exclaimed, "*People who live in grass houses shouldn't stow thrones.*"

Officialese Clichés

Within our language there exist many kinds of specialized jargon used as abbreviations for complex concepts or as terms for special activities. Biologists, lawyers, journalists, copywriters, actors, sociologists, and a host of other professionals have created and coined these terms for their own use. Poets have sensed the power of contrasting these terms to the terms of daily human existence and have capitalized upon the irony of setting the official tone against human, personal needs. A widely used technique in contemporary poetry is that of Miller Williams' poem *Sale*, where he parodies a classified advertisement.

Another kind of official jargon is that used by literary editors in the delicate ritual of rejecting unsolicited manuscripts. Philip Dacey has compiled a number of stock rejection-slip phrasings which, rather than offer the reader a clear and direct refusal, sidestep and obfuscate the issue in a language born out of evasion and compromise. Dacey's compendium contradicts itself and confuses the rejection with apologies. Here is the first stanza:

> *Form Rejection Letter*
> We are sorry we cannot use the enclosed.
> We are returning it to you.
> We do not mean to imply anything by this.
> We would prefer not to be pinned down about this matter.
> But we are not keeping—cannot, will not keep—
>   what you have sent us.
> We did receive it, though, and our returning it to you
>   is a sign of that.
> It was not that we minded your sending it to us
>   unasked.
> That is happening all the time, they
>   come when we least expect them,
>   when we forget we have needed or might yet need
>   them,
>   and we send them back.
> We send this back.
> It is not that we minded.
> At another time, there is no telling ...
> But this time, it does not suit our present needs.

Clichéd Ideas

Sometimes a poet will expose an unexamined attitude by stripping it down to a basic prejudice and presenting it as a self-evident truth. For instance, in Ira Sadoff's poem *A Concise History of the World* the speaker maintains the superiority of white Americans over the rest of the world, thus revealing himself to be a paranoid xenophobic fool. Similarly, Judith Kroll's poem *Dick and Jane* parodies the primers that millions of Americans read in the elementary grades. The purpose of this approach is to expose sexual stereotypes and propose a line of action:

> *Dick and Jane*
> Dick is the one with the weenie
> who gets to be doctor
> and never cries,
> in love with mechanics and motion.
>
> Jane is the one with nothing under her skirt,
> so soft and weepy,
> in love with rulers of earth.
>
> Dick gulps his soup and burns his tongue.
> Jane blows and blows to cool hers,
> it takes so long
> she has ages to see

that Dick is just a boy
with a rubber jiggler.
She can take his tongue on hers and cool it off.
She can cut his thing off at the root.
She can tuck him in bed and sing him to sleep.
She can leave him alone.

See COLLOQUIALISM, DEAD METAPHOR, FILL-IN-THE-BLANKS POEM, FLAT STATEMENT, FOUND POEM, JARGON, ORIGINALITY VS. NOVELTY, STOCK CHARACTER. See also *clichés* in APPENDIX 1, and *control and diction* in APPENDIX 1.

climax (Greek for "ladder") a rhetorical figure of repetition that extends ANADIPLOSIS through three or more clauses that rise in intensity or in the order of importance; e.g., "Day brings joy, joy brings night, / Night brings peace, peace brings day." In terms of dramatic structure, the c. can be said to occur at the height of the action where the reader's interest and emotions peak. See *figures of repetition* in APPENDIX 2.

closed couplet two lines of verse joined by RHYME and METER that make complete logical and/or grammatical sense; e.g., Pope's "Instruct the planets in what orbs to run, / Correct old time, and regulate the sun." The term "closed" refers to the independent, autonomous quality of the two lines in relation to the surrounding context. The c.c. can be end-stopped or enjambed. See COUPLET. See also *forms* in APPENDIX 1.

closed ending: See WESTERN ENDING.

closed-field composition a poem with obvious referential limits that form a complete frame of reference through structure, strategy, and content. The term is used to distinguish this traditional type of poem from contemporary poems of OPEN-FIELD COMPOSITION.

close-up shot (see CINEMATIC TECHNIQUES) a type of scene in which details are seen at close distance. This view has the effect of pulling the audience into the visual field or content of the poem. See also *cinematic terms* in APPENDIX 1.

closure the structural and thematic ending of a poem. A poem can end in several general ways: It can have (1) a *closed ending*, dependent upon a DEDUCTIVE STRUCTURE, in which the last line(s) of the poem form(s) a dramatic, finalized conclusion; (2) an *open ending*, dependent upon an INDUCTIVE STRUCTURE, which is somewhat "soft" and inconclusive (common in Asian poetry); or (3) a *leaping ending* in which levels of diction, aesthetic texture, or domains of thought are jumped without the aid of transitional devices. See EASTERN ENDING, CIRCULAR STRUCTURE, DEDUCTIVE-INDUCTIVE STRUCTURE, INDUCTIVE-DEDUCTIVE STRUCTURE, LEAPING POETRY, and WESTERN ENDING. See also *closure* in APPENDIX 1.

coda (from Latin *cauda*, for "tail"; also called "cauda" or "tail") an independent or subordinate line or short passage that recapitulates the themes or motifs of earlier lines or stanzas. The TAIL-RHYME STANZA or RIME COUÉE, popular in medieval romances, has its shorter lines in rhyme, as in the formula aa^{4}b^{3}cc^{4}b^3. Ezra Pound wrote a number of epigrammatic poems entitled c. which summarize his perception of an implied experience. A line that functions as a c. often incorporates images and sounds that are complementary to the main body of verse. See also STOCK.

cognitive meaning (*cognitive*, from Latin for "knowledge") a factual reference to reality that is known, shared, or agreed upon by most people, and which does not express an attitude or emotion: e.g., "rocks are hard." C.m. is the opposite of EMOTIVE MEANING. See CONNOTATION and DENOTATION. See also *meaning* in APPENDIX 1.

cola: See COLON.

collage /kəläzh′/ (French for "a gluing, a pasting") originally, an artistic composition of disparate materials pasted together on a single surface. The term has been borrowed by literary critics to indicate the use of ALLUSION, foreign expressions, and quotations in a literary body of work as in that of Milton, Lamb, Joyce, Eliot, or Pound.

The surrealist painter Max Ernst was interested in the element of surprise that could be created by the chance juxtapositioning of disparate objects (see CHANCE POETRY and JUXTAPOSITION). He described the c. technique as "the pairing of two realities that apparently cannot be paired on a plane apparently unsuited to them." The experience of the c. removes the viewer from known identities and the tyranny of memory. When the accidental meets up with the needs of the subconscious, the viewer is faced with an experience that speaks to him in a language of immediacy.

In a sense, the c. carried the idea of the Cubists' fragmented surface a step further by employing actual three-dimensional objects on a canvas instead of painted representations (see CUBISM). The use of real objects and the interplay of their functions, textures, and patterns gives a three-dimensional quality to painting that locates the c. composition half-way between painting and sculpture. A refinement of the c. technique is used by Robert Francis in his *Silent Poem*, which incorporates a patchwork of words with heavy sound values (shape, texture, density, and intensity) and high image content. See *forms* in APPENDIX 1.

collective unconscious a term coined by Carl Gustav Jung to stand for innate shared experiences. He said that ". . . all human beings possess similar inborn tendencies to form certain general symbols, and that these symbols manifest themselves through the unconscious mind in myths, dreams, delusions and folklore." Archetypal images, such as the sea, the stars, and the moon, are used as symbols in poetry and are said to originate in the c.u. See ARCHETYPAL MYTH, ARCHETYPE, and MYTH.

colloquialism (from Latin for "to converse") an informal expression of speech considered to be proper in spoken language but unacceptable in formal usage because it differs in pronunciation, grammar, vocabulary, imagery, or connotative quality. This "lower" level of diction, such as "Hold on a minute!" can be used to make poetry seem more natural in rhythm and content, and is currently being exploited by a number of contemporary poets for its musical richness. See CLASSICAL FALLACY, DIALECT, and LOCAL COLOR. See also *clichés* in APPENDIX 1.

colon (Greek for "limb" or "portion of a strophe") a standard rhythmical period in Classical prosody that is made up of a variable number of feet, metrical groups, or clauses in a line, sentence, or stanza. It may be scanned in FREE VERSE according to PHRASING, or in Classical metrical verse according to a general number of short syllables (*morae*) that usually ranges from 16 to 25. Cola (the plural of "colon") can be combined into larger units called periods.

colophon /kol'-/ (Greek for "summit, finishing touch") the distinctive sign or emblem of a publisher, which is called an *imprint* when it appears at the front of a book; also, the information at the end of a book describing its publisher, printer, date and place of publication, typeface, type of paper, etc. In the 15th century, at its earliest known occurrence, it was used as a reverential address to the reader, and it appeared at the back of the book. The words "the end" or "finis" following a text can also be considered a c.

comedy (of obscure derivation, but having to do with revelry and singing) a piece of literature that through WIT, humorous action, and sympathetic characters amuses the audience and ends happily. Although some comedies, such as those of Dante and Chekov, are nearer to TRAGEDY than the plethora of lighter forms, it is best to say that c. begins in difficulty which is later resolved congenially. *Low c.* is crude, *high c.* is subtle. The genre differs from *burlesque* and farce in that its plot is more closely woven, its dialogue is more skilled, and its characterization is more believable. The protagonists of comedy are usually literal-minded or tend to interpret events by way of their senses. The rise of great c., fifth and fourth centuries B.C. in Greece and the 16th and 17th centuries in Europe, was accompanied by the rise of great tragedy. Various general types of c. include: (1) the *c. of humors*, which exposes the artificial conventions and proprieties of high society; and (3) the *situation c.*, which depends upon the sometimes complex manipulations of PLOT. See *humor* in APPENDIX 1.

committing word (a similarly used term is TRIGGERING WORD) a contemporary term used to indicate a word that sets off by association or reasoning a subsequent image, action, metaphor, or concept. The author may or may not be aware of the function of the word that commits him to develop a subsequent part of the poem; nevertheless, the committing word's effect is powerful whether or not it is consciously intended. See *diction* in APPENDIX 1.

common meter or common measure (also called "hymnal stanza" or "common time") a type of STANZA that often is used in hymns. Like the BALLAD METER, the c.m.o.c.m. consists of four lines rhyming abab (or sometimes abcb); lines one and three are iambic tetrameter, and two and four are iambic trimeter. Unlike the ballad meter, however, the c.m.o.c.m. uses full rhymes and strict iambics. Some literary theorists claim that this stanza was a ballad stanza adapted to the hymn. See *forms* in APPENDIX 1.

common rhythm a term used by Gerard Manley Hopkins in his preface to *Poems* (1930) to designate a class of rhythms measured by feet of two or three syllables. Each FOOT has a principal STRESS as well as one or two unstressed syllables. The term is similar to RUNNING RHYTHM, the usual rhythm of English verse, and Hopkins contrasts it to SPRUNG RHYTHM. See ACCENTUAL-SYLLABIC VERSE, METER, and RHYTHM.

commoratio (Latin for "a delaying, a dwelling") a figure of argumentation that bolsters one main point with various disparate expressions: "You can't leave us. You're the foundation of the house. How can it stand without you? Would a lioness leave her cubs unprotected?" See *figures of argumentation* in APPENDIX 2.

companion poems a group of poems by the same or different authors which complement one another in style and/or theme. Christopher Marlowe's *The Passionate Shepherd to His Love* and Sir Walter Raleigh's *The Nymph's Reply to the Shepherd* are well know c.p, as well as Matthew Arnold's *Dover Beach* and Anthony Hecht's *The Dover Bitch*.

comparative criticism: See FORMAL CRITICISM.

comparison the basic intellectual and intuitive activity of simile-making in which the attributes of one thing, action, or idea are related to the attributes of a separate entity. See METAPHOR, as well as separate entries treating the figures of comparison (see APPENDIX 2).

compensation (from Latin for "counterbalance") a form of SUBSTITUTION used to make up for TRUNCATION or the extra syllable(s) in a HYPERMETRIC line. The omissions are usually one or more unstressed syllables, though sometimes a whole foot is involved. A syllable missing in one foot may be added to another; or a loss in one line may be made up in the subsequent line. Another use of c. is that of a pause other than CAESURA—a rest or hold (as in music) that has durational value. SPRUNG RHYTHM is a form of uncompensated rhythm.

complaint (from Latin for "a bewailing") a type of LYRIC that presents the speaker's misery. The type was common in the RENAISSANCE and the Middle Ages. Chaucer's *To His Empty Purse*, Surrey's *Complaint of a Lover Rebuked*, and Spenser's *Complaints* are well-known examples.
   Complaints are usually monologues, either serious or humorous, that ask for earthly or divine guidance. If a c. is serious and mournful, it is known as a LAMENT. Many of John Berryman's *Dream Songs* are complaints. See *forms* in APPENDIX 1.

complexio: See SYMPLOCE.

complex metaphor (also called "telescoped metaphor") a type of TROPE in which the *vehicle* of one metaphor becomes the tenor of another metaphor. For a fuller discussion, see METAPHOR.

composite verses poems made up of a mixture of metrical feet, e.g., dactylo-trochaic. See *forms* in APPENDIX 1.

comprobation (from Latin for "to approve") a figure of ETHOS or character in which the speaker uses the strategy of rewarding his audience for its actions of character: "You jurors will show, by your decision today, your good judgment and sense of justice." See *figures of ethos* in APPENDIX 2.

computer poetry a recently developed form of poetic composition in which data-processing machines are used to generate new sequences of words. There are basically two types of c.p.: *formulary* and *derivative*. In formulary c.p., the programmer gives the computer a syntactical structure and a list of words to fill in the structure. In derivative c.p., the programmer gives the computer lines of existing poems and the computer alters them in a systematic way.

Alberta Turner used her *Returner* poems to write verse based on derivations of the original (Alberta Turner, '*Returner*' *Re-turned*, in *Midwest Quarterly*, 13, 1972). See *forms in* APPENDIX 1.

conceit (from Latin for "to seize") a TROPE that establishes a striking and elaborate parallel. The term was originally derogatory but is now neutral in tone. As the term is used now, there are two basic types of c.: (1) The *Petrarchan c.* was used by Petrarch in his love poems and was widely imitated in Europe during the RENAISSANCE. The comparisons were applied to a cold, beautiful mistress, and to the despair of her lover (see COURTLY LOVE). Sir Thomas Wyatt, in his sonnet *My Galley Charged with Forgetfulness* compares the lover to a ship in a storm . A familiar type of Petrarchan c. is the OXYMORON describing the simultaneous fever and chills of a person wracked by love. (2) The *metaphysical c.* was used by the METAPHYSICAL POETS of the 17th century, and in particular by John Donne. The metaphysical c. is, as Dr. Johnson described it, "a kind of *discordia concors*; a combination of dissimilar images, or discovery of occult resemblances in things apparently unlike .... The most heterogeneous ideas are yoked by violence together." With the revival of the Metaphysical Poets in the early 20th century, many modern poets renewed the use of conceits. Examples are T.S. Eliot's comparison of evening to "a patient etherized upon a table," and the sequence of surprising figures in Dylan Thomas' *After the Funeral*. The popularity of the metaphysical c. caught on in popular songs, e.g., in Cole Porter's *You're the Tops* and *You're the Cream in My Coffee*. See also FIGURES OF SPEECH and METAPHOR.

concessio (Latin for "a yielding") a figure of argumentation similar to PAROMOLOGIA in that it concedes points to the opposition, but in a jesting or ironic style whose conclusion is meant to wound the opponent; e.g.:

> Lady, your good looks give you power over men,
> Your sweet voice is a weapon over them,
> But age will cure you of your health.

See *figures of argumentation* in APPENDIX 2.

concrete poetry (*concrete*, from Latin for "to grow together") a poem whose TYPOGRAPHICAL ARRANGEMENT and selection of typeface express a message complementary to or beyond the semantic meaning of the poem. See ALTAR POEM and CARMEN FIGURATUM. See also *forms* in APPENDIX 1.

concrete terms: See ABSTRACT TERMS AND C.T.

concrete universal (also known as "organic universal") Hegel's theoretical term for a specific detail that contains universal significance. The other half of Hegel's theory of reality in art deals with the *abstract universal* which contains generality: e.g., the word "man" is abstract and is an accumulation of traits, whereas a set of particular details that can be experienced can signify concretely the abstract universal term "man." In order to qualify as c.u., a term must have (1) variety of parts, (2) coherence among its parts, (3) a sense of completeness in detail, (4) unity among its parts, (5) autonomy, and (6) self-sufficiency. W.K. Wimsatt in *The Verbal Icon* maintains that the c.u. unifies the particular and the general, and that an accumulation of the particulars results in an organic totality analogous to the dimension of CONNOTATION which contains universal significance. The literary theory of the c.u. is particularly useful in analyzing poems that are seen as having been arranged by some central ORGANIZING PRINCIPLE. See ABSTRACT TERMS AND CONCRETE TERMS.

concretion the process of making an abstract term more concrete and vivid, according to Denise Levertov who coined the term. In her poem *The Son*, e.g., Levertov revises the word "hastens" into the more concrete compound noun "rockleaping." See ABSTRACT TERMS AND CONCRETE TERMS.

conditional metaphor equation a METAPHOR that has a qualified mathematical base upon which it is constructed. For example, in substituting "man" for the attributes of "rock" ("He is a rock"), a qualifying condition or set of conditions may be added, as in the *if/then* formula: "If he is opposed, then he will become a rock." Other common kinds of conditional metaphor equations take the form of *when/then* or *not A, but B*, or *yet A, if C*. See SI . . . QUAND.

Confessional poetry an autobiographical form of poetry whose name was created by 20th-century literary critics, and which was applied to poets such as John Berryman, Robert Lowell, Sylvia Plath, Anne Sexton, and W.D. Snodgrass. The term has become more diffused in popular use and has come to refer to autobiographical or personal poetry in general. Although it has been resented by poets to whom it was applied, the term is not pejorative per se but is meant to classify a genre of poetry which, some critics maintain, is limited to the self in nature and subject matter. For an interesting study of the topic, see A. Alvarez's *The Savage God*.

conflict (from Latin for "a striking together, a fight") the thematic tension between characters or their actions upon which PLOT is based. There are four main kinds of c.: (1) *elemental* or *physical c.*, in which man pits himself against nature; (2) *social c.*, in which man is challenged by another man or society; (3) *internal* or *psychological c.*, in which a man's desires are in conflict with his conscience; and (4) *providential c.*, in which man is in conflict with the decrees of fate or some deity. See DRAMATIC STRUCTURE.

connotation (from Latin for "to mark [a thing] with or in addition to [another]") the associative responses to a word that are beyond its DENOTATION or *lexical* meaning. For example, a star is defined denotatively as "any of the heavenly bodies seen as small, fixed points of light in the night sky," but its connotative meaning suggests ideas of success, brilliance, hope, and desire. These associations may arise from contexts ranging from the personal to the racial to the universal; even the TONE COLOR, texture, and typography of a word or its context can evoke c. The connotative meaning, according to aesthetic theory, is a secondary level of meaning which is implicit in the word or its surrounding context. See ANAGOGICAL VISION and FOUR SENSES OF INTERPRETATION. See also *Diction* in APPENDIX 1.

consonance (from Latin for "harmony") the close REPETITION of similar or identical consonants of words whose main vowels differ (as in the *t* sounds of "total," "late," and "stop"). Half-rhyme is c. of the final consonants, as "mast" and "paste." *Complete* or *rich c.* is the twinning of consonants both at the beginnings and ends of words with different main vowels (as in "mast/mist") and is sometimes referred to as *consonantal dissonance*. Rich c. is, in effect, a complex form of consonantal ALLITERATION and half-rhyme. As a replacement for PERFECT RHYME, it can be very effective. Modern poets, such as Dylan Thomas and Gerard Manley Hopkins, whose work depends on the sonic aspect of poetry (see MELOPOEIA) have made notable use of this complementary device to ASSONANCE. See RHYME.

consonants those alphabetical letters whose sounds are produced in the mouth or nose, as opposed to vowels, letters whose sounds are produced in the larynx. The basic c. are *b, c, d, f, g, h, j, k, l, m, n, p, q, r, s, t, v, w, x, z*, and, sometimes, *y*. They group themselves according to the area of the mouth (and/or nose) in which they are primarily made. The groups include *fricatives* (*f, s, sh, th, dth, zh, h, z, v*), *plosives* (*p, t, d, b, j, ch, k, g*), *nasals* (*ng* and, sometimes, *m* and *n*), *liquids* (*r, l*), and *glides* (*w, y*). The sound of a consonantal letter may vary according to the way in which it is pronounced; e.g., *th* in "thing" (th) is pronounced differently from *th* in "that" (dth). It is even possible to arrange c. according to their musical PITCH. See MELOPOEIA, SIBILANTS, and SIGMATISM. See also *melopoetics* in APPENDIX 1.

contemporary poetry literature of the recent past (approximately the last 25 years) or the work of a living writer. As a generic term, c.p. refers to Post-Modernist poetry. See POST-MODERNISTS.

contentio: See ENANTIOSIS.

context (from Latin for "to weave together, to compose") the accumulation of denotative and connotative meaning surrounding a particular part of a passage that puts into perspective the aim and direction of the TEXT. Proper literary interpretation depends on an understanding of the c. in which something is stated. See FOUR SENSES OF INTERPRETATION.

contextualism a form of CRITICISM that interprets a literary work as being self-referential and independent of external practical applications. Conversely, the more popular use of the term indicates criticism that applies or ascribes its interpretation to the social, political, or economic milieu of the poet, the poet's personal life, the domain of the symbols he has used, or the poetics extant in his age. See *criticism* in APPENDIX 1.

continuum poetry (*continuum*, Latin for "an uninterrupted thing") poetry that imitates the movement of the writer's mind as its DIALECTIC is reflected in the writing process itself. The term has been borrowed from painting to indicate this unconventional subject matter. The painter Jackson Pollack created his painting *Autumn Rhythm* by dripping and splotching colors of paint from various angles and heights. Stanley Kunitz, a noted American poet, dubbed this painting a "choreographic composition," indicating the dance or quality of movement in it. This genre of continuum painting excludes the specific image and concentrates on the process of painting as its subject matter. Kunitz remarked of this method: "In the fifties a painting began to look like a scarred battleground in which there was as much evidence of destruction as of creation. The corrections, the rejections, the mistakes had become incorporated into the final work. It was as though the artist were intent on showing us the painting as a process rather than a thing."

Similarly, John Ashbery's poetry does not focus on a conventional, representational subject but on the process of recording how the mind works through the fluid medium of language. His work seeks to explore his subconscious, and it has that quality of active self-discovery which the inquisitive mind displays. The time jumps, the leaps and fusion of content, the fluctuating tones, syntax, and diction record the synchronic capacity of the mind in a process that naturally relates events and impressions through a rapid, associational series of connections. He said of his work: "My poems are a record of the thought process—the process and thought reflect back and forth on each other." Just as Einstein intuited and sought evidence of a basic physical reality, a continuum between the electromagnetic and gravitational forces in the universe, Ashbery links the discrete contents of his poems through the unifying process of the mind's conscious movement. What one sees as dissociated, random, disjointed patterns in his work, Ashbery sees as a dialectic. It is an extension, it would seem, of Charles Olson's maxim: "One perception must immediately follow another perception." Just as Einstein's conception of time, space, and mass is that they are elastic and measured in relation to events and objects around them, so, in Ashbery's work, the images and suggestions of plot must be interpreted in the context of the speaker's evolving consciousness. The absolute for Einstein is the speed of light, for Ashbery it is the movement of the mind.

For complementary discussions of composition, see CENTRIPETAL-CENTRIFUGAL STRUCTURE and OPEN FIELD COMPOSITION.

contrapuntal (from Latin for "point against point") a technique in poetry in which two or more separate themes, systems of imagery or sound, lines of logic, or subjects are stated next to one another in leapfrog fashion. The term has been borrowed by critics from music that uses the device synchronically. See CONTRAST and COUNTERPOINT. See also CUT-AND-SHUFFLE POEM.

contrast (from Old French for "to resist, to oppose") the JUXTAPOSITION, rhetorically speaking, of one idea or image with another to produce enhancement, synthesis, or tension. Used in imagery, the device can evoke deep sensuous response; used in ideas, it can evoke powerful abstract reasoning; used melopoetically, it can produce a varied aesthetic texture; used in actions, it can produce ironic or sharply etched characterization. For instance, the following couplet states the same concept in concrete terms (line 1) and in abstract terms (line 2):

> The bats fly away like bits of paper
> in a slipstream.
> I have no thoughts.

contrast cut (see CINEMATIC TECHNIQUES) a cinematic type of editing that juxtaposes opposite types of actions or situations in order to produce thematic or plot tensions. See also *cinematic terms* in APPENDIX 1.

control (from French for "to oversee") the artistic and skillful manipulation of language and insight to effect the appropriate experience of a work of art. For defects in c., see BURIED THEME, DIGRESSION, DISTRACTING DETAIL, MIXED MESSAGE, MOOD PIECE, OBSCURITY, OVERDECORATION, OVERREPETITION, OVERWRITING, and STRAIN BEHIND THE POEM.

controlling image (also known as "central image") an image that dominates, controls, unifies, and often gives impulse to a poem. The poem, either implicitly or explicitly, continually refers to the c.i. It functions as a thematic and structural device, a function much larger than that associated with images. See CONTROLLING METAPHOR. See also *imagery* in APPENDIX 1.

controlling metaphor a METAPHOR that dominates, controls, unifies, and often gives impulse to a poem, and one that runs through the work. See also CONTROLLING IMAGE.

convention (from Latin for "assembly") an established technique, style, or device that is commonly and implicitly agreed upon and practiced. The term includes the structure of verse (lines, stanzas, forms, syntax, etc.), contents (tropes, rhetorical constructions and expressions, genres, logic, elements of time, narration techniques, etc.), the aesthetics of an age, and an assumed readership. The INVENTION of one age often becomes the c. of another age. See ORIGINALITY VS. NOVELTY. See also *clichés* in APPENDIX 1.

conversational rhythm an internally imposed, organic set of rhythms that stress the natural speaking voice over strict metrical form. These colloquial rhythms contain more variation and are closer to natural speech patterns than their more formal metrical precursors in poetry, but they have remained unclassified since no satisfactory system of scansion has been devised to categorize them. See RHYTHM for a fuller discussion. See also LOGAOEDIC, PROSE RHYTHM, and SENTENCE SOUNDS.

coronach /kor'ənak/ (from Gaelic for "wailing together") a funeral song or LAMENT of Ireland and Scotland which is usually sung by the wives and daughters of the deceased. The Hebrew prayer for the dead, *Kaddish*, is similar to a c. See DIRGE. See *forms* in APPENDIX 1.

correlative verse /-rel'-/ (*correlative*, from Medieval Latin for "referring together") a third-century-B.C. epigrammatic form of verse in which the relationships among the words of one group are parallel and in balance with the relationships among the words of a second group. For example, a Greek epigram from the *Anthologia Graeca* offers this simple and wise c.v.: "You [wine are] boldness, youth, strength, wealth, country / to the shy, the old, the weak, the poor, the foreigner." See *forms in* APPENDIX 1.

counterplot: See SUBPLOT.

counterpoint (from Latin for "[song or music] pointed-against") a rhythmic SYNCOPATION in which variations of a metrical line occur so that two distinct rhythmical patterns appear to intertwine. This variation is accomplished by substituting a duple foot for a triple foot (or vice versa), or by the addition or subtraction of stresses from a foot, as in the spondaic and pyrrhic substitutions in these iambic lines from Pope:

> Whĕn Á / jăx strĭves / sŏme roćk's / vást weíght / tŏ thrŏw
> Thĕ líne / tóo lá / boŕs ănd / thĕ woŕds / móve slŏw.

The use of this device can easily reverse the direction of an ASCENDING RHYTHM or a FALLING RHYTHM. Other elements of a poem (theme, PLOT, CHARACTER, SETTING, etc.) can also be counterpointed. See CONTRAPUNTAL, CONTRAST, and SUBPLOT.

couplet /kup'lyt/ or /kō͞oplā'/ (French for "two things coupled") two lines of verse, rhymed or unrhymed, that share the same base meter and which usually form a complete grammatical and logical structure. *Open c.* refers to two lines that share a common grammar and logic, but in which the second line is enjambed. *Closed c.* refers to two rhyming lines sharing the same meter, and containing a complete statement. The *short c.* is written in iambic or trochaic tetrameter and thus is octosyllabic. The most common English c. is written in rhyming iambic pentameter. A *Heroic c.*, the favorite meter of Chaucer, is composed of iambic pentameter lines rhyming in pairs. HUDIBRASTIC VERSE is rhymed iambic tetrameter with the use of feminine and multiple rhymes, and includes ludicrous rhyme words. As a structural element, the c. constitutes a major unit of verse in Western literature. It can be an autonomous epigrammatic form, a stanza length, or a unit within a stanza. Poets from Chaucer to the contemporary poet John Logan have employed it. See also DISTICH.

courtly love the genteel and sophisticated philosophy of love invented by the troubadours of the 11th and 12th centuries in the Provençal area, in southern France (see TROUBADOUR). It was based on an interpretation of Ovid's *The Remedies of Love* and called for an idealization of the woman for whose chaste state one might suffer physical and spiritual trials in order to win her favor. Whether or not this complex code reflected actual social behavior or was simply a literary CONVENTION is unknown. But examples from *Sir Gawain and the Green Knight* to the works of the Elizabethan poets reflect this philosophy of man-woman relationships, which, it seems, is a view very different from that of sexual equality in contemporary American society.

Cowleyan ode /kou′lē·ən/ (also know as "irregular ode") an ODE in which the rhyme scheme, length of lines, number of lines in each stanza, and general parallel structure are irregular. It was named after the 17th-century English poet Abraham Cowley, but the best known examples are, perhaps, those of Dryden. See *forms* in APPENDIX 1.

crasis (Greek for "mixture, combination") a grammatical form of SYN-AERESIS that contracts two words, syllables, or vowels into one sound, as in "seer" for "see-er." The device particularly refers to the slurring of the vowels at the end of one word with those at the beginning of the next word. For other forms of contraction, see ELISION, SYNALEPHA, SYNCOPE, and SYZYGY. See *grammatical constructions that are technically incorrect* in APPENDIX 2.

Creationism a post-World-War-I aesthetic movement that called for a new creed that would substitute past literary conventions with the creation of poems of daring invention. According to Vicente Huidobro, a Chilean poet, the movement called for poetry composed as naturally as the products of nature and as startlingly varied in its effects. Other Spanish and French poets, such as Pierre Reverdy, attempted this new, "purer" poetry, whose creed is imbedded in the following poetic dogma by Huidobro:

> Why do you sing the rose, O, poets?
> Make it flower in the poem.
> Only for you.
> Live all things under the sun.
> The poet is a small God.

The movement *Ultraism* was a successor to C.

cretic /krē′tik/ (from Greek for "Cretan"): See AMPHIMACER.

crisis (Greek for "decision") a structural PLOT device made up of opposing forces that meet and create dramatic tension. The CLIMAX refers to the reader's emotional response, and there may be one or more crises in a plot. See DRAMATIC STRUCTURE. See also *Dramatic terms* in APPENDIX 1.

critical feedback an informal contemporary WORKSHOP term indicating the analytical, interpretive, and appreciative remarks offered in discussing the craft of a poem. See CRITICISM. See also *criticism* in APPENDIX 1.

criticism (from Greek for "decision, judging") a branch of literary study that defines, interprets, analyzes, and judges a work according to a variety of different aesthetic systems, and which results in the laying down of certain principles. The two main Classical systems are: (1) *Aristotelian c.*, which seeks to unearth the values of a work without relationship to other life activities; it is logical, formal, and objective in its view; (2) *Platonic c.*, which seeks to apply the values of a work of art in relation to its usefulness to life; thus it is a moral tool and considered the more subjective of the two Classical systems of c.

Four other types of c. interpret a work via outside references or develop principles from the work in order to apply them to other works: (3) *relativistic c.* uses any system of outside references to aid in interpreting a work; (4) *absolutist c.* applies a standard set of principles to any and all work; (5) *theoretical c.* attempts to formulate permanent principles from the study of a specific work in order to determine what, in general, differentiates literature from other disciplines and to define standards of quality for poetry; (6) *practical c.* applies implied, but external, principles to a specific work and aims to improve future works of literature.

The intentions of c. are to define and explain underlying principles; to justify the risks and imaginative aspects to an ignorant or skeptical audience; to set down rules of craft and propriety; to make a work accessible to the public; to judge the quality and merit of a work; to discover and apply the principles of excellence in art.

Other systems of critical classification include: (7) *impressionistic c.* (or *subjective c.*), which emphasizes how a work affects a critic; (8) *historical c.*, which compares a work with its age and the author's life; (9) *textual c.*, which attempts to reconstruct a work from the original manuscript; (10) *formal c.* (or *comparative c.*), which examines a work in relation to the genre in which it belongs; (11) *judicial c.*, which judges the work by a definite set of standards; (12) *moral c.* (or *ethical c.*), which evaluates a work in relation to human life (see *Platonic c.*); (13) *mythic c.* (or *archetypal c.*), which explores the nature and significance of symbology in a work (see ARCHETYPE and MYTH); (14) *technical c.*, which guides the writer in the actual craft of writing; (15) *social c.*, which acts as a public-relations, good-will tool in sponsoring the merits of a good writer or quality piece of literature; (16) *mimetic c.*, which seeks to reflect the human condition and which judges a work according to its success or failure in that aim; (17) *pragmatic c.*, which judges the effect of a work on an audience and judges whether or not the work has thereby succeeded in its aim of instructing, entertaining, evoking, etc.; (18) *expressive c.*, developed by the ROMANTICS and popular today, which relate to the work in terms of its author's form or style of expression (whether it is sincere, merely clever, noble, deeply felt, etc.); and (19) *objective c.*, which is a kind of Aristotelian critical descendent that has become widely used and judges a work without reference to its author, age, or audience, but by a set of criteria deemed proper to good writing. Many of these critical systems or points of view overlap or parallel one another. See AESTHETICISM, CHICAGO CRITICS, and NEW CRITICISM. See also *criticism* in APPENDIX 1.

critique /kritĕk′/ (French, from Greek for "to judge, to decide") an oral or written evaluation of a work. It can be studied or extemporaneous and is often synonymous with the term *review*. The c. is one of the main features of the creative writing WORKSHOP.

cross-acrostic a puzzle poem displaying an oblique ordering of key letters beginning with the first letter of the first line, the second letter of the second line, the third letter of the third line, etc., until the accumulated letters reveal a hidden name or message. For example, Poe's *A Valentine* spells out the name of his lover, F-r-a-n-c-e-s-S-a-r-g-e-n-t-O-s-g-o-o-d. See ACROSTIC. See also *forms* in APPENDIX 1.

crosscut (see CINEMATIC TECHNIQUES) a cinematic editing technique that depicts two or more simultaneous scenes or actions. D.W. Griffith, a noted film director, first employed the device. It is similar in effect to the cut-and-shuffle structure of certain poems. See also *cinematic terms* in APPENDIX 1.

crossed rhyme or interlaced rhyme full rhyme of internal and external words in a long couplet with those of another couplet. Because of the long length of the lines, they may be heard as a series of shorter lines, as in this example from Swinburne:

> Will ye bridle the deep sea with *reins*, will ye chasten the
>   high seas with *rods*?
> Will ye take her to chain her with *chains*, who is older than
>   all ye *Gods*?

The terms are not to be confused with CROSS-RHYME, which is the rhyming of an end-word with a word in the middle of the subsequent line. See RHYME.

cross-rhyme the rhyme of an end-rhymed syllable or word with one in the middle of the next line: "He of the soft and empty *purse* / Will live to *curse* his spendthrift ways." The term is not to be confused with CROSSED RHYME OR INTERLACED RHYME, which interlinks separate couplets. See RHYME.

crown of sonnets seven sonnets linked together by the first and last lines of consecutive stanzas; that is, the last line of the first stanza is also the first line of the second stanza, the last line of the second stanza is the first line of the third stanza, etc. The sequence is usually composed of Italian sonnets and no rhyme is repeated twice (see ITALIAN SONNET). It was first seen in Italy, but the best-known example is Donne's *Holy Sonnets* whose *La Corona* is a c.o.s. acting as an introduction to the work's other sonnets. Other examples include Dante's *Vita Nuova*, Petrarch's *Canzoniere*, Longfellow's *Divina Commèdia*, Millay's *Fatal Interview*. See SONNET SEQUENCE. See also *forms* in APPENDIX 1.

Cubism a painting term invented by Henri Matisse who in 1908 mockingly characterized the new work of Picasso and Braque with the term. It was borrowed by the poets Apollinaire and Pierre Reverdy who used the technique to reveal the inner perspective of nature and its forces. The rearrangement of texture and surface created a new synthesis which, in turn, reflected the fragmented consciousness of modern man and his preoccupation with scientific inquiries into the structure of nature. e.e. cummings often used this technique by employing split syllabication and new concoctions of punctuation to inform his reader of complex emotional states.

The poet Frank O'Hara, who lived and worked closely with New York painters, adopted this method of composition. In his poem *War* O'Hara uses metaphorical phrases based on war to create the multifaceted fragments of his poem which abruptly switches levels of focus from nature to cityscape to domestic interests. Because feelings and events occur simultaneously within and around an individual, O'Hara forces the reader to see this "confusion" of forces by attacking his theme from different perspectives and by shifting the order of his phrases. A good example of this new, self-conscious syntax, which speaks as much about the actual composition of a poem as about the poem's subject matter, is Gertrude Stein's *Lifting Belly*. This gentle and precise sexual poem seems filled with nonsequiturs and switches of attention, yet its effect is mind-opening. The poem brings out a high level of language consciousness, a rarified atmosphere which delights and surprises. The poem begins:

> Kiss my lips. She did.
> Kiss my lips again she did.
> Kiss my lips over and over and over again she did.
> I have feathers.
> Gentle fishes.
> Do you think about apricots. We find them very beautiful.

See *movements and schools of poetry* in APPENDIX 1.

culteranism: See GONGORISM.

curtal-sonnet (*curtal*, from French for "short") Gerard Manley Hopkin's shortened version of a SONNET. It is composed of ten-and-a-half lines: two stanzas of six lines and four lines, respectively, with an added *tailpiece* of half a line in the last stanza. The rhyme scheme is abcabc in the SESTET and dcbdb or dcbdc in the tailed QUATRAIN. Hopkins wrote only two curtal-sonnets, and both contain SPRUNG RHYTHM. See *forms* in APPENDIX 1.

cut-and-shuffle poem a poem whose structure consists of alternating lines or stanzas of different subject matters, themes, actions, or characters. The structure takes its name from the common method of mixing playing cards in which the left- and right-hand piles are alternately stacked into a common pile. Both poetry and film have used this form of organization in order to coordinate two or more disparate but associated themes or subjects. (In music, the structure is called a *fugue*.) There are three general types of this construction: (1) *dovetailed stanzas* (2) *fused subjects*, and (3) the *sandwich construction*.

(1) The *dovetailed stanzas* construction juxtaposes mutually exclusive, simultaneous scenes which, when put together, synthesize a productive tension between two scenes. For example:

> *scene 1*
> A woman slips into bed.
> She turns on some soft music
> and lazily reads a book.
> She turns out the light
> and lets go of her thoughts.
> She lies on her back daydreaming.
> She gently falls asleep.
>
> *scene 2*
> A man slides onto his motorcycle.

He kicks the engine over
and guns the throttle.
He skids on the wet pavement
going around a corner.
He hits a siderail and goes over.

scenes 1 and 2 shuffled together
A woman slips into bed.
A man slides onto his motorcycle.
She turns on some soft music
and lazily reads a book.
He kicks the engine over
and guns the throttle.
She turns out the light
and lets go of her thoughts.
He skids on the pavement

going around a corner.
She lies on her back daydreaming.
He hits the siderail and goes over.
She gently falls asleep.

By alternating the actions and characters of each scene, an implied relationship is built into the synthesized version, and the reader assumes that there is a dependency between the woman's gentle indifference and the man's aggressive action.

(2) The *fused subjects* construction uses a pivotal word or phrase that acts as a common denominator for disparate scenes, actions, or characters. In the following example, scene 1 depicts a night cityscape which is smoothly fused to a domestic scene (scene 2) with the use of the word "down":

I was an intruder in the emptiness of the streets
where the moon, like a searchlight, kept everything

"Down," I said startling her. It is only me.
I want to talk with you. Sit down."

The fused form seems to have a single line of development rather than the simultaneity of the dovetailed type.

(3) The *sandwich* construction is composed of an outer frame which is interrupted by an inner frame. In the example below two scenes are sandwiched together; William Stafford's *Vacation* poem uses this construction to contrast opposing textures and themes so that an implied moral becomes apparent:

One scene as I bow to pour her coffee:—
Indians in the scouring drouth
huddle at a grave scooped in gravel,
lean to the wind as our train goes by.
Someone is gone.
There is dust on everything in Nevada.
I pour the cream.

These two events literally pass by one another and are interrelated not only by their spatial proximity, but fused together by the wind of the onrushing train. The themes of suffering and luxury are typographically separated by the indentation of the middle stanza.

The c.-a.-s. p., it should be noted, is not composed as mechanically as the analytical examples here might indicate. But for illustrative purposes, it is simpler to present the technique in its basic, crude stages rather than try to capture the complex interplay of associations that occur in the poet's mind during the actual creative process. For a related discussion, see *cuts* under CINEMATIC TECHNIQUES. See also *forms* in APPENDIX 1.

cutting to continuity: See JUMP CUT.

cycle (from Greek for "circle") a group of poems, plays, or narratives about a central heroic character, theme, or major event, as in accounts of the Trojan War, the Charlemagne epics, and the romances of King Arthur and Knights of the Round Table. It is usually written by one author, though a group of Greek poets, known as the *cyclic poets*, were the authors of the Trojan War cycle which was intended to supplement Homer's account. See *forms* in APPENDIX 1.

cynghanedd /kin-/ (Welsh for "harmony") originally, a strictly metered form of Welsh poetry that featured ALLITERATION, INTERNAL RHYME, and stresses that chimed (as Gerard Manley Hopkins described it) through interlinked correspondences in sound and rhythm. There are two kinds of cynghanedds: (1) the *consonantal c.*, which relies on alliteration and rhyme, and (2) the *lusg c.*, which relies mainly on an internal rhyme. The meter is based on the syllabic system and the relation between WORD ACCENT and CAESURA: "the rock-wracked, pock-backed bay" would be an English approximation of c. See *forms* in APPENDIX 1.

D

dactyl /dak'təl/ (from Greek for "finger") a FOOT of three syllables, marked ´˘˘, more common in Classical poetry than in modern. See ACCENTUAL-SYLLABIC VERSE, FALLING RHYTHM, and METER.

Dada /dä'də/ or /dä'dä/ (also called "Dadaism") a nihilistic movement in art and poetry founded by Tristan Tzara in Zurich during World War I. D. glorified disorder as a normal state, and used satirical violence to protest the limitations of logic, religion, and morality of 19th-century European society which had led, they claimed, to the war. The *Dadaists* said that, like the eye of a hurricane, order lies within disorder. Everything was considered D.: a man buying a loaf of bread is D., but children throwing bread at each other is more faithfully in keeping with Dada's ambience. The Dadaists printed shocking pictures, nonsensical poems and manifestoes, and performed strange theatrical presentations. Marcel Duchamp sent a toilet as a sculpture to be exhibited in Paris, but it was returned by the more conventional-minded organizers of the show.

When asked how the D. movement was founded, Hans Arp half-seriously formalized its inception and exemplified its tone with the following reply: "I hereby declare that Tristan Tzara found the word Dada on February 8, 1916, at six o'clock in the afternoon: I was present with my twelve children when Tzara for the first time uttered this word which filled us with justified enthusiasm. This occurred in the Café de la Terrasse in Zurich and I was wearing a brioche in my left nostril."

The final value of Dada's teaching was in showing the usefulness of jokes as a didactic tool in modern poetry and the part that chance, as opposed to premeditated order, could play in aesthetic endeavors. More specifically, the wild aesthetics of D. opened the way for the more refined aesthetics of SURREALISM. See *humor* in APPENDIX 1.

dead metaphor (see METAPHOR) a figure of speech that is no longer recognized as such, but rather is accepted in a literal sense. Some common dead metaphors are "table leg," "nightfall," "break of day," "telecast," and "baker's dozen."

A d.m., like a CLICHÉ, has been so overused that it has lost its original freshness. Thousands of these constructions litter the language, surviving mainly because of their convenience. When they are closely examined for their originality, they often seem startlingly imaginative, but because they are victims of their own brilliance and popularity, they have lost their impact. A skillful writer can use them to flavor a poem with colloquial character or to find a new twist to the d.m. James Wright, in his poem *Redwings*, uses the d.m. "Ohio was already going to hell" as a thematic

75 decasyllabic verse

statement that balances the striking images of the disintegration of Ohio's natural landscape. See also COLLOQUIALISM and *clichés* in APPENDIX 1.

débat /däbä'/ (French for "debate") one of the most popular literary forms of the 12th and 13th centuries, in which two characters debate a topic of theology, politics, morality, or love. After a lengthy argument, the characters refer the question to a judge, who often postpones or hedges on the decision. The form was possibly influenced by the PASTORAL contests in Theocritus and Virgil. The best example in English of a d. is Nicholas of Guildford's *The Owl and the Nightingale* (12th century) which expresses the conflict between DIDACTIC POETRY and love poetry. See *forms* in APPENDIX 1.

Decadence /dek'-/ or /dikā'-/ (from Latin for "falling away") originally, the Greek Hellenistic period (ca. 300–30 B.C.), but now any period of literary history considered inferior to the preceding period. The "Silver Age" of Latin literature was *decadent* compared to the "Golden Age" when Virgil, Horace, Livy, and Ovid wrote. Similarly, the period of English Literature after Shakespeare, characterized by sensationalism, low morals, and comparative lack of serious purpose, was also decadent.

In the modern age, D. usually refers to the 19th-century literary movement, originating in France, that emphasized the autonomy of art, the hostility of the artist to middle-class values, the superiority of artifice to nature, and the search for sensual experience. The *Decadents* based their aesthetic principles on the art and literature of the late Roman Empire and the Byzantine era (like Europe at the end of the 19th century, two cultures that were past their vigorous prime). The precepts of D. were summarized by Gautier in the notice he attached to an edition of Baudelaire's *Les Fleurs du Mal* (1868), and were represented by the bizarre subject matter and exuberant style of J.K. Huysman's *Against the Grain* (1884).

D. was introduced to England by Walter Pater with his emphasis on careful artifice and stylistic subtlety. George Moore in *Confessions of a Young Man* (1888) included a manifesto proclaiming D., which thereafter became identified with AESTHETICISM. Both movements were represented in the 1890s by Oscar Wilde, Arthur Symons, Ernest Dowson, and Lionel Johnson, as well as by the visual artist Aubrey Beardsley.

Some critics claim that the BEATS were part of an American decadent movement.

See FIN DE SIÈCLE.

decasyllabic verse (*decasyllabic*, from Greek for "ten" plus "syllable") lines of ten syllables, a form used by Dante, Petrarch, Chaucer, Milton, Pope, Wordsworth, and Wallace Stevens, among others. Chaucer helped the ten-syllable line become associated with the five-stress line, which made possible the rise of the great English verse forms (SONNET, HEROIC COUPLET, BLANK VERSE, etc.). The actual number of syllables per line in d.v. may be nine, ten, 11, or 12, depending upon pronunciation and POETIC LICENSE. See *line forms* under *forms* in APPENDIX 1.

décima (Spanish for "tenth") a Spanish stanzaic form that consists of any ten-line STANZA. See *stanzaic forms* under *forms* in APPENDIX 1.

decorum (Latin for "that which is proper or fitting") the principle of suiting the STYLE to the subject. D. is most important in the genre of drama, in which the writer does not usually speak except through the voices of the characters (See CHARACTER). The writer must modify his style to fit the characters, as well as modifying his TONE to fit the SUBJECT MATTER and MOOD. For example, in *Paradise Lost* the fallen angels speak in a highly dignified and rhetorical manner. See *diction* in APPENDIX 1.

The roots of d. lie in Classical theory, especially Horace's verse-essay *Ars Poetica* (lines 89-127). According to Horace, a speaker's words should never be discordant with his station in life, and comic and tragic themes should rarely, if ever, be mingled. Aristotle is said to be speaking of d. when he tells the poet to visualize every scene so there will be nothing inappropriate.

In Horace, as well as later theorists, d. is interchangeable with propriety and harmony. The style should be appropriate to the speaker, the occasion, and the subject matter. Renaissance writers took care that kings spoke in a "high" style, old men in a "grave" style, clowns in prose, and shepherds in a "rustic" style. In other words, character type determined quality of speech.

Milton's *Tractate of Education* calls for clear distinctions between poetic genres, characters who are consistent, and careful attention to the Classical hierarchy of style (grand, moderate, plain). Writers of the Neo-Classical Age, following the theory and practice of Milton and Horace, raised d. to the controlling literary principle of their age. Wordsworth's revolt against the "false refinement" and "poetic diction" of the poetry of the previous age is seen as a reaction against the principles of d. See DICTION.

dedication (from Latin for "to declare, to proclaim, to devote") a subscript of a title that offers the poem to, for, or after an event or person. D. is also used to indicate a writer's devotion to his art.

deduction (from Latin for "to lead, bring off or away") a form of logical reasoning that first establishes a conclusion of general nature, and then shows that it conforms to a specific premise. The development of the argument or line of reasoning is from the general to the particular, whereas *induction* moves from the particular to the general. See DEDUCTIVE STRUCTURE and INDUCTIVE STRUCTURE.

deductive-inductive structure a form of argumentative development that begins by using general statements of deduction, procedes toward the particular by using supporting details, then completes its development with general statements at the CLOSURE of the poem. Pablo Neruda's poem *Walking Around* exemplifies the structure that can be schematically represented by this shape: ⟩ ⟨. See CENTRIFUGAL-CENTRIPETAL STRUCTURE, CENTRIFUGAL STRUCTURE, CENTRIPETAL STRUCTURE, DEDUCTIVE STRUCTURE, INDUCTIVE-DEDUCTIVE STRUCTURE, and INDUCTIVE STRUCTURE.

deductive structure (*deductive*, from Latin for "to lead, bring off or away") an argumentative development that uses DEDUCTION, the movement from general to particular, to shape its reasoning. Alan Dugan's *Love Song: I and Thou* begins with a general statement that is subsequently supported by various concrete examples. The shape of the poem's argument of self-martyrdom narrows down to the last line in which the last word, "wife," seals up the poem. This kind of dramatic ending is sometimes referred to as a WESTERN ENDING, a dramatic finale that has the same effect as slamming a door shut. The d.s. can be schematically represented as: (v)
See CENTRIFUGAL STRUCTURE, CENTRIPETAL-CENTRIFUGAL STRUCTURE, CENTRIPETAL STRUCTURE, DEDUCTIVE-INDUCTIVE STRUCTURE, INDUCTIVE-DEDUCTIVE STRUCTURE, and INDUCTIVE STRUCTURE.

deep focus shot a term borrowed from cinema, used to describe the effect of a wide-angle lens enabling the viewer to see background, middleground, and foreground clearly. This view is not normally possible with either the naked eye or with the conventional lens. The d.f.s. was first used by Orson Welles in *Citizen Kane*. See CINEMATIC TECHNIQUES. See also *cinematic terms* in APPENDIX 1.

deep image a term widely used in contemporary discussions of poetry, but which no one has specifically defined. In general the term refers to an IMAGE that connects the physical world with the spiritual world, and in this way is synonymous with the much older term ANAGOGE. Some of the contemporary associations of d.i. can be glimpsed in the following quotation from Robert Bly in an essay on Francis Ponge (*The Georgia Review*, Spring 1980, p. 107):

> Something surprising happens often during the writing (of the prose poem). It is as if the object itself, a stump or an orange, has links with the human psyche, and the unconscious provides material it would not give if asked directly. The unconscious passes into the object and returns. The union of the object with the psyche moves slowly , and the poem may take four to five years to write.

See ANAGOGICAL VISION and LEAPING POETRY. See also *imagery* in APPENDIX 1.

deesis /dē-ē'sis/ (Greek, denoting a relation to a "god") a figure of emotional speech in which the speaker fervently desires something for the sake of God or mankind. See *figures of pathos* in APPENDIX 2.

defective foot a line of conventional verse that lacks one or more unstressed syllables, as in:

Thís iš thĕ / fórešt přim / évăl

Here the last foot is "defective" because it lacks the extra unstressed syllable that would make it conform to the dactylic METER of the rest of the line. Actually the term d.f. is a misnomer since complete metrical regularity can be boring, and metrical variation, skillfully used, is desirable. See CATALEXIS and TRUNCATION.

definition poem: See FILL-IN-THE-BLANKS POEM.

deletion (from Latin for "to blot out or efface") the process of REVISION in which some part of a poem is taken out, thus making the revision subtractive.

denotation (from Latin for "to mark out") the exact, specific meaning of a word, independent of the associated attitudes and feelings that the word might invoke. For a fuller discussion, see the opposite term CONNOTATION. See also *diction* in APPENDIX 1.

dénouement /dänōōmäN′/ (French for "an untying") an element of PLOT in which the main dramatic complications are resolved. D. refers usually to the events following the CLIMAX, and especially to the last scene in which the mysteries are unraveled. In Shakespeare's *Midsummer Night's Dream*, e.g., the d. is the final rearrangement of the pairs of lovers and their subsequent marriages. See DRAMATIC STRUCTURE. See also *closure* and *dramatic terms* in APPENDIX 1.

density (from Latin for "thickness") the degree of compression (or *thickness*) in the language of a poem that is achieved through sound, RHYTHM, imagery, figures, concepts, structure, syntax, or any combination of these elements. For example, Wallace Stevens' poems could be said to have a high degree of d. in their imagery and concepts, Dylan Thomas' poems in their sound patterns, John Berryman's poems in their syntax, and e.e. cummings' poems in their TYPOGRAPHICAL ARRANGEMENT and POINT OF VIEW. The so-called *plain style* in contemporary poetry has a low degree of d.

description (from Latin for "sketching off in writing or painting") the type of writing or speaking that relates how something looks, smells, sounds, feels, or acts. Its purpose is to portray a sense impression and thereby indicate a mood. D. is usually not an end in itself, but rather is used as a complement to narration or exposition. Since the best d. is made of graphic and concrete details, it depends on the writer's ability to select and arrange images. See IMAGERY.

deus ex machina /dā′əs eks mäk′-/ (Latin for "god from a machine") a device that originates unexpectedly outside the plot and which is meant to resolve the forces of conflict in a work. Because of its seemingly forced appearance and application, critics such as Aristotle have condemned the device by claiming the d.e.m. must be prepared for by having it grow out of the action of the plot itself. The device was a convention of Classical Greek drama, as used by Euripides in about half of his plays. See DRAMATIC STRUCTURE. See also *dramatic terms* in APPENDIX 1.

deuteragonist /dyōōtərag′-/ (from Greek for "second actor") the character who is second in importance to the PROTAGONIST in Classical Greek drama. Often the d. is the ANTAGONIST. The term is currently used to designate a character of secondary importance, such as Claudius in *Hamlet*. See *Dramatic terms* in APPENDIX 1.

devotional poetry (devotional, from Latin for "dedicated by a vow") a GENRE of poetry that directs and restricts its attention to the praise of God and his works. The genre was popular from antiquity to the early 20th century, but it has now dwindled in use, although it can still be found to thrive among avocational poets of the American South and Southwest. See *forms* in APPENDIX 1.

diacope /dī·ak′əpē/ (Greek for "cleft" or "a cutting through") a figure of repetition that uses the various semantic senses of a word for special effect. D. is similar to EPIZEUXIS but places words between the word repeated, e.g., "When I put life into the life I led / My life was never so well fed." See *figures of repetition* in APPENDIX 2.

diaeresis /dī·er′əsis/ (Greek for "a dividing"; also spelled "dieresis") literally, a division. There are three different meanings of d.: (1) a figure of division that divides something of a general nature into its specific parts or terms, as in the Aristotelian "genus into species" classification, e.g., "For weapons we have daggers, guns, rockets / and the will of the people in our pockets"; (2) the distinct pronunciation of two successive vowels so that they occur as separate sounds, e.g., in the word "cooperation"; and (3), in Classical prosody, the place where a word and metrical foot simultaneously end. The pause within a line that occurs when d. takes place is called a d.-pause, which creates a longer pause and gives unity and emphatic pacing to the line. An example is Milton's

> Hăd cást / hĭm oút / frŏm Héav'n / wĭth aĺl / hĭs hóst.

See *figures of division* in APPENDIX 2.

dialect (from Greek for "speaking together") the spoken language of a people whose specific geographical location, cultural heritage, or position in society makes their DICTION, PHONETICS, and grammar distinct from those of other peoples. D., in DIALOGUE or speech, is a major technique of CHARACTERIZATION and has been used effectively by writers from Chaucer to Robert Frost. It makes the education, social status, and geographical location of a character obvious, and is said to have been derived from a community's isolation and resultant homogeneity. Denis Johnson's poem *The Boarding* portrays the character and voice of a New York Jewish lady whose complaint is made more poignant because of the d. in which it is spoken:

> "Watch det my medicine one second for me will you dolling,
> I'm four feet and det's a tall bus you got and its hot
> and I got every disease they are making these days,
> My God, Jesus Christ, I'm telling you out of my soul."

When d. occurs within a small region of a country, as in the Northeast United States where people of Maine and New York states maintain different idioms and habits of speech, it is termed a *subdialect*. Generally speaking, the difference in speech is a difference in sound and not in semantics. See *diction* in APPENDIX 1.

dialectic *rhetorically*, the logical movement of ideas in an ARGUMENT, and a major technique used by debators to undermine an opponent's argument by stating it, then pointing out its deficiencies, and then proceeding to state the strengths of the proponent's point of view. The d. moves through a series of positive and negative statements either shuffled together or stated in separate groupings. *Stylistically*, d. is usually connected by a number of transitional words or phrases, such as "on the other hand," "nevertheless," or "in addition to," which lend direction and coherence to the essay or speech. In prose and poetry, the d. moves by way of the *hypotactic style*, which uses connecting words such as "when," "then," or "so." It moves the ideas and plot forward by pointing out the logical relationships between ideas and events. The *paratactic style* features the JUXTAPOSITION of events, ideas, or images without any intervening connecting words, and thus forms a kind of disjointed d. Poets such as Richard Hugo use the paratactic method of d. See *figures of argumentation* in APPENDIX 2, and *structures of arguments* in APPENDIX 1.

dialogismus (from Greek for "speaking together") a figure of definition by division that uses "subject and adjunct" and comes under the class of *enargia* in which there is a vivid description of someone absent. D., also known by the Latin term *sermocinatio*, is the representation of fictional speech with imagined persons. See *figures of subject and adjunct* in APPENDIX 2.

dialogue a narrative and dramatic device that represents characters exchanging opinions. D. is used in a poem to advance the action or PLOT, to establish relationships between characters (See CHARACTER), to give an impression of naturalness, to present an interplay of ideas, to vary SYNTAX, DICTION, and RHYTHM, to lighten the TONE of a serious passage, or any combination of these purposes.

　　D., simply enough, is the device of characters speaking together. Thus, it differs from a MONOLOGUE, where one character is speaking, and from an address, which starts the main character on his speech. The most famous classical verse dialogues are by Horace. In modern poetry, Yeats' *Dialogue of Self and Soul*, Dylan Thomas' *Under Milkwood*, and Frost's *West-Running Brook* and *The Death of the Hired Man* are well-known examples of d. See SOLILOQUY. See also *dramatic terms* in APPENDIX 1.

dialysis /dī·al′-/ (Greek for "separation, dissolution") a figure of argumentation that divides its terms by first stating a major premise, then listing reasons that end with a summary conclusion. It is similar to the DILEMMA argument. See *figures of argumentation* in APPENDIX 2.

dianoia /dī·ənoi′ə/ (Greek for "reflective knowledge") a term, according to Northorp Frye, that Aristotle uses to refer to the THEME of the poem. D. is one of three elements in a work of literature, the other two being MYTHOS (the story or PLOT), and ETHOS (the CHARACTERIZATION).

diaphora /dī·af′-/ (Greek for "difference") a figure of repetition that first uses a word in its designated general sense, followed by its use in a qualifying sense. The figure is used for a sense of progression and emphasis: "What *man* never shed a tear? / A *man* who holds nothing dear." See *figures of repetition* in APPENDIX 2.

diastole: See SYSTOLE AND DIASTOLE.

diasyrmus /dī·əsur′məs/ (from Greek for "ridicule") a figure of argumentation that refutes an opponent's argument by an outright rejection using an absurd comparison: "For you to marry my daughter would be like mating a dove with a baboon." See *figures of argumentation* in APPENDIX 2.

diatyposis /dī·ə-/ (Greek for "vivid description") the originating of rules to live by that are meant for one's immediate audience or for posterity: "To women on the tendencies of men: / the more powerless you seem, / the more power men will give you." See *types of testimony* in APPENDIX 2.

diazeugma /dī·əzoog′mə/ (Greek for "double yoking") a grammatical construction (technically incorrect) that uses one noun applied to more than one verb. D. is used for the sake of melody and brevity: "The king kissed his queen, mounted his horse, and rode off to join the crusade." See *grammatical constructions* in APPENDIX 2.

dibrach /dī′brak/ (from Greek for "two short") in Greek and Latin prosody, a metrical FOOT consisting of two short syllables (˘˘). See METER and PYRRHIC.

dicaeologia (from Greek for "plea in defense") a figure of argumentation that uses an excuse showing an absolute necessity by the doer: "I confess I stole a loaf of bread, but my family was starving." See *figures of argumentation* in APPENDIX 2.

diction (from Latin for "mode of expression") the choice and arrangement of words in a work of literature. D. can be analyzed by examining the level to which the word choice is abstract or concrete, colloquial or formal, common or technical, literal or figurative, and Latinate or Anglo-Saxon. Sometimes d. is described in terms of four levels of language: (1) *formal*, as in serious discourse; (2) *informal*, as in relaxed but polite conversation; (3) *colloquial*, as in everyday usage; and (4) *slang*, as in impolite and newly coined words (see NEOLOGISM). It is generally agreed that the qualities of proper d. are appropriateness, correctness, and accuracy. A distinction is usually made between d., which refers to the choice of words, and STYLE, which refers to the manner in which the words are used.

Since the poetry of almost every age has been written in a special language which includes words, phrases, syntactical constructions, and FIGURES OF SPEECH not found in the ordinary conversation of the time, the term POETIC D. has come to refer to the use of artifice in the language of literature. In particular, the term poetic d. is usually applied to the work of Neo-Classical writers such as Thomas Gray who claimed that "the language of the age is never the language of poetry." Neo-Classical d. was derived in part from the widespread imitation of Virgil, Spenser, and Milton as well as common acceptance of the principles of DECORUM. According to these principles each GENRE required a certain level of d.

Formal SATIRE, e.g., Pope's *Epistle to Arbuthnot*, required language that resembled the speech of a cultured gentleman; while other genres, such as EPIC, TRAGEDY, and ODE, required a special d. in order to raise the style to the level of the form. Characteristics of Neo-Classical d. include the use of EPITHET, ARCHAISM, INVOCATION, PERSONIFICATION, and PERIPHRASIS. The last characteristic device was overused to such an extent that many later writers point to its use during this period as representative of the dangers of thinking of the language of poetry as being far removed from ordinary language. James Thomson's *The Seasons* has been particularly singled out for ridicule for his heavy dependence on periphrasis. Thomson writes "the finny tribe" for "fish," "the bleating kind" for "sheep," and when he means "she removed her stocking" he writes "from the snowy leg . . . the inverted silk she drew."

In the preface to *Lyrical Ballads*, Wordsworth attacked the Neo-Classical ideal of a refined language for poetry by claiming that there is no "essential difference between the language of prose and metrical composition." He called the Neo-Classical poetic diction "artificial," "vicious," and "unnatural." Wordsworth went on to establish the criteria of an appropriate d. for poetry: It should be the result of a "spontaneous overflow of powerful feelings," and it should be based on the speech of a "humble and rustic life."

In the 20th century, the debate between the adherents of a "poetic diction" and the adherents of a "natural diction" continues. Although Wordsworth's idea that poetry should be based on everyday speech is widely accepted, many poets, e.g., Wallace Stevens, use a wide range of d. that is far removed from the everyday language of shopkeepers and college students. Even the work of a poet like William Carlos Williams, who tried to capture the common idioms of the American language, displays a wide range of d.

See ABSTRACT TERMS AND CONCRETE TERMS, BARBARISM, BILLINGSGATE, CLASSICAL FALLACY, CLICHÉ, COLLOQUIALISM, DIALECT, EUPHEMISM, EUPHUISM, FLAT STATEMENT, JARGON, LOCALISM, NEO-CLASSICISM, OVERWRITING, PLAIN STYLE, PRECIOUSNESS, PURPLE PATCH, REGIONALISM, and SLACKNESS. See also *diction* in APPENDIX 1.

didactic poetry /dīdak'-/ (*didactic*, from Greek for "apt at teaching") poetry that seeks to instruct. In its earliest form it grew from the PROVERB. D.p. is concerned more with moral instruction or practical and philosophical information than with imaginative purposes. From the Middle Ages to the 18th century, the form enjoyed much popularity, though it can be traced back to Virgil and Lucretius. Other famous works of d.p. include Pope's *Essay on Criticism*, Ovid's *Art of Love*, Chaucer's *Nun's Priest's Tale*, Dante's *Divine Comedy*, and Milton's *Paradise Lost*. Most critics agree on the existence of d.p. as a genre, but many disagree on which specific works could be classified as such since the decision is a subjective one. Although the genre is currently unfashionable because of changes in religious and aesthetic values, notable examples of d.p. can still be found in the work of poets such as Pablo Neruda, Denise Levertov, and Allen Ginsberg, among others. See ALLEGORY, APHORISM, DEVOTIONAL POETRY, FABLE, and SATIRE. See also the antonym, AUTOTELIC.

dieresis: See DIAERESIS.

diffused focus a cinematic technique adopted as a critical term that refers to a blurry or slightly incoherent image or set of images meant to lend a soft, impressionistic aura, so that a confused or emotional quality is imbued. As a defect in uncontrolled writing, it represents a lack of focus behind which is a confused message and a bewildered intention. See CINEMATIC TECHNIQUES and MOOD PIECE.

digression (from Latin for "to go aside") a passage that is not closely related to the logical development, basic theme, or central plot of the rest of a work. Although there are forms of acceptable digressions, such as the EPIC SIMILE, they are usually seen as a defect in CONTROL. An extended d. is known as an *excursus*, and writers such as Swift have capitalized upon it as a humorous device. See *defects in control* in APPENDIX 1.

diiamb /dī·ĭ′amb/ or /dī·ĭ′am/ (from Greek for "two iambs") a combination of two iambic feet considered as one metrical unit; also known as *iambic dimeter*. The general term for this fusion is SYZYGY. The ancient Greeks commonly used four-syllable feet such as the d., but modern metrical scansion favors dividing these feet into two duple units.

dilemma (Greek for "double proposition") a figure of argumentation composed of a two-part SYLLOGISM. It usually begins with a conditional or hypothetical word or phrase, such as "if" or "when," but maintains mutually exclusive terms. For example: "If you lived here, / you'd be home now. / If you were home, / You'd be here now." The d. is often used intentionally as an element of PLOT, such as when a CHARACTER has two equally unfavorable choices of action. Joseph Heller's novel *Catch 22* depends on the ironic use of d. See CRISIS. See also *figures of argumentation* in APPENDIX 2.

dimeter /dim′ətər/ (from Greek for "two measures") a term that, according to Classical prosody, originally meant a measure of four feet, but which is interpreted by modern prosodists as a two-foot line. The third and fourth lines of a LIMERICK are usually in d. See METER.

diminishing metaphor a type of METAPHOR in which something known (the *vehicle*) is identified with something unknown (the *tenor*) in a disparaging frame of reference. Usually, the device takes the form of an intellectualized metaphor, a CONCEIT. This favorite skeptical substitution was used by METAPHYSICAL POETRY, as can be seen in the following verse from John Donne, in which the vehicle is the serpent and the tenor is the woman:

> But as some Serpent's poyson hurteth not,
> Except it be from the live serpent shot,
> So doth her vertue need her here, to fit
> That unto us; she working more than it.

According to this classification, a type of metaphor in which the vehicle flatters the tenor might be called an *expanding metaphor,* as in this anonymous couplet:

> As the rays of the sun gladden the sight,
> So will my death abide in light.

Dinggedicht /ding'gedisht/ (German for "poem of things") a school of poetry that attempts to describe the inner state of an object. D. was developed as an aesthetic stance by Rainer Maria Rilke who, as secretary to the sculptor Rodin, was so impressed by the vitality of the latter's works that he devoted himself to writing about them. In Rilke's *Torso of an Archaic Apollo,* based on the figure of Apollo in the Archaic Room of the Louvre Museum, the poet speaks in the mask of Rodin about the object's pattern of existence which is so full of energy and light that it requires us to change our lives. The poem's translator is C.F. MacIntyre:

> *Torso of an Archaic Apollo*
> Never will we know his fabulous head
> where the eyes' apples slowly ripened. Yet
> his torso glows: a candelabrum set
> before his gaze, which is pushed back and hid,
>
> restrained and shining. Else the curving breast
> could not thus blind you, nor through the soft turn
> of the loins could this smile easily have passed
> into the bright groins where the genitals burned.
>
> Else stood this stone a fragment and defaced,
> with lucent body from the shoulders falling,
> too short, not gleaming like a lion's fell;
>
> nor would this star have shaken the shackles off,
> bursting with delight, until there is no place
> that does not see you. You must change your life.

dipody /dip'-/ (from Greek for a "combination of two feet") a prosodic unit of two feet. Classical prosody often measured two similar or identical metrical feet as a single unit: that is, two iambs would be counted as one d., and four iambs would be two dipodies. Often, there may be a variation in rhythmical stress in one half of the d., making the two halves rhythmically similar but not identical. See *forms* in APPENDIX 1.

dirge /durj/ (from *dirige,* the first word of the Latin ANTIPHON *Dirige, Domine, Deus meus, in conspectu tuo viam meam*) a song or poem lamenting the dead and meant to commemorate them. While the name is of Latin origin, the genre is Greek. In Shakespeare's *The Tempest,* Ariel's song of Ferdinand's lost father is a d.

The Greek THRENODY and MONODY are forms of d.; but the modern ELEGY is more meditative than the outpourings of the d. The Latin forms of d. are written in hexameters or the elegaic distich. In popular usage, the term has come to denote any kind of solemn, mournful song or poem. In Classical Greece, Pindar employed the form, and the Latin poets Catullus and Propertius perfected it. See LAMENT. See also *forms* in APPENDIX 1.

dirimens copulatio a figure of logic subsumed under the category of "comparisons of greater, equal, and less." The figure states a condition that is followed by a greater cause or reason, as in this couplet from Whitman's *Song of Myself*:

> Dazzling and tremendous how quick the sun-rise would kill me,
> If I could not now and always send sun-rise out of me.

See *figures comparing greater, lesser, or equal things* in APPENDIX 2.

disemic /dīsē'-/ (from Greek for "two time-units") in Classical Greek and Latin prosody, the duration of a long syllable equal to two shorter syllables, a practice still common in musical notation. Thus in QUANTITA-TIVE METER, the word "crows" in the following example is equal in duration to "are not" and "wise":

> Crows ăre nŏt wise.

dispondee /dīspon'dē/ (from Greek for "two spondees") double spondees measured as a single unit or DIPODY, as in the following example:

> oĺd bláck coĺd stóve

The foot never occurs in a series and is seldom found as an independent foot in English poetry. See METER and SCANSION.

dissociation of sensibility T.S. Eliot's term (*Metaphysical Poets*, 1921) for the failure of certain 18th-century poets to integrate feelings and intellect. Eliot claimed that the influence of Dryden and Milton was to a large degree responsible for this failure. The d.o.s. is the opposite of what Eliot called the *unified sensibility*, which fuses mind and emotions. Critics of Eliot see his dichotomy as an artificial schism designed to justify the particular poetics held by Eliot. See METAPHYSICAL CONCEIT and META-PHYSICAL POETRY. See also *criticism* in APPENDIX 1.

dissonance (from Latin for "disagreement in sound") discordant sounds and rhythm produced by CONSONANCE, OFF-RHYME, or harsh-sounding syllables. Donne, Browning, Swinburne, and Hopkins used it effectively; but the device often shows up in less skillful hands as a defect. See CACAPHONY and EUPHONY.

dissyllabic foot: See DUPLE FOOT.

distance and involvement the degree of detachment or empathy a reader maintains toward a poem. The more involved a reader becomes in a work of art, the less concerned he is with personal or practical matters peripheral to the work. Oftentimes a reader's degree of involvement in a poem is proportionate to the degree of involvement or distance on the part of the poem's speaker. See AESTHETIC DISTANCE.

distich /dis'tik/ (from Greek for 'two lines of verse"; a similarly used term is CLOSED COUPLET) two metrically regular lines that develop a complete thought in end-rhyme form. Pope employed the d., as well as Milton who wrote the following d.: "These pleasures, Melancholy, give, / And I with thee will choose to live." Greek and Latin prosody of the Classical period used the ELEGIAC D., a line of dactylic hexameter followed by a line of dactylic pentameter.

The modern rhymed d. is more often called a COUPLET.

distinction (from Latin for "separation, division") a logical argument based on the meaning or notation of a word, as in the following: "You say I should be sorry for what I've done. If by 'sorry' you mean regretful, yes, I regret ever having met you; if by 'sorry' you mean miserable, then, yes, you've made me that." See *figures of notation and conjugation* in APPENDIX 2.

distracting detail a detail that indicates an arbitrary or nonfunctional use of images in a setting. It is the opposite defect of overly general writing since it tends to accumulate too many specific images that obscure or submerge the thematic development of a poem. See *defects in control* in APPENDIX 1.

distributed stress (similarly used terms are HOVERING STRESS or "resolved accent") two consecutive syllables of undeterminable but approximately equal DURATION and STRESS. The syllables in question could be forced into regular metrical scansion and be termed *spondaic*, but because there is some doubt as to their equality, prosodists feel it is more accurate to indicate that slight qualitative difference by using the term d.s. In the following line by Tennyson, the syllables marked by a slur exemplify the use of the rhythm:

There is sweet music here that softer falls . . .

disyllabic foot: See DUPLE FOOT.

dithyramb /dith'iramb/ or /dith'iram/ (derivation unkown) a Greek choric hymn structured in strophes about Dionysus or Bacchus. Later on, the form used subjects from all periods of Greek mythology, and in more recent times the d. loosened up into a dittylike quality, as in these satirical lines from Dryden's *Alexander's Feast*:

> With ravished ears
> The monarch hears,
> Assumes the god,
> Affects to nod,
> And seems to shake the spheres.

dithyrambic /-ram'-/ a wildly enthusiastic lyric or poem whose style evolved from the original Greek choric hymns to Dionysus and Bacchus. Shelley's *Ode to the West Wind*, Blake's prophecies, and poems by Swinburne, Hugo, and Christopher Smart exemplify the rhapsodic or possessed quality of the d. In contemporary poetry, works by Michael McClure, Ginsberg, and Robert Duncan, among others, illustrate the mode. See *forms* in APPENDIX 1.

ditrochee /dītrō'kē/ (from Greek for "two trochees") double trochees measured as a single unit or DIPODY.

divine afflatus (*afflatus*, Latin for "breathing, inspiration") the period before composition when a poet is said to be inspired by the MUSE. The idea is often ascribed to Plato, though today it has fallen out of fashion and is often used sarcastically. See INSPIRATION and LOCATION.

dizain /dizeN′/ or /dizān′/ (French for "a collection of ten") a French *fixed form* of ten lines composed of eight or ten syllables each, rhyming ababbccdcd. As an autonomous form, it resembles the EPIGRAM. Consecutive dizains with an added ENVOY could form a BALLADE or CHANT ROYAL. See FIXED FORMS. See also *forms* in APPENDIX 1.

doggerel (from *dog*) trivial LIGHT VERSE written in an uneven, irregular style usually containing obvious rhyme and rhythm. The form, in the hands of masters such as John Skelton, Samuel Butler, and Jonathan Swift, can be effective as a parodic vehicle. The EPITAPH on Shakespeare's tomb illustrates the genre:

> Good friend, for Jesus' sake forbear
> To dig the dust enclosed here!
> Blest be the man that spares these stones,
> And cursed be he that moves my bones.

See HUDIBRASTIC VERSE, parody, and SKELTONIC VERSE. See also *forms and humor* in APPENDIX 1.

domain of thought (also known as "frame of reference") a method of classifying metaphors based upon things common to a particular area of concern, such as nature, science, religion, or art. In 19th-century France the method of d.o.t. was developed to describe the matrix or grounding of a metaphor, or group of metaphors; and this system was further refined by German linguists into the *Domain Trait* formula which attempted a point-by-point analytical comparison of the terms within metaphors.

domestic poetry a contemporary term, probably borrowed from 18th-century English drama (the DOMESTIC TRAGEDY), which denotes a genre of poetry concerned with the everyday life of common people. Critics have, at times, used the term contemptuously to indicate the low position and limitations in dramatic scope of such concerns. See *forms* in APPENDIX 1.

domestic tragedy poetic drama concerning the lives of middle- or lower-class characters. It was first developed on the Elizabethan stage in plays such as *Arden of Feversham* and *A Woman Killed with Kindness*, but it was not until the 18th century that it won acceptance as a dramatic genre. See *dramatic terms* in APPENDIX 1.

dominant impression the general thematic lesson of importance that a poem conveys. For instance, T.S. Eliot's *The Lovesong of J. Alfred Prufrock* conveys the d.i. of society's overbearing restrictions placed upon a weak soul. Although less accurate in its specificity, the term is similar to the critical term THEME.

Doric (from *Doris*, a Greek town where the *D.* dialect was spoken) a simple and unpretentious style, especially of the PASTORAL poets writing in the Greek dialect. The style is said to be somewhat rustic but characterized by the strength of straightforwardness. Later writers who adopted the voice include Milton in *Lycidas*, Wordsworth in his nature poems, and Tennyson in his *Dora*. The contrasting term is ATTIC.

double ballade a poem composed of six octaves, instead of three octaves as in the BALLADE, and composed of only three or four rhymes. There is usually a REFRAIN, but no ENVOY. Alfred Noyes wrote a *triple ballade* of nine octaves with an envoy. Variations of the form include poems written in ten-line stanzas. See *forms* in APPENDIX 1.

double ending a poem that closes twice. The technique is common in classical music in which multiple endings are stated. For example, Stanley Kunitz's *The Portrait* creates a double, reflexive closure; the first ending, that of the mother slapping her son, is reflected upon by the last two lines of the second ending. Oftentimes, the structure of the d.e. is created by an editorial comment on the part of the speaker who explains or enhances the dramatic action. See *closure* in APPENDIX 1.

double entendre /doo′bläNtäNd′r/ or /dub′əl-/ (French for "double understanding") the use of any word to refer to two meanings. Other types of d.e. are the EQUIVOQUE, in which a word contains different discordant meanings, as in the Elizabethan word "die" (both to lose one's life and to reach sexual orgasm), and the PUN, a play on words that are spelled or pronounced differently, as in "they went to the *ball* and ended up *bawling*." See also EQUIVOCATION.

double rhyme (also called "double full rhyme") a pair of words in which evenly stressed (and sometimes rhymed) syllables are followed by identical unstressed syllables, as in "dreaming" and "steaming." See FEMININE RHYME and RHYME.

draft a version of a poem still in its stages of REVISION. The d. can exist as scattered, disjointed notes or images, or as a completed, polished poem, a *final d.* The process of writing multiple drafts of a poem is not merely analytical, or critical; it can be as creative a process and as complex a procedure as the freer, originating impulse of the poem. See SHAPING.

dramatic convention the acceptance by the audience of a certain literary practice that simulates reality, e.g., the compression of REAL TIME in a poem or play, the invention of masks and personae as representing real speakers, and the representation of thought as seen in the DRAMATIC MONOLOGUE. See CONVENTION. See also *dramatic terms* in APPENDIX 1.

dramatic dialogue two or more characters (the speaker of the poem may be counted as one) speaking alternately to one another so that plot and theme are developed ideally to a point of climax or resolution. The speakers may be equal or unequal in importance, and it is possible to have monologues indirectly answer or enhance one another. Robert Frost's *West Running Brook*, composed of dialogue expressing the contrasting characters of a man and woman, is a good example of the d.d. See *dramatic terms* in APPENDIX 1.

dramatic irony (also know as "tragic irony") a situation in which the audience is aware of information or action that the characters in the piece of literature are not aware of. Therefore, what is spoken has a double meaning to the audience but a single meaning to the character. D.i. depends more upon structure than DIALOGUE. For instance, in *Hamlet* there is a play-within-a-play structure in which characters mime the killing of Hamlet's father by Claudius. While Hamlet, Claudius, and the reader of the play are aware of this mirror-effect, other characters in *Hamlet* do not understand the double meaning of what they are witnessing. See IRONY. See also *dramatic terms* in APPENDIX 1.

dramatic lyric: See DRAMATIC MONOLOGUE.

dramatic monologue a type of SOLILOQUY in which a character (not the poet) addresses a silent listener, and in his speech reveals his own nature, the nature of the conflict in his situation (see DRAMATIC SITUATION), and the period and setting of the poem or play. Robert Browning perfected the form in *My Last Duchess* and *Soliloquy of the Spanish Cloister*, and Eliot used the technique notably in *The Lovesong of J. Alfred Prufrock*. Robert Browning's synonymous term is *dramatic lyric*. See *dramatic terms* in APPENDIX 1.

dramatic poetry poetry that employs dramatic techniques in order to achieve poetic ends, or, conversely, drama that employs verse. The term is meant to indicate the inclusion of one form within another. There are many plays that use verse, including all of Shakespeare's plays; and Browning's poetic work employs conventions of drama such as the DRAMATIC MONOLOGUE. The DRAMATIC SITUATION, BLANK VERSE, and poetic DICTION are other techniques used in d.p.

dramatic situation the representation through NARRATION, IMAGERY, META-PHOR, or DIALOGUE of a situation that contains forces of conflict. The d.s. answers the question "What is happening?" and can be reduced to a prose summary. The d.s. acts as a springboard toward philosophical specul-ation, the psychology of a character, the morality of an action or event, or the celebration of an emotion. See *dramatic terms* in APPENDIX 1.

dramatic structure the plan that creates and resolves conflict in a piece of literature. Ideally, it is made up of five parts: (1) the *introduction*, which puts forth the SETTING, the background, the characters, and the TONE; (2) the *rising action*, in which an event or series of events complicates the PLOT; (3) the *climax*, in which the action reaches a dramatic peak; (4) the *falling action*, in which an event or action by an antagonistic character leads to tragedy; and (5) the *catastrophe*, in which the protagonist is killed or dies, eventually resulting in a new order or a restoration of order (see DÉNOUEMENT). Although most plays do not fit this five-part scheme based on Elizabethan tragedy, the term is still useful to point to the abstract pattern of rising and falling conflict in a piece of literature. See *dramatic terms* in APPENDIX 1.

dramatis personae /dram'ətis persōn'ē/ (Latin for "persons [literally, masks] in the play") the characters in a play. Usually, play programs head the list of characters and relationships with this Latin phrase. See *dramatic terms* in APPENDIX 1.

dream allegory or dream vision a narrative device, popular in the 12th and 13th centuries, in which a major character falls asleep and dreams the events of the story. Usually, the characters have allegorical names such as Pride, Humility, or Death, and their actions are symbolic. The major character is usually guided through the dream by another human (as Dante is led by Virgil in *The Divine Comedy*) or by an animal (as Dorothy is led by Toto in *The Wizard of Oz*). There is a wide range of variations of the d.a.o.d.v., including *Piers Plowman*, Chaucer's *The Book of the Duchess*, Dante's *Divine Comedy*, *Alice's Adventures in Wonderland*, and *The Wizard of Oz*. The d.a.o.d.v. probably originated with Cicero's *Somnium Scipionis* in his *Republic*. See ALLEGORY, SYMBOL, and VISION. See also *forms* in APPENDIX 1.

dream poetry poetry either directly or indirectly based on dreams, or written in the ASSOCIATIONAL LOGIC of the dream. In the early 20th century, the Surrealists felt that the dream state should be exteriorized without being filtered through or subjected to analytical thought. André Breton and Paul Eluard wrote about the power of the subconscious during sleep in *Notes sur la Poesie*:

> In the poet
> It is intelligence waking that kills;
> It is sleep that dreams and sees clearly.

Possibly the most satisfying way to interpret Surrealist poetry is to experience it through the body's senses, not the intellect. There is a clarity and primitiveness to dream imagery that modern biologists have come to believe harkens back to a time in man's evolution when all the senses were fused and unfiltered, when they channeled through one another (see SYNAESTHESIA). Images produced sounds; odors created images; textures produced sensations in all the other senses. The Surrealists maintained that by the innate nature of man and his gift to dream, everyone who dreams is a Surrealist. The dreamer "experiences" his dream (even though one of his selves may be watching him dream), so that his subconscious understanding of the dream is complete. In a sense, he understands the dream because he *is* the dream, but he may have a difficult time transforming the experience into language. See DREAM ALLEGORY and DREAMSCAPE. See also *forms* in APPENDIX 1.

dreamscape the IMAGERY in a dream indicating SETTING, ATMOSPHERE, MOOD, characters, and, often, psychology of the speaker. See LOCATION.

dream vision: See DREAM ALLEGORY.

duende /dōō·en′da/ (Spanish for "ghost," though in the Andalusian dialect the word signifies "demonic inspiration") Federico García Lorca's term for "black sounds" through which the feeling of a struggle with death emanates, and about which he felt that "there is no greater truth." By striving to transcend the power of darkness within the soul, the artist encounters a struggle with d., an event in song or poetry "not in the throat ... [but] up from the very soles of the feet." See García Lorca's lyrical essay *The Duende: Theory and Divertissement*.

duple foot (also called "dissyllabic foot" or "disyllabic foot") any metrical unit of two syllables, such as an iamb, trochee, pyrrhic, or spondee. The d.f. is derived from the original Greek four-syllable foot, which in English has been broken in half, a separation caused by heavy stresses. The d.f. can occur in a line of any length.

duration (from Latin for "a hardening, an enduring") the Classical Greek quantitative measurement that considers the time it takes to say one or more syllables. In this system of SCANSION, as in musical notation, two short syllables are equal in quantity to one long syllable. While d. in English verse is a qualitative function of pronunciation, it is not used as a scansion unit since most metrical poetry is based on stress rather than time. See DISEMIC and QUANTITATIVE METER.

E

earned pertaining to the proper preparation or groundwork made by a poem in order to introduce an IMAGE, METAPHOR, statement, or CHARACTER. This contemporary critical term can also refer to the writer's AUTHORITY of VOICE and STYLE in presenting the experience of the poem. See *expressive criticism* under CRITICISM.

Eastern ending the CLOSURE of a poem that continues to develop quietly and to complete itself in the reader's mind after the actual printed ending of the poem has been read. Many Chinese and Asian FIXED FORMS display this type of ongoing ending, thus the derivation of the term. The following haiku's meaning develops slowly after the poem has ended (pay special attention to the phrase "city fields"):

> In the city fields
> Contemplating cherry trees
> Strangers are like friends.

See WESTERN ENDING, the opposite of E.e. See also LEAPING POETRY, and *closure* in APPENDIX 1.

echo allusion a twisting of a well-known saying, often for ironic effect, as in Oscar Wilde's PARODY of Abraham Lincoln's phrase: ". . . but democracy means simply the bludgeoning of the people by the people for the people." See ALLUSION.

echo rhyme subtle effect of rhyming produced by placing similar or identical sounds at distances that present an auditory shadow effect. It can result from the use of ALLITERATION, ASSONANCE, consonance, OFF-RHYME, REPETEND, or REFRAIN, and it can take place at various positions in lines. As a formal device, it can be a means of structuring a poem by way of its music. In the following lines the rhyme "sighs it" and "quiet" has enough distance between these words so that the effect is softly echoed rather than brashly coupled: "She *sighs it*, and men in lonely rooms / turn toward their window, suddenly *quiet*." See RHYME.

echo verse poetry or LIGHT VERSE in which the last syllable(s) of one line is (are) repeated in the next line but with a different meaning. The form was popular in Renaissance France, Italy, and England, and was used extensively in PASTORAL POETRY. George Herbert's *Heaven* employed the device, and it is skillfully presented in the following lines of Swift's *A Gentle Echo on Woman*:

> What most moves women when we them address?
> A dress.

Say, what can keep her chaste whom I adore?
                    A door.

See *forms* in APPENDIX 1.

eclipsis: See ELLIPSIS.

eclogue /ek'log/ (from Greek for "to select, to choose") originally, because of the influence of Virgil's *Eclogues,* a PASTORAL poem that followed the form derived from the idylls of Theocritus. By the 18th century, critics distinguished the e. from the pastoral, and e. came to be synonymous with a dramatic poem that uses plot and characters. An e. can be in the form of a DIALOGUE or SOLILOQUY. Modern examples are Frost's *Build Soil,* MacNeice's *Eclogue from Iceland,* and Auden's *Age of Anxiety.* See *forms* in APPENDIX 1.

ecphonesis /-nē'-/ (Greek for "exclamation"; also known as "exclamation") a figure of emotion that uses exclamatory speech. The device is often found in Elizabethan tragedies, such as *Macbeth* and *King Lear.* See *figures of pathos* in APPENDIX 2.

edition (from Latin for "to give out") the form of a book or any printed matter in its original version. Revisions in size, shape, and content constitute a new e. See *publishing format* under *forms* in APPENDIX 1.

editorial intrusion as an intentional device, an author's interruption of the poem's speaker or its narration in order to explain, sum up, or add a perspective otherwise unattained by the poem. As an unintended break in the development of the poem, the device is a *defect in control* (see APPENDIX 1).

Edwardian Period a period of English literature between Queen Victoria's death (1901) and the beginning of World War I (1914) when King Edward VII reigned. Noteworthy poets of the period include Thomas Hardy, W.B. Yeats, Alfred Noyes, and Rudyard Kipling. The E.P. was preceded by the VICTORIAN PERIOD and followed by the MODERN PERIOD.

effectiveness (from Latin for "a working out, an accomplishing") a judgment as to how well an author communicates an experience, argument, or state of mind. E. is, of course, dependent upon technical matters such as STRATEGY, DICTION, or RHYTHM, as well as subjective matters such as the quality of perception, imagination, and knowledge of human behavior. See *pragmatic criticism* under CRITICISM.

efficient cause a form of logical argumentation using two terms, an agent and his instrument, that are linked together through usage, as in Whitman's *Song of Myself:* "The carpenter dresses his plank ... the tongue of his foreplane whistles its wild ascending lisp." See *figures of argumentation* in APPENDIX 2.

elaboration (from Latin for "producing by labor") the use of repetition, restatement, added detail or tropes to complete an ARGUMENT or IMAGE. Other references of the term apply to OVERDECORATION, the use of too

many words or images. See AMPLIFICATION. See also *figures of repetition* in
APPENDIX 2.

elegiac distich /eləjīe'ək/ or /əlē'ji·ək/ originally, a Greek COUPLET (DISTICH)
of the dactylic hexameter line followed by a line of dactylic pentameter.
Homer, Ovid, and Catullus used the form, which was derived from eighth-
century songs about war and love. English poets such as Spenser, Sidney,
and Swinburne imitated the form. It was used for the THRENODY in
Classical Greece. See *forms* in APPENDIX 1.

elegiac stanza (also know as "elegiac quatrain," "heroic quatrain," and
"Hammond's meter") an iambic pentameter STANZA of four lines rhym-
ing abab, popularized by Shakespeare's sonnets and Thomas Gray's *Elegy
Written in a Country Churchyard*. See ELEGY. See also *forms* in APPEN-
DIX 1.

elegant variation elaborations, usually in the form of epithets, used to
describe an aforementioned person, place, or thing for the purpose of
avoiding repeating the name. Sir Arthur Quiller-Couch coined the term,
although Shakespeare used the device effectively hundreds of years earlier
in describing England:

> This royal throne of kings, this scepter'd isle,
> This earth of majesty, this seat of Mars,
> This other Eden, demi-paradise,
> This fortress built by Nature for herself . . .

See *figures of repetition* in APPENDIX 2, and *diction* in APPENDIX 1.

elegy /el'-/ (from Greek for "lament") a long, formal poem mourning the
dead. The original form was the ELEGIAC DISTICH, but the e. has been used
by Elizabethans and moderns in other forms, and has come to indicate a
type of mood poem rather than a form. Famous elegies include Gray's
Elegy Written in a Country Churchyard, Shelley's *Adonis*, Tennyson's *In
Memoriam*, Milton's *Lycidas*, Whitman's *When Lilacs Last in the Dooryard Bloom'd*, Rilke's *Duino Elegies*, Auden's *In Memory of W.B. Yeats*,
and Roethke's *Elegy for Jane*. See DIRGE, MONODY, and THRENODY. See
also *forms* in APPENDIX 1.

elision (from Latin for "a striking out") the omission of the final unstressed
syllable in a regular line of verse (see CATALEXIS); also, the contraction of a
word ("ne'er" for "never"). Similarly used terms are SYNAERESIS and
SYNCOPE. See the related terms SYNALEPHA and SYZYGY. See also *grammatical constructions that are technically incorrect* in APPENDIX 2.

Elizabethan /-bē'thən/ or /əliz'-/ a period of English Literature during the
Renaissance when Elizabeth I reigned (1558–1603). During this age,
England reached great nationalist and literary powers. It is known as
"The Golden Age of English Literature" due to the work of writers such
as Shakespeare, Marlowe, Sidney, Spenser, Raleigh, Jonson, and Donne.

ellipsis (Greek for "a coming short, a leaving out"; also known as "ellipse"
and "eclipsis") a figure of speech and a grammatical device in which

words of a sentence are left out for the sake of brevity, emphasis, grace, or ambiguity. The omitted words can easily be inferred from their previous context and from their grammatical compatibility. Many 20th-century poets such as Pound, Auden, Williams, and Eliot have used the device. In a similar figure, APOSIOPESIS, there is a sudden breaking off of a sentence, but the exact omitted words may not be easily inferred from the context. Usually e. dots (...) are used to indicate omissions in thought or quotations. See *devices of poetic license* in APPENDIX 2.

emblem (from Greek for "insertion"; also, more immediately, from 15th-century engravings in England and France) a visual or linguistic SYMBOL expressing a moral or abstract quality. The term originally referred to images in poetry that were derived from engravings (as in Shakespeare's *Merchant of Venice* and in poems by Spenser, Donne, and Blake). In contemporary usage, the term often signifies a schematic presentation of a poet's most frequently used images throughout the author's body of work; e.g., Sylvia Plath's e. is made up of flowers, bees, fire, and images of entrapment. In this sense, synonyms for the term are *totem* and *icon*. See *imagery* in Appendix 1.

embryonic rhyme /embri·on′ik/: See OFF-RHYME.

emotive language language that uses IMAGERY, selected details, sound, rhythm, ambiguity, and other devices to produce an emotional response in a reader toward a subject or theme. While e.l. may also carry information, purely factual information is thought of as a contrasting mode known as *referential language*, such as that found in newspapers, scientific reports, and other forms of expository writing. I. A. Richards in *The Meaning of Meaning* and *Principles of Literary Criticism* popularized the distinction between language meant to convey emotion (creative writing forms) and language meant to convey facts (dictionaries, reports, and research essays). For related terms, see COGNITIVE MEANING, and EMOTIVE MEANING.

emotive meaning the emotional level of interpretation contained in poetry or dramatic language, as opposed to the COGNITIVE MEANING, the referential or denotative level of interpretation that pertains to fact. The e.m. is usually located in the connotative, associative levels of words (see CONNOTATION), and also in characterization, dramatic action, and dialogue. See EMOTIVE LANGUAGE. See also *meaning* in APPENDIX 1.

emotive thrust the driving force of emotion that develops and completes a poem. Yeats's *Sailing to Byzantium* develops out of a man's feelings of his limitations in old age and fear of his oncoming death. See LOCATION and the associated term DIVINE AFFLATUS.

empathy (loan translation of German *Einfühlung*, for "a feeling into") a merging with the physical sensations and emotions of someone or something, the ultimate expression of involvement on the part of a reader or writer. The term, coined by Hermann Lotze in 1858 (in his *Microcosmus*), distinguishes this type of involvement from *sympathy* which runs parallel to, but does not fuse with, another person or object. Thus e. strikes actively on the physical level and moves the reader closer to the poem's experience. Keats said "If a sparrow comes before my Window, I take part of its existence and pick about the gravel." Theorists maintain that e. is not only essential to poetry, but is the basis for devices such as METAPHOR, PERSONIFICATION, and other stratagems of identity and substitution. Francis Ponge's *The Voice of Things*, a poetic dictionary composed of inanimate and animate characters, is a good example of sustained e. See AESTHETIC DISTANCE and DISTANCE AND INVOLVEMENT.

emphasis (from the Greek for "significance" [literally, "a showing in mid-voice"]) a rhetorical principle that calls on the writer or speaker to give important elements important positions and adequate development. E. can be achieved through the skillful use of repetition, contrast, elaboration, climactic ordering, selection of detail, and mechanical devices such as typeface and punctuation. The term e. also denotes a rhetorical device that substitutes an intangible quality for a more concrete term, as in "She is not vain, but vanity itself." See *figures comparing greater, lesser, or equal things* in APPENDIX 2.

emphatic line ending a type of LINE ENDING that highlights, underscores, or emphasizes character, theme, or plot by the use of simple repetition, juxtaposition, or semantic ambiguity. While the line in which this type of ending occurs can be end-stopped or enjambed, the device acts to reinforce previously stated content. See also *line endings* in APPENDIX 1.

emphatic sentence: See IRMUS.

enallage /ənel′-/ (from Greek for "exchange") a figure of exchange in which a grammatical form in case, number, gender, mood, or tense is transformed, as in the verb/noun exchange in Shakespeare's "But me no buts," or as in the verb number change of "A gaggle of people go about shopping." The last example uses a plural verb form instead of singular form called for by the collective noun because the element of melody is better served. See ANTHIMERIA and HENDIADYS. See also *grammatical figures of exchange* in APPENDIX 2, and *figurative expressions* in APPENDIX 1.

enantiosis /-ti·ō′-/ (Greek for "contradiction"; also know as "contentio") a form of IRONY that uses opposites, often in different clauses, as in "She was delicate in awkward matters, / awkward in delicate ones." For more information on rhetorical balance, See CHIASMUS. See also *contraries and contradictories* in APPENDIX 2.

encomiastic verse (*encomiastic*, from Greek for "eulogy") a type of occasional verse praising people, objects, or abstract ideas. Pindar's odes praise the winners of Olympic games, and Wordsworth's *Ode to Duty* glorifies the notion of responsibility. Many epigrams in this genre have been written. See ENCOMIUM. See also *forms* in APPENDIX 1.

encomium (from Greek for "eulogy") originally a Greek choral song praising the winners of the Olympic games. In the Classical period, Isocrates was famed for writing encomiums (alternative plural: encomia).

Currently, the term applies to poems of a laudatory nature. See EULOGY and PANEGYRIC.

See also *figures of subject and adjunct* in APPENDIX 2.

end-rhyme a RHYME occurring at the ends of lines. Both the full rhyme and off-rhyme help unify rhythm and idea, add emphasis and melody, and at times are used to produce a tension through the opposition of meaning and sound, as in the *ironic rhymes* of T.S. Eliot.

end-stopped petaining to a LINE ENDING that completes the line's syntax, meaning, and rhythm and thus stops the movement into the next line. Although this type of line ending can occur independently, it is usually found related to one or more previous or subsequent lines, as Pope's CLOSED COUPLET form:

Hope springs eternal in the Human breast:
Man never is, but always to be blest.

This rhymed, e.-s. couplet creates unity, completeness, and coherence by accenting the end words. The opposite of e.-s. is *enjambed*; see AUTONOMOUS LINE and ENJAMBMENT. See also *line endings* in APPENDIX 1.

English sonnet (also known as "Shakespearian sonnet"; see SONNET) a FIXED FORM composed of three quatrains and an autonomous couplet in iambic pentameter, each unit containing different rhymes of abab, cdcd, efef, and gg. The usual format for the content of an E.s. is to state a problem or proposition in the first twelve lines, and then solve or conclude it in the climactic couplet. See also FIXED FORMS.

enigma (from Greek for "to speak elusively or obscurely") a figure of division in the form of a riddle that intends to obscure rather than reveal, as in "This son is father to his sister," meaning a protective older brother rather than one involved in an incestuous relationship. See *figures of division* in APPENDIX 2.

enjambment /ənjamb′mənt/ (from French *enjambement*, from *enjamber*, for "to encroach, to stride"; also known as "run-on line") a line ending in which the syntax, rhythm, and thought are continued and completed in the subsequent line. Used in a couplet, the device creates the *open couplet*. The e. evokes suspense and anticipation in the reader, furthers the smooth development of a poem, and allows for variation in rhythm, syntax, and semantics. The opposite of e. is an END-STOPPED line. See LINE ENDING for a fuller discussion. See also *line endings* in APPENDIX 1.

enthymeme /en′thimēm/ (from Greek for "to think, to infer"; also known as "aetiologia") a *figure of argumentation* in the form of a SYLLOGISM which (1) makes a statement followed by a statement for that cause, as in "I will be glad to go to court / because then justice will be done," (2) poses contrary propositions in order to refute, as in "If pleasing people leads toward love, then to displease people leads toward loneliness," (3) omits a major or minor premise that is implied, as in this remark by Clarence Darrow: "When I was a boy I was told that anybody could become

President. I'm beginning to believe it." The last, contracted proposition leaves out the premise that whoever happened to be President in Darrow's day wasn't doing a good job. See *figures of argumentation* in APPENDIX 2.

enumeration (from Latin for "to number") a figure of division that considers a subject in terms of (1) its characteristics, (2) its circumstances leading up to the subject, or (3) the effect of the subject on causes or events that come after it. For example, (1) *characteristics*—"A man is part God, part mule, part king, part fool," (2) *antecedents*—"The Bible's version of the creation of the earth records that it took seven days," (3) *effects*—"God struck the stone of darkness against the shadow of death; thus light issued forth." See *figures of division* in APPENDIX 2.

envelope a structural pattern of REPETITION in which a line or stanza repeats itself in order to enclose other material and enrich its meaning. In the eighth Psalm the first and last lines are "O Lord, our Lord, how excellent is thy name in all the earth!" When first stated, it is an emotional but vague statement; however, when the sentence is repeated at the end of the psalm after an enumeration of God's actions and powers, the repeated line takes on powers from the enhancement. In Blake's *The Tyger*, the first and last stanzas are identical and form a frame for the poem. E. differs from the REFRAIN in that it reflects meaning on what it encloses, whereas the refrain sums up or reflects upon material that leads up to it. See *closure* and *forms in* APPENDIX 1.

envoy (from French for "to send forth"; also spelled "envoi") the concluding stanza of four to seven lines of the BALLADE and CHANT ROYAL. Originally, the Provençal troubadours used the e. to dedicate the poem to a patron or other important person, and repeated both the main MOTIF and REFRAIN in a bcbc RHYME SCHEME. The device has variations in the SESTINA form and in longer forms used by Chaucer. Scott, Southey, and Swinburne worked with the e. Other poets, such as Ezra Pound, used the stanza form as a separate and autonomous poem that is meant to send a book off in a celebratory fashion. The device has also been used in prose. See *closure* and *forms* in APPENDIX 1.

eolic: See AEOLIC.

epanadiplosis: See ANADIPLOSIS.

epanalepsis /-lep'-/ (Greek for "a taking up again") originally, a repetition of a word or phrase interrupted by other words. In modern rhetoric, the term indicates a construction in which a word or phrase both begins and ends a line, a clause, or a sentence, as in Shakespeare's "Blood hath brought blood, and blows have answer'd blows: / Strength match'd with strength, and power confronted power." Walt Whitman in *Leaves of Grass* employed e. (in the original sense) in some 40 percent of his lines. See grammatical *devices of rhythm and balance* and *figures of repetition* in APPENDIX 2.

epanaphora: See ANAPHORA.

epanodos /əpan'-/ (Greek for "a rising, a return") originally, a logical figure of division that states a general proposition followed by its parts, adds a figure of repetition to it, and then incorporates a figure of climax, as in:

> Nature is a mirror of time: temporary, cyclical, generational, and eternal. It is temporal as a falling leaf, cyclical as a leaf that falls each fall, generational as the seed which bears the tree, and eternal as the never-ending process.

Other definitions of the term include (1) the repetition of a sentence in an inverse order, and (2) a return to the regular thread of discourse after a DIGRESSION. See *figures of division* in APPENDIX 2.

epanorthosis /-thō'-/ (Greek for "a setting straight again") a logical figure of division that relates what already has been stated for the sake of greater or lesser comparison, e.g., "He only looked at me, but his look threw daggers."
    See *figures of division* in APPENDIX 2.

epergesis (Greek for "additional explanation") a grammatical construction that uses a qualifying opposition, e.g., "That man, the fool who loves you, just called." See *figures of repetition* in APPENDIX 2.

epic (from Greek for "word, narrative, song") in strict critical usage, a long NARRATIVE POEM in an elevated style whose PROTAGONIST is a heroic or quasi-divine figure on whose actions depend the fate of a tribe, a nation, or the human race. More generally, e. is one of the two basic types of narrative poetry (BALLAD being the other), and the term is often used to describe any poem, novel, or play that is grand in scope and style.
    The e. is the most ambitious of poetic types, making tremendous demands on a poet's imagination, craft, and knowledge to sustain the grandeur, scope, and variety of a poem that encompasses the entire world of its day and a large part of its learning. It contains shorter forms within its boundaries; e.g., the PANEGYRIC appears in the heroic contests, and the ELEGY in the death of heroes. In the last 3,000 years, many poets have attempted to compose epics, but in the Western tradition we have no more than a half-dozen epic poems of indubitable greatness. Renaissance critics ranked the e. as the highest genre of all (though Aristotle ranked it second to tragedy).
    Certain conventions have come to be associated with the e. For example, the poet begins by stating the ARGUMENT or THEME, gives an INVOCATION to a muse to inspire him in his great task, then addresses to the muse a question, the answer to which inaugurates the narrative. The narrative usually starts IN MEDIAS RES ("in the middle of things"). The poet often digresses from the narrative in order to give a catalogue of the principle characters and to give elaborate descriptive comparisons called epic similes (see EPIC SIMILE).
    Other typical qualities of the genre include: a cosmic setting ranging from heaven to the underworld; an encyclopedic scope of themes which use an enormous mass of traditional knowledge; action that involves superhuman deeds in battle; and characters that include gods and other

supernatural beings. The poem is traditionally a ceremonial performance deliberately distanced from ordinary speech and proportioned to the grandeur and formality of the heroic subject and epic architecture.

Scholars usually distinguish between two types of epics: (1) *traditional epics* (sometimes called *primary* or *folk epics*), which are shaped by a poet from historical and legendary materials developed earlier in the oral traditions of his or her culture during a period of warfare; examples include the *Iliad* and *Odyssey*, *Beowulf*, *El Cid*, *Gilgamesh*, *Chanson de Roland*, *Nibelungenlied*, the East Indian *Mahabharate*, and the Finnish *Kalevala*; (2) *literary epics* (sometimes called *secondary epics*), which are composed by a sophisticated craftsperson in deliberate imitation of the traditional form; e.g., Virgil based *The Aeneid* on Homer's epics; *The Aeneid*, in turn, became the chief model for Milton's *Paradise Lost*, which became the model for Keats' *Hyperion*; *Paradise Lost* was also the model for Blake's prophetic books (*The Four Zoas*, *Milton*, *Jerusalem*) which translated Milton's Biblical design and subject matter into Blake's own mythic terms.

Many Americans have attempted writing literary epics; two well-known examples are Longfellow's *Hiawatha* and Benét's *John Brown's Body*.

The term e. is often applied to works that differ in many respects from the Homeric prototype, but manifest the e. spirit in the magnitude of their scope and the importance of their subjects. Dante's *Divine Comedy*, Spenser's *Faerie Queene*, Melville's *Moby Dick*, Tolstoy's *War and Peace*, and Whitman's *Song of Myself* have all been called epics. Northrop Frye, complaining about the inadequacy of modern critical terminology, points out that the term has become JARGON for any long poem (just as LYRIC has become jargon for any short poem). Browning's *The Ring and the Book* is often called an e., although it has virtually none of the e. conventions described above. Similarly, we call Shelley's *Epipsychidion* a lyric, though it has many of the qualities of an e. See *forms* in APPENDIX 1.

epicede: See EPIDEICTIC POETRY.

epicrisis /-krī'-/ (also known as "parachresis") a rhetorical expression in the form of testimony that uses a quotation (see APOMNEMONYSIS) and then procedes to comment upon or judge that quotation. See *types of testimony* in APPENDIX 2.

epic simile an elaborate comparison developed in a lengthy passage. More ornate than a simple METAPHOR, the e.s. develops the *vehicle* into an independent set of images that exclude the *tenor*, as well as temporarily obscuring the main thread of the *narrative*. The e.s. is sometimes called an *Homeric s.* because of its frequent use in the *Iliad* and *Odyssey*. For example, in the *Iliad* (4.275) the Greek host led by Ajax is compared to a storm cloud. The image of the ominous cloud is developed until it almost obscures the real war. See EPIC.

epideictic poetry /-dīk'-/ (*epideictic*, from Greek for "to show") poetry that is in praise or blame of something. The term was used by Aristotle to describe the third category of RHETORIC, that which is demonstrative in nature. Common e.p. types include, among others, ENCOMIUM, EPITHA-

LAMION, and *epicede* (a funeral oration). E. was popular during the Classical decadence: Statius' *Silvae* is a collection of e.p. See *forms* in APPENDIX 1.

epigram (from Greek for "inscription [on a tomb or monument]") any short, terse poem, especially if it is ingenious or pointed. The form is characterized by balance, polish, and wit, and often uses ANTITHESIS as a thematic structure. Greek poets used the form widely; the best examples are in *The Greek Anthology*. Among Roman poets, Martial set the model for the *caustic e.*, which was widely imitated by 16th- and 17th-century English poets. Among the Romantics, Blake's *Miscellaneous Epigrams* and *Gnomic Verses* provide examples, and Coleridge defines the term while providing an example when he calls an e. "A dwarfish whole / Its body brevity, and wit its soul." See *forms* in APPENDIX 1.

epigraph a motto or quotation at the beginning of a book or poem. See *forms* in APPENDIX 1.

epilogue /ep'-/ (from Greek for "conclusion" [literally, "upon" plus "speech"]) a section concluding a long poem or play. E. is related to *peroration* (eloquent conclusion of a speech) and is the opposite of *prologue*. Though epilogues are rarely found in modern literature, in the Renaissance well-known poets were paid to write epilogues for plays— much as prefaces are written today. An example of an e. is Puck's speech in *A Midsummer Night's Dream*, in which he entreats the audience to have good will and the critics to give the play "courteous treatment." See *closure* in APPENDIX 1.

epilogus /-log'əs/ a figure of argumentation that hypothetically supposes that if certain events were to occur then other events would follow. The speaker of Andrew Marvell's *To His Coy Mistress* hypothesizes a better world in order to remind his lady of the limitations of this one: "Had we but world enough and time, / This coyness, lady, were no crime." See *figures of argumentation* in APPENDIX 2.

epimone a figure of argumentation that repeats the same words or uses a REFRAIN, as in the following three lines from William Blake's *The Tyger*:

> What the hammer? What the chain?
> In what furnace was thy brain?
> What the anvil? What dread grasp?

See *figures of argumentation* in APPENDIX 2.

epiphany /əpif'-/ (from Greek for "appearence, manifest") the name of a Christian festival celebrated on January 6th commemorating the magi; also, more importantly, a theological term signifying a manifestation of God's presence, as in the e. of Yahweh in the burning bush. James Joyce adopted the term in *Stephen Hero* to describe an experience of sudden radiance and revelation while looking at an ordinary object or scene. Though many critics have seized on Joyce's use of the term as being an important breakthrough in literary theory, there is actually very little evidence that Joyce's e. differs significantly from what earlier writers called "the moment." Shelley in his *Defense of Poetry* spoke of the "best and happiest moments ... arising unforeseen and departing unbidden." Wordsworth spoke of "spots of time," and often his poems, e.g. *The Solitary Reaper* and *The Two April Mornings*, represent a single moment of revelation. His long poem *Prelude* is a sequence of such visions. See ANAGOGICAL VISION, ANAGOGE, and OBJECTIVE CORRELATIVE. See also *narration* in APPENDIX 1.

epiphonema (Greek for "a mentioning, a speaking out") an exclamation that summarizes or concludes a discourse or action. The e. is often spoken with moral intent:

> You value what has been stolen
> When the thief has come and reached,
> But the deeper crime that will haunt you
> Is the sanctum breached!

See *figures of pathos* in APPENDIX 2.

epiplexis (Greek for "a striking at, a reproving") a rhetorical figure of emotion that scolds fiercely or exposes the speaker's grief. See *figures of pathos* in APPENDIX 2.

epiploce /əpip′losē/ (from Greek for "a plaiting together") in Classical prosody, a term indicating the plausibility of dual metrical interpretations. For example, a series of rising iambic feet could also be considered trochaic. The term e. further denotes a figure of rhetoric in which one aggravation, or striking circumstance, is added in due graduation to another (*The Tempest*, III. ii. 88–91):

> There thou mayst brain him,
> Having first seiz'd his books; or with a log
> Batter his skull, or paunch him with a stake,
> Or cut his wezand with thy knife.

See *figures of repetition* in APPENDIX 2.

episode (from Greek for "a coming in besides") originally, in Greek drama, that part of a tragedy presented between two choruses. The term has come to mean the presentation or narration of an event with its own completed structure set within the larger framework of long verse or prose piece, e.g., the story of Aeneas' journey to Hades in *The Aeneid*. See EPISODIC STRUCTURE and STORY-WITHIN-A STORY.

episodic structure a narrative form consisting of a series of incidents rather than a cohesive plot structure. Usually, the e.s. has little or no central PLOT, though the Italian romantic epic has both e.s. and a complicated main plot; and *metrical romances* and the picaresque novel have e.s., but they hang together through a chronological sequence of events occurring to a single character. Tennyson's *Idylls of the King* is an example of a long poem using e.s. See EPISODE. *See also narration, forms*, and *dramatic terms* in APPENDIX 1.

epistle /əpis′əl/ (from Greek for "a sending in") a letter in verse form meant to give moral instruction or to evoke an emotion. Horace originated the form in his *Epistles* which were written in hexameter and in simple diction. Several books of the Bible contain the form in prose, and poets such as Johnson, Burns, Shelley, Byron, and Donne have used the e. for purposes of dedication or preface. Contemporary poets have used the form for two basic purposes: as an opportunity for prophecy, such as MacLeish's *Epistle To Be Left in the Earth*, and as an opportunity for intimate personal statement, such as James Wright's *Epistle to Roland Flint* and Richard Hugo's letter poems to friends. See *forms* in APPENDIX 1.

epistrophe /əpis′trəfē/ (Greek for "a turning toward, a return") a figure of repetition that repeats the same word or phrase at the end of subsequent clauses or sentences. E. is used for melody, emphasis, and progression of thought. Whitman uses the device often. See *figures of repetition* in APPENDIX 2.

epitaph /ep′-/ (from Greek for "[writing] on a tomb") a work suitable for inscription on a gravestone, though the verse may not be intended to be actually inscribed. The e. is an abbreviated ELEGY, found in a wide range of tones, which includes the name of the dead person, vital statistics, and a comment on or summary of his or her life. The Egyptians originated the form by making it more personal and verselike, as in the EPIGRAM. The major classical collection of epitaphs is found in book four of *The Greek Anthology*. Modern examples include Masters' *Spoon River Anthology* and Yeats' epitaph for himself which concludes his poem *Under Ben Bulben*. See EPIGRAM.

epitasis /əpit′-/ (Greek for ("a stretching") the part of a play following the main action (*protasis*) in which the action rises and the plot thickens. See DRAMATIC STRUCTURE.

epithalamion /-lā′-/ (from Greek *epithalamios*, for "upon the bridal chamber"; also known as "epithalamium") a poem celebrating a marriage, originally meant to be sung outside the bedroom of the bridal couple. Sappho originated the form, which can vary in length, but it is usually celebratory in tone, as in Spenser's famous lyric, and sometimes solemn, as in the Song of Solomon. Epithalamia (or epithalamiums) became widely practiced during the English Renaissance, the first known instance being Sidney's great lyric celebrating his own marriage (1580). Others who have used the form include Donne, Jonson, Herrick, Shelley, Tennyson, Housman, and Auden. See *forms* in APPENDIX 1.

epithet /ep′-/ (from Greek for "something added") an adjective or adjectival phrase characterizing a person or thing, as in "the fleet-footed Achilles." As it is taken from Homer, it is also called *Homeric e.* Sometimes the e. takes the form of a noun or noun phrase, as in "Jack-the-Ripper" and "Rudolph the Red-nosed Reindeer." The device, at its best, is musical, imagistic, evocative, and fresh. A TRANSFERRED e. is an adjectival phrase in which the adjective does not modify the noun but shows an effect, as in "laughing gas," or as in Milton's "blind mouths."

The Latin term for the device is *epitheton*. See EPONYM. See also *figures of subject and adjunct in* APPENDIX 2, and *diction* in APPENDIX 1.

epitome /əpit′omē/ (Greek for "incision, abridgement") a condensed summary of a literary work or a characterization in epigrammatic form of a person, event, or thing.

epitrope /əpit′rope/ (Greek for "reference, arbitration") a figure in which the speaker either ironically or sincerely gives up something that an opponent wants. See *figures of ethos* in APPENDIX 2, and *figurative expressions* in APPENDIX 1.

epizeuxis /epizook′sis/ (Greek for "a fastening upon"; also known as "subjunctio") a rhetorical figure by which a word is repeated with vehemence or emphasis. Whitman uses this device often, as in his *Song of Myself*: "Urge and urge and urge, / Always the procreant urge of the world." See *grammatical constructions that are technically incorrect* in APPENDIX 2.

epode /ep′ōd/ (from Greek for "additional song, aftersong") a Greek choral invention meant to be sung while standing still, or a lyric in which a long line is followed regularly by a short line. Archilochus probably invented the form for the purpose of INVECTIVE and SATIRE. The PINDARIC ODE contains the e. as a stanza form. Horace's *Iambi* was the first instance of the form in Latin literature. See ANTISTROPHE and STROPHE. See also *dramatic terms* and *forms* in APPENDIX 1.

eponym /ep′-/ (from Greek for "to a name") a quality so closely associated with a character or event that it comes to stand for that character or event, as in "beauty" for Helen of Troy, or "Holocaust" for the Nazi genocide of Jews. See EPITHET and METONYMY.

epos /ep′os/ (Greek for "word, song") verse or song presented orally before an audience. See *forms* in APPENDIX 1.

epyllion (Greek for "little epos, scrap of poetry") a short NARRATIVE POEM, written in dactylic hexameters, containing ornate description, allusions, mythology, and digressions. Its subject was usually love, and its form often offered psychological insights into the love relationship. The form was cultivated in the Alexandrian period, but other cultures have adopted it. Many modern lyrics fit the description of this form. See *forms* in APPENDIX 1.

equivalence (from Latin for "equal worth") in Classical prosody, the principle of substituting two short syllables for one long syllable, or substituting a number of syllables in one metrical foot for those of an equal number in another foot (e.g., anapestic for dactylic). See DISEMIC and SUBSTITUTION.

equivocation (from Latin for "to call by the same name") a fallacious form of argumentation that uses a word of two meanings that apply to a single situation: "The poet said there is no profit in making money, / But I have made much profit in making money." Often the device is used with the intention to deceive. See DOUBLE ENTENDRE, EQUIVOQUE, and PUN. See also *figures of argumentation* in APPENDIX 2.

equivoque /ek′wivōk/ a type of DOUBLE ENTENDRE that offers two different and discordant meanings. For example, the word "plot" can be used to signify a section of land or a surreptitious plan. When e. is used with the intent to evade or deceive, it is called EQUIVOCATION. See PUN. See also *contraries and contradictories* in APPENDIX 2.

erotema (Greek for "question") a figure of emotion that asks a question not for the purpose of soliciting an answer but for the purpose of asserting or denying something. For examples, see RHETORICAL QUESTION. See also EROTESIS; ALSO *figures of pathos* in APPENDIX 2, and *figurative expressions* in APPENDIX 1.

erotesis /-tē′-/ (Greek for "a questioning") a figure of emotion in which the speaker, in the form of a question, boldly asserts the opposite of what is asked. For example, Emily Dickinson's poem beginning "Is Bliss then, such Abyss" asserts that the utterly happy state of "Bliss" is a quagmire into which she is willing to step. See *figures of pathos* in APPENDIX 2.

esemplastic (coined by Coleridge in *Biographia Literaria*, chapter 10, from Greek words for "to shape into one") the active unifying creative impulse as opposed to the more passive IMAGINATION which Coleridge considered "a repetition of the finite mind of the eternal act of creation in the infinite *I am*." See SHAPING.

establishing shot (see CINEMATIC TECHNIQUES) a term borrowed from cinema describing a long-range view of a scene. See also *cinematic terms in* APPENDIX 1.

ethical criticism: See MORAL CRITICISM OR E.C.

ethopoeia /ēthopē′yə/ (from Greek for "character representation") a GENRE of poetry that vividly characterizes someone in terms of praise or reproach by examining his quality of mind, habits, or vices. The genre ranges widely in style, from Pope's satiric *Epistle to Dr. Arbuthnot* to Eliot's tragic *The Love Song of J. Alfred Prufrock*. Originally, the term indicated a rhetorical figure of speech in which certain persons are sketched. See *figures of subject and adjunct* in APPENDIX 2.

ethos /ē′-/ (Greek for "character") a term used by Aristotle (*Rhetoric II*, xii-xiv) and adopted by many later writers to refer to one or more of the following applications: (1) the moral stature of a major character in a piece of literature as described by his actions rather than by his thought or emotion—e.g., the frequent soliloquies of Hamlet indicating his indecisive character; (2) the characteristic spirit, principles, and beliefs of a people or community—e.g., the democratic e. of the American people; (3) the principles of aesthetics and rhetoric of the ancient world—e.g., the Platonic distinction between reality and appearance. For related terms, see DIANOIA and MYTHOPOEIA. See *figures of ethos* in APPENDIX 2.

etymological accent: See ACCENT.

eucharista /yo͞okəris'tə/ (from Greek for "grateful") a figure of ETHOS or character in which the speaker lauds his benefactors for the good he has received and belittles himself in an effort to pay back that goodness. For example, in *The Taming of the Shrew*, lines 146–155, Kate advises headstrong women to place more value on their husbands by being obedient and servile. See *figures of ethos* in APPENDIX 2.

euche /yo͞o'kā/ a figure of testimony that uses a solemn promise or vow, as in this line from Whitman: "By God! I will accept nothing which all cannot have their counterpart of on the same terms." See *types of testimony* in APPENDIX 2.

eulogy (from Greek for "praise"; a similarly used term is ENCOMIUM) a formal speech in praise of someone, especially high praise in honor of the recently deceased, as in Mark Anthony's e. for Brutus in *Julius Caesar*. The form is common today, as it was in ancient times, in funeral orations and in elegies such as Auden's *In Memory of W.B. Yeats*. Related terms are DIRGE, ELEGY, MONODY, PANEGYRIC, and THRENODY. See *figures of pathos* in APPENDIX 2.

euphemism (from Greek "to speak well [of something or someone]") an indirect reference to something distasteful, untoward, or indelicate— indirect in order to make the subject more acceptable. For instance, the dead are called "the departed," and the mad are called "a bit touched." These forms of discretion are looked upon as weaknesses in good writing because modern literary principles and practices call for sincerity and forthrightness. See PARRHESIA. See also *figures of ethos* in APPENDIX 2, and *clichés* and *diction* in APPENDIX 1.

euphemismus a kind of speech that prophesies good fortune, as in these lines from Robert Browning's *Rabbi ben Ezra*: "Grow old along with me! / The best is yet to be, / The last of life, for which the first was made . . ." See *types of testimony* in APPENDIX 2.

euphony /yo͞o'-/ (from Greek for "well-sounding") a pleasing combination of sound and RHYTHM, the opposite of CACOPHONY—harsh and jarring sounds. Generally, the use of a high percentage of vowel sounds and unaccented syllables in combination with a low percentage of consonants and accented syllables tends to produce e. In terms of phonetics, middle vowels, liquid consonants, and semivowels tend to be more pleasant than other combinations. See PITCH for a discussion of the melody of language. See also MELOPOEIA, SONICS, and SOUND SYSTEMS; also *melopoetics* in APPENDIX 1.

euphuism /yo͞o'fo͞o·izm/ (from Greek for "well-grown") a term, adapted from John Lyly's prose romance *Euphues: The Anatomy of Wit* (1578), that is used to indicate a highly ornate literary style characterized by latinate diction, rhetorical balances, heavy sound values and density, elaborate arguments and comparisons, and serialized figures of speech. This analytical style fully explored both the wit and the expressive capacity of the English language. The style influenced many writers of the

16th and 17th centuries, most notably Shakespeare and Sidney, the former using it for wit and satire, the latter reacting against its contrivances. See GONGORISM and PURPLE PATCHING. See also *devices of poetic license* in APPENDIX 2.

eustaphia a form of speech that asserts one's support and loyalty, as in Lady Macbeth's welcome to King Duncan. Sometimes the e. is in the form of an INVOCATION as in the first line of the fifth section of Whitman's *Song of Myself:* "I believe in you my soul . . . the other I am must not abase itself to you." See *types of testimony* in APPENDIX 2.

eutrepismus a naming of parts in their correct or logical order, as in Henry Reed's poem *Naming of Parts*.
   See *figures of division* in APPENDIX 2.

even accent (also known as "level stress") a nonmetrical term that describes the equal amount of stress given two or more syllables in a word or phrase, e.g. "blackjack," "hard core," "night light." When the e.a. occurs in metrical scansion, it is termed DISTRIBUTED STRESS. See also ACCENT, CADENCE, and RHYTHM.

exclamation: See ECPHONESIS.

exegesis /-jē′-/ (Greek for "explanation") an interpretation of a passage, particularly one from the Bible. During the Middle Ages, such exercises of analysis were an important branch of rhetorical practice. In current use the term is interchangeable with EXPLICATION.

exemplum (Latin for "example") a short tale or narrative that illustrates a moral lesson. For example, the principal and secondary narratives in Chaucer's *The Pardoner's Tale* instruct against avarice, and the contemporary allegorist Russell Edson illustrates the absurdity and confusion of 20th-century man in his sequence of short prose pieces dealing with apes and men. See also ALLEGORY, ANECDOTE, DIDACTIC POETRY, FABLE, and PARABLE.

exergasia (Greek for "a working out") a figure of equal comparison that works incrementally by setting down a series of metaphorical equivalents similar in meaning but not in form. The series, as illustrated here, usually progresses climactically: "This island is a jewel in an emerald sea, / a star in the darkest night, a fantasy, / a dreamer's delight." Usually the *tenor* has more than one *vehicle*. See SYNONYMIA. See also *figures comparing greater, lesser, or equal things* in APPENDIX 2.

experimental poetry generally, any poetry that attempts to broaden the experiencer's conventional concepts of language, consciousness, or poetic form. Edward Lucie-Smith's *Primer of Experimental Poetry* is a collection of modern e.p. For discussions of specific types, see ABSTRACT POETRY, CADAVRE EXQUIS, CARMEN FIGURATUM, CHANCE POETRY, COMPUTER POETRY, CONTINUUM POETRY, FOUND POEM, FREE VERSE, LEAPING POETRY, MONTAGE, OPEN FIELD COMPOSITION, PROSE POEM, READYMADE, STREAM-OF-CONSCIOUSNESS, and TRANS-SENSE VERSE. For discussions of modern movements in art and literature that have challenged conventional poetic modes, see AESTHETICISM, CUBISM, DADA, FUTURISM, POP ART, SURREALISM, and VORTICISM.

explication (from Latin for "to unfold") originally a pedagogic device in French schools where students were required to explain the meaning and style of a traditional text. Currently the term refers to the approach to explaining literature that was used by the New Critics (1920s and 1930s), which analyzes and organizes into a whole the context, devices, semantics, and form of a piece of literature. The attempt takes into consideration not only the summary of the piece in question but also the various levels of resonance on which the work operates. The New Critics assume that poetry displays the qualities of autonomy, unity, and complexity and avoids outside practical applications to the poet's intention or social milieu. Some important critical texts that use e. include Laura Riding and Robert Graves' *A Survey of Modernist Poetry* (1928), I.A. Richards' *Practical Criticism* (1929), William Empson's *Seven Types of Ambiguity* (1930), Cleanth Brooks and Robert Penn Warren's popular *Understanding Poetry* (1939). A number of contemporary critical journals publish explication, including most notably *The Explicator*. See AFFECTIVE FALLACY, CRITICISM, EXEGESIS, EXPRESSIVE FALLACY, INTENTIONAL FALLACY, and NEW CRITICISM. See also *criticism* in APPENDIX 1.

Expressionism originally an artistic movement in the early part of the 20th century among German dramatists, film-makers, painters, and composers. The term has come to refer generally to the deliberate distortion of reality in order to portray the artist's feelings. *Expressionist* art is often outrageous, demanding, or explosive in tone and reflects the mechanical rhythm of the industrial and postindustrial ages. Often the artist who uses the style tends to create a self-portrait as seen through the surface features of an object, an extension of the earlier movement of IMPRESSIONISM. The aesthetics of the movement reduced to a set of stylistic devices are commonly accepted in, and are considered an important element of, contemporary American poetry. See *movements and schools of poetry* in APPENDIX 1.

Expressive criticism a school of CRITICISM, developed by the ROMANTICS, that applies the writer's attitude as a main element in the analysis of the work. See *criticism* in APPENDIX 1.

expressive fallacy the New Critics' view that however intense an author's feelings may be, they are not sufficient, in themselves, to produce adequate expression in the poem. Yvor Winters and R.P. Blackmur claim that considering the author's original emotional thrust tends to blind both poet and critic to wider, more objective criteria in evaluating the text. See AFFECTIVE FALLACY, CLASSICAL FALLACY, CRITICISM, INTENTIONAL FALLACY, PATHETIC FALLACY, and REDUCTIVE FALLACY.

external rhyme: See TERMINAL RHYME.

extrametrical: See HYPERMETRIC.

exuscitatio (Latin for "arousal, awakening") a figure of PATHOS that excites an audience either positively or negatively through the speaker's tone. See *figures of pathos* in APPENDIX 2.

eye-rhyme (also know as "sight rhyme") a type of RHYME in which words or the final parts of words are spelled alike but not pronounced alike, as in "chive/live", "blood/mood" and "through/cough." Sometimes, as in this example from Alexander Pope, the paired words were originally rhymes, but have come to be pronounced differently: "Some fold the sleeve, whilst others plait the gown; / And Betty's praised for labours not her own." See HISTORICAL RHYME.

F

fable (from Latin for "to talk, to discourse") a short, unadorned story, often using animals as characters who exemplify human morality or behavior. Fables, thought to have originated in the allegories of tribal societies, were orally passed on and were often improved in the hands of skilled writers (see ALLEGORY). Aesop, a sixth-century-B.C. Greek about whom very little is documented, is renowned for his beast fables which offer lessons in prudence, vanity, greed, etc., as in his stories about the hare and the turtle, the king of the frogs, and the fox and the grapes. The oldest known f. is Hesiod's poem of the hawk and the nightingale (eighth century B.C.). Other fabulists throughout history include Phaedrus (first century A.D.), Marie de France (ca. 1200 A.D.), Jean de la Fontaine (1621–95), and American 20th-century poets such as Marianne Moore and Russell Edson. See FABLIAU. See also *figures of similarity and dissimilarity* in APPENDIX 2.

fabliau /fab′li·ō/ (Old French for "fable"; also spelled "fableau") a short, metrical verse (usually octosyllabic) popular in 12th- and 13th-century England and France. The form crudely satirized, sometimes to the point of obscenity, the foibles of the Church, the station of women, and the values of the middle and lower classes. Although many fabliaux were written anonymously, Chaucer in his *Canterbury Tales* made famous the fabliaux of the Friar, the Miller, the Reeve, the Cook, and the Manciple. Other writers in the genre include Rutebeuf, Philippe de Beaumanoir, and Jean Bodel. In contemporary American poetry, the work of Charles Bukowski displays many of the characteristics of the f. See FABLE.

fallacy of expressive form: See EXPRESSIVE FALLACY.

falling action that part of DRAMATIC STRUCTURE in which an event or action by an antagonistic character leads to tragedy. See *dramatic terms* in APPENDIX 1.

falling foot a metrical FOOT descending from stressed to unstressed syllables, such as the trochee (´‿), the dactyl (´‿‿), and the antibacchius (´´‿). Although this type of foot has often been used for poems of a sombre mood, the foot can also be used for lighter moods. See FALLING RHYTHM, FEMININE ENDING, RISING FOOT, and RISING RHYTHM.

falling rhythm a metrical or FREE VERSE rhythm in which each unit or measure begins on an accented syllable and ends on an unaccented syllable, as in trochaic meter (´‿) or dactylic meter (´‿‿). See METER, RHYTHM, RISING RHYTHM, and SCANSION.

false pronoun: See MASKED PRONOUN OR F.P.

fancy and imagination terms that originally were used synonymously to indicate functions of the mind that reorder and synthesize elements from dreams and reality, a process different in kind from that of reason or RATIOCINATION. Through history, many schools of thought have sought to make distinctions in quality, range, and function between f. a. i. Samuel Taylor Coleridge (*Biographia Literaria*, 1817) set the standard for the definition of these terms as they are used today by critics and poets. For Coleridge, both functions depend upon the primary imagination, but fancy is more limited in scope than imagination, more arbitrary in nature, and less able to control its meaning and direction. The fancy mechanically reorders sensual information given by memory or experience into a new order that is unrelated to its original frames of spatial or temporal reference. The fancy is said to produce a lighter, more fleeting, less responsible sort of creation than the imagination. On the other hand, the imagination is a process that has the power to change the character of its individual parts, and to synthesize and unify them into an organic whole that is related to the quality of perception of an experience or memory. The imagination has the power to lead to or to grow a new creation from parts that are integrally related to and inextricable from the whole. Coleridge claims that Milton had an imaginative mind, while Cowley had a fanciful mind. In contemporary American poetics, Denise Levertov's well-known critical essays on ORGANIC COMPOSITION are based on Coleridge's distinction. See ESEMPLASTIC and FANTASY. See also *stylistic elements* in APPENDIX 1.

fantasy (from Greek for "appearance, perception") a term that was originally synonymous with the term and process of *imagination*, and the word from which *fancy* has been contracted. Current usage of the word denotes the results of an undirected daydream or a sensed object or feeling conjured up by a speaker or writer, a result different in depth, quality, and range from that of the imagination. See FANCY AND IMAGINATION.

fatras (also called "fatrasie," "fratrasie," and "resverie") a whimsical form of medieval verse written in 11-line stanzas replete with wildly connecting ideas and word play. Apparently, the French invented the form, whose contents often made no attempt at sense. All this was done in the spirit of and for the sake of gamesmanship. See *forms* in APPENDIX 1.

felt thought a style of writing characterized by an emotionally charged intellectual, philosophical, and often analytical perspective of consciousness. This half-felt, half-thought style of expression, which Herbert Read termed the "emotional apprehension of thought," is attributed to poets such as Lucretius and the Metaphysicals (Donne, Marvell, Crashaw, etc.) and to 20th-century poets influenced by the Metaphysicals (Eliot, Tate, Ransom, etc.). The style is often a defect in younger writers whose urge toward statement in poetry overpowers the aesthetic and musical aspects of a poem. In this sense, the mode stands opposite to that of the LYRIC. See METAPHYSICAL POETRY, and the related term DISSOCIATION OF SENSIBILITY. See also *meaning* in APPENDIX 1.

felt time a rhythmical and narrative effect that communicates to the reader a sense of the temporal experience of the poem, as opposed to the "actual" time it takes to read a poem. The aesthetic texture of a piece of literature, made up of devices such as sound, rhythm, stanzaic patterns, etc., obviously affect the quality of f.t. See REAL TIME.

feminine ending (also called "light ending") an unstressed syllable at the end of a regular metrical line of iambics or anapests, added for its music. The placement of this FALLING FOOT was commonly employed as a variation in BLANK VERSE, as in the second and third lines of this example by Shakespeare:

> O! I could play the woman with mine eyes
> And braggart with my tongue. But gentle heávens
> Cut short all intermíssion.

feminine rhyme (Similarly used terms are DOUBLE RHYME and LIGHT RHYME) a dissyllabic pair of rhyming words, as in "table/fable."

figurative language the creative manipulation of the syntax, semantics, structure, effects, or associations of normal language used to arrive at vivid expressions and innovative ideas. Some critics divide the term, which is the opposite of denotative language (see DENOTATION), into two main categories: *tropes*, which work through turns of thought to affect the normal meaning of words, and *figures of speech*, which work through a reorganization of the normal syntax and rhetorical use of words. For specific examples of devices, see FIGURES OF SPEECH and TROPE. See also *figurative expressions* in APPENDIX 1.

figures of speech generally, words that depart from normal syntactical, rhetorical, or grammatical usage. Quintilian distinguishes f.o.s. from figures of thought (tropes), the former being new expressions brought about by a change in the grammatical or rhetorical use of language. His classification includes those created by the addition of elements (such as ANAPHORA and POLYSYNDETON), by the subtraction of elements (such as ASYNDETON and ZEUGMA), and by the use of parallel constructions (such as ANTITHESIS and PARONOMASIA). Longinus claimed that f.o.s. functioned differently in rhetoric and poetry, but during the Middle Ages the ideas of Cicero were revived, and the argument that poetry is a category of rhetoric was put forth. During the RENAISSANCE, the identification and classification of f.o.s. grew enormously, and Puttenham cleared up this confusion by classifying specific devices within the genre according to whether they appealed to the ear, the eye, or both. Renaissance theorists proposed that f.o.s. should be used with attention paid to their grace, clarity, and appropriateness. In the 19th century, Coleridge argued that all of the f.o.s. aspire, like tropes, toward metaphor and even metaphysical reference. The multitude of specific f.o.s. are categorized according to elements of grammar, diction, syntax, rhythm and balance, and transformation in construction. See *figurative expressions* in APPENDIX 1, and *devices of poetic license* in APPENDIX 2.

fill-in-the-blanks poem (also known as "definition poem") the contemporary term for a type of poetry that states a subject or informs the reader of a general condition and then is supported by a series of lines that define the subject of the poem. Usually, the beginning of the poem focuses on its subject and what follows is an imaginative and highly selective list of characteristics concerning the poem's subject. For instance, Louis Simpson provides a definition of American poetry in his poem of the same title:

(title & subject)	*American Poetry*
(general condition)	Whatever it is, it must have
(list of objects & actions)	A stomach that can digest
	Rubber, coal, uranium, moons, poems.
"	Like the shark, it contains a shoe.
"	It must swim for miles through the desert
"	Uttering cries that are almost human.

The body of the f.-i.-t.-b.p. can be composed of objects, actions, observations, or descriptions; but the development or strategy of the poem is deductive in nature (see DEDUCTIVE STRUCTURE). It begins with a general subject which is then supported by and defined with specific references to that subject. The form's most salient feature is that it is simply a list that coheres around a stated subject. The CATALOGUE VERSE, which is another form of poetic listing, differs from this form in that cataloguing has a much larger, freewheeling accumulative style. In terms of challenges, this form presents a good test of the poet's capacity to imagine because its stripped-down quality demands that the list be inventive, interesting, and directly related to the theme of the poem. See LIST POEM. See also *forms in* APPENDIX 1.

fin de siècle /feN′dəsyak′əl/ (French for "end of the century") usually, the last ten years of the 19th century, a transition period in which writers and artists tried to abandon old ideas and to establish new aesthetic ideals. DECADENCE (as in the lives and works of Oscar Wilde and Aubrey Beardsley) and REALISM (as in the works of George Bernard Shaw and George Moore) were two major movements of the period. The 1890s were also marked by a number of seminal social movements, among them women's suffrage. See AESTHETICISM.

final cause a rhetorical figure of logic that, through argument of cause and effect, takes into account the intention of a certain thing or person, as in Emily Dickinson's *There's a Certain Slant of Light*, in which an oppressive afternoon light comes to menace. See *figures of cause and effect* in APPENDIX 2.

fixed forms any set of regularly rhyming and metrically patterned verse forms, e.g., the SONNET, originating in Italy, the GHAZAL, originating in the Middle East, and the HAIKU, originating in Japan. Most f.f. in English originated in France, thus the term FRENCH FORMS is sometimes synonymous with f.f. For a list of *f.f.*, see APPENDIX 1.

fixed image and free image *fixed image:* a specific, detailed picture or series of pictures created and presented by the poet in an effort to control the reader's imagination and act as a guide as the complication and complexity of the poem develop. The *free image* is a more generalized, impressionistic picture which depends upon the reader's subjective experience, memory, or imagination for its specificity. Since this type of *floating image* supposedly relies more on the reader's participation, the poem with free imagery is thought to have a more personal effect and to offer the sort of looseness of control and structure appropriate to the aesthetics and philosophy of the 20th century. On the other hand, the fixed image is said to produce a stronger sense of unity, completeness, and coherence in a poem. However, most poems employ a combination of the two types. See IMAGE and IMAGERY. See also *imagery* in APPENDIX 1.

flashback (see CINEMATIC TECHNIQUES) a narrative device used to depict events that occurred previous to the opening of a work. It can be used to heighten the drama of the present, to supply necessary information, or to connect the past with the present and future. It functions primarily as an economical and versatile way to package chronological time. See CINEMATIC EDITING and FLASHFORWARD. See also *cinematic terms* and *dramatic terms* in APPENDIX 1.

flashforward (see CINEMATIC TECHNIQUES) a narrative device used to depict events that occur after the present action of a work. The device certifies forces acting within the present temporal framework of the poem, and heightens that action by interesting the reader in how such events could come into being. W.S. Merwin's poem *For the Anniversary of My Death* uses this device. See CINEMATIC EDITING and FLASHBACK. See also *cinematic terms* and *dramatic terms* in APPENDIX 1.

flat character: See STOCK CHARACTER.

flat statement a phrase or line that, taken out of context of the poem, appears to be unpoetic, has little aesthetic texture and RESONANCE, and is devoid of IMAGERY. In the context of the poem, the f.s. stands as a powerful contrast to its surrounding lines. There are various, specific ways in which the device functions: (1) as a *contrast to thickly textured language*, in which the uncluttered purity and simplicity of the f.s. counterpoint the matrix of rich sounds and rhythms, as in the sentence "The king is dead" in Marianne Moore's poem *No Swan So Fine*; (2) as a *contrast to the poem's imagery* (which may be parallel to the poem's theme), as in the last line ("I have wasted my life") of James Wright's *Lying in a Hammock at William Duffy's Farm in Pine Island, Minnesota*; (3) as a *thematic statement*, which centers and highlights the poem's theme, as in John Skoyle's line "The lights go on and go off" in his poem *Burlesque*; (4) as a *structural focusing device*, upon which the dramatic forces of conflict pivot, as in W.S. Merwin's line "So that is what I am" in his poem *Fly*; (5) as a *strategy in aesthetic texture*, which employs flat statements to create a

PLAIN STYLE of writing or a simple surface, as in William Stafford's poem *Passing Remark*; (6) as a *syntactical device* that stands in contrast to surrounding forms of syntax, as in e.e. cummings' last three lines of *Me Up At Does;* (7) as a *simple base* for a typographically twisted statement, as in D.J. Enright's epigram "The trypewriter is cretin / a revulsion in peotry." See ASCHEMATISTON and CLICHÉ. See also *diction* in APPENDIX 1.

Fleshly School of Poetry the title of a critical essay published in the *Contemporary Review*, October 1871, signed by Thomas Maitland but actually written by Robert W. Buchanan. The article is an attack on Swinburne, Morris, and Rossetti in the guise of a review of Rossetti's poems. Buchanan accuses the three poets of forming a "Mutual Admiration School." Rossetti replied with an essay entitled "The Stealthy School of Criticism" in the *Athenaeum*, December 16, 1871. The term "fleshly" was meant to demean the attention that the three poets were paying to the subject of the human body. See PRE-RAPHAELITES.

fliting: See FLYTING.

floating image: See FIXED IMAGE AND FREE IMAGE.

flourish (from Latin for "flower") a nonessential word or phrase that serves to deliberately interrupt the regular meter, rhythm, or syntax of a poem, and which thus acts as a rhythmical COUNTERPOINT or SYNCOPATION in the poem. Flourishes are often used for ELEGANT VARIATION or as a means of delaying the final and complete sense of a line for the sake of dramatic buildup. See *grammatical devices of rhythm and balance* in APPENDIX 2.

flyting (from Middle English *flit*, for "fleet, flight"; also spelled "fliting") repartée in which two poets abuse each other with rounds of crude and scandalous verses. Sixteenth-century Scottish verse has flytings that are fresh and powerful. This Scottish tradition extends from William Dunbar (ca. 1460–1520) to the contemporary poet Hugh MacDiarmid. A similar, though less crude, form appears in the showdown offered by Gregory Corso in his *Poets Hitchhiking on the Highway*. See STICHOMYTHIA. See also *forms, humor,* and *light verse* in APPENDIX 1.

focus (Latin for "hearth") as an organizational element, the center of attention from which and to which all parts of a poem can be traced. The f. can be an IMAGE, a DRAMATIC SITUATION, a FLAT STATEMENT or line of DIALOGUE, an action, an element of SYNTAX, a psychological viewpoint, a SETTING, CHARACTERIZATION, TONE, or even a structural element from which the THEME of a poem develops. In the work of Richard Hugo, the speaker's feelings about the setting acts as a f. In e.e. cummings' poems, the TYPOGRAPHICAL ARRANGEMENT of words and lines serve as a focusing device. W.S. Merwin's poems often use an AMBIENCE or TONE to serve this purpose. As an element in the creative process of writing a poem, the term denotes CONTROL over the poem's composition. See DIFFUSED FOCUS.

folk ballad an anonymous narrative poem passed down orally in a culture from generation to generation. See BALLAD, ORAL POETRY, and POPULAR BALLAD.

folk epic an anonymous narrative of substantial length that grew out of early national history and which often focused on a noble hero or important historical event. Examples of the genre, also known as *primary epic*, include *Beowulf*, *The Iliad*, *The Odyssey*, and *El Cid*. An ART EPIC is a conscious imitation of a f.e. See EPIC and ORAL POETRY.

folklore (loan translation of German *Volkskunde*, from Anglo-Saxon *folc*, for "people," and *lar*, for "learning") various forms of cultural information, shared in the oral tradition, which explain, demonstrate, or instill in a people their most important values and beliefs. F. can take the form of songs, children's games, dramas, poems, riddles, stories, legends, myths, proverbs, fairy tales, or jokes. The English term was first used by W.J. Thomas in 1846 as a substitute for the phrase "popular antiquities." Even in postindustrial societies such as ours, new f. material is being created and passed on in examples such as The Urban Cowboy, The Liberated Woman, The Miss America Pageant, and stories from the protest gatherings of the 1960s. See BALLAD, BEAST EPIC, BLUES, FABLE, FABLIAU, FOLK SONG, FOLK TALE, and ORAL POETRY.

folk song an anonymous SONG featuring mnemonic devices such as RHYME and METER that relates a story about well-known events or historical or legendary figures or centers on universal themes of love, loss, or struggle. Examples include *John Henry* and *Frankie and Johnny*. During the 1960s, many protest and social-issue songs were written by composers such as Bob Dylan, Tom Rush, and Phil Ochs. See BALLAD, BLUES, FOLK BALLAD, FOLK EPIC and ROCK LYRIC.

folk tale a verse or prose narrative celebrating a historical event, hero, belief, or mode of behavior among culturally homogeneous people. The form was originated and passed on orally in stories, fairy tales, legends, and other forms. American folk tales include stories about Davy Crockett, Daniel Boone, Johnny Appleseed, and Paul Bunyan. See FOLK BALLAD, FOLK EPIC, FOLKLORE, and FOLK SONG.

foot a metrical unit of measurement in ACCENTUAL-SYLLABIC VERSE or QUANTITATIVE METER. The term includes duple, triple, and quadruple syllables such as the IAMB ($\smile\prime$), the ANAPEST ($\smile\smile\prime$), and the IONIC ($\smile\smile\prime\prime$), and is used to count the length and kind of meter in a line of verse. See METER and SCANSION.

foreshadowing a dramatic element in a piece of literature that hints at later developments in the PLOT. For example, the riddles spoken by the three witches in *MacBeth* prepare the reader for the fate that later befalls MacBeth. See NARRATIVE HOOK and PROLEPSIS.

form (from Latin for "shape") a widely and sometimes loosely used critical term describing many aspects of a piece of literature: (1) The term is often used as a substitute for the word GENRE or type of poetry that can be categorized according to its kind of theme, structure, concerns, meter, or devices. For example, a SONNET is a fixed form designated by its external metrical structure and argumentative development, while another work, such as an ALLEGORY, is classified according to the symbolic devices it uses. (2) Another sense of the term f. refers strictly to the design structure of the work; e.g., a PROSE POEM uses no line endings and thus appears to be prose. Stichic and strophic verse refer to the stanzaic form of a poem. (3) The process of composition, as it relates to the poet's method and mode of perception, is yet another application of the term f. For example, STREAM-OF-CONSCIOUSNESS poetry, DREAM POETRY, and COMPUTER POETRY are defined by their modes of composition. (4) At times, f. designates the quality of emotion used in a poem, as in the LYRIC, the DIRGE, and the ODE. (5) Sometimes the time of day and mood dictate a separate classification, as in the AUBADE and the NOCTURNE. (6) Scholars of myth use f. to refer specifically to one of several recurring plot shapes that a myth might explore, such as renewal, initiation, or identity. (7) In its most central sense, the term f. is used to describe the harmony of elements in a poem (direction, rhythm, sound, development, imagery, devices, etc.) which unite to form its ORGANIZING PRINCIPLE, an idea that Aristotle's *Poetics* explores. This ideal INSCAPE, which develops a poem from within, is what Coleridge refers to as "organic f." as opposed to the preconceived, external shape of a poem. NEW CRITICISM uses the word STRUCTURE synonymously with this sense of the term f. See FIXED FORMS, ORGANIC COMPOSITION, STICH, and STROPHE.

formal cause a rhetorical figure of logic that proves the self-contained identity of a thing and which separates a thing from all other things. The f.c. recognizes that which makes a certain thing no other than itself, and what the difference is between that thing and any other thing. William Shakespeare's definition of what love is and is not in *Sonnet 116* is an example. The poetic dictionary-maker Francis Ponge (*The Voice of Things*) created many examples of definition by f.c. See *figures of cause and effect* in APPENDIX 2. See also FILL-IN-THE-BLANKS POEM.

formal criticism (also known as "comparative criticism") criticism that examines and evaluates a piece of literature in terms of the standards of the genre to which it belongs. See CRITICISM. See also *criticism* in APPENDIX 1.

formal limitations the specific elements that control a poem, e.g., structural design, type of argument, quality of imagery, line lengths, diction, or types of figurative and rhetorical devices. A FILL-IN-THE-BLANKS POEM is defined by its list of actions, characteristics, or attributes; and a PROSE POEM is defined by its lack of line endings. F.l. can be dictated by traditional requirements or created as innovations by the poet.

format (from Latin [*liber*] *formatus*, for "[a book] formed in such a way") the physical qualities of a book, such as its size, shape, quality of paper, type of binding, amount of margin space, or typefaces. The term has also come to refer to how a book is organized according to thematic sections, chronological sequences, episodic structure, etc. In addition, f. can be used to indicate the traditional information concerning what the book contains in terms of notations peripheral to the text, such as its EDITION, number of printings, its COLOPHON, table of contents, or dust jacket blurbs. See *publishing formats* under *forms* in APPENDIX 1.

formative energy the impulse that creates a harmonic order among the parts of a poem, or that energy which externalizes in the language of a poem the holistic perceptions of experience and memory on the part of the poet. See DIVINE AFFLATUS, FORM, INSPIRATION, and ORGANIC COMPOSITION.

form dissolve (see CINEMATIC TECHNIQUES) a CINEMATIC EDITING technique, also used in poetry, that provides a smooth transition by fusing two images with the same shape, texture, or color. See also *cinematic terms* in APPENDIX 1.

Found Art art created from materials that are GIVEN and used in their unaltered states. The artist's act of aesthetically perceiving the object gives it a higher meaning and the status of art. At times, an artist will combine common objects, as in Marcel Duchamp's famous *Bicycle Wheel* which contains the upside-down fork and wheel of a bicycle inserted into a stool. The result is a humorous statement that forces the viewer to see mundane objects as aesthetic designs. But the essential component of a piece of F.A. is that it is discovered, not created. Ronald Gross (*Pop Poems*) works in this genre. See FOUND POEM, MINIMALISM, POP ART, and READYMADE.

found poem a piece of writing that, without change in conception or major reorganization or substantial distortion, could be considered a poem. Usually, the f.p. is wrested from a mundane domain (street signs, business notices, newspaper advertisements) and isolated so that it takes on an ironic, dramatic, or multilayered meaning. For instance, the Massachusetts Department for Motor Vehicles sent this notice to a man whom it did not know to be a poet:

Notice
You have twenty days in which to correct
your vision.

For further elaboration, see FOUND ART. See also MINIMALISM, POP ART, and READYMADE. See also *forms* in APPENDIX 1.

four meanings of a poem four expressive elements that I.A. Richards (*Practical Criticism*, 1929) found germane to communication in general and poetry in particular: (1) *sense*, or information supplied in the language; (2) *feeling*, or emotions supplied by diction, statement, or devices; (3) TONE, the writer's attitude toward his subject matter and/or audience; and (4) *intention*, what the writer hopes to achieve by creating the piece of literature. Each genre of writing, of course, will emphasize different aspects of its communication, but the distinctions delineated above are helpful in analyzing and discussing a literary work. See CRITICISM. See also *meaning* in APPENDIX 1.

four senses of interpretation four levels of meaning that can be gleaned from a passage or work: (1) the *literal*, or informational; (2) the *allegorical*, which interprets concrete images in terms of abstract values that lie outside the work; (3) the *moral*, which takes into consideration the values, beliefs, and modes of behavior of the work's characters; and (4) the *anagogical*, which interprets the spiritual values and symbols in a piece of literature. Originally, this four-part system of interpretation was applied to readings of scripture but has been extended to the realm of literature. See ALLEGORY, ANAGOGICAL VISION, ANAGOGE, COGNITIVE MEANING, CRITICISM, and LITERAL VISION VS. ANAGOGICAL VISION. See also *criticism* in APPENDIX 1.

fourteeners another term for iambic heptameter, a seven-foot iambic meter. The term applies to the amount of syllables in a line of this verse. See ACCENTUAL-SYLLABIC VERSE and HEPTAMETER. See also *forms* in APPENDIX 1.

fractured narrative a narrative technique whose STRATEGY is to fragment intentionally the development and STRUCTURE of a story. The STYLE is probably a reflection of the way in which a writer apperceives the PLOT and THEME of his story. In terms of classifications, it appears there are two basic types of fractured narratives: those based upon *episodic structures* and those that work by way of ASSOCIATIONAL LOGIC. The following illustrations are meant to show the major forms of this type of narrative.

Episodic Structure
This type of f.n. forms itself according to the selection of plot material taken from memory or created from the imagination and structured according to discrete plot units which define and explore their subjects and themes. The strategy is one of accumulating and layering meaning through progressive episodes of action, character, and detail. Jack Driscoll's *Memories of My Deaf Mother* employs scenes that manipulate action, noise, and silence so that the quality of experience and memory itself are equated:

> My mother takes down her hair
> long and heavy
> like so many nights of snow.
>   In bed she dreams
> me knocking sound from these boards, each nail
> a whisper driven deep into her ear. I am building
> a coffin, my dead voice trying hard to call her back
> through all this silence.
>   * * *
> The deaf have poor balance. Undressing
> by the stairs she always imagined falling, fear
> alive in her spine. I was nine
> the first time I saw her naked, her pale arms
> hugging the railing like a neck.
>   * * *
> I learned to talk with my hands, to close them
> sometimes in anger, a door
> slamming in my throat. I remember
> how often water on the stove whistled itself dry,
> how the pickup's horn stuck one night
> while my mother, smiling, parked it full of hay
> in the barn. I woke, ran barefoot through the cold,

found four stalls battered, the horses
crazier than fire.

* * *

My father died dragging bales
through the deep snow. My mother, finding him,
exhaled a single word;
I choked it down,
listened to it thaw for years.

* * *

I am always coming home, wind
stuttering on the lip of a hill.
There is a cow;
she pulls her tongue across a saltlick,
where my mother opened her fur coat,
pulled my mouth around her nipple
like a scream.
         All winter
I curled next to her, dreamed
absence was a sound, the moon
tapping in her blind ear.

* * *

For the last time
I step into childhood,
unfold these memories, notes
pushed like a groan across the snow
         where she is hauling water
on a sled. I follow,
ringing a bell for the horses
who step now from under the pines.

Another sort of episodic f.n., used in the classic Japanese film
Rashomon, is that of the *retake*, which proposes different versions of an
event, and which sometimes uses switches in the story's POINT OF VIEW (see
SYNCHRONICITY). In Laurie Davie's poem *Revision*, the accumulation of
retakes of the basic dramatic situation between a man and a woman forms
a large thematic framework that reveals the speaker's character and
emotional need:

I actually spoke once:

We were in a giant green
tree, that breathed in and
out when we did. There was
a crazylace pattern of sun-
light over your face—
we were safe and I said
         Behave yourself. No,

I was sitting in your car,
reapplying lipstick and feeling
perfect and crystalline; you
drove, your face reflected
the stars and hope—
you embraced the night and I said
         There are a limited number
of good moments.   No,

I was at home, knitting possibilities
together, dreaming into the fire
and drinking scotch. You

blew in, flushed with victory,
your white scarf so dashing and I said
        My desires are insufferable,
please leave.   No,
We were riding across the
plains and into the sunset,
sweaty and tired but
competent: comrades—we
stopped to rest, you shook
off your hat and under the
wide spotlight looked
flaxen and bronze, immobile
and eternal   so beautiful
and did I say
I want you I need you let's go home.

Associational-Logic Structure

This type of f.n. uses slanting forms of logic which associate with one another through LOGIC OF THE METAPHOR (comparison, substitution, or identity) in order to coherently fuse disparate entities. In Albert Goldbarth's *Family/Watch*, the fragmentation of the surface texture (plot, time frames, details, and scenes) works in productive tension with the underlying theme and is, in fact, a structural reflection of the theme. The poet is able to carry three levels of meaning throughout his narrative by using techniques of JUXTAPOSITION, PUN, and ASSOCIATIONAL LOGIC in his PROSE POEM:

There is a pleiosaur at the Dallas-Fort Worth airport, its bonesnout jetstyled by the earth's work. I'm from the dawn of time too, having wakened at 6 for an 8 a.m. flight, the alarm having excavated me from the ground floor of sleep. It was found by the construction crew. Then pieced long and low bone by bone. I bumbled through the bathroom's few ablutions, everything blurred as if the world were caught on film set to a different time than mine. I wound up the heirloom. Its face, despite the sleek lines, is anachronism; crowds form, something like runway crews helping a jet dock into a later time zone. It was Grandma Rosie's, filligree gold from a time of dented chickensoup pots every gray ghetto day and parasol Sunday evenings. My father gave it to me just a week ago, passing it down, I could feel the individual bones in his handshake move minutely through their element. 100,000 years ago; the steppe must have shook when it crashed. So early, and such a fog—of course I dropped it. The crystal broke. Everything shook light sharp on its edges. Of course I would; when I was thirteen, a truculent manchild being groomed for bar mitzvah, didn't I snicker at the Passover table? They went from a great ton winch to tweezers, and here it is now silent and commanding while, outside, motors shiver the air. You'd have to know Daddy Irv, his salesman's bluster, his smile set in like fixative: so that, when he suddenly wept, the first time ever in public, our whole tribe smashed like a plate. It wasn't much later, she died—though I have given her at least a gift of seeing her only grandson bar mitzvahed. Everything stopped for a moment, I ran across the room and cradled his head. What would be flesh is something plaster-looking—the skeleton, though, is true, and awesome, and makes its own flesh around it: the power of

architecture. Time reversed a moment: he was the child. Light in
fragments down his cheeks. And so I stood there, holding the
broken face. That's what it is really—a stopped clock. Dead, it
says its life forever. Says gneiss, says coal, says crystal forming.
Here I am, with my baggage. You can't stop time but you can stop
a time. This time, this one. I've never been good with faces. I think
it forgives me, this looking thing with the motors far behind us, its
empty eyes, its story full of repairwork.

One other type combines both the episodic and associational modes;
that is, the discrete surface structures of plot and form hold together by the
deeper structures of logic and argument. In Michael Simms' early draft of
his poem *The Explanation*, he establishes a common ground that, by
means of selected examples, links up the natural processes of growth in
nature, the spontaneity and clarity of a child's innocent perception of the
world, and their relation to the creative process underlying mature art:

> I think there is a likeness in all things.
> The woods always seem to be waiting
> for us to move on, so the trees
> may resume their patient chemistry.
>
> A painter friend tells me
> he can't paint a tree
> except by becoming the tree, nor a boy
> except he'd been a boy.
>
> My stepson is playing marbles,
> learning the activities of light.
> His mind opens the fable:
> what occurs once, occurs often.
>
> I think we remain children always
> and the world a child's toy.
> Last night we watched the moon rising
> in the transparent darkness, the air
>
> filling with birds, the smell of pine and hay,
> and Christoper came out with a line
> jotted by a poet fifty years before—
> The moon, the moon is at the door
> and silence was the explanation.

The following techniques and devices of narrative relate to the f.n.:
CENTRIFUGAL STRUCTURE, CUT-AND-SHUFFLE POEM, FLASHBACK, FLASHFOR-
WARD, LEAPING POETRY, and SANDWICH CONSTRUCTION.

frame the design element of a poem, such as its RHYTHM, PLOT, STRUC-
TURE, DOMAIN OF IMAGERY, or SOUND SYSTEM. The f. provides an
abstract enclosure within which the poem is displayed. It is regarded as a
formalizing element in the poem and can be an ORGANIZING PRINCIPLE in
terms of FOCUS and UNITY. I.A. Richards thought that the artificial nature
or effect of rhythm in poetry acted as a f. in the same manner that the
borders of a painting set off a canvas. See FORM.

frame of reference: See DOMAIN OF THOUGHT.

frame story a narrative structure that contains other, usually shorter, narratives. The f.s. of Chaucer's *Canterbury Tales* is that of the pilgrims' meeting each other and taking turns relating their tales. Chaucer's structure, as well as many of the tales themselves, were borrowed from Boccaccio's *Decameron*, in which the f.s. is a group of young people singing, telling stories, and reciting poetry while they hide from the ravages of the black plague. Probably the best known of frame stories is that of Scheherazade, the newlywed who staves off her execution by weaving the intricate tales of *A Thousand and One Arabian Nights*. See PLAY-WITHIN-A-PLAY and STORY-WITHIN-A-STORY. See also *forms* in AP-PENDIX 1.

free association a process of logic linked to the sub- or unconscious level of the mind in which a series of chainlike associative connections are made between one thing or idea and another. The process probably works by comparison or contrast of attributes much in the way that metaphors are created. This type of logic is commonly thought to stand opposite that of RATIOCINATION or normal reason and judgment, and is used extensively in DREAM POETRY, LEAPING POETRY, and STREAM-OF-CONSCIOUSNESS.

free image: See FIXED IMAGE AND F.I.

free verse (loan translation of French VERS LIBRE) unmetered and often irregularly lined-out unrhymed verse that depends upon extensive variation in rhythm, balanced phrasing, syntactical repetition, and typographical and grammatical oddness to achieve its effects. Pacing or CADENCE, a unit of measure that is larger than the metrical foot, is used. As a form, its strength lies in the variation and subtlety of effects which it can achieve in contrast to the more limited possibilities of regularly metered, rhymed, and structured verse. While the line or stanza acts as a basic unit or measurement in f.v., these guides may depend upon a number of more specific, formative units of pacing, such as (1) the *syntactical unit*, which measures a line according to units of grammar, as in these lines of Galway Kinnell:

> We walk across the snow,
> The stars can be faint,
> The moon can be eating itself out,
> There can be meteors flaring to death on earth,
> The Northern Lights can be blooming and seething
> And tearing themselves apart all night,
> We walk arm in arm, and we are happy.

(2) the *breath unit*, which measures a line according to duration of a normal breath, as in these lines from Allen Ginsberg:

> I saw the best minds of my generation destroyed by madness,
>   starving hysterical naked,
> dragging themselves through the negro streets at dawn,
>   looking for an angry fix . . . .

(3) the *sense* or *thought unit*, which builds lines by parceling out discrete ideas, images, or other sensual perceptions, as in these lines by Louise Glück:

> One sound. Then the hiss and whir
> of houses gliding into their places.
> And the wind
> leafs through the bodies of animals.

(4) the *conversational unit*, which creates phrases and line lengths according to commonly spoken language, as in these lines by Ira Sadoff:

> I miss the peace and quiet of Chicago
> that's the kind of guy I am

and (5) the *rhetorical unit*, which molds lines according to the emphasis in meaning and semantics that the poet intends, as in these lines by Philip Dacey:

> Thirty candles and one
> to grow on. My husband
> and son watch me
> think of wishes.

Any one of these formal rhythmical elements has the potential either singly or in combination to dominate and form the rhythm and lineation of a poem.

F.v., an invention of the 19th-century French poets whose system of QUANTITATIVE VERSE adapted itself naturally to the new form, has revolutionized the English ACCENTUAL-SYLLABIC VERSE by loosening the somewhat mechanical restrictions inherent in STRESS PROSODY. In intention and effect, f.v. has claimed a middle ground between prose and metered verse which has brought poetry closer to the spoken idiom of various languages. Central to its use in American poetry is William Carlos Williams' theory and use of the VARIABLE FOOT in which the customary metrical units of measurement are expanded to include more unaccented syllables, words, and phrases, so that the line or stanza, the new unit of measurement, is dependent upon a sense of pacing, of COUNTERPOINT and rhythmical improvisation, rather than metrical feet. In general, f.v. creates an air of familiarity, accessibility, and naturalness. In terms of language models that f.v. reflects, it is based on (1) *verse written toward the style of prose*, as in Philip Levine's *Fixing the Foot: On Rhythm*:

> Yesterday I heard a Dutch doctor talking to a small girl
> who had cut her foot, not seriously, and was very frightened
> by the sight of her own blood. "Nay! Nay!" he said over and
> over. I could hear him quite distinctly through the wall
> that separated us, and his voice was strong and calm, he
> spoke very slowly and seemed never to stop speaking . . .

(2) *verse structured on semiformal speech rhythms*, as in Philip Larkin's *Poetry of Departures*:

> Sometimes you hear, fifth-hand,
> as epitaph:
> He chucked up everything
> And just cleared off,
> And always the voice will sound
> Certain you approve

This audacious, purifying,
Elemental move.

or (3) *verse written toward the style of the common idiom* or *low diction*, as in Charles Bukowski's *no charge*:

> this babe in the grandstand
> with dyed red hair
> kept leaning her breasts against me
> and talking about Gardena
> poker parlors

The King James version of the Bible has been very influential in revealing the possibilities in nonmetrical verse. Walt Whitman imitated its use of CATALOGUE VERSE, and its Psalms and Song of Solomon acted as ancient models for new forms. Long before the new form became conventional, poets such as Milton and Blake were using metrical verse that resembles f.v.

See BALANCE, EXPERIMENTAL POETRY, IMAGISM, LINE ENDING, LINE, MNENOMIC DEVICE, OPEN FIELD COMPOSITION, ORGANIC COMPOSITION, PACE, PARALLELISM, PHRASING, POLYRHYTHMIC, PROSE POEM, PUNCTUATION, REPETITION, RUNNING RHYTHM, SPRUNG RHYTHM, and TRIADIC STANZA. See also *rhythm* in APPENDIX 1.

French forms a set of regularly rhyming and metrically patterned verse forms that originated in Southern France during the 12th and 13th centuries when the troubadours were extant. Some of the forms include BALLADE, bref double, CHANT ROYAL, kyrielle, LAI, lai nouveau, LIMERICK, RIME COUÉE, RONDEAU, RONDEL, RONDELET, SESTINA, terzanelle, TRIOLET, VILLANELLE, and VIRELAY. For a related term, see FIXED FORMS.

Fugitives a group of well-known poets from Vanderbilt University who celebrated the mores and values of the South and espoused the power of the specific, concrete image. Among its adherents were Allen Tate, Robert Penn Warren, John Crowe Ransom, and Donald Davidson who edited and wrote for the short-lived literary magazine *The Fugitive* during 1922–25. Tate, the school's most vociferous spokesman, linked economics and social behavior to poetry, and spoke against antirural values of the North. The Fugitive's ideas are best put forth in a collection of their essays on poetry, history, and socioeconomics entitled *I'll Take My Stand, the South and the Agrarian Tradition by Twelve Southerners*. See *movements and schools of poetry* in APPENDIX 1. See also NEW CRITICISM, a movement often associated with the F.

full rhyme: See PERFECT RHYME.

functional metaphor (also called "organic metaphor" or "structural metaphor") a metaphor whose tenor is implicitly carried within its vehicle (see TENOR AND VEHICLE) and thus acts symbolically. The form is common in Shakespeare's work, as in the following lines in which the soul is depicted as a king surrounded by rebelling forces of the body: "Poor soul, the centre of my sinful earth, / Thrall to these rebel pow'rs that thee array." In Metaphysical Poetry, the f.m. is referred to as CONCEIT. See METAPHOR.

fundamental image: See CONTROLLING IMAGE; see also FUNCTIONAL METAPHOR.

Futurism a movement in art and poetry of early 20th-century international postsymbolists in France, Germany, Italy, Russia, and Spain who called for an unwavering commitment to action in art and life, even if that action means destruction of the past and leads to anarchy and war. The *Futurists* disavowed everything associated with the past in order to concentrate on experiments with the unknown. Their call, like that of the *Cubists* (see CUBISM), was meant to invent a new means of expression, at times without literal meaning, which would release its followers from the bonds of tradition in a new world. The Russian poet Anton Lotov pushed language toward its aural limit when he composed his *Melody of an Easter City*, which, through the medium of sound alone, tried to recreate the brash atmosphere of a Russian Bazaar. It represented a type of poetry like Lewis Carrol's *Jabberwocky* which is known as NONSENSE VERSE, but which the Russian Futurists termed TRANS-SENSE VERSE.

Mayakovsky in Russia, Filippo Marinetti in Italy (who wrote the first *Futurist Manifesto* in 1909), and Guillaume Apollinaire in France all tried to revolutionize the poem through this short-lived movement. Apollinaire in his own manifesto called for "exaltation of aggressive movement, feverish insomnia, gymnastic pace, perilous jump, etc.—glorification of war—the only hygiene of the world—militarism, patriotism, the destructive gesture of the anarchist, and scorn of woman." F. created a hysteria meant to break the calm and innocent surface of the prewar Georgian state of mind. It was, in fact, an artistic gesture that foreshadowed the spectre of World War I. See BEAST LANGUAGE, CUBISM, DADA, EXPRESSIONISM, IMAGISM, SURREALISM, and VORTICISM.

G

generational rhythm a theory of rhythmic composition that is based on developing a series of ever-changing linear improvisations rather than being based on regular meter or base rhythms. The unity of the rhythm is found in the GESTALT or whole feeling of the poem which accumulates through the continual slanting and evolution of new rhythmic patterns. The strategy is to create a free-wheeling, ongoing dialectical rhythm whose coherence depends upon previous and subsequent lines. The form exists in theory only, at this point, but its creation seems plausible since jazz musicians have already spawned such forms using rhythmic and sound patterns that are manipulated away from a set melody line. For an extensive discussion of g.r., see RHYTHM.

generative content vs. ornamental content *generative content*: the seminal content of a poem, such as its DRAMATIC SITUATION, CONTROLLING METAPHOR or IMAGE, or central idea, which gives rise to further elaborations of content. The *ornamental content* is a much less important component of the poem as a whole and may be found in the form of descriptive detail, rhythmic flourishes or variations, or minor action. In Yeats' *Sailing to Byzantium*, the references to art and old age act as generative content, while the image of the "mackerel-crowded seas" acts as ornamental content.

generative metrics metrical theories that arose in the 1960s and 1970s out of studies in transformational-generative linguistic theory. Just as transformational-generative grammar attempted to distinguish vigorously between grammatical and nongrammatical utterances, g.m. tried to set apart metrical and nonmetrical rhythms. Both use a formalism based on modern mathematics and, in particular, set theory. The first study to use g.m. was by Morris Halle and Samuel Jay Keyser (1966) and focused on Chaucer's meters. The important contribution of g.m. is the idea that a line is considered as a set of positions having strengths or weaknesses in accent, rather than as a set of feet. Most of the studies to date have been on iambic pentameter which is seen as having ten positions. See *musical* and *acoustic scansion* under SCANSION.

genre /zhäN'r/ or /zhän'rə/ (French for "kind, type") originally, any literary type based on an ideal abstract model that describes a group of works with common form, method of presentation, technique, subject matter, or mood. For instance, the four main literary genres have traditionally been categorized as COMEDY, *romance*, TRAGEDY, and SATIRE, while verse has been classified according to its length as in the EPIC, and the EPIGRAM. Over the centuries, the notion of genres has consistently lost favor so that critics now see the function of the term more as an arbitrary method of labeling a work than as a truly functional device in recognizing an aesthetic. See FORM.

Georgian pertaining to two periods in England: the reigns of George I to George IV (1714–1830) and the reign of George V (1910–36). The G. POETS, a group of English poets who described rural subjects in a delicate style, arose during George V's reign. See PERIODS OF ENGLISH LITERATURE.

Georgian poets a group of poets writing between 1910 and 1936 under the reign of George V of England. Their subject matter was BUCOLIC and their various styles were delicate, refined, and set in traditional forms. The group, anthologized by Edward Marsh five times between 1912 and 1922, included Rupert Brooke, Walter de la Mare, Ralph Hodgson, W.H. Davies, John Masefield, and W.J. Turner. Others associated with them include D.H. Lawrence, Robert Graves, and James Stephens. See GEORGIAN.

Georgic poetry in which the rural life is praised. The *Georgics* (first century B.C.) of Virgil discuss animal husbandry, weather forecasting, and other skills, so that the term has come to connote a DIDACTIC POETRY concerning agrarian ways. Addison's *Essay on the Georgic* (1697) distinguishes this didactic element in the G. form from the PASTORAL poem which is not necessarily instructional. The earliest example of the form is Hesiod's *Works and Days* (750 B.C). The form was much admired in the 17th and 18th centuries in England.

gestalt /gəshtält/ or /gestôlt′/ (from German *Gestalt*, for "whole") a term borrowed from psychology, describing the holistic effect of a piece of literature, that is, the thoughts and feelings aroused by the accumulation of interrelationships between rhythm, image, structure, sound, etc., an effect that cannot be explained by an examination of its parts. The term was originally used by German psychologists who studied human behavior in units of g. The element of VOICE in poetry is best described in terms of g. rather than by its particular components.

geste /jest/ (from Latin for "deeds, exploits"; also spelled "gest") a romance in verse form celebrating the exploits and heroes of important wars, as the *Gest Historiale of the Destruction of Troy* in the 14th century and the *Gesta Romanorum* in the 13th century, a sourcebook on Roman adventures. See CHANSON DE GESTE.

ghazal /gaz′əl/ (Arabic; also spelled "ghasel") a Near Eastern verse form celebrating love and drinking, and composed of five to 12 couplets, the last of which contains the author's name. The eighth-century form was popularized in the West by German Romanticists.

The original love poem form in Arabia fused a COURTLY LOVE motif, similar to that of Medieval Europe's, with an erotic ENVOY, as in the following anonymous poem from the *Dā al-tirāz* (House of Embroidery) volume:

> Sometimes a young girl appears like the full moon rising.
> What a breast on a branch of laurel!
> Her leaves are a garment more red than the rose.
> She spent the night while singing:
>> "My darling, make up your mind. Arise! Hurry and
>> Kiss my mouth. Come embrace
>> My breast and raise my ankles to my earrings.
>> My husband is busy."

See FIXED FORMS and FRENCH FORMS. See also *forms* in APPENDIX 1.

given any one of the linguistic, aesthetic, and technical assumptions made by a piece of literature. For instance, language assumes a certain order of words; specific forms of poetry assume conventions of structure and meter; and the experience of literature itself makes assumptions about the compression of FELT TIME as opposed to chronological REAL TIME. A second use of the term refers to a poet's receiving an inspired line or whole poem seemingly without conscious effort, as in the example of Coleridge's fragment *Kubla Khan*. See *clichés* in APPENDIX 1.

gloss (from Greek for "language, tongue," or "a word needing explanation") notes of translation, interpretation, or explanation inserted between the words or in the margins of a text. The practice arose primarily in translated works in which Latin Scholars commented upon Greek works, and, in turn, Medieval scholars commented upon Latin texts. Eventually, it became common for editors and scholars to comment on texts in their own language, and for writers to add *marginalia* to their own books, as in the case of Coleridge's *Rime of the Ancient Mariner*. A popular, pejorative meaning of the term connotes the oversummarizing or misinterpretation of a work (see REDUCTIVE FALLACY).

gnomic writing /nō′mik/ (*gnomic*, from Greek for "dealing in maxims, sententious") short aphoristic statements that purport the truth about ethical situations. Ancient cultures, such as the Chinese, Egyptian, Indian, and Greek, developed the form to a high degree. The *Gnomic poets* of Greece (sixth and seventh centuries B.C.) serialized lines of gnomic verse much as the contemporary American poets W.S. Merwin, Mark Strand, W.H. Auden, and Archibald MacLeish have done. Other famous sayings included in the genre are those of Francis Bacon, Ben Franklin, Emerson, Thoreau, and Robert Frost. See APHORISM, APOTHEGM, and PROVERB.

Goliardic verse /gōlyär′dik/ (*Goliardic*, from Old French for "gluttony") satiric and profane lyrical verse written by itinerant scholars, jesters, and students in Northern Europe during the 12th and 13th centuries. The term, supposedly derived from the name of a famous Latin poet, Golias, denotes verse whose themes describe the pleasures of love, drinking, and merriment. The most famous collection of this type of verse is *Carmina Burana* (published in Germany in 1847). The Medieval Goliardic poets created the *Goliardic measure*, a stanzaic form containing four lines of 13 syllables apiece, and occasionally ending in a six-foot line quoted from a Classical source. See *forms* in APPENDIX 1.

Gongorism (also called "culteranism") an overdecorated, bombastic style of verse that affects learnedness through the use of *puns, conceits,* and *paradoxes*. The style is named after Luis de Gongora y Argote, a contemporary of the 17th-century English writer John Lyly who became famous for the demands he made on grammar, phrasing, and his reader's patience. See *devices of poetic license* in APPENDIX 2, and *defects in control* in APPENDIX 1. See also EUPHUISM.

Gothic a style of writing featuring primitive settings, violent action, and gloomy moods. The term, derived from the ancient Germanic Goth tribe, originally indicated barbaric qualities, but came to be closely associated with the architectural style of the Medieval period. Popularly, the term refers to literature such as Mary Shelley's *Frankenstein* and the novels of the Brönte sisters.

gradual verse: See RHOPALIC VERSE.

grammatical accent: See ACCENT.

graphic scansion a system of metrical analysis that considers the accented and unaccented syllables in a meter. It is the most common form of SCANSION in the English language.

Graveyard School a group of 18th-century English poets whose work is often set in graveyards. The poems' themes deal with the inevitability of death and a longing for immortality, and their moods range from meditative to despairing. The group includes Thomas Gray, Thomas Parnell, Edward Young, Robert Blair, among others. Thomas Gray's *Elegy Written in a Country Churchyard* (1751) is probably the most important poem of the type. Edith M. Sickel's *The Gloomy Egoist* (1932) traces the genre from its inception through the Romantic period.

ground rhythm (also called "base rhythm" or "matrix rhythm") the ideal or abstract metrical RHYTHM, stated or unstated, that lies behind the rhythmical variations in a poem. For instance, many poems are based on iambic pentameter as a g.r., but that meter may be only hinted at or loosely referred to in the actual improvised meter of a poem.

H

habbie stanza: See BURNS STANZA.

hack (from *hackney*) a writer who has creative ability but who produces unimaginative, unoriginal, or nonscholarly work for the sole purpose of financial gain. Writers of advertisements, romance and detective novels, occasional verse, and greeting cards are often placed in this class. See HACKNEYED. See also *Clichés* in APPENDIX 1.

hackneyed a pejorative term referring to an uninspired, unimaginative style of writing. See HACK. See also *Clichés*, *Control*, and *Diction* in APPENDIX 1.

haiku /hī′kōō/ (from Japanese for "starting verse"; also spelled "haikai" and "hokku") a 16th century Japanese form of lyric, syllabic verse composed of 17 syllables in three lines of five, seven, and five syllables, respectively. According to traditional form, the IMAGERY in the poem must be from nature; the poem must contain the name of or reference to a season; it must allude to religious beliefs or historical events; it must contain no rhymes; it must create an emotional response in the reader; and it must penetrate to the heart of its theme in a sudden EPIPHANY known as *satori*. The following is a h. by Basho:

> Lightning in the sky!
> In the deeper dark is heard
> A night-heron's cry.

Ezra Pound, Amy Lowell, and John Gould Fletcher, the Imagists, were influenced by the form (see IMAGISM). See *forms* in APPENDIX 1.

half-rhyme: See OFF-RHYME.

hamartia (Greek for "sin, fault") in Greek TRAGEDY, the character flaw, error of poor judgment, or human weakness that shows up in the action of a PROTAGONIST who is, therefore, doomed by fate. Ambition, impulsiveness, fecklessness, ignorance, jealousy, and greed are examples of such weakness.

Hammond's meter: See ELEGIAC STANZA.

headless line (see CATALEXIS) initial TRUNCATION, that is, a line that is metrically incomplete because it is missing its initial syllable or syllables.

head rhyme (see ALLITERATION) the repetition of the initial consonants or vowels in two or more words. See also BEGINNING RHYME.

hemiepes /hemi·ep′ēz/ (Late Greek for "half-verse, half-word") a truncated, three-foot dactylic measure (-⌣⌣ / -⌣⌣ / -) used as a stock unit of rhythm in Classical Greek metric verse.

hemistich /hem′istik/ (from Greek for "half line") a half or incomplete line of verse. Usually, the term applies to the section of a line before or after the medial CAESURA. When it is used as a metrically incomplete length of line, it is meant to show disruption, quickness of pace, and emotional upheaval. Both Anglo-Saxon verse and Classical Greek prosody used it as a stock device in rhythm. *Hemistichomythia* indicates verse composed of a series of half-lines.

hendecasyllabic verse (hendecasyllabic, Greek for "eleven-syllabled"; also called "phalaecean," after the Greek poet Phalaikos) an 11-syllable line composed of trochees or spondees in its first and last feet, a dactyl in its second foot, and trochees in its third and fourth feet (′⌣/′⌣⌣/′⌣/′⌣/′⌣). Created by Catullus who based the form on Classical pentameter, the verse was mostly used by Latin, Greek, and Italian poets and seldom used in English in its strict form, except by Swinburne and the following lines by Tennyson who credits his source: "Look, I come to the test, a tiny poem / All composed in a metre of Catullus." See *forms* in APPENDIX 1.

hendiadys /-dī′ə-/ (from Greek *hen dia dyion*, for "one by a means of two") a figure of speech that links up substantives or a substantive and genitive by using the conjunction "and," as in Virgil's "We drink from cups and gold." The device compresses and makes equivalent different attributes of a thing into one grammatical unit. Modern examples of its use abound in clichés such as "good and hot," "nice and warm," or "tried and true." See *grammatical figures of exchange* in APPENDIX 2.

heptameter /-tam′-/ (from Greek for "seven-foot"; a similarly used term is SEPTENARY) a seven-foot duple meter used in Classical prosody and in much English narrative verse by Wordsworth, E.B. Browning, and Coleridge. See FOURTEENERS. See also *forms* in APPENDIX 1.

heresy of paraphrase the critical tenet that a poem can never be satisfactorily expressed in a paraphrase. The term was put forth by Cleanth Brooks (*The Well Wrought Urn*, 1947) who explained that the infrastructure of drama, tone, and other devices in a poem makes its form and content so inextricably interdependent that any attempt to present less than the complete work of art (such as its argument or plot summary) does the poem a disservice. Brooks and his mentor, I.A. Richards, were and remain very influential in promoting the integrity of poetry through their criticism. See NEW CRITICISM. See also *criticism* in APPENDIX 1.

hermeneutics /-nōō′-/ (from Greek for "interpretation, translation," and eventually perhaps from *Hermes*, god of speech and writing) originally, the Church practice of interpreting the scriptures to an audience not familiar with ancient languages such as Latin or Hebrew. Later, h. was applied to texts in literature that attempted to interpret poetry or POETICS. See CRITICISM and EXEGESIS.

hermeticism generally, any poetry that uses occult SYMBOLISM. H. was named after Hermes Trismegistus, the Egyptian god of letters, to whom several books on the subject are attributed. The theory behind the poetry is to strip words of their usual logical meanings in order to increase their musical impact, to heighten the dramatic impact and function of silences in the poem, and to put forth the esoteric, symbolic power of the words. This subjective aesthetic eschewed the usual structural elements of narrative and argument in order to arrive at a *naked poetry*. Practitioners include the symbolists Novalis, Poe, Baudelaire, Mallarmé, Rimbaud, and Valéry (see SYMBOLISM). Yeats, Apollinaire, Strindberg, Ibsen, Ungaretti, Quasimodo, and Montale were also influenced by the possibilities of occult symbolism.

hero (from Greek for "protector") originally, a man—or woman, **heroine**—whose superior abilities and character raised him—or her—to the level of a god, demigod, or warrior-king. The current popular notion of the term similarly indicates one of high moral character whose courage, physical exploits, and nobility of purpose make him or her singularly admired. The term is often incorrectly used as a synonym for the main character in literature. See ANTAGONIST, DEUTERAGONIST, and PROTAGONIST. See also *dramatic terms* in APPENDIX 1.

heroic couplet a two-line, rhymed form of verse in iambic pentameter. Chaucer introduced the form into English (*The Legend of Good Women* and the *Canterbury Tales*). The name h.c. is derived from its use in heroic epic poetry and drama. Intermittently used in the RENAISSANCE, the form reached its popular height in the 17th century and took on a very fixed character in the NEO-CLASSICISM period which used both END-STOPPED lines and closed syntactical units in each line. There are two main types: the CLOSED COUPLET, in which the second line is generally the end-stopped line, and the OPEN COUPLET, in which the second line is enjambed so that the sense and/or syntax are continued into the next couplet. The utility of the form lies in its succinctness and its flexibility when the CAESURA is shifted from one position to another. It allows for much manipulation of rhetorical balance in the JUXTAPOSITION of lines and hemistiches. See also *forms* in APPENDIX 1.

heroic drama tragic and tragicomic drama, often in verse, developed in the RESTORATION period and characterized by HYPERBOLE, BOMBAST, HEROIC COUPLET, violent action, exotic settings, and heroic characters. According to Dryden, this operatic form was developed by Sir William Davenant (*The Siege of Rhodes*, 1656). George Villiers' *The Rehearsal* (1671) is a notable SATIRE of the form. See *forms* in APPENDIX 1.

heroic line the iambic pentameter line used in epic verse. See HEROIC COUPLET and HEROIC STANZA.

heroic quatrain: See ELEGIAC STANZA.

heroic stanza a verse composed of four lines of iambic pentameter rhyming aabb, or, as in Thomas Gray's *Elegy Written in a Country Churchyard*, rhyming abab. See HEROIC COUPLET. See also *forms* in APPENDIX 1.

heroic verse the ALEXANDRINE Old French line of hendecasyllabics used in Romances about Alexander the Great, such as *Roman d' Alexandre*.

heuristic /hyo͞oris'-/ (from Greek for "to discover") events that cause a character or the reader to come upon the truth. The function of art is said to be h. since it generally stimulates thinking about the nature of man and the world around him.

hexameter /-am'-/ (from Greek for "six measures") originally, in Greek QUANTITATIVE METER a six-foot line that used dactylic and spondaic syllables. The first four feet are dactylic or spondaic, the fifth foot dactylic, and the sixth spondaic (ˊ˘˘/ˊ˘˘/ˊ˘˘/ˊ˘˘/ˊ˘˘/ˊˊ) as in Longfellow's *Evangeline*. English accentual-syllabic versions of the foot have tended to lose the form's quicker Greek pacing and flexibility by not substituting spondees for dactyls. Greek and Latin poets used the verse for epic and didactic forms, but current use of the term generally refers to any verse of six feet. Poets such as Spenser, Sidney, Coleridge, Tennyson, and Swinburne have used the h. form extensively. See *forms* in APPENDIX 1.

hiatus /hī·ā'-/ (Latin for "gap, opening") a term referring to (1) a pause between the pronunciations of consecutive vowels (as in the word "poem"), the opposite of ELISION; (2) a part missing in a line of verse; and (3) steps of reasoning omitted from an argument or syllogism. As an element of SCANSION in SYLLABIC METER, h. was commonly found as a device in Greek epic poetry and French syllabic verse.

hipallage: See HYPALLAGE.

historical criticism a form of literary analysis that compares a work with its age and its author's life. See CRITICISM. See also *criticism* in APPENDIX 1.

historical rhyme words that once rhymed with each other in a former period of history, but which have come to be pronounced differently, as in the eye-rhymes "love/prove" and "mood/blood." Other rhymes that have lost their twinning sound values are not necessarily eye rhymes, as in Pope's "Good-nature and good-sense must ever join; / To err is human, to forgive, divine." See EYE-RHYME and RHYME.

hokku: See HAIKU.

homeric epithet: See EPITHET.

homiologia a rhetorical device of narration, sometimes thought of as a vice or defect, that presents a tedious and unpleasant dragging out of a story. The "shaggy dog story" is one type of h., and many of the short stories of Raymond Carver use the device ironically. See *devices of poetic license* in APPENDIX 2, and *diction* in APPENDIX 1.

homoeomeral /hōmē·om'ərəl/ (from Greek for "having like parts") referring to verse containing metrically similar parts, as STROPHE and ANTISTROPHE, or the same stanzaic form repeated.

homoeosis /hōmē·ō'sis/ (from Greek for "resemblance") a rhetorical expression for figures that seek to persuade through a comparison of their similarities. There are four types: (1) ICON, a comparison of persons or things through imagery, as in "His eyes were burning coals, / His tongue flicked like a snake's"; (2) PARADIGMA, the comparison of two examples of note in an argument, as in "Romeo loved Juliet as Troilus loved Creseyde. / Will our love also be disastrous?" (3) PARABLE, a brief story teaching a moral lesson through a metaphorical example that may or may not be fictitious, as in Christ's example of the laborers in the vineyard; and (4) FABLE, a parable that uses animals as characters, as in the story of the *Three Little Pigs*. See *figures of similarity and dissimilarity* in APPENDIX 2.

homoeoteleuton /hōmē·ōtelōō′ton/ (from   Greek   for   "having   like endings") precursors of rhyme that used similar sounding suffixes at the ends of clauses, as in "Living in the cit*y*, a woman must look prett*y*." Inflected languages such as Greek and Latin use the device extensively. See *grammatical devices of rhythm and balance* in APPENDIX 2.

homostrophic (from Greek for "same strophe") verse that uses the same stanzaic pattern throughout. For example, Keats' *Ode to Autumn* is composed of three stanzas of 11 lines each with five feet in each line. The term is synonymous with HORATIAN ODE when speaking of odes. See PINDARIC ODE. See also *forms* in APPENDIX 1.

Horatian Ode philosophical or meditative verse written in HOMOSTROPHIC form. Horace's notion of the ode implied the use of informal poems usually written in stichic form. Examples of the H.O. are Marvell's *Horatian Ode upon Cromwell's Return from Ireland* and Keats' *Ode on a Grecian Urn*. For further discussion, see ODE.

horismus (from Greek for "a marking by boundaries") a rhetorical figure of definition in which a term is defined through ELABORATION, as in "The soul is eternal, an essence which is infinite, / A spirit which temporarily takes human form." See SYSTROPHE. See also *figures of definition* in APPENDIX 2.

hovering stress (see DISTRIBUTED STRESS; a similarly used term is HOVERING ACCENT) a term originated by Cleanth Brooks and Robert Penn Warren to refer to two consecutive syllables of indeterminate but approximately equal STRESS.

hudibrastic verse a specific type of DOGGEREL consisting of octosyllabic couplets in iambic tetrameter. The term takes its name from Samuel Butler's *Hudibras*. See *light verse* in APPENDIX 1.

huitain /wēteN′/ or /wētän′/ (French for "a collection of eight") a French verse form, popular in the first half of the 16th century, consisting of eight-line strophes of eight to ten syllables. There are three rhymes in each strophe with one used twice in the fourth and fifth lines. François Villon's *Lais* is an example of the form, as well as *The Monk's Tale* in *Canterbury Tales*. See *forms* in APPENDIX 1.

hymnal stanza: See COMMON METER OR COMMON MEASURE.

hypallage /hipal′əjē/ (Greek for "exchange"; also spelled "hipallage") a rhetorical figure of grammatical construction that reorganizes normal word order to pervert the sense of something, as in "Give your ears to my words." Usually, an EPITHET commonly associated with one noun is associated with another noun, as in Virgil's "the trumpet's Tuscan blare" (rather than "Tuscan trumpet's blare"). The device is also used for PARODY, as in this example from Shakespeare: "I see a voice. Now will I to the chink, / To spy and I can hear my Thisby's face." Spenser and Milton used the device fairly often. See HYPERBATON. See also *grammatical constructions* in APPENDIX 2, and *figurative expressions* in APPENDIX 1.

hyperbaton /hīpur'-/ (Greek for "an overstepping, a transposition") a generic name for rhetorical figures that work through a reorganization of normal word order for the sake of emphasis or humor. Specific types include ANASTROPHE, EPERGESIS, HYPALLAGE, HYSTERIOLOGIA, HYSTERON PROTERON, PARENTHESIS, and TMESIS. See *grammatical constructions* in APPENDIX 2.

hyperbole /hīpur'bolē/ (Greek for "an overshooting, an excess") a rhetorical form of comparison using exaggeration or obvious overstatement for comic or dramatic effect. The opposite term is LITOTES, a form of UNDERSTATEMENT used ironically or comically. Andrew Marvell's *To His Coy Mistress* used ironic hyperboles, and contemporary poets such as Richard Hugo, James Wright, and Sylvia Plath often use the device. See *figures comparing greater, lesser, or equal things* in APPENDIX 2, and *diction* and *figurative expressions* in APPENDIX 1.

hypercatalectic: See HYPERMETRIC.

hypermetric (from Greek for "beyond the measure"; also called "extra-metrical" and "hypercatalectic") a line of verse having one or more extra syllables at the end, or an unexpected extra syllable in the regular metrical pattern. In Yeats' ten-syllable pattern below, the second line substitutes triple feet for its normal duple iambic meter:

> Once out / of na / ture I / shall ne / ver take
> My bo / dily form / from a / ny na / tural thing. . . .

See CATALEXIS and TRUNCATION.

hyporchema: See AMPHIMACER.

hypocorism (from Greek for "pet name" or "to play the child") a nickname or pet name derived from a more formal name, such as "Jimmie" for "James," or "Stevie" for "Stephen." The diminution of the formal name is meant as an endearment or EUPHEMISM where something distasteful or difficult is being mentioned, as in "potty" for "toilet."

hypothetical proposition a logical figure of rhetoric that shows the consequences of proposed action: "If you learn about men, you will be wise. / If you learn about women, you will be wiser." See ANTISOGOGE. See also *figures of cause and effect* in APPENDIX 2.

hypotyposis /-tīpō'sis/ (Greek for "sketch, outline"; also spelled "hypotiposis") the general rhetorical term, under the category of "subject and adjunct," designating a description of an imaginative and fictional character, object, or scene. Specific forms of h. include CHARACTERISMUS, CHRONOGRAPHIA, DIALOGISMUS, MIMESIS, PRAGMATOGRAPHIA, PROSO-GRAPHIA, PROSOPOPEIA, TOPOGRAPHIA, and TOPOTHESIA. See *figures of subject and adjunct* in APPENDIX 2.

hypozeugma /-zo͞og′mə/ (Greek for "subordinate [last]" plus "yoking") a rhetorical construction of grammar that for the sake of drama, grace, and efficiency places the utility word of a sentence in the last line or section of a sentence, as in the verb "turns" below:

> The house you built on dreams,
> The dreams you built your life on,
> The life you built around yourself
> Soon *turns* common and contemptible.

See ZEUGMA. See also *grammatical constructions that are technically incorrect* in APPENDIX 2.

hypozeuxis /-zo͞ok′sis/ (Greek for "a joining") a rhetorical construction of grammar that for the sake of emphasis and melody repeats a key verb or noun throughout a series of clauses. See *figures of repetition* in APPENDIX 2.

hysteriologia (from Greek for "lagging word") a rhetorical construction of grammar that reorganizes normal word order by interrupting a prepositional phrase with another phrase in such a way that the preposition seems more related to the preceding verb than to the object of the preposition: "She jumped in, rolling and tumbling, the sea." See *grammatical constructions* in APPENDIX 2.

hysteron proteron /his′təron prot′-/ (from Greek for "later earlier") a rhetorical construction of grammar that for the sake of dramatic emphasis or comic effect reverses the time sequence of two actions, as in "I started the engine and got into the car." See HYPERBATON. See also *grammatical constructions* in APPENDIX 2.

I

iamb /ī'amb/ or /ī'am/ (also called "iambus" /ī·am'bəs/) a duple metrical foot composed of an unaccented syllable followed by an accented syllable (⌣ ⁄) in ACCENTUAL-SYLLABIC VERSE, or a short syllable followed by a long syllable in QUANTITATIVE METER. The i. is probably the most frequently used foot in English verse and, used in combination with anapestic feet, is said to be most like ordinary speech. BLANK VERSE (unrhymed iambic pentameter) is considered to be the meter best suited to our language. See METER.

icon /ī'kon/ (from Greek for "likeness, image") a pictorial or sculptural representation, often referring to religious art. In rhetorical usage, subsumed under the general name HOMOEOSIS, i. compares persons or things through the vehicle of IMAGERY, as in "His eyes were burning coals. / His tongue flicked like a snake's." In contemporary critical discussions, the term is sometimes used to indicate a composite of the most frequently used images in an author's work, and thus is synonymous with the term EMBLEM. See *figures of similarity and dissimilarity* in APPENDIX 2.

ictus (Latin for "blow, stroke, thrust") in CLASSICAL PROSODY, the i. denotes only the accent that falls on a stressed syllable, not the stressed syllable itself. See ARSIS AND THESIS and ACCENT.

id (loan translation of German Es, which, like the Latin *id*, means "it") a term that, through Freud, has come to be associated in psychology and literature as the part of the psyche that is supposedly the source of action, supplying pleasure-seeking impulses. These impulses, in turn, are thought to be controlled by the higher functions of the ego and superego.

identical rhyme repetition of the same word used as an END-RHYME. If the i.r. does not function as an emphatic element, then it may be considered redundant. Recurrence of two words that sound alike but contain different meanings is called RIME RICHE, as in this example from Chaucer: "The holy blisful martir for to seke [seek], / That hem hath holpen whan that they were seeke [sick]." See RHYME.

identity (from Latin for "same") one of the two main functions of METAPHOR that equates one thing with another, as in "Hope is a bird." SUBSTITUTION is the other process in metaphor.

idiograph /id'-/ (from Greek, for "personal mark"; also called "idiogram") a mark or character representing an idea, action, or thing, rather than the more indirect use of words or speech. The Chinese system of idiographs and the ancient Egyptian hieroglyphics were stylized forms of idiographs.

138

idiolect /id′ē·əlekt/ (from Greek for "personal" plus "speaking") the personal speech pattern of an individual at a specific time in his life. Theoretically, everyone's speech patterns differ, and there are significant differences even among the speech patterns within different periods of an individual's lifetime. See *diction* in APPENDIX 1.

idiom (from Greek for "to make one's own") word or speech usage or syntactical constructions of a language that are not translatable into another language, such as the expression "to put your best foot forward" and "barking up the wrong tree." Linguists call these expressions *opaque* because the whole phrase is different in meaning from the sum of its parts, whereas expressions that are translatable and are no different in effect from the sum of their parts are described as being *transparent.* See DIALECT. See also *diction* in APPENDIX 1.

idyll /ī′dəl/ (from Greek for "a little image," also "a short descriptive poem"; also spelled "idyl") literature that renders rustic settings accompanied by uncomplicated, idealistic, happy themes. Theocritus' *Idylls* (third century B.C.) developed the form which differs from the more mournful PASTORAL poetry. Other works in the genre include Marlowe's *The Passionate Shepherd to his Love,* Tennyson's *Idylls of the King,* Wordsworth's *The Solitary Reaper,* John Greenleaf Whittier's *Maud Miller,* and a number of lyrical poems by Renaissance writers. See ARCADY and GEORGIC. See also *forms* in APPENDIX 1.

illuminated manuscript a medieval parchment copy of earlier works replete with brightly colored drawings, letter designs, and printing done by hand. Among the most famous extant illuminated manuscripts is the Irish *Book of Kells.* See *publishing formats* under *forms* in APPENDIX 1.

image (from Latin for "likeness, conception, semblance") a pictorial likeness, literal or figurative, that illustrates an idea, object, or action by appeal to the senses. Most images in poetry are specific and carefully selected and contain an implied or explicit statement organically connected to the rest of the poem. Generally, images are of two types: *fixed i.,* in which the picture conveys a concrete and specific meaning throughout its various levels of interpretation, and *free i.,* in which the i. creates a general meaning to be subjectively interpreted in various ways by readers. The i., one of the basic and essential devices in poetry, directly expresses a sensual experience and is not used decoratively in good poetry. See DEEP IMAGE, FIXED IMAGE AND FREE IMAGE, IMAGERY, and IMAGISM. See also *imagery* in APPENDIX 1.

imagery the use of pictures, figures of speech, or description to evoke action, ideas, objects, or characters. The term ranges in meaning from the use of a single IMAGE or detail to the accumulative effect of a poem's figurative devices that imply THEMATIC STRUCTURE. In Shakespeare's *Macbeth,* the repeated pattern of allusions to red images shows the emotional state of Macbeth and the theme of violence begetting more violence. Thus a LEITMOTIF is built up through i. In Robert Hayden's *Those Winter*

Sundays, images of coldness represent the indifference and ingratitude of the son toward his father. See *imagery* in APPENDIX 1.

imagination the faculty of producing ideal creations consistent with reality, as distinct from the power of creating decorative imagery. For a more detailed discussion, see FANCY AND I.

imaginative transformation the movement and process of change in which an idea, situation, image, or figure is transformed through the IMAGINATION into a new condition. The i.t. applies not only to a single process of change but also to a series of changes that form a chain or sequence. For instance, in Matthew Arnold's *Dover Beach*, the sound and image of the sea is transformed into the sound of ancient human misery, then into the ebb and flow of religious faith, and finally into a battlefield. See CONCEIT, SLANT IMAGERY, and *telescoped metaphor* under METAPHOR.

Imagism /im'-/ a poetic movement from 1909 to 1917 in England and America that, as a reaction to the more abstract, rhetorical, and sentimental poetry of the VICTORIAN period, called for the use of the clear, concrete IMAGE, the apt metaphorical equivalent, syntactical efficiency, strict control of form in FREE VERSE, and RHYTHM based on the model of common speech. Its members include Ezra Pound, Amy Lowell (its founder), T.E. Hulme (its theoretician), Richard Aldington, John Gould Fletcher, H(ilda) D(oolittle), and more peripheral luminaries such as D.H. Lawrence, T.S. Eliot, James Joyce, William Carlos Williams, and Robert Frost. The movement, basic to the tenets of modern poetry, called for a stripped-down, "no frills" aesthetic, a poetry "burned to the bone"—a principle that was promulgated through Pound's *ABC of Reading*, Amy Lowell's anthology *Some Imagist Poets*, and *Des Imagistes* (1914), an early collection of their work. The aesthetic of the school is substantially based on the Japanese HAIKU form. See VORTICISM. See also *imagery* and *movements and schools of poetry* in APPENDIX 1.

imitation (from Latin for "to copy") *philosophically*, a reflection of the nature of things. Aristotle claimed that all arts attempt to imitate nature (MIMESIS), and that this act is their highest function. Plato, on the other hand, saw this function as a defect that distances art from reality. Much later, ROMANTICISM revised the position of i. in art by saying that the function of art is to express emotions or acts of the imagination, thereby decreasing the value of i. With the advent of the Modern CHICAGO CRITICS, the term was restored to its original propriety and meaning. *Technically*, the term is used to categorize genres of literature in relation to the models on which each is based (drama, EPIC, TRAGEDY, COMEDY). *As a writing technique*, the practice of i., of copying earlier masters has been condoned; Cicero, Quintilian, and Horace recommended that young Latin writers imitate the form and spirit of previous works by Greek writers. Renaissance and Neo-Classical writers continued the practice as a method of composition. Alexander Pope's *Imitations of Horace* is a notable and successful use of the technique. The practice came under fire with the Romantics who felt that spontaneity and originality suffer under the technique's restrictions.

In contemporary poetic practice, the MIMETIC THEORY OF ART is again fashionable, and in workshops students are often assigned imitation exercises as a method of learning fixed and free forms of verse. In fact, *adaptions* and *free translations* are both based on i. See TRANSLATION.

imitative fallacy I.A. Richards' term for the attempt to make a poem's form (and its effect) reflect its content. The term is not necessarily derogatory, for the use of the technique is often effective in typographically arranged verse (see CARMEN FIGURATUM and CONCRETE POETRY). But the fallacious aspect of the strategy can be pointed out by asking, "Should a poem about confusion be confusing?" For other types of fallacies, see AFFECTIVE FALLACY, CLASSICAL FALLACY, EXPRESSIVE FALLACY, INTENTIONAL FALLACY, PATHETIC FALLACY, and REDUCTIVE FALLACY.

imitative words: See ONOMATOPOEIA.

immediacy (from Latin for "directness") the qualities of directness, vividness, and freshness in a poem. As an aesthetic standard, i. measures how closely a poem approaches the quality of lived experience, and to what degree the reader becomes involved in the poem so that the artifice and conventions of art disappear. See SUSPENSION OF DISBELIEF and VERISIMILITUDE.

imperfect rhyme: See OFF-RHYME.

impossibilia: See ADYNATON.

imprecation (from Latin for the reverse of "to pray") a cursing or damning of a person, as King Lear does to Cordelia. See MALEDICTION. See also *types of testimony* in APPENDIX 2.

Impressionism a 19th-century movement in art that based its technique (in painting) on what the eye alone sees in an object. Its aesthetic stance stood in opposition to the earlier, idealized, sentimentalized stance of the Romantic and Neo-Classical movements. Influenced by scientific discoveries about the nature of light, *Impressionists* created a style that was not so much concerned with the shapes of things as with their color, hue, intensity, and texture. While this school recreated the warm glows, sparkling surfaces, and misty, atomized textures of nature, it often made objects appear formless, as if they were disintegrating. The Impressionists were concerned with the overall subjective feeling they experienced when looking at an object. Their perspective was, as critics termed it, a "subjectification of the objective." It was REALISM expressed in an individualized, subjective form.

The French SYMBOLISTS in poetry were Impressionists who rejected the verbal, denotative meaning of words in favor of their aural qualities. Intoxicated with the possibility of opening up the secrets of nature as their scientific counterparts had, the Symbolists proposed to use the SYMBOL as a vehicle with which to idealize beauty. Some of its proponents envisioned a revolution of the senses in order to write a *pure poetry*. In the lives of some of these poets, such as Arthur Rimbaud, the most precocious and, perhaps, the greatest of the Symbolists, the debauching of his senses eventually led him into exile and death. His poem *Morning of Drunkenness* is a good example of the brilliant delirium of the senses he desired. Symbolism and I. dematerialized objects and pointed the way toward subjective, psychological stances and a kind of intelligibility that in its many forms has irked art fanciers who were comfortable with the realism of representational art. For movements in arts and literature that were influenced by I., see CUBISM, DADA, EXPRESSIONISM, IMAGISM, REALISM, SURREALISM, and VORTICISM.

impressionistic criticism or subjective criticism a form of literary evaluation that bases its critical principle upon how and to what degree a work affects a critic. See CRITICISM. See also *criticism* in APPENDIX 1.

incantation (from Latin for "chanting [a magical formula] over and over") the half-sung utterance of words deemed to have special or supernatural powers over nature or events. The early cultures of Africa, Asia, and America included spell-casting within and outside of religious rituals. Notable examples are found throughout the literature of primitives (*Technicians of the Sacred*, 1969) and in some of Shakespeare's works, such as *The Tempest* and *Macbeth* in which the three witches complete a spell using numerology. See CATALOGUE VERSE, CHARM, and LITANY.

incremental repetition (*incremental*, from Latin for "increasing") a repetitive structural device found in anonymous English and Scottish ballads whose lines or stanzas are repeated with key changes in important words. Francis B. Gummere (*The Popular Ballad*, 1907) named this device, which slowly and suspensefully unfolds the narration of ballads such as *The Demon Lover, Lord Randal,* and *Edward, Edward.* See REFRAIN and REPETEND.

inductive-deductive structure a rhetorical structure of reasoning that fuses the inductive mode of argument to the deductive mode, moving from particular to general to particular, so that the specific diamond shape ($\Diamond$) is achieved. Charles Bukowski's poem *The House* is an example of the i.-d.s. See CENTRIFUGAL STRUCTURE, CENTRIPETAL-CENTRIFUGAL STRUCTURE, CENTRIPETAL STRUCTURE, DEDUCTIVE-INDUCTIVE STRUCTURE, DEDUCTIVE STRUCTURE, and INDUCTIVE STRUCTURE.

inductive structure a rhetorical structure of reasoning moving from particular to the general. Many poems accumulate their ultimate meaning by enlarging their subject and theme through added details until the specific upside-down funnel-shape ($\wedge$) of i.s. is achieved. See CENTRIFUGAL-CENTRIPETAL STRUCTURE, CENTRIFUGAL STRUCTURE, CENTRIPETAL-CENTRIFUGAL STRUCTURE, CENTRIPETAL STRUCTURE, DEDUCTIVE-INDUCTIVE STRUCTURE, DEDUCTIVE STRUCTURE, and INDUCTIVE-DEDUCTIVE STRUCTURE.

inflection (from Latin for "to bend inward"; also spelled "inflexion") morphological changes in the endings of a word that transform its grammatical function. For instance, the addition of "s" or "es" to most English nouns changes the word from singular to plural. In many other languages, particularly the Romance languages, a change in the form of a word can denote the gender of nouns, pronouns, and adjectives, the conjugation of verbs, and the order and/or degree of adjectives and adverbs. A second use of the term refers to the changes in PITCH, DURATION, and STRESS that words spoken aloud may undergo.

initial rhyme: See BEGINNING RHYME.

initial truncation: See ACEPHALOUS LINE.

initiating action; initiating event: See CATALYTIC EVENT.

initiating image an image that catalyzes the development of other elements in a poem. In Thomas Hardy's *The Self-Unseeing*, the poet writes about revisiting his childhood home and uses the image of the floor as i.i. to unfold further elements of plot. It is not necessary that the i.i. come at the beginning of a poem. See CATALYTIC EVENT. See also *imagery* in APPENDIX 1.

in medias res /in mē′di·əs rēz/ (Latin for "in[to] the middle of things") a narrative technique that engages the reader by starting a story in midaction. At some further point in the story, flashbacks are added to complete the missing initial action of the story. The *Iliad*, e.g., begins in the tenth year of the Trojan war. Many EPIC poems and pieces of drama and fiction have used the convention. See *dramatic terms* in APPENDIX 1.

In Memoriam stanza an iambic tetrameter QUATRAIN rhyming abba, purportedly invented by Tennyson and named after his poem *In Memoriam*. Three hundred years earlier, Ben Jonson used the form, but Tennyson elaborated its form and content. See ENVELOPE. See also *forms* in APPENDIX 1.

inner reflections elements within a poem that reinforce meaning by echoing nuances back and forth. As a technique of composition, the method achieves a sense of fullness and depth in a poem by relating image to action, structure to plot, dialogue to setting, etc. Other devices, such as SLANT IMAGERY, the OBJECTIVE CORRELATIVE, the STORY-WITHIN-A-STORY convention—in fact, any device in poetry—can add i.r. to a poem. The following devices are offered as examples of strategy: (1) *Reflection of the setting*, in which the setting acts both as a catalytic agent and metaphor within the poem, as in this first stanza from Richard Hugo's *Degrees of Gray in Philipsburg:*

> You might come here Sunday on a whim.
> Say your life broke down. The last good kiss
> you had was years ago. You walk these streets
> laid out by the insane, past hotels
> that didn't last, bars that did, the tortured try
> of local drivers to accelerate their lives.
> Only churches are kept up. The jail
> turned 70 this year. The only prisoner
> is always in, not knowing what he's done.

(2) *Metaphorical reflection*, in which a metaphorical identity is set up

between characters or other elements in a poem, as in William Stafford's
Moles:

> Every day the moles' dirt sky
> sags upon their shoulders,
> and mine too sags on many a day,
> pinned by heavy boulders.

(3) *Symbolic reflection*, in which a symbol reflects real-life activity, as in
the following stanza by Allison Hunter who uses a trophy to enhance and
highlight the relationship between mother and daughter:

> The rooms cleaned by noon, you dusted
> the trophies on my desk, each one a portrait
> of my posture, miles away: horse welded to rider.
> The silver trembled as your cloth rubbed it alive.

(4) *Typographical reflection*, in which the form or structure of a poem
imitates its theme, plot, or characters (see IMITATIVE FALLACY), as in the
following stanza by John Ebert:

> checking myself
> CHECKING MYSELF
>
> The light is out
> The light is out
> The light is OUT
> OUT
> OUT
> OUT
> dash out the door

See TRIGGERING TOWN.

innuendo /inyo͞o·en′dō/ (Latin for "by hinting") an interpolated explanation
of a word or text. Usually, the TONE is suggestive and understated, as in
Robert Frost's symbolic concluding lines from *Stopping by Woods on a
Snowy Evening*: "And miles to go before I sleep, / And miles to go before I
sleep." See AMBIGUITY and IRONY.

inscape Gerard Manley Hopkins' term indicating "the principle of physical
distinctiveness in a natural or artistic object," that is, the exterior
reflection of essence of "thisness" of a thing or poem. The forces that hold
these qualities together he termed *instress*. See DINGGEDICHT, GESTALT,
ORGANIC COMPOSITION, and TAUTOLOGY.

inspiration (from Latin for "breathing into") the need to write, originally
credited to deities who breathed the soul into the poet. Modernists of
psychological bent tend to think that the urge to write emanates from the
subconscious of the poet. Poets themselves generally credit a particular
mood, image, rhythm, event, or idea for the initial impulse or catalyst of a
poem. Coleridge used the term *initiative* as being synonymous with i. See
DIVINE AFFLATUS and MUSES.

intelligence (from Latin for "understanding") specifically, the effect and
meaning of a poetic device considered by itself. RHYTHM, DICTION, SYNTAX,
TROPE, IMAGERY, rhetorical constructions, and STRUCTURE, each in itself,

are modes of expression that communicate discrete meaning to the overall poem. Robert Frost's concept of SENTENCE SOUNDS, the abstract feel and pacing of a sentence stripped of its words, is a notable example of one of the separate but organic intelligences of a poem. See also *meaning* in APPENDIX 1.

intensity (from Latin for "stretched, strained, tight") the force of mind and/or passion that permeates good poetry. Latin critics viewed i. in terms of ecstatic power, the ability of the poet to transcend the normal self; the Romantics sought a poetry whose passions, insights, and powerful images would create a pure poetry. Since the capacity to penetrate and to reveal is considered paramount in poetry, the element of i. must be considered essential.

intentional fallacy W.K. Wimsatt, Jr., and H.C. Beardsley's term (*The Verbal Icon*, 1954) for the error of interpreting a literary work by considering its author's intentions. They maintained that the work itself, without inferential or external remarks concerning what the author intended, is the most important criterion by which to evaluate it. D.H. Lawrence echoed this idea with "Never trust the artist. Trust the tale." Other critics have argued that biography and other peripheral statements may, indeed, have a very large bearing on interpretation, but generally critics tend to take both text and peripheral material into consideration in discussing a poem. See AESTHETICISM, AFFECTIVE FALLACY, CLASSICAL FALLACY, EXPRESSIVE FALLACY, IMITATIVE FALLACY, PATHETIC FALLACY, and REDUCTIVE FALLACY.

interior monologue writing that reveals the thoughts of a character who is undergoing intense physical, emotional, or psychological experiences. The expression of the i.m. assumes the character is not actually speaking, but that his mind's voice is being exposed to the reader who overhears it. Sometimes, as in the poems of W.S. Merwin and in the prose of William Faulkner, the i.m. functions in the same manner as the DRAMATIC MONOLOGUE. A specific type of i.m. is STREAM-OF-CONSCIOUSNESS. See SOLILOQUY. See also *dramatic terms* in APPENDIX 1.

interlaced rhyme: See CROSSED RHYME OR I.R.

interlude (from Latin for "between play") an interruption in the development of a piece of literature. It can be in the form of another work meant to relieve the intensity of the work that it breaks up, or in the form of a space of time between acts in a play or sections of a poem. Renaissance English plays often employed a *farce* as an i. See *forms* in APPENDIX 1.

internal rhyme a rhyme that occurs within a metrical line in order to create a musical or rhythmical effect different from that of END-RHYME. Donald Hall's *Name of Horses* uses this type of rhyme to effect the feeling of repetitive work. See RHYME.

interpretation (from Latin for "to explain, to translate") the general explanation of a text's meaning. More specific types of i. are EXEGESIS, EXPLICATION, and HERMENEUTICS. See CRITICISM.

inter se pugnantia a rhetorical figure of division in which there is a scolding of an opponent for his lack of character or high-mindedness. The figure is usually couched in contradictory terms, such as "Physician, heal thyself." See *figures of division* in APPENDIX 2.

invective (from Latin for "reproachful, abusive") the denunciation of a person or idea through the use of epithets that demean, as in Shakespeare's *Henry IV* in which Prince Hal ridicules Falstaff: "This sanguine coward, this bed-presser, this horseback-breaker, this huge hill of flesh...." In Dryden's *Discourse Concerning Satire*, the differences between direct i. and indirect IRONY is pointed out:

> How easy it is to call rogue and villain, and that wittily! But how hard to make a man appear a fool, a blockhead, or a knave, without using any of those opprobrious terms.... There is ... a vast difference between the slovenly butchering of a man and the fineness of a stroke that separates the head from the body, and leaves it standing in its place.

See ANTIPHRASIS, EPIPLEXIS, INTER SE PUGNANTIA, LAMPOON, ONEDISMUS, SATIRE, and WIT. See also *humor* in APPENDIX 1.

invention (from Latin for "discovery") originally, in Greek and Latin Classical rhetoric, the discovery of one's argument. In the RENAISSANCE and NEO-CLASSICAL periods, the term was generally used as a substitute for the elements of WIT and IMAGINATION in a piece of literature. In modern times, i. refers to originality in form and/or content. Generally, the i. of one period becomes a CONVENTION of subsequent periods.

inversion (from Latin for "to turn outside in") the reversing of normal word order, stressed and unstressed syllables, or the direction of an argument. *In grammar*, the normal word order is often reversed to preserve form or to emphasize certain words in a line, as in Coleridge's "A damsel with a dulcimer / In a vision once I saw." (see ANASTROPHE). *In prosody*, the INVERTED FOOT (the reversal of accented and unaccented syllables) creates interesting variations in rhythm and usually occurs at the beginning of a line, as in Theodore Roethke's

> Ă kít / tĕn cán
> Bíte wĭth / hĭs feét

(see SUBSTITUTION). *In rhetoric*, i. refers to the turning of an opponent's argument against him. Various forms of argumentative reversals are APODIOXIS, CONCESSIO, DIASYRMUS, METASTASIS, PAROMOLOGIA, and PRO-CATALEPSIS. See *grammatical constructions* and *figures of argumentation* in APPENDIX 2.

inverted accent (also called "inverted stress") a type of metrical reversal in which a stressed syllable is replaced by an unstressed syllable, as in this example:

> Whĕn the blúe / wáve rólls níght / lў oň deép / Gálĭlée
> Ănd the eyés / oř the sléep / eřs waxed deád / lў ănd chíll

Multiple substitutions and inversions of feet create a rhythmical prose cadence termed LOGAOEDIC. See the related term INVERTED FOOT.

inverted foot (also called "reverse foot") a form of SUBSTITUTION in which a foot is replaced by its opposite, that is, an IAMB for a TROCHEE, a DACTYL for an ANAPEST, or a PYRRHIC for a SPONDEE. See INVERTED ACCENT.

inverted stress: See INVERTED ACCENT.

inverted syntax: See INVERSION.

invocation (from Latin for "to call upon, to implore") a literary convention in which the poet implores a deity for assistance in or inspiration for the completion of his task. The *Odyssey*, the *Iliad*, the *Aeneid*, *Paradise Lost*, Hart Crane's *The Bridge*, and St. Perse's *Amers* all begin by appealing to the MUSE for aid. Mock epics employ *mock invocations*. The RENAISSANCE and NEO-CLASSICISM used invocations extensively in lyric and narrative poetry. See *forms* in APPENDIX 1.

ionic /ī·on'ik/ (from the *Ionians*, a Greek tribe) a Classical Greek quantitative foot consisting of two long syllables followed by two short syllables (⁻⁻ᵛᵛ; called *major* or *greater i.*). The i. was originally associated with the Ionian Dionysian songs and the tragedies of Euripides, but is most commonly associated with the Latin poet Horace, who used the meter frequently. See METER.

irmus (also known as "periodic sentence" or "emphatic sentence") a grammatical sentence construction of RHYTHM and BALANCE in which the last part of the sentence completes the sense. The effect of the grammatical device is to highlight important parts of thought or perception. Whitman uses the device frequently; e.g., the first 22 lines of *Out of the Cradle Endlessly Rocking* are one sentence whose sense is not completed until the last three lines which contain the subject, the predicate, and the object. See *grammatical devices of rhythm and balance* in APPENDIX 2.

ironic rhyme rhyming words that make an ironic comment upon a situation, character, or action, as in Eliot's "Should I, after tea and cakes and *ices*, / Have the strength to force the moment to its *crisis*?" See IRONY and RHYME.

irony (from Greek for "a dissembling") a rhetorical TROPE that names or states one thing but intends another, and which is conveyed through a TONE of voice or contradiction between words and the matter at hand. The term originated with the Greek comedic character Eiron who, by cleverness and deception, triumphed over the bully Alazon, a character who could not understand the subtle implications between Eiron's assertions. Generally, there are two major types of i.: that which is created by an author through a clear contradiction between intention and statement, and that which is created by the disparity between appearance and reality. There are many specific types of i.: *verbal* or *rhetorical i.*, in which there is an obvious discrepancy between what a speaker asserts and what he intends to mean, as in Mark Anthony's "For Brutus is an *honorable* man; so are they all *honorable* men"; (2) *dramatic* or *tragic i.*, in which the reader or audience is aware of a conflict in meaning but the character speaking or acting is not aware of the conflict, as in the example of Oedipus who wants to punish the murderer of his father and is not aware that he himself is the murderer; (3) *structural i.*, the consistent use of i. in a piece of literature, particularly that in which the author of a work and his audience share knowledge that the speaker of a work is denied, as in Browning's *Soliloquy of the Spanish Cloister*; (4) *Socratic i.*, named after Socrates who pretended an ignorant point of view in order to bring out the error or truth of a position; (5) *Romantic i.*, in which the audience is privy to the faults and foibles of an author who after being overserious in his task, role, and emotions concedes the humor of his situation (e.g., Byron's *Don Juan*); (6) *cosmic i.*, in which the deities or fate frustrate the goals, actions, or expectations of a character, as in Shelley's *Ozymandias*; and (7) *i. of situation*, in which characters find themselves in compromising, humorous, or paradoxical situations, as the speaker of Robert Frost's *The Road Not Taken*. See ANTIPHRASIS, CHARIENTISMUS, EPITROPE, HYPERBOLE, INNUENDO, MIMESIS, MYCTERISMUS, PARADOX, PARALIPSIS, PARODY, PUN, and UNDERSTATEMENT. See also *contraries and contradictories* in APPENDIX 2, and *figurative expressions* in APPENDIX 1.

irregular ode: See COWLEYAN ODE.

isochronism /īsok′-/ (from Greek for "equal in time") the equal DURATION of metrical feet, stanzas, or sections in a poem. I. is a musical conception of language that is carried to extremes in the theory of linguists who contend that English is an *isochronous* language and thus lends equivalency to duple and triple feet. In Classical Greek and Latin prosody, such a concept was useful since their QUANTITATIVE METER measures the duration of syllables rather than stresses.

isocolon /īsokō′-/ (Greek for "of equal members of clauses") a rhetorical device of rhythm and balance in which parallel elements of a sentence are similar in structure and length, as in "A hard man may be hard with men, soft with women. / But a soft man being soft with men, is hard with himself." Another example, using serial phrasing, is "His purpose was to impress the ignorant, to perplex the dubious, and to confound the scrupulous." See other *grammatical devices of rhythm and balance* in APPENDIX 2.

Italian sonnet (a similarly used term is PETRARCHAN SONNET; see SONNET) a fixed verse form divided into an OCTAVE rhyming abbaabba and a SESTET rhyming cdecde or cdcdcd. Petrarch often wrote in the form, as did Dante. Well-known examples in English include Milton's *On His Blindness*, Wordsworth's *Composed upon Westminster Bridge*, and Keats' *On First Looking into Chapman's Homer*. See *fixed forms* under *forms* in APPENDIX 1.

ivory tower a pejorative reference to an author who has isolated himself from the mainstream of life or literature. The term is taken from Sainte-

Beuve's *tour d'ivoire* which characterized the author Vigny in comparison to Victor Hugo. The image itself is taken from literature, e.g., Milton's *Il Penseroso*, in which the tower symbolizes ideal contemplation and indifference.

J

Jacobean age /kōb'-/ the reign of James I (1603–25), known as the greatest period of English drama, when Shakespeare produced his tragedies and tragi-comedies, the King James version of the Bible was translated, and writers such as Jonson, Beaumont, Fletcher, Webster, Middleton, Donne, and Drayton flowered. This period moved toward realism in characterization and plot, and saw the gap between Cavalier and Puritan literature widen. See PERIODS OF ENGLISH LITERATURE.

jargon /jär'-/ (Old French for "the warbling of birds" or "chatter") originally the intermixing of dialects or languages to make nonsense words. Currently, the term indicates the highly specialized terminology and phrases of a particular profession, such as the legal or medical professions. The use of j. as a poetic device can lend humor, authority, or specificity to a work. See *clichés* and *diction* in APPENDIX 1.

jeremiad /-mī'əd/ (from the *Lamentations of Jeremiah* in the Old Testament) writing that complains about the distressing state of man, forcefully mourns a loss, or rants prophetically about coming doom. As a genre of writing, j. is exemplified by works such as Jonathan Edwards' *Sinners in the Hands of an Angry God*, Allen Ginsberg's *Howl*, and Galway Kinnell's *The Book of Nightmares*. See COMPLAINT and LAMENT. See also *types of testimony* in APPENDIX 2, and *forms* in APPENDIX 1.

jeu d'esprit /zhœdesprē'/ (French for "spirit of play") a clever playing with words, or a light, happy-spirited verse. Ben Franklin's *Bagatelles* and Lewis Carroll's verse are marked by this sporting tone. See LIGHT VERSE.

jingle light mnemonic verse full of rhyming sounds and simple, repetitive rhythms, as characterized by nursery rhymes: "Hickory, dickory, dock" and "To market, to market," among others. Sometimes, the term is used pejoratively to refer to verse that is unimportant or simpleminded. See LIGHT VERSE and SKELTONIC VERSE. See also *forms, humor,* and *light verse* in APPENDIX 1.

jongleur /zhôNglœr'/ or /jong'glər/ (French for "minstrel, juggler") an eighth-century term describing musicians, acrobats, jesters, jugglers, actors, and poets who wandered through France and Norman England from the fifth to the 15th centuries. The TROUBADOUR, who succeeded the j., came to be known as one who wrote his own verse, while the j. recited traditional pieces in set forms. The Anglo-Saxon SCOP is the early Teutonic counterpart to the j. See also TROUVÈRE.

journal (Old French for "day-book") originally, a book in which daily, personal recordings of observations and events were written. This diary-like process has been carried on by artists and writers through the ages and is a common practice among student writers in contemporary workshops. Another meaning of the term relates to newspapers or literary reviews that appear regularly. See LITTLE MAGAZINE. See also *publishing formats* under *forms* in APPENDIX 1.

judicial criticism a form of literary evaluation that judges a work by a definite set of standards. See CRITICISM. See also *criticism* in APPENDIX 1.

jump cut (also called "cutting to continuity"; see CINEMATIC TECHNIQUES) a cinematic-editing term used to describe the compression of time in the narration of an event. See also *cinematic terms* in APPENDIX 1.

juncture (from Latin for "joining, joint") a salient sound-word that joins two phrases and which often acts as a *"squinting modifier"*; that is, the word could modify either what comes before or what comes after it, depending upon punctuation or phrasing: "My father drove home *hurriedly* thinking of us." The term j. also refers to a point in time that is critical because of circumstances.

juvenalian pertaining to work characteristic of the Roman satirist Juvenal (60–140 A.D.), who wrote with INVECTIVE and WIT. Jonathan Swift and the contemporary American poet Russell Edson, who use biting SATIRE, have produced work that could be called j. See *form* and *light verse* in APPENDIX 1.

juxtaposition (from Latin for "placing side by side"; also called "parataxis") the placing of a word or phrase directly against another word or phrase without any transitional word connecting the two halves. J. is often used to enhance, contrast, change, or synthesize an IMAGE. For example, if the words "moon" and "streetlight" are brought together, the j. gives the reader a sense of harmony because of the similarity of the two images. If the words "dog" and "wolf" are brought together, the j. creates a sense of MOVEMENT in the images from domesticity to wildness—the second term builds on the first term. When the words "sun" and "asteroid" are brought together, the difference between the two images, even though they share a common cosmic environment, creates tension which a poet might use to maintain interest. And finally, if we bring together the words "tiger" and "baby," the concept of danger is synthesized by the clash between the image of ferocity and the image of vulnerability. The poet does not have to overstate his meaning by explicitly saying there is danger in the situation; he allows the reader to develop that idea. So j. can be seen as a form of UNDERSTATEMENT because the poet deletes the logical steps between the terms.

As a craft technique, j. is similar to the use of the CAESURA and the LINE ENDING. Because both of these rhythmical devices are places in the poem where the reader's mind synthesizes, recapitulates, and contemplates the material, they provide opportunities to juggle meaning. The best contemporary poets who use effective juxtapositioning also use effective line endings and midline pauses.

J. can be used to portray character, create plot movement, amplify a theme, or furnish the poem with associated imagery. It could be claimed that juxtapositions, like virtually all poetic devices, are actually abbreviated forms of METAPHOR or SIMILE. Juxtapositions reinforce, oppose, or extend what has come before, thereby creating a larger context of imagery.

Pierre Reverdy explains the relationship between opposing or balancing images when he states: "The image cannot spring from any comparison but from the bringing together of two more or less remote realities. . . . The more distant and legitimate the relation between the two realities brought together, the stronger the image will be . . . the more emotive power and poetic reality it will possess." There is a sense of leaping from image to image, or concept to concept, which is the reason that poets such as Robert Bly refer to this style of writing as LEAPING POETRY. It is a poetry without transitions. After poets work with this technique for years, after they have learned to control the various nuances in meaning, the device becomes a means of perception, a method of thinking or seeing. It gives the poem a force and vitality, an immediacy that more rationally organized poetry does not have.

Here is a list, tentatively offered, of variations in juxtapositioning and the ways in which they function:

(1) *Juxtaposing equal images:* Because there are more similarities in the following terms than there are differences, they are, in a sense, equal:

> Sheep sleep on the hill.
> White pebbles in the grass mark the way home.

(2) *Juxtaposing images in contrast:* The sharp reversal in the contrasting images of these two lines stimulates the reader into a new sense of reality:

> The mirror reflected the whole sky
> in a thousand jagged pieces.

In this example the contrast is between unity and fragmentation, whereas in the following example the images are in contrast, and the second term of the j. acts to further the plot of the poem:

> He drove a spike into the ground. A worm
> glided to the muddy surface.

Notice that the phrase "a worm" is both a j. and a line ending. Surprise and expectation are created both by the leaping imagery and the hesitation at the end of the line.

Now let's look at the jump from an image to an abstraction (see ABSTRACT TERMS AND CONCRETE TERMS). Concepts or abstractions are often simply the result of concrete images being fused together. In a language-learning experiment with chimpanzees, one primate tasted a radish, which the dictionary describes abstractly as "pungent," and the chimpanzee signed via Ameslan the emotional concrete j. "cry-hurt-food." A human adult might call the radish "bitter" or "tangy," while chimpanzees, as well as human children, being closer to their emotions and the sensual world around them, tend to use more concrete terms.

(3) *Juxtaposing equal image and concept:*

> The bats fly away like bits of paper in a slipstream.
> I have no thoughts.

The strange connection between the image of bats and the lack of thoughts is an unstated simile: The thoughts that have left the speaker's mind are like bats that fly away.

(4) *Juxtaposing equal concepts:* Sometimes concepts can be juxtaposed in the same way as images. Notice how Mark Strand (in *Keeping Things Whole*) states a simple observation, then restates the same idea in a different way:

> In a field
> I am the absence
> of field.
> This is
> always the case.
> Wherever I am
> I am what is missing.

(5) *Juxtaposing an image in contrast to a concept:* It is also possible to contrast an image against a concept, as in

> The blue wings of angels fanned the flames
> of his sins.

Here, the image of angels contrasts with the concept of sins.

(6) *Juxtaposing concepts in contrast:* The most difficult form of j. is that of abstraction against abstraction, as in this example by Charles Olson: "What does not change / is the will to change." This paradox sets a state of nonchange against a state of continual change and is part of a genre of rhetoric called an *absolute*. Another example of this type of word play is the absolute statement "Nothing is absolute."

Aside from the quality of the relationship between juxtapositions, they also function as devices to indicate the plot, theme, and characters of a poem.

(7) *Juxtapositioning to indicate character:* In the following example, the words "he was" are equivalent to the first term of the j. and also show the aggressive nature of Clifford Hill, a brutal football coach (from *First Practice* by Gary Gildner):

> he was Clifford Hill, he was
> a man who believed dogs
> ate dogs, he had once killed

The juxtaposition of "ate dogs" against "he had once killed" becomes a synthesis in the reader's mind, implying that Clifford Hill had a wild, doglike character and was possibly given to eating dogs. The exaggeration demonstrates the vicious character of the man.

(8) *Juxtapositioning to indicate theme:* The THEME of a poem, rather than being explicitly stated, might be imbedded in the poem's imagery, its dialogue, the plot, or, as in the example below, in the poem's juxtapositions. Philip Dacey's *The Birthday* contains the major theme of a woman's concern about aging, and a minor theme about her fight to be independent from her husband. The j. he creates quietly states the poem's subtheme:

> Thirty candles and one
> to grow on. My husband
> and son watch me
> think of wishes.

The j. of "grow on" and "husband" implies that the woman is dependent on her spouse. But by the end of the poem, the woman has realized that only she can make herself happy and fulfilled, and this realization frees her from her dependency on her husband. Her new freedom allows her to make the wish she couldn't think of before:

> the impossibly thin
> membrane this side
> of nothing. Husband
> I wish I could tell you.

Here, the j. of "nothing" with "husband" implies that the woman has gained independence from her spouse. Her character has evolved, and that evolution has been indicated by juxtaposing the word "husband" with two different words.

(9) *Juxtaposing images to develop plot:* The development of PLOT takes place anytime the action is incited, furthered, or changed. In Richard Hugo's poem *The Only Bar in Dixon* he portrays some derelict Indians who go into a store to buy cheap Thunderbird wine. Hugo puns on the word "Thunderbird," which originally referred to an Indian symbol, by associating it with flying high on wine. Both the original meaning of the word and the brand name have to do with high spirits, an ironic comment in light of the depressed Indians:

> Another buying
> Thunderbird to go. This air
> is fat with gangsters I imagine.

The plot of this poem moves forward through a series of associational leaps in meaning. The poet is actually thinking out his story, not by logical narration but by a series of resemblances that trigger each other.

(10) *Juxtaposing abstractions to develop plot:* The development of plot through the j. of abstractions is extremely difficult to create and maintain. In Diane Wald's poem *Take Yourself Back*, a continually transforming series of ideas evolve and thus create the plot:

> Please keep these comments in sequence: I have to move
> by the end of next week: the fact that time grows shorter
> is just another imperative I can resent. Take yourself back
> to whatever you were doing this date in 1953.

The speaker is talking about living a short life backwards through memory. She resents the passing of time and the disappearance of people she loves; so she prefers to live in the happier past. The first line juxtaposes her plea to maintain order against her statement of the impending disruption of her life. The association between language and space develops the plot in the first line. The thought of order in language gives rise to the contrasting disorder of her life, which, in turn, gives rise to the sense that time is short. The irreversibility of time, which she resents, is associated with the contrasting phrase "take yourself back" which means both a movement backward through time and an erasure of her personal existence, both of which fit the theme of the poem. The juxtapositions in the first three lines are both in contrast and equivalency, and they also function as a device to keep the plot moving.

In order to understand how the various types of j. described here can work together in a single poem, let us examine the several kinds of associations present in the poetic sequence *Bantu Combinations*. The poem is originally African and is taken from *Technicians of the Sacred*, edited by Jerome Rothenberg:

> 1.
> I am carving an ironwood stick.
> I am still thinking about it.
>
> 2.
> The lake dries up at the edges.
> The elephant is killed by a small arrow.
>
> 3.
> The little hut falls down.
> Tomorrow, debts.
>
> 4.
> The sound of a cracked elephant tusk.
> The anger of a hungry man.
>
> 5.
> Is there someone on the shore?
> The crab has caught me by one finger.
>
> 6.
> We are the fire which burns the country.
> The Calf of the Elephant is exposed on the plain.

The first couplet equates a physical activity with a mental activity. The whittling of the stick and the implied difficulty of solving its design problems are equal in nature. The couplet creates an equivalency between image and concept. The second group of lines presents two equal but distant physical images. The lake slowly evaporates in the same manner as the elephant slowly dies from a small arrow wound. The third couplet is a good example of a physical image juxtaposed equally with an abstract statement. The reader can infer a cause-and-effect relationship between the two lines, though the two incidents can be interpreted as separate disasters. The fourth stanza equates the physical sound of a tusk breaking with the abstract name of an emotion. Since the sound is translated into an emotion, the j. is synaesthetic in effect (see SYNAESTHESIA). Since the actions are in sequence, the reader can infer another cause-and-effect relationship, that is, a rudimentary PLOT: the tusk may have been broken by the angry man. The fifth pair of lines contrast with one another in image and concept. The man is surprised by a crab just as he is surprised by the feeling that there is someone on the shore. And finally, the sixth couplet contains contrasting images. The emptiness of the plain and the lone figure of the elephant calf standing in relief are opposing images. Again, the j. implies a rudimentary plot: A tribe of hunters burns the high grass in order to trap an elephant calf.

J. is often used as one of the formal elements in the following rhetorical devices (see APPENDIX 2): the *grammatical constructions* EPIZEUXIS, HYPO-ZEUGMA, PROZEUGMA, SCESIS ONOMATON, and ZEUGMA; the *grammatical devices of rhythm and balance* ASYNDETON, BRACHYLOGIA, and POLYSYNDE-TON; the *grammatical figure of exchange* HENDIADYS; the *figure of repetition* CLIMAX; the *figure of definition* TAXIS; and the *figure of argumentation* SORITES.

Other terms that relate to the device of j. include AESTHETIC SURFACE, ASSOCIATIONAL LOGIC, CATALOGUE VERSE, CINEMATIC TECHNIQUES, COUN-TERPOINT, CUT-AND-SHUFFLE POEM, ENJAMBMENT, FREE ASSOCIATION, KEN-NING, and OPPOSING IMAGE OR BALANCING IMAGE. See also *cinematic terms* in APPENDIX 1.

K

kenning (from Old Norse *kenna*, "to perceive, to name") a phrasal figure of speech, common in ANGLO-SAXON VERSE, in which two or more words are yoked in order to form a conventional reference to a person, place, object, or office. For example, one name for the sea in the Anglo-Saxon poem *Beowulf* is "whale-road," while a poem is the "divine mead of inspiration," a boat is a "wave-traveller," and darkness is the "helmet of night." The k., a common device in the poetry of "primitive" cultures, is often a concrete JUXTAPOSITION that stands for a more abstract term. See EPITHET and KENNING METAPHOR. See also *diction* in APPENDIX 1.

kenning metaphor a concrete compound noun or phrase that acts as a metaphor for something more general or abstract. For instance, Native Americans are said to have called whiskey "fire-water." See *noun metaphor* under METAPHOR. See also KENNING.

L

lacuna (Latin for "hollow, hole") a gap in a manuscript. The plural *lacunae* refers to illegible parts of an ancient text that has been subjected to inevitable wear or abuse. For a related term, see HIATUS.

lai /lā/ (also spelled "lay") originally, a short narrative or lyric meant to be sung. The oldest extant l. narrative on record is Marie de France's from the 12th century. The oldest extant lyric l. is Gautier de Dargies' from the 13th century. In form, the l. verse is composed of octosyllabic couplets. The *Provençal l.*, a love poem sung to a popular tune, contains greater metrical variety than the usual French l. The *Breton l.* is best exemplified by Chaucer's *Franklin's Tale*. In popular usage, the term l. has come to be synonymous with SONG. See *forms* in APPENDIX 1.

Lake Poets an early-19th-century group of English poets, including Wordsworth, Coleridge, and Southey, so called because of their habitation in the northwest lake region of England. That area gave rise to the subject of their poetry—nature—and to the serene tone and simple diction which Lord Byron ridiculed. See ROMANTICISM.

lament (from Latin for "wailing, weeping") a nonnarrative poem expressing deep grief, a form found in most cultures. Examples include The Lamentations of Jeremiah in the Old Testament, the Anglo-Saxon poem *The Wanderer*, Deor's *Lament*, and Shelley's *Lament*. See COMPLAINT, DIRGE, ELEGY, JEREMIAD, MONODY, THRENODY, and "UBI SUNT" FORMULA. See also *forms* in APPENDIX 1.

lampoon (from French for a "drinking song") prose or verse intended to ridicule a person, character, office, or type of behavior. It was common in the 17th and 18th centuries (Pope's *Epistle to Dr. Arbuthnot*) as a form of SATIRE, but was cautioned against by one of its most effective practitioners, Dryden. Due to modern libel and slander laws, the genre has fallen out of general use, though there are several contemporary magazines that publish lampoons including *National Lampoon, Harvard Lampoon, Mad*, and *Punch*. See INVECTIVE and WIT. See also *humor* and *light verse* in APPENDIX 1.

landscape a painter's term designating inland scenery as opposed to a seascape or portrait. See SETTING.

lapidary: See PARNASSIANS.

l'art pour l'art /lär′pōōr′lär′/: See ARS GRATIA ARTIS.

latent form (a similarly used term is INSCAPE) the final, ideal form toward which an unfinished or defective poem tends to mold itself. See ORGANIC COMPOSITION.

laureate /lô′ri·ət/ (from Latin for "crowned with laurel") a name given for achieving high distinction in a specific field. In ancient times, warriors who were victorious and other personages of great accomplishments were crowned with a wreath of laurel to signify honor. See POET L.

lay: See LAI.

leap (from Robert Bly's *leaping poetry*) an abrupt change from one topic, domain of imagery, mode of thought, or level of consciousness to another. The switch usually occurs through ASSOCIATIONAL LOGIC with no accompanying transition or editorial comment by the writer. The poem's metaphorical or symbolic level, or overall CONNOTATION allows the surface disparities on the literal level to cohere. These jumps in content can occur within a line, between lines, or between stanzas. In Cesar Vallejo's *Poem To Be Read and Sung*, translated by James Wright and Robert Bly, the images contain metaphorical statements that act as a unifying matrix on a deep level of the poem, but which seem irrational on a literal level. The poem begins:

> I know there is someone
> looking for me day and night inside her hand,
> and coming upon me, each moment, in her shoes.
> Doesn't she know the night is buried
> with spurs behind the kitchen?

See ANAGOGICAL VISION, ANAGOGE, DEEP IMAGE, and JUXTAPOSITION.

leaping poetry Robert Bly's term for poems that display a "leap from the conscious to the unconscious and back again, a leap from the known part of the mind to the unknown part and back to the known" *(Leaping Poetry: An Idea with Poems and Translations,* 1975). The associational quality of the poet's imagination continually transforms the objects, the development of thought, and even the structure of a poem so that an ongoing sense of surprise at the poem's surface is experienced. The *leaping poet* attempts to expose the essential inner quality of an experience through a series of metaphorical transformations that become both the strategy of the poem and evidence that the poet has broken through levels of consciousness. The first stanza of Pablo Neruda's *The Ruined Street* uses PERSONIFICATION, JUXTAPOSITION, METAPHOR, and agents that cause transformation to create a surreal and powerfully descriptive setting:

> A tongue from different eras of time is moving
> over the injured iron, over the eyes
> of plaster. It's a tail of harsh
> horsehair, stone hands stuffed with rage,
> and the house colors fall silent, and the decisions
> of the architecture explode,
> a ghostly foot makes the balconies filthy,
> so slowly, with saved-up shadow,
> with face masks bitten by winter and leisure,

the days with their high foreheads drift between
the houses with no moon.

Bly maintains that at the center of great works of art in all cultures there is "a great, floating leap," signifying a change in consciousness. In addition, he lists, in diminishing order, the levels of this switch in consciousness from (1) *leaping*, to (2) *hopping*, to (3) dull poets who give off a *steady light*. See ANAGOGICAL VISION, ANAGOGE, DEEP IMAGE, and LEAP.

legend (from Latin for "to read") originally, a story concerning the life of a saint, but now any fictitious tale about a real person, place, or event, closely related to the genres of MYTH and FABLE. Chaucer's *Legend of Good Women* contains both mythological and historical figures (Medea and Cleopatra), and certain American legends such as those of Paul Bunyan, Casey Jones, and John Henry, were originally based on historical figures but have become mythological in scope. See FOLK LORE and FOLK TALE.

leitmotif /līt'motēf/ (from German *Leitmotif*, for "leading motive") originally, a musical term indicating a THEME associated throughout a work with a particular person, situation, or sentiment. The term is related to *idée fixe* and DOMINANT IMPRESSION in that a theme, stated in various forms, recurs at appropriate times in a work, e.g., the theme of nostalgia for his boyhood that weaves itself through James Wright's work, and the TONE of tough cynicism in the work of Alan Dugan. The l. can be present in a single work of literature or in a body of work. See MOTIF. See also *forms* in APPENDIX 1.

leonine rhyme (from the 12th-century French poet *Leoninus* who used the form extensively) a form of INTERNAL RHYME in which the last word in a line echoes the last word before the CAESURA. The device has been favored in the EPITAPH, as in "Here lies *John* who's both here and *gone*." See RHYME.

level stress: See EVEN ACCENT.

lexical (from Greek for "pertaining to words") referring to the denotative or dictionary meaning of a word, as opposed to the connotative meaning. See *diction* in APPENDIX 1.

lexical accent: See ACCENT.

lexicography (from Greek for "writing about words") the process of writing and compiling a dictionary. The task consists of compiling a list of headwords, syllabifications, pronunciations, derivations, alternative spellings, inflected forms, meanings, illustrations, historical applications, and other considerations. See *publishing formats* under *forms* in APPENDIX 1.

light ending: See FEMININE ENDING.

light rhyme rhyme in which the final rhyming syllable of a word is unstressed, as in the last two lines of Robert Herrick's *Corinna's Going A-Maying*: "Then, while time serves, and we are but decaying, / Come, my Corinna, come, let's go a'Maying." The term is also used to indicate a rhyme in which one syllable of the rhyming word is unstressed, as in this stanza from the anonymous BALLAD *The Demon Lover*:

> "O hold your tongue of your weeping," says *he*
> "Of your weeping now let me *be*;
> I will show you how the lilies grow
> On the banks of Ital*y*."

The device occurs often in ballads and is used to relieve the monotony of full rhyme. See RHYME.

light stress a metrical stress that falls on a word or syllable not emphasized in normal speech, as in Shakespeare's "Those are pearls that *were* his eyes." See METER.

light verse VERSE that is light-hearted in TONE and which displays obvious formal characteristics of METER, RHYME, and STRUCTURE. Good l.v. runs the gamut from French FIXED FORMS such as the TRIOLET, the BALLADE, and the RONDEAU to VERS DE SOCIÉTÉ, CLERIHEW, LIMERICK, NURSERY RHYME, DOGGEREL, SKELTONIC VERSE, and NONSENSE VERSE. Generally, the function of l.v. is to entertain with wit, grace, and intelligence. But l.v. is also used for serious purposes in forms such as the PARODY, SATIRE, and OCCASIONAL VERSE.

The CAVALIER POETS of the 17th century used the form extensively, as did Edward Lear, Lewis Carroll, Alexander Pope, Ogden Nash, and Theodore Roethke, among many others. W.H. Auden's *Oxford Book of Light Verse* is a well known source of l.v.

Common devices used in l.v. include ALLITERATION, ASSONANCE, RHYME, METER, TYPOGRAPHICAL ARRANGEMENT, PUN, rhythmical variation, ACROSTIC, RIDDLE, and humorous JUXTAPOSITION. See also CARICATURE, JINGLE, and LAMPOON; also *forms, light verse,* and *humor* in APPENDIX 1.

l'image juste /limäzh′zhYst′/ (French for "the right image") an IMAGE that aptly and accurately fits a particular place in a poem.

limerick (from the town of *Limerick* in Ireland, possibly from the custom in which guests at a party extemporaneously sing NONSENSE VERSE in round-robin fashion, each performance followed by the chorus "Will you come up to *Limerick?*") a form of LIGHT VERSE composed of anapestic lines rhyming aabba, the first, second, and fifth being anapestic trimeter, and the third and fourth lines being anapestic dimeter. The genre wittily considers human behavior and values, or, as in the example below, attempts to render a risqué or bawdy situation for the sake of entertainment:

> There was a young girl from St. Paul.
> Who wore a newspaper dress to a ball,
> But the dress caught on fire
> And burned her entire
> Front page, sporting section, and all.

The first appearance of the form is said to be Loane's *History of Sixteen Wonderful Old Women* (1821). One of the most famous collections of limericks is Edward Lear's *Book of Nonsense* (1846). As a fixed form, the l. is used solely for light verse, and has evolved its argumentative structure into the convention in which the fifth line is used for witty reversal. See *forms* in APPENDIX 1. See also *humor* and *light verse* in APPENDIX 1.

limited edition an EDITION of a book limited to a small number of copies, usually less than a thousand. The publisher might limit an edition because he or she anticipates a small audience or because the limited number of copies increases the value of each individual copy. Usually each copy is sequentially numbered, the first 25 or so signed by the author. Most contemporary poetry is issued in limited editions, and it is common for these publications to be beautifully produced with fine paper, fine binding, and carefully chosen typefaces. See BROADSIDE, CHAPBOOK, COLOPHON, FORMAT, and LITTLE MAGAZINE. See also *publishing formats* under *forms* in APPENDIX 1.

line (from Greek and Latin for "flax, thread") a structural unit of measurement in verse that, by its length and rhythm, adjusts the reading speed and overall CADENCE of a poem. In metrical verse, the l. is characterized by the number of feet it contains—monometer, dimeter, trimeter, etc.—and by the type of meter employed—iambic, trochaic, dactylic, etc. (see FOOT and METER). In ACCENTUAL VERSE the length of the l. is determined by the number of accented syllables, and in SYLLABIC VERSE the length is determined by a specific syllable count. In FREE VERSE, which may contain base metrical rhythms, the l. may be formed phrasally by conversational rhythmic units, syntactical units, breath units, rhetorical units, sensual units, or thought units (see RHYTHM), depending upon the nature of the experience being expressed.

  In a symposium on the concept and use of the l. in contemporary poetry (published as part of *Field Guide to Contemporary Poetry & Poetics*, edited by Stuart Friebert and David Young, 1980, Longman Inc., New York) John Haines maintains, "It is the voice of the poet that determines the lines, the rhythm, structure, everything." Sandra McPherson defines the l. as "a module of interest, surprise, or direction, which offers itself as distinct from what precedes and follows." In response to her explanation, Louis Simpson notes, "The line is a unit of rhythm. The poet is moved by impulse of rhythm which he expresses in lines of verse. Impulse determines when each line breaks, and the impulse of the poem as a whole determines the look of the poem on the page or its sound in the air." Charles Simic, in explaining the instinctual aspect of creating the l., says, "Content imposes a time scale: I have to say x in x amount of time." He goes on to say that the l. creates visual and dramatic effects and is technically important in creating resonance between images.

  Although the term VERSE is sometimes used synonymously for l., the former is usually thought of as a larger unit that contains lines; its original meaning of "turning" indicates an essential quality that the l. offers, a specific length of words that can be viewed both autonomously and in relation to previous and subsequent units of words. Generally, the ends of lines are either end-stopped or enjambed. For a detailed discussion of the classifications, see LINE ENDING. See also AUTONOMOUS L., BLANK VERSE, ENJAMBMENT, FORM, STRUCTURE, and VOICE.

lineation the composition of or the creation of a line or lines. See LINE, LINE ENDING, RHYTHM, and SHAPING.

line ending the terminal point of a line of poetry (see LINE). Traditionally, line endings have been classified as being either END-STOPPED or enjambed (see ENJAMBMENT). But this rough characterization doesn't take into account the internal semantic movement of line endings that exists within the syntactical structure of a group of lines and forms a separate INTELLIGENCE in the poem. This intuitive system is a key element in the poem's movement of thought, its RHYTHM, its thematic development, and other basic elements such as PLOT, CHARACTER, and AESTHETIC SURFACE. The type of l.e. affects the sculptural quality of a poem, the feeling that experience via language has been given an organic, living form.

This essay attempts to describe this intuitive SHAPING by classifying line endings into two categories: (1) those that function by affecting the syntactical and semantic *movement* of the lines, and (2) those that function by affecting the syntactical and semantic *character* of the lines. Although these two functions often occur simultaneously, for the sake of clarity they are treated here as separate phenomena. We also warn the reader that we offer these categories tentatively, realizing the inherent paradox of subjecting an intuitive process to descriptive analysis.

The Movement of the Line Ending

THE END-STOPPED LINE: ———————————|
This is the simplest and most traditional l.e. unit, the l.e. most often used in poetry and song before the Renaissance. The line simply stops at its last word, and the last word's semantic meaning contains no internal movement backward or forward. Here's a stanza from an anonymous 13th-century song:

> Now the summer's come again!
> Loud sing, cuckoo!
> Seed a-growing! Mead a-blowing!
> Green grow the woods too.
> Sing, cuckoo!

THE END-STOPPED REFLEXIVE LINE: ←———————————|
Here the basic end-stopped line is complicated by the addition of a semantic movement that refers the reader backward to something previously stated in the line. Its syntax stops, but its meaning moves backward, as can be seen in the following lines taken from various poems by Richard Hugo: "My eyes were like this photo. Old." "These dirt mounds make the dead seem fat." "The day is a woman who loves you. Open."

THE ENJAMBED LINE:———————————→
This is the second major type of l.e. movement. In its simplest form, the l.e. carries over syntactically to the next line, but the last word contains no semantic movement to nudge the reader forward or backward or make

him or her hesitate. Here are some sample lines from a poem by Thomas Lux:

> Fifty thousand crack troops
> prepare to dash
> over a cliff.

THE ENJAMBED AND END-STOPPED LINE: ——————————|————→

This is a combination of the two primary types. It acts as a flashing red light controlling the flow of traffic; it makes the reader stop and then go forward by manipulating syntax and semantics. Because the phrase or sense unit at the end of each line is semiautonomous within the larger syntactical structure of the sentence, and because the semantics of the last word contain internal movement, a productive ambiguity in meaning (and thus in movement) is created. The reader is forced to hesitate at the end of each line before he can go on. Auden's *Musée des Beaux Arts* contains many of these enjambed and end-stopped line breaks:

> About suffering they were never wrong,
> The Old Masters: how well they understood
> Its human position; how it takes place
> While someone else is eating or opening a window or just walking
>   dully along

THE ENJAMBED AND REFLEXIVE LINE: ←——————————————→

This l.e. refers forward syntactically and refers backward semantically. In Richard Hugo's lines below, the last word at the end of lines 2, 3, 4, 5, 7, and 8 contains double entendres that work on the literal, metaphorical, and symbolic levels so that its meaning refers backward but its syntax goes forward:

> You might come here Sunday on a whim.
> Say your life broke down. The last good kiss
> you had was years ago. You walk these streets
> laid out by the insane, past hotels
> that didn't last, bars that did, the tortured try
> of local drivers to accelerate their lives.
> Only churches are kept up. The jail
> turned 70 this year. The only prisoner
> is always in, not knowing what he's done.

THE ENJAMBED, REFLEXIVE, END-STOPPED LINE: ←—————————|————→

This line contains a combination of forward, backward, and end-stopped signals on the semantic and syntactical levels of reading. The degree of movement depends upon how much emphasis the reader places on the syntactical break and the denotative and connotative meanings of each last word in a line. Again the example lines are from Hugo's poetry:

> Isn't this your life? That ancient kiss
> still burning out your eyes? Isn't this defeat
> so accurate, the church bell simply seems
> a pure announcement: ring and no one comes?

The Character of Line Endings

Aside from the kinesthetic aspects of line endings brought about externally by syntax or internally by semantics, there are dramatic characteristics of line endings that are affected by grammatical transformations, ambiguity, and indefiniteness. By holding back information, employing multiple meanings, or emphasizing information at the ends of lines, poets can manipulate the reader in order to imitate the experience upon which the poem is built. In studying line endings in order to characterize their effects, three main groups emerge: the *anticipatory l.e.*, the *transformational l.e.*, and the *emphatic l.e.* Each of these types has more to do with the mind's reaction to a line-break word than to its movement in relation to the context. Each type has a distinctly different effect upon the reader which is meant to guide him or her toward the deeper levels in a poem. Also, what holds true for the line break also holds true for the stanza break.

THE ANTICIPATORY LINE ENDING:

This type of l.e. creates suspense in the poem by holding back or delaying either syntax or sense necessary to the complete understanding of a sentence. The last word in the line is meant to increase the reader's curiosity. This type is always enjambed and is formed by cutting off from completion a phrase or sense unit. Any part of speech can be used to end the line, e.g.,

> She [*pronoun*]
> She went [*verb*]
> She went into [*preposition*]
> She went into the [*article*]
> She went into the store to [*infinitive particle*]
> She went into the store to see who [*relative pronoun*]

The opening of May Swenson's poem *Watch* uses the anticipatory l.e. technique:

> When I
> took my
> watch to the watch fixer I
> felt privileged but also pained to watch the operation. He
> had long fingernails and a voluntary squint. He
> fixed a magnifying cup over his
> squint eye. He
> . . . .

THE TRANSFORMATIONAL LINE ENDING:

This type employs end-words that change their grammatical or semantic value, or jump levels of meaning, unexpectedly. The transformation is either a function of manipulating a stock response to phrasing, or a function of using a misleading grammatical structure. The transformational line ending usually uses descriptive words of general character that quickly change their meaning or quality in the context of the subsequent line(s). Upon first reading the l.e., the reader becomes aware of the resonant, connotative possibilities, but as soon as the subsequent line is read, the previous line shrinks in character because its secondary use is simple modification. The two most common types of transformational endings are composed of adjectives that at first glance appear to be nouns, and of present participles that transform themselves into adjectives. Some other types of transformational endings do not change their grammatical functions but are transformed in meaning in various ways by the context of the subsequent line. Here are some examples of the various types: Grammatical changes:

> She walked into the dark [*noun/adjective change*]
> hallway

Change from general to specific:

> She said it was as easy as walking
> away

Synaesthetic change (see SYNAESTHESIA):

> He made the horseshoes ring [*auditory/visual change*]
> his campfire

Ambiguities (see AMBIGUITY):

> He kissed her until she yelled "Stop
> fooling around and get down to business."

Literal/metaphorical changes:

> He was lost in the forest
> of her hair

Fused syntax:

> She reached for Tom and Jim
> laughed at her

Emotional/physical changes:

> When an actor does well I melt
> into the gray light and change places with him.

Puns:

> The death-row inmates were holding out
> a rose to the warden.

THE EMPHATIC LINE ENDING:
This type uses simple repetition to reinforce character, theme, or plot in the line in which it appears; but it also acts as a link to the context in the subsequent line. Because this type of line is so obviously enjambed, many readers don't pause at the end of the line to catch the implications and subtlety that the line contains. Here is an example:

> Although Hitler was a tyrant, he was
> a man who enjoyed art.

In certain authors' work, for example that of Milton and W.C. Williams, we can see the full spectrum of l.e. techniques. The movement and character of the line endings contribute to the overall effects of rhythm, plot, character, and theme. Furthermore, juxtapositioning of words with multiple meanings in the syntactical and thematic context creates resonance between individual lines. Here, terminal juxtapositioning and effective line endings are often the same technique. In fact, the craft of shaping line endings can be seen as a metaphor for the experience that the poem represents. See also AUTONOMOUS LINE, CADENCE, CAESURA, CATALEXIS, DOUBLE ENTENDRE, EMPHASIS, EQUIVOCATION, EQUIVOQUE, FREE VERSE, LINEATION, LINE LENGTH, METER, MOVEMENT, PROSE POEM, PUN, RHYTHM, STANZA, TYPOGRAPHICAL ARRANGEMENT, and VOICE. See also *line endings* in APPENDIX 1.

line length a measure of the number of syllables, feet, or words in a line. Line lengths range from a single letter to whatever the margins of a page might contain (as in the PROSE POEM), and they may vary or be regular with a single poem. See LINE, LINE ENDING, METER, and RHYTHM. See also *line endings* in APPENDIX 1.

linguistic associations the ideas and emotions that a word or phrase evokes through DENOTATION and CONNOTATION, IMAGE, SYMBOL, RHYTHM, SONICS, and universal/personal experience (see COLLECTIVE UNCONSCIOUS.) For example, the word "horse" etymologically may derive from a word meaning "to run" and denotes an equine, four-legged beast of burden and sport. But archetypally, the word is perceived as a symbol of sexual desire. In addition to these evocations, the word commonly summons up images of speed and grace; and the reader may also have vicarious and personal experiences associated with the word or the animal it represents. A multiplicity of l.a. come into play consciously and subconsciously during word-recognition processes. See ASSOCIATIONAL LOGIC. See also *meaning* in APPENDIX 1.

linked rhyme a type of RHYME, common in early Welsh verse, in which the last syllable of a line is joined by rhyme to the first syllable of the subsequent line, as in the opening lines of G.M. Hopkins' *Spring*.

linked verse a poetry game of the Chinese T'ang Dynasty played in an impromptu round-robin fashion. After agreeing upon subject and meter, each poet takes a turn at improvising lines toward creating a group poem. See *game forms* under *forms* in APPENDIX 1.

list poem a contemporary, foreshortened version of CATALOGUE VERSE. Usually the poem's intention is to define something by listing its characteristics, actions, or effects, and so is closely related to the DEFINITION POEM and the FILL-IN-THE-BLANKS POEM in its strategy and format. For instance, the Mexican poet Jáime Sabines has created his poem R_x from a list of medicinal forms and their effects within the larger metaphorical structure of the moon as a cure-all. It begins:

> The moon can be taken by the spoonful
> or in capsule form, one every two hours.
> It is a good hypnotic and sedative,

and it also alleviates
those intoxicated with philosophy.

See *forms* in APPENDIX 1.

litany (from Greek for "to pray, to plead") originally, a form of prayer in which the clergy and the congregation take part alternately, with recitation of supplications and fixed responses. But now the term usually refers to any lengthy, syntactically repetitive work, such as the Book of Psalms or Whitman's *Song of Myself*. In contemporary poetry, the term indicates a chantlike list (see LIST POEM) meant as an INCANTATION or highly emotional CATHARSIS, as in the third section of Allen Ginsberg's *Kaddish*. The form has been widely used in contemporary poetry.

literal (from Latin for "by the letter") referring to the denotative meaning of a word as opposed to the connotative meaning. The l. meaning of a word is usually thought of as the basic meaning or, sometimes, the lowest level of meaning, and the term *l. language* is often used as an antonym of FIGURATIVE LANGUAGE. See ANAGOGE, CONNOTATION, DENOTATION, DICTION, FIGURES OF SPEECH, FOUR SENSES OF INTERPRETATION, LITERAL VISION VS. ANAGOGICAL VISION, and LEXICAL. See also *diction* in APPENDIX 1.

literal vision vs. anagogical vision levels of meaning and modes of perception used in literary interpretation and composition. The term *literal vision* refers to the *denotative* level of meaning in the use of a word, e.g., "He ate an apple," in which the noun is used simply to indicate a type of fruit. The *anagogical vision* is a kind of layered perception through which the writer expresses himself on multiple and simultaneous levels. Flannery O'Connor, addressing fiction writers, urged her audience to develop this coordinated type of vision:

> The kind of vision the fiction writer needs to have or to develop, in order to increase the meaning of his story is called *anagogical vision*, and that is the kind of vision that is able to see different levels of reality in one image or one situation.

See ANAGOGICAL VISION, ANAGOGE, CONNOTATION, DENOTATION, FOUR SENSES OF INTERPRETATION, LITERAL, and VISION.

literary ballad: See ART BALLAD.

literary epic: See ART EPIC.

litotes /lī′tətēz/ or /lit′-/ (Greek for "something plain or simple") a rhetorical figure of speech in which something is asserted positively in the form of a negative contrary, as in St. Paul's remark about his Roman citizenship: "I am a citizen of no mean city." The device is often used to diminish and understate a perception or fact and therefore is akin to MEIOSIS and stands as an opposite to HYPERBOLE. See FIGURATIVE LANGUAGE and UNDERSTATEMENT. See also *contraries and contradictories* in APPENDIX 2, and *figurative expressions* in APPENDIX 1.

little magazines literary journals with small circulation and small finances.

L.m. typically produce work of an experimental nature, or represent an identifiable school or movement in art or literature. Often they are short-lived, uneven in quality, and produced as a labor of love by their editors. The 1920s saw a plethora of l.m. in America and Europe; and journals such as *The Dial, The Little Review, Blast, The Yellow Book, The Fugitive,* and *Poetry: A Magazine of Verse* published the first works of luminaries in 20th-century literature: T.S. Eliot, Ezra Pound, Ernest Hemingway, William Faulkner, Gertrude Stein, e.e. cummings, Hart Crane; and sketches by artists such as Georges Braque and Pablo Picasso. In contemporary American letters, magazines such as *Antaeus, The American Poetry Review,* and a host of fine university-sponsored reviews carry on the tradition of offering new writing on limited budgets. For a wide-ranging dialogue between major poets and publishers on the present state of l.m., trade publication, and the livelihood of the WRITER, see *The Publication of Poetry and Fiction: a conference* published by the Library of Congress, 1977. Stanley Kunitz, Donald Barthelme, James Laughlin, and David Godine, among many others, participated in the discussion of the economic, political, and historical aspects of the publishing of literature in the United States. See JOURNAL. See *publishing formats* under *forms* in APPENDIX 1.

loading the poem the process of freighting a poem with an abundance of poetical and rhetorical devices, so that a crafted bass resonance reverberates throughout the poem. See INNER REFLECTIONS.

local color language that creates the character of a particular time and place. The effect can be promoted subtly or vividly by details of speech, description, gesture, tone, or setting. The works of Robert Frost (New England), Richard Hugo (the Northwest), Robert Penn Warren and James Dickey (the South), and Carl Sandburg (the Midwest), among others, contain these elements of l.c. See DIALECT, LOCALE, and LOCALISM.

locale /lōkal'/ (from Latin for "place") a SETTING in a particular region. For instance, many of the poems of Robinson Jeffers are set on the Northwest coast, while the stories and novels of William Faulkner are set in Mississippi, and the fiction of John Cheever and John Updike typically transpire in New England suburbs. Although the use of l. lends itself to specificity, it does not necessarily limit the universality of a work. See LOCAL COLOR.

localism the DIALECT or subdialect of the people of a particular region. For instance the contraction "ya'll," the verb form "might could've," and the drawn-out pronunciation of monosyllabic words are characteristics of language spoken in the southern United States. The term may also refer to ideas, interest, or sympathies peculiar to a specific region, such as Californians' contemporary penchant toward creating innovative types of life-styles. See LOCAL COLOR. See also *diction* in APPENDIX 1.

location a cinematic term denoting SETTING. The term has been borrowed by contemporary poets to indicate the particular perspective of consciousness from which a poem arises, be it intellectual, emotional, or spiritual. By locating the type of consciousness from which the poem is derived, critics find it easier to speak about the intention of the writer. For example, T.S. Eliot's *The Love-Song of J. Alfred Prufrock* is located in an existential ennui colored by romanticism. See TRIGGERING TOWN.

logaoedic /log′ə·ēdik/ (from Greek for "prose-poetic") a word (adjective and noun) coined by Latin metricians to indicate a rhythm lying somewhere between PROSE and VERSE. L. is created by combinations of trochees and dactyls, or by the use of an unusually large number of unaccented syllables. The contemporary use of the term is looser and generally refers to the mixture of various feet used in FREE VERSE, such as the series of monomic, duple, and triple feet employed by Walt Whitman in *When Lilacs Last in the Dooryard Bloom'd*:

> Whĕn lílačs lást ĭn tĥe dóoryárd blóom'd,
>
> Aňd tĥe gréat stár eárlў dróop'd ĭn ĩhe wésteřn sǩy ĭn tĥe níght,
>
> Í mouřn'd, aňd yĕt shăll moúrn wĭth éveř rĕtuřnĭňg sprĭng.

L. verse stands in opposition to classical *choreic* verse which employs the trochee as its regular foot. The term is also somewhat related to ANACRUSIS, the use of unaccented syllables at the beginning and end of a line. See PROSE RHYTHM and RHYTHM. See also *forms* in APPENDIX 1.

logic (from Greek for "pertaining to speaking or reason") the system, philosophy, or art of reasoning leading toward the truth or falsity of an argument. Generally speaking, there are two main systems of l. used in poetry: (1) RATIONAL L. (RATIOCINATION) bases its argumentation upon assumptions, premises, and assertions through modes of deduction, induction, comparison, testimony, and definition, among others. Common errors within this system take the form of fallacies such as oversimplification, sequence as cause, holiness or guilt by association, genetic fallacy, begging the question, non sequitur, faulty analogy, or circular reasoning. (2) ASSOCIATIONAL L., a system that finds its best use in art forms, is based on intuitive connections made between things not normally linked together. These connections are achieved through processes of resemblance, archetypal connotation, and juxtaposition. In general, rational l. works through analysis while associational l. relies on synthesis. For argumentative structures used in poetry, see CENTRIFUGAL-CENTRIPETAL STRUCTURE, CENTRIFUGAL STRUCTURE, CENTRIPETAL STRUCTURE, DEDUCTIVE-INDUCTIVE STRUCTURE, DEDUCTIVE STRUCTURE, INDUCTIVE-DEDUCTIVE STRUCTURE and INDUCTIVE STRUCTURE. For associational forms of logic, see ARCHETYPE, AUTOMATIC WRITING, CADAVRE EXQUIS, CHANCE POETRY, DEEP IMAGE, DREAM POETRY, FREE ASSOCIATION, JUXTAPOSITION, LEAPING POETRY, STREAM-OF-CONSCIOUSNESS, SURREALISM, and SYMBOLISM. For a history of the use of logic to persuade, see RHETORIC.

logical stress (also called "rhetorical stress," "rhetorical accent," or "sense stress") stress that is created by the meaning, importance, or function of a word in a line, as opposed to *etymological* or *metrical stress*. In the following line the verb "is" would not normally be stressed unless attention needed to be paid to the fact that the statement is, indeed, true: "The cat is in the tree." See ACCENT.

logical structure the concise prose paraphrase of a poem's argument or thematic development. See ARGUMENT, FORM, HERESY OF PARAPHRASE, LOGIC, and STRUCTURE. See also *structures of arguments* in APPENDIX 1, and *figures of argumentation* in APPENDIX 2.

logic of the metaphor (see ASSOCIATIONAL LOGIC, LOGIC, and METAPHOR) a phrase first used by Hart Crane in a letter to Harriet Monroe.

logopoeia /-pē′ə/ (Greek for "word-creation") a critical term used by Ezra Pound to indicate that "dance of ideas" created by the interplay of words when their meanings are used in unexpected ways. Pound points to Jules Laforgue's work as an example of this often playful, ironic, and multidimensional type of writing. MELOPOEIA is Pound's term for the musical quality of poetry, and PHANOPOEIA is his term for the use of imagery in poetry. These three aspects of poetry, along with ARCHITECHTONICS, the structural harmony of the whole, form the basis of all writing.

logorrhea /-rē′ə/ (Greek for "flow or discharge of words") speech that is chaotic, meandering, repetitive, verbose, and equivocating, as in Polonius's speeches in *Hamlet*. Some contemporary poets, e.g., Russell Edson, use l. in order to create comic situations and to satirize the characters who speak in this manner. See BOMBAST.

long measure: See LONG METER.

long meter a stanzaic form composed of four lines of iambic tetrameter. Used by Robert Burns, among others, the form is a variant of the HYMNAL STANZA (also known as COMMON METER or COMMON MEASURE) which is composed of four lines of alternating iambic tetrameter and trimeter (4,3,4,3). See BALLAD METER. See also *forms* in APPENDIX 1.

loudness an empirical element of PROSODY that measures the amount of sound made when a syllable is pronounced. Other aspects in the prosodic measurement of a syllable are DURATION, STRESS, and PITCH. It is important to keep in mind that loudness and stress can be mutually exclusive; that is, a stressed syllable may be pronounced softly and an unstressed syllable may be pronounced loudly. See SCANSION.

low angle shot (see CINEMATIC TECHNIQUES) a cinematic term, sometimes used in literary criticism, that indicates the upward viewing of a scene, which makes subjects and settings seem larger than life. See also *cinematic terms* in APPENDIX 1.

lyric (from Greek for "lyre," an ancient stringed instrument) originally, poetry meant to be sung, accompanied by music from the lyre or lute. The term now refers to a category of poetry (distinct from NARRATIVE POEM and DRAMATIC POETRY) that is short in form, concentrated in its expression, subjective in its observations, personal in subject matter, and songlike in quality. In fact, its musical thrust and aura form the aesthetic of its type, which may include forms such as the ODE, the ELEGY, the meditation, and the ARGUMENT. Its range of expressions include deeply felt emotion, states of mind, statements of moral, philosophical, or ethical values, and systems of thought. Most often, its strategy is to create a private expression intended to be overheard; if the l. is directly addressed to another person, it is called a DRAMATIC L. or DRAMATIC MONOLOGUE. In the 20th century, the l. is the dominant poetic form; and promulgated by the aesthetics of the Romantics and other poets such as E.A. Poe, the term has come to be synonymous with the word "poetry." Donald Hall has described the contemporary l. as having "one goal and one message, which is to urge the condition of inwardness, the 'inside' from which its structure derives." An array of famous lyrics include Keats' *Ode on a Grecian Urn*, Ben Jonson's *Drink to Me Only with Thine Eyes*, Wordsworth's *Tintern Abbey*, Marvell's *To His Coy Mistress*, Eliot's *The Love Song of J. Alfred Prufrock*, and Dylan Thomas' *Fern Hill*. See *forms* in APPENDIX 1.

M

macron (Greek for "long") in classical prosody and QUANTITATIVE METER, the mark (-) used to indicate a long syllable. The BREVE (˘) indicates a short syllable. For accentual verse symbols, see ACCENT, ARSIS AND THESIS, ICTUS, and PROSODIC SYMBOLS.

macronic verse poetry that intersperses the words of one language into another. Usually, the writer mixes his own language with an older language. Although the technique is probably as old as poetry itself, some scholars credit its invention to the 16-century poet Tisi degli Odassi who introduced his native Italian into Latin poetry. The form has often been used to satirize various elite groups. See BARBARISM and SOLECISMUS.

madrigal (of obscure derivation; possibly from Italian for "herd" or from Greek for "fold") originally a 14th-century Italian pastoral LYRIC sung by a chorus and accompanied by a stringed instrument. At that time, the m. took the form of a six- to 13-line stanza employing three rhymes. In Renaissance England, the form reached a brief height of popularity and was characterized by intricate harmonies and rhythms. Shakespeare's comedy *Measure for Measure* contains a m. The form, at times, was also adapted as a satirical vehicle aimed at elite groups in the church and society. See *forms* in APPENDIX 1.

malapropism (from French for "inappropriate") a ludicrous misuse of words caused by ignorance or by a confusion over similar-sounding words. The term is taken from the name of a character, Mrs. Malaprop, in Sheridan's play *The Rivals* (1775). Shakespeare also used this humorous device in *Much Ado about Nothing* in which Dogberry, the constable, habitually misstates his thoughts so that his words stand opposite his meaning. The television character Archie Bunker is often guilty of using malapropisms. See CACOZELON and SPOONERISM. See also *devices of poetic license* in APPENDIX 2, and *diction* in APPENDIX 1.

malediction (from Latin for "to speak ill of") a form of speech that reviles, curses, or slanders. See DOGGEREL, and IMPRECATION.

Marinism a flamboyant style of writing, named after the Italian poet Giovanni Marino (1569–1625) who employed wild tropes and rhetorical devices in his work. His style influenced some METAPHYSICAL POETRY: that of George Herbert who was fond of creating chains of conceits, and Richard Crashaw whose hyperbolic, intense, overdecorated metaphors and similes are exemplified in the following description of a woman's eyes filling with tears: "Two walking baths, two weeping motions, / Portable

173

and compendious oceans." See BOMBAST, EUPHUISM, and GONGORISM. See also *devices of poetic license* in APPENDIX 2.

martyria (from Greek *martyr*, for "witness") a rhetorical expression of testimony in which one uses one's own experience as authority: "My own hands know the feeling of an axe. / What dictionary could tell me that?" See *types of testimony* in APPENDIX 2.

masculine ending a verse ending in which the last syllable is stressed. The m.e. is usually part of a RISING FOOT and stands in opposition to the FEMININE ENDING. See MASCULINE RHYME.

masculine rhyme a form of rhyme that occurs in a set of stressed monosyllabic words. When a set of rhymed words ends in unaccented or unstressed syllables, it is termed FEMININE RHYME or DOUBLE RHYME. See MASCULINE ENDING and RHYME.

mask (probably from Medieval Latin *masca*, for "witch, specter") an identity or voice adopted by a poet that represents the speaker in a poem. The term was popularized in CRITICISM by W.B. Yeats who used the example of the masks in traditional Japanese Nō theater to illustrate the process of imagination that enables a writer to adopt different voices. The m. as a literary device was originally derived from the Italian, French, and English *masques* in which royalty and commoners dramatized their conflict with one another. Those who were commoners or antisocial were dubbed the ANTIMASQUE, a parallel to today's antiheroes in literature and film. Ben Johnson defined the m. as being divided between words that function as illuminations of the soul, and the spectacle of scenery and dancing that refers back to the body. In contemporary times, the poetic m. has been refined down to words alone, unless one includes opera, musicals, and plays as poetic forms. In contemporary poetry the POINT OF VIEW is generally referred to as the m. of a poet. For instance, the "I" point-of-view in a poem is the poet's m., not the poet himself, even though the poem may be factually autobiographical. The m. is the poet's vehicle for materializing his perceptions and emotions. The human is so complex and variable that it would be impossible to truly say that anyone's identity has been fixed on the page. When repeatedly asked if a number of characters created by Saul Bellow weren't really he, Bellow answered: "I would have to suffer from dissociation of personality to be all these people in the books. I can't possibly be all of them. I lend a character, out of pure friendship, whatever he needs, that's all." In the same way, poets lend parts of themselves to their poems through the m. By writing out of a particular attitude on a sharply focused theme, and by selecting and intensifying the poem's contents, the poet presents an identity in high relief from the background of human behavior. The editing and revision processes exclude the possibility that what we see on the page is the poet's identity. Those poets who have been labeled *Confessional* (see CONFESSIONAL POETRY) would not agree that their lives and identities are in their poems even though what they have to say through their masks is highly personal and autobiographical.

Oftentimes the m. is used synonymously with the term PERSONA, but some critics distinguish between the two narrative devices in terms of the degree to which the speaker of a poem differs from its writer. Thus an anonymous "I," or "you," or "he" voice in a poem would be termed a m., while a speaker who is easily recognized as being different from the poet (another character, an animal, or an inanimate object) is termed a persona. See ANTIMASQUE, MASKED PRONOUN OR FALSE PRONOUN, and MASQUE. See also *dramatic terms* in APPENDIX 1.

masked pronoun or false pronoun a pronoun that grammatically refers to one point of view but which in reality intends another (see POINT OF VIEW). For instance, a poem written in the second person ("you") may refer to the speaker of the poem, the individual reader, or a general audience, while a poem written in the first person ("I") may refer not to a first-person character but to the poem's audience. Oftentimes poets will use this technique as a formal device in getting closer to their subjects or in gaining perspective on their own perceptions. For example, Richard Hugo's *Degrees of Gray in Phillipsburg* uses the second person to objectify the speaker's experience:

> *You* might come here Sunday on a whim.
> Say *your* life broke down. The last good kiss
> *you* had was years ago.

See ANTIMASQUE, MASK, and MASQUE. See also *grammatical constructions that are technically incorrect* in APPENDIX 2.

masque (a variant of *mask*) a Renaissance spectacle of entertainment involving mime and songs performed by heavily costumed and masked characters. The form, probably of Italian or French origin, featured conflicts among royal characters. The ANTIMASQUE featured conflict among common characters. Leonardo da Vinci designed settings for some masques in Italy, and Ben Jonson and his collaborator, Inigo Jones, produced masques in England. Jonson (*Hymenaei*, 1606) maintained that the aspects of design and words in the m. pertained to the soul, while the elements of song, mime, and dance symbolized the body. Famous examples of the m. in literature include Milton's *Comus* (1634), act IV of Shakespeare's *The Tempest*, and brief parts of his *Romeo and Juliet*, *The Winter's Tale*, and *Cymbeline*. The contemporary term MASK refers to the identity of a poem's speaker.

material cause a rhetorical figure of definition that works by antecedent and consequent in first speaking of a thing and then speaking of the material from which it is made; e.g., "A house of wood, a fence of stone, a cup of gold, / a mind of reason." See *figures of cause and effect, antecedent and consequent* in APPENDIX 2.

matrix (Latin for "womb") a general critical term referring to various kinds of background material or aesthetic texture in a poem, such as its GROUND RHYTHM, DOMAIN OF THOUGHT, IMAGERY, and BOND DENSITY, or other considerations such as social milieu, historical period, or regional DIALECT. See AESTHETIC SURFACE, REGIONALISM, and RHYTHM.

matrix rhythm: See GROUND RHYTHM.

measure a unit of rhythm referring to a FOOT, two feet (DIPODY in Greek Classical prosody), or, in contemporary prosody, the cadenced parts of a line, units of lines, or stanzaic forms (as in W.C. Williams' TRIADIC STANZA). The term is often used interchangeably with METER. See RHYTHM.

medela (possibly from Latin for "middle") a rhetorical figure of emotion or ethics that recognizes something negative but attempts to better conditions through kind or approving words. See PATHOPOEIA. See also *figures of pathos* in APPENDIX 2.

meiosis /mī·ō′-/ (Greek for "a lessening") a rhetorical figure of definition that substitutes a word of lesser degree for one of greater degree, as in "My excommunication is nothing but a *leave-of-absence.*" The device is often a form of humorous or ironic UNDERSTATEMENT similar to LITOTES, and one that has the opposite effect of AUXESIS. Auden's *Musée des Beaux Arts* and *The Unknown Citizen* use entire strategies composed of m., and Shakespeare's *King Lear*, in its most tragic moments, uses the device. See *figures comparing greater, lesser, or equal things* in APPENDIX 2, and *figurative expressions* in APPENDIX 1.

melic poetry /mel′ik/ (*melic*, from Greek for "song") an Aeolian and Dorian verse of the seventh to the fifth century B.C. accompanied by music from a string or wind instrument. At times the verse was written for solo presentation as in the lyrics of Sappho, Alcaeus, and Anacreon; at other times, the verse was written as choral composition, as in the lyrics of Pindar and others. The term was used by Greeks to refer generally to any lyric poetry. See *forms* in APPENDIX 1.

melodrama /mel′-/ (from Greek for "song" plus "drama") originally an Italian Renaissance operatic form containing music, song, and a simple plot. In the 18th century, the term referred to a play that depended heavily on its musical background and spectacle of scenery and costumes (see MASQUE), and contained a conflict between stereotypical characters of high virtue and villainy. In modern times, the term has come to refer to a piece of literature, usually drama or film, displaying an exaggerated style of emotional expression (SENTIMENTALISM, BATHOS, etc.) tending more toward a CARICATURE of vice and virtue than toward realistic portrayal (see REALISM). The form flourished in the 19th century in England and was typified by plays such as *Ten Nights in a Bar-room* (1858), and in contemporary times can be seen daily on television soap operas.

melopoeia /-pē′yə/ (from Greek for "song" plus "a making") a term used by Ezra Pound (*ABC of Reading*, 1934) to indicate the musical or sound qualities of a poem. Poets such as Dylan Thomas and Gerard Manley Hopkins depended almost exclusively for their effects upon this aspect of their poetry. The other two "qualities of poetic creation" that Pound categorized are LOGOPOEIA, the combined effect of ideas, rhythm, and syntax, and PHANOPOEIA, the imagistic aspects of a poem (see IMAGISM). See also *melopoetics* in APPENDIX 1.

melopoetics: See MELOPOEIA and SONICS.

melos (from Greek for "song") the quality of sound and rhythm in a poem created by the use of SOUND SYSTEM and degrees of stressed syllables. For instance, in Dryden's *Alexander's Feast*, rising iambic feet combined with plosives and fricatives (see CONSONANTS) and SLANT RHYME create a very musical effect:

> 'Twas at the royal feast, for Persia won
> By Philip's warlike son:
> Aloft in awful state
> The godlike hero sate
> On his imperial throne;
> His valiant peers were placed around;
> Their brows with roses and with myrtles bound:
> (So should desert in arms be crowned).
> The lovely Thais, by his side,
> Sate like a blooming Eastern bride
> In flower of youth and beauty's pride

The term refers to effects in rhythm, as in the staccato *River* section of Hart Crane's *The Bridge*, as well as to a wide spectrum of sound effects ranging from the impacted, clashing sound systems of Gerard Manley Hopkins to the subtle musical qualities of poets such as Wyatt and Poe. See BOND DENSITY, MELOPOEIA, and SONICS.

mempsis a rhetorical figure of emotion in which a speaker both complains and seeks help: "Don't go away in my hour of need. I am troubled. Be with me." See *figures of pathos* in APPENDIX 2.

mesostich /mes'ostik/ (from Greek for "middle" plus "line of verse") a form of ACROSTIC poem in which the middle letters in the lines of verse, read vertically, form a hidden or key word in a poem. A *true acrostic* employs the first letters of succeeding lines of verse, a *telestich* uses the last letters, and a CROSS-ACROSTIC uses an obliquely ordered sequence of letters to spell out its message. See *forms* in APPENDIX 1.

mesozeugma /-zōōg'mə/ (from Greek for "middle" plus "yoking") a rhetorical construction of grammar, used for the sake of grace, brevity, or ambiguity, in which a key verb placed in the middle of a sentence links up preceding and subsequent clauses, as in this line from the *Maitri Upanishad*, a Hindu scripture: "A plunging bird he *is*, a swan of surpassing splendor." See HYPOZEUGMA, PROZEUGMA, and ZEUGMA. See also *grammatical constructions that are technically incorrect* in APPENDIX 2.

metabasis /metab'-/ (Greek for "a passing over") a rhetorical construction of rhythm and balance used as a device of transition. Usually, the term refers to a speaker who in balanced and parallel clauses moves from the past to the present to the future, as in

> Once you were where promises were traded,
> Now you stand where promises are faded,
> Soon you'll be where promises are evaded.

See *grammatical devices of rhythm and balance* in APPENDIX 2.

metacriticism discourse about CRITICISM that attempts to elaborate, interpret, or evaluate the discipline of literary study. The form, important in modern letters, ranges in scope from doctoral dissertations that discuss various critics' opinions relevant to a particular thesis about a work or group of works to theoretical considerations of the role and function of criticism, such as Northrop Frye's *The Anatomy of Criticism* (1957). See *criticism* in APPENDIX 1.

metalepsis /-lep′-/ (Greek for "participation") a rhetorical figure of definition, subsumed under FINAL CAUSE, that shows a present effect created by a remote cause, as in this example from Goethe's *Theory of Colors*: "The eye, if it were not orbed like the sun, / Could never view the light the sun creates." Here, Goethe is arguing that the reason we can see is that the eye is essentially like the sun. See *figures of cause and effect*, and *antecedent and consequent* in APPENDIX 2.

metaphor /met′əfər/ or /met′əfôr/ (from Greek for "to transfer, to carry across") a rhetorical figurative expression of similarity or dissimilarity in which a direct, nonliteral substitution or identity is made between one thing and another: *similarity*, as in "Johnny's belly is a pink balloon" or *dissimilarity*, as in "the President's proposed budget is an overinflated balloon." When a m. merely illustrates something that could be more accurately described by means other than m., it is termed *decorative*. But if a m. expresses a thought so precisely or subtly that it could not be so well expressed by other means, it is termed *organic, structural,* or *functional*. I.A. Richards (*The Philosophy of Rhetoric*, 1936) broke down the m. into two aspects: the *tenor*, or referential word which is usually stated first and is often of a general or abstract nature ("*Hope* is a bird"), and the *vehicle*, usually the second term and commonly more concrete or specific ("Hope is a *bird*"). The meaning of the tenor is transformed and adjusted by passing through the connotations of the vehicle which, in turn, energizes the original tenor. In longer metaphorical constructions, such as the *controlling, extended,* and *subtractive m.*, the original tenor almost disappears from attention when the vehicle assumes command of the imagination. Richards spoke of the way in which the mind functions when it riffles through the qualities that things or ideas possess: "The mind is a connecting organ, it works by connecting any two things in an indefinitely large number of different ways. Which of these it chooses is settled by reference to some larger whole or aim, and though we may not discover its aim, the mind is never aimless."

In Laurence Perrine's essay *Four Forms of Metaphor*, Richards' terms "tenor" and "vehicle" are substituted by "literal" and "figurative," respectively, and then elaborated into a classification of metaphors based upon whether the parts are named or implied.

The poet James Dickey analyzes the making of a metaphor into a four-step process (*Metaphor as Pure Adventure*, 1968) which begins with (1) making picture comparisons in the mind, (2) discovering the threads of continuity that run through these pictures and which create a "narrative of dramatic action," (3) recombining these elements so that they undergo a "fruitful interchange of qualities, a transference of energies, an informing of each other", and (4) translating this process into the medium of language. Although metaphors do not have to occur in the idiom of images, Dickey's process of metaphorical conceptualization is probably accurate. Paul Ricoeur (*The Rule of Metaphor*, 1977) defines the process of metaphor-making as a three-step process of *selection, substitution*, and *language formation*. In other words, the creation of m. is akin to a three-dimensional starburst of associations in which the imagination splits, fuses, and refines images and concepts. Although linguists draw a definite line between the process of comparison, which defines the basic activity of creating a SIMILE, and the process of substitution, which is the replacement role of the vehicle in a m., it seems obvious that we are involved in making resemblances so that we can then substitute the vehicle for the tenor. But the act is so fluid and instantaneous that we are unaware of its workings and find it impossible to analyze. Resemblance and substitution are probably two complementary sides of the same act of thinking which, as Dickey points out, is not just a way of understanding the world, but a way of recreating it.

The History of Metaphors
Some linguists claim that the first grammatical unit of language was the verb, not the noun, because verbs already contain nouns within them by implication: The word "run" implies that someone or something must be engaged in the activity. Thus, although the verb seems to be a more complex and highly evolved unit of language than the noun, studies have shown that the verb m. in poetry is older than the noun m. (Christine Brooke-Rose, *A Grammar of Metaphor*, 1965).

Just how difficult it is to analyze and organize metaphors into any comprehensive system can be seen by the number and kind of attempts that have been made by prominent minds since Aristotle's time. Each major effort has failed to capture the full range of the complexity of form and function in the m. Aristotle devised a descriptive system known as the "Genus/Species Classification," which is the same classification of family characteristics that biology uses. His organization includes four classes of metaphors: (1) particular to general ("sparrow/bird"), (2) general to particular ("tree/oak"), (3) particular to particular ("sparrow/pigeon"), and (4) analogical or proportional metaphors (A:B as C:D). Aristotle's classification describes the level of relationship in which the terms of a m. exist, but it does not explain how metaphors function technically. His successors, such as Quintilian, devised other descriptive systems. Quintilian's "Animate/Inanimate Classification" is similar in form to that of Aristotle's, and it includes also four classes: (1) animate to inanimate ("leg of the chair"), (2) inanimate to animate ("books are a man's best friend"), (3) animate to animate ("Beatrice is a rose"), and (4) inanimate to inanimate ("your glasses are a gas"). In 19th-century France a system was developed that described the matrix or grounding of a m. according to its DOMAIN OF THOUGHT—from the world of science, nature, religion, etc. And this method, in turn, was refined by German linguists into the *Domain Trait formula*, which is a point-by-point analytical comparison of the terms of a metaphorical construction. The last major attempt to characterize metaphors took into account the metaphor's intention, that is, whether it is meant to entertain, inform, or proselytize, or some other intention, a system that has little value to either scholars or writers. Therefore, perhaps it is best to look at the way in which metaphors function grammatically. The bulk of the following grammatical considerations are based on the painstaking work of Christine Brooke-Rose *A Grammar of Metaphor*, 1965.

Grammatical Construction of Metaphors
The *noun m.*, structurally speaking, is one of the most primitive types of m., especially in the compound noun or KENNING form which dominated ANGLO-SAXON VERSE and is often found naturally in the speech of children. It is an attempt to synthesize or fuse two different qualities of a thing into one concept. In Western films, we often hear Indians call whiskey "firewater," which defines the form and effect of the drink. In the famous chimpanzee experiments that Beatrice and Robert Gardner performed (Carl Sagan, *Dragons of Eden*, 1977), primates with a working vocabulary of 100 to 200 words were able to describe through Ameslan a duck as a "water-bird," a watermelon as "drink-fruit," and a radish as "cry-hurt-food." Although the noun m. may seem simple in terms of its explicitness of expression, it is also complex because of the resonance or multiple attributes that it contains. If we say, "My mother is a flower," which is the simplest kind of metaphorical noun substitution, we are also implying free-floating associations of weather, landscape, temperament, emotional relationships, and temporal and spiritual time dimensions. Another simple form of the noun m. is the *appositional phrase* in which the vehicle further defines or explains the tenor that immediately precedes it: "My mother, *a rose among weeds.*" The apposition can also be extended into a phrasal form or even a series of phrases that defines a tenor in a number of ways. In the following noun-phrase series, the tenor "scars" is elaborated by a series of appositions: "Poverty had left its scars on him: the empty pocket, the furrowed face, the slow-motion gestures of futility." The *vocative* and APOSTROPHE, which are foreshortened forms of the appositional m., leave out the referential term or tenor, and simply state: "My flower," or "Oh Rose," in which the first half of the m., "You are," is unstated. Surrounding context supplies what's missing. A compromised form of the noun m. is one that depends upon an adjectival word or phrase that qualifies and modifies the noun m. in a specific manner. In fact, the *qualifying adjective* is really a disguised prepositional phrase that shows what realm the noun belongs to. For example, the term "the eternal sleep" connotes death and was originally derived from "the sleep of eternity," or "the eternity of sleep." Also, the *possessive-noun m.* is another disguised prepositional phrase: "the clouds' tears," meaning rain, was originally constructed as "the tears of the clouds." But sometimes the modified noun m. can be confusing because the reader may not know which noun is being described in the m. and, therefore, what person or thing the adjective is affecting. For instance, the phrase "laughing gas" used without sufficient context may confuse someone new to the term since it could refer to the effect of the gas on a patient or the emotional instability of the gas itself.

At this point, it is important to discuss the choice of verbs that link the two terms of a simple noun m. If we use the linking verb (*copula*) "to be" in any of its forms, we will set up a very direct but static form of replacement and identity. In saying, "God is our father," there is a direct identity without any sense of process, transformation, or development. The writer might want to use a more energized form of linking verb that demonstrates an active state of change. This kind of linking verb can be termed *transformational* because half of its function is to show change. Verbs such as "create," "become," "turn," and "make" accomplish the same thing as the verb "to be," but include process. Another kind of linking verb is the *representational verb*, such as "seem," "call," and "represent," which function halfway between being a pure linking verb and a transformational verb. They show a kind of identity that is tentative and also imply the potential of transformation rather than the actual process of change.

The *verb m.* is the most highly charged form of m. because it fuses together a description and an action, whereas the noun m. fuses together a description and a thing. Some verb metaphors are derived from verbs, some from adjectives, and some from compressed noun phrases. The sentence "I have blinded myself with optimism" could have been derived from either the verb "to blind" or the adjective "blind." We can transform the noun simile "He ran away as fast as a rocket can fly" into the verb m. "He rocketed away," which is known as buried or implied m. because the noun m. ("He is a rocket") is never explicitly stated. Within the metaphorical use of the verb there is both a pure action and a description of the quality of that action. The following example relates different qualities of the same basic communication: "The police *hammered* away at me with questions," and "The police *needled* me with questions." Both give out the same basic information in terms of pure action, but the quality of those actions differ. Other kinds of abbreviated verb metaphors can be found in HYPERBOLE and UNDERSTATEMENT. If a worker has slowed down his pace on the job, his boss might yell, "Don't die on me," which is really a compressed form of the SYLLOGISM "Because you are working so slowly, you seem to be dying." While many verb metaphors relate only to one noun in a sentence ("She ducked the ball," in which "ducked" relates only to "she"), some uses of verb metaphors transform both the subject and object of a sentence. If we say, "He burrowed through the crowd," the "he" is likened to a burrowing animal and "the crowd" is likened to something like soil. Usually the effect of the verb m. is implicit. The substitution, comparison, or identity is implied. But many verb metaphors in extended forms (the CONCEIT, the CONTROLLING METAPHOR, and the *extended metaphor*) take their cue from an explicit noun m. For example, if life were compared to a card game, we could elaborate the original noun m. of "Life is a card game" by building up additional buried verb metaphors: "In the game of life, you *draw* a limited number of breaths, then *fold*, when you're *bumped*."

The *preposition m.* is the quickest and easiest kind of m. to construct. Basically, it tells the derivation of something—how it is possessed, what it is possessed by, what it is related to, where it is located, or from what it is derived. The genitive, as it is properly termed, has the basic formulation of "A is the B of C," as in "She is the sun of my day." Here the vehicle "sun" is equated with the tenor "she," and the third term "day" completes the figure by providing it with the larger metaphorical and literal framework. The prepositional m. is really a verbal idea and can be expressed as such. "She is the sun of my day" easily translates into "You light up my life." Many times poets find it unnecessary to state the first general term of the m. because the context of the poem or the obviousness of the subject takes on that responsibility. In the metaphorical cliché "We have a wolf in sheep's clothing" someone whom the context would identify is equated with an animal. Sometimes there is no first term at all, simply a "B of C" formula, as in "I know the bitterness of defeat." Here the term "defeat" is acting as a vehicle to an unstated tenor.

Other prepositional metaphors show ownership, as in "the knife of pain," which could also be constructed as (1) a verb plus a preposition ("the knife thrown by pain"), (2) as a possessive adjective ("pain's knife"), or (3) as an adjective or adjectival participle ("the knife-like pain" or "the kniving pain").

The *adjectival m.*, in terms of its grammatical derivation, lies somewhere between a noun and a verb. If we say, "Writing is a *sweaty* occupation," we are implying both the act of sweating and sweat itself. While the adjective has tremendous versatility in modifying any noun, that very strength is also its weakness. The adjective can be applied indiscriminately to any noun and not change its own meaning. "A sweaty occupation" or a sweaty anything at all have the same meaning. But if we were to use the same root word in verb form, then in noun form, its meaning would change somewhat: "He veiled his thoughts" has a slightly different meaning from "His thoughts were a veil." So the adjectival m. should be used sparingly and only when it gives the exact shade of meaning to a noun that the imagination calls for. The adjectival m. is like the ubiquitous oxygen atom which is easily dispersed because it is too easily attracted to and combined with other elements.

The *adverbial m.* is less universally applicable than the adjectival m. because it usually qualifies a bland action in order to make it more specific. In other words, a highly specific and charged verb can replace the adverbial m. Examples of the form are "He ran blindly after his desires" and "She read the dime novel sheepishly." Running and reading are fairly innocuous actions in terms of their specificity and vividness, so they need sharpening and refinement with adverbs. At times the adverbial m. is capable of coloring both an action and a noun, as in "He walked woodenly," which, like some verb metaphors, portrays both the "he" and the way he walked, both subject and verb. And in some instances, the adverbial m. can be used to state a PARADOX, as in "He was fiercely quiet, outrageously still." The adverb can exaggerate and distort a state of being because in these cases it overpowers the relatively bland adjective that it modifies. In rarer cases, the adverb can transform the entire meaning of a noun. In the following example from Dylan Thomas a noun denoting an emotion (grief) becomes a noun denoting time when the adverb "ago" is added: "A grief ago . . . ."

Metaphorical Equations
Because metaphors are based upon substitution and identity, they can be

expressed in mathematical terms as equations, a form that becomes useful if we want to examine the substructure of metaphorical relationships, or if we are trying to construct a m. that seems confusing when it is not broken down.

The simplest kind of m., the base of all metaphorical relationships, is "A = B," as in the example "Desires (A) are birds (B)." The "A = B" formula can also be expressed phrasally, as in the Biblical quotation "As the lily among thorns, so is my love among the daughters," though this is spoken of as an ANALOGY. Using the simple identity as a base formula, we can increase its complexity by adding on another term, C: "A = B + C," as in "Desires are birds and harbingers of Fall." Here the A term must be completed by the complete weight of meaning in both the B and C terms.

A variation of the "A = B + C" formula is the genitive or prepositional m., which calls for the formula

$$A = \text{the B } \begin{matrix} \text{in} \\ \text{of} \\ \text{for} \end{matrix} \text{ C}$$

as in "Desires are birds of prey." We can even extend the formula by adding on another prepositional phrase: "Desires are the birds of prey of reckless lives."

We can also extend our simple "A = B" formula into a *compound m.* in which the term C qualifies how A = B. The formula is "A = B = C. Therefore, A = C." This translates into "Desires (A) are Birds of prey (B) who are their own victims (C)." Or, "A = C": "Desire is its own victim." A variation of the "A = B = C" formula is the parallel series "A = B, as C = D," in which two new terms are added to the basic m. equation and which reinforce or further describe how A is related to B, as in the example "Desires (A) are birds of prey (B) as thoughts (C) are the mind's marauders (D)."

Conditional Metaphorical Equations
There are many interesting types of "A = B" equations that have special conditions attached to them. These conditional metaphors, which are sometimes expressed in analogical terms, make statements in the subjunctive mood. Their states of being are either assumed or not in force. It is a projection that allows the writer to transform events into other possibilities so that their consequences can be known or guessed.

Taking the basic "A = B" formula in "My eyesight is glue," we can make a conditional m. whose structure depends upon the words "since" and "then": "since A = B, then . . . ." or "Since my eyesight is like glue, you won't be able to unwrap that present." This conditional m. was actually spoken by a ten-year-old in a more complex form which used a verb m. In fact, his statement is much smoother than the examples cited above: "I don't think you'll be able to unwrap that present because my eyes are so glued to it." There are many other kinds of conditional metaphors whose set-ups include formulations such as "when/then" and the negative type of "not A but B, yet A, if C."

The Controlling Metaphor
This is sometimes referred to as a central m., but the name "controlling m." better describes its importance and function. It is probably the most widely used type of elaborated m., if we discount the CONCEIT which is similar but is more of an intellectual construction rather than an intuitive one. The controlling m. systemizes a poem with its pervasive nuances and is actually a form of internal control that keeps the poem focused. It usually opens the poem by stating a m., and then the poem proceeds to create a number of subordinate images and metaphors that are directly relatable to the controlling m. It is the rightness of the controlling metaphor that makes it more than just the ruler of the poem, which makes it the progenitor of the contents. Alan Dugan's poem *Love Song: I and Thou* uses the technique of the *controlling m.* in which the speaker's life is expressed in the figure of a badly built house.

The Telescoped Metaphor
This m. probably takes its name from the way in which pocket telescopes pull out from themselves when we extend their concentric tubes. In fact, the telescoped m. is often referred to as an extended m. It's a complex, permutating m. whose vehicle becomes the tenor for the next m., and that second tenor gives rise to a vehicle which, in turn, becomes the tenor for the next m. It is a serially transforming m. which becomes, in effect, the strategy of a poem that uses it. A famous example is Caesar's speech to Antony in Shakespeare's *Antony and Cleopatra*:

> Let not the peece of Vertue which is set
> Betwixt us, as the Cyment of our love
> To keepe it builded, be the Ramme to batter
> The fortune of it . . .

The virtue becomes a kind of cement which, in turn, becomes a battering ram.

The Conceit
The CONCEIT is an intellectualized form of controlling m. whose elaborations are based upon an abstract concept rather than upon the senses. There are two types: the PETRARCHAN CONCEIT, which exaggerates the attributes of a m. by presenting highly contrasting images, and the METAPHYSICAL CONCEIT, whose intellectualizations of the second term in the m., the vehicle, have little obvious resemblance to the proper term or tenor. In the following DEFINITION POEM by Francis Ponge, he considers the movement of fire and metamorphoses its qualities into the movements of animals. The vehicles of the amoeba, the giraffe, and butterflies are wildly unrelated images that cohere under the intellectualized movement of fire:

Fire
Fire has a system: first all the flames move in one direction
. . .
> (One can only compare the gait of fire to that of an animal: it must first leave one place before occupying another; it moves like an amoeba and a giraffe at the same time, its neck lurching, its foot dragging) . . .

Then, while the substances consumed with method collapse, the
escaping gasses are subsequently transformed into one long flight
of butterflies.

Ponge's poem is a form of PERSONIFICATION in which an inanimate entity
takes on the characteristics of something living, which is one of
Quintilian's classes of metaphors. In fact, many poetic devices, when
considered, are really forms of metaphors.

Mark Strand employs a Metaphysical conceit that begins with the
speaker's identity as an absence. The poem then intellectually manipulates
the negative spiritual possibilities inherent in the premise of matter viewed
as space:

> *Keeping Things Whole*
> In a field
> I am the absence
> of field.
> This is
> always the case.
> Wherever I am
> I am what is missing.
>
> When I walk
> I part the air
> and always
> the air moves in
> to fill the spaces
> where my body's been.
>
> We all have reasons
> for moving.
> I move
> to keep things whole.

The Subtractive Metaphor
This type of m. is a kind of definition m. that sets up implied expectations
and then subtracts parts of the m. in order to define its subject. Yehuda
Amichai uses such a subtractive m. in speaking about the difference
between what a man is and what he has to work with. The narrator of the
poem is a father who is speaking about his son's knowledge of him:

> He thinks I'm a sailor,
> But knows I have no ship.
> And that we have no sea.
> Only vast distances, and winds.

The Reverse Metaphor
This type of m. is similar to the subtractive m. in that it defines something
in negative terms; but the reverse m. does not subtract from its premise, it
compares the tenor of its m. to what is unlike it, so that the vehicles
become contrasts rather than identities with the tenor. In Emily
Dickinson's poem *It Was Not Death, For I Stood Up*, she defines her sense
of despair and loss in terms of what it was not like.

The Mixed Metaphor
The mixed m., which combines opposing domains of thought within one
metaphorical expression, creates a confusion in the primary attributes of

the tenor and vehicle. The common types of mixed metaphors result from (1) adding a prepositional phrase to a m., as in "He is the shepherd *of his garden,*" which implies wrongly that flowers are sheep; (2) adding a second noun m. to a preceding m. without an interceding phrase or word to set up the second m., as in "He is the polestar, the cloud I stand on," which could be saved if the two metaphors were separated widely enough and prepared for by interceding phrases; and (3) adding a literal verb to metaphorical noun, as in "She is the flower that walks beside me." It is also easy to mix metaphors by simply not paying attention to the poem's emblem or complex of attributes, as in "Her lips were rust-colored," in which the unwanted connotations of rust overtake the shade of color the writer has tried to describe. Other examples of mixed metaphors can be found in examples of exaggeration (see PLEONASM), such as "It's raining buckets." There are many examples of mixed metaphors from Shakespeare to the French Surrealists that work because of their imaginative power and authority. When to use or not use a mixed m. depends upon the writer's sense of risk as well as his or her skill.

The Dead Metaphor
This m., like the CLICHÉ, has been so overused that it has lost its original freshness. Thousands of these constructions litter the language and persist mostly because of their convenience. When they are closely examined for their originality, they seem startlingly good. But because they are victims of their own brilliance, they have lost their impact. It would take a very skillful writer to renew them, one who is interested in flavoring his poem with colloquial character or one who has found a new twist to the dead m. Here are some examples of dead metaphors: "Time marches on," "The boss chewed him out," "I'm in a stew," "You look like hell." Another common type of metaphorical cliché is the genre of food metaphors used for women—"sweetie pie, dish, tomato, peach, sugar, dumpling, prune, lemon," etc.

See *figurative expressions* in APPENDIX 1, and *figures of similarity and dissimilarity* in APPENDIX 2.

metaphorical dissolve a device of transition, borrowed from film, in which separate actions or images are fused by means of their similar, implied meanings. For instance, a transition is often made between lovers in the throes of passion and an onrushing train. Poetry employs the device through JUXTAPOSITION between lines or the beginning and ends of stanzas. See CINEMATIC TECHNIQUES. See also *cinematic terms* in APPENDIX 1.

metaphorical equation an extended form of METAPHOR whose structure is based on a mathematical model or conditional construction. See CONDITIONAL METAPHOR EQUATION.

metaphorical objectivity a Surrealist phrase indicating a subconscious, imaginative state of mind through which everyday objects spontaneously take on universal meaning in a context of unconventional associations. See AUTOMATIC WRITING, DREAM POETRY, and SURREALISM.

metaphorical reflection a technique of composition, based on the use of METAPHOR, which enhances and deepens meaning in a poem. See INNER REFLECTIONS.

Metaphysical conceit (see CONCEIT and METAPHOR) an extended metaphor, often used in METAPHYSICAL POETRY (see FELT THOUGHT), in which a subtle and surprising connection is made between things in order to illuminate a thought or feeling. The M.c. is typically a PARADOX.

Metaphysical Poetry Dr. Johnson's term (expanding upon a comment made by Dryden in *Discourse of Satire*, 1693, which noted that John Donne's poetry "too much affects the metaphysics") designating the poetry of the 17th-century English writers Donne, Marvell, Cleveland, and Cowley, and the religious verse of Crashaw, Herbert, and Vaughn. Their work is characterized by the use of elaborate CONCEIT, PUN, IRONY, PARADOX, somewhat strained or surprising METAPHOR, everyday images, and ordinary speech often salted with scientific terms. Their analytical themes centered on religion, mysticism, philosophy, and post-Elizabethan unconventional views on love. Because the school's style displayed intellectual perception posited in modes of argumentation, the term has come to refer popularly to poetry that is analytically philosophical in outlook as opposed to the more emotional and simpler lyric poem. After suffering a degree of ignominy during the Neo-Classical and Romantic periods, M.P. in the 20th century was promoted by H.J.C. Grierson's anthology *Metaphysical Lyrics and Poems of the Seventeenth Century*. The poetry came to be intensely admired by and influential in the styles of poets such as T.S. Eliot, John Crowe Ransom, and Allen Tate. See *forms* in APPENDIX 1.

metastasis /mətas′-/ (Greek for "a placing in another way, a change") a rhetorical figure of argumentation that by digression turns an opponent's accusations back against him. See *figures of argumentation* in APPENDIX 2.

metathesis /mətath′-/ (Greek for "transposition") in grammar, an interchange in the position of letters, syllables, or sounds; e.g., the Old English word "brid" has become "bird" in modern usage. In rhetoric, the term denotes the transposition of words in a sentence. The SPOONERISM has the same effect as grammatical m. but does not reflect the historical change in usage. See MALAPROPISM. See also *grammatical constructions* in APPENDIX 2.

meter (from Greek for "measure") measurement in poetry based on any of the following systems of count: (1) the number of accented syllables in a line of verse (STRONG-STRESS M.); (2) the number of accented and unaccented syllables in a line of verse (ACCENTUAL-SYLLABIC VERSE); (3) the number of syllables in a line of verse (SYLLABIC M.); and (4) the DURATION of short and long syllables in a line of verse (QUANTITATIVE M.)

In contemporary times, m. has come to be viewed as an externally imposed, abstract set of recurring rhythms that mark the passage of time in a poem. There are specific forms (see *types of feet* below) that easily lend themselves to technical analysis, and which create a stable frame for the poem. I.A. Richards spoke of the isolating effect of m. as that of a frame around a painting: "Through its very appearance of artificiality metre produces in the highest degree the 'frame' effect, isolating the poetic experience from the accidents and irrelevancies of everyday experience." M. marks not only the tempo and speed of time passing in a poem but also the quality of that time in terms of particular human experiences. While m. can be described as a concept, intellectually conceived, RHYTHM is a precept, experientially felt (see FELT TIME). Richards maintains that rhythm in any poetic form is based upon *expectations, satisfactions, disappointments,* and *surprises.*

Some meters, such as Anglo-Saxon strong-stress and Elizabethan BLANK VERSE, were originally formed from the language of their respective periods, which would make them organically derived; but most metrically controlled poems in the modern era are formal experiments in which the metrical rhythm is adapted artificially from a former period. This is not to say that metrical and conversational rhythms are merely decorative aspects of poetry, for they are as intrinsic and functional in an expressive sense as are the figurative and denotative words in a poem.

Types of Scansion and Meters
Meters can be analyzed or scanned (see SCANSION) by using *graphic, musical,* or *acoustic* methods of notation. Each system offers particular strengths and displays weaknesses or gaps, and it must be noted that because there are emotive nuances (inflections) embedded in *stress, pitch, loudness,* and *duration* of words, scansion cannot approach the sensitivity of the human ear:

(1) STRONG-STRESS M. has two main features: the marking of only strongly stressed syllables that usually employ ALLITERATION, and the indication of major pauses (caesuras) in each line's m. The form was popular in Anglo-Saxon verse. It does not take into account unaccented syllables. The caesura may be initial, medial, or terminal, and each half-line (HEMISTICH) contains two major stresses, although these fixed elements often vary. The following lines from *Beowulf* exemplify the system:

> Often Scyld Scefing ‖ seized mead benches
> from enemy troops, ‖ from many a clan

Coleridge's *Christabel* also uses this m. (see CHRISTABEL METER).

SPRUNG RHYTHM, a more modern strong-stress system invented by G.M. Hopkins, begins each foot with a stressed syllable but does not take into account the position or number of unaccented syllables. It features a clashing, impacted rhythmic effect, as can be seen in Hopkins' *The Windhover.*

(2) *Syllabic-stress m.* (ACCENTUAL-SYLLABIC VERSE) takes into account both accented and unaccented syllables in a line. It is the most commonly used system of measurement in English metrics, and bases its measurement on groups of syllables organized according to the FOOT. Typically, there can be from one to eight feet in a line, though some verse contains up to 14 feet. The number of feet in a line are termed:

monometer	one-foot line
dimeter	two-foot line
trimeter	three-foot line
tetrameter	four-foot line
pentameter	five-foot line
hexameter	six-foot line
heptameter	seven-foot line
octameter	eight-foot line

Syllabic-stress feet are scanned according to the graphic system that considers both accented and unaccented syllables, along with an indication of the major pauses in a line. The syllables range in degree of accent from heavy to unaccented.

heavy or primary	´
medium or secondary	`
light or tertiary	'
unaccented	˘

Accents in verse are determined according to (1) loudness of pronunciation (WORD ACCENT), (2) the relative grammatical importance of words (GRAMMATICAL ACCENT, which counts nouns, verbs, and adjectives heavier than prepositions and articles), (3) the semantic emphasis placed on a word (LOGICAL STRESS), and (4) the accents predicted by previous meters in a verse (METRICAL ACCENT) (see ACCENT). When word accent and metrical accent conflict so that a word is pronounced unusually, it is termed WRENCHED ACCENT or RECESSIVE ACCENT. Feet are diacritically separated by use of a virgule (/, see PROSODIC SYMBOLS), and major pauses or caesuras are indicated by parallel lines (‖). Usually, only the primary accented syllables and the unaccented syllables are scanned. Even though the system can differentiate degrees of stress, it tends to assume that syllables have no durational value or pitch. The lines below demonstrate the graphic system first in its commonly used form, and then in its more elaborate form:

Doĕs thís / maǩe á / nў seńse / tŏ yóu?

Doĕs thís / ‖ màke a᷄ / nў seńse / ‖ tŏ yóu?

After marking off the syllables and pauses, the rhythmic combinations are then identified as units of measurement termed *feet*:

the iamb (iambic)	hĕlló
the trochee (trochaic)	ońlў
the anapest (anapestic)	uňdĕrstánd
the dactyl (dactylic)	cánŏpў
the spondee (spondaic)	woŕk sóng
the pyrrhic	tŏ ă
the tribrach (tribacchic)	iňtŏ ă
the molossos	sóft waŕm rúg
the antibacchus (antibacchic)	fíve doźeń
the amphibrach (amphibrachic)	iňténdĕd

the cretic	óne oň óne
the antipast (antipastic)	ăt hárd lábŏr
the choriamb (choriambic)	sońg ŏf tȟe wińd
first epitrite (epitritic)	ă lońg cóld dáy
second epitrite	ȟe wăs haŕd preśsed
third epitrite	ńo óne cŏŭld téll
fourth epitrite	bláck hót eńgiňe
ionic a majore	ȟe stártĕd ĭo
ionic a minore	ĭo oŭr friéndshĭp
first paeon	ińtĕreštiňg
second paeon	ińcrédĭbȟe
third paeon	cŏmpȟehénsĭve
fourth paeon	iňtŏ tȟe niǵht

Those feet that end in an accented syllable are called rising feet, while those that end in unaccented syllables are called falling feet. If a rising foot ends a line, then the line has a MASCULINE ENDING; if a line breaks on a falling foot, then it has a FEMININE ENDING. An accent whose qualitative differences are difficult to determine is termed DISTRIBUTED STRESS or HOVERING STRESS. Generally speaking, a line's m. can be distinguished by ascertaining what the last foot in a line is, and then scanning backwards to the first foot. Devices of variation such as INVERSION, TRUNCATION, and *acatalexis* in lines often make this rule of thumb difficult to follow.

(3) SYLLABIC M. is composed of and analyzed according to the number of syllables in a line of verse. It may strictly maintain the same number of syllables in a line or vary them according to a preset pattern. This meter was brought to perfection in 18th-century France. During that time, the French line of poetry typically featured a uniform number of syllables and an evenness in the position of the lines' stresses. It is difficult to write syllabic poetry in English since our language is more suited to stress count, while in less heavily accented languages, such as French, the syllabic method is more commonly used.

(4) QUANTITATIVE M., native to Classical Greek and Latin poetry, measures the duration of time it takes to pronounce a stressed or unstressed (long or short) syllable. Since the Classical languages have rules that govern the length of a syllable according to its position or traditional pronunciation, and the English language does not, English-speaking poets have found quantitative m. an almost impossible system to use effectively and naturally. Perhaps the best method of scanning verse written in the quantitative m. system is the musical method, which emphasizes the duration of various syllables. It should be noted that Robert Frost, among others, expressed disdain of this method, but Elizabethan poets such as Sidney and Spenser, as well as Coleridge, Tennyson, Longfellow, and Bridges, used quantitative m.

Many modern and contemporary poems are not based strictly on m. but on CADENCE or rhythm. For a fuller discussion of these types of rhythmic structures, see RHYTHM. See also ALEXANDRINE, FOURTEENER,

FREE VERSE, and SPRUNG RHYTHM. See *Meter* in APPENDIX 1 for a list of related terms.

metonymy /miton'-/ (from Greek for "change of name") a rhetorical figure of speech under the category of "subject and adjunct" that replaces the subject for its characteristic(s), or its characteristic(s) for its subject. For example, the states of Mississippi, Alabama, and Louisiana are so closely associated with their geographical location, vegetation, dialects, and economies that they are called "The South." M., which uses nonliteral or figurative meaning, often shows up in the form of an object closely associated with a person; e.g., an athlete is known as a "jock," and a king is often called the "crown," and military officers are known as "brass." Other instances of its use communicate abstract ideas by means of concrete terms; e.g., the leader of a group is usually referred to as its "head," and the expression "blood, sweat, and tears" commonly stands for a sacrifice of hard labor on someone's part. The closely related device of SYNECDOCHE differs from m. in that it divides a part from the whole rather than working its association from something separately related.

M. is widely used in poetry. In his poem *Out, Out—*, Robert Frost describes a boy holding up his hand injured by a buzz saw "as if to keep / The life from spilling." And Emily Dickinson uses M. in the closure of her poem *She Sights a Bird*. See HYPALLAGE and METAPHOR. See also *figures of subject and adjunct* in APPENDIX 2, and *figurative expressions* in APPENDIX 1.

metrical accent (also called "metrical stress") the accenting of syllables determined by the meter in which a poem is set. Thus, if a poem is composed in iambic pentameter, excepting variations in the meter, the words that are accented will fall into that metrical pattern. For considerations of other types of STRESS PROSODY, see ACCENT and METER.

metrical filler syllables, words, or phrases that are employed for the sole purpose of completing or meeting the requirements of a specific, fixed meter. For instance, in the NURSERY RHYME *Mary Had a Little Lamb*, the phrase "was sure to" fills out the iambic trimeter meter. See *control* in APPENDIX 1.

metrical pause the pause that occurs at the end of a line or stanza when a metrical unit has been completed. While the *caesura* is scanned in metrical analysis because it takes place *within* a line of verse, the m.p. is not indicated because it takes place *outside* of the line. In fact, whether the term and its notion have any value at all is debatable since there is an automatic pause at the end of every line and stanza regardless of meter. Some critics, such as Laurence Perrine, use m.p. to indicate "a pause that replaces an accented syllable." See LINE ENDING. See also *grammatical devices of rhythm and balance* in APPENDIX 2.

metrical romance an adventure story in verse form. The term *romance* originated in France and indicated literature written in the French vernacular as opposed to Latin. Examples of the genre include *Sir Gawain and the Green Knight*, Chaucer's *The Knight's Tale*, Sir Walter Scott's *The*

Lady of the Lake and *Marmion*, and Byron's *Bride of Abydos*. The form usually employs exotic settings and/or distant eras, and appeals to sentimental or "romantic" feelings. See *forms* in APPENDIX 1.

metrical stress: See METRICAL ACCENT.

metrical variations INVERSION, TRUNCATION, or SUBSTITUTION of syllables or feet in a regular line of metered verse. See ACATALECTIC, CATALEXIS, and METER.

metrics techniques of composing or analyzing (see SCANSION and METER) the rhythmic patterns of verse and the theories relating to their nature. For instance, verse may be rhythmically patterned according to STRONG-STRESS METER, ACCENTUAL-SYLLABIC VERSE, SYLLABIC METER, SPRUNG RHYTHM, or QUANTITATIVE METER. In FREE VERSE prosody, units of measurement other than the FOOT or METER are used, so the term m. is generalized into the term PROSODY. For a discussion of free verse rhythms, see RHYTHM.

metron (from Old French *meter*, for "measure") a Classical prosodic unit that measures units of feet according to the number of morae (units measuring the durational value of long and short syllables) contained in the foot (see MORA). In Classical QUANTITATIVE METER, certain feet, such as the iamb, the trochee, and anapest (see METER) are measured not by the single foot but as dipodic units; thus, the m. for these meters is composed of two feet (see DIPODY). Other meters, such as the dactyl, the cretic, and bacchic have for their m. the single foot. For foot units based on similarities in sound, see DISEMIC and SYZYGY.

Middle English period 1100–1500, after the Norman Conquest (1066) when the English language gained enough complexity in dialects and additions from Romance languages to make it closer to "modern English." Until this period, English had been primarily Germanic; it then took on an Anglo-Norman quality. While the English upper class spoke in a French dialect, by the 15th century, literature was directed toward the middle and lower classes in the form of songs, folk ballads, and tales. The second half of the 14th century produced works such as *The Pearl* (ca. 1350–80) and *Sir Gawain and the Green Knight*, the Scottish poems of King James I and Robert Henryson, William Langland's *Piers Plowman* (ca. 1360–99), the works of John Gower, and, of course, the greatest work of the period, Chaucer's *Canterbury Tales* (ca. 1387). See PERIODS OF ENGLISH LITERATURE.

Miles Gloriosus originally, an obnoxiously loud-mouthed and cowardly soldier in Plautus' play *Miles Gloriosus* (ca. 254–184 B.C.). The character was used by Shakespeare (Falstaff and Pistol) and other writers in the Renaissance and became a comedic STOCK CHARACTER even in contemporary Western films which feature the role of a bragging but somewhat victimized *sidekick* to a hero. See CHARACTER. See also *clichés* and *dramatic terms* in APPENDIX 1.

Miltonic sonnet a form of sonnet invented by Milton and based on the PETRARCHAN SONNET. The form consists of a Petrarchan octave rhyming abbaabba and a sestet (with no stanza break) of variable rhyme scheme. Milton's form contributed a tighter sense of unity to the sonnet because of frequent ENJAMBMENT, stichic form, and its positioning of the TURN somewhere between the ninth and 11th lines, which is somewhat after the normal Petrarchan turn. The variable turn creates room for a less forced, more natural resolution, and usually the poem depends for its coherence and unity upon emotional thrust rather than structural organization. See ENGLISH SONNET and SONNET.

mimesis /məmē′-/ or /mīmē′-/ (Greek for "imitation"; also called "Mimetic Theory of Art") a theory of art invented by Aristotle (*Poetics*, ca. 350 B.C.) in which art is seen as having its base in an artistically arranged imitation of nature and human nature. The theory of m. is still a force in poetics, e.g., the Surrealists (see SURREALISM) imitate the workings of the unconscious. See CRITICISM, and IMITATION. See also *figures of subject and adjunct* in APPENDIX 2.

mimetic criticism: See CRITICISM.

Mimetic Theory of Art: See CRITICISM and MIMESIS.

mindscape a poem whose LOCATION, TONE, and *subject matter* pertain to psychological states of mind. The term, parallel in function to LANDSCAPE and seascape, seems to have become necessary in the solipsistic, existential, psychological WELTANSCHAUUNG of the 20th century. Poets such as W.S. Merwin, John Ashbery, and Mark Strand often work in this subgenre.

miniature (from Italian for "illumination [of a manuscript]"; literally, "coloring with red [lead]") originally, a small painting; later, any diminutive work of art. In poetry the term refers to short poems of limited range and depth that are succinct and oftentimes precious (see PRECIOUSNESS). See *publishing formats* under *forms* in APPENDIX 1.

Minimalism (from the Latin for "least, smallest") a 20th-century aesthetic movement, arising from SURREALISM, which erased the context of an object or image so that its details could be seen in high relief. Marcel Duchamp's readymades (ca. 1951) ignited the seminal ideas of the school. In poetry, the *Minimalists* telescoped the Surrealist's notion of PURE POETRY by dismissing literariness in an image or language and displaying the subject's singular properties in a nonrelative environment. This sort of existential art form is not open to interpretation in the way that most conventional art is. The viewer must approach M. in the same way that he approaches dream material, experientially (see DREAM POETRY), although in most instances there is a controlling concept behind the piece of art. The following poem by Aram Saroyan combines Minimal and *Conceptual Art* theories:

aaple

The word itself, isolated from context, is not static or inscrutable, but demonstrates a transformational process based on the word "apple." The humor of the poem is in the fusion of language as "food for thought," and the fact that as the reader "digests" the word, a bite has been taken out of the object. Additionally, the pronunciation of the word physically makes the reader's mouth receptive to biting into an apple. See FOUND ART, FOUND POEM, and POP ART.

Minnesinger /min'ə-/ (German for "singer of love") a member of a group of 12th-to-14th century German poets who wrote love poems. Known as *German troubadours*, the most famous of the group is Walter von der Vogelweide. Longfellow wrote of them, "Round the Gothic spire, Screamed the feathered Minnesingers."

minstrel (from Old French for "official, servant, musician") originally, an entertainer or musician paid by patrons or royalty to perform on occasion. In medieval Europe (13th to 15th century), the itinerant m. recited poems or stories while accompanying himself on an instrument, and he often served as a clearing house for the news of the day. Forms such as the CHANSON DE GESTE, the LYRIC, the AUBADE, the MADRIGAL, and the *minstrel romance* were performed. By the early 15th century, the increase in literacy due to the advent of printing (ca. 1430) made the minstrel's primary function, that of mnemonic recitation, obsolete although the institution still exists today in the evolved form of the street poet and folksinger. The figure of the m. was ennobled and romanticized by poets such as James Beattie (1735–1803), who wrote *The Minstrel*, a history of the m. written in Spenserian stanzas, and Sir Walter Scott (1771–1832), whose *Lay of the Last Minstrel* (1805) gained him his first reputation. See JONGLEUR, TROUBADOUR, and TROUVÈRE.

miscellanies an Elizabethan term for an ANTHOLOGY of verse by various authors. Richard Tottle's *Songs and Sonnets* (1557), usually known as *Tottle's Miscellany*, collected the major works of Wyatt and Surrey. Sometimes these poetical miscellanies exhibited elaborate titles, such as Richard Edwards' *The Paradise of Daynty Devises* (1576). Even though the poetical miscellanies often miscredited or slighted their authors by using only initials, it was through this vehicle that the best Elizabethan verse was published. Nowadays, the anthology is a staple of literature which, through discriminating selection of authors, periods, genres, styles, and themes, offers informative surveys of poetry. See *publishing formats* under *forms* in APPENDIX 1.

mixed figures mixed attributes in a figure of speech, or the fusion of two different figures of speech or sayings, such as "You can lead a horse to water, but a fool and his horse are soon parted," or "Once more at dawn I drive / The weary cattle of my soul to the mudholes of your eyes." See MALAPROPISM, MIXED METAPHOR, and SPOONERISM. See also *defects in control* in APPENDIX 1.

mixed message a defect in writing due to lack of focus in the control of a poem's composition. This defect usually creates a confused or unproductive AMBIGUITY in a poem's thematic statement. The m.m. is not to be confused with transformational poetry which purposefully creates smoothly developed changes in tone, plot, and theme. See *defects in control* in APPENDIX 1.

mixed metaphor or **confused metaphor** the mixing of incongruous or illogically connected metaphors (see MIXED FIGURES), or the clashing of attributes between the tenor and vehicle within a single metaphor. For a fuller discussion, see METAPHOR. See also *defects in control* in APPENDIX 1.

mnemonic device (*mnemonic*, from Greek for "mindful, remembering") any poetic or rhetorical element of GENRE, STRUCTURE, PROSODY, AESTHETIC SURFACE, etc., that aids in memorizing a verse or poem. Specifically, the conventions of REFRAIN, METER, RHYME, TYPOGRAPHICAL ARRANGEMENT, PLOT, etc., can be employed as m.d. Their use was particularly necessary to cultures dependent upon oral literature whose function it was to pass on instruction or information through the recounting of myths, history, religious beliefs, and morality. See *mnemonic devices* in APPENDIX 1. See also ORAL POETRY.

mock epic (*mock*, from Old French for "deride"; also referred to by the adjectival phrase "mock heroic") a long, narrative verse on a trivial subject written in an elevated style and using the conventions of the EPIC genre (INVOCATION, EPIC SIMILE, CATALOGUE VERSE, macrocosmic setting, historical allusions, etc.). The purpose of the form is to deride a subject by overdignifying its presentation. For instance, Pope's heroic-comical poem, *The Rape of the Lock* (1712), tries to mitigate an intense family feud ignited by the unwarranted cutting of a lock of Miss Arabella Fermor's hair by mocking the event. The Greek *Batrachomyomachia* ("battle of frogs and mice") is probably the earliest model for the style. Other well-known mock epics include Chaucer's *The Nun's Priest's Tale*, Dryden's *Macflecknoe*, Pope's *Dunciad*, Swift's satiric prose, and various works by Kenneth Koch. See BURLESQUE, PARODY, SATIRE, and TRAVESTY.

Modern Period (*modern*, from Latin for "just now") a period commonly thought to begin with World War I (1914), offering a dazzling array of invention in both English and American literature and criticism. The genealogy of American poetry in this period is usually said to begin with Ezra Pound, but critics and poets often cite Walt Whitman and Emily Dickinson as precursors of the experimental modern modes. Major British and American poets of the period include Yeats, Frost, Eliot, Pound, Stevens, Auden, Lowell, Thomas, Graves, and critics such as I.A. Richards, F.R. Leavis, Lionel Trilling, the *New Critics*, and, again, T.S. Eliot. For topics germane to the period, see CHICAGO CRITICS, CINEMATIC TECHNIQUES, COLLECTIVE UNCONSCIOUS, CONFESSIONAL POETRY, CONTEXTUALISM, CRITICISM, DISSOCIATION OF SENSIBILITY, DISTANCE AND INVOLVEMENT, FREE ASSOCIATION, FREE VERSE, FUGITIVES, IMAGISM, IRONY, OBJECTIVE CORRELATIVE, OPEN FIELD COMPOSITION, ORGANIC COMPOSITION, POSTMODERNISTS, REALISM, SENTENCE SOUNDS, STRUCTURALISM, TENOR AND VEHICLE, and VORTICISM.

monody /mon'-/ (from Greek for "singing alone") originally a lyric ODE sung by a single performer, as opposed to lyrics sung by a *chorus*. The form was also often used by Greek poets in performing the funeral DIRGE. In terms of form, the m. is composed of identically structured strophes. Milton's *Lycidas*, and Matthew Arnold's *Thyrsis*, commemorating his poet-friend Arthur Hugh Clough, are well-known examples of this lyric LAMENT. See THRENODY. See also *forms* in APPENDIX 1.

monologue (from Greek for "speaking alone") a speech in verse or prose uttered by one speaker as part of a larger work or as an independent work in itself. Eliot's *The Lovesong of J. Alfred Prufrock* is an INTERIOR M. which exposes Prufrock's psychology; the Bible often uses monologues, such as Jeremiah's LAMENT over Jerusalem. Browning's *My Last Duchess* and other pieces repopularized the form for 20th-century poets such as Pound, Eliot, and Frost. See DRAMATIC MONOLOGUE, LOGORRHEA, SOLILOQUY, and STREAM-OF-CONSCIOUSNESS.

monometer /mənom'ətər/ (from Greek for "one measure"; also called "monopody /mə'nop'ə·dē/") a line of verse composed of one FOOT in ACCENTUAL-SYLLABIC VERSE (see METER and SCANSION). In Greek Classical prosody, which often measures more than one foot in a meter (see METRON), the m. could be made up of several feet. Although the meter is not common in English verse (see AMPHIMACER), one of the most famous examples is Robert Herrick's *The Bridegroom; Upon His Departure Hence.* See DIPODY and DISEMIC. See also *forms* in APPENDIX 1.

monorhyme (from Greek for "one rhyme") lines of verse that share the same rhyme. The device is often used for satirical or comic effect. Although this type of rhyme is rare in English poetry, it is common in the more highly inflected Romance and Slavic languages which display a multitude of words ending in the same suffix. St. Augustine wrote a PSALM of 288 lines ending on *e* or *ae* rhymes. See RHYME.

monostich /mon'əstik/ (from Greek for "one line of verse") a one-line stanza, poem, or EPIGRAM. As a form, the m. calls for succinctness, grace, thrust, and penetration. See *forms* in APPENDIX 1.

monostrophe /mon'əstrōfē/ or /mənos'trōfē/ or /mon'əstrōf/ (from Greek for "one stanza") a poem consisting of one stanza, or a poem composed of metrically identical stanzas, such as the HEROIC COUPLET, LAI, OTTAVA RIMA, and PANTOUM. See also *forms* in APPENDIX 1.

monosyllabics /-lab'-/ (from Greek for "one syllable") words or lines consisting of one syllable, as in Robert Lax's poem *Novel/*. The term is also used to refer to poems that use many one-syllable words for emphasis and pacing, and it stands opposite the term POLYSYLLABICS. See also *forms* in APPENDIX 1.

montage /montäzh'/ (French for "a mounting"; borrowed from the film term *thematic montage*; see CINEMATIC TECHNIQUES) a technique in which disparate images, references, or levels of thought are brought into a coherent and unified whole. The device of the INTERIOR MONOLOGUE, as used in John Ashbery's poetry, and the concept of SYNCHRONICITY, as seen in Ezra Pound's *Cantos* and Frank O'Hara's Cubist constructions, are strategies of the m. Robert Francis' *Silent Poem* offers a "patchwork quilt" of "fragmented surfaces" held together by sound, emotional thrust, and setting:

backroad	leafmold	stonewall	chipmunk
underbrush	grapevine	woodchuck	shadblow
woodsmoke	cowbarn	honeysuckle	woodpile
sawhorse	bucksaw	outhouse	wellsweep
backdoor	flagstone	bulkhead	buttermilk
candlestick	ragrug	firedog	brownbread
hilltop	outcrop	cowbell	buttercup
whetstone	thunderstorm	pitchfork	steeplebush
gristmill	millstone	cornmeal	waterwheel
watercress	buckwheat	firefly	jewelweed
gravestone	groundpine	windbreak	bedrock
weathercock	snowfall	starlight	cockcrow

See COLLAGE and IMPRESSIONISM. See also *forms* in APPENDIX 1.

mood the ATMOSPHERE prevailing in a piece of literature. Elements such as TONE, SETTING, THEME, VOICE, and STYLE combine to create the general m. of a poem. For example, in many of the poems and short stories of E.A. Poe, the m. is gloomy; in many of the poems of Southey, Spenser, Lovelace, and Herrick, the m. is bright and lively. See CONTROLLING IMAGE, DOMINANT IMPRESSION, and LOCATION.

mood piece a poem in which the main intention is to effect a MOOD or general emotional feeling. As a technique of composition attempting to evoke, as music does, a special moment or emotion, the focus of the poem must not wander undirected or it will be considered a defect in composition. For other problems in control, see BURIED THEME, DIGRESSION, DISTRACTING DETAILS, EDITORIAL INTRUSION, MIXED MESSAGE, OVERDECORATION, OVER-REPETITION, OVERWRITING, and STRAIN BEHIND THE POEM. See also *defects in control* in APPENDIX 1.

mora (Latin for "delay") in Greek Classical prosody the unit of duration of a short syllable diacritically marked by a BREVE (-). The *morae* (that is, two *mora*) is the Greek QUANTITATIVE METER term for a long syllable marked by a MACRON (-). These durational time units, in which two short syllables are equal to one long syllable, are parallel to the accent marks in English stress prosody. See DIPODY, DISEMIC, METER, and METRON.

moral criticism or ethical criticism a type of CRITICISM that sees the value related in a work as instructive to the reader. Traditionally, poetry is said to inspire people to virtuous action by representing the beauty of virtue. Virgil, e.g., saw the EPIC genre as a potential lesson in ethics and politics. This critical viewpoint is the exact opposite of that taken by AESTHETICISM. See PRAGMATIC THEORY OF ART. See also *criticism* in APPENDIX 1.

morpheme /môr′fēm/ (from Greek for "form, shape") the smallest unit of meaning in language. It may range from a letter showing negativity ("*amoral*") or plurality ("boy*s*") to prefixes, suffixes, root words ("child," "pin," etc.), and even to accents that determine the grammatical function of a word ("cóntent," a noun; "conteńt," a verb or adjective). Any word is composed of one or several morphemes. The term differs from *allomorph*, which shows the transformational character of words ("sleep, slept"). The m. in semantics is parallel to the function of the PHONEME, the smallest meaningful unit of sound in language.

motif /mōtēf'/ (from Latin for "to move"; also called "topos") a theme, device, event, or character that is developed through nuance and repetition in a work. Classic motifs include the "UBI SUNT" FORMULA, which laments the passing of something or someone, and the CARPE DIEM m., which exhorts one to "seize the day." STOCK CHARACTER motifs include MILES GLORIOSUS (the braggart soldier), the pauper-turned-prince, and the ugly-girl-turned-princess. As a design element, the m. may appear as a repeating statement. According to Cleanth Brooks (*The Well-Wrought Urn*, 1947), all literature of any import contains an identifiable m. See LEITMOTIF and THEME.

movement a group of writers sharing the same aesthetics, techniques, style, or period, such as the SYMBOLISTS, the POST-MODERNISTS, and the Romantics (see ROMANTICISM). The term also refers to the development of PLOT or the separate events within a plot, or the relative strength in dramatic action or narrative; and it is also applied to the viewer's angle of vision or m. relative to the scene being viewed, as in PAN, *zoom-in*, or *zoom-out* (see CINEMATIC TECHNIQUES). See MOVING SHOT and NARRATION.

moves a contemporary poetry-workshop term borrowed from sports to indicate loosely the tactics and techniques within a poem's development. LEAP, JUXTAPOSITION, transformational LINE ENDING, etc., are all metaphorically referred to as moves. See INTELLIGENCE and STRATEGY.

moving shot (see CINEMATIC TECHNIQUES) a term borrowed from cinema indicating the camera MOVEMENT (viewer's speed and direction) toward or away from the action in a scene. See also *cinematic terms* in APPENDIX 1.

multeity /-tē'itē/ (from Latin for "much, many") Coleridge's literary term (*Biographia Literaria*, 1847) referring to the complex of CONNOTATION and DENOTATION within a single, harmonized work of literature. Contemporary use of the term more specifically refers to purposefully disparate images, tones, and levels of thought within a unified work, as in the poetry of Pablo Neruda, Allen Ginsberg, and John Ashbery, among others. See COLLAGE and MONTAGE. See also *meaning* in APPENDIX 1.

multiple meanings: See AMBIGUITY.

multiple rhyme or polysyllabic rhyme a rhyme of three or more syllables. The device is used more commonly in romance languages than in English although Lord Bryon used it comically in *Don Juan*:

> But—Oh! ye lords of ladies *intellectual*,
> Inform us truly, have they not *hen-pecked you all*?

See MONORHYME, RHYME, and TRIPLE RHYME.

muses (from the Greek *Muses*, whose name may have been derived from a word meaning "to remember") originally, the nine daughters of Zeus who were thought to have lived on the peak of Mt. Pieria near Mt. Olympus in Greece, and who later were said to reign over particular arts and sciences: *Calliope* (chief among them), muse of epic poetry; *Clio*, muse of history; *Erato*, muse of love poetry; *Euterpe*, muse of lyric poetry; *Melpomene*, muse of tragedy; *Polyhymnia*, muse of songs to gods; *Terpsichore*, muse of music and dance; *Thalia*, muse of comedy; and *Urania*, muse of astronomy. INVOCATION to a particular muse was ceremonially performed in longer works, such as epics, to enlist her aid; writers including Milton, Spenser, Sidney, Gray, Homer, and Shakespeare have used the device, and it has held the title to books on poetics by Robert Graves (*The White Goddess*, 1948) and Wallace Stevens (*The Necessary Angel*, 1951). In modern times, the muse tends to refer to the force that inspires a poet. See DIVINE AFFLATUS, DUENDE, INSPIRATION, and PEGASUS.

musical scansion (see SCANSION) a specific system of analysis, borrowed from musical notation, that takes into consideration the relative PITCH and DURATION of syllables in a poem. See METER. See also *melopoetics* in APPENDIX 1.

mycterismus (from Greek for "to sneer at") a rhetorical figure of emotion in which the speaker replies to a remark with a mocking, scowling tone. See PATHOPOEIA. See *figures of pathos* in APPENDIX 2.

mysticism (from Greek for "to initiate into religious rites") a particular mode of mental perception that lies beyond the range of normal processes of reason, and one that is so subjective in nature that it cannot be objectively tested or analyzed. The language of m. is usually metaphorical or symbolic, leaving only general impressions in the mind of one who has not experienced such insight or vision into the workings of nature and the cosmos. But poets throughout recorded history have expressed their understanding of the phenomenon, and great works from Herbert, Crashaw, Cowper, Wordsworth, Shelley, Blake, Coleridge, Emerson, Thoreau, and Whitman are embedded in this religious matrix. For a detailed analysis of the mystical experience revealed in the work of Whitman, see Malcolm Cowley's introduction to *Leaves of Grass*, 1976. See VISION.

myth (from Greek *mythos*, "for story" [of true or false nature]) a supernatural narrative of unknown authorship that seeks to hand down an explanation of natural events such as death, geological occurrences, and the creation of the universe. The term also refers the beliefs of a homogeneous people about their origin, history, and fears and the existence of natural phenomena. In the late Classical period, the m. was not thought to be a true recounting of events but rather an inventive, symbolic means of expressing phenomena and ideas, as in Plato's philosophical musings in the *Myth of Er* (*The Republic*, Book X). The oracular form of the m. engendered smaller types of literature such as the LEGEND, the FOLK TALE, the FAIRY TALE, the PARABLE, and the APHORISM.

The term also refers to types of plots or motifs in literature: the initiation, the quest, the rite of passage, etc., and to whole tonal genres (COMEDY, TRAGEDY, and SATIRE) that are said to be derived from myths about the seasons and used as weapons against foes or used as instruments of instruction.

In modern times, the development of psychology brought a new dimension to the ancient form of m. Freud, who did so much to uncover the meaning of dreams and the irrational, interprets myths in a metaphorical or symbolic way. His disciple Carl Jung, who pointed out the literalness of the imagination, suggests that what is unearthed in a m. stands for innate shared experiences that are part of our COLLECTIVE UNCONSCIOUS. He defined the term by saying: "... all human beings possess similar inborn tendencies to form certain general symbols, and ... these symbols manifest themselves through the unconscious mind in myths, dreams, delusion, and folklore." Jung called these symbols archetypes (see ARCHETYPE). But there are other theorists who see the images of the sun, the sea, an old man, a virgin, etc., not as genetically transmitted engrams, but as experiences that every human undergoes as he or she grows up. While some m. scholars argue that the narrative of a m. is more important than its accompanying ritual, others, such as the Structuralist Lévi-Strauss (see STRUCTURALISM), subsume content to form and interpret the relationship of episodes to one another and the dynamics between characters as more meaningful than what is actually being said in the m. And still other theorists see m. as a form of symbolic communication; and these adherents, in turn, are countered by arguments that the m. is not a symbol but the thing itself. There is no definite consensus as to what a m. is, what it contains, nor how to interpret it. Yet despite the ravages of intense analysis, myths have survived as a form of human expression and, indeed, are still being created. By this fact alone, we know that they are vital in pointing out the origin, state of being, and destiny of a culture, and that they are created, as the best art is created, out of need. They are not merely products of fantasy; they are acts of IMAGINATION.

Myths have gone through three general stages of evolution. In the distant past of Neolithic man, the myths of primitive societies tended to reflect in a literal sense the society from which they arose. In the Iron and Bronze Ages, they began to take on an allegorical and symbolic form. The familiar Greek Homeric and Roman myths are examples of this kind of story which began to turn away from experience itself and reorient mythic expression toward rational and poetic modes of thinking. The final stage of m.-making involved creating myths as pure symbolic language. Out of this conceptualization of experience-as-symbol came philosophy and science—the speculative and pragmatic branches of human thought that reflect our outer and inner worlds. While primitive man interpreted the chaotic appearance of the world in literal and exaggerated terms, philosophy and science assumed there was a rational and ordered INSCAPE behind the surface randomness of reality. It is by their persistent, and in some cases triumphant, inquiries that the old order of myths has fallen.

Some characteristics of m. can be generally stated. The speculative and explanatory myths about how the natural world was organized (the Egyptian Sun religion) or how man came to be (Genesis) usually aimed to fix the fleeting and indiscernable present to a traditional and comprehensible past. Myths such as hymns and prayers rehearsed the origins of man and praised a higher authority so that man would remain in favor with his God or gods. Other myths are cathartic. They help purge man of individual or collective mental and physical ills, prepare him for challenges ahead, or keep the group intact. They are, ultimately, finalized forms of language and ritual that reflect the emotions, structure, morality, and actions of a culture.

But modern man has been left with the debris of outmoded mythologies and images. The Classical myths do not seem germane to our needs. So myths are being created by writers to express the isolation and disjointedness of society. They are efforts to explain, enforce, discover, or change modern man's ideology. They may take the form of moral allegories on the nature of the world or the world of nature; they may externalize archetypal, universal responses in our psyche; they may be the vehicle for religious or philosophical insights; or they may simply exist to instruct or entertain. The ceremonies of birth, initiation, marriage, installment, passage, and burial are old themes dressed in new forms. The new myths seek, as the old ones did, to raise our social, political, spiritual, and intellectual consciousness by allegorizing the tribe's history. But what is new in this abstracting of human behavior is the exteriorizing of personal mythic structures by writers who have created their own sense of personal history and identity, not by choice, but because they were born into a society that has not supplied the nourishing matrix of mythological structures. These writers are recapitulating the ancient and basic function of the shaman/poet, to create once again common terms of understanding that form the substructure of culture.

There are many artificial systems of m. classification. Some are organized by subject matter, some by theme, some by function or use, some by ethnic and geographical origin. James G. Frazer's poetic and classic text on myths, *The Golden Bough*, contains over 160 myths grouped according to major figures, themes, genres, and rituals. Apparently, the literature is too sprawling to yield an inherent organic order. For our purposes in poetry, the authors have limited the categories to mythic poems that demonstrate a strong sense of LOCATION, a term that can be defined as the anchoring level of a poem. These groups include poems arising from the areas of personal, religious, social, political, archetypal, natural, and ritual concerns. They form a natural hierarchy but are not meant to be either all-embracing or definitive categories.

The Personal Myth
This kind of m. is a self-portrait that reflects the writer's self-image and his or her relationship to the outside world. It is exemplified by Anne Sexton's *Self in 1958*: She is the one who is unreal, who can't feel, and who can be bought in any dimestore. From her self-deprecating doll metaphor, her world becomes transformed into a cardboard setting, outside of which flesh-and-blood people determine her fate. The poem begins:

What is reality?
I am a plaster doll; I pose
with eyes that cut open without landfall or nightfall
upon some shellacked and grinning person,
eyes that open, blue, steel, and close.
Am I approximately an I. Magnin transplant?
I have hair, black angel,
black-angel-stuffing to comb,
nylon legs, luminous arms
and some advertised clothes.

The Spiritual Myth

An example can be found in Yehuda Amichai's *King Saul and I,* where he rehearses in an almost hymnal form both the greatness of the Old Testament's King Saul and the smallness of his own life in comparison to that of Saul. Although the exaggerated descriptions of Saul belittle Amichai's speaker, we sense, when looking behind the poem to discover its motivation, that at one time the speaker thought he had possessed at least the possibility of being as great as Saul. The strategy of the poem is to parallel the speaker's character and actions with Saul's.

1
They gave him a finger, but he took the whole hand
They gave me the whole hand: I didn't even take the little finger.

While my heart
Was weightlifting its first feelings
He rehearsed the tearing of oxen.

My pulse-beats were like
Drips from a tap
His pulse-beats
Pounded like hammers on a new building.

He was my big brother
I got used to his clothes.

2
His head, like a compass, will always bring him
To the sure north of his future.

His heart is set, like an alarm clock
For the hour of his reign.
When everyone's asleep, he will cry out
Until all the quarries are hoarse.
Nobody will stop him!
Only the asses bear their yellow teeth
At the end.

3
Dead prophets turned time-wheels
When he went out searching for asses
Which I, now, have found.
But I don't know how to handle them.
They kick me.

I was raised with the straw,
I fell with heavy seeds.
But he breathed the winds of this histories.
He was anointed with the royal oil
As with wrestler's grease.

He battled with olive trees
Forcing them to kneel.

Roots bulged on the earth's forehead
With the strain.
The prophets escaped from the arena;
Only God remained, counting:
Seven ... eight ... nine ... ten ...
The people, from his shoulders downwards, rejoiced.
Not a man stood up.
He had won.

The Social Myth

Philip Larkin's ironic treatment of contemporary social appearances leads him to expose the social myths of his youth, and the delusions of middle age. The poem, which may have been triggered by envy of the current sexual revolution, achieves a transcendent experience of release when Larkin's speaker comes to an understanding of the natural social history of the youthful and aging groups he is comparing. The term "progress" in that sense is illusory:

High Windows
When I see a couple of kids
And guess he's fucking her and she's
Taking pills or wearing a diaphram,
I know this is paradise

Everyone old has dreamed of all their lives—
Bonds and gestures pushed to one side
Like an outdated combine harvester,
And everyone young going down the long slide

To happiness, endlessly, I wonder if
Anyone looked at me, forty years back,
And thought, *That'll be the life*;
No God any more, or sweating in the dark

About Hell and that, or having to hide
What you think of the priest. He
And his lot will all go down the long slide
Like free bloody birds. And immediately

Rather than words comes the thought of high windows:
The sun-comprehending glass,
And beyond it, the deep blue air, that shows
Nothing, and is nowhere, and is endless.

The Political Myth

Denise Levertov's scathing understatement for the American imposition in Vietnam mythologizes the Vietnamese way of life. Her last answer as to whether or not the Vietnamese speech was like singing ("It is silent now") reinforces the power of the m. she has built:

What Were They Like?
1) Did the people of Viet Nam
   use lanterns of stone?
2) Did they hold ceremonies
   to reverence the opening of buds?
3) Were they inclined to quiet laughter?

4) Did they use bone and ivory,
  jade and silver, for ornament?
5) Had they an epic poem?
6) Did they distinguish between speech and singing?

1) Sir, their light hearts turned to stone.
  It is not remembered whether in gardens
  stone lanterns illumined pleasant ways.
2) Perhaps they gathered once to delight in blossom,
  but after the children were killed
  there were no more buds.
3) Sir, laughter is bitter to the burned mouth.
4) A dream ago, perhaps. Ornament is for joy.
  All the bones were charred.
5) It is not remembered. Remember,
  most were peasants; their life
  was in rice and bamboo.
  When peaceful clouds were reflected in the paddies
  and the water buffalo stepped surely along the terraces,
  maybe fathers told their sons old tales.
  When bombs smashed those mirrors
  there was time only to scream.
6) There is an echo yet
  of their speech which was like a song.
  It was reported their singing resembled
  the flight of moths in moonlight.
  Who can say? It is silent now.

Rites of Initiation

Cesare Pavese's poem *Atavism* externalizes the sexual fears that a young boy must overcome in order to pass into manhood. Behind the seemingly simple façade of the poem's plot is the ancient theme of ceremonial possession of one's sexual identity and place in nature. The poem ends:

> People with bodies shouldn't hide them. But the boy
> isn't sure that everyone has a body. The grizzled
> old man who went by that morning is too pale and pitiful
> to have a body, to have anything as scary
> as a body. And not even grown-ups are naked;
> not even mothers who give their breasts to their babies
> are really bare. Only boys have bodies.
>
> The boy is afraid to look at himself in the dark,
> but he knows for a fact his body must soak up the sun
> and get used to the sky, before he can be a man.

The Nature Myth

William Stafford's *The Animal That Drank Up Sound* invents a mythological structure based on the lack of atmosphere and sound on the moon.

> 1
> One day across the lake where echoes come now
> an animal that needed sound came down. He gazed
> enormously, and instead of making any, he took
> away from, sound: the lake and all the land
> went dumb. A fish that jumped went back like a knife,
> and the water died. In all the wilderness around he
> drained the rustle from the leaves into the mountainside
> and folded a quilt over the rocks, getting ready
> to store everything the place had known; he buried—

thousands of autumns deep—the noise that used to come there.
Then that animal wandered on and began to drink
the sound out of all the valleys—the croak of toads,
and all the little shiny noise grass blades make.
He drank till winter, and then looked out one night
at the stilled places guaranteed around by frozen
peaks and held in the shallow pools of starlight.
It was finally tall and still, and he stopped on the highest
ridge, just where the cold sky fell away
like a perpetual curve, and from there he walked on silently,
and began to starve.

When the moon drifted over that night the whole world lay
just like the moon, shining back that still
silver, and the moon saw its own animal dead
on the snow, its dark absorbent paws and quiet
muzzle, and thick, velvet, deep fur.

2
After the animal that drank sound died, the world
lay still and cold for months, and the moon yearned
and explored, letting its dead light float down
the west walls of canyons and then climb its delighted
soundless way up the east side. The moon
owned the earth its animal had faithfully explored.
The sun disregarded the life it used to warm.
But on the north side of a mountain, deep in some rocks,
a cricket slept. It had been hiding when that animal
passed, and as spring came again this cricket waited,
afraid to crawl out into the heavy stillness.
Think how deep the cricket felt, lost there
in such a silence—the grass, the leaves, the water,
the stilled animals all depending on such a little
thing. But softly it tried—"Cricket!"—and back like a
river from that one act flowed the kind of world we know,
first whisperings, then moves in the grass and leaves;
the water splashed, and a big night bird screamed.

It all returned, our precious world with its life and sound,
where sometimes loud over the hill the moon,
wild again, looks for its animal to roam, still,
down out of the hills, any time.
But somewhere a cricket waits.

It listens now, and practices at night.

See ARCHETYPAL MYTH, MYSTICISM, *mythic criticism* under CRITICISM,
MYTHOPOEIA, and NARRATION.

myth criticism a system of literary analysis that evaluates, interprets, and
categorizes a work according to its symbolic narrative structure and
elements. Major texts representing this type of writing include James
Frazer's *The Golden Bough* (1890–1936, 12 vols. and supplement) and
Northrop Frye's *Anatomy of Criticism* (1957). See ARCHETYPE, CRITICISM,
MYTH, and MYTHOPOEIA. See also *criticism* in APPENDIX 1.

mythopoeia /-pē′ə/ (Greek for "making of myths") a type of writing that
employs myth for structural and interpretive reasons, as in the poetry of
Blake, Yeats, Joyce, and Eliot, and in the fiction of Melville and Faulkner.
See MYTH and MYTH CRITICISM. See also *forms* in APPENDIX 1.

N

narration (from Latin for "to relate, to recount"; also called "narrative") a rhetorical mode that consists of a telling of events linked by a cause-and-effect relationship. For instance, E.M. Forster's famous paradigm "The King died, then the Queen died" does not constitute n. since there is no cause-and-effect relationship between the actions. However, "The King died, then the Queen died *of grief*" constitutes a true PLOT since the second action is caused by the first action. In literature, the following forms depend on n.: *anecdote*, EPIC, EXEMPLUM, FABLE, FABLIAU, *fairy tale*, FOLK TALE, LEGEND, METRICAL ROMANCE, MYTH, *novel*, *short story*, and TALE. In modern rhetoric, n. represents one of the four types of rhetorical modes, the other three being *argumentation, description,* and *exposition.* For other terms related to n., see ANAGOGICAL VISION, ANTECEDENT ACTION, CARPE DIEM, CHARACTERIZATION, CINEMATIC TECHNIQUES, CONFLICT, DIALECTIC, DOMINANT IMPRESSION, DRAMATIC SITUATION, EPISODIC STRUCTURE, FRAME STORY, GENERATIVE CONTENT, IN MEDIAS RES, LEITMOTIF, MOOD, MOTIF, NARRATIVE HOOK, NARRATIVE POEM, NARRATOR AGENT, OBLIGATORY SCENE, POINT OF VIEW, PSYCHIC DISTANCE, SETTING, SPEAKER, STOCK CHARACTER, STORY-WITHIN-A-STORY, SUBPLOT, SUB-THEME, TONE COLOR, and TRANSITION.

narrative hook a device intended to arouse the reader's interest, such as IN MEDIAS RES, PARADOX, EPIGRAPH, heightened action, DRAMATIC SITUATION, or dramatic statement. In Russell Edson's fables, the first sentences often pose an absurd or unusual situation which creates anticipation in the reader. Consider the following narrative hooks that begin Edson's works: "Some coffee had gotten on a man's ape." "His daughter had broken." "A man had a son who was an anvil." "Grandpa had invented how to make artificial grandpas." And "A man splits into two who are an old woman and an old man." See NARRATION.

narrative poem a nondramatic poem that tells a story. See ART BALLAD, ART EPIC, AUBADE, BALLAD, BEAST EPIC, BOASTING POEM, CHANSON DE GESTE, DOMESTIC POETRY, DREAM ALLEGORY, DREAM POETRY, EPIC, EXEMPLUM, FABLE, FABLIAU, FOLK BALLAD, FOLK EPIC, FOLK SONG, FOLK TALE, FRAME STORY, GENRE, IN MEDIAS RES, LEGEND, LEITMOTIF, LYRIC, METRICAL ROMANCE, MOCK EPIC, MYTH, NARRATION, NARRATIVE HOOK, NARRATOR AGENT, ODE, PARABLE, PASTORAL, PASTORAL ELEGY, POPULAR BALLAD, PROSE POEM, ROMANTIC EPIC, STORY-WITHIN-A-STORY, SYMBOLIC NARRATIVE, THEMATIC MONTAGE, and THEMATIC STRUCTURE.

narrator agent a character assigned by an author to speak for him. There may be an OMNISCIENT POINT OF VIEW organizing the FRAME of a story or poem, but within this structure various characters may extend or multiply the viewpoint (see POINT OF VIEW) so that a feeling of SYNCHRONICITY is achieved. In the Japanese film *Rashomon* several different characters relate their versions of the same incident, each according to the dictates of his own prejudice, so that the final truth can be interpolated by the reader. See NARRATION, NARRATIVE HOOK, and *view* under CINEMATIC TECHNIQUES.

Naturalism a deterministic MOVEMENT in 19th-century artistic theory that considers natural causes the author of "all movements of mind and matter." Emile Zola's *Roman expérimental* sets forth the tenets of N. in recommending that the writer investigate social reality, as a scientist would investigate phenomena in order to promote change and progress; thus the link between N. and socialistic theories. Zola's aesthetics, designed to apply to the novel, were also applied to poetry (*Les Poètes contemporains*, 1878). His ideas were considered radical, especially in that he dared poets to cast aside all conventions. In the 1880s of Germany, N. designated a particular school of poetry. Karl Henckell's anthology *Dichtercharaktere* (1884) tries to find characteristic images of social struggle in the work of German poets. Arno Holz and Richard Dehmel are the two most important poets in the German N. movement.

nature myth (see MYTH) a supernatural story explaining the existence of a natural phenomenon or event. See *forms* in APPENDIX 1.

near rhyme: See OFF-RHYME.

negative capability a phrase used by Keats in a letter to his brothers (December 21, 1817) referring to the ability of a poet to receive truth and beauty passively. He maintained that the poet must be "capable of being in uncertainties, Mysteries, doubts, without any irritable reaching after fact and reason." Keats affirmed the autonomy and integrity of poetry whose highest aim is to express beauty and discard lesser forms of knowledge: ". . . with a great poet the sense of Beauty overcomes every other consideration. . . ." His famous maxim as to the nature of the poet expresses the sympathetic relationship between the artist and his work: "If poetry comes not as naturally as leaves to a tree it had better not come at all." The phrase n.c. has come to stand for a writer's objectivity, that is, an attitude of accepting whatever may be received while in a state of intense, heightened awareness. See AESTHETIC DISTANCE and OBJECTIVE CORRELATIVE.

negative image an image that is not explicitly presented, but indirectly discussed or referred to, as the image of the gift in Sylvia Plath's *A Birthday Present*. See IMAGE, IMAGERY, SUBSTITUTE IMAGE, and *subtractive metaphor* under METAPHOR.

Neo-Classicism 17th- and 18th-century revival of Greek and especially Latin stylistic qualities of balance, decorum, polish, thoroughness, and accuracy, as espoused in Horace's *Ars Poetica*. The N.-C. aesthetic holds that poetry should focus on social man as its subject; it should be written in strict forms such as the CLOSED COUPLET; and it should be used to instruct and delight—a set of poetics radically different from those of ROMANTICISM and the tenets of AESTHETICISM (see ARS GRATIA ARTIS). The school's major writers include Dryden, Pope, Addison, Johnson, Goldsmith, and Swift. Although their ideas on art included an escape valve for writers of "natural genius" (Shakespeare and Homer), they tended to see man as limited and thus having to work within FIXED FORMS (the HEROIC COUPLET, for example) which sought a perfect expression of man's state. The term N.-C. has also come to mean any reconstitution or renewal of an earlier style. The period is usually divided into three ages: the RESTORATION age (1660–1700), the AUGUSTAN AGE, sometimes called the Age of Pope (1700–45), and the AGE OF SENSIBILITY, sometimes called the Age of Johnson (1745–98). See CLASSICAL POETICS and PERIODS OF ENGLISH LITERATURE.

neologism /nē·ol′-/ (from Greek for "new word") a word or doctrine newly created, often by a known author. Writers of the Renaissance, depending on Greek or Latin root words, added many new words to the English language in a conscious effort to enrich it. Milton is credited with being the greatest inventor of neologisms. Modern examples include Hopkins, Hart Crane, and, most of all, Ezra Pound who used Greek terminology to express ideas of the Imagist movement. And, of course, modern science has invented a plethora of new terms to express ideas, functions, and names in its ongoing discipline. Overuse of the device leads to OBSCURITY and pendantry. See EUPHUISM, GONGORISM, KENNING, and PORTMANTEAU. See also *devices of poetic license* in APPENDIX 2, and *diction* in APPENDIX 1.

New Criticism a school of CRITICISM whose adherents included Allen Tate, Robert Penn Warren, Yvor Winters, W.K. Wimsatt, Jr., Kenneth Burke, and John Crowe Ransom, all associated with Vanderbilt University. Ransom coined the term (*New Criticism*, 1941), which called for the aesthetic evaluation and interpretation of poetry to be based upon close reading of the text and its surface complications rather than making judgments dependent upon peripheral social, biographical, or historical contexts (see PRAGMATIC THEORY OF ART). This principle of a work's autonomy (see AESTHETICISM) led to a highly developed system of poetic EXPLICATION, and a loosely organized set of guiding principles put forth by critics such as I.A. Richards (*Principles of Literary Criticism*, 1924; *Science and Poetry*, 1926) and William Empson (*Seven Types of Ambiguity*, 1930) which have influenced modern poetry and poetics. Other well-known critics and explicators such as R.P. Blackmur, Cleanth Brooks (*Understanding Poetry*, 1938, coedited with Robert Penn Warren), and Laurence Perrine (*Sound and Sense*, 1956) have systematically carried forward the practice of contemporary explication. The N.C. is best suited to the analysis of shorter, lyrical works rather than longer, dramatic or narrative verse; however, the long poems of T.S. Eliot lend themselves well to this type of objective critical view. See AFFECTIVE FALLACY, AMBIGUITY, AUTOTELIC, INTENTIONAL FALLACY, and OBJECTIVE THEORY OF ART. See also *criticism* in APPENDIX 1.

New York Poets a school of poetry, arising out of New York City in the 1950s, that included Frank O'Hara, Kenneth Koch, James Schuyler, and John Ashbery, who sought to break the strong influence of T.S. Eliot and Robert Lowell's Modernism by creating a more open, chaotic, and informal aesthetic. The N.Y.P. founded their various styles on the work and spirit of Whitman and William Carlos Williams who offered a more Americanized type of poetry. Frank O'Hara and John Ashbery's knowledge of contemporary painting techniques and styles informed their stance which reflected concepts from CUBISM, SURREALISM, CONTINUUM POETRY, and *Abstract Expressionism.* They produced a difficult and, at times, inaccessible poetry which was at odds with their contemporaries Robert Bly and James Wright, among others. But other movements such as the BEATS and the *Black Mountain School* paralleled their search for freer forms and more lively attitudes than those prevalent in the more formal, academic mode of the Modernists.

nocturne /nok'turn/ or /nokturn'/ (from Latin for "night") a song or poem expressing romantic and lyrical emotions evoked by nighttime moods. Gray's *Elegy Written in a Country Churchyard*, Sandburg's *Nocturne in a Deserted Brickyard*, and Coleridge's *The Nightingale* exemplify the genre. See AUBADE. See also *forms* in APPENDIX 1.

noema /nō·ē'mə/ (Greek for "the understanding") a rhetorical figure of expression categorized under "notation and conjugates" in which a jest, PUN, or RIDDLE lies in the DIALECTIC of a speech rather than in a single word or phrase; e.g., "If you are a stranger in a strange land, Sir, / Then you should feel you've come home at last." See *figures of notation and conjugation* in APPENDIX 2.

nom de plume /nomdəploom'/ or /nôN'dəplYm'/ (French for "pen name") the author's signed name when it is different than his true, given name. Writers, as well as actors, use pseudonyms to evoke CONNOTATION, to hide their sex, origin, or professional identity, or to dissociate their former views or style of writing from their newly evolved ideas. Famous examples include George Orwell (Eric Blair), Lewis Carroll (Charles Lutwidge Dodgson), and Voltaire (François Marie Arouet). (N.d.p. is now the term used in English; the term that the French prefer is *nom de guerre.*)

nonce word (*nonce*, from Middle English for "one [purpose, occasion, etc.]") a word or phrase coined for its use in a specific work or for a specific occasion. Lewis Carroll's *Jabberwocky* and James Joyce's *Finnigan's Wake* feature the device. See NEOLOGISM, NONSENSE VERSE, PORTMANTEAU, and TRANS-SENSE VERSE. See also *devices of poetic license* in APPENDIX 2, and *diction* in APPENDIX 1.

nonsense verse a form of LIGHT VERSE that is used to amuse or instruct (PARODY, SATIRE, etc.) through the creation of highly rhythmic, melopoetic, and onomatopoetic verse in which sense is subordinated to sound. Well-known practitioners include Edward Lear and Lewis Carroll whose *Jabberwocky* employs the technique brilliantly. See CLERIHEW, DOGGEREL,

JINGLE, LIMERICK, MACRONIC VERSE, NONCE WORD, NURSERY RHYME, OCCA-
SIONAL VERSE, PARODY, SKELTONIC VERSE, and TRANS-SENSE VERSE. See also
diction, humor, and *light verse* in APPENDIX 1.

novelty: See ORIGINALITY VS. N.

nuance /n(y)o͞o′äns/ or /nYäNs′/ (French for "shade of color") subtle
touches of description, gesture, dialogue, and connotative detail that
deepen and shade the meanings of a poem. See *meaning* in APPENDIX 1.

number (also called "numbers") a Renaissance term for poetry in general.
The term owes its origin to the harmonic nature of Classical verse and to
the fact that Classical prosody described poetry in strict terms of meter
and form. See METER and STRESS PROSODY.

nursery rhyme a children's verse form of highly mnemonic style used to
entertain and instruct. Some one-quarter to one-half of the extant nursery
rhymes are said to be at least 200 years old. Famous examples of English
nursery rhymes, once called *Tommy Thumb's Songs,* include *Humpty
Dumpty, This Little Piggy, Ride a Horse to Banbury Cross, Yankee Doodle
Went to Town,* and many others to be found in anthologies such as *Tommy
Thumb's Pretty Song Book* (1744) and *Mother Goose's Melody* (1765).
Material for the genre derives from oral folk forms, as well as religious
and secular events. Some nursery rhymes are of known authorship, e.g.,
Jane Taylor's *Twinkle, Twinkle Little Star* (18th century).

Poets, such as Anne Sexton, Sylvia Plath, and Elizabeth Bishop, have
modeled their serious work upon nursery rhymes in order to produce
aesthetic tension. For instance, Donald Justice's *Counting the Mad*
is based on the children's toe-counting game *This Little Piggy.* See
DOGGEREL, JINGLE, LIMERICK, NONSENSE VERSE, and TRANS-SENSE VERSE. See
also *humor* and *light verse* in APPENDIX 1.

O

objective correlative a term used by T.S. Eliot in his critical study of *Hamlet* (*Hamlet and His Problems*, 1919) in which he faulted the play for its unjustifiable use of emotions in relation to events surrounding them. He defined the term by saying: "When the external facts, which must terminate in sensory experience, are given, the emotion is immediately evoked." Other critics, especially the *New Critics*, have used the term to indicate a specific emotion evoked in a reader through a series of details, actions, or situations which are objectively presented. Originally, the term o.c. was used by Washington Allston (*Lectures on Art*, 1850) to describe how "the external world produces pleasurable emotion" on the part of the viewer. Eliot's theory of the o.c. has been debated widely. Critics of the device contend that emotion can't be created formulistically, and that an o.c. cannot be truly objective since its use and meaning are directly laden with emotion. The device has been widely applied by poets who prefer specificity and directness. See AESTHETIC DISTANCE, DISTANCE AND INVOLVEMENT, NEGATIVE CAPABILITY, and OBJECTIVITY VS. SUBJECTIVITY.

objective criticism a form of literary analysis and evaluation that bases its judgment of a work on factors that exclude the age in which the work is written, the life of its author, and other pragmatic considerations. See CRITICISM. See also *criticism* in APPENDIX 1.

Objective Theory of Art M.H. Abrams' term (in *The Mirror and the Lamp*, 1953) referring to the poem as an autonomous art object separate from the reality it describes. In this sense, neither the author's intentions nor his effect on his audience (see INTENTIONAL FALLACY and *expressive criticism* under CRITICISM), nor the style of the work, nor its social or historical matrix (see PRAGMATIC THEORY OF ART) affects the independent nature of the creation. See AUTOTELIC, NEW CRITICISM, OBJECTIVE CORRELATIVE, OBJECTIVISM, OBJECTIVITY VS. SUBJECTIVITY. See also *criticism* in APPENDIX 1.

Objectivism a school of poetry in the early 1930s that proposed that a poem be seen as an art object unrelated to considerations of theory, historical contexts, or authorial intention. The movement, never widely popular, included George Oppen, Louis Zukofsky, Charles Reznikoff, Lorine Niedecker, and William Carlos Williams. Their work was anthologized in *An Objectivist's Anthology* (1932), and it concentrated on the presentation of images, a method of composition succinctly expressed by Williams in his poem *A Sort of a Song* with "No ideas but in things." He maintained that an image or object should be selected for the statement that it makes by itself without editorial comment or intrusion by the author. His famous poem *The Red Wheelbarrow* highlights the aesthetic value of the object and is a precursor to SUPERREALISM. See AESTHETIC DISTANCE, DISTANCE AND INVOLVEMENT, NEGATIVE CAPABILITY, OBJECTIVE CORRELATIVE, OBJECTIVE THEORY OF ART, and OBJECTIVITY VS. SUBJECTIVITY.

objectivity vs. subjectivity generally, the DISTANCE AND INVOLVEMENT toward subject matter on the part of an author. The terms were derived by 19th-century English critics from late 18th-century German metaphysicians. *Objectivity* implies an unemotional, impersonal detachment indisposed either to judge what is written or to promote particular beliefs. Examples of this voice in English and American poetry include Browning's *My Last Duchess*, Eliot's *The Love-Song of J. Alfred Prufrock* and *Sweeney among the Nightingales*, and Wallace Stevens' *Sunday Morning*. *Subjectivity*, on the other hand, implies a close emotional involvement on the part of an author who obviously invests his work with personal testimony and value judgments. Most lyric poetry, including that of the Romantics, the Symbolists, and Post-Modernists, fall into this category. A general case could be made that much Classical literature is objective, and that much Romantic poetry is subjective, although there is such disagreement over the meaning of these terms that the argument becomes academic. See AESTHETIC DISTANCE, NEGATIVE CAPABILITY, OBJECTIVE CORRELATIVE, OBJECTIVE THEORY OF ART, OBJECTIVISM, and SUBJECTIVITY. See also *criticism* in APPENDIX 1.

obligatory scene (also known in French as "scène à faire") a dramatic convention that calls for a climatic scene that is expected by the audience due to the RISING ACTION and preparation made toward it in the text. For instance, in *Macbeth* the three witches prophesy the fall of Macbeth's castle at a time when a man "not born of woman" arises and when the forest literally moves toward the castle, "Till Birnan wood remove to Dunsinane." Thus scenes iv and viii of act V need to be enacted in order to satisfy the prophecy. See OBLIGATORY WORD. See also *dramatic terms* in APPENDIX 1.

obligatory word a word that must appear so that a complete sense of an image, action, or dramatic situation is achieved. See COMMITTING WORD and OBLIGATORY SCENE. See also *diction* in APPENDIX 1.

oblique rhyme: See OFF-RHYME.

obscurity (from Latin for "covering, hide") a defect in the control of writing created by diffused theme, idiosyncratic symbols and word usage, or lack of specificity. When poets and critics speak negatively of a poem's being "difficult," the term is usually meant as a synonym of "obscure." In terms of poetics, o. may be a result of mishandling complex issues and emotions or, as some critics believe, the natural effect of the DISSOCIATION OF SENSIBILITY which began in the late Renaissance. Other critics, with some justification, point to o. as the result of the writer's not knowing what he wants to say. For other problems in control, see BURIED THEME, DIGRESSION, DISTRACTING DETAILS, EDITORIAL INTRUSION, MIXED MESSAGE,

MOOD PIECE, OTIOSE, OVERDECORATION, OVERREPETITION, OVERWRITING, and STRAIN BEHIND THE POEM. See also *control* in APPENDIX 1.

obsessive image a phenomenon frequent in contemporary poetry in which a single image dominates and reappears throughout an author's work so that it comes to control the context with the strength of a SYMBOL. Images of bees and fire in Sylvia Plath's poetry, emptiness and stones in W.S. Merwin's work, and detritus and bears in Galway Kinnell's poems form part of these poets' emblems which, like musical leitmotifs, reach the realm of the idée fixe (see EMBLEM and LEITMOTIF). The term applies to an author's body of work as well as to the works of poets in a particular period, such as contemporary poetry which uses the "stone" as a gnomic o.i. (see the works of Galway Kinnell, Robert Bly, W.S. Merwin, Gregory Orr, Philip Levine, Larry Levis, Jack Myers, and Mark Strand). See *imagery* in APPENDIX 1.

occasional verse light or serious poetry arising out of historical occasions, holidays, deaths, marriages, honor days, dedications, informal gameplay, etc. The LIMERICK and VERS DE SOCIÉTÉ are sometimes forms of light o.v., and the ODE, the ELEGY, the ENCOMIUM, and the *political poem* are sometimes forms of serious o.v. Famous poems in the genre include Milton's *On the Late Massacre in Piedmont*, Hopkins' *The Wreck of the Deutschland*, Yeats' *Among School Children*, Burns' *To a Louse*, Pope's *Rape of the Lock*, Spenser's *Epithalamion*, Marvell's *An Horation Ode upon Cromwell's Return from Ireland*, Tennyson's *The Charge of the Light Brigade*, Auden's *September, 1939*, Byron's *The Destruction of Sennacherib*, Hart Crane's *The Bridge*, Roethke's *Elegy for Jane*, and Dylan Thomas' *After the Funeral*. See POET LAUREATE. See also *light verse* in APPENDIX 1.

octameter /oktom'-/ (from Greek for "eight measures"; also spelled "octometer") an eight-foot line of verse. The pure form is rare in both Classical and English verse—Swinburne's *March: An Ode* is said to be the only true octametric poem written in English. Poe's *The Raven* sometimes holds the form, as in the opening line:

> Onće ŭp / oń ă / mídníght / dréarȳ / whíle Ĭ / pónderĕd /
> wéak ańd / wéarȳ

Some poems of Tennyson approach the line length, but most English verse tends to break into two lines of tetrameter. See METER and OTTAVA RIMA.

octastich /ok'tǝstik/ (from Greek for "eight lines") a STROPHE or STANZA composed of eight lines, as in the OTTAVA RIMA form in Yeats's *Sailing to Byzantium*. Sometimes the eight-line form is referred to as an *octet*. See HUITAIN and OCTAVE. See also *forms* in APPENDIX 1.

octave (also called "octet"; a similarly used term is OCTASTICH) a stanzaic form of eight lines (see OTTAVA RIMA and HUITAIN). The term is often used to describe the first eight lines of a PETRARCHAN SONNET in which a proposition or question is posed and then answered in the subsequent SESTET.

octometer: See OCTAMETER.

octosyllabic verse lines composed of eight syllables in ACCENTUAL-SYLLABIC VERSE or SYLLABIC METER. Usually the line is created from duple feet (iambic or trochaic), as in the HUDIBRASTIC VERSE of Samuel Butler's *Hudibras*. The form is very well suited to NARRATIVE VERSE, possibly because the duple foot and line length approach natural thought units and conversational rhythms (see RHYTHM). See also *forms* in APPENDIX 1.

ode /ōd/ (from Greek for "song") originally, a Greek form set by Pindar (522–442 B.C.) who modeled his verse after the movement and song in Classical Greek drama: (1) STROPHE, in which the chorus moved from left to right, (2) ANTISTROPHE, in which the chorus moved from right to left, and (3) EPODE, in which the chorus stood still. The PINDARIC ODE (also known as the *regular ode*) is written in one form for the strophe and antistrophe, and another form for the epode, as in Thomas Gray's *The Progress of Poesy: A Pindaric Ode*, which is in praise of poetry (see ENCOMIASTIC VERSE).

While the Pindardic ode tends toward OCCASIONAL VERSE, the *Horatian* or *homostrophic ode*, after Horace (65–8 B.C.), tends to be more meditative and personal, and is composed of equally formal stanzas with some variation allowed, as in Keats's *Ode on a Grecian Urn*, Shelley's *Ode to the West Wind*, Marvell's *An Horatian Ode upon Cromwell's Return from Ireland*. The *Cowleyan* or *irregular ode*, a loose form close to the LYRIC in its personal and emotional nature, is composed of varying line and stanza lengths and thus is similar to free verse odes. It is the most common type of ode in English. Typically, the ode in its various forms is thought of as a complex, long lyrical poem displaying emotion. Donald Justice's *Three Odes* is a tour de force consisting of the three forms of the ode: *Cool Dark Ode* in Pindaric form, *Warm Flesh-Colored Ode* in Horatian form, and *Pale Tepid Ode* in irregular form. See *forms* in APPENDIX 1.

off-rhyme (also called "approximate rhyme," "embryonic rhyme," "half-rhyme," "imperfect rhyme," "near rhyme," "oblique rhyme," "para-phone," "pararhyme," "partial rhyme," and "slant rhyme") a general term for harmonic sound values that are not *full rhymes* assonantally or consonantally (see ASSONANCE and CONSONANCE), but are partial rhymes, as in "blood/good," "hour/saw," "tuck/look," and "poem/sum." Often the rhyming quality of o.-r. depends upon the use of terminal consonance. Poets sometimes prefer to use the pleasing twinning effect of o.-r. in order to avoid the predictable and dulling effect of full rhyme. The sense of cohesion experienced in a poem that uses o.-r. can be a result of the device being used either ornamentally or structurally. Once thought of as a defect resulting from a lack of skill, o.-r. has been widely practiced for the freedom, grace, and bonding qualities that it allows. Poets who have used the device include Hardy, Yeats, Dickinson, Dylan Thomas, and, in more contemporary writing, Kinnell, Levine, Justice, Hugo, and Bishop. Shelley's *Adonais* and Hopkins' *Spring and Fall* are poems that exemplify the practice. See BOND DENSITY, MELOPOEIA, RHYME, SONICS, and SOUND SYSTEMS.

Old English the language spoken in England from 450 A.D., the invasion of the Angles, Saxons, and Jutes, to about 1100 A.D., after the Norman Conquest (1066). Shortly after the Anglo-Saxon conversion to Christianity in the seventh century, the Latin alphabet was adopted. Poems such as *Beowulf* (eight century), *The Wanderer*, and *The Seafarer* reflected pre-Christian values. Monastic scholars such as Bede and Alcuin translated Latin texts and portions of the Bible into O.E., and religious poets (known as *cynewulf*) created devotional poetry. In the latter part of the ninth century, Alfred the Great chronicled important historical events in the *Anglo-Saxon Chronicle*. O.E., a Germanic dialect, contained approximately 50,000 words and achieved its subtlety and range through the use of compound nouns or kennings, such as the fusion of "God" and "spell" into "Godspell," which in modern English is "gospel." See ANGLO-SAXON VERSE, KENNING, OLD ENGLISH VERSIFICATION, and PERIODS OF ENGLISH LITERATURE.

Old English versification (see ANGLO-SAXON VERSE) the Old English system of PROSODY and POETICS. See also ACCENTUAL VERSE, ALLITERATIVE METER, METER, OLD ENGLISH, and STRONG-STRESS METER.

Omar stanza (also known as "Omar Khayyam quatrain"; a similarly used term is RUBAIYAT, Persian for "quatrains") four-line stanzas composed of ten-syllable lines usually rhyming aaba. Edward FitzGerald's loose translation of Omar Khayyam's *Rubaiyat*, done in the 19th century, gave the form its name, and poets such as Swinburne and Pound (Canto LXXX of the *Pisan Cantos*) have used the form. The Persian word *ruba'ai* refers to a different lyrical form. See *forms* in APPENDIX 1.

ominatio (Latin for prophecy) a rhetorical figure of logic given in the form of testimony that prophesies the consequences of an evil act or vice. See *types of testimony* in APPENDIX 2.

omniscient point of view an all-knowing narrative POINT OF VIEW that allows an author to explain actions, expose characters' thoughts and feelings, intrude editorially, and range through time and place. The technique is used frequently in novels and plays, seldom in lyric poetry, but has been employed in epics such as the *Iliad*, the *Odyssey*, the *Aeneid*, *Paradise Lost*, *The Wasteland*, and Pound's *Cantos*. Although there is obvious freedom to be gained in using the o.p.v., it restricts the emotional intensity to be found in more subjective stances.

onedismus a rhetorical figure of ethics that scolds an opponent for his miserable character. Shakespeare's *King Lear* contains examples of this figure, as does Edgar Lee Masters' *Spoon River Anthology* in which the deceased inhabitants of a town reveal each other's petty and immoral lives. See *figures of ethos* in APPENDIX 2.

onomatopoeia /on'əmatəpē'yə/ (from Greek for "the making of a name") the formation of words whose sounds and/or rhythm imitate the referential sound itself ("tinkle," "bow-wow," "slap," etc.), or whose sound and/or rhythm both imitate a sound and the name of the source of that sound ("bobwhite," "peewit," "cuckoo," etc). (The adjectives are *onomatopoeic* /-pē′ik/ or *onomatopoetic* /pō·et′ik/.) O., in its general sense, offers mimicry as an approximation of a sensual experience. In its more specifically imitative sense, o. echoes the sound it names. There is disagreement among critics as to whether o. is simply a musical, decorative effect or a technically important device. See ABSTRACT POETRY, ALLITERATIVE VERSE, AMPHIGORY, NONSENSE VERSE, and TRANS-SENSE VERSE. See also *devices of poetic license* in APPENDIX 2, and *figurative expressions* in APPENDIX 1.

open couplet two lines of rhymed or unrhymed verse that share a common grammar and logic, but which are enjambed (see ENJAMBMENT and LINE ENDING). See COUPLET. See also *forms* in APPENDIX 1.

open ending (see EASTERN ENDING) the CLOSURE of a poem that continues to develop quietly and to complete itself in the reader's mind. For an opposite term, see WESTERN ENDING. See also *closure* in APPENDIX 1.

open field composition (a similarly used term is PROJECTIVE VERSE) Robert Duncan's term for a poetic composition with open boundaries that allows for disparate, associational subject matter from various angles of thought to enter the poem spontaneously and create its unique organic form (see ORGANIC COMPOSITION). Duncan says: "This exposed, open form ("Projective Verse," [Charles] Olson named it in poetry) began to appear in the 1940's. With the *Pisan Cantos* of Ezra Pound and *Paterson* of William Carlos Williams, with the *Symphony in Three Movements* of Stravinsky, I began to be aware of the possibility that the locus of form might be in the immediate minim of the work, and that one might concentrate upon the sound and meaning present where one was, and derive melody and story from impulse not from plan." See CENTRIFUGAL STRUCTURE, CLOSED-FIELD COMPOSITION, and PROPRIOCEPTION.

opposing image or balancing image an image placed next to an image whose function is to enchance, contrast with, parallel, or elaborate the first image. For a fuller discussion, see JUXTAPOSITION.

optatio (Latin for "wish, desire") a rhetorical figure of emotion that appeals to God or man that the speaker's wishes be granted. The device was used frequently in past ages but has generally fallen out of favor. In his essay *The Poet*, Emerson appeals to future poets to reach their full potential: "Doubt not, O poet, but persist. Say 'It is in me, and shall out.' Stand there, balked and dumb, stuttering and stammering, hissed and hooted, stand and strive, until at last rage draws out of thee that *dream*-power which every night shows thee is thine own ..." See *figures of pathos* in APPENDIX 2.

oral poetry formulaic spoken verse spontaneously improvised during and for a specific occasion (see OCCASIONAL VERSE). The *shaman*, the BARD, the *pencerdd* (chief of songs), *cynewulf* (religious poet), JONGLEUR, TROUBADOUR, and other precursors of the modern poet spent long apprenticeships memorizing the general forms upon which they would base their oral improvisations. Generally, there are three classifications of o.p., all of whose lines are developed by JUXTAPOSITION: (1) NARRATIVE, such as the BALLAD, EPIC, FABLE, FOLKLORE, and *romance*; (2) LYRIC, such as the love song, ODE, and LAMENT; and (3) *ritual,* such as the *work song, sea chantey,* CHARM, *spell, spiritual, toast,* RIDDLE, oracle, and INCANTATION, and songs for specific occasions.

orcos a rhetorical form of testimony swearing an oath that supports or denies what one has already said. For example, in *A Song for Bolivar* Pablo Neruda praises the great South American hero and swears to work for a world of peace and plenty. See *types of testimony* in APPENDIX 2.

O.R.E. /ôr/ an acronym standing for *originality, risk,* and *excellence,* the standards for judging international ice-skating competition, which might generally be used as standards for evaluating poetry.

organic composition writing in which the impulse and form are derived directly from the inner forces of experience. In writing about *organic form,* Denise Levertov said:

> A partial definition, then, of organic poetry might be that it is a *method of apperception,* i.e., of recognizing what we perceive, and is based on an intuition of an order, a form beyond forms, in which forms partake, and of which man's creative works are analogies, resemblances, natural allegories. Such a poetry is exploratory.

This Platonic ideal (see PLATONIC CRITICISM) of composition is the general ORGANIZING PRINCIPLE behind FREE VERSE, although poets such as Coleridge and Hopkins, among others, inched toward a body of poetics upon which later modern poets would base their free-verse aesthetics. See INSCAPE, INSTRESS, GENERATIVE CONTENT VS. ORNAMENTAL CONTENT, OPEN FIELD COMPOSITION, PROJECTIVE VERSE, and RHYTHM.

organic metaphor: See FUNCTIONAL METAPHOR.

organic universal: See CONCRETE UNIVERSAL.

organizing principle a set of aesthetics or poetic rules that inform and organize the composition process. Such guidelines may appear as (1) the formal limitations in a fixed form such as the BALLADE, VILLANELLE, and TRIOLET; (2) the argumentative development and THEMATIC STRUCTURE of a poem such as the LIST POEM; (3) the aesthetic principles of a movement such as OPEN FIELD COMPOSITION, ORGANIC COMPOSITION, and SURREALISM; or (4) the philosophy of an age, such as NEO-CLASSICISM, ROMANTICISM, and the MODERN PERIOD. So the term's application can range from the use of a device or technique to a mode of perception or a philosophy of art.

originality, risk, and excellence: See O.R.E.

originality vs. novelty *originality:* the effect of independent, creative thinking that constructs through innovative expressions, devices, techniques, strategies, modes of perception, and poetic theories that stand the test of time and thus themselves become conventions (see CONVENTION and INVENTION). *Novelty,* on the other hand, emerges from whim and fancy (see FANCY VS. IMAGINATION) and does not carry the imaginative weight of originality. The poet Dave Smith succinctly set the differences between the two terms in saying, "Novelty is a hula hoop, is 3-D vision. Originality is Picasso." In modern and contemporary poetry, originality has been both raised to an ideal by experimentalists and scorned as an affected and useless device by traditionalists.

ornamental content: See GENERATIVE CONTENT VS. O.C.

oscillographic representation the video presentation of sonic and rhythmic wavelengths on an instrument called the *oscilloscope*. The scope, used by linguists and speech therapists, can determine the PITCH, compression, overtones, and rhythmic flow of human speech. See SCANSION.

otiose /ō'shē·ōs/ or /ō'tē·ōs/ (from Latin for "at leisure") pertaining to a style of writing that is useless for its irrelevancies, repetitions, superfluousness, and lackadaisical manner. See SLACKNESS. See also *defects in control* in APPENDIX 1.

ottava rima /ôtä'və rē'mə/ (Italian for "eighth rhyme") an Italian stanzaic form composed of eight lines of iambic pentameter rhyming abababcc. Boccacio is credited with having created the form, and poets such as Spenser, Milton, Keats, Byron, and Yeats have used it. The form is suited to narrative and lyric verse, and has come to be associated with parodic verse (see PARODY) since its most famous employment by Byron in *Don Juan*. But the form has been used in serious poetry, too, as in Yeats' *Sailing to Byzantium*. The form probably originated as a SESTET with an added HEROIC COUPLET. For other eight-line stanzas without fixed rhyme schemes, see OCTASTICH and OCTAVE. See also *forms* in APPENDIX 1.

overdecoration a defect in composition caused by seeing substance in a clutter of details, metaphorical debris, sound and rhythm excesses, and irrelevant digressions. No amount of formal structure can mask o. For other defects in writing, see BURIED THEME, DIGRESSION, DISTRACTING DETAILS, EDITORIAL INTRUSION, MIXED MESSAGE, MOOD PIECE, OBSCURITY, OTIOSE, OVERREPETITION, OVERWRITING, and STRAIN BEHIND THE POEM. See also *control* in APPENDIX 1.

overreading a defect in critical reading arising from a strained "reading into" or overextension of the references and semantics of a text. This can apply to the thematic structure of a book as well as to specific passages. See *meaning* in APPENDIX 1.

overrepetition a defect in writing in which unnecessary repetition of a word, phrase, or image takes place. O. is sometimes used for effective humor in NONSENSE VERSE and PARODY. For the uses of REPETITION, see LEITMOTIF, OBSESSIVE IMAGE, and REFRAIN. Another term relating to o. is OTIOSE. See *figures of repetition* in APPENDIX 2, and *defects in control* in APPENDIX 1.

overstress the additional effect of ALLITERATION, *word accent*, or *grammatical accent* on an already metrically stressed syllable. See ACCENT and SPRUNG RHYTHM.

overwriting a defect in style characterized by "loud" cacophonous words (see CACOPHONY), jammed or impacted phrasing, melodramatic emotion, and a general lack of sensitivity to language. See BOMBAST, EUPHUISM, GONGORISM, OTIOSE, OVERREPETITION, and PURPLE PATCH. See also *control* in APPENDIX 1.

oxymoron /-mō'-/ (Greek for "[obvious] foolishness") a rhetorical figure that works by efficiently linking opposite and contradictory attributes that result in a PARADOX, such as Roethke's "Dark, dark my light." The device differs from paradox in that an oxymoron's meaning turns within a phrase, while the paradox's meaning turns within a whole statement. O. is used for wit, compression, and surprise; it differs from ANTITHESIS, which divides and categorizes, by yoking characteristics into one succinct phrase. Other examples of the device are "black sun," "thunderous silences," "beggarly riches," "cold heat," and "cruel kindness." The late Renaissance was taken with the oxymoron's power to evoke mystery and depth in relation to questions of religious faith. See CATACHRESIS and SYNAESTHESIA. See also *contraries and contradictories* in APPENDIX 2, and *figurative expressions* in APPENDIX 1.

P

pace rhythmically, the speed at which large units of rhythm or lines move. Generally, short-lined poems move more slowly than long-lined poems which tend to read in the manner of prose. In FREE VERSE, accumulating units of measurement other than METER are described rhythmically by their tempo or p. In terms of the narrative or dramatic development of a text, if there is a substantial amount of DIGRESSION, complication, and DIALOGUE, a piece will tend to move more slowly than a more straightforward PLOT. The elements of TONE and MOOD can also affect the tempo. The lyric poem, even in its longer forms, tends to move faster than its narrative and dramatic counterparts. See CADENCE.

paean /pē′ən/ (also spelled "pean"; see also PAEON) originally Paian, the Homeric name of the physician of the gods as used in the *Iliad* to address Apollo to heal the Achaeans of the plague he sent upon them. The form became less restricted and was used for any chant, HYMN, INCANTATION, ODE, or song of victory addressed to Apollo. In more modern usage, the term has been employed by Tennyson, Shakespeare, Pope, Lyly, and Lytton to refer to any song of praise, joy, or thanksgiving or any shout of exultation. The full form in its ancient sense was used by Pindar and Sophocles (in *Antigone*), among others. See *forms* in APPENDIX 1.

paeanismus a rhetorical expression of emotion that is full of joy because some goodness is attained or some evil avoided. In the 23rd section of *Song of Myself*, Whitman uses p.: "Divine am I inside and out, and I make holy whatever I touch or am touched from." See *figures of pathos* in APPENDIX 2.

paeon /pē′on/ (from *Paian*; see also PAEAN) a Classical Greek quadruple metrical FOOT found in QUANTITATIVE METER and composed of one long and three short syllables in varying order: *first p.*, ‒ ˘ ˘ ˘; *second p.* ˘ ‒ ˘ ˘; *third p.*, ˘ ˘ ‒ ˘; and *fourth p.*, ˘ ˘ ˘ ‒. The meter was used in hymns to Apollo and also by Sophocles in *Electra*. It is too long a foot to use in English ACCENTUAL-SYLLABIC VERSE, though G.M. Hopkins' system of SPRUNG RHYTHM found sporadic use for it in *The Windhover* and *The Wreck of the Deutschland*. See METER for other quadruple feet.

palimbacchius: See ANTIBACCHIUS.

palindrome /pal′indrōm/ (from Greek for "running back again") a word, line of verse, or sentence that reads the same way backwards and forwards; e.g., "mom," "pop," and "Madam, I'm Adam" are palindromes, as well as this reference to Napoleon: "Able was I ere I saw

Elba." The form is said to have been invented by the Greek poet Sotades and is thus also known as *sotadies*. See ACROSTIC and ANAGRAM. See also *forms* in APPENDIX 1.

palinode /pal'inōd/ (from Greek for "a singing over again") a poem that recants or retracts something written earlier. The term is derived from an ODE by the Greek poet Stesichorus who apologized for his attack on Helen of Troy. Other poets, such as Chaucer in his *Legend of Good Women*, which retracts his comments about women in *Troilus and Criseyde*, and Ovid in *Remedia Amoris*, which recants *Ars Amatoria*, have used the form. See *forms* in APPENDIX 1.

pan (see CINEMATIC TECHNIQUES) a cinematic term indicating the horizontal sweeping movement over a SETTING by a stationary camera. The lateral view is an aid in establishing MOOD, SELECTED DETAIL, and elements of history and geography. See also *cinematic terms* in APPENDIX 1.

panegyric /panəjir'ik/ (from Greek for "public assembly or festival") a rhetorical expression classified as *epideictic* consisting of thanksgiving in praise of victories after battles, and of important personages and gods (see PAEAN). The genre has come to include speeches eulogizing formal occasions, such as that of Pliny the Younger when he assumed his consulship. In modern times, the term has taken on a derogatory connotation because it has been closely connected with political speeches and dust-jacket blurbs which tend to make false tributes for favor or gain. See ENCOMIUM, EPIDEICTIC POETRY, and EULOGY.

pantoum /-tōōm'/ (from Malay *pantum*) a Malay verse form imitated by the French and English. The Malayan form consisted of a quatrain rhyming abab in which the second couplet contained the meaning and the first couplet consisted of a distantly related SIMILE. In the hands of Europeans, the verse took on a formal repetitive character similar to the VILLANELLE in which specific lines are repeated (called *répétons*): Lines two and four of the first stanza recur respectively as lines one and three of the succeeding stanza, and sometimes lines two and four of the last stanza are the same lines as one and three of the first stanza. Poets such as Victor Hugo, Charles Baudelaire, and Austin Dobson have used the form, which relates to older French FIXED FORMS even though the p. is a much later adaption. See *forms* in APPENDIX 1.

parable /par'-/ (from Greek for "a putting next to, a comparison, an analogy") a short, fictitious narrative employing an allegorical comparison or parallel between the parts of its story and the moral or philosophical issue that the author is illustrating. Usually, the events in the p. are natural and are meant as analogies to religious values, as in Jesus' p. of the sower. See ALLEGORY, ANALOGY, APOLOGUE, and FABLE. For other examples of rhetorical comparisons, see *figures of similarity and dissimilarity* in APPENDIX 2.

parachresis: See EPICRISIS.

paradiastole /-dī·as'tolē/ (Greek for "a putting together of dissimilar things") a rhetorical expression that uses comparison to soothe, flatter, or assuage. In his essay *The Poet*, Emerson flatters all men in an attempt to defend poetry: "For we are not ... porters of the fire and torch-bearers, but children of the fire, made of it ..." See *figures comparing greater, lesser, or equal things* in APPENDIX 2, and *figurative expressions* in APPENDIX 1.

paradiegesis a rhetorical expression in the form of an argument in which a speaker mentions a thing or person in order to introduce his own special purpose or meaning. P. is one of the most common argumentative devices, and examples abound. To choose one: In his essay *Domestic Life*, Emerson introduces his topic by stating as fact the questionable thesis that intelligent people are less interested in "the study of fossils, the history of meteors, the genesis of nebulae" than in the "usual things" that are immediately around them. See *figures of argumentation* in APPENDIX 2.

paradigma /-dig′mə/ (Greek for "pattern, example") a rhetorical expression of logic under the category of HOMOEOSIS that argues by comparing two well-known examples to a present situation: "Romeo loved Juliet as Troilus loved Criseyde. / Will our great love also be disastrous?" See *figures of contraries and contradictories* in APPENDIX 2.

paradiorthosis /-dī·ôrthō′-/ (Greek for "false correction") a rhetorical type of testimony in which the speaker twists a well-known quotation without crediting its author: "In times of high inflation, a penny spent is a penny saved." See *types of testimony* in APPENDIX 2.

paradox (from Greek for "contrary to received opinion or expectation") a rhetorical figure of speech that tells its truth through a self-contradicting assertion in the whole of its meaning, or an assertion of strange quality that contradicts popular opinion. It is similar to the OXYMORON and classified as a *contradictory* but differs from an oxymoron in that the meaning of a p. turns on the whole meaning of its statement rather than on a few juxtaposed words. The device has been widely used by poets since antiquity. Examples include Shakespeare's "Cowards die many times before their deaths" and Wordsworth's "The child is father of the man." Some critics, such as Cleanth Brooks, maintain "the language of poetry is the language of paradox." The device is often used in the EPIGRAM and METAPHYSICAL POETRY for the elements of WIT, surprise, compression, BALANCE, and ANTITHESIS. Extended forms of p. such as the METAPHYSICAL CONCEIT and the PASTOURELLE use the device as a strategy. See EPIGRAM and HYPALLAGE. See also *contraries and contradictories* in APPENDIX 2, and *figurative expressions* in APPENDIX 1.

paraenesis /paren′-/ or /parē-/ (Greek for "exhortation, advice") a figurative expression that warns or berates: "It is easier for a camel to pass through the eye of a needle than for a wealthy man to enter the Kingdom of God." See *types of testimony* in APPENDIX 2.

paragoge /-gō′jē/ (Greek for "a leading past") grammatically, the addition of a syllable at the end of a word that may or may not add any more sense to the word: "right*o*" for "right," and "peasan*t*" for "peasan." Hebrew often uses the device to modify the meaning of words. Its adjectival form, *paragogic*, is used as a derogatory term for speech that extends words without adding any meaning to them. See *grammatical constructions that are technically incorrect* in APPENDIX 2.

paralipsis /-lip′-/ (from Greek for "omission, a passing by") a rhetorical figure of contradictories in which a speaker emphasizes a point by ironically pretending to pass it by. The device is usually introduced with phrases such as, "I won't mention . . ." or ". . . to say nothing of . . ." Mark Antony's famous speech in *Julius Caesar* contains p. See LITOTES. See also *contraries and contradictories* in APPENDIX 2, and *figurative expressions* in APPENDIX 1.

parallelism /par′-/ (from Greek for "beside one another") a rhetorical device of grammar in which words, phrases, or ideas of equivalent value share a similar grammatical structure, thus creating an inherent comparison among them. The term also applies to the larger aspects of development in literary works: the manner in which abstractions and images are used, the various manipulations that JUXTAPOSITION presents in the form and content of NARRATION, and the balancing of description and DIALOGUE. Although all good writing has elements of p. in it, some writers rely on it more than others; and some writers, such as John Berryman, systematically break expected patterns of p. in order to create surprise and emphasis. Walt Whitman, who based his CATALOGUE technique on the book of Psalms, uses the p. as the ORGANIZING PRINCIPLE in his work, as in the following example from *Song of Myself*:

> Stop this day and night with me and you shall possess
>   the origin of all poems.
> You shall possess the good of the earth and sun, (there are
>   millions of suns left,)
> You shall no longer take things at second or third hand,
>   nor look through the eyes of the dead, nor feed
>   on the spectres in books,
> You shall not look through my eyes either, nor take
>   things from me,
> You shall listen to all sides and filter them from your self.

See ASYNDETON, BALANCE, BRACHYLOGIA, ISOCOLON, and REPETITION. See also *grammatical devices of rhythm and balance* in APPENDIX 2.

paramythia (from Greek for "to encourage, to console") a rhetorical figure of emotion or logic, subsumed under the general category PATHOPOEIA in which a speaker tries to mitigate the misery of someone who is suffering: "Woman, your painful labor will bring forth a beautiful child." See *figures of pathos* in APPENDIX 2.

paraphone: See OFF-RHYME.

paraphrase /par′-/ (from Greek for "to tell the same thing in other words") a restatement of a TEXT using different words in order to clarify or elaborate it. The device is often necessary as an outline of complex and subtle development of ideas but, according to critics and writers, is never a substitute for the original work (see *heresy of p.*). The *New Critics* condemned the tendency to substitute a p. for the work itself.

paraphrasis /pəraf'resis/: See PERIPHRASIS.

pararhyme: See OFF-RHYME.

parataxis: See JUXTAPOSITION.

parecbasis a rhetorical argument using greater, equal, or lesser ideas in the form of an oblique DIGRESSION that intensifies the argument: "This man should get murder in the first degree, not the second degree, for he has slain one of our most conscientious and law-abiding citizens. His victim was a man of substance and worth which makes the crime even more heinous." See *figures comparing greater, lesser, or equal things* in APPENDIX 2.

parelcon a rhetorical device, usually thought of as a "tolerable vice" of language, that introduces an extraneous word into a sentence but which adds nothing to the sense except, perhaps, an affectation in tone: "If *that* I meet you, I hope we will be friends." See PARAGOGE. See also *devices of poetic license* in APPENDIX 2, and *diction* in APPENDIX 1.

parenthesis (Greek for "insertion") in rhetoric, a grammatical construction under the category of HYPERBATON (irregular or inverted word order) in which a word, phrase, or clause interrupts the normal flow of SYNTAX and ideas in order to introduce a tangential thought or comment (see DIGRESSION). The device is used as a stylistic strategy in e.e. cummings' *much i cannot*). The aside or editorial remark is usually indicated by p. marks ( ) or with commas, dashes, brackets, or white spaces and has been used effectively by writers such as Joyce and Faulkner. See PUNCTUATION. See also *grammatical constructions* in APPENDIX 2.

pareuresis a rhetorical form of argumentation that refutes an accusation by showing premeditated reasons that are strong enough to dismiss objections to the deed. Emerson and Thoreau, among others, used this strategy to defend the morality of civil disobedience, as in Emerson's essay *Politics*: "Every actual State is corrupt. Good men must not obey the laws too well." See MEDELA and PROECTHESIS. See also *figures of argumentation* in APPENDIX 2.

parimion: See ALLITERATION.

parison /par'-/ (Greek for "even balance") in rhetoric, a grammatical construction of rhythm and balance composed of a series of equally constructed clauses that effect a sense of grace: "It is the time of war, it is the time of care, / It is the time of courage, it is the time of fear." Whitman uses this device often in *Song of Myself*. See ASYNDETON, BALANCE, BRACHYLOGIA, ISOCOLON, PARALLELISM, and REPETITION. See also *grammatical devices of rhythm and balance* in APPENDIX 2.

Parnassians (from *Parnassus*, a mountain in Central Greece, sacred to Apollo and the Muses, thus a term used to refer to literature, especially poetry) a 19th-century French school of poetry extant between ROMANTICISM and the SYMBOLISTS that called for the objective treatment of subject matter, THEME, and TONE in poetry so that a sculptural quality of hardness and clarity (sometimes referred to as *lapidary*) could be achieved. Led by Théophile Gautier, and including Albert Glatigny, Banville, Sully-Prudhomme, and Anatole France, the group called for ART FOR ART'S SAKE (see ARS GRATIA ARTIS), and thus could be considered a precursor to AESTHETICISM. They rebelled against the subjectivism of Victor Hugo, Vigny, and Lamartine and the latter's tendency to apply art toward activist concerns of society, politics, and history. Their style eventually influenced the work of Swinburne, Dobson, Lange, and Pound, among others.

parody (from Greek for "beside a song") an ancient device of comic IMITATION or sustained ALLUSION meant to satirize previous works or ideas for the sake of humor or serious criticism by using the original form and/or content as a model. There are four basic types of p.: (1) Imitation of a sacred or highly esteemed text in order to satirize the hypocrisy of those who claim to uphold its principles. For instance, Mark Twain's *Battle Hymn of the Republic* (*Brought Down to Date*, 1900) is a p. of the famous patriotic song in which Twain satirizes the greed and jingoistic national spirit that led to the American invasion of the Philippines. Twain keeps the same rhyme scheme, meter, and structure, changing only a few key words in each line and substituting *near-homophones* ("Mine eyes have seen the *orgy* of the *launching* of the *Sword*"). (2) P. of a well-known song or poem in order to entertain in the form of LIGHT VERSE. For example, X.J. Kennedy's *In a Prominent Bar in Secaucus One Day* is a take-off on *Sweet Betsy from Pike*. Kennedy's version turns the original female folk heroine into a prostitute who tells her story as a lesson to young girls. He maintains the original form but changes the characters, setting, and tone to effect a BURLESQUE. (3) P. of a well-known poem or song in order to create a serious poem. For example, Donald Justice's *Counting the Mad* is a p. of *This Little Piggy*, the children's toe-counting game song. By borrowing the sonic form and the repetitive structure of the children's poem, Justice increases the terror and irony of his description of various types of madness. (4) P. of a highly esteemed text in order to satirize the principles that it espouses. For example, in Anthony Hecht's *The Dover Bitch*, Hecht models his piece after Matthew Arnold's *Dover Beach* in order to tell the story from a modern woman's point of veiw. The effect is comic, but the point—that life is too short to live it sadly—is serious. The contemporary poetry journal *Poultry* is devoted solely to p. See CARICATURE, COMPANION POEMS, LAMPOON, SATIRE, TRAVESTY, and WIT. See also *humor* and *light verse* in APPENDIX 1.

paroemia /pərē′mi·ə/ (from Greek for "proverb") a rhetorical figurative expression of testimony commonly known as a PROVERB, a moral saying usually of anonymous source or authorship: "A bird in the hand is worth two in the bush." See APOMNEMONYSIS, APOTHEGM, CHRIA, EPICRISIS, and PARADIORTHOSIS. See also *types of testimony* in APPENDIX 2.

paromologia (Greek for "partial admission") a rhetorical figure of argumentation in which one gives in to gain an advantage over an opponent's argument by subsequently bringing out reasons that overturn the previous concession: "It's true he has a pleasant speech and a strong mind. He may, as you say, have even done some good in his life. But what are these against his betrayal to the State?" See *figures of argumentation* in APPENDIX 2.

paronomasia (Greek for "formation of a word by a slight change") a rhetorical expression, under the category of "notation and conjugates," in the form of a PUN that creates AMBIGUITY from similar-sounding words, or by changing a letter in a previously stated word: "Don't *wrest* my *rest* from me." The effect, according to John Donne, creates "humor or a double meaning." See ANTANACLASIS, DOUBLE ENTENDRE, NOEMA, and SYLLEPSIS. See also *figures of notation and conjugation* in APPENDIX 2, and *figurative expressions* in APPENDIX 1.

parrhesia (Greek for "a speaking beyond," thus "frankness") a rhetorical figure of character or ethos used as a strategy in speech that (1) shows humility, or respect for real or imagined offenses, as in this passage from a letter by Vincent Van Gogh: "I am a man of passions, capable of and subject to doing more or less foolish things, of which I happen to repent, more or less, afterwards"; (2) shows boldness, freedom of expression, and frankness—a device widely used in modern literature in describing physiological and sexual activities openly, as in this selection from Charles Bukowski's *a 340 dollar horse and a hundred dollar whore*: "and the biggest blonde of all / all ass and breast, hardly anything else / went to the payoff window with me." See the opposite term EUPHEMISM. See also *figures of ethos* in APPENDIX 2.

partial rhyme; part rhyme: See OFF-RHYME.

pastiche /-tĕsh′/ (French, from Italian for "pie [of meat, macaroni, etc.]"') originally, the French term for PARODY or take-off of another literary work's style, form, or content; e.g., Amy Lowell's *A Critical Fable* (1922) is a p. of James Russell Lowell's *A Fable for Critics*. Eventually the word came to connote a potpourri of extracts from one or more authors (see CENTO). The etymology of the term is rooted in the Italian pastry chef's habit of combining various ingredients into one whole taste so that it produced a new entity. See BURLESQUE, CARICATURE, IMITATION, LAMPOON, and TRAVESTY. See also *forms* in APPENDIX 1.

pastoral (from Latin *pastor*, for "shepherd") a form originated by the third-century Sicilian poet Theocritus who adapted ritual laments for Adonis for the depiction of the lives of shepherds he knew. Later on, the Roman poet Virgil conventionalized the form in his *Eclogues* (see ECLOGUE). Generally, the classic p. describes rural life in simple, serene, nostalgic, and idealized terms, almost implicitly criticizing urban life. The conventional formats include (1) a DIALOGUE or singing contest between two shepherds, (2) a MONOLOGUE in which a single dreamy shepherd extols BUCOLIC values, (3) requited or unrequited rural love lyrics, and (4) the lament of the death of a fellow shepherd (see PASTORAL ELEGY). By the time of the RENAISSANCE, the genre had taken on an artful, contrived nature either using rural and Biblical allusions to state a serious message or using these elements of setting and tone for satirical purposes, as in Spenser's *Shepheardes Calender* (1579) and John Gay's *Shepherd's Week* (1714). Other poets used the form to portray a simple kind of existence, e.g., Milton's *Lycidas*, Shakespeare's comedies, Marlowe's lyric *The Passionate Shepherd to His Love*, Wordsworth's *Michael, a Pastoral Poem*, and Whitman's lament for Abraham Lincoln, *When Lilacs Last in the Dooryard Bloom'd*. In 1950 William Empson (*Some Versions of Pastoral*) widened the definition of the genre by claiming that it generally attempts to contrast the simple rural life with the more complex urban life, and often uses INVERSION, the stating of complex ideas through simple characters. In light of this definition, poets such as E.A. Robinson, Dylan Thomas, and Robert Frost might be considered p. poets. See BUCOLIC and IDYLL.

pastoral elegy a form of PASTORAL that uses a rural setting and simple diction to lament the death of a fellow shepherd. The conventions of the form include an INVOCATION to the MUSES, the use of mythological or biblical ALLUSION, PATHETIC FALLACY, a blaming of the deities or demigods who oversaw the once-living shepherd, the attendance of other mourners as a chorus, a diatribe against the injustice of the death and the values of the times, a ceremonial placing of flowers on the grave, and an epiphanic reversal or consolation. The classic poem containing all of these elements is Milton's *Lycidas* which displays simple, formal diction and a solemn rhythm. Other pastoral elegies include Shelley's *Adonais* and Matthew Arnold's *Thyrsis*. See BUCOLIC, ECLOGUE, ELEGY, and IDYLL.

pastourelle /pastōōrel'/ (French for "little shepherdess") a medieval PAS-TORAL dialogue framed by a situation in which a shepherdess is being courted by a knight or other man of high standing. The form is probably derived from Theocritus' *Idyll #27*. See BUCOLIC, ECLOGUE, and IDYLL.

pathetic fallacy a form of PERSONIFICATION in which nature is credited with human feeling or behavior. The term was coined by John Ruskin in 1856 (*Modern Painters*, Vol. III) and thought by him to be a negative device used by fanciful or emotional artists to reflect artistic truths rather than reality, e.g., in Coleridge's *Christabel*: "The one red leaf, the last of its clan, / That dances as often as dance it can." Ruskin made exceptions to his dislike of the p.f. when it was used by great poets such as Shakespeare and Chaucer, a view that would deny the work of a great many fine poets. In fact, Ruskin thought of Wordsworth, Keats, Coleridge, and Tennyson as second-rank writers. Today, the term is used to describe loosely any display of human values, behavior, or feelings on the part of something not human. The device is not as common as it once was in the 18th and 19th centuries. See BATHOS and PATHOS. For other fallacies, see AFFECTIVE FALLACY, CLASSICAL FALLACY, EXPRESSIVE FALLACY, IMITATIVE FALLACY, INTENTIONAL FALLACY, and REDUCTIVE FALLACY.

pathopoeia /-pē'yə/ (from Greek for "a stirring of passions") the rhetorical generic name given to figures of emotion such as ANAMNESIS, APOCARTE-RESIS, APOSIOPESIS, APOSTROPHE, ARA, BDELYGMIA, CATAPLEXIS, CATEGORIA, DEESIS, ECPHONESIS, EPIPLEXIS, EROTEMA, EROTESIS, EULOGY, EXUSCITATIO, MEDELA, MEMPSIS, MYCTERISMUS, ONEDISMUS, OPTATIO, PAEANISMUS, PARA-MYTHIA, PROCLEES, SARCASMUS, and THRENOS. See *figures of pathos* in APPENDIX 2.

pathos /pā'-/ (Greek for "suffering, passion") the depth of feeling in a skilled work that arouses a sympathetic passion in its audience. The great Shakespearean tragedies share p., but if it is used in an exaggerated form, as much VICTORIAN literature has used it, the device becomes bathetic or sentimental. See BATHOS, EMPATHY, PATHETIC FALLACY, PATHOPOEIA, and SENTIMENTALISM. See *figures of pathos* in APPENDIX 2.

pause: See CAESURA.

pean: See PAEAN.

Pegasus /peg'-/ the winged horse fabled to have sprung from the blood of Medusa when slain by Perseus. With a strike of its hoof, P. is said to have opened the Hippocrene fountain on Mt. Helicon, the wellhead of inspiration for the MUSES. In modern times, the mythological figure is symbolic of poetic inspiration. See DIVINE AFFLATUS.

pentameter /-tam'-/ (from Greek for "five measures") a line of verse containing five metrical feet. In Classical Greek PROSODY, the measure consisted of hemistiches of two feet sharing a medial SPONDEE ($\smile\smile$/$\smile\smile$/$\smile\smile$/$\smile\smile$, called *dactylospondaic*). In English ACCENTUAL-SYLLABIC VERSE the p. line is usually composed of five iambic feet and has been the most commonly used meter in the language. See BLANK VERSE, ELEGY, HEROIC COUPLET, and METER. See also *forms* in APPENDIX 1.

pentapody /-tap'-/ (from Greek for "five feet") in Classical Prosody a line or lines occurring in five feet. Pentapodies are usually composed of dactylic, iambic, and trochaic feet. A line with one foot is a *monopody*; two feet, a *dipody*; three feet, a *tripody*, four feet, a *tetrapody*, etc. Some of Sappho's verse is written in pentapodies. See PENTASTICH. See also *forms* in APPENDIX 1.

pentarsic (from Greek for "of five rises") a Classical Greek prosodic term for a measure or line having five long syllables. See ARSIS AND THESIS and PENTAMETER.

pentastich /pen'təstik/ (from Greek for "five lines") a group of lines or a stanza or a poem consisting of five lines, such as the LIMERICK and the CINQUAIN. The five-line stanza is also called a QUINTAIN. See also *forms* in APPENDIX 1.

penultimate (from Latin for "almost last, the last but one") the next-to-last position of a line or word in a line. The third-to-last position is referred to as the *antepenultimate*.

perfect rhyme (also called "true rhyme" or "full rhyme") the twinning sound values of stressed vowels and subsequent consonants (the initial un-stressed consonants are discounted), as in "glow/blow" (single p.r.), "people/steeple" (double p.r.), "furious/curious" (triple p.r.), and "combination/domination" (quadruple p.r.). Words that are spelled differently but pronounced the same are considered a form of p.r. called RIME RICHE. See OFF-RHYME and RHYME.

periergia /peri·ur'gē·ə/ (from Greek for "overcareful work") a rhetorical device, known to be a "tolerable vice," that contains a repetitive grandiloquence belaboring its point with high diction in order to sound fine. See BOMPHIOLOGIA, CACOZELIA, PERISSOLOGIA, and SORIASMUS. See also *devices of poetic license* in APPENDIX 2, and *diction* in APPENDIX 1.

periodic sentence: See IRMUS.

Periods of English Literature the *periods* into which English literature is divided for convenience. The exact dates of these periods vary, according to literary historians, but the following periods (and *ages*) are generally agreed upon:

> 450–1100—Old English or Anglo-Saxon period
> 1100–1500—Middle English period
> 1500–1660—Renaissance period
> 　1558–1603—Elizabethan age
> 　1603–1625—Jacobean age
> 　1625–1649—Caroline age
> 　1649–1660—Commonwealth period (Puritan Interregnum)
> 1660–1798—Neo-Classical period
> 　1660–1700—Restoration age
> 　1700–1745—Augustan age (the Age of Pope)
> 　1745–1798—Age of Sensibility (the Age of Johnson)
> 1798–1832—Romantic period
> 1832–1901—Victorian period
> 1901–1914—Edwardian period
> 1910–1936—Georgian age
> 1914 to present—Modern period

For more detailed information, see the entries for specific periods.

peripeteia /peripətē'yə/ (from Greek for "sudden change"; also called "peripety" /pərip'-/) a sudden change in the events of a work. Aristotle's example of p. is the point in *Oedipus Rex* when the first messenger attempting to allay Oedipus' fears reports that the parents who have died are really Oedipus' foster parents, a fact that exponentially increases his fears. See ANAGNORISIS, CLIMAX, and CRISIS.

periphrasis /perif'-/ (Greek for "roundabout expression") a rhetorical figure classified under "subject and adjunct" that substitutes many words for a single word or proper name. This type of circumlocution, used to avoid sounding ordinary, is often heard in political speeches and decorous poetry. Used in its positive sense, the device may add drama and dignity to an otherwise flat word, as in this sentence referring to the Bible: "It is the word of God preserved." This device was especially popular in the NEO-CLASSICAL PERIOD; such works as James Thompson's *The Seasons* relied on it heavily. Shakespeare's Polonius, as well as many characters from Dickens, is guilty of inflated p., and shows the skillful use of the device which might otherwise be thought of as a defect in style. The opposite figure of p. is ANTONOMASIA. See EUPHEMISM and EUPHUISM. See also *figures of subject and adjunct* in APPENDIX 2, and *figurative expressions* in APPENDIX 1.

perissologia /-lō'jē·ə/ (Greek for "speaking too much") a rhetorical device usually thought of as a "tolerable vice," in which a FLOURISH oı extraneous clause is added to a sentence in order to supply grace and/or emphasis. Functionally speaking, the p. adds no new sense to the sentence: "I give this gift to you, / *handing it to you* / with a glad heart." See PLEONASM. See also *grammatical devices of rhythm and balance* and *devices of poetic license* in APPENDIX 2.

peristasis /pəris'-/ a rhetorical figure of definition under the category of "subject and adjunct" that defines a thing or person through circumstance: "He is of royal ancestry, meticulous education, / and has a noble and poetic turn of mind." Emerson begins his essay *Politics* by reminding his reader of the lack of any inalienable right that a government has other than the collective will of its citizens. See *figures of definition* and *figures of subject and adjunct* in APPENDIX 2.

persiflage /pur'sifläzh/ (French for "banter") unimportant banter or jesting repartee as found in some of Shakespeare's comedies and the works of Oscar Wilde and Eugene Ionesco (who used it for the sake of SATIRE). The device is used for comedic purposes. See FLYTING and STICHOMYTHIA.

persona (Latin for "mask, person"; see MASK) the speaker of a poem who is easily recognized as being different from the poet. The p. might be an animal, an inanimate object, or a character as in W.S. Merwin's *Noah's Raven*. P. is sometimes differentiated from the mask in terms of the degree to which the speaker is removed from the writer. See *dramatic terms* in APPENDIX 1.

personal myth (see MYTH) the imaginative construct that reflects the writer's self-image and relationship to the outside world.

personification (a similarly used term is PROSOPOPOEIA) originally a rhetorical device of definition grouped under "subject and adjunct" and incorporated within the general term HYPOTYPOSIS, imaginative description of a vivid and fictional nature. As a poetic device, p. lends human qualities to abstractions and animate or inanimate objects, and is designed to evoke emotion. Most poets since ancient times have used the device in their works. The following example, in the form of an APOSTROPHE, is from Keats' *Ode on a Grecian Urn*:

> Thou still unravished bride of quietness,
> Thou foster child of silence and slow time,
> Sylvan historian, who canst thus express
> A flowery tale more sweetly than our rhyme

It is said that p. has its origins in the displacement of primitive myth-making, is contemporaneous with the advent of ALLEGORY, and is an egoistic form of EMPATHY. See PATHETIC FALLACY. See also *figures of subject and adjunct* in APPENDIX 2.

Petrarchan conceit (see CONCEIT; see also *Petrarchan sonnet* under SONNET) a figure of comparison that establishes a striking and elaborate parallel. The device was used by Petrarch in his love poems and widely imitated in Europe during the RENAISSANCE. See COURTLY LOVE.

Petrarchan sonnet: See SONNET.

phalaecean: See HENDECASYLLABIC VERSE.

phanopoeia /fānōpē'yə/ Ezra Pound's term for the imagistic or visual aspect of poetry, as opposed to the melopoetic and logical aspects of a work. Pound maintained that the success of an image depends upon the "utter precision of word" and that IMAGERY is one of the elements in poetry that survives translation. The two other terms that Pound used to speak technically about poetry are LOGOPOEIA, which indicates the JUXTAPOSITION of ideas arising out of word usage, and MELOPOEIA, the sonic and rhythmical texture in a poem. Pound's poem *Phanopoeia* exemplifies a singular use of the device. See FIXED IMAGE AND FREE IMAGE, IMAGE, and IMAGERY. See also *imagery* in APPENDIX 1.

phoneme /fō'nēm/ (from Greek for "sound") the smallest particle of sound whose form is meaningful in terms of its recognition as a word feature. For example, the sound difference between "nurse" and "curse" (*n/c* difference) represents one form of phonemic variation; another form is that of the range found within a single letter, such as the range of sound in the letter *o* at the end of the word "to" (phonemically spelled /t/ + /o͞o/ + /wä/). Units of phonemes make up morphemes which concern themselves with semantics rather than pure sound values. Intonation, duration, accent, and pitch (see SOUND SYSTEM) determine the quality of a p. See also EQUIVALENCE, PHONETICS, and SOUND-SIGNS.

phonemics /fonē'miks/ the study of phonemes, the recognizable word-sound unit. See EQUIVALENCE, PHONEME, and SOUND SYSTEM.

phonetic equivalence the existence of echoing sounds in the SONIC STRUCTURE throughout a poem, as in ALLITERATION, RHYME, ASSONANCE, CONSONANCE, and REPETITION. The twinning sound values may not be identical, only approximate, since the proximity of other sounds, along with other variables, affects the quality of EQUIVALENCE. See ECHO RHYME, PHONEME, REPETITION, SOUND SYSTEM, SYZYGY, and TONE COLOR.

phonetics the analysis and classification of sound in language. See PHONEME and SOUND SYSTEM.

phonics a method of teaching reading based on the sounds of the letters rather than on the word as a unit. See PHONEME, PHONETICS, and SOUND.

phrase metaphor a CLICHÉ. For a more detailed discussion, see METAPHOR.

phrasing (from Greek for "diction, telling") the syntactical, sonic, semantic, and rhythmical relationships among a group of words. The PACE of phrases, clauses, and sentences lends dramatic effect and sculptural quality to experience transmitted via language. For instance, in Edwin Honig's translation of Fernando Pessoa's *If They Want Me To Be a Mystic, Fine. So I'm a Mystic*, the combinations of monosyllabics, rhythm, and declarative statements within a structure of variation and COUNTERPOINT makes p. a chief element of the poem:

> If they want me to be a mystic, fine. So I'm a mystic.
> I'm a mystic, but only of the body.
> My soul is simple; it doesn't think.
>
> My mysticism consists in not desiring to know,
> In living without thinking about it.
>
> I don't know what Nature is; I sing it.
> I live on a hilltop
> In a solitary cabin.
> And that's what it's all about.

See CADENCE, FREE VERSE, RHYTHM, and SENTENCE SOUNDS.

physical distance: See AESTHETIC DISTANCE.

physicality/physicalness the quality of concreteness effected by the various elements of poetry, such as IMAGE, RHYTHM, SELECTED DETAIL, and TYPOGRAPHICAL ARRANGEMENT. Dylan Thomas, in speaking of p./p. of word-sounds, explained how as a child he loved "the shape and shade and size and noise of the words as they hummed, strummed, jigged and galloped along." See ABSTRACT TERMS AND CONCRETE TERMS.

Pindaric Ode (also known as "regular ode") an ODE composed of a STROPHE and ANTISTROPHE in one stanzaic form, and an EPODE in a different stanzaic form. See ODE.

pitch (of obscure derivation) a musical term indicating the frequency of sound of a syllable (see *musical scansion* under SCANSION). John Frederick Nims's *Western Wind* presents the following *Scale of English Vowel Sounds* in ascending order:

```
                                              ē
                                         ā  (bee)
                                       ī    (bay)
                                    i  (buy)
                                  e  (bit)
                                a  (bet)
                             ur  (bat)
                            u  (bird)
                           ä  (bud)
                        ou  (bar)
                      oi  (bough)
                    ô    (boy)
                  oo   (bought)
                 o  (book)
            oo  (bone)
         (boo)
```

One could also create a scale for the consonant groups (see CONSONANTS)

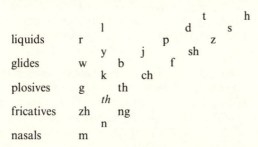

It would be impossible to combine coherently all five consonant groups into one pitch scale because of their mutually exclusive qualities and complex composites of phonemic tones. But by using general guidelines of p., DURATION, LOUDNESS, and STRESS, it is possible to create a "heavy" and "low" feeling using nasals, low vowels, low plosives, and glides, or to create a very "light" feeling by using high plosives, high vowels, and fricatives. P. is very important in evoking drama and emotion, and while much of it can be created or varied only by spoken intonation, the innate p. quality of consonants and vowels can be transmitted in written language. See also PHRASING and SOUND SYSTEMS.

plain style a contemporary term referring to a conversational style of poetry that is uncluttered, easily readable, and accessible. It represents the opposite style of the ornate, pyrotechnic, complex aesthetic surface of writers such as G.M. Hopkins or Wallace Stevens. As a movement in poetry, the style is currently found in the work of young contemporary poets such as Larry Levis. See AESTHETIC SURFACE, CACOPHONY, COLLO-QUIALISM, DENSITY, FLOURISH, IMMEDIACY, LOCATION, OBSCURITY, OVERWRITING, PROSY, TONE, and VOICE. See also *diction* in APPENDIX 1.

planh an exaggerated form of DIRGE or funeral LAMENT in Provençal verse that eulogizes the qualities of the deceased and denigrates those of his survivors. It is a variation of the SIRVENTES. Ezra Pound's poem *Planh for the Young English King*, which laments the death of Prince Henry Plantagenet, is an ADAPTATION of a work by the Provençal poet Bertrans de Born.

Platonic Criticism (also known as "Platonism") the philosophies of Plato (fourth century B.C.) and those who have adopted his idea that the temporal world is a mere reflection of the ideal world. In this system, art (including poetry) is mere illusion, an imitation of the temporal world which, in turn, is an imitation of the ideal, actual world. In *The Republic*, Plato banned artists from his ideal society because they make falsehoods. He believed (*Dialogues*) that the function of art is to serve the public good, to encourage positive, higher moral values through imitation of the manifestations of this world of the divine. See *Aristotelian Criticism* under CRITICISM. See also *criticism* in APPENDIX 1.

play-within-a-play a dramatic structural convention that sets a smaller play within the confines of a larger play, oftentimes so that DRAMATIC IRONY results. Shakespeare used the narrative device in both *Hamlet* and *The Taming of the Shrew*. Fiction writers and poets have also successfully used the concentric strategy in a variety of ways. See FRAME STORY and STORY-WITHIN-A-STORY. See also *dramatic terms* in APPENDIX 1.

pleonasm /plē'ōnazəm/ (from Greek for "superfluous, redundant"; also called "pleonasmus") a rhetorical device of POETIC LICENSE that displays needless repetition or redundancy for the sake of mellifluousness, pleasing phrasing, or emphasis: "We should be together and *not separate* / or choose *different paths.*" See PERISSOLOGIA, PLOCE, and TAUTOLOGY. See also *devices of poetic license* in APPENDIX 2.

ploce /plō'sē/ (Greek for "complication") a rhetorical figure of repetition, usually of a proper name, that repeats the same name with differing meanings:

> When I put Death against his adversary, Death,
> I knew that there would be nothing left.

See PARADOX. See also *figures of repetition* in APPENDIX 2.

plot the selection and orchestration of the incidents that relate a story, reveal character, and affect unity in a work. Known by Aristotle as the "soul of tragedy," the device of p. offers the possibility of achieving complexity, depth, and emotional range within its DRAMATIC STRUCTURE. In terms of tragedy, the classic five-part form displays (1) an *exposition* or *introduction*, explaining the setting, characters, and past events; (2) *rising action (complication)*, introducing new material along with the element of conflict; (3) *climax*, which peaks the action; (4) *falling action*, pointing toward the tragic fall of a character; and (5) *catastrophe (dénoument)*, leaving the PROTAGONIST to his final fate. Other elements often used in p. are: *intrigue*, action of a subversive nature aimed by one character at another; *suspense*, hints that create audience anticipation toward future events; *surprise*, unpredictable but not unprepared-for turns in the p.; *double plot* (SUBPLOT), action that parallels or contrasts the main p.; and PERIPETEIA, sudden changes in the assumed direction of the p. Most well-known dramatists writing in a five-act structure use these elements. P. is also an essential element in the rhetorical mode of NARRATION. See *dramatic terms* in APPENDIX 1.

plurisignation (from Latin for "several distinguishing marks") the producing of multiple directions of thought from the use of double entendres. This skillful use of AMBIGUITY produces IRONY or PARADOX, and is often employed in poetry.

poem (from Greek for "thing created") an artistically organized use of language that cannot be replaced by PARAPHRASE. Generally speaking, a p. will use all or some of the following: RHYTHM, IMAGERY, SONICS, *rhetorical and poetical devices* (see APPENDIX 2), TYPOGRAPHICAL ARRANGEMENT, selective DICTION, economical PHRASING, LINE ENDING, and qualities of imagination, emotion, and insightfulness. Oftentimes, the term is not used to designate an art form, but a high level of perception in any medium. Donald Hall (*Goatfoot, Milktongue, Twinbird*, 1980) defined a p. as "one man's inside talking to another man's inside." Emily Dickinson said she knew she was reading poetry when she felt as if the top of her head were taken off. Carl Sandburg (*Good Morning America*, 1928) in his *Tentative (First Model) Definitions of Poetry* attempted 38 imaginative definitions of poetry. William Blake defined poetry as "allegory addressed to the intellectual powers"; Coleridge maintained it is "the identity of knowledge." Most critics and writers agree on its power to move its readers with its depth of penetration, but few agree upon a specific definition. See HERESY OF PARAPHRASE and VERSE.

poesy /pō′əzi/ (also spelled "poesie"; romantic variation of POEM) an archaic synonym for poetry. Ben Jonson defined the term as the poet's "skill, or crafte of making," while the poem, he said, "is the work of the poet." Most contemporary writers and critics use the term in a derogatory or humorous sense.

poet (from Greek for "maker") one who is artistically gifted and skilled in producing imaginative, rigorously organized, songlike language for the sake of entertainment, instruction, or discovery. On being a p., Margaret Atwood said: "Being a poet isn't something you are or choose. It's something that happens to you at irregular intervals and with no guarantee it will happen again." Poets have taken on a number of roles, sometimes in contemporary poetry called masks or voices, from lover to political satirist, from stand-up comedian to prophet and soothsayer. See *names for poets* under APPENDIX 1.

poetaster /pō′ət-/ (from *poet*, plus *aster*, a Latin suffix for "not authentic") one who uses the art and devices of poetry in a trivializing or inferior manner. See HACK. See also *clichés* in APPENDIX 1.

poetic a quality of mind or a quality of perception produced by the devices reserved for poetry. See POEM and POET. See also *diction* in APPENDIX 1.

poetic attachments the peripheral addenda of a poem, e.g., CODA, DEDICATION, EPILOGUE, and PRELUDE.

poetic closure (see CLOSURE) the conclusion or ending of a poem. Generally, poems can end effectively with the use of a resolution of conflict, summary or concluding statement, repetition, refrain, or structural balance. The p.c. can be open, as in the EASTERN ENDING style, or closed, as in the finality of the WESTERN ENDING. For an in-depth study on how poems end, see Barbara Smith's *Poetic Closure: A Study of How Poems End*, University of Chicago, 1971. See structural possibilities under THEMATIC STRUCTURE. See also *closure* in APPENDIX 1.

poetic diction (see DICTION) the use of heightened, carefully selected words combined with rhetorical and poetical devices to effect grace, brevity, music, and imaginative insight. P.d. in modern times lies midway between prose and the p.d. of the 19th century. Over the years there have been many arguments for and against the use of p.d. so that fluctuating views have formed an ongoing DIALECTIC in poetics. Aristotle's *Poetics* argues that poets should use "metaphors, unusual words, and various stylistic ornaments." Romantics such as Wordsworth held that p.d. should reflect the colloquial language of men "in a state of vivid sensation." In CONTEMPORARY POETRY, the old conventions of p.d. used by the Elizabethans, the Augustans, the Romantics, etc., are looked upon as artificially contrived or overly ornate uses of language not fitting today's sparer sense of poetics, except, perhaps, for the uses of humor or SATIRE. See also *diction* in APPENDIX 1.

poetic drama   verse plays, usually composed of BLANK VERSE or, as in the case of HEROIC DRAMA, written in heroic couplets (see HEROIC COUPLET). The term includes the great tragedies, comedies, and histories of Shakespeare as well as minor, occasional poetic dramas of community theater.

poetic justice   Thomas Rhymer's critical phrase in the 17th century indicating the moral function of literature to punish wrong-doing and to reward virtue. This concept of fate stemming from one's actions is not closely observed in either Classical or modern literature since it is not reflective of life in general. But certain critics observing the dictates of DECORUM (see NEO-CLASSICISM) felt that p.j. is a natural outcome and obligatory element of drama.

poetic license   the violation of conventional word usage, fact, logic, or reality for the sake of achieving an aesthetic effect or for fulfilling an established pattern. The range of elements included in p.l. extends from "tolerable vices" in the use of rhetorical and poetical devices (grammatical constructions, repetitions, contradictions) to technical distortions (the wrenching of rhythm, rhyme, and pronunciation for the sake of meter, rhyme scheme, grace, or brevity) to states of consciousness (the disparities of the Surrealists, Cubists, etc.). The imaginative writer has the right to employ this "license" since, from ancient times, poets have been known primarily as inventors (the word "poet" literally means "maker"). Critically speaking, the use of p.l. is judged to be successful by the degree of effect it achieves. See ARCHAISM, FIGURATIVE LANGUAGE, INVERSION, and PLATONIC CRITICISM. Terms that fall under the rhetorical category of "tolerable vices" are ACYRON, AMPHIBOLOGIA, ASCHEMATISTON, BOMPHIOLOGIA, CACEMPHATON, CACOSYNTHETON, CACOZELIA, CACOZELON, HOMIOLOGIA, PARELCON, PERIERGIA, PERISSOLOGIA, PLEONASM, SOLECISMUS, SORIASMUS, TAPINOSIS, and TAUTOLOGIA. See also *devices of poetic license* in APPENDIX 2.

poetic prose   intensified and elaborate PROSE that uses *rhetorical and poetical devices* (see APPENDIX 2) and elements of aesthetic texture (sound, rhythm, imagery, etc.). P.p. is not to be confused with the PROSE POEM, which intends itself to be poetry in a prose format. Fiction writers such as Herman Melville, William Faulkner, Lawrence Durrell, D.H. Lawrence, Gertrude Stein, James Joyce, Oscar Wilde, and Henry Miller, among others, have achieved success with p.p. See POLYPHONIC PROSE and PROSE RHYTHM.

poeticism a word or phrase with an archaic poetical heritage used to decorate a poem; e.g., in modern literature the words "harken" and "beckon" would be seen as poeticisms. See ARCHAISM and POETIC DICTION. See also *diction* in APPENDIX 1.

poetics theories dealing with the nature, composition, or criticism of poetry; also, a specific tract on poetry. Poets and critics for at least 23 centuries have written principles, theories, rules, and technical studies extolling their various views; e.g., Aristotle's *Poetics* begins:

> Our subject being poetry, I propose to speak not only of the art in general but also of its species and their respective capacities; of the structure of plot required for a good poem; of the number and nature of the constituent parts of a poem; and likewise of any other matters in the same line of inquiry. Let us follow the natural order and begin with the primary facts.

There follows a discussion of theories on the study and writing of poetry which includes writers from former periods of Greek literature, from a plethora of aesthetic stances and movements. In modern times, Ezra Pound and T.S. Eliot heavily influenced the direction of modern poetry, and in contemporary times, the theories of Robert Bly have made their mark. See *theoretical criticism* under CRITICISM. See also the BIBLIOGRAPHY for a list of important contemporary books that discuss the subject.

poet laureate /lô′ri·ət/ the English honorary title bestowed upon a poet chosen by the King to represent him. In former times, the p.l. was paid for composing occasional verse glorifying and entertaining the royal household. Eventually, this public-relations function was dropped, possibly because it produced so many mediocre works. Thus the office came to be stipended solely as an honorary award. The first officially recognized royal poet was Ben Jonson (1573–1637), and the first poet to be titled p.l. was John Dryden (1688). Other poets laureate have included Wordsworth, Tennyson, Robert Bridges, and John Masefield. The origin of the title derives from the Greek ceremony of placing a wreath of laurel on the head of one who had attained excellence in sports or oratory. During the Medieval period, universities awarded the title to students who excelled in Latin rhetoric. The United States has a p.l. in the office of the Poet of the Library of Congress, and several states have their own p.l. For a history of the politics of the office of the p.l. in England, see John Tieman's unpublished Master's thesis *The Politics of the Poet Laureateship: Antecedents to Dryden, Dryden to Tennyson* (SMU, 1979). See *names for poets* in APPENDIX 1.

poetry (see POEM) a highly organized, artistic genre of oral or written expression that seeks to instruct, inform, or entertain. Some contemporary writers make a distinction between writing poems and writing p.; that is, the former produces a discrete objet d'art, and the latter is an ongoing process, which can be arbitrarily stopped at any point. It has been said that Pablo Neruda wrote p. not poems.

poetry therapy the use of poetry writing as a prescriptive method of resolving or alleviating psychological disorders. Because much poetry writing depends on the vehicles of memory and the subconscious, it is possible to use the poetic process to track down original traumatic events and through self-exploration make these events conscious and thus more manageable. See GESTALT.

point of view the physical, mental, or personal perspective an author maintains toward the events he recounts. The *physical p.o.v.* is the angle of view (see CINEMATIC TECHNIQUES) and time frame from which a story is told. The *mental p.o.v.* is the perspective of consciousness (see LOCATION) and emotional attitude (see TONE) an author maintains toward his story. The *personal p.o.v.* indicates the distance an author maintains between his speaker (writer as narrator or NARRATOR AGENT) and his story. If the story is told in the *first-person p.o.v.* ("I" or "we"), the speaker is a participant and has the emotional, subjective power of an involved witness (much contemporary poetry in the lyric mode has this p.o.v.). The *second-person p.o.v.* ("you") allows more distance, thus more objective freedom, and carries a demanding, sometimes accusatory, tone. The "you" voice often represents a MASKED PRONOUN OR FALSE PRONOUN since it can substitute for "I" or "he." The *third-person p.o.v.* offers different kinds of freedom: (1) that of the *omniscient p.o.v.*, in which the speaker freely roams in and among his characters and their thoughts and actions, either intruding with editorial comments (see EDITORIAL INTRUSION) or remaining impersonal; and (2) that of the *limited p.o.v.*, in which the speaker limits himself to the view of one character's thoughts and actions, sometimes reporting objectively the state of consciousness of that character (see STREAM-OF-CONSCIOUSNESS). See NARRATION.

political myth (see MYTH) an imaginative construct meant to point out political problems.

polyphonic prose (*polyphonic*, from Greek for "variety of tones or speech") poetry written in the format of prose. The term was coined by John Gould Fletcher, and the first p.p. of its type is found in Amy Lowell's *Can Grande's Castle* (1918) although the genre had its precursor in the French PROSE POEM of the 19th century. As with prose poems, the form is intended to be poetry, and to contain the devices and freedom of poetry with the exception of the line break. A similar form, POETIC PROSE, is intended to be prose with the inclusion of poetic devices. See also *prose forms* in APPENDIX 1.

polyptoton /-tō′ton/ (from Greek for "many" plus "falling") a rhetorical figure of repetition that repeats either (1) the same root word in its various forms: "Wouldn't it be nice to spend one's *life* / earning a *living* by learning how to *live?*" or (2) the repetition of an identical syllable in semantically unrelated words: "*Al always al*igned his thoughts." See *figures of repetition* in APPENDIX 2.

polyrhythmic (from Greek for "many rhythms") prose or verse forms containing various rhythmic systems based on meter or free rhythms. The strophic movements of the ODE and the base and generational rhythms of

FREE VERSE (see RHYTHM) display these changes in pacing and rhythm. See CADENCE, LOGAOEDIC, METER, and PROSE RHYTHM.

polysyllabic rhyme: See MULTIPLE RHYME OR P.R.

polysyllabics (from Greek for "many syllables") a style of writing that employs words containing three or more syllables, or lines containing a large amount of words with multiple syllables. The style effects speed, lightness, and WILDNESS, as opposed to the slower, more emphatic monosyllabic type of line. Writers from early times to modern times have been noted for use of p. See MONOSYLLABICS.

polysyndeton /-sin′-/ (from Greek for "binding many together") a *grammatical device of rhythm and balance* in rhetoric that employs the repetition of conjunctions to effect measured thought and solemnity:

> Time moves by seconds, and by minutes, and by hours,
> and by years, and by centuries, and by millenia.

The device is the opposite of ASYNDETON and BRACHYLOGIA which omit the conjunction between words and clauses. See *grammatical devices of rhythm and balance* in APPENDIX 2.

Pop Art a 20th-century movement in poetry and painting that turns language or images from "popular" culture into aesthetic objects. Andy Warhol's *Campbell Soup Can* painting simply depicts a can of the commercial product, but the art is in the painting not the object. The artist means to call our attention back to objects, especially overly familiar objects, so that we may reexperience them. The style is a combination of the old master's use of still lives and a form of revitalizing a dead CLICHÉ (see *dead metaphor* under METAPHOR). See FOUND ART, MINIMALISM, and READYMADE.

popular ballad a BALLAD that has an anonymous author and has been passed down orally through the generations (see ORAL POETRY). Usually, the form is simple, unpretentious, and replete with MNEMONIC DEVICES such as meter, rhyme, and refrains. In America, songs of love and loss are still sung in Appalachia by descendants of the English, Irish, and Scotch; and Western ballads of heroism and travail (*Frankie and Johnny, John Henry, The Streets of Laredo,* etc.) are still extant in films, stage plays, and live performances. See ART BALLAD, BALLAD METER, FOLK BALLAD, and FOLK SONG.

portmanteau /pôrtman′tō, pôrtmantō′/ (from French for "cloak carrier") a word synthetically invented by combining the sounds of two distinctly different words, thus fusing their meanings. The word p. refers to a British trunk composed of two halves. The term was brought into literary criticism by Lewis Carroll (*Through the Looking Glass*) whose Humpty Dumpty explained the use of the p. in the poem *Jabberwocky*. James Joyce in *Ulysses* and *Finnigan's Wake* used such conglomerates as "bisexcycles," and Ogden Nash was fond of the device. See NEOLOGISM, and SPOONERISM. See also *devices of poetic license* in APPENDIX 2, and *diction* in APPENDIX 1.

Post-Modernists a post-World-War-II international poetry movement heavily influenced by the fiction techniques of NARRATION, POINT OF VIEW, and PHRASING, which relaxed the dictates of economy in modernist theory by introducing the increased use of loose lineation, FLAT STATEMENT, and colloquial diction. The availability of good translations has, as much as any set of poetics, affected the new style. Poets such as James Wright in North America, Cesare Pavese in Italy, and Julio Cortazar in South America are major figures in the movement. See CONTEMPORARY POETRY, MODERN PERIOD, and TRANSLATION.

poulter's measure /pōl'tər/ (from *poultry*; also called "poulterer's measure") a fanciful name for a meter composed of alternating 12- and 14-syllable lines (ALEXANDRINE and FOURTEENERS) extant in the 16th century. The term derives from the egg merchant's custom of giving 12 eggs in the dozen bought, and 14 in the second dozen bought. The form is very close to the SHORT MEASURE OR SHORT METER of English hymns. Poets such as Wyatt, Surrey, and Sidney employed variations of the p.m. Because of the monotony of the form, it fell into disuse. See also *forms* in APPENDIX 1.

practical criticism a form of applied criticism that seeks to set already formulated theories to the study of specific works. It is the opposite of THEORETICAL CRITICISM. See CRITICISM and PRAGMATIC THEORY OF ART. For a list of important works of p.c., see the BIBLIOGRAPHY. See also *criticism* in APPENDIX 1.

Pragmatic criticism a form of literary evaluation judging the success of a work according to the effect it has on an audience. See CRITICISM. See also *criticism* in APPENDIX 1.

Pragmatic Theory of Art the aesthetic concept holding that a work of art must primarily function for practical, social purposes rather than for the effects of the work itself (see AESTHETICISM and ARS GRATIA ARTIS). William James, a 19th-century American leader of the theory, held that a true conception's whole meaning "expresses itself in practical consequences, either in the shape of conduct to be recommended, or of experiences to be expected. . . ." The theory is a natural outgrowth of NATURALISM and REALISM, both of which tauted social reform. The opposite of P.T.o.A. is the OBJECTIVE THEORY OF ART. See CRITICISM, DIDACTIC POETRY, PRACTICAL CRITICISM, and PROPAGANDIST LITERATURE. See also *criticism in* APPENDIX 1.

pragmatographia a rhetorical form of imaginative description that colorfully recounts the story of a fictitious event. See HYPOTYPOSIS. See also *figures of subject and adjunct* in APPENDIX 2.

preciousness (from French for "costly, valuable"; also known as "preciosity") a highly refined, light and delicate style of writing that employs an affected type of daintiness of subject matter and imagery, as in Alexander Pope's satirical *The Rape of the Lock*. P. differs from EUPHUISM and GONGORISM in that the latter are forms of OVERWRITING that employ superfluous figures, rhythm, images, and sound devices. See PURPLE PATCH. See also *control* and *diction* in APPENDIX 1.

précis /prāsē′/ (French for "concise"; a similarly used term is PARAPHRASE) a summary of the events and themes in a work. See HERESY OF PARAPHRASE and POEM.

predictability (from Latin for "to say beforehand") the characteristic that is designed to satisfy explicit or implied expectations set up by the PLOT, EMOTIVE THRUST, ARGUMENT, or THEMATIC STRUCTURE of a work. Unless an author is writing in a humorous or ironic genre such as PARODY, BURLESQUE, or SATIRE, too much dependence upon the element of p. becomes a defect in writing and tends to elicit a STOCK RESPONSE from the reader. Usually, writers try to maintain a balance between p. and *surprise* in order to effect a sense of both satisfaction and tension. See CLICHÉ, COMMITTING WORD, OBLIGATORY SCENE, and SURPRISE ENDING.

prelude /prel′yōōd/ (from French *prélude*, for "preliminary play") a short work meant to introduce a longer one. Sometimes the p. functions as an independent work, as it does in musical compositions and poems such as Wordsworth's *The Prelude* and T.S. Eliot's *Preludes*. See EPILOGUE, PROLOGUE, and PROEM. See also *sections of poems* under *forms* in APPENDIX 1.

preposition metaphor a METAPHOR in the grammatical form of a prepositional phrase, as in "the summer of my delight."

Pre-Raphaelites a mid-19th-century reactionary aesthetic movement founded in 1848 by painters and poets who attempted to recapture the spirit of devotion and simplicity extant in the religious art of the Italian Renaissance painter Raphael (1483–1520). The group, first known as the "Pre-Raphaelite Brotherhood," came to include Dante Gabriel Rossetti, Christina Rossetti, William Morris, John Millais, Algernon Swinburne, and William Holman Hunt. In their paintings and poems, they employed intricate and sensuous detail, symbols, and rhythms; but they came under ridicule by critics such as Robert W. Buchanan who accused the group of being a "Mutual Admiration School"; he contemptuously termed the group the FLESHLY SCHOOL OF POETRY because it often depicted nakedness.

primary accent the most heavily stressed syllable in a meter or foot. See ACCENT, METER, and STRESS.

procatalepsis /-lep′-/ (Greek for "anticipation") a rhetorical *figure of argumentation* in which a speaker undermines an opponent's argument by anticipating and answering it. See *figures of argumentation* in APPENDIX 2.

process of metaphor-making (see METAPHOR) the mental functions of identity, substitution, and comparison that produce *figurative expressions*.

proclees /prok′lēs/ a rhetorical *figure of ethos* in which a speaker provokes conflict by finding fault with an opponent, or by demanding reasons for certain behavior. See *figures of ethos* in APPENDIX 2.

product vs. process a DIALECTIC that describes the dual nature of a poem as well as a struggle between opposing camps in contemporary poetics. On the one hand, a poem is a *product*, an object of art, for the *reader* to experience; on the other hand, a poem is the fossilized imprint of the *poet's process* of creation and discovery—furthermore, some critics have suggested that reading a poem is an act that re-creates the poem and process of composition. The opposing camps in contemporary poetry (PROJECTIVE VERSE VS. NEW CRITICISM) have essential differences in their choices of styles, subjects, and philosophical and social viewpoints, and, indeed, even in the life-styles and livelihoods of the poets themselves. But the debate between the two camps cannot be dismissed as differences in temperament and personality, for the arguments have their paradigms in the differences between Aristotle's view of the poem as an aesthetic artifact (see CRITICISM) and Longinus' view of the poem as an absorption in ecstasy; that is, an on-going struggle (see DUENDE). In the 19th century, the debate between the adherents of process and those of product was manifested by the dialectics between the Romantics and Neo-Classicists, and later between the two major outgrowths of Romanticism: symbolism and REALISM.

proecthesis /prō·ek′-/ (from Greek *ekthesis*, for "exposition") a rhetorical figure of argumentation by excuse that gives good reason why one should not be blamed for transgressions of authority. See *figures of argumentation* in APPENDIX 2.

proem /prō′əm/ (from Greek for "before a song or poem") an introductory passage to a longer work. Some critics have used the term as a PORTMANTEAU, combining the words "prose" and "poem" into p., but the term did not originally refer to the PROSE POEM. See EPILOGUE and PRELUDE.

Projective Verse (a similarly used term is OPEN FIELD COMPOSITION) a theory of FREE VERSE, promulgated by the Black Mountain School of poets: Charles Olson, Robert Creeley, Robert Duncan, Edward Dorn, and Denise Levertov, among others. P.V. called for an openness of form and an ORGANIC COMPOSITION process in order to allow for flexible rhythms based on the poet's breath (similar to Allen Ginsberg's "mind-breath"), as well as to allow disparate associations and allusions to enter the field of the poem. P.V. is an extension of Ezra Pound's and W.C. Williams' poetics which call attention to the creative process of making a poem: "The HEAD, by way of the EAR, to the SYLLABLE .... the HEART, by way of the BREATH, to the LINE," according to Olson. In his essay *Projective Verse* (1951), Olson calls for the poem to discharge high energy through this "proprioceptive act: One perception must immediately and directly lead to a further perception." This mode of composition or apperception is based on Robert Creeley's "law" that "form is never more than an extension of content." These dicta are in reaction to what the Projectivists saw as the prescriptions of "closed verse" espoused by the NEW CRITICISM of the '30s and '40s. The spiritual mentor of P.V. is Walt Whitman; the technical mentor is Ezra Pound. Critics disagree as to whether the practitioners of P.V., especially Olson, have, in fact, manifested their theories into actual poems, but the movement is generally credited with having opened up mid-20th-century American poetry to new freedoms and ideas of composition. See PRODUCT VS. PROCESS and PROPRIOCEPTION.

prolepsis /-lep'-/ (Greek for "preconception" or "anticipation") a rhetorical *figure of division* in which a matter is stated in a brief summary and then its parts are listed in detail: "Nature is a mirror of time. It is temporary, cyclical, generational, and eternal." The term is also used for a representation of something accomplished that actually lies in the future, e.g., Hamlet exclaiming upon being wounded, "Horatio, I am dead." Another use of the figure is as a synonym for PROCATALEPSIS, the anticipation and answering of an opponent's argument; further, as a synonym for *prochronism* or *anachronism*, a chronological displacement in which a person or event is assigned a date other than the correct one. See *figures of division* in APPENDIX 2.

prologue the introduction to a poem or play. See PROEM. See also *forms* in APPENDIX 1.

propagandist literature didactic or political works that seek to persuade a reader to take a particular stand or action on practical issues such as race relations, religious tolerance, war protest, or other sociopolitical issues. Allen Ginsberg's and Denise Levertov's anti-Vietnam and antinuclear poems and the feminist poems of Adrienne Rich, among others, make practical and moral statements. See DIDACTIC POETRY, NATURALISM, PRAGMATIC THEORY OF ART, and REALISM.

proposito /-poz'-/ (from Latin for "a thing proposed") a rhetorical *figure of division* that defines by briefly outlining what is about to follow in detail:

> Life is a matter of three things: observing keenly,
> experiencing deeply, then remembering what one forgot.

See PROLEPSIS. See also *figures of division* in APPENDIX 2.

proprioception Charles Olson's term (*Proprioception*, 1965) for the body's sensation of itself. He extended the term to refer to a kinesthetic theory of composition in which a poem is transformed from outer reality into language which, in turn, is projected into the reader and causes him to experience. Olson maintains that a poem is a "high energy construct" which dictates its own development, form, and message; and that its final form is the only possible form for a particular set of experiences and content. See OPEN FIELD COMPOSITION, ORGANIC COMPOSITION, and PROJECTIVE VERSE.

prosapodosis a rhetorical *figure of argumentation* (see APPENDIX 2) that lists reasons for some purpose, does not omit any reasons, and reinforces each reason as it is spoken. Usually, this argumentative device carries with it a tone of reproval or unpleasantness:

If you don't believe me, you are calling me a liar;
If I do not answer, silence is the scabbard of my guilt.

See APOPHASIS. See also *figures of argumentation* in APPENDIX 2.

prose (from Latin *prosa*, "straightforward [discourse]") written language generally lying midway between verse and spoken language. Although some critics have defined p. as containing nonrecurrent or irregular rhythms, and containing no formal line breaks, other critics have pointed out the highly developed sense of improvisational and counterpointed rhythms in the works of skilled writers throughout literary history. Coleridge showed the differences between p. and poetry in his advice to young poets by saying: "... prose—words in their best order; poetry—the best words in their best order," implying that p. contains an inferior choice or more relaxed selection of words. Interestingly, p. is a language development that took place in most cultures after the emergence of poetry. Northrop Frye notes that poetry contains an unconscious associative sound-image process which discursive prose lacks. But for every rule, principle, or definition for p. and poetry, there are notable and skilled exceptions which make a clear and fast definition impossible. See POETIC P., POLYPHONIC P., P. POEM, P. RHYTHM, RHYTHM, and VERSE.

prose poem (sometimes incorrectly referred to with the portmanteau PROEM) a form of poetry in prose format that contains the devices and modes of perception of lined-out poetry. The real roots of the p.p. go back as far as the origins of poetry itself since the line break is a relatively recent invention—neither the ancient Greeks nor the Anglo-Saxons in their original manuscripts employed line endings. But the earliest forms of the p.p., as a separate genre, appear in the Old Testament, early folk tales, fables, and parables which used ALLUSION, SYMBOL, and IMAGERY in a less diluted form than is usually found in PROSE. There are also early traces of prose poetry in the Chinese *rhyme-prose* in the Fu form, which incorporates rhythmical and metrical patterns in prose form. This process of word association was called the "time of inspiration" when the poet flew from one word to another, or as the Chinese called it, "riding on dragons" (see LEAPING POETRY).

But the recognized beginning of prose poetry was in 19th-century France where the French Academy's rigid rules of versification drove some great poetic originators into prose. The first widely known prose poems are those of Charles Baudelaire who was initially influenced by Aloysius Bertrand who wrote his "new genre of prose" using rural subject matter. Baudelaire adapted the form to urban settings and produced *Petits Poèmes en Prose*, or *Spleen de Paris* (published posthumously, in 1869) which combines vivid imagery and humorous philosophical observations on his fellow Parisians. Baudelaire asks: "Which one of us, in his moments of ambition, has not dreamed of the miracle of a poetic prose, musical, without rhythm and without rhyme, supple enough and rugged enough to adapt itself to the lyrical impulses of the soul, the undulations of reverie, the jibes of conscience?" Other French SYMBOLISTS, such as Arthur Rimbaud, Stephane Mallarmé, and Paul Valéry also wrote in this new form. The emergence of the p.p. in the United States was slow. Even in the *International Index to Periodicals* it is not until July of 1934 that a reference is made to the p.p. as a peripheral form, and not until April of 1946 that it appears as a separate entry. Because the p.p. is a larger and looser form than lined poetry, it can carry more information and often shows a close interest in everyday affairs. Prose has been the traditional link between popular audiences and literature (discounting oral poetry). In response to both a felt need for a more accessible, wider form and criticism that poetry had devolved into a pure craft which was written for its own sake, the p.p. was welcomed by American poets who sensed the need for more plot and characterization as elements of style. On the other hand, the German poet and critic A.W. Schlegel in the early 1800s thought of prose poetry and POETIC PROSE as interchangeable, saying that ". . . it springs from poetic impotence and it tries to unite the prerogatives of prose and poetry, missing the perfection of both." Once again, the ultimate issue is not one of form but one of substance. Whether a prose piece can be designated as poetic prose or as a p.p. should depend upon the quality of the writer's perceptions.

In its current general use, the p.p. is meant to instruct or entertain. Usually, it is composed of organic associations that move from an implied or stated premise. Many of these premises are wild observations or conditions that are worked into logical proofs by means of rational, linear logic. The level of language is often colloquial, but in some cases it is "mock formal," pretending to be serious but ending in PARODY, a style that masquerades in the voice of authority and expertise. There is a great deal of internal rhythmical and syntactical movement in the poem which takes up the SLACKNESS in formal tension that is the inevitable result of not using line endings. The p.p. rhythm follows that of well-crafted prose sentences which use the phrase as its smallest unit of rhythm, although there is sometimes the REPETITION and COUNTERPOINT that we usually associate with poetry. But, if a steady and predictable rhythm were to be used in the p.p., the natural fluidity of the form would be stultified and the work would seem wooden. Many times the TONE of the p.p. is witty, skeptical, or self-consciously playful, a tone that evolved from the early Symbolist prose poems. The form represents an especially refreshing change from the seriousness and tight form control of most American poetry that follows the Pound and Eliot Modernist tendencies. This is not to say that the p.p. will replace the lined form of poetry, but it has already exerted a healthy effect on international poetry by opening up the range of its subject matter and moods.

A formal definition of the p.p. in recent times, by the poet and anthologist Michael Benedict (*The Prose Poem*, 1976), states: "It is a genre of poetry, self-consciously written in prose, and characterized by the intense use of virtually all the devices of poetry, which includes the intense use of devices of verse. The sole exception to access to the possibilities, rather than set priorities of verse is, we would say, the line-break."

There is a tremendous variety of prose poems being written in countries around the world. One need not write exclusively in this form in order to gain the benefits offered by it. If nothing else, the form opens up the imagination and allows the writer a larger area in which to play. See POETIC PROSE, POLYPHONIC PROSE, PROSE RHYTHM, and VERSE. See also *prose forms* in APPENDIX 1.

prose rhythm a discursive, sinewy type of rhythm that may be irregular but may also contain the larger rhythmical elements of rhetoric such as BALANCE, COUNTERPOINT, PARALLELISM, and CONTRAST. Usually, the p.r. differs from verse rhythm in that it lacks the repetitive rhythmical patterns of poetry and depends upon the larger units of the phrase, the clause, the sentence, and the paragraph rather than the syllable, the measure, the line, and the stanza. The sense of freedom of range and the lack of rigorous rhythmical organization and variation gives the p.r. its identity. See LOGICAL STRESS, PHRASING, PROSE POEM, and RHYTHM.

prosodic symbols marks of metrical notation that indicate the DURATION, STRESS, PAUSE, and RHYME SCHEME of verse:

accents	´	primary accent (ICTUS)
	`	secondary accent
	ˈ	tertiary or light accent
	˘	unaccented syllable (ARSIS)
duration	-	long syllable (MACRON)
	˘	short syllable (BREVE)
	⁀	slurred phrase (DISTRIBUTED STRESS)
pauses	‖	CAESURA
	^	rest or PAUSE
	/	VIRGULE (LINE ENDING or PAUSE)
		line break (WHITE SPACE)
	//	stanza break
rhyme scheme	×	unrhymed syllable
	a,b,c,	sequence of rhymes
	A,B,C,	rhymed refrains
	A1,B1,A2 B2,A3,B4	sequence of refrains

See ACCENT, ARSIS AND THESIS, METER, PROSODY, PUNCTUATION, and SCANSION.

prosody /pros′-/ (from Greek for "tone or accent of a syllable") the study of the theory, principles, and notation of verse, especially the musical aspects of rhythm and sound, and sometimes including rhetorical devices and structure. According to the critic Harvey Gross, the job of p. in the hands of the poet is not to mimic experience in an onomatopoetic sense, but to give "a curve of feeling, the shape of an emotion." Thus the cumulative effect of RHYTHM, SONIC STRUCTURE, devices, PHRASING, rhetorical emphasis, semantic nuance, DICTION, and micro- and macrostructure as experience effect the reader. The two main categories that p. falls into are *literary p.*, which studies the artifical effect of language as used in artistic compositions, and *linguistic p.*, which accounts for the common rhythmical and structural elements found in everyday language. See METER, PROSODIC SYMBOLS, and SCANSION.

prosographia (from Greek for "toward" plus "to write") a rhetorical figure of definition under the category of "subject and adjunct" that vividly describes someone who is not present but who is spoken of as if he were present. See HYPOTYPOSIS. See also *figures of subject and adjunct* in APPENDIX 2.

prosopopoeia /-pē'yə/ (from Greek for "toward" plus "to make"; a similarly used term is PERSONIFICATION) a rhetorical figure of definition that through vivid and imaginative description lends human qualities to an abstraction, or to an animate or inanimate object. Another use of the term refers to the vivid description of a nonexistent, absent, or dead person (see PROSOGRAPHIA). See also *figures of subject and adjunct* in APPENDIX 2, and *figurative expressions* in APPENDIX 1.

prosy a pejorative term derived from the discursive nature of PROSE and indicating a SLACKNESS or rambling quality in a line or selection of verse. Usually, *prosiness* is a result of lack of precision and selectivity in DICTION, RHYTHM, and IMAGE. See *defects in control* and *diction* in APPENDIX 1.

protagonist (from the Greek for "first to lead") in Greek Classical drama, the actor who plays the first part. The term has come to refer to the chief or central character in a work of literature, but one who may not be the hero of a work. The protagonist's opposite with whom he is in conflict is the ANTAGONIST. See AGON, and DEUTERAGONIST. See also *dramatic terms* in APPENDIX 1.

protrope /-trōp'/ (from Greek for "first to turn") a rhetorical *figure of argumentation* that commands or promises, and then offers reasons for doing what is commanded. See *figures of argumentation* in APPENDIX 2.

proverb a short saying commonly used, usually pertaining to advice on how to conduct one's life. Generally, the form displays simple diction, rhetorical devices of brevity, and AMBIGUITY, IMAGE, and METAPHOR, and is usually of unknown authorship: "If ye knew how little people noticed ye, / Ye'd worry less about what they noticed." In his essay *Compensation,* Emerson claimed that proverbs are "the sanctuary of the intuitions" and should be regarded as important as sacred books because both are "statements of absolute truth without qualification." Some proverbs of known authorship include The Book of Proverbs, ascribed to Solomon, closed couplets by Alexander Pope, and those in *Poor Richard's Almanac* by Benjamin Franklin. See APHORISM, GNOMIC WRITING, and PAROEMIA.

prozeugma /-zōog'mə/ (from Greek for "first" plus "yoking") a rhetorical grammatical construction that for the sake of brevity and grace uses a verb in one clause that is understood to apply in the succeeding clause(s): "Her voice *pierced* my ears; her words, my heart." See HYPOZEUGMA, and ZEUGMA. See also *grammatical constructions that are technically incorrect* in APPENDIX 2.

psalm /säm/ (from Greek for "a twitching [of the strings of a harp]") a religious lyrical song extolling the glory of God and used in conjunction with prayer or worship. The p. can be considered in a general sense any song of a sacred nature. The Book of Psalms, attributed to King David of Israel, is a collection of some of the oldest extant psalms.

pseudonym: See ALLONYM.

psychic distance: See AESTHETIC DISTANCE; see also DISTANCE AND INVOLVEMENT.

pun (probably shortened from Italian *puntiglio*, for "fine point") a word used in a witty way so that its similarity to another word is emphasized. In *Romeo and Juliet*, Mercutio, who is about to die, says: "Ask for me tomorrow and you shall find me a *grave* man." The Elizabethan dramatists often used the word "die" to mean both "loss of life" and "sexual climax." The device in its various forms is ancient and was not used solely for humorous purposes until the 18th century. Today, the device is considered a low form of humor though writers such as James Joyce have used extensive verbal play in a serious manner. Modern poems that depend on pun include Langston Hughes' *Cross*, Siegfried Sassoon's *Base Details*, and Bill Knott's *A Sudden Departure*. Specific forms of the pun are AMPHIBOLOGIA, ANTANACLASIS, ANTHIMERIA, ANTONOMASIA, DOUBLE ENTENDRE, EQUIVOQUE, HYPALLAGE, NOEMA, PARONOMASIA, POLYPTOTON, PLOCE, RIME RICHE, and SYLLEPSIS. See WIT. See also *figurative expressions* and *humor* APPENDIX 1.

punctuation (from Latin *punctus*, for "point") a system of marks that separate and organize words into groups of phrases, clauses, and sentences. P. marks speed, flow, emphasis, direction, and emotional impulse of written language, and can indicate the duration of a pause, the setting up of a sequence, and the amount and quality of energy that a syntactical unit possesses. The following English p. is commonly used:

comma	,	indicates a slight pause
semicolon	;	indicates a heavy pause, or clauses, or a series containing commas
colon	:	indicates a heavy pause; introduces a list, explanation or quotation
period	.	indicates a full stop at end of sentence or abbreviated word
ellipsis	. . .	indicates missing content
dash	—	indicates a breaking-off pause
hyphen	-	connects morphemes and compound words
quotation marks	" "	indicate quoted or unusual material
	' '	indicate a quotation within a quotation
slash (VIRGULE)	/	indicates a line or foot ending
exclamation point	!	indicates emphasis or emotion
question mark	?	indicates a request for information
parentheses	( )	indicate an aside
brackets	[ ]	indicate an editorial comment
italics	*italics*	indicate emphasis, foreign words, or titles

In using p. in poetry, critics and writers generally agree that it is best to use a consistent system; the same rule of thumb applies to using no punctuation at all—there should be a consistent lack of it.

Because poetry has built-in elements of control that can take over the function of p. (syntax, words, lineation, and rhythm), many poets find the use of p. redundant. They feel it clutters the purity of the line and poem. For some of these poets, traditional p. does not give the poem the exact sense of timing it requires. Just as certain Asian, blue-grass, and jazz-rock music calls for a bending of the notes, so some contemporary poetry requires a slurring or fusion of normally end-stopped clauses and sentences. Along with this break in the tradition of standard p., poets such as e.e. cummings pioneered in altering the expected capitalization of words. The Chinese language of ideograms (word-pictures and symbols) contains a number of different picture-words that stand for the letter "I." One is the picture of a man holding his arms out wide as if to proclaim his greatness or receive a great spirit; another is that of a man with his hand over his mouth, as if he were abashed. In poetry, we have the symbols of the self-aggrandizing "I" and the self-effacing "i," which follow the same two meanings of the Chinese ideograms. Poets such as cummings have paid close attention to the implications these symbols contain.

As long as the poem has a consistent, uniform set of p. principles that are organically related to the theme, the reader should have no problem interpreting the way the poem should be read. This is true whether the p. is traditional or experimental.

Here are a few ways poets have circumvented the use of traditional p.:

single comma	rules, = rules
	(using a short space or line ending after it)
multiple commas	rules, rules, rules, = rules rules rules
	or rules
	rules
	rules
dash and colon	rules—Let's change them = rules
	Let's change them
	rules: let's change them
quotation marks	He said, "Rules." = He said Rules.
	(Content replaces the need for " ")
question mark	"Why not?" he asked = Why not he
	asked
	(Content replaces need for "?")
parentheses	Rules (let's change them) = Rules
	Let's change them
	(indentation shows subordinate character).

See PROSODIC SYMBOLS and TYPOGRAPHICAL ARRANGEMENT.

pure poetry poetry that depends for its effect more on music than on statement. E.A. Poe (1809–49) first suggested the term (*The Poetic Principle*) as representing the condition to which poetry should aspire. The French SYMBOLISTS came closest to practicing the style although writers such as Dylan Thomas and Wallace Stevens might fit the prescriptive mold of p.p. Pushed to its limits, p.p. would tend toward the style of ABSTRACT POETRY or NONSENSE VERSE.

purple patch (also known as "purple prose") a gaudy or ornate passage in a work. The term originated in Horace's *Ars Poetica* which spoke of the p.p. as a heightened intrusion of extraneous material. As a defect, p.p. is characterized by excesses of sound, rhythm, balancing devices, overwrought diction, POLYSYLLABICS, clotted imagery, and a sense of forced contrivance. As an intended effect, the device seeks to parallel a rise in emotion or heightened action. See BOMBAST, EUPHUISM, GONGORISM, and PRECIOUSNESS.

pyrrhic (a similarly used term is DIBRACH) a Classical Greek metrical foot composed of two short (or unaccented) syllables (˘˘), or a duple extrametrical foot (ANACRUSIS) (from Greek *pyrrhiche*, an ancient martial dance). The term p. is also used as an indication of something won at too great a cost—a "p. victory" (from *Pyrrhus'* victory over the Romans in Apulia in 279 B.C. where he lost his best men). See METER.

pysma (from Greek for "question") a rhetorical form of argument that forcefully repeats many accusing questions, one after another. See *figures of argumentation* in APPENDIX 2.

pythiambic (from *Pythian*, or "Delphic," plus *iambic*) the name of a Classical composite meter used by Horace and consisting of a dactylic hexameter followed by either an iambic dimeter (*first p.*) or an iambic trimeter (*second p.*):

‒˘˘/‒˘˘/‒˘˘/‒˘˘/‒˘˘/‒˘˘/ ˘‒/˘‒/ or ˘‒/˘‒/˘‒

Q

quantitative meter the Classical Greek metrical system based on the duration of a syllable rather than on its amount of stress as in ACCENTUAL-SYLLABIC VERSE. Other languages that have used this prosody are Latin, Hebrew, and occasionally French and English. For a fuller discussion, see METER, QUANTITY, and SCANSION.

quantity the unit of rhythm, based on duration, in Classical PROSODY. In this system, a long syllable (-) is equal in duration to two short syllables (‿‿). This mathematical equivalency forms the basis for SUBSTITUTION and variation in QUANTITATIVE METER. The English ACCENTUAL-SYLLABIC VERSE does not mark off durational units, but uses accentual units instead. Obviously q. is implied though it is not explicitly recognized in the English system of prosody. See METER and SCANSION.

quatorzain /kətôr'zān/ (French for "a collection of fourteen") an archaic term for SONNET. But it has come to indicate any poem in any form composed of 14 lines. See *forms* in APPENDIX 1.

quatrain /kwät'rān/ (French for "a collection of four") a poem or stanza of four lines, usually with alternating rhyme scheme (abab, aabb, abba, aaba, abcb). It is the most common stanzaic form in English and is used in forms such as EPIGRAM, long ballad, short ballad, ART BALLAD, FOLK BALLAD, HYMNAL STANZA, heroic q., IN MEMORIAM STANZA, PANTOUM, BOB AND WHEEL, ALCAICS, SAPPHIC, brace stanza, REDONDILLA, SONNET, RUBAIYAT (or OMAR STANZA), and a number of irregular and unrhymed forms.

quintain /kwin'tən/ (French for "a collection of five"; also called "quintet"; a similarly used term is PENTASTICH) a poem or stanza in five lines, rhymed or unrhymed. Specific forms include BOB AND WHEEL, CINQUAIN, LIMERICK, QUINTILLA, and TANKA. See also *forms* in APPENDIX 1.

quintilla a Spanish five-line octosyllablic stanzaic form rhyming ababb, abbab, abaab, or aabba, and containing no more than two consecutive rhymes. See PENTASTICH. See also *forms* in APPENDIX 1.

R

range (see CINEMATIC TECHNIQUES) the full extent of the skill and VISION of a poet, especially as exhibited in particular works; also, the position, angle, and movement of a viewer. See also *cinematic terms* in APPENDIX 1.

ratiocination (from Latin for "a calculating or thinking") logical reasoning in steps that argue from induction, deduction, cause-and-effect, definition, comparison, or testimony (see ARGUMENT). The term was first adapted from logic to literature by Coleridge (*Literaria Biographia*) who referred to the range "of eloquence from the ratiocinative to the declamatory."

rational logic: See RATIOCINATION.

readymade an already manufactured object or found article ready for use. Although the term goes back to 19th-century England, it was revived in painting, sculpture, and poetry to refer to FOUND ART, objects or language that could be used as art when the proper aesthetically isolating frame was applied. Marcel Duchamp's *Bicycle Wheel* (1951), created by placing the front wheel and stem of a bicycle upside-down through a kitchen stool, was one of the precursors of *Junk Art*. By taking mundane objects out of their usual context, and sometimes combining them with other common objects or bits of language, the artist forced the viewer to see these objects as aesthetic designs and statements. In poetry, advertising and instruction manuals have proved to be rich sources of readymades. See MINIMALISM and POP ART.

Realism originally, the doctrine of the objective existence of "universals" as espoused, e.g., by Thomas Aquinas. Later, the philosophical term referred to an independent and objective outer reality apart from the perceiver. In literature, R. implies VERISIMILITUDE in subject matter and technique, that is, the use of vivid and precise details and idiomatic speech in an attempt to portray ordinary events and characters as truthfully as possible. Thus, the term became the name for the 19th-century movement—especially influential on fiction writers—that embraced this approach and which included such major figures as Henry James and Mark Twain. Sometimes the term implies the use of unpleasant or sordid details and is contrasted with the idealized aesthetics of both ROMANTICISM and NEO-CLASSICISM. Similarly, R. is often contrasted to IMPRESSIONISM which is seen as a precursor to EXPRESSIONISM and SURREALISM. In poetry, writers such as Jonathan Swift, Robert Browning, Walt Whitman, E.A. Robinson, Robert Frost, Carl Sandburg, and, more recently, James Wright and Philip Levine, have been adherents of R. See DIALECT, LOCAL COLOR, NATURALISM, and PRAGMATIC THEORY OF ART.

real time the existence of a simultaneity between the time an event takes to report and the amount of time the event takes to occur, as opposed to FELT TIME, the illusory sense of time that a reader is made to experience through the conventions of narration. A third sense of time that might be called *actual time* can be used to indicate the time it takes to read a work of literature. R.t. is sometimes used as a technique of REALISM.

recessive accent a type of WRENCHED ACCENT that for the sake of ease in pronunciation and metrical regularity moves the accent in a two-syllable word from the terminal to the initial position, as in this example from Shakespeare: "Or I with grief and *éxtreme* rage shall perish." With the advent of FREE VERSE, this kind of forced metrical regularity has disappeared.

reciprocus versus (Latin for "back and forward verse") balanced verse that metrically reads the same forward and backward. R.v. is the rhythmical equivalent of the PALINDROME. See *forms* in APPENDIX 1.

redaction (from Latin for "to bring back, to collect, to reduce") a REVISION, or the SHAPING of a work (usually subtractive or reductive editing) into final form. In the 19th century, an editor was sometimes referred to as a *redacteur* or *redactor*.

redondilla (diminutive of Spanish for "round") a Spanish stanzaic form composed of four trochaic lines of six or eight syllables and rhyming abba. The form was very popular in lyric and romance poetry of 19th-century Spain. See *forms* in APPENDIX 1.

reductive fallacy a fallacy of substitution and paraphrase, according to the critic Harold Bloom, "by which we first explain a phenomenon in terms more elementary than its own, and then replace the discredited phenomenon by our own explanation." For other fallacies, see AFFECTIVE FALLACY, CLASSICAL FALLACY, IMITATIVE FALLACY, INTENTIONAL FALLACY, and PATHETIC FALLACY.

reflexive line ending (see LINE ENDING) a line break whose last word or phrase refers back semantically or syntactically to previous content.

refrain /rəfrān′/ (from Latin for "to break back, to break again"; similarly used terms are BURDEN, CHORUS, and REPETEND) a phrase, line, or stanza recurring regularly at the end of stanzas, or irregularly throughout a song or poem. The r. may be used to state action, time, SETTING, ATMOSPHERE, or TONE; to emphasize conditions or CHARACTER; to accumulate PLOT or information; to editorialize; to create UNITY; or to maintain RHYTHM or melody. In ballads such as *John Henry*, identical REPETITION after plot verses often deepens the meaning of the r. In poems such as Spenser's *Epithalamion*, slight changes in the r. (see REPETEND and INCREMENTAL REPETITION) indicate changes in time, mood, and circumstance.The PANTOUM, VILLANELLE, and SESTINA make use of elaborate forms of r. See also *forms* in APPENDIX 1.

regionalism literature that realistically characterizes the DIALECT, ATMOS-

PHERE, behavior, beliefs, values, history, or SETTING of a particular geographical area. Although the term has often been used pejoratively to describe the limitations of certain literary works, good regional literature transcends its particularity. Poets such as Robert Burns, Dylan Thomas, Robinson Jeffers, Richard Hugo, Robert Penn Warren, Robert Frost, and Robert Lowell, among many others, have reached universal audiences while concentrating their focus on a specific time and place. See DIALECT, LOCAL COLOR, and REALISM.

regular ode: See PINDARIC ODE.

relativism in criticism the use of external references as an aid in the interpretation and evaluation of a literary work. Although popular among European critics, this approach has been considered out of fashion by many American critics. For instance, Saul Bellow humorously pointed out the absurdity of viewing *Moby Dick* through specialized psychoanalytical literary theory (Moby Dick as "the Mother"), through Marxist literary theory (the ship as a "factory"), or through mythic literary prototypes (the journey toward the "self"). But, generally speaking, r.i.c. has given insight, range, and value to the views of works of literature. See CRITICISM. See also *criticism* in APPENDIX 1.

relativistic criticism any form of literary analysis and evaluation that uses references outside of the work itself to judge that work. See CRITICISM. See also *criticism* in APPENDIX 1.

Renaissance /ren′əsäns/ or /rənəsäns′/ (French for "rebirth") the great revival of art, literature, and learning in Europe in the 14th, 15th and 16th centuries, based on Classical Greek and Latin sources. The R. began in Italy and spread gradually to other countries, and it marked the transition from the Medieval world to the modern. Discoveries in science and increases in economic activity, both probably due in part to the new trade routes to the East, affected every phase of life. The period produced great writers such as Dante, Petrarch, Boccaccio, Erasmus, Machiavelli, Rabelais, Montaigne, Cervantes, Shakespeare, Spenser, Marlowe, Jonson, Donne, and Milton. The term R. is also used to refer to any dramatic increase in the arts of a certain time and place, such as the San Francisco Renaissance during the 1950s, the Southern Renaissance during the 1920s and 30s, and the Texas Renaissance during the 1970s and 80s. See PERIODS OF ENGLISH LITERATURE.

render (from Latin for "to give back") to reproduce or represent, especially by artistic means. Ezra Pound's *ABC of Reading* (1934) popularized this old critical term in exhorting would-be writers to *render* or present an event rather than indirectly describing it.

repetend /rep′ətend, repətend′/ (from Latin for "that which is to be repeated") an irregular or partial REPETITION of a word, phrase, or line. The term represents a variation of the REFRAIN, which repeats itself regularly and in its entirety. In E.A. Poe's *Annabel Lee*, the "Annabel Lee" lines and the "kingdom by the sea" lines are repetends as are the "shadow" and "Eldorado" lines in his *Eldorado*. Coleridge and Eliot, among others, used the device, which offers the contrasting elements of surprise and PREDICTABILITY. Other figures and terms of repetition include ALLITERATION, ANADIPLOSIS, ANAPHORA, ANTIMETABOLE, ASSONANCE, BALANCE, CATALOGUE VERSE, CLIMAX, CONSONANCE, DIACOPE, DIAPHORA, EMBLEM, EPANALEPSIS, EPISTROPHE, LEITMOTIF, METER, OBSESSIVE IMAGE, PARALLELISM, PLEONASM, PLOCE, POLYPTOTON, RHYME, RHYTHM, SYMPLOCE, and TAUTOLOGY. See also *forms* in APPENDIX 1.

repetition a fundamental aesthetic, structural, and rhetorical element in poetry that can occur in RHYTHM, FORM, SONIC STRUCTURE, and SYNTAX and which affects PREDICTABILITY, UNITY, coherence, emphasis, and surprise. R. is the basis of any form of variation in the poem. It is the MNEMONIC DEVICE common to every form of poetry. For specific kinds of r., see ALLITERATION, ANADIPLOSIS, ANAPHORA, ANTIMETABOLE, ASSONANCE, BALANCE, CATALOGUE VERSE, CLIMAX, CONSONANCE, DIACOPE, DIAPHORA, EMBLEM, EPANALEPSIS, EPISTROPHE, LEITMOTIF, METER, OBSESSIVE IMAGE, PARALLELISM, PLEONASM, PLOCE, POLYPTOTON, REPETEND, RHYME, RHYTHM, SYMPLOCE and TAUTOLOGY. See *figures of repetition* in APPENDIX 2.

répétons: See PANTOUM.

requiem /rek'wi·əm/ (Latin for "rest," from the introduction in the Mass for the dead: *Requiem aeternam dona eis, Domine* . . ., for "Give eternal rest to them, O Lord") a CHANT praying for peace for the dead, or a DIRGE or LAMENT solemnly singing for the soul's rest. Stanley Kunitz' translation of Anna Akhmatova's *Requiem* is a highly regarded contemporary example of the form. See also PSALM.

resolution (from Latin for "to loosen, to dissolve") in drama, the knitting together of plot elements during the FALLING ACTION (see DRAMATIC STRUCTURE). Metrically, the term indicates the SUBSTITUTION of one foot for another; e.g., in Classical prosody two short syllables are often replaced by one long syllable (see MORA and PROSODY), and in modern metrics it is common to vary duple feet with triple feet. See also *closure* in APPENDIX 1.

resolved accent: See DISTRIBUTED STRESS.

resonance (from Latin for "echo") the effect of increasing the emotional content of a poem by relying on the REPETITION of words and sounds or the deepening of meaning through the manipulation of SYNTAX, FIGURES OF SPEECH, or IMAGE. More specifically, the term refers to the magnetic effect of METAPHOR which organizes the elements of a poem into a harmonic code. This technique is loosely referred to in contemporary poetics as "loading" or "packing" the poem, a technique that stems from ANAGOGICAL VISION. Sometimes, the term is used simply to express a sense of thematic fullness in a poem. See INNER REFLECTIONS.

rest a musical notation indicated by the symbol for a pause (∧ or ‖), or the pause itself (see CAESURA) in metrical or free rhythms. See COMPENSATION, PROSODIC SYMBOLS, and SCANSION.

restoration an age in English literature that began in 1660 with the restoration of the Stuart line to the English throne in the person of Charles II and ended in 1688 when parliament regained power. Sometimes the period is said to extend until the end of the 17th century. The writing of the period reflects the lively reaction against Puritanism, the influence of French literature and culture, and the increasing interest in Classical poetics. Drama was revived and became for a short while the period's most important genre. Major writers include John Dryden, John Milton, John Locke, and Samuel Butler. See NEO-CLASSICISM and PERIODS OF ENGLISH LITERATURE.

restraint a form of compositional CONTROL or UNDERSTATEMENT that, through subtle implication and NUANCE in the elements of PLOT, CHARACTER, NARRATION, FIGURES OF SPEECH, and IMAGERY, holds back an explicit expression of emotion, so that the reader may create that passion for himself. Many critics maintain that such a form of control is ultimately more powerful than more direct expression (see HYPERBOLE) and that r. is characteristic of great writing. See also *diction* in APPENDIX 1.

restrictio (Medieval Latin for "limitation") a rhetorical figure of definition that works through division by stating the general as a condition and then excepting a part of the general:

> We are forsaken, but not lost;
> We are alone, but have each other;
> We have death to face, but eternal life hereafter.

See *figures of division* in APPENDIX 2.

resverie: See FATRAS.

reverse foot: See INVERTED FOOT.

reverse metaphor a METAPHOR that compares, substitutes, or identifies one thing with another thing in contrast to it. In Michael Ryan's poem *The Blind Swimmer*, the comparison between the ocean and the lives of the characters is denied:

> The ocean doesn't stand for
> our lives, calm and regular, but we still fear
> drowning.

revision (from Latin for "to look again") the process of examining a work in progress with the aim of improving or correcting that work. Generally, the two most common types of r. are the *subtractive process*, which requires compression, deletion, and distillation of material, and the *additive process*, which calls for the more difficult task of creating new material or elaborating what is already written. The process of r., most critics and poets maintain, is as necessary and as creative as the original writing process; therefore, it is equally difficult to categorize or describe. Many poets offer a check list of elements by which beginning students may assess the effectiveness of their poetry: diction, rhythm, logical development, structure, appropriateness of imagery and figures, etc. The r. process joins critical and creative faculties, and calls for the poet to be both involved and distant from his work so that the effect of the poem can be judged. The most important element in the r. is that of allowing oneself time, though peer criticism can accelerate the process. It is common for poets to work on as many as 25 to 40 drafts of their poems. Some poets, such as Donald Hall, take up to three years to complete (or abandon) a work; other poets, such as Allen Ginsberg, maintain that they do not revise their initial writing at all. See ORGANIC COMPOSITION, REDACTION, and SHAPING.

rhetoric /ret'-/ (from Greek "*rhetor*, for "orator, teacher of oratory") language use that creates and organizes arguments and argumentative devices and delivers these in an effective style of expression. The founder of r. is said to be Corax of Syracuse (fifth century B.C.) who described and laid down principles of argumentation by which Sicilians might legally recover their property from the estate of the deposed despot Thrasybulus, but none of Corax' work is extant. Sophists, such as Gorgias of Leotini and Isocrates, taught r. and philosophy as professional teachers and orators, but many of the sophists gained a less-than-impeccable reputation because they used their argumentative skills to the service of their pockets and ambitions. Thus Socrates (470–399 B.C.) came to consider r. as a means of hiding, not exposing, the truth. Plato (427–347 B.C.), Socrates' disciple, viewed r. in the same light as he did poetry, feeling both uses of language lent themselves more to illusion and decoration than to pragmatic and effective vehicles of instruction for the public good (see PLATONIC CRITICISM).

It was left to Aristotle (384–322 B.C.) to dignify the art of r. In his *Rhetoric* and his *Poetics*, he assigns the characteristics of truth and intellect to r., and emotion and imagination to poetry; to r. he also assigns the practical arts of persuasion and logic, and to poetry the aesthetic art of imitation (see MIMESIS). He defined r. as "the faculty of discovering all the available means of persuasion in any given situation." He maintained that there are three types of persuasion, all based on the classification of time: (1) *deliberative persuasion*, which considers the future in matters of social and political policies; (2) *forensic persuasion*, which considers the past actions of men and which applies to judicial and moral decisions; and (3) *epideictic persuasion*, which concerns itself with ceremonially commemorating the present with praise or blame of men's actions (see EPIDEICTIC and PANEGYRIC).

Among the Latin rhetoricians, Cicero (106–43 B.C.) had the greatest influence. He saw little or no difference in the aims of rhetoric and the aims of poetry, both depending on these five steps: (1) *inventio*, the creation of arguments; (2) *dispositio*, the organization of those arguments; (3) *elocutio*, the style and diction of language; (4) *memoria*, the memorizing of the discourse; and (5) *pronuntiatio*, the performance of the speech, including the use of the voice and the body. As a skillful orator, Cicero synthesized the high style of the *Asiatics* with the plainer style of the *Atticists* and called for the orator to be liberally educated and morally responsible. The *Ad Herennium* (86-82 B.C.), a study of rhetorical figures that is the earliest extant Latin work on r., was thought for a millennium to have been written by Cicero, but is now thought to be of anonymous origin.

Besides Cicero, other Latin rhetoricians had a lasting influence, including Quintilian (M. Fabius Quintilianus, 35–95 A.D.), who was Cicero's most important disciple. His principal work is probably the *Institutio Oratoria*, a treatise on education and literary criticism which, in its insistence on moral and intellectual veracity in r., dominated pedagogical theory and practice until the Renaissance. Horace (65–8 B.C.), in his *Art of Poetry*, maintained that the rhetorical function of the poet is pragmatic, to instruct or delight the reader; his set of practical guidelines has influenced poets from his own time until the present, and was especially influential on 18th-century poets. Another Latin rhetorician, Longinus (210–273 A.D.), wrote *On the Sublime*, which is an important work of literary criticism and theory. The work attempts to indicate the essentials of a noble style by discussing figures of speech, nobility of diction, and elevation of word order. He defended enthusiasm as a respectable resource and insisted that sublimity is "the echo of a great soul."

During the Middle Ages, r. became one of the requirements in the *trivium* (grammar, logic, and rhetoric), which every student mastered. The study of r. usually focused on the genres of letter-writing and sermons, and drew on the works of Cicero and Horace as stylistic and moral models.

During the Renaissance, three schools of rhetoricians existed: (1) *traditionalists*, who followed the five-part study of Cicero; (2) *ramists*, who focused only on style and delivery and left the creation and organization of arguments to the study of logic; and (3) *figurists*, who classified, renamed, and defined figures of speech and grammatical constructions. Among the last group, two names are worth mentioning: Henry Peacham and George Puttenham. Peacham's *The Garden of Eloquence* (1577) lists 184 figures of speech. Puttenham's *The Arte of English Poesie* (1589) lists 107 figures adapted from Classical sources which he renamed and categorized according to their appeal to the ear (the *auricular*), the mind (the *sensable*), and the mind and ear (the *sententious*).

After the Renaissance, the elaborate citing of figures was streamlined, categories became blurred, and much accuracy in classification was lost. By the 17th century, r. and poetics began to be considered as one, and by the 18th century these once important arts became relegated to aspects of eloquence. In the early 19th century, r. and poetry were looked upon solely for their expressive effect on an audience, and serious scholarly interest in r. was depleted even further by the 1920s school of Objective Criticism which viewed the poem as an autonomous object, separate from its author and reader (see NEW CRITICISM). Most rhetoricians and literary critics have followed the lead of I.A. Richards who, in *The Philosophy of Rhetoric* (1936), concentrated on the emotive and semantic thrust of language and disregarded its persuasive elements. According to Kenneth Burke, Classical r. set forth conscious and deliberate designs on the reader's opinions and emotions; the "new r." worked on its audience through unconscious appeal. Thus, the expressive aspects of r., especially

VOICE and IMAGE, have become all-important in a rhetorical view of modern poetry, while the types of grammatical constructions, modes of logic, and figures of speech have been neglected.

Since the 1950s new areas in r. have come to the fore. Noam Chomsky's *transformational grammar* which focuses on the mathematical structure of language, the work of clinical and Jungian psychologists who have called attention to the symbolic elements in language, and the impact of the aural and visual media as persuasive forms of communication will occupy rhetoricians for the rest of this century. As will be noted by readers of this dictionary, the authors have included a good number of Puttenham's constructions, figures, and argumentative devices in the hope that they will not be lost and might prove valuable to contemporary writers and critics. See APPENDIX 2 for a list of *rhetorical, poetical*, and *logical devices*. See also ARGUMENT, LOGIC and RHETORICAL FIGURES.

rhetorical accent: See LOGICAL STRESS.

rhetorical figures the effective organization of words for the purpose of influencing or persuading an audience. R. f. differ from FIGURES OF SPEECH or tropes (see TROPE) in that they do not attempt to change the usual meaning of words, but rather change their usual order or arrangement. Alexander Pope is known as the greatest master of r.f. because of his syntactical and expressive manipulations within the CLOSED COUPLET. Some specific types of r.f. include APOSTROPHE, CHIASMUS, INVOCATION, RHETORICAL QUESTION, and ZEUGMA.

rhetorical question a rhetorical figure in question form that asks not in order to obtain an answer but in order to make a point, elicit a desired response, or create an effect. Specific forms include (1) EROTEMA, which functions to assert or deny something and thus influence the audience—"Do you expect me to drop everything and come running whenever you call?" and (2) ANACOENOSIS, which poses a question in order to create an effect, as in the closing lines of Shelley's *Ode to the West Wind*:

> O, Wind,
> If Winter comes, can Spring be far behind?

The device is frequently used in all periods and genres of poetry. See *figures of argumentation* in APPENDIX 2.

rhetorical stress: See LOGICAL STRESS.

rhopalic verse /rōpal′ik/ (*rhopalic*, from Greek for "cudgel thicker towards one end"; also known as "gradual verse") verse in which each word in a series contains one more syllable than the word preceding it, as in: "I rally efficient machinery." The *Iliad* contains examples of the form.

rhyme (variant of *rime*; perhaps from Greek *rhythmos*, for "measured motion, time, proportion") the harmony or identity of sound values. HOMOETELEUTON, in which the suffixes of words sound alike, is an ancient Greek precursor of r., although Greek poetics did not employ r. as it is known today. It is thought to have been developed in the ceremonies of the Catholic church for mnemonic purposes. The Anglo-Saxons, who also did not utilize r., did develop ALLITERATION, the repetition of the initial CONSONANTS in a series of words (see HEAD-R.). Alliteration is a type of CONSONANCE, the repetition of similar or identical consonants. Rich consonance is the twinning of consonants at the beginnings and ends of words with different vowels ("mast/mist"). VOWEL R. or ASSONANCE is the rhyming of only the vowel sounds in words ("late/stay"). SINGLE R. (also known as MASCULINE R., PERFECT R., or RIME SUFFISANTE) is the repetition of stressed vowels and their subsequent consonants ("glow/blow"); DOUBLE FULL R. (also known as FEMININE R. or LIGHT R.) has two syllables ("people/steeple"); TRIPLE R. has three syllables ("furious/curious"). OFF-R. (also known as *approximate, embryonic, half-, imperfect, near, oblique, para-, partial, part,* and *slant r.,* also *paraphone*) is a general term for r. that depends on partial vowel r. and terminal consonance ("good/mud"). G.M. Hopkins, W.B. Yeats, and Dylan Thomas are major innovators of this device. EYE R. (also known as SIGHT R. or HISTORICAL R.) contains words whose final parts are spelled alike but pronounced differently ("chive/live"), "through/cough," "mood/blood"), an effect that is usually the result of an etymological change in pronunciation.

R. is categorized not only according to the sounds and number of syllables, but also according to the position of rhyming words in a line. Thus END-R. occurs at the ends of lines and is common in most fixed forms. The use of full or partial rhymes in these positions helps unify rhythm and idea, and adds emphasis and melody to the lines. INTERNAL R. occurs within the lines and creates a cohesive, dense effect. A combination of end-r. and internal r. creates LEONINE R. in which the last word in a line echoes the last word before the CAESURA, as in "Here lies John who's both here and gone." Other variations include ANALYZED R. (or SUSPENDED R.) which shuffles the order of rhyming vowels and consonants of words ("run/hunt," "fin/splint"), and which, if strung over a number of lines, produces ECHO R., a subtle auditory effect used frequently in contemporary poetry. Another variation, APOCOPATED R., combines full and double r. to produce an off-balance effect, as in "find/blinder." Position also rules LINKED R., a Welsh invention, in which the last syllable of a line is rhymed to the first syllable of the subsequent line, and BROKEN R., in which a rhyming word is broken at the end of a line, leaving the rhyming syllable at the line break and its remaining syllables at the start of the next line. CROSS-R., not to be confused with CROSSED R. OR INTERLACED R., rhymes the end syllable or word in a line with another in the middle of the succeeding line. Crossed r. or interlaced r. features the full rhyming of internal and end words in one long couplet with those in another couplet.

INDENTICAL R. simply repeats the same word in the same or different lines, and RIME RICHE repeats identically sounding words with different meanings. BOUTS-RIMÉS is a Parisian game in which an arbitrary set of rhymes is established and fitted to any desired fixed form. CHAIN R. or CHAIN VERSE is a type of verse whose lines are interlinked through rhyme or repetition, and whose last syllable in a line is repeated in a new meaning in the succeeding line. SYNTHETIC R., common in LIGHT VERSE, occurs when one of the rhyming words is made to sound equivalent by a process of distorting the word through contraction or protraction. Finally, the semantic content of rhyming words is taken into consideration in IRONIC R. in which the two or more rhyming words contain a conflict between what is being stated and what is intended (see IRONY).

Compared with the Romance languages, which offer a multitude of similar suffixes, English is a relatively r.-poor language. Thus, poets writing in English tend to be more experimental in their use of sound, and some, such as Lewis Carroll and Ogden Nash, have purposefully wrenched the sounds of words for humorous effect. Aside from the pleasurable sonic qualities of r., poets use it as a unifying element in structure and meaning, as decorative element for grace, as a device for rhetorical emphasis, and as an aid in memorizing verse. The use of DISSONANCE and CACOPHONY, the opposite of EUPHONY, produces effects of tension, chaos, and harshness. See RHYME-COUNTERPOINT, RHYME SCHEME, and SONICS. See also *mnemonic devices* in APPENDIX 1.

rhyme-counterpoint verse composed of unrhymed lines of equal length and rhymed lines of unequal length. Poets such as Donne, Vaughan, and Herbert used this irregular form. See RHYME, RHYME SCHEME, and STANZA.

rhyme royal: See CHAUCER STANZA.

rhyme scheme the formal arrangement of rhymes throughout a poem or stanza. The most common position is at the end of a line, but many variant forms have been created (see RHYME). Generally, the pattern of rhyme in a verse is notated by alphabetical letters (see PROSODIC SYMBOLS), as in this scheme of the SPENSERIAN STANZA: ababbcbcc. Rhymes of refrain lines are capitalized and numbered A^1A^2, B^1B^2, and unrhymed lines are symbolized by an "x." Some verse forms repeat entire words, as in the SESTINA, or entire lines, as in the TRIOLET and VILLANELLE. See REFRAIN and REPETEND.

rhythm (from Greek *rhythmos*, for "measured motion, time, proportion) the sense of movement attributable to the pattern of stressed and unstressed syllables in a line of PROSE or POETRY or to the DURATION of syllables in QUANTITATIVE METER. In VERSE, r. is determined by metrical pattern, whereas in prose or FREE VERSE it is the effect of an arrangement of words in a pattern that creates a CADENCE based on conversational phrasing. Here, only the r. of free verse will be discussed, the r. of metered verse being discussed in other entries (see especially METER, PROSODIC SYMBOLS, and SCANSION).

Free verse makes use of an internally imposed, organic set of rhythms that stress the natural speaking voice. Generally characterized, the rhythmical base of VERS LIBRE has been described by A.M. Dale as one that:

> emancipates itself from structural principle and proceeds arbitrarily, with none but empirical elements; the subtlety of its rhythms is not a formal complexity but arises from the fusion of a number of indeterminates ....

These colloquial rhythms contain more variation and are closer to everyday speech than the externally imposed, formal rhythms of metrical verse. As a form, conversational rhythms have remained uncategorized because no satisfactory system of scansion or analysis has yet been devised for them. However, some of the elements that go into the making of conversational rhythms in free verse can be listed. As in metrical verse, conversational rhythms are made up, in large part, of two elements, *stresses* and *pauses*. There are many discernible degrees of stress, ranging from heavy to light. The length and position of pauses before and after syllables and the duration of the syllables themselves are also highly variable and add considerable musical complexity to poetic speech. Another element that is closely allied to the stress of a syllable is its *loudness*. It must be remembered that stress and loudness can be mutually exclusive: It is possible to pronounce a heavily stressed word softly, and a lightly stressed word loudly. Some other variable elements that determine free rhythms are differences in PITCH of syllables, LINE ENDING, line length, overall appearance of the poem on the page, and the amount of WHITE SPACE or silence that determines the FELT TIME in a poem.

The tension between the reader's expectation and the poem's fulfillment of that expectation is the underlying dialectic that determines the successful effect of the poem's r. In metered verse, recurring stresses in a predetermined pattern provide that sense of expectation and fulfillment. In free verse, units that are larger than the metrical foot provide that sense. A free-verse poem might depend on syntactical units, breath units, conversational units, thought units, sensual units, rhetorical units, or the rhythmical unit of the line itself to provide coherence and organization to the movement of the poem.

If we have no predetermined, recurring meter to maintain a definite sense of expectation and fulfillment (which are the major affective attributes of r.), then what elements keep free-verse rhythms coherent and organized? As we will see, other, larger units in free-verse composition can create rhythms, such as:

Syntactical Units (Galway Kinnell):

> We walk across the snow,
> The stars can be faint,
> The moon can be eating itself out,
> There can be meteors flaring to death on earth,
> The Northern Lights can be blooming and seething
> And tearing themselves apart all night,
> We walk arm in arm, and we are happy.

Breath Units (Allen Ginsberg):

> I saw the best minds of my generation destroyed by madness,
>   starving hysterical naked,
> dragging themselves through the negro streets at dawn,
>   looking for an angry fix,

Conversational Units (Ira Sadoff):

> I miss the peace and quiet of Chicago
> that's the kind of guy I am

Thought and Sensual Units (Louise Glück):

> One sound. Then the hiss and whir
> of houses gliding into their places.
> And the wind
> leafs through the bodies of animals

Rhetorical Emphasis (Philip Dacey):

> Thirty candles and one
> to grow on. My husband
> and son watch me
> think of wishes.

Incremental Development Units (W.C. Williams):

> A Negro Woman
> carrying a bunch of marigolds
> wrapped
> in an old newspaper:
> she carries them upright,
> bareheaded,
> the bulk
> of her thighs
> causing her to waddle
> as she walks
> looking into
> the store window which she passes
> on her way.

Any of these formal rhythmic elements has the potential either singly or in combination to dominate the r. and lineation.

In *Sound and Form in Modern Poetry* (1964), Harvey Gross states that the job of prosody is not to mimic in an onomatopoetic sense, but to give "a curve of feeling, the shape of an emotion." In that sense, prosody informs us with its own kind of "nondiscursive communication," and the meaning of the words themselves will, conversely, often create the potential form of the prosody in a particular poem. The tension between rhythmic form and lexical meaning can indicate the speaker's state of mind or his sense of the world. Even the type of grammar and punctuation that a line or sentence exhibits can convey a meaning that, beyond the denotative sense of the words involved, gives the reader a rhythmic line of feeling to follow. In a letter to John Bartlett, Robert Frost spoke of the nonlexical meaning, the dramatic character, that the form of a sentence can carry, when he said: "A sentence is a sound in itself on which other sounds called words may be strung." He felt these SENTENCE SOUNDS could and should be taken selectively from everyday conversation, and that the reader should recognize the emotional and ethical contextual matrix from which these phrasings arose and bring to the poem that indefinite meaning embedded in the sound. Whatever the rhythmical pattern, or system that it is based upon, we must remember that in both metrical verse and free verse the rhythmical patterns are used as devices of expression that give us the quality of an experience. The experience of a poem is more important than the recognition of the poem's pattern, and we understand the effect of r. by experiencing it with our bodies.

So, in general, free verse creates an air of familiarity and accessibility, and it is characterized by a lack of obvious rhyming (particularly end rhyming), by a lack of metrical regularity, by repetitive syntax and phrasing, by significant line endings, and by the use of syncopation and other rhythmic modifications such as improvisation.

In terms of the language systems that free verse is based upon, we can say that it reflects three types of speech models corresponding to levels of formality in diction—(1) *formal*: verse written toward the style of prose; (2) *informal*: verse structured on conventional speech rhythms; and (3) *idiomatic*: verse structured on colloquial speech rhythm.

Now that we have looked at some of the elements that go into the making of conversational rhythms in free verse, let us examine two types of sustained rhythms that are commonly used by poets: ground rhythms and generational rhythms.

A GROUND R. is a rhythmic pattern or continuum that is fairly easy to detect underneath a conversational poetic voice. It maintains a nominal regularity and surfaces once in a while in its ideal form, or appears as variations of its ideal form. The ground r., or matrix, can be deduced from its variations and is formed through the use of both fixed and variable elements. This irregular patterning in r. gives the ground r. both a formal and natural character. The ground rhythm's predictability resides in its units of r.; its variety lies in the order and proportion of rhythmical elements that interrupt or vary the base r. The establishment of a set ground r. as a controlling element in the poem places the technique somewhere between the recurring, external rhythms of metrical poetry (in which there is often much deviation from predetermined form) and the dialectical rhythms of generational free-verse rhythms (see GENERATIONAL R.), discussed below.

The composition of ground r. is analogous to the improvisation of jazz melodies in which a formal line of notes is stated and then transformed, by turns, in the varying restatements of several individual musicians. However, in poetry the use of counterpoint and syncopation is more difficult to follow than in music because music usually employs both melody and rhythm lines at the same time, elements that both contain r., and the two can play off of one another without straying too far from the terms of the composition. Only one line of r. can be carried in poetry, and because there is no simultaneity, the missing base r. has to be imagined or felt by the reader.

Sometimes a crossover from one ground r. to another occurs. This change usually takes place slowly through small, refined maneuvers. An analogy from the visual arts will help us to understand this process: If we begin rounding the four sides of a square, which represents one matrix r., and if we begin squaring the circumference of a circle, which represents the second matrix r. to which we will cross over, then at a certain point there will be a proportional harmony (visually in painting, aurally in poetry) which forms a bridge between the two rhythmic dimensions. In other words, we can slant one r. toward another until the new r. is established. In Fernando Pessoa's poem *If They Want Me To Be Mystic, Fine. So I'm Mystic,* translated by Edwin Honig, we see an anapestic GROUND R. that undergoes considerable variation in PHRASING through the use of COUNTERPOINT and SYNCOPATION:

> If they want me to be a mystic, Fine. So I'm a mystic.
> I'm a mystic, but only of the body.
> My soul is simple; it doesn't think.
> My mysticism consists in not desiring to know,
> In living without thinking about it.
>
> I don't know what Nature is; I sing it.
> I live on a hilltop
> In a solitary cabin.
> And that's what it's all about.

A GENERATIONAL R. has no predetermined recurring ground r. or regular meter; instead, its development proceeds by a series of single variations composed upon each line's predecessor. The r. is formed through a chain reaction in which a line is stated and the next line improvises upon the former line. Thus, the new line enhances, contrasts, or slants off the older line; and there is no detectable ground r., but rather an on-going evolutionary process. Just as two parents determine the range or limits of genetic possibilities in their children, but cannot predict the exact characteristics of those children, so in generational rhythms the reader's ear can sense the rightness of the evolving rhythms but cannot predict their exact form. In order to understand the process of the generational r., the reader must feel the DIALECTIC, the ontogeny of the rhythmic development. The whole poem forms a GESTALT that each line attempts to arrive at; there is usually no recapitulation of earlier rhythms. Although this process sounds difficult, it is actually easy to experience; for as I.A. Richards points out in *Principles of Literary Criticism,* it is not so much a matter of our perceiving the r. in a poem as it is a matter of our becoming patterned to the poem through our senses. In successful poems, rhythms not only reach out to us, but we become their rhythms.

The generational r. is linear in effect and construction, and contains an exponential number of possible variations. The success of this evolutionary strategy lies in the many creative opportunities it presents. Although the reader cannot rely on the predictability of recurring patterns and close harmonizing patterns, the freewheeling development is in itself a dependable characteristic. The form's coherence stems from the rhythmic relation between lines. In a larger sense, generational rhythms reflect 20th-century man's new perception of time and space which is based on the ideas of relativity. As Harvey Gross notes, "Our apprehension of modern rhythm goes deeper than our physical reactions: it lies in fundamental matters of coherence, perception, and how we conceive the structure of space and time." In W.S. Merwin's poem *In the Winter of My Thirty-Eighth Year,* each line transforms the previous line's r., thereby echoing the uncertainty in the poem's tone and theme. Although it can be rightly argued that Merwin's poem represents a ground-based rhythmic model, the improvisational impulse pushes the development of the poem into the sphere of the generational rhythmic model:

> It sounds unconvincing to say *When I was young*
> Though I have long wondered what it would be like
> To be me now
> No older at all it seems from here
> As far from myself as ever
> Walking in fog and rain and seeing nothing
> I imagine all the clocks have died in the night
> Now no one is looking I could choose my age
> It would be younger I suppose so I am older
> It is there at hand I could take it
> Except for the things I think I would do differently
> They keep coming between they are what I am
> They have taught me little I did not know when I was young
>
> There is nothing wrong with my age now probably
> It is how I have come to it
> Like a thing I kept putting off as I did my youth
>
> There is nothing the matter with the stars
> It is my emptiness among them
> While they drift farther away in the invisible morning

See ACCENT, ASCENDING R., FALLING R., PROSE R., PROSODY, ROCKING R., and SPRUNG R. See also *grammatical devices of rhythm and balance* in APPENDIX 2, and *rhythm* in APPENDIX 1.

rhythmical pause a metrical or extrametrical PAUSE within a line of verse. Sometimes, the r.p. is counted as an initial, medial, or terminal CAESURA in metrical verse; other times, it is outside of the pattern of formal rhythm and occurs because of punctuation, emphasis of meaning, or syntactical phrasing. See RHYTHM.

rich rhyme: See RIME RICHE.

riddle a statement or question partially describing or outlining in the coded language of tropes or images a word, object, mood, or judgment. Usually, there is an implied or explicit comparison between what is presented sensually and conceptually, and what is left to conjecture. This form of puzzle was powerfully and extensively used in Anglo-Saxon verse (see KENNING), and Western literature from the Middle Ages to the present has made use of the curiously in-wrought aesthetics of the genre. Riddles are fairly common in contemporary poetry: W.S. Merwin, Charles Simic, Donald Justice, and Rita Dove have written them.

Northrop Frye points out in *The Anatomy of Criticism* that the r. functions as descriptive containment: A circle of words is drawn around the subject; that is, the subject is circumscribed. In simple riddles, the central subject is an image or a concept; the reader is supposed to guess the subject. In more complicated poems, such as those of the 19th-century Symbolist poets, a mood rather than an image or a concept is circumscribed. Probably the most complicated form of the r. is the emblematic vision, which circumscribes not a mood but rather a visionary experience (see ANAGOGICAL VISION and VISION). Emblematic visions appear extensively in religious texts such as the Indian *Rig Veda*, the Buddhist *I Ching*, and the Bible. Other puzzle and game poems include the ACROSTIC, CADAVRE EXQUIS, CARMEN FIGURATUM, CHANCE POETRY, LINKED VERSE, NONSENSE VERSE, and SI . . . QUAND. See also *light verse* in APPENDIX 1.

rime couée /rēmkōō·ā'/ (French for "tail rhyme"; a similarly used term is TAIL-RHYME STANZA) a stanzaic form featuring a group of long lines closing with a shorter line that rhymes with a preceding short line, as in the first stanza of Shelley's *To Night*. The BURNS STANZA is a fixed form that also includes rhyming shorter lines. For a related variation, see RHYME-COUNTERPOINT. See also *forms* in APPENDIX 1.

rime riche /rēmrēsh'/ (French for "rich rhyme") a RHYME that repeats identically sounding words with different meanings ("threw/through").

rime royal /rēmrô·äyäl'/ (French for "royal rhyme"): See CHAUCER STANZA.

rime suffisante /rēmsōōfēzänt', rēmsYfēzäNt'/ (French for "sufficient rhyme"; see *full rhyme* under RHYME) the repetition of stressed vowels and their subsequent consonants, as in "glow/blow."

rising action the events in PLOT preceding the CLIMAX. See DRAMATIC STRUCTURE. See also *dramatic terms* in APPENDIX 1.

rising foot (Similarly used terms are ASCENDING RHYTHM, MASCULINE RHYTHM, and RISING RHYTHM) a metrical FOOT that ends in a stressed or long syllable, such as the iamb (˘ ´) and the anapest (˘ ˘ ´). See also FALLING FOOT and METER.

rising rhythm: See ASCENDING RHYTHM.

risk the possibility of failure or transcendence in art. R. is an important element of AMBITION, especially in poetry that strives for originality, a goal that may lead the poet to the sublime or to the ridiculous. R. is one of the pillars of the modern acronymic trivium O.R.E. (*o*riginality, *r*isk, and *e*xcellence).

rites of initiation (see MYTH) an important THEME or MOTIF in the literature of every culture and period. Rites of initiation center on actions, events, or ceremonies that introduce a character to a cultural, spiritual, physical, or psychological stage of development.

rocking rhythm a triple FOOT whose stressed middle syllable is flanked by two unstressed syllables, as in the AMPHIBRACH (˘ ´ ˘). The foot was named by G.M. Hopkins to characterize its rhythmical effect. Possibly, the quadruple foot, the ANTISPAST (˘ ´ ´ ˘), could be termed a r.r. At any rate, the foot as a regular meter is rare in English verse. See METER and SPRUNG RHYTHM.

rock lyric rhymed or unrhymed verse set to rock-and-roll music. Usually, this genre is rhythmically characterized by heavy stresses, and features topics of love, sex, alienation, adventure, and protest. Through the commercial use of modern electronic media, rock lyrics have formed a universal tribal community of youth around the world. The range in quality of rock lyrics is wide. Although most of them would not qualify, nor indeed were intended by their authors to be judged as poetry, some popular recording artists such as Bob Dylan, Joni Mitchell, and James Taylor write lyrics close to the quality of the poetry that appears in contemporary literary journals. Such musician-composers can be considered to be carrying on the TROUBADOUR tradition. See BALLAD, FOLK BALLAD, FOLK SONG, and ORAL POETRY.

romantic epic a RENAISSANCE form of narrative verse synthesized by combining the form of the METRICAL ROMANCE with the restraint and conventions of the Classical EPIC. Spenser's *The Faerie Queene* adapts the mode of earlier Italian models of Pulci, Boiardo, and especially Ariosto. One of the major poetic devices used in the form is ALLEGORY.

romantic irony a self-conscious VOICE that verges on self-pity but is balanced by the restraints of self-mockery. Byron's *Don Juan* is usually regarded to be the greatest poem that uses this device. Also, many modern and contemporary poets whose work focuses on the self-as-speaker (see CONFESSIONAL POETRY) employ the tone. See IRONY.

Romanticism a period in English literature from 1789 (the beginning of the French Revolution) or 1798 (publication of Wordsworth's and Coleridge's *Lyrical Ballads*) to 1832 (passage of the first Reform Bill) or 1837 (accession of Queen Victoria). The movement began in reaction to the restraints of AESTHETIC DISTANCE and formalism of NEO-CLASSICISM, and called for a poetics and philosophy centered on the individual's feelings and imagination. Philosophically, the movement maintained that (1) man is born good and is later corrupted by experience in society, (2) the inner man's spirit and emotions are proper vehicles for poetry, and (3) evolutionary spiritual change can be brought about by exalting nature over civilization, revolution over status quo, and energy over restraint. In terms of poetics, the movement called for (1) the colloquializing of DICTION, (2) the use of resource material such as folk tales, myths, autobiography, and visionary experience (see VISION), (3) the use of nature as a catalyst to meditation and feeling, (4) innovation and ORGANIC COMPOSITION as opposed to externally imposed forms such as the HEROIC COUPLET and the ODE; and (5) an AMBITION to transcend the typical and ordinary.

The period is known as one of the golden ages in poetry, and it includes poets such as Wordsworth, Coleridge (see LAKE POETS), Shelley, Keats, Byron, and Blake. Sometimes the period is extended back in time to include earlier poets such as Robert Burns, who have romantic tendencies, or forward in time to include Victorian poets such as the Brownings, Tennyson, Arnold, and the *Pre-Raphaelites*, all of whom were influenced by R. Yeats, who showed an early influence from Blake and Shelley, has been called "the last of the great romantic poets."

In America, the Romantic period stretched from 1830 to 1865. Whitman's *Leaves of Grass* (1855) was the paradigm of American

Romantic poetry because it exhibited idealism, *organic form*, open feeling, informal diction, and celebration of nature. Other American writers of what has come to be known as the first golden age of American literature include Bryant, Irving, Cooper, Hawthorne, Melville, Stowe, Poe, Whittier, Longfellow, Lowell, Thoreau, Emerson, and Holmes.

The term "Romantic" was first used by the German writer Friedrich von Schlegel in describing literature of the fancy (see FANCY AND IMAGINATION) related to early romances and opposite in kind from Classical literature. As a general descriptive term for literature it lacks specificity but implies the use of emotion and imagination over reason (see ASSOCIATIONAL LOGIC). In Romanticism's focus on the uniqueness and personality of the individual can be found the roots of the modern emphasis on VOICE. See also CLASSICAL POETICS, NATURALISM, REALISM, and SYMBOLISTS.

rondeau /ron′dō, rondō′/ (French for "little circle") a special form of the RONDEL written in syllabic meter consisting of 15 lines (sometimes fewer) set down in a QUINTAIN (aabba), a QUATRAIN (aabR), and a SESTET (aabbaR). The entire poem rests on one refrain which appears twice and echoes, in part or whole, the first line, and two rhymes. François Villon practiced the form. Sir Thomas Wyatt introduced the form into English. See RONDEAU REDOUBLÉ, and RONDELET, and ROUNDEL. See also *forms* in APPENDIX 1.

rondeau redoublé /rədoōblā′/ (*redoublé*, French for "double") a French FIXED FORM based on the RONDEAU. The r.r. is written in SYLLABIC METER and consists of five quatrains and a last quintet which employ two alternating rhymes and five refrains modeled on the lines of the first stanza. In addition, the first half of line one is repeated in line 25; the whole first line reappears as line eight in the second stanza; line three as line 16 in the fourth stanza; and line four as line 20 in the fifth stanza. The form is used in English primarily for LIGHT VERSE and has been practiced by Louis Untermeyer and Dorothy Parker. See FIXED FORMS, ROUNDEL, RONDEL, and ROUNDELET. See also *forms* in APPENDIX 1.

rondel /ron′dəl/ (from French for "round") a French FIXED FORM based on the RONDEAU. The r. consists of 13 lines (a *rondel prime* has 14 lines) in two quatrains and a final quintet. The meter and rhyme scheme are not fixed, but the poem turns on two rhymes and two REFRAIN lines: The first and second lines reappear as seven and eight, and the last line mirrors the first line (ABba, abAB, and abbaA). See RONDEAU REDOUBLE', RONDELET, and ROUNDEL. See also *forms* in APPENDIX 1.

rondelet /ron′dəlet/ (French diminutive of RONDEL; a similarly used term is ROUNDELAY) a seven-line French FIXED FORM consisting of two rhymes and a REFRAIN: Line one is repeated as lines three and seven (all are four syllables). Lines two, four, five, and six are composed of eight syllables. The RHYME SCHEME is AbAabbA. See RONDEAU, RONDEAU REDOUBLÉ, RONDEL, and ROUNDEL. See also *forms* in APPENDIX 1.

round character a three-dimensional CHARACTER described in depth through NARRATION and DIALOGUE. The AUDIENCE enters into an empathetic relationship with the r.c. as if he or she were a real person. The r.c. stands in opposition to the STOCK CHARACTER (also known as the STEREOTYPE or FLAT CHARACTER) who represents a known type and who possesses predictable attitudes and characteristics. In contrast, the r.c. is described in such a way as to be understandable and yet surprising; the audience perceives the r.c. as a fully realized individual rather than as a literary SYMBOL. See *dramatic terms* in APPENDIX 1.

roundel /roun'dəl/ (from French *rondel*; see RONDEL) an accentual-syllabic form invented by Swinburne and based on the rondeau. The r. consists of 11 lines in three stanzas turning on two rhymes and a REFRAIN: a QUATRAIN (RbaR), a TRIPLET (bab), and a quatrain (abaR). The refrain is taken from the initial part of the first line and rhymes with lines 2, 5, 7, and 9. See RONDEAU, RONDEAU REDOUBLÉ, RONDELET, and ROUNDELAY. See also *forms* in APPENDIX 1.

roundelay /roun'dəlā/ (from French *rondelet*) a LYRIC with a REFRAIN, or the music or dance set to such a lyric. The term has also been used as a synonym for RONDEAU, RONDEL, and ROUNDEL. See RONDEAU REDOUBLÉ and RONDELET. See also *forms* in APPENDIX 1.

Rubaiyat /rōōbī'yät/ (from Arabic for "quatrain"; see OMAR STANZA) an abbreviation for *Rubaiyat of Omar Khayyam*, poems by the 11th-century Persian poet and astronomer (first translated in full by Edward Fitz-Gerald). Sometimes any poem that exhibits qualities similar to FitzGerald's translation is called a R.

rubric /rōōb'rik/ (from Latin for "red") a title, heading, or instruction in a manuscript or a book. The r. is usually written or printed in red or otherwise distinguished from the text. See GLOSS. See also *publishing formats* under *forms* in APPENDIX 1.

runes (from Old English for "mystery") the letters of the earliest Teutonic alphabet, usually carved on stones, drinking horns, weapons, and ornaments. The alphabet is thought to have been developed during the second or third centuries A.D. by Germanic tribes who used it primarily for the purpose of recording magical incantations, and it died out when the Latin alphabet gained importance with the rise of Christianity. Emerson, among others, used the term to refer to any song or poem, and in modern usage the term implies a poem that uses a magical or incantatory style, e.g., W.S. Merwin's *Runes for a Round Table*. See CHARM.

running rhythm a term coined by G.M. Hopkins to indicate the common RISING RHYTHM and FALLING RHYTHM of English meters written in feet of two or three syllables (iambic, trochaic, dactylic, anapestic, etc.). See COMMON RHYTHM, ROCKING RHYTHM, and SPRUNG RHYTHM. See *rhythm* in APPENDIX 1.

run-on line: See ENJAMBMENT.

S

saga (Old Norse and Icelandic for "narrative, story, history," related to *say*) originally, a long prose narrative recounting traditional Norwegian or Icelandic history. The term has come to mean any long story of heroic adventure. The word "saw," as in the saying "an old saw" is etymologically related to s. Longfellow's *Saga of King Olaf* is based on the ancient s. *Heimskringla*. See EPIC.

sandwich construction (see CUT-AND-SHUFFLE POEM and FRAME STORY) a narrative structure featuring an outer frame into which an inner frame is inserted. See also *forms* in APPENDIX 1.

Sapphic the meter and stanzaic forms of the Greek poetess of Lesbos, Sappho. The S. stanza consists of three *lesser Sapphics*, 11-syllable lines with a dactyl in the third foot ($-\smile/-\smile/-\smile\smile/-\smile/-\smile$), followed by an ADONIC ($-\smile\smile-\smile$). The *greater S.* is a logaoedic (proselike) couplet whose first line has seven syllables ($-\smile-\smile\smile-\smile$) and whose second line has 15 syllables ($-\smile-\smile\smile\ -\smile\smile\ \|\ -\smile\smile-\smile\smile$). Many poets, including Sappho's contemporary Alcaeus, as well as Catullus, Horace, Swinburne, and some Renaissance poets, have practiced the form. See *forms* in APPENDIX 1.

sarcasmus (from the Greek for "to speak bitterly," literally "to tear flesh") a rhetorical figure of emotion, similar to MYCTERISMUS, but which employs a more cutting and bitter retort: "How can you judge others when you are incapable of judging yourself?" See *figures of pathos* in APPENDIX 2.

satire /sat'ī·ər/ (from Latin *satura*, a dish containing mixed fruit or other ingredients, related to *satis*, for "enough") a style, tone, or technique that moralistically diminishes, by way of ridicule or scorn, the failings of an individual, institution, or society. Archilochus (seventh century B.C.) was perhaps the first Greek literary satirist. Traditionally, the approach is divided into two major types: formal s. and indirect s.

Formal s. is a direct attack in which the satirist, represented by an "I" point of view, addresses the *adversarius* whose failings are the object of attack and whose technical function is to steer the speaker's comments. The *Horatian s.* presents a worldly and amused speaker whose speech is informal and whose attitude is generous toward the folly he speaks of (as in Pope's *Moral Essays* and in the work of certain contemporary American poets such as Alan Dugan, James Tate, Thomas Lux, and Russell Edson). The *Juvenalian s.* presents a grave speaker who views folly as a serious threat, and thus hopes to elicit serious reaction from his readers (as in the work of Johnson as well as the contemporary poets William Everson, Robinson Jeffers, and Denise Levertov).

Indirect s., usually presented in the third-person point of view, uses narration that exposes the folly of characters by depicting their action, thoughts, and dialogue (sometimes with authorial comments). The *Menippean* (or *Varronian*) *s.* is a form of indirect s. that presents a running dialectic by a gathering of learned people whose dignity is undermined by the ridiculous speeches they make: Petronius' *Satyricon*, Voltaire's *Candide*, Lewis Carroll's two *Alice* books, and Jerzy Kozinksky's *Being There* are examples of this subtype.

Historically, the manner has employed an array of devices, genres, and styles of writing, such as BEAST EPIC, BURLESQUE, CARICATURE, FABLIAU, HEROIC COUPLET, INVECTIVE, IRONY, LAMPOON, MYCTERISMUS, PARODY, and SARCASMUS. Humor is more of a strategy than an expected response. Writers who are well known for their use of s. besides those mentioned above include Aristophanes, Martial, Shakespeare, Jonson, Dryden, the Earl of Rochester, Goldsmith, Swift, Thackeray, Burns, Blake, Rabelais, Huxley, Eliot, Auden, and the contemporary writers Robert Lowell and Philip Roth. See *humor* and *light verse* in APPENDIX 1.

satiric poetry /sətir′ik/ (see SATIRE) a verse offering witty or humorous moral criticism as in the work of Byron, Pope, Dryden, and others.

scansion /skansh′ən/ (from Latin for "a climbing") a system analyzing conventional metrics by employing the use of visual symbols or graphs. The most common types of s. are (1) graphic, (2) musical, and (3) acoustic. Each system offers its own particular strengths and weaknesses, and it must be noted that because there are emotive nuances in the use of STRESS, PITCH, LOUDNESS, and DURATION of words, which have no schematic representations, s. cannot approach the accuracy and sensitivity of the trained ear.

The *graphic* system is the most widely used method of s. in the English language. It considers, primarily, both the stressed and unstressed syllables in a poetic line, and, secondarily, the number of feet and the position and number of caesuras (initial, medial, or terminal pauses). Even though graphic s. can differentiate between primary, secondary, and tertiary stressed syllables, it tends to assume that syllables have no durational value or pitch, and that they maintain one of four positions on a scale of stress, when in fact the quality and degree of accent can be infinitely divided. The four symbols are:

heavy	´
medium or secondary	`
light, or tertiary	ˈ
unstressed	˘

The division between feet is indicated by / and caesuras or major pauses are indicated by ||. In the question "Does this make any sense to you?" the words "this," "sense," and "you" would be marked with *primary* accents or stresses; the *y* in "any" and the word "to" would be marked as unstressed; the word "does" and the *an* in "any" would be marked as *secondary* stresses; and the word "make" would be marked as a *tertiary* stress. There are two caesuras in the line: an initial one after "this," and a terminal pause after "sense." At this point, it is easy to mark off the positions and amount of feet in the line. Because stresses generally come after unstressed syllables in the line, it contains a RISING RHYTHM or meter which breaks down and builds up after each stress. This type of very common foot is called iambic (see IAMB), and although there are metrical variations in the line (the *an* in any is not a true primary accent, but is counted as one) the base meter of the line contains four feet; thus, it is iambic tetrameter and would be scanned in the following way:

Does this / ‖ make an / y̆ sense / ‖ to you?

To indicate the rhyme scheme of a STANZA and the number of feet per line, letters are used to represent rhymes, and numbers to indicate the amount of feet in a line. An iambic tetrameter set of four lines, rhyming every other line would thus be: abab4. If the number of feet varied in each line, then a subnumeral would indicate how many feet were in that line.

The *musical* system of s., less common than the graphic, has been adapted from methods of notation in music. It highlights the speed or duration of syllables by using 1/8 notes, 1/4 notes, 1/2 notes, whole notes, and rests (𝄾). The graphically scanned line above would appear as:

Does this 𝄾 make any sense 𝄾 to you?

It's possible to indicate the relative pitch between syllables by positioning them as if they were on a musical staff:

Does　this　make　an　y　sense　to　you?

The slur marks above the words indicate phrasing or cadence. The weakness of musical s. is that it does not account for the degree and quality of stress of each syllable.

The *acoustic s.* is used mainly by linguists, not metricists. By means of a machine such as the oscillograph or the kymograph, it is possible to "see" voice patterns as words are pronounced. It is even possible to analyze the particles of sound called phonemes. While this system can account for the duration and emphasis of syllables, it is extremely complex to read.

Another, less common, method used by those who reject the conventional systems of scansion is the CADENCE s. which marks off the general phrasing of a line with wavy lines or brackets:

[　　][　　][　][　　]
Does this make any sense to you?

One of the most important aspects of poetry read aloud is the combination of the quality of voice and the interpretation of the poem. These color the sounds and silences, but have not been represented in any of the above systems. See also METER, PROSODIC SYMBOLS, PROSODY, and RHYTHM.

scene (from Greek for "tent" or "stage") originally, the floor and backdrop of the stage in Greek and Roman theater. Currently, the term denotes (1) the performance on stage, (2) a subdivision of an act in a play, (3) the setting for the play's action, (4) the pictorial representation of a real or imagined place, or (5) a real or dramatized emotional encounter. Shakespeare, it should be noted, did not divide his plays into scenes; these divisions were added by later editors. See DRAMATIC STRUCTURE and NARRATION. See also *dramatic terms* in APPENDIX 1.

scène à faire /sen′äfer′/: See OBLIGATORY SCENE.

scesis onomaton /sē′sis ənom′əton/ a grammatical construction that omits the verb: "A man huge in stature, soft in voice, graceful in manner." See *grammatical constructions are technically incorrect* in APPENDIX 2.

schematismus /skēm-/ (from Greek *schema*, for "form, figure") a rhetorical figure of circuitous speech created by suspicions. Its planned meaning is understated or left unspoken for the sake of safety, modesty, or grace, as in these words of a small to a larger man: "History teaches us that large men often use force to get their way. But I see from your demeanor, sir, that you depend upon reason and what is right." See *figures of notation and conjugation* in APPENDIX 2.

scop (from Old High German *schof*, for "poet") an Anglo-Saxon BARD or MINSTREL, the precursor of the modern POET LAUREATE, whose function was to relate history, particularly in the form of the SAGA, compose OCCASIONAL VERSE, and entertain royalty. The scops were usually itinerant, though the luckier ones were considered part of the household of a noble family. See JONGLEUR, TROUBADOUR, and TROUVÈRE.

Scottish stanza: See BURNS STANZA.

selected details skillfully chosen images, events, dialogue, or allusions that, minor in themselves, add to the establishment of CHARACTER, SETTING, THEME or other major elements in a poem. The astute use of s.d. can provide depth, comment, saliency, and nuance.

semantics (from Greek *sema*, for "sign") the study of the meaning and etymology of words, or the relationship between signs or symbols and their meaning. I.A. Richards' *Principles of Literary Criticism* (1925) contains an influential discussion of s. (Historical s. is also called *semasiology*.) See SEMIOTICS. See also *meaning* in APPENDIX 1.

semiotics in linguistics, the application of formal rules to any type of visual communication that does not use the standard alphabet; in poetics, the study of implicit conventions (SYNTAX, line ending, devices of POETIC LICENSE, etc.) governing meaning in a form or genre. (The related term *semiology* or *semeiology* refers to the use and interpretation of sign language.) See also SEMANTICS.

senhal a form of affectionate and imaginative address in the conventions of Provençal TROUBADOUR verse.

sense stress: See LOGICAL STRESS.

sense transference: See SYNAESTHESIA.

sensibility an 18th-century doctrine stressing EMPATHY with others as opposed to the doctrine, put forward by Hobbes and others, that man is inherently selfish. The movement in philosophy is a precursor of ROMANTICISM in which appreciation of nature and emotion took precedence. The term DISSOCIATION OF S. indicates the split between emotions and thought (see METAPHYSICAL POETRY). The phrase "the poet's s." refers to the type of VOICE and VISION of a particular poet. Carried to its extreme, s. becomes SENTIMENTALISM which is looked upon as a defect in TONE. See also AGE OF SENSIBILITY.

sentence sounds the sculptural and dramatic qualities inherent in the rhythm and syntax of sentences without regard to the sound or meaning of the words in those sentences. The term was coined by Robert Frost, in letters to John Bartlett and others, to refer to the nonlexical sense of meaning (aesthetic impact) that the form of a sentence can carry. He said: "A sentence is a sound in itself on which other sounds called words may be strung." Thus, the sentence's construction is a GIVEN, as the denotations of the words are, and acts as one of the elements in the INTELLIGENCE in the poem. Frost recommended that s.s. could and should be taken selectively from everyday conversation, and that the reader would recognize the contextual matrix from which these phrasings arose. Thus, the reader brings to the poem that indefinite, gestaltlike meaning embedded in the s.s. See FLAT STATEMENT, PROSE, PROSE RHYTHM, and RHYTHM.

sentimentalism a pejorative term indicating an excess of emotion in a poem and a lack of critical judgment in a poet. As a defect in writing, s. is not seen primarily as emotional overindulgence but as the use of the slack and dull language of clichés. Also, what is judged appropriate in one age and culture may not be acceptable in the conventions of another age. For example, some of the GRAVEYARD SCHOOL of poetry is considered maudlin and sentimental by proponents of the NEW CRITICISM. Certain popular genres, such as soap operas and romance novels, inevitably are examples of s. since they pander to stock responses with stock characters, and are concerned with surface effect rather than genuineness. For related terms, see EMPATHY and SENSIBILITY. See also *defects in control* in APPENDIX 1.

septenary (from Latin for "seven of each"; similarly used terms are HEPTAMETER and FOURTEENERS) a seven-foot line usually in trochaic rhythm. The English *Poema Morale* (*Moral Ode*, 1200–50) is an early example of rhymed couplets in the s. form. The term s. also refers specifically to Medieval Latin verse and other religious works written in the vernacular, such as the *Ormulum* (1200s), a 10,000-line poem by Orm, an Augustinian monk who paraphrased the gospels for services. See *forms* in APPENDIX 1.

septet (from Latin for "seven") a STANZA of seven lines. The RHYME SCHEME and METER may vary. A specific form of the s. is the CHAUCER STANZA (also known as RHYME ROYAL or TROILUS STANZA) used by Chaucer, Shakespeare, and King James I of Scotland, among others. See also *forms* in APPENDIX 1.

sestet (from Latin for "six") a poem composed of six lines, or a stanza of six lines, as in the ITALIAN SONNET. Specific s. stanza forms include the *stave of six*, written in iambic tetrameter; the *Venus and Adonis* stanza, named after Shakespeare's poem of that title; RIME COUÉE (or TAIL-RHYME STANZA) of mixed iambic tetrameter and trimeter; and the BURNS STANZA. See SESTINA. See also *forms* in APPENDIX 1.

sestina (Italian for "sixth") an unrhymed fixed form consisting of six sestets with a concluding three-line ENVOY. In addition, the six end-words of the first stanza are repeated in the following stanzas in a special order, as exemplified in Robert Francis' *Hallelujah: A Sestina*:

> A wind's word, the Hebrew Hallelujah.
> I wonder they never gave it to a boy
> (Hal for short) boy with wind-wild hair.
> It means Praise God, as well it should since praise
> Is what God's for. Why didn't they call my father
> Hallelujah instead of Ebenezer?
>
> Eben, of course, but christened Ebenezer,
> Product of Nova Scotia (hallelujah).
> Daniel, a country doctor, was his father
> And my father his tenth and final boy.
> A baby and last, he had a baby's praise:
> Red petticoat, red cheeks, and crow-black hair.
>
> A boy has little say about his hair
> And little about a name like Ebenezer
> Except that he can shorten either. Praise
> God for that, for that shout Hallelujah.
> Shout Hallelujah for everything a boy
> Can be that is not his father or grandfather.
>
> But then, before you know it, he is a father
> Too and passing on his brand of hair
> To one more perfectly defenseless boy,
> Dubbing him John or James or Ebenezer
> But never, so far as I know, Hallelujah,
> As if God didn't need quite that much praise.
>
> But what I'm coming to—Could I ever praise
> My father half enough for being a father
> Who let me be myself? Sing halleluhah.
> Preacher he was with a prophet's head of hair
> And what but a prophet's name was Ebenezer,
> However little I guessed it as a boy?

The complicated form is thought to have been invented by the Provençal TROUBADOUR Arnaud Daniel and later was brought into English versification. With variations, it has been used by many poets, including Sydney, Swinburne, Kipling, Auden, Pound, Donald Justice, and W.D. Snodgrass. The *double s.* is a variant form consisting of 12 stanzas. For other specialized forms, see FIXED FORMS and FRENCH FORMS. See also *forms* in APPENDIX 1.

setting the environment (including physical place, historical period, AMBIENCE, and cultural class) of a literary work. The Greek term *opsis* (SCENE) describes the physical manifestations of the place in which the action occurs; a general s. creates the entire frame of the work, and specific settings are attached to the various episodes within the work. For example, in Eliot's *The Love Song of J. Alfred Prufrock*, the general s. is said to be that of Haymarket Square in Boston. Within this environment, apartments, the rooms of a museum, other houses, and a beach make up specific settings. The air of defeat and boredom (see MOOD) that permeates the poem, and the upper-class characters add to the s. See ATMOSPHERE, DRAMATIC STRUCTURE, LOCAL COLOR, LOCALE, NARRATION, and REGIONAL-ISM. See also *dramatic terms* in APPENDIX 1.

Shakespearean sonnet: See ENGLISH SONNET and SONNET.

shaping the act of gradually forming a poem through REVISION. See FORM, LINE ENDING, REDACTION, STANZA, and STRUCTURE.

short couplet a pair of rhymed lines in iambic or trochaic tetrameter, so-called because it is shorter than the HEROIC COUPLET of iambic pentameter lines. See COUPLET and TETRAMETER. See also *forms* in APPENDIX 1.

short measure or short meter an iambic QUATRAIN rhyming abcb with lines one, two, and four in iambic trimeter, and line three in iambic tetrameter:

> My girl, thou gazest much
> Upon the golden skies:
> Would I were heaven! I would behold
> Thee then with all mine eyes!

The *short hymnal stanza* rhymes abab in the same metrical pattern. The form takes its name from the LONG METER, COMMON METER OR COMMON MEASURE, or HYMNAL STANZA which rhymes abcb all in iambic tetrameter. The long *ballad stanza* rhymes either abab or abcb in iambic tetrameter. A corresponding form is the POULTER'S MEASURE, composed of alternating 12- and 14- syllable lines. See BALLAD METER.

sibilants (from Latin "to hiss, to whistle") consonants that make a hissing sound, such as /s/, /z/, /j/, and /sh/. The term *sibilance* refers to a prevalance of these sounds in a passage of literature; and the term SIGMATISM (repetition of the /s/ sound) refers to a defect in the sound of a poem because of a prevalence of whistling sounds (see CACOPHONY). The use of sibilants can have a musical effect: E.A. Poe, e.g., used the /s/ sound in 27 of the lines of the *Valley of Unrest*. Traditionally, the sound is said to symbolize evil and to evoke the sound of a snake. See ASSONANCE and CONSONANCE.

sight rhyme: See EYE-RHYME.

sigmatism (from the 18th letter of the Greek alphabet, *sigma*, which is equivalent to the English *s*) generally, lisping; in literature, a defect in the sonic quality of a passage because of the prevalence of hissing sounds. Tennyson called his efforts to keep the /s/ sound at a minimum, "kicking the geese out of the boat." See SIBILANTS. See also ASSONANCE and CONSONANCE.

simile /sim'ilē/ (from Latin for "like") a rhetorical and poetical figure of speech in which particular attributes of one thing are explicitly compared with particular attributes of another thing, usually using the words "like," "as," or "as if" to link up TENOR AND VEHICLE. The main differences between the s. and METAPHOR are that (1) the s. does not attempt to use its vehicle as an identity or substitution, but simply as a comparison, (2) s. is a form of extension while metaphor is a form of compression, and (3) the construction of s. displays a characteristic tentativeness, while the metaphor displays a sense of directness and certainty. The s. is comparatively rare in Anglo-Saxon literature and became popular as a TROPE during the English Medieval period. See EPIC S. See also *figurative expressions* in APPENDIX 1.

simultaneity /sīmultənē′itē/ (from Latin for "at the same time") the presentation of two or more styles, voices, themes, or plots at the same time. The term also refers to the Buddhist concentric sense of time, as found in the *I Ching*, in which nonrecurrent, recurrent, and eternal time frames coexist. See the related terms COLLAGE, MULTEITY, and THEMATIC MONTAGE.

Si ... quand /sē′käN′/ (French for "if ... when") a variant of the CADAVRE EXQUIS ("exquisite corpse") poetry game invented by French Surrealists. As André Breton described s.q.:

> Each of a number of players writes on a piece of paper a hypothetical phrase beginning with "if" or "when." On another he writes a proposition in the future or conditional tense. The game consists simply in bringing together one of the first phrases with one of the second. What results is a sentence containing two clauses impeccably related from the grammatical point of view but—having been associated by a chance process acknowledging no rights in accepted logic—not satisfying to the demands of rational sequence:

> > If there were no guillotine,
> > Wasps would take off their corsets.

> > If octopuses wore bracelets,
> > Boats would be drawn by flies.

> When aeronauts will have attained the seventh heaven,
> Statues will order themselves cold suppers.

For other poetry games, see ACROSTIC, BOUTS-RIMÉS, CARMEN FIGURATUM, CHANCE POETRY, FLYTING, LINKED VERSE, and NONSENSE VERSE. See also *forms* in APPENDIX 1.

sirventes /sēr′väNt/ (Provençal for "services"; the connection to the poetic form is unclear) a Provençal satirical poem or LAI, often written to current popular songs, that poked fun at politicians and other unpopular figures. Usually, the form carried a didactic or moral message. The contemporary analogue to this Medieval form is the work of the Washington satirist Mark Russell who composes witty barbs and diatribes against national political figures. See DIDACTIC POETRY, INVECTIVE, PARODY, and SATIRE.

situation the DRAMATIC S., the circumstances containing drama or conflict that precedes the unfolding of a PLOT; also, any set of conditions (MOOD,

SETTING, RISING ACTION, CLIMAX, or DÉNOUMENT) in which a *character* is involved. See DRAMATIC STRUCTURE, GIVEN, and NARRATION.

skald /skôld, skält/ (a ninth-century Old Norse or Icelandic term for "poet"; also spelled "scald") a Scandinavian poet (Norwegian or Icelandic). The term was used in Viking days from the ninth through the 12th centuries. Neither these poets' function nor the character of their work is known. Other terms for poets include BARD (Welsh), JONGLEUR (French), POET LAUREATE (modern English), SCOP (Old English) and TROUBADOUR (Provençal).

Skeltonic verse (also called "tumbling verse," "skeltonics," and "skeltoniads") satiric, roughly hewn verse of revolt written by John Skelton (1460–1529) and consisting of short, irregularly lined and rhymed verses. The form, aimed at the formalists, politicians, and clergymen of his period, resembles DOGGEREL in effect and intention. See also *forms* and *light verse* in APPENDIX 1.

slackness a defect due to the lack of economy, efficiency, tension, and verbal acuity in the form and content of a line or poem. In some literary periods, more s. was tolerated than in the modern and postmodern periods. See *defects in control* in APPENDIX 1. See also IMAGISM and NEW CRITICISM for modern poetic schools that believed writers should avoid s.

slant imagery the oblique rhyming of visual images to show both identity and transformational processes. For instance, in the series of images "chandelier, constellation, fireflies," the identity stems from all three being objects that give off light, and the transformation moves from manufactured, inorganic, static object to natural, organic, kinetic object. Thus, a buried or implied plot develops in the JUXTAPOSITION of images that, in a poem, would link disparate elements into a complex, self-defining system. See IMAGE, IMAGERY, INNER REFLECTIONS, and OFF-RHYME. See also *imagery* in APPENDIX 1.

slant rhyme: See OFF-RHYME.

social criticism a form of literary CRITICISM that undertakes to promote and thereby to create an audience for a work that it judges to be successful. See *criticism* in APPENDIX 1.

social myth (see MYTH) an imaginative construct meant to point out social problems.

solecism /sol'-/ (from Greek for "to speak incorrectly") a rhetorical figure of exchange categorized by Puttenham under "tolerable vices of language" in which a speaker misuses normal grammatical rules of case, gender, tense, etc. The defect extends to the violation of a language's IDIOM even if the rules of that idiom are in terms of formal usage. But many writers, such as John Berryman, Charles Bukowski, and James Wright, effectively use solecismus to reflect MOOD and CHARACTER. See BARBARISM, DIALECT, ENALLAGE, LOCAL COLOR, POETIC LICENSE, and SORIASMUS. See also *devices of poetic license* in APPENDIX 2.

soliloquy /səlil'əkwē/ (from Latin *soliloquium,* coined by St. Augustine from Greek *sonologia,* for "monologue"; also called "autologue") a dramatic convention in which a CHARACTER speaks to himself in an extended speech for the purpose of revealing emotion or information to the audience, or the character develops a philosophical argument or a narrative unrelated to him- or herself. The DRAMATIC MONOLOGUE uses a speaker who addresses a silent listener and thus exposes his nature and the DRAMATIC SITUATION in which he finds himself. The INTERIOR MONOLOGUE functions in the same way as the dramatic monologue, except that the reader is hearing the character's thoughts instead of actual speech. STREAM-OF-CONSCIOUSNESS writing represents the unbroken, uncensored flow of a character's thoughts and usually works by ASSOCIATIONAL LOGIC. Some of the most moving pieces in literature have been written in the form of soliloquies as exemplified by Shakespeare's tragedies, Marlowe's *Dr. Faustus,* and works by T.S. Eliot and W.H. Auden. See *dramatic terms* in APPENDIX 1.

song a LYRIC verse, usually short, accompanied by music. Usually, the lyric is simple, direct, and conventional so as not to compete with the music. Specific forms include the AUBADE, BALLAD, BLUES, CHANSON, CHANTEY, *dance s.,* DIRGE, *drinking s.,* EPITHALAMION, FOLK S., *hymn,* INCANTATION, JINGLE, LAI, *love s.,* MADRIGAL, NOCTURNE, NURSERY RHYME, PASTORAL LYRIC, PSALM, ROCK LYRIC, ROUNDELAY, *war s.,* and *work s.* See also *musical scansion* under SCANSION, and TONE COLOR.

sonics (also called "melopoetics") generally, acoustics; in poetry, the study of the systems, structures, and values of sound in a poem. Linguists and writers take into account the phonemes, phonetics, consonants, vowels, and sound systems in a poem in order to analyze the complex sounds that form speech or contribute to a work's aesthetic effect. In the past 40 years, sophisticated equipment, such as the oscilloscope and spectrograph, has enabled scientists in the field of *acoustic phonetics* to visually examine sound particles' frequencies and patterns, and has, in fact, been able to reproduce the human voice through computers. It has long been known that sound has an emotional and psychological effect on living things. Indian mantras, e.g., have in their various forms induced specific states of consciousness, and poets have long known the value of selectively arranging the types and patterns of sounds in a poem so that meaning and effect are enhanced. See ABSTRACT POETRY, BOND DENSITY, ONOMATOPOEIA, PHONEME, SOUND POEMS, SOUND-SYMBOLISM, SOUND SYSTEM, and TONE COLOR.

sonic structure Denise Levertov's term for the sound patterns and texture in a poem. For example, the sonic structures of Dylan Thomas and G.M. Hopkins might be described as thick, complex, impacted, and heavy, while the sonic structures of Donald Justice and Mark Strand might be said to be light, smooth, and harmonic. See AESTHETIC SURFACE, ASSONANCE, CONSONANCE, CONSONANTS, MELOPOEIA, METER, PHONEME, PHONETICS, RHYTHM, SCANSION, SONICS, SOUND POEMS, SOUND SYSTEM, TONE COLOR, and VOWELS.

sonnet /son'ət/ (from Italian for "little song, little sound") a 14-line lyrical fixed form, typically in iambic pentameter, characteristically using one of several specific rhyme schemes and expressing a single theme or emotion. A number of variations have evolved from the two basic types of sonnets: (1) The PETRARCHAN S. (or ITALIAN S.) was developed in 13th-century Italy and perfected by Petrarch in the 14th century. (For a description of the *Petrarchan conceit*, an important device in the Renaissance, see CONCEIT). The Petrarchan s. consists of 14 lines divided into an OCTAVE (RHYMING ABBAABBA) AND A SESTET (rhyming cdecde, cdcdcd, or cdedce). Usually, the s. is thematically divided into four sections: The first QUATRAIN states the proposition; the second quatrain elaborates upon it; the succeeding TERCET presents an example or ruminates upon the theme; and the last three lines create a final turn in the logical exposition. Keats' *On First Looking into Chapman's Homer* exemplifies the type:

opening of theme	Much have I travelled in the realms of gold,	a
	And many goodly states and kingdoms seen;	b
	Round many western islands have I been	b
octave	Which bards in fealty to Apollo hold.	a
	Oft of one wide expanse had I been told	a
elaboration of theme	That deep-browed Homer ruled in his demesne;	b
	Yet did I never breathe its pure serene	b
	Till I heard Chapman speak out loud and bold;	a

turn

example of theme	Then felt I like some watcher of the skies	c
	When a new planet swims into his ken;	d
	Or like stout Cortez when with eagle eyes	c
sestet	He stared at the Pacific—and all his men	d
conclusion of theme	Looked at each other with a wild surmise—	c
	Silent, upon a peak in Darien.	d

The form is uncommon in English, but has been used by Sidney, Wyatt, Wordsworth, D.G. Rossetti, Auden, and Berryman.

The MILTONIC S. is a variation on the Petrarchan s. The form consists of a Petrarchan octave rhyming abbaabba and a sestet with variable rhyme scheme with no major thematic turn between the octave and the sestet. Milton's variation on the form contributed a tighter sense of unity to the s. because of frequent ENJAMBMENT and the positioning of the turn somewhere between the ninth and 11th lines, which is somewhat later than the normal Petrarchan turn. The freedom of the position of the turn creates room for a less forced, more natural resolution, and usually the poem depends for its coherence and unity upon emotional thrust rather than structural organization.

(2) The SHAKESPEAREAN S. (or ENGLISH S.) consists of three quatrains (ababcdcdefef) and a concluding CLOSED COUPLET (gg). The turn in the theme occurs between the third quatrain and the final couplet. It differs significantly in the argumentative shape from the Petrarchan s. in that 12 lines are given over to stating the problem and only two to resolving it. Usually, the first three quatrains contain repetition and variation of the theme, as in Shakespeare's REVERSE METAPHOR S. (which, incidentally, is a

parody of the Petrarchan conceit popular with many of Shakespeare's contemporaries):

presentation of theme	My mistress' eyes are nothing like the sun;	a
	Coral is far more red than her lips' red;	b
first quatrain	If snow be white, why then her breasts are dun;	a
variation	If hairs be wires, black wires grow on her head.	b
variation	I have seen roses damasked, red and white,	c
second quatrain	But no such roses see I in her cheeks,	d
variation	And in some perfumes is there more delight	c
	Than in the breath that from my mistress reeks.	d
variation	I love to hear her speak, yet well I know	e
third quatrain	That music hath a far more pleasing sound;	f
variation	I grant I never saw a goddess go—	e
	My mistress, when she walks, treads on the ground:	f
turn		
closed final couplet resolution	And yet, by heaven, I think my love as rare	g
	As any she belied with false compare.	g

The SPENSERIAN S. is a variation on the Shakespearean s. The form consists of interlocking quatrains (abab, bcbc, cdcd), which create a close-knit exposition, and a final closed couplet (ee), which must be strong enough to balance the previous complicated 12-line development. The form is reputed to be the most demanding type of s. because of its intricate rhyme scheme and quick turn.

In general, the s. has enjoyed much attention by many poets over the past 500 years. Its strict form challenges the poet, and its set rhyme scheme provides a pleasant music for the reader. Furthermore, the brevity of the form demands concentrated expression of the emotion or idea. See CROWN OF SONNETS, CURTAL S. METER, RHYME, and S. SEQUENCE. For other fixed forms, see BALLADE, CHANT ROYAL, LAI, LIMERICK, RIME COUÉE, RONDEAU, RONDEL, ROUNDELET, SESTINA, TRIOLET, and VILLANELLE. See also *forms* in APPENDIX 1.

sonnet sequence (also called "sonnet cycle") a series of sonnets linked by form and theme. Petrarch's love poems for Laura and Sidney's *Astrophel and Stella* (1580) are among the early well-known examples that cohere through thematic development of love relationships. Other examples include Spenser's *Amoretti* (1595), Shakespeare's 154 sonnets, Rossetti's *The House of Life*, Elizabeth Barret Browning's *Sonnets from the Portuguese*, Dylan Thomas's *Altarwise by Owl-Light*, and the early sonnets of John Berryman. See a specialized s.s., CROWN OF SONNETS. See also *forms* in APPENDIX 1.

soriasmus a rhetorical figure, similar to CACOZELIA, classified by Puttenham (1520?–1601?) as a "tolerable vice of language," featuring speech that incorporates a number of foreign expressions:

My "tsoris," mi amigo, is in not finding "le mot juste" to say "arrivederci" to "mon cher." Kapish?

See BARBARISM, CACOZELON, and SOLECISM. See also *devices of poetic license* in APPENDIX 2, and *diction* in APPENDIX 1.

sorites /sorī′tēz/ (from Greek for "heap") a rhetorical figure of argumentation based on a series of enthymemes in which the content of a previous clause supplies content for the succeeding clause until a chain or *climbing argument* is achieved:

> An insect scared the cat; the cat scared the child;
> The child scared the mother; the mother scared the father;
> The father scared the neighbors; the neighbors scared
> The town; therefore, an insect scared the town.

The term is applied to Greek sophists (see RHETORIC), who practiced such logic that works against common sense. See *figures of argumentation* in APPENDIX 2.

sotadies: See PALINDROME.

sound poems poems that depend on the element of sound for the major portion of their meaning. The genre includes ABSTRACT POETRY, NONSENSE VERSE, TRANS-SENSE VERSE, and the device of AMPHIGORY.
  Aram Saroyan has created a "Minimal poem" (see MINIMALISM) based on the name of an insect and the sound it makes. During the development of the poem, the word turns itself inside out, going from the linguistic concept of the cricket through pure onomatopoetic sound (see ONOMATOPOEIA) and then back into the conceptual word again. When the last word in the poem has been read, the reader experiences that word as a sensual entity:

> crickets
> crickess
> cricksss
> cricssss
> crisssss
> crssssss
> csssssss
> sssssss
> ssssssts
> ssssssets
> sssskets
> sssckets
> ssickets
> srickets
> crickets

See BOND DENSITY, PHONEME, SONICS, SONIC STRUCTURE, SOUND-SYMBOLISM, SOUND SYSTEM, and TONE COLOR.

sound-signs: See phoneme.

sound-symbolism a modern linguistic term, related to ONOMATOPOEIA, referring to the general capability of speech sounds to imitate physical qualities; e.g., in the consonant grouping, the sounds /l/ and /r/ are termed *liquids* for their flowing, mellifluous quality, the large *fricative* group (voiced /v/, /z/, /zh/, /th/; voiceless /f/, /s/, /sh/, /th/, /h/) contains sounds that suggest speed and friction, the *plosives* (/b/, /d/, /g/, /j/; /p/, /t/, /k/) feature hard, explosive sounds, the *nasals* (/m/, /n/, /ng/) display satisfying inward sounds, and the *glides* (/w/, /y/) offer the sense of duration and weight. The term s.-s. is used simply to describe the close relationship between sound and sense in language and poetry. See CACAPHONY, EUPHONY, SONICS, AND SOUND SYSTEM.

sound system the conscious or intuitive arrangement of various consonant and vowel groupings. The s.s. of a poem supplies a texture that conveys meaning through the experience of sound; this meaning is integral to the overall experience of the work but separate from the denotative meaning of the work (see DENOTATION and CONNOTATION). For example, the two lines below contain each a different and specific experience due to their sounds, yet the paraphrasable meaning is essentially the same:

> (plosives)   *Two black bats bit twenty people.*
> (fricatives)   *Fifteen black bats bit six peasants.*

The short, clipped vowels and hard plosives of the first line contribute to the experience of violence. The fricatives of the second line add an element of anguish. Compare these two lines with a line that uses long, open vowels as well as nasals, glides, and liquids:

> One's home has a monumental hold on the heart.

For a closer look at how a master sound technician uses textural sound systems, let us look at Dylan Thomas' *After the Funeral*. At the time that Thomas wrote the poem he was using sound systems that tended to clot together and become isolated from the total experience of the poem. His later work was less inconsistent, more homogenized in its MELOPOEIA. But for the purpose of illustrating dense sound systems, his early work is the best place to turn to:

> *After the Funeral*
> (In memory of Ann Jones)
> After the funeral, mule praises, brays,
> Windshake of sailshaped ears, muffle toed tap
> Tap happily of one peg in the thick
> Grave's foot, blinds down the lids, the teeth in black,
> The spittled eyes, the salt ponds in the sleeves,
> Morning smack of the spade that wakes up sleep,
> Shakes a desolate boy who slits his throat
> In the dark of the coffin and sheds dry leaves,
> That breaks one bone to light with a judgment clout,
> After the feast of tear-stuffed time and thistles
> In a room with a stuffed fox and a stale fern,
> I stand, for this memorial's sake, alone
> In the snivelling hours with dead, humped Ann
> Whose hooded, fountain heart once fell in puddles
> Round the parched world of Wales and drowned each sun
> (Though this for her is a monstrous image blindly
> Magnified out of praise; she would lie dumb and deep
> And need no druid of her broken body).
> But I, Ann's bard on a raised hearth, call all
> The seas to service that her wood-tongued virtue
> Babble like a bellbuoy over the hymning heads,
> Bow down the walls of the ferned and foxy woods

That her love sing and swing through a brown chapel,
Bless her bent spirit with four, crossing birds.
Her flesh was meek as milk, but this skyward statue
With the wild breast and blessed and giant skull
Is carved from her in a room with a wet window
In a fiercely mourning house in a crooked year.
I know her scrubbed and sour humble hands
Lie with religion in their cramp, her threadbare
Whisper in a damp word, her wits drilled hollow,
Her fist of a face died clenched on a round pain;
And sculptured Ann is seventy years of stone.
These cloud-sopped marble hands, this monumental
Argument of the hewn voice, gesture and psalm,
Storm me forever over her grave until
The stuffed lung of the fox twitch and cry Love
And the strutting fern lay seeds on the black sill.

Without an explication of the poem, the reader can sense the poem's emotional meaning through sound alone. Let's examine some of the more obvious sound systems:

>   Tap
> Tap happily of one peg in the thick
> Grave's foot,

The combination of plosives and short vowels give the onomatopoetic effect of a peg being nailed into a coffin, or of a cross being hammered into place.

> Morning smack of the spade that wakes up sleep,
> Shakes a desolate boy who slits his throat

In these lines the fricatives, plosives, and long vowels have a cold and startling quality that is appropriate to the meaning of the words.

> That breaks one bone to light with a judgment clout.

Here, again, the heavy plosives have the impact of a hammer. Notice that the word "light," which is made of a liquid and a high vowel, goes against the heavy sounds of the line. The sound flashes out from the somberness of the line in the same terrifying way the image of the bone is revealed.

> After the feast of tear-stuffed time and thistles
> In a room with a stuffed fox and a stale fern,

Here the heavy layer of fricatives in these lines makes the reader aware of the discomfort and anguish contained in the room. The sound echoes the images of tears, thistles, a dead fox, and stale fern.

> In the snivelling hours with dead, humped Ann
> Whose hooded, fountain heart once fell in puddles
> Round the parched world of Wales and drowned each sun

Here there is a feeling of a body being crammed into a small space. The short vowels and nasals of the first line, which create this effect, telescope fluidly into the larger, rounder, heavier effects of the next system, which is made up of long vowels, glides, and liquids.

> She would lie dumb and deep
> And need no druid of her broken body.

Here Thomas switches back to the heavy, thudding plosives, as if he were having to force Ann's body back into her coffin.

> her wood-tongued virtue
> Babble like a bellbuoy over the hymning heads

Although Thomas is using plosives in these lines, their usually heavy effect is lightened by the polysllabics which create a light rhythm. These plosives have speed instead of striking power. So rhythm is yet another device to control sound.

> I know her scrubbed and sour humble hands
> Lie with religion in their cramp, her threadbare
> Whisper in a damp word,

The short vowels, nasals, and plosives in these lines again give the reader the feeling of being cramped and numbed. All the sounds are blunted, except for the word "Whisper," whose sibilance (see SIBILANTS) is the same counterpoint technique that Thomas used with the word "light" in our earlier example.

> Her fist of a face died clenched on a round pain;

the fricatives and diphthongs here make a violent sound, as if in his frustration over her death the poet is seeking revenge. The word "whisper," which breaks the deadening sound of the previous inward and cramped s.s. is the COMMITTING WORD that signals the advance of the fricatives and diphthongs.

> marble hands, this monumental
> Argument of the hewn voice, gesture and psalm,
> Storm me forever over her grave

The system here has an enlarging and sculptured effect. Thomas is now speaking as a bardic orator, a voice that magnifies Ann's presence in the reader's mind by employing vowels of long duration, nasals, which also have long duration, and r's, which add solidity and a sense of strain.

> The stuffed lung of the fox twitch and cry Love
> And the strutting fern lay seeds on the black sill.

The word "grave" in the penultimate s.s. is another committing word whose high /ā/ vowel signals an imminent rise in emotion. It peaks and breaks in the anxious fricatives of the last two lines, just as the apparently dead fox is startled into speech.

The study of sound builds an appreciation for the shape and feeling of words, their physicality (See PHYSICALITY/PHYSICALNESS). Just as an accomplished pianist can free himself from having to pay attention to his hands, an accomplished poet learns to select words for his poems without having to study them while in the process of writing. So it is important to play with the sounds of words, learn what they are saying beyond their meaning in terms of the sound they make. See also ABSTRACT POETRY, BOND DENSITY, CACOPHONY, EUPHONY, ONOMATOPOEIA, PHONEME, SONICS, SONIC STRUCTURE, SOUND-SYMBOLISM, and TONE COLOR, as well as *melopoetics* in APPENDIX 1.

speaker the identified or unidentified NARRATOR of a poem. See CHARACTER, MASK, NARRATION, NARRATOR AGENT, PERSONA, POINT OF VIEW, and VOICE.

specious simile (coined by the French Surrealist poet Raymond Roussel) a SIMILE "that tells one less than one would know if the thing were stated flatly"; e.g., instead of flatly stating that something is out of favor, Roussel might say "as anachronistic as the sky." The point of the s.s. is to create an unspecific maze of connections in order to enlarge the realms of possibility and suspense. John Ashbery, who has closely studied the work of Roussel, has cultivated the device. See REVERSE METAPHOR. See also *negative metaphor* and *subtractive metaphor* under METAPHOR.

Spenserian sonnet Edmund Spenser's 14-line sonnet form in iambic pentameter rhyming abab, bcbc, cdcd, ee. See SONNET.

Spenserian stanza Edmund Spenser's stanzaic creation invented for his six-part PAEAN to Queen Elizabeth, *The Faerie Queene* (1596). The form consists of nine lines: The first eight are in iambic pentameter and represent a variation of OTTAVA RIMA; the ninth is in iambic hexameter (ALEXANDRINE); and the rhyme scheme is ababbcbc^{5}c^6, as in the following stanza from part i of *The Cave of Despair:*

> Ere long they come, where that same wicket wight
>   His dwelling has, low in a hollow cave,
> Farre underneath a craggie clift ypight,
>   Darke, dolefull, drearie, like a greedie grave,
>   That still for carcases doth crave:
> On top whereof aye dwelt the ghostly Owle,
>   Shrieking his baleful note, where ever drave
> Farre from that haunt all other chearefull fowle;
> And all about it wandring ghostes did waile and howle.

This flexible form adapts well to a balance between succinctness and ELABORATION, and became popular in Romantic poetry. Keats (*The Eve of St. Agnes*), Shelley (*Adonais*), and Byron (*Childe Harold's Pilgrimage*), among others, have used this form which is said to be based on Chaucer's ottava rima and linked octave which he employed in *The Monk's Tale*. For other stanzaic forms, see STANZA. See also *forms* in APPENDIX 1.

spiritual myth (see MYTH) an imaginative construct that is meant to reflect the speaker's system of spiritual and moral values.

spondee /spon'dē/ (from Greek for "solemn drink-offering"; the staid FOOT used in early Greek religious verse) a duple foot of two long syllables in QUANTITATIVE METER or two accented syllables in ACCENTUAL-SYLLABIC VERSE, such as "óh, nó" or "hót dóg." In Classical prosody, the s. was used as a base rhythm, but in English verse it is usually used as a SUBSTITUTION for iambic, trochaic, or triple feet. See METER.

Spoonerism (named after the Rev. W.A. Spooner, of New College, Oxford, who was inordinately guilty of this mistake) a form of MALAPROPISM, in which there is an accidental transposition of the parts of two or more words, such as, "drown beer" for "brown deer," or "moppish food" for "foppish mood." See CACOZELON and METATHESIS. See also *devices of poetic license* in APPENDIX 2, and *diction* in APPENDIX 1.

sprung rhythm an impacted ACCENTUAL-SYLLABIC VERSE popularized by Gerard Manley Hopkins (1844–89), calling for feet of equal DURATION containing a first accented syllable standing alone or followed by one to three unaccented syllables. This kind of rhythm (see LOGAOEDIC) is common in nursery rhymes and, according to Hopkins, emulates the natural rhythms of emotional speech. Its strengths are in its power of expression, intensity of emotion, and range of rhythmical variations. Wanting a strong and urgent tone, Hopkins saw the accent as the key to his new meter. He said: "Why, if it is forcible in prose to say "lashed rod," am I obliged to weaken this in verse, which ought to be stronger, not weaker . . .?" Contemporary FREE VERSE tends to use a less highly accented conversational rhythm. See ACCENT, METER, PROSODY, RHYTHM, ROCKING RHYTHM, and RUNNING RHYTHM.

stance (from Old French for "post, position, station") the LOCATION, POINT OF VIEW, or TONE of the SPEAKER of a poem. See MASK.

stanza (Italian for "stopping place" or "room"; similarly used terms are STROPHE and STAVE) a fixed (HOMOSTROPHIC), or variable (ASTROPHIC) grouping of lines that is organized into thematic, metrical, rhetorical, musical, or narrative sections. Although much contemporary FREE VERSE contains stanzas roughly equivalent in length, rhythm, and number, variation is common. Other recognized stanzaic forms include BALLAD, BALLADE, BARZELLETA, BLOCK POEM, BURDEN, BURNS S., CHAUCER S., CINQUAIN, CLOSED COUPLET (DISTICH), CODA, CANTO, COWLEYAN ODE, DÉCIMA, DIZAIN, ELEGIAC DISTICH, ELEGAIC S., ENVELOPE S., EPIGRAM, EPODE, FATRAS, HAIKU, HEROIC COUPLET, HEROIC S., HORATIAN ODE, HUDIBRASTIC VERSE, IN MEMORIAM S., LAI, LIMERICK, MONOSTROPHE, OCTAVE, OCTASTICH, OPEN COUPLET, OTTAVA RIMA, PINDARIC ODE, QUATRAIN, QUINTET, QUINTILLA, REDONDILLA, RHOPALIC VERSE, RIME COUÉE, RONDEAU, RONDEL, RONDELET, RUBAIYAT S., SAPPHIC, SEPTET, SESTET, SESTINA, SONNET, SPENSERIAN S., TANKA, TERCET, TERZA RIMA, TRIADIC S., TRIOLET, VERSE PARAGRAPH, and VILLANELLE.

stave (from *staff*) a verse or STANZA of a poem, particularly verses of hymns or ballads (18th and 19th centuries).

stereotype /ster'ē-ōtīp/ (from Greek for "solid" plus "type") clichéd characterization of a person, concept, SETTING, or event without development or nuance. A s. depends upon the reader's STOCK RESPONSE. See CLICHÉ, MILES GLORIOSUS, STOCK CHARACTER, and STOCK SITUATION. See also *control* in APPENDIX 1.

stich /stik/ (from Greek for "row, line, verse") a measured line of verse. The term *stichic* refers to successive lines of verse containing the same METER, the Greek form of recitative poetry, as opposed to the *strophic* or *stanzaic* form, which was meant to be sung. A half-line is referred to as a *hemistich*, a single line as a MONOSTICH, a couplet as a DISTICH, a tercet or triplet as a TRISTICH, etc. See also MESOSTICH, PENTASTICH, PROSODIC SYMBOL, STICHOMYTHIA, STROPHE, STANZA, and TELESTICH.

stichomythia /stikōmith'ē·a/ (from Greek for "line" plus "speech") in Classical Greek drama, single alternating lines of DIALOGUE during a dispute or heated exchange between two characters. Their speech in this form displays rhetorical elements of contrast (see ANTITHESIS), repetition, and PARALLELISM; current usage of the term includes all repartee or *cut and thrust* dialogue. Shakespeare's *Richard III* shows a vivid example of s. in the exchange between Richard and Queen Elizabeth (IV. iv). See also AMOEBEAN VERSES and FLYTING.

stock (from Old English for "tree trunk, log," "stick,"; also probably related to the meaning of provisions to be drawn upon as the occasion requires) the use of the repeating last line in the refrain of a BALLADE.

stock character a conventional character or STEREOTYPE whose traits have been established by many authors and whose recognition by the audience relies on STOCK RESPONSE. Examples include the villain, the ne'er-do-well, the fair lady in distress, the rich fop, the wicked stepmother, the braggart soldier (MILES GLORIOSUS), the hermit, the taciturn father, and the hard-bitten yeoman. In lyric poetry since the Romantic era (see ROMANTICISM), the lyric monologuist tortured by his passions, memories, and losses has come to be a s.c. Ancient Greek comedy offers three stock characters: the *alazon* (the posturing braggart), the *eiron* (the self-deprecatory character), and the *bomolochos* (the buffoon). Northrop Frye has revived these terms and added a fourth: the *agroikos* (the "hayseed" who is easily led astray). See ANTAGONIST, CLICHÉ, DEUTERAGONIST, PLOT, and STOCK SITUATION. See also *clichés* and *dramatic terms* in APPENDIX 1.

stock response (probably coined by I.A. Richards in *Practical Criticism*, 1930, chapter 5) the predictable, shallow reaction to standard and conmmonly recognized characters, settings, situations, or symbols. Writers who are not working in COMEDY, SATIRE, or in genres such as MELODRAMA, soap opera, popular verse, etc., usually avoid stock responses by fully developing their content. The GRAVEYARD SCHOOL poets are known for their dependence on easily triggered emotions, although some of these poets, such as Thomas Gray (*Elegy in a Country Churchyard*), created works of lasting artistic merit. See CLICHÉ, PLOT, SENTIMENTALISM, STEREOTYPE, STOCK CHARACTER, and STOCK SITUATION. See also *clichés* in APPENDIX 1.

stock situation a PLOT element that presents a standard CONFLICT or predicament that is easily recognized by the audience. Examples of stock situations include the secret tryst, the journey of the prodigal son, the haunted-house exploration, the exchange of identities, the poor-boy-makes-good, the search for revenge, the seductive vamp beguiling the innocent man, the gold digger endearing herself, and the surburban ennui. Depending on how imaginatively the characters of the s.s. are developed, the s.s. may produce a solid framework for vivid drama or a boring and predictable work. See ARCHETYPE, CLICHÉ, CONVENTION, DRAMATIC SITU-ATION, MOTIF, MYTH, PLOT, SENTIMENTALISM, SITUATION, STEREOTYPE, STOCK CHARACTER, and STOCK RESPONSE. See also *clichés* and *dramatic terms* in APPENDIX 1.

story-within-a-story a conventional device of NARRATION that inserts a vignette or telling incident inside the larger FRAME STORY in order to deepen exposition, PLOT, or CHARACTER. Often this device is accomplished by means of FLASHBACK, DIGRESSION, or the STOCK SITUATION in which a character is obliged to relate his story, as in Chaucer's *Canterbury Tales* and in certain episodes of Twain's *The Adventures of Huckleberry Finn*. See PLAY-WITHIN-A-PLAY.

straight cut (see CINEMATIC TECHNIQUES) a CINEMATIC EDITING device in which cuts are made to further PLOT or THEME in a straightforward way. This type of cutting gives the work a natural sense of movement and a logical chronology. See also *cinematic terms* in APPENDIX 1.

strain behind the poem a defect in the creative process represented by an unconscious intrusion on the part of the author whose attitude either toward the writing process itself or toward something outside the aesthetic framework of the poem finds its way into the work at hand. Undetected, these unaffiliated emotions or attitudes may become transferred to the poem and inappropriately tinge it, an effect that reflects upon the writer's lack of CONTROL. For other defects in control, see BURIED THEME, DIGRESSION, DISTRACTING DETAILS, MIXED MESSAGE, MOOD PIECE, OBSCURITY, OVERDECORATION, OVERREPTITION, and OVERWRITING. See also CONTROL in APPENDIX 1.

strategy (from Greek for "office or command of a general") the tactical plan of a poem's development; that is, the terms through which the poem accomplishes its purpose. This plan includes the larger vehicles such as METAPHOR, FORM and STRUCTURE, RHYTHM, TONE, and ARGUMENT, as well as the smaller components that make up the AESTHETIC SURFACE, such as sound system, rhetorical figures, imagery, and DICTION. The s. of a poem may also include special devices such as CARMEN FIGURATUM, FILL-IN-THE-BLANKS POEMS, or ABSTRACT POETRY.

stream-of-consciousness a narrative technique, developed by the French novelist Edouard Dujardin in 1888 and named by William James (*Principles of Psychology*, 1890), representing the unbroken flow of thought of a character's conscious and subconscious mind. The cohesive force in the seemingly random and ungrammatical stream of language is ASSOCIATIONAL LOGIC, which works by means of JUXTAPOSITION (*parataxis*) rather than the usual conventional framework of grammar, which indicates logical relationships. The overriding sense is one of quickly arriving at some epiphanic experience (see EPIPHANY). The s.-o.-c. manner of representing the mind's workings appears spontaneous, unedited, and uncensored although, in fact, its success rests on a process of careful selection.

André Breton, formulating his ideas on SURREALISM, described s.-o.-c. as AUTOMATIC WRITING, and he called for "the dictation of thought in the absence of any control exercised by reason, beyond aesthetic or moral preoccupations." He said, "Write quickly, without a preconceived subject, quickly enough not to remember and not to be tempted to reread." By looking at an everyday object through the subconscious mind in order to arrive at a *metaphorical objectivity*, the Surrealists hoped to touch upon the universal in man's nature. Many writers, such as William Faulkner, James Joyce, Virginia Woolf, and Allen Ginsberg, have successfully employed the technique to reveal the INTERIOR MONOLOGUE of a character. See ARCHETYPE, CHANCE IMAGERY, COLLECTIVE UNCONSCIOUS, CONCRETE UNIVERSAL, DADA, DEEP IMAGE, DREAM POETRY, DREAMSCAPE, FANCY AND IMAGINATION, FIN DE SIÈCLE, FREE ASSOCIATION, LEAPING POETRY, LOGIC OF THE METAPHOR, MINDSCAPE, SIMULTANEITY, and SYMBOLISM.

stress (a similarly used term is ACCENT) the amount of force or emphasis placed on a syllable in a metrical FOOT or other unit of rhythm. Prosody in English verse rests on the s. See ACCENTUAL-SYLLABIC VERSE, CADENCE, ICTUS, METER, PROSODIC SYMBOLS, PROSODY, RHYTHM, SCANSION, and STRESS PROSODY.

stress prosody rhythmical systems of versification that rely upon STRESS as their basic unit of measurement, as in ACCENTUAL-SYLLABIC VERSE, SKELTONIC VERSE, and SPRUNG RHYTHM. See ARSIS AND THESIS, CADENCE, ICTUS, METER, PROSODIC SYMBOLS, PROSODY, RHYTHM, SCANSION, and STRONG-STRESS METER.

strong-stress meter (see METER) a system of metrics that depends upon rhythmical stresses in a FOOT. See also ARSIS AND THESIS, CADENCE, ICTUS, PROSODIC SYMBOLS, PROSODY, RHYTHM, SCANSION, SPRUNG RHYTHM, and STRESS.

strophe /strō'fē/ (Greek for "a turning") originally, the first section of metrically identical lines in Greek choral odes in which the chorus moved from right to left, followed by the metrically similar ANTISTROPHE, in which the chorus moved from left to right, and then followed by the metrically different EPODE during which the chorus stood still (see ODE). In contemporary usage, the term usually refers to any stanzaic unit containing irregular lines, whereas STANZA refers to a grouping of metrically regular lines (see HOMOSTROPHIC). *Stichic verse* usually refers to a poem without stanzaic divisions. See also *forms* in APPENDIX 1.

Structuralism a form of literary critical analysis, based on linguistics, that highlights the relationship of language to poetic form. S. in literary CRITICISM owes much to Lévi-Strauss' analysis of legends and folk stories (see MYTH) and Roman Jakobson's study of poetry, especially Shakespeare's sonnets. The movement stems from studies in language and anthropology in France during the mid 20th century. See CRITICISM. See also *criticism* in APPENDIX 1.

structural metaphor: See FUNCTIONAL METAPHOR.

structural reflection (see INNER REFLECTIONS) the external shape of a poem that imitates its content.

structure (see FORM) a general and ambiguously used term that may refer to the arrangement of stanzaic patterns, typography, PLOT elements, argument, FIXED FORMS, systems of images or metrics, and/or genre of verse. The NEW CRITICISM used the term synonymously with form and those aspects of a poem that could be paraphrased; the CHICAGO CRITICS, on the other hand, used the term to refer to the final dramatic rendering and effect of the poem which stems from its form, the devices that contribute to its emotional thrust. New Critics used the term in contrast to TEXTURE, those elements of a poem that are lost in paraphrase (see HERESY OF PARAPHRASE).

style (from Latin for "pointed instrument for writing," or "manner of speaking or writing") the manifestation in language of a writer's individual VOICE and VISION that are derived from his or her character; or, a particular tone of writing (formal, informal, objective, emotional, etc.); also, a specific manner of writing influenced by the movements or fashions of a period (Surrealist, Romantic, Baroque, Neo-Classical, etc.). Recognizable patterns of s. are formed by habits and preferences in choice of DICTION, TONE, IMAGERY, statement, STRUCTURE, SYNTAX, SONICS, rhetorical devices, and forms of emotional and logical appeal—all of which organically refer back to the natural or assumed sensibility and stance of a writer (see LOCATION). Conventions of development, such as exposition, NARRATION, JUXTAPOSITION, and DIGRESSION, also form patterns that define s. See also FORM and TEXTURE, as well as *Stylistic elements* in APPENDIX 1.

subdued metaphor (also called "buried metaphor" or "implied metaphor") a METAPHOR that is not explicitly stated but is expressed in an implied manner through compression, as in the *verb metaphor* "He high-tailed it home"; also, elaboration, as in the indirect CONCEIT from Eliot's "Streets that follow like a tedious argument / Of insidious intent." Often a s.m. forms part of an *extended metaphor* or a TELESCOPED METAPHOR. Also, within a metaphor, the TENOR AND VEHICLE may be implied or subdued.

subject/subject matter what or who is being discussed in a work of literature. S./s.m. forms the *referential substance*, as opposed to the THEME, which forms the *propositional substance*.

subjectivity (see OBJECTIVITY VS. S.) an emphasis on the personal perspective of consciousness in a work that incorporates an author's own experiences, values, emotions, and point of view. Usually, in a subjective poem, e.g., Coleridge's *Frost at Midnight*, we are invited to identify the speaker of the poem with the poet himself, whereas in an objective poem, e.g., Browning's *My Last Duchess*, the speaker is fictional and the author himself remains detached. The distinction between objective and subjective was probably imported into English ciriticism from the German critics of the late 18th century, and has been objected to by many critics, such as John Ruskin, for the vagueness of the terms. However, if we keep in mind that every effective work of art contains both personal and universal applications, then the two terms are useful to describe the opposite extremes between which a poem can be located. Autobiographical writing (see CONFESSIONAL POETRY) and the poetry of ROMANTICISM tend to be subjective, while the poetry of NEO-CLASSICISM tends to be objective. It should also be pointed out that sometimes s. is a derogatory term referring to an author's solipsism as displayed in a work. See AESTHETIC DISTANCE, DISTANCE AND INVOLVEMENT, DRAMATIC LYRIC, DRAMATIC MONOLOGUE, *impressionistic criticism* under CRITICISM, NEGATIVE CAPABILITY, OBJECTIVE CORRELATIVE, OBJECTIVE THEORY OF ART, OBJECTIVISM, and SURREALISM.

subjunctio: See EPIZEUXIS.

subplot (also known as "counterplot") a series of events subordinate in focus, importance, and function to those of the main PLOT in a work of literature. The s. may parallel or be in contrast to the main plot, thereby enhancing and emphasizing it; or the s. may be more or less unrelated to the main plot, thereby acting as a device of COMIC RELIEF. For example, in Shakespeare's *Hamlet*, the play focuses mainly on the antagonism between Hamlet and Claudius, and secondarily on the s. of the struggle between Hamlet and Laertes. See DRAMATIC STRUCTURE and SUB-THEME. See also *dramatic terms* in APPENDIX 1.

substitute image (see *cinematic techniques*) the replacement of an expected image with one that is unexpected. See also NEGATIVE IMAGE, and *subtractive metaphor* under METAPHOR; also *cinematic terms* in APPENDIX 1.

substitution in metrics, the replacement of one type of rhythmic FOOT with another. In QUANTITATIVE METER two short syllables can be replaced by one long syllable or by two different short syllables (see EQUIVALENCE). In ACCENTUAL-SYLLABIC VERSE, variations by s. are common; e.g., an IAMB may replace a TROCHEE (see INVERTED FOOT), or any duple foot may be substituted by a triple foot, thereby leaving the line in CATALEXIS or in HYPERMETERICAL TENSION. In terms of METAPHOR, s. is one of the primary steps in the analogue process; it converts the characteristics of the known TENOR into the attributes of unknown VEHICLE (see TENOR AND VEHICLE), a leap absolutely essential to revealing the poet's mode of perception. In IMAGERY, the SUBSTITUTE IMAGE acts as a means of manipulating STOCK RESPONSE and of furthering theme and plot. See COMPENSATION, INVERSION, INVERTED ACCENT, METER, PROSODY, and SCANSION. See also *grammatical constructions* in APPENDIX 2.

sub-theme an order of ideas subordinate to the main THEME in a work of art. The s.-t. is usually intimately related to the structure and thought of the main theme and may surface at regular intervals in the form of a LEITMOTIF throughout the NARRATION. For example, the s.-t. of fate in *Macbeth* emerges in the witches' prophecies and reappears at varius intervals through the play. See COUNTERPLOT, DRAMATIC STRUCTURE, and MOTIF.

subtractive metaphor a METAPHOR that sets up a comparison, then subtracts specific parts or characteristics and thereby manipulates the reader's expectations or stock responses:

> He thinks I am a fisherman,
> but knows I have no boat, no line, no sea.

See NEGATIVE IMAGE, STOCK RESPONSE, and SUBSTITUTE IMAGE.

Superrealism a contemporary movement in the visual arts in which the aesthetic motive is to represent nature and man with photographic accuracy. Although the art movement has had little or no influence on contemporary poetry, some poets such as Michael Ondaatje (*The Collected Works of Billy the Kid*) have carried the tenets of Realism to an extreme, and thus they could be called Superrealists. For related terms, see CHANCE IMAGERY, CHANCE POETRY, CONTINUUM POETRY, CUBISM, DADA, EXPRESSIONISM, FOUND ART, FUTURISM, IMAGISM, MINIMALISM, POP ART, OBJECTIVISM, REALISM, SURREALISM, and VORTICISM.

supporting details specific textural, structural, or metaphorical elements that enhance the plot, characters, and theme of a work of art. For example, an accurate IMAGE makes its own statement and also is integrally related to the whole poem of which it is part. S.d. include specific devices of RHETORIC, METAPHOR, and SONICS, as well as large-scale strategies such as NARRATION, ARGUMENT, VOICE, and TYPOGRAPHICAL ARRANGEMENT. See SELECTED DETAILS, STRATEGY, and SUPPORTING IMAGE.

supporting image a subordinate IMAGE or METAPHOR that deepens and elaborates a larger, more dominant image or metaphor. In Theodore Roethke's love poem *I Knew a Woman*, the CONTROLLING METAPHOR of the natural world acts as an analogue to love; and within that comparison, supporting images of objects, animals, and vegetation specify the proposition. See SELECTED DETAILS and SUPPORTING DETAILS. See also *imagery* in APPENDIX 1.

surprise ending a CLOSURE containing a sudden and unexpected TURN that catches the reader off-guard. Such a conclusion is a TRICK ENDING, and thus a defect in structure, unless it has been subtly and carefully prepared for by FORESHADOWING. An effective s.e. can be seen in James Wright's poem *Lying in a Hammock at William Duffy's Farm in Pine Island, Minnesota*. See *closure* in APPENDIX 1.

Surrealism /sərē′əlizəm/ (from French for "superrealism")   art that goes beyond what we think of as "the real." The term was coined by Guillaume Apollinaire in 1917, six years before André Breton founded the Surrealist movement with the publication of his *Manifeste du Surréalisme*. The Surrealists, as well as poets such as Tristan Tzara and Hans Arp, were associated with DADA, which shared Surrealism's goal of revolutionizing art by rejecting traditional forms and embracing the random anarchy extant in European society during and directly after World War I. But while S. was primarily concerned with inventing new aesthetic principles that would incorporate the wild associations found in dream images (see DREAM POETRY), Dada's major goal was destruction of traditional art and aesthetics, and, as some critics claim, Dada may not have contributed much toward inventing new art principles. According to Breton, S. was influenced by the dream theories of Freud, the writings of Hegel and De Sade, and, most importantly, the poetry of Rimbaud, Lautréamont, Baudelaire, Bertrand, Mallarmé, Valéry, Apollinaire, and other Symbolist and post-Symbolist poets. S. counted some of the best postwar poets in France among its members: Breton, Tzara, Arp, Louis Aragon, Pierre Reverdy, Paul Éluard, and Robert Desnos.

The movement is claimed to have expressed the actual functioning of thought, including the illogical associations and even the nonsense that form the normal patterns of our conscious and unconscious lives. AUTOMATIC WRITING, in which one opens the subconscious and lets mind and writing hand go where they will, is an essential element in the Surrealist creative writing process. Leaping from image to image through ASSOCIATIONAL LOGIC, automatic writing is said to have led to profound discoveries in the self, language, and reality. The Surrealists felt that reality was not of a fixed order but rather a negotiable agreement, a way of looking at a continually changing world.

Michael Benedikt (*The Poetry of Surrealism*, 1974) says that although Surrealist poetry varies widely in form and effect, its IMAGERY is a conglomerate of normally disparate things, which when brought together produce a lucid, heady, and unearthly feeling in the reader (see SYNAES-THESIA). The odd and sometimes randomly chosen images imply comparisons that are multilayered and which contain great distances between them. The TONE is usually mixed, ranging from the humorous to the serious, from the noble to the absurd, from the lyrical to the ironic, from the mysterious to the obvious—a variety that means to reflect the ephemeral shadings of man's moment-to-moment experiences. Surrealist DICTION tends toward the vernacular but is also formal at times, oppositions that may occur in the same line. The RHYTHM and METER is irregular and sometimes even convulsive with formal metrics juxtaposed against irregular rhythms. It is a mixture intended to represent the actual functioning of thought. One of the central themes of Surrealist poetry is *mutability*, that is, the longing for change. It is expressed intensely, and the element of desire (sometimes sexual desire) frequently leads toward the satire of figures who wish to restrict desire, a theme reminiscent of the ancient motif that condemns everything that separates one from his beloved. The Surrealist poem often compares the world to the beloved, and the two are often seen as being identical. But the SUBJECT MATTER of the poems, focusing on the mind's processes, is really the way that the poet looks at both poem and mind. Nothing is seen as being outside the scope of the poem, including words and images that could be considered vulgar. Surrealist FORM also reflects the way in which the mind moves. Each poem demands its own individual form, which is to be discovered in the writing. There is often a certain randomness fostered at the beginning of the poem in order to allow the form to stand out. The whole notion of traditional forms is irrelevant to the Surrealist who would not write a SONNET unless his mind spontaneously happened to rediscover the form. A poem might be written half in PROSE, half in DIALOGUE; or it might visually represent the CENTRAL IMAGE (see CONCRETE POETRY). These explorations of forms are not ends in themselves, but means by which the poet breaks down boundaries between, say, the world and the mind, waking and dreaming, or art and life.

The aim of S. was nothing less than to free mankind from the bondage of the past and the stifling familiarity of rational language. By dismissing conventional logic and by surrendering himself to his subjective experience, the Surrealist hopes to discover the key to his subconscious. According to Breton, S. would "enable the mind to leap the barrier set up for it by the antinomies of reason and dreaming, reason and madness, feeling and representation, etc., which constitute the major obstacles in Western thought." Such masters as García Lorca, Vallejo, Neruda, Celan, Alberti, Michaux, and Char have accepted the Surrealist aesthetic enthusiastically. In the United States, James Wright, Frank O'Hara, John Ashbery, Robert Bly, and many others show the influence of French S.

It is still too early to tell whether S. achieved the high aims that Breton had in mind for it; however, it is certain that the French Surrealist movement has had a tremendous effect on modern poetry. See EXPERIMENTAL POETRY, FUTURISM, SI . . . QUAND, and STREAM-OF-CONSCIOUSNESS.

suspended rhyme: See ANALYZED RHYME.

suspension of disbelief a form of reader EMPATHY in ignoring the artifice of art and the improbability of whatever events occur in a work. The term was first used by Coleridge (*Biographia Literaria*, 1817) in the phrase "that willing suspension of disbelief for the moment, which constitutes poetic faith." See VERISIMILITUDE.

syllaba anceps /sil'əbə an'seps/ (Latin for "twofold syllable") a form of POETIC LICENSE in which a syllable may be counted as long or short, accented or unaccented, according to the dictates of the regular meter in which it appears. The device represents a wrenching into form. See METER, QUANTITATIVE METER, SUBSTITUTION, and WRENCHED ACCENT. See also *grammatical constructions that are technically incorrect* in APPENDIX 2.

syllabic meter (also called "syllabic verse") a system of verse organized according to the number of syllables (rather than according to accents or durational units) in a line. The form fits comfortably into French verse and has been used with success by English and American poets (Auden, Marianne Moore, and James Tate, among others); but due to the accentual nature of English prosody, s.m. remains fairly uncommon in this language. See METER.

syllabic-stress meter: See ACCENTUAL-SYLLABIC VERSE.

syllepsis /silep'/ (Greek for "a taking together") a grammatical and rhetorical device of POETIC LICENSE in which one word in a sentence may loosely refer to two or more words in that sentence. Usually, the *utility word* agrees most accurately to the word nearest it, but can be applied also to the word farthest away, as in the word "rests" in the following:

> Each creature sleeps on what is fitting:
> The gull *rests* on his rock, I upon my bed.

Sometimes, the term governs the ambiguous use of a *squinting modifier* which applies equally to two or more words in equal proximity, as with the word "frequently" below:

> He asked *frequently* to give him a call.

S. differs from ZEUGMA in that the latter always contains a grammatically incorrect application, whereas the former may be grammatically correct. See *grammatical constructions that are technically incorrect* and *devices of poetic license* in APPENDIX 2, and *figurative expressions* in APPENDIX 1.

syllogism /sil'ojizəm/ (from Greek for "a reckoning all together, a collection") a formula for presenting a logical argument that offers two propositions called the *major* and *minor premises* (containing a common term), and a third proposition called the *conclusion*, the seemingly logical deduction of the first two statements. For example:

major premise	All students are intelligent.
minor premise	John is a student.
conclusion	John is intelligent.

syllogismus a contracted form of SYLLOGISM in which one word resonates throughout the sentence and implies the full form of a syllogism, as in the word "mountains" in "Paul Bunyan stepped over mountains." (Implying he was very big.) The full syllogism would be:

major premise	Anyone who steps over mountains is big.
minor premise	Paul Bunyan stepped over mountains.
conclusion	Paul Bunyan is big.

See *figures of argumentation* in APPENDIX 2.

symbol (from Greek for "to throw together, to compare") a TROPE in which a word, phrase, or image represents something literal and concrete and yet maintains a complex set of abstract ideas and values that are usually interpreted according to the surrounding context but which may mean a number of things depending upon who is interpreting the s. In terms of the dynamics of semantic energy flow (see SEMANTICS), the s. works in the opposite way of a METAPHOR: While the metaphor gives off meaning to its context, the s. absorbs meaning from its context. For example, in the *metaphorical* expression "He is a mountain of a man," the word "mountain" throws off semantic energy onto the man and thus defines his stature; but in the following *symbolic* use of the word "mountain" the word takes its religious meaning from the language surrounding it: "A rich man cannot buy the mountain a pious man builds." A system of symbols strung along a narrative forms an ALLEGORY, which is read both literally and in reference to its abstract level of meaning.

Generally speaking, there are three generic forms of symbols: (1) the *archetypal s.* (see ARCHETYPE and MYTH), in which a natural object refers to a limited number of interpretations that transcend cultural barriers, as in sun representing energy, a source of life, and the male active principle; (2) the *general s.*, which appeals to a smaller audience but which contains more associative meanings, as in the Christian cross and the Nazi swastika; and (3) the *private s.*, created in an author's imagination and conveying any number of meanings in the guiding context, as in Yeats' "holy city of Byzantium."

Of course, language is a symbolic system in and of itself and has developed in order to symbolically communicate human experience. In this way, the term s. can refer to any unit of any literary structure. But the term should be distinguished from *sign* in that the latter communicates only one meaning (a crosswalk, e.g.) while the former embodies a complex of associative meanings. See ABSTRACT TERMS AND CONCRETE TERMS, COLLECTIVE UNCONSCIOUS, IMAGE, IMAGERY, SIMILE, SYMBOLIC ACTION, SYMBOLIC NARRATIVE, SYMBOLIC REFLECTION, SYMBOLISM, and SYMBOLISTS. See also *figures of similarity and dissimilarity* in APPENDIX 2, and *figurative expressions* in APPENDIX 1.

symbolic action a dramatic gesture or movement meant to stand for a complex set of abstract values or attitudes, as in the variations of the Chinese idiograms of the word "I"—a man with his hand over his mouth, or a man standing with arms outstretched. S.a. is also Kenneth Burke's term indicating the very act of writing as a symbolic means of understanding, exploring, and revering human behavior and the world around us. See ARCHETYPE, COLLECTIVE UNCONSCIOUS, and SYMBOL.

symbolic narrative a story that proceeds by and is based upon a series of symbols or symbolic actions, as in the ALLEGORY. See also *archetypal myth* under MYTH, ARCHETYPE, COLLECTIVE UNCONSCIOUS, DREAM POETRY, PARABLE, and SYMBOLIC REFLECTION.

symbolic reflection (See INNER REFLECTIONS) the action of a SYMBOL reflecting action in real life.

symbolism the use of symbols to express either public or private values. In a SYMBOLIC NARRATIVE, such as the PARABLE and the ALLEGORY, associated symbols are used linearly in the story, whereas in the lyric poetry of many modern poets symbols are used in clusters. The meaning of symbols may be obvious and derived from public knowledge, or their significance may be idiosyncratic and GNOMIC, arising out of the realms of the subconscious and unconscious (see SURREALISM). For a discussion of the movement that focused on s., see SYMBOLISTS. See also ARCHETYPAL MYTH, ARCHETYPE, COLLECTIVE UNCONSCIOUS, SYMBOLIC ACTION, and SYMBOL RELECTION.

Symbolists the group of French artists and writers who constituted the 19th-century movment that came as a reaction to REALISM and to the *Salon Poetry* of the French PARNASSIANS. The movement included such poets as Arthur Rimbaud, Baudelaire, Mallarmé, Verlaine, Maeterlinck, and Laforgue. It came into being with Baudelaire's *Fleurs du Mal* (1857), which shows an appreciable influence from Baudelaire's own translation of the work of Edgar A. Poe. According to Jean Moréas' 1886 manifesto on the S., the Symbolist is a poet who seeks to express a primordial idea through concrete phenomena. Subjective expression, even to the point of unintelligibility, was encouraged and promoted because PATHOS, the movement maintained, is best expressed through the suggestive medium of private symbols. Stylistically, the movement eschewed sentimentality, ornament, exposition, rhetorical devices, and practical applications of the work to any historical, political, religious, or social context. The meaning of the poem does not exist outside the poem; the images of the poem do not point to anything other than the other images of the poem, and as a whole they evoke the mood of the poem. The best poems of the S. carry a rich suggestiveness, a medley of metaphor, and music that resembles magical incantation.

The Symbolist movement had a tremendous influence on poets throughout Europe during the FIN DE SIÈCLE, and it was certainly the single most influential force in British, Irish, and American poetry of the 20th century. Certain devices common in the Symbolists' poetry, e.g., SYN-AESTHESIA, have become a familiar part of the repertoire of most modern poets. Yeats, Eliot, Pound, Stevens, Dylan Thomas, and e.e. cummings are among the poets writing in English who show an influence from the S., and Rilke, Valéry, and Apollinaire should also be mentioned as poets who showed a direct, early influence from the S. See AESTHETICISM, DECADENCE, IMAGISM, IMPRESSIONISM, PURE POETRY, SYMBOL, and SYMBOLISM. See also *movements and schools of poetry* in APPENDIX 1.

symploce /sim'plosē/ (Greek for "an interweaving"); also known as "complexio") a rhetorical figure of repetition that represents a combination of ANAPHORA and EPISTROPHE in that the first and last words (or phrases) in a clause or sentence are repeated in successive clauses or sentences: "*What* are joys but an imaginary *world.* / *What* is pain but the condition of the *world.*" See PLOCE. See also *figures of repetition* in *Appendix* 2.

synaeresis /siner'-/ (from Greek for "a drawing together") a contraction or slurring of two words, syllables, or vowels into one, e.g., "can't" for "can not," or "seer" for "see-er." Originally, the device was used in QUANTITA-TIVE METER to compress separate vowels into one vowel in order to fit the regular meter. See CRASIS, ELISION, SYNALEPHA, SYNCOPE, and SYZYGY. See also *grammatical constructions that are technically incorrect* in APPEN-DIX 2.

synaesthesia (from Greek for "to feel or perceive together"; also spelled "synesthesia"; also known as "sense transference") the translation of a physical sensation from one sense into another, e.g., images simultaneously experienced as sound and texture or sight and smell. It has been estimated that about ten percent of the United States' population are natural *synaesthetes* and that most people retain this confluence of the senses to some degree into their adult years. Some anthropologists and linguists maintain that early man did not have compartmentalized senses, but through evolution we lost the ability to experience s. The device in poetry can be found as far back as Homer, although the 19th-century

SYMBOLISTS were the ones who most thoroughly concentrated on it as a technique. Rimbaud's poem *Voyelles* and Baudelaire's *Correspondences* are two well-known examples. Others who have used the device include Poe, Stevens, Shelley, Keats, Horace, and Shakespeare. Although synaesthetes may not agree on the specific associations summoned by specific stimuli, s. occurs commonly enough to have extended the fabric of our everyday language: "a loud dress," "a cool color," and "sunny laughter" are clichés that exhibit s. Usually s. occurs as a combination of several images, although s. can occur as an abstract statement as in the expression "Touching is the first language we know." The term, for the technique, first appears in Jules Millet's *Audition Colorée* (1892). See AUDITION COLORÉE. See also *devices of poetic license* in APPENDIX 2.

synalepha /sinəlē′fə/ (from Greek for "to melt or smear together"; also spelled "synaloepha" and "synalephe") a specific form of ELISION or SYNAERESIS that obliterates the vowel at the end of one word and leaves the initial vowel of a succeeding word, as in much 19th-century poetry which suppressed the vowel *e* in "the": "th' empire . . ." In the classical prosody of QUANTITATIVE METER the device was used to regulate rhythm. See CRASIS, SYNCOPE, and SYZYGY. See also *grammatical constructions that are technically incorrect* in APPENDIX 2.

synathroesmus /-thrēs-/ a rhetorical figure of division that accumulates descriptive phrases or gathers together previous points dispersed throughout a speech. See *figures of division* in APPENDIX 2.

synchoresis /kərē′-/ (Greek for "a going together") a figure of argumentation that features a speech made in a confident tone, the conclusion to which the audience is left to create: "Since he swore and has witnesses to swear that he was in another place at the time of the crime, I leave it to you to determine his guilt or innocence." See *figures of argumentation* in APPENDIX 2.

synchronicity (see CINEMATIC TECHNIQUES) a device of narration, using narrator agents, in which simultaneous points of view or events are offered in a parallel or intersecting pattern. William Faulkner's *As I Lay Dying* uses this device. See FRACTURED NARRATIVE, POINT OF VIEW, and SIMULTANEITY. See also *cinematic terms* in APPENDIX 1.

syncoeciosis a rhetorical figure of *contraries and contradictories* that accumulates opposite statements: "What I did not need, I needed most. / What I hated most, I loved. / What I wanted most was loneliness. / I lost myself in crowds." See *contraries and contradictories* in APPENDIX 2, and *figurative expressions* in APPENDIX 1.

syncopation (from Greek *synkope*, "a cutting up") a rhythmic effect brought about by the SUBSTITUTION of an accented syllable for an unaccented syllable, or vice versa. Usually, it is accomplished by cutting across a regular, established meter with LOGICAL STRESS or word accent so as to produce a slightly off-balance effect. For example, if we set up the metrically iambic phrase

Ĭs Geórge ăt hóme?

we can rhetorically accent the word "is" so that the veracity of his being there is emphasized; thus we get the s.:

Ís Geórge ăt hóme?

See ACCENT, COUNTERPOINT, METER, PROSODY, RHYTHM, and SCANSION. See also *grammatical devices of rhythm and balance* in APPENDIX 2.

syncope /sing'kəpē/ the deletion of a letter in the middle of a word, such as "o'er" for "over," "ne'er" for "never," etc., for the sake of maintaining music and regular meter in verse. See the related forms of CRASIS, ELISION, SYNAERESIS, SYNALEPHA, and SYZYGY. See also *grammatical constructions that are technically incorrect* in APPENDIX 2.

syncrisis /sing'krisis/ (Greek for "comparison") a rhetorical figure of *subject and adjunct* that contrasts opposing persons and things in one statement: "A wise man sees beauty for what it is; a foolish man is blinded by beauty and never sees it." See *figures of subject and adjunct* in APPENDIX 2.

synecdoche /sinek'dəkē/ (Greek for "a receiving jointly") a figure of division in which a part stands for the whole in any one of four ways: (1) the general for the specific—"Here comes the law" (meaning a policeman); (2) the specific for the general—"He's nothing but a cutthroat" (meaning a murderer); (3) the part for the whole—"All hands on deck" (hands meaning sailors); and (4) the material for the object made from it—"He is my own flesh and blood" (meaning genetically related). Robert Graves uses s. in his poem *The Naked and the Nude* when he refers to a doctor as a "hippocratic eye." And Eliot uses it in *The Love Song of J. Alfred Prufrock* when he refers to a crab as "a pair of ragged claws." S. differs from METONYMY in that the former is always a part of the whole, while the latter may be outside of or only associated with the reference in question. Also, s. differs from *partitio* or *merismus* in which the whole is distributed into its parts. See *figures of division* in *Appendix* 2 and *figurative expressions* in APPENDIX 1.

synesthesia: See SYNAESTHESIA.

syngnome /sinōm', sinō'mē/ (from Greek for "a knowing together") a rhetorical figure of *ethos* or *character* in which one puts aside the wrongs of one's adversaries and asks that they be treated leniently: "Forgive them, Father, for they know not what they do." See *figures of ethos* in APPENDIX 2.

synonym /sin'-/ (from Greek for "a naming together") a word or words whose denotative sense may be equalled or substituted by that of another word, e.g., "countryman" and "compatriot," "sweets" and "candies," "contrary" and "opposite," "encourage" and "promote," etc. Of course, the associational and connotative levels of meanings in synonyms will differ, but English with its mix of root languages (Anglo-Saxon, Latin, Greek, and French being the principle ones) contains a rich opportunity to use synonyms. See CONNOTATION and DENOTATION.

synonymia /-nim′ē·ə/ a rhetorical figure comparing a series of things equal in meaning but differing in form: "Is he dead, / The one I saw immobile as a rock, / The one whose eyes looked inward, / The one from whom all rhythm and reason have escaped?" See *figures comparing greater, lesser, or equal things* in APPENDIX 2.

synopsis (Greek for "a seeing together") a PRÉCIS or SUMMARY of a work so that a quick overview is possible. See HERESY OF PARAPHRASE and REDUCTIVE FALLACY.

syntax (from Greek for "an arranging together") sentence structure; that is, the grammatical ordering into the conventional patterns of usage of words in their appropriate forms. The simple declarative sentence usually has a subject-verb-object pattern, while the interrogative usually is based on a verb-subject-object pattern. In poetry, the order, length, and inclusion of subordinate elements, as well as the stripping down, counterpointing of, and elaborating on, the basic sentence forms affect integrally both form and content. For instance, note the way in which Roger Weingarten's *Night Signals* smoothly develops THEME, SCENE, CHARACTER, and PATHOS in one sentence:

> Most of our neighbors, if they haven't
> been cut down or carried off, are bone-tired
>
> and huddled in the muddy run-off
> of last night's rain, where grandmother, the post
>
> and beam of our people, sick
> or in need of counsel, climbed up
>
> into the gunpowdered dark to comb what remains
> of the rock-swollen high meadows, avoiding
>
> the level quicksand for an apron
> round with leaves and fresh grasses we must
>
> swallow against hunger.

Generally speaking, the s. should derive naturally from VOICE and LOCATION and be a harmonic part of the whole poem. See AESTHETIC SURFACE, SENTENCE SOUNDS, and STYLE.

synthesis /sin′-/ (Greek for "a placing together") the fusion of various elements in a poem so that *sound, sense*, SYNTAX, IMAGERY, tropes, LOGIC, TYPOGRAPHICAL ARRANGEMENT, and other patterns and devices harmonize into a complete and unified work of art. See ORGANIC COMPOSITION.

synthetic rhyme false RHYME produced by deleting, expanding, or in some way wrenching the letters of words so that they rhyme, as Ogden Nash's "Jellyfish/sellyfish" offering. The device often appears in LIGHT VERSE but has been used by poets such as Byron and Spenser. For other forms of word changes, see SYNAERESIS, SYNALEPHA, SYNCOPE, and SYZYGY.

systole and diastole /sis′tolē/ or /dī·as′tolē/ (*systole*, Greek for "contraction"; *diastole*, Greek for "expansion") *systole*: a form of ELISION common in QUANTITATIVE METER in which a naturally long syllable is shortened.

Diastole is its opposite. For related terms, see SYNAERESIS, SYNALEPHA, SYNCOPE, and SYZYGY.

systrophe /sis′trofē/ a rhetorical *figure of definition* representing a conglomerate definition composed of descriptions that are derived from diverse classes of things:

> Love laughs at risk, is stronger than machines of war,
> softer than a summer's eve, and shames the light of suns;
> it is a gift passed on endlessly and enlarged by use.

See HORISMUS. See also *figures of definition* in APPENDIX 2.

syzygy /siz′ijē/ (from Greek for "yoke, pair") originally, the fusing of two separate foot units into a single dipodic unit (see DIPODY), so that some prosodists have become accustomed to using the term synonymously with METER. Modern and contemporary use of the term refers mainly to *phonetic s.* (coined by J.J. Sylvester, *Laws of Verse*, 1870), a device in which the terminal letter of one word is fused to the initial letter of a succeeding word, as in "fair Ruth." This consonantal pairing is similar to the vowel pairing occurring in SYNAERESIS. Other forms of letter changes are CRASIS, ELISION, SYNALEPHA, SYNCOPE, and SYSTOLE AND DIASTOLE. See *grammatical constructions that are technically incorrect* in APPENDIX 2.

T

tail: See CODA; see also *forms* in APPENDIX 1.

tailed sonnet a SONNET that includes extra lines. There are tailed sonnets of 15, 16, 18, and 20 lines. Alan Dugan draws attention to his use of the form in the CLOSURE of his 15-line poem *To a Red-Headed Do-Good Waitress*. See also CAUDATE SONNET and CODA.

tail-rhyme stanza (see RIME COUÉE) a stanzaic form that includes a rhyming short line. The usual form is aa^{3}b^{3}cc^{4}b^3. See also BURNS STANZA, CAUDATE RHYME, CODA, RHYME-COUNTERPOINT, and TAILED SONNET.

tale (from Old English for "speech") a true or fictitious NARRATIVE in which the impetus is to relate PLOT events and focus on their conclusion or RESOLUTION. Famous examples include Chaucer's *Canterbury Tales* and Swift's *A Tale of a Tub*.

tanka (also known as "waka" or "uta") a seventh-century Classical Japanese fixed form of verse, similar to the HAIKU, composed of five lines of 31 syllables (5, 7, 5, 7, 7). The style is formal in DICTION and MOOD, and the THEME centers on lyrical subjects of nature, love, and loss, as in the following poignant example by a tenth-century poet, Lady Izumi Shikibu:

> Lying here alone,
> So lost in thinking of you
> I forgot to comb
> My tangled tresses—oh for
> Your hand caressing them smooth!

Usually in the t. and haiku there is a quick TURN near or at the poem's CLOSURE. See CINQUAIN, GHAZAL, IDIOGRAPH, and IMAGISM. See also *forms* in APPENDIX 1.

tapinosis (from Greek for "lowness [of style]") a rhetorical device of POETIC LICENSE in which slang is used in formal circumstances. The effect is usually humorous or satiric: "I told the king he wore some beautiful rags." The term also refers to pejorative epithets. See BURLESQUE, DICTION, EPITHET, INVECTIVE, MEIOSIS, and SATIRE. See *devices of poetic license* in APPENDIX 2, and *diction* in APPENDIX 1.

tautologia (from Greek for "a repeating what has been said") a device of POETIC LICENSE that uses the same idea repeatedly, or the same word in different phrases. See BOMPHIOLOGIA, HOMIOLOGIA, OVERREPETITION, PARELCON, PERIERGIA, PERISSOLOGIA, PLEONASMUS, and TAUTOLOGIA. See also *devices of poetic license* in APPENDIX 2.

tautology /tôlol'-/ the needless REPETITION of the same words, or of the same idea in other words, without clarification, EMPHASIS, or elucidation: "I wrote this *love poem* which expresses *my desire for you in verse form.*" T. is usually considered a defect in STYLE. Other devices of OVERWRITING include BOMPHIOLOGIA, HOMIOLOGIA, OVERREPETITION, PARELCON, PERIERGIA, PERISSOLOGIA, PLEONASMUS, and TAUTOLOGIA. See *figures of repetition* in APPENDIX 2, and *defects in control* in APPENDIX 1.

taxis (Greek for "division, arrangement") a rhetorical *figure of definition* that expresses the most salient features of things:

> God created the mountain for height,
> The water for flow,
> The earth for nourishment,
> And man for knowledge.

See ANTONOMASIA, EPITHETON, METONYMY, PERIPHRASIS, PERISTASIS, and SYNECDOCHE. See also *figures of definition* in APPENDIX 2.

technique /teknēk'/ (French for "technical skill," from Greek for "pertaining to art or craft") the acquired and intuitive skills that go into the making of a work of art. The poet has a method or procedure that has many steps, including the establishing of a STANCE (see LOCATION) during the conception of the poem, the working out of LOGIC, the making of tropes (see TROPE) and other poetic and rhetorical devices, the shaping of the AESTHETIC SURFACE (sonics, rhythm, imagery, DICTION, and SYNTAX), as well as the forming of the structure of the poem (LINEATION, LINE ENDING, JUXTAPOSITION, TYPOGRAPHICAL ARRANGEMENT, RHYME SCHEME, etc.) Northrop Frye defines t. as "an habitual and unconscious skill."

telescoped metaphor: See COMPLEX METAPHOR.

telestich /təles'tik, tel'əstik/ (from Greek for "end of a line of verse") an ACROSTIC in which the vertical pattern of the last letters in consecutive lines of the poem form a word, name, message, or recognizable pattern. See ABECEDARIUS, ALTAR POEM, CARMEN FIGURATUM, CONCRETE POETRY, and MESOSTICH. See also *forms* in APPENDIX 1.

tenor and vehicle (coined by I.A. Richards, *The Philosophy of Rhetoric*, 1936) the two parts of a METAPHOR. The *tenor* is the subject to which the vehicle refers. For example, in the metaphoric phrase "sands of time," "time" is the tenor and "sands" is the vehicle. The tenor is usually of a general and denotative nature, and the vehicle is of a specific, imagistic, and connotative nature. The vehicle carries the weight of the comparison, lending its energy to the tenor. This semantic exchange of identity represents a synthesis unobtainable in language that attempts to communicate information rather than experience. Laurence Perrine uses *literal term* and *figurative term* for *tenor* and *vehicle*, respectively. See IMAGERY and SYMBOL.

tension (from Latin for "a stretching") the action of the cohesive forces that unify a work of art. The effect is felt as a result of the existence of contrasting or contrary elements, such as meter against propositional sense, rhythm against counterrhythm (see SYNCOPATION), diction against action, abstract statement against concrete image, general against specific, what is said against what is meant (see IRONY), and appearance against reality. The NEW CRITICISM focuses on this term, embodied in the ideas of Allen Tate ("Tension in Poetry," *On the Limits of Poetry*, 1948), who explains t. as the pulling and pushing of the literal level of language (*extension*) against the connotative or metaphorical levels of language (*intension*). More specifically, according to Robert Penn Warren, *conflict structures* expressed in the technique of the poem (METER VS. SENTENCE SOUNDS, formal limits vs. variations, etc.) create both the paths toward the poem's expression and the means by which to judge and evaluate the poem. While the New Critics elaborated the meaning and uses of the term, the concept is as old as art itself and has had a number of theoreticians, including Coleridge, T.E. Hulme, and Henry James, who discuss the principles it represents. See also ABSTRACT TERMS AND CONCRETE TERMS, AMBIGUITY, CHICAGO CRITICS, COGNITIVE MEANING, CONFLICT, COUNTER-POINT, CRITICISM, CROSSCUT, DIALECTIC, DISSOCIATION OF SENSIBILITY, DISSONANCE, FORMATIVE ENERGY, FOUR SENSES OF INTERPRETATION, FREE VERSE, INNER REFLECTIONS, INNUENDO, INSCAPE, INTENSITY, INVERSION, JUMP CUT, JUXTAPOSITION, LATENT FORM, LEAPING POETRY, LINE ENDING, LITERAL VISION VS. ANAGOGICAL VISION, LOADING THE POEM, MULTEITY, ORGANIC COMPOSITION, ORGANIZING PRINCIPLES, SIMULTANEITY, SLACKNESS, SOUND SYSTEM, STRUCTURALISM, and UNDERSTATEMENT.

tercet /tur′sət, turset′/ (from Italian for "third") a three-line stanza having external rhyme, usually aaa, bbb, etc., as in Robert Herrick's *Upon Julia's Clothes*. Sometimes an unrhymed three-line stanza, for instance W.C. Williams' TRIADIC STANZA is called a t. See TERZA RIMA, TRIPLET, and TRISTICH. See also *forms* in APPENDIX 1.

terminal rhyme (also known as "external rhyme"; see END-RHYME) the identity or close similarity of assonantal and/or consonantal sounds at the ends of lines of verse. See also RHYME and RHYME SCHEME.

terza rima /ter′tsä rē′mä/ (Italian for "third or triple rhyme") a fixed form, invented by Dante in his *Divine Comedy* and introduced into English by Chaucer in his *Complaint to His Lady*, consisting of iambic (usually pentameter) tercets rhyming aba bcb cdc ded, etc.—a RHYME SCHEME that pushes the reader through the poem, as can be seen from the first section of Shelley's *Ode to the West Wind*. Although the form is somewhat ill-fitted to English because of the demanding rhyme scheme, poets such as Browning, Yeats, Byron, MacLeish, Auden, and Eliot, among others, have successfully employed it, often with variations in RHYME and METER. See PENTAMETER and TRIPLET. See also *forms* in APPENDIX 1.

tetrameter /tətram′-/ (from Greek for "four measures") originally, in Classical prosody (see QUANTITATIVE METER), a DIPODY composed of two pairs of feet. In ACCENTUAL-SYLLABIC VERSE, the term refers to a line composed of four feet such as four iambs, trochees, anapests, dactyls, etc. Aside from iambic pentameter, iambic tetrameter is the most widely used MEASURE in English poetry. The meter achieves power and succinctness, as can be seen in the opening stanza of Byron's *She Walks in Beauty*. See METER, RHYTHM, and SCANSION. See also *forms* in APPENDIX 1.

text /from Latin for "fabric, structure, text") the specific words of a literary work. See EXPLICATION and TEXTUAL CRITICISM.

textual criticism the study of an original manuscript for the purpose of restoring it to its original state; also, the analysis of a literary work by scholars to determine its authoritativenes or its meaning. See CRITICISM and TEXT. See also *criticism* in APPENDIX 1.

texture (from Latin for "to weave") originally, the surface constitution of a painting or sculpture. In poetry, according to the NEW CRITICS which used the term frequently, t. refers to the unparaphrasable elements of a poem. Some of the most important of these elements include AESTHETIC SURFACE, DRAMATIC STRUCTURE, FORM, IMAGERY, IRONY, LINEATION, METER, RHYME, RHYTHM, SOUND SYSTEM, and TYPOGRPHICAL ARRANGEMENT. See also HERESY OF PARAPHRASE.

thematic content the paraphrasable statements on which a work of literature is built, and those elements of *texture* that color the abstract ideas of the work. See AESTHETIC SURFACE, CRITICISM, HERESY OF PARAPHRASE, THEMATIC STRUCTURE, and THEME.

thematic montage (see CINEMATIC TECHNIQUES) a series of selected images and statements that relate either progressively or centrifugally to a stated or unstated THEME. See also *cinematic terms* in APPENDIX 1.

thematic structure the abstract geometrical shape of a theme's development. Poems, like expository writing, contain geometrical thematic shapes that develop in various ways according to the ARGUMENT or thesis under consideration. They can progress from the general to the specific, the specific to the general; they can move outward or inward from a central thematic statement; they can present a circular, self-contained structure or a combination of structural types. There isn't any one best argumentative type of structure, but the most suitable inner shape of a poem should be formed from the poet's sense of aesthetic order. The thematic shape should accurately reflect the imagination's movement through its material so that it is a kind of Platonic abstraction, or INSCAPE, of the poet's perceptions.

The poem's inner t.s. does not literally have to mirror the TYPOGRAPH-ICAL ARRANGEMENT of the poem on the page. In other words, it is possible for an OPEN FIELD t.s., which allows for a large range of perceptions in the poem, still to be physically represented as a BLOCK POEM; and, conversely, it is entirely possible for a straight-line inductive argument to have unequal line lengths, variegated indentations, and unusual word spacings. But poets will consciously or intuitively correlate the inner and outer (thematic and typographical) structures of a poem so that they are in harmony or some kind of productive TENSION with one another.

For specific forms of t.s., see CENTRIPETAL-CENTRIFUGAL STRUCTURE, CENTRIPETAL STRUCTURE, CIRCULAR STRUCTURE, DEDUCTIVE-INDUCTIVE STRUCTURE, DEDUCTIVE STRUCTURE, INDUCTIVE-DEDUCTIVE STRUCTURE, and INDUCTIVE STRUCTURE. See also ARGUMENT, CLOSURE, LOGIC, and THEMATIC CONTENT; also *closure* in APPENDIX 1.

theme (from Greek for "proposition" or "to put, to place") the paraphrasable main idea(s) of a piece of literature, that is, what the work is about. For example, a GLOSS of *Hamlet* might briefly summarize the play by saying it is about the irreconcilable tragedy of human indecisiveness in the face of duty. What is left beyond the t. is the TEXTURE. See CARPE DIEM, CHARACTER, DRAMATIC STRUCTURE, LEITMOTIF, MOTIF, THEMATIC CONTENT, THEMATIC MONTAGE, THEMATIC STRUCTURE, and "UBI SUNT" FORMULA.

theoretical criticism literary analysis that strives to formulate permanent and universal principles from the study of literature in order to determine the character of the discipline and to set standards of quality. Aristotle's *Poetics* is the most lasting and influential text of t.c. Modern critics in the field include I.A. Richards, the New Critics, and Northrop Frye. For related terms, see CRITICISM. See also the BIBLIOGRAPHY for a list of important books in the field; also *criticism* in APPENDIX 1.

thesis /thē′sis, thes′is/ (Greek for "a placing, a proposition") in logic and rhetoric, a proposition or assertion to be proven or defended. See THEME. For Classical prosodic meaning, see ARSIS AND THESIS. See also *figures of argumentation* in APPENDIX 2.

threnody /thren′-/ (from Greek for "dirge song") a LAMENT sung for the dead. Originally, in Classical poetry, the t. was sung in the form of a choral DIRGE. Modern examples of written threnodies include Tennyson's *In Memoriam*, Longfellow's *The Jewish Cemetery at Newport*, and Emerson's *Threnody*. See also ENCOMIUM and MONODY.

threnos /thrē′nəs/ (Greek for "dirge") a rhetorical *figure of pathos* (*or emotion*) in which one laments one's own or another's suffering. See DIRGE, ENCOMIUM, LAMENT, MONODY, PATHOPOEIA, and THRENODY. See also *figures of pathos* in APPENDIX 2.

timbre /tim′bər/ or /teNbr/ (Old French for "small bell') the characteristic quality of sound that distinguishes one voice or musical instrument from another. T. is determined by the harmonics of sound and is distinguished from INTENSITY and PITCH. Sometimes in musical terminology, t. refers to the emotional associations with each instrument, e.g., power with the tympany, grief with the violin, and triumph with the trumpet. In poetry, the term refers both to the aural and EMOTIVE THRUST of language. See AESTHETIC SURFACE, TEXTURE, and TONE COLOR. See also *melopoetics* in APPENDIX 1.

titles (from Latin for "inscription, label, title, sign") the name or description placed in front of or above a piece of literature.

There has been very little written about the subject of making t., except for a few perfunctory remarks which urge writers to catch the fickle attention of their readers through humor or drama, to be specific enough in focus to frame the body of work which follows the title, and to be honest enough so as not to disappoint the expectations of the reader.

While this essay is by no means an exhaustive treatment of the subject, we intend here to put forth some of the ways in which t. are created, to determine some of the decisions involved in choosing a title, and to give examples of the directions that t. have taken in literature.

T. function both as an introduction and a simple reference to poems. They can be stated in concrete, abstract, literal, metaphorical, or conversational terms. Their characters, like those of people, can display as many variations as there are human responses. They can be assertive, cautious, dry, impressionistic, daring, formal, predictable, incomprehensible, intriguing, silly, sensitive, fanciful, humble, wild, tense, or wise or have any other value the writer feels is applicable.

After we have read a poem, a title often takes on deeper significance because it begins to resonate in sympathy with the contents of the poem. It takes on new layers of meaning in the context of the poem's physical, emotional, intellectual, metaphorical, and spiritual themes. As a name can summon up the character, actions, and locale of someone we have come to know, so t. can re-create a piece of literature.

Depending upon the poet's motives toward his poem and reader, he may choose to formulate his title in direct relation to the poem's contents, to the reader, or to an outside reference. The title may be structurally important, as when it acts as a necessary springboard into the poem; aesthetically pleasing, as the decorative grace note in a piece of music; or ceremonially included, as in the "topping off" of a building with a living plant. Sometimes the poet will use a title to manipulate the reader, and at other times the idiosyncrasy or facelessness of a poem's title will indicate the writer didn't have a reader in mind at all. Close reading of a poem will often reveal whether a title was created before or after the poem was written. This revelation may be important in determining whether or not the title fits the poem. If the poet creates his title first, he may feel obligated to stay within its confines and possibly force the creative process, or he might miss an opportunity to name more fully what he has created. Titling the poem after its completion, by far the most common order, could cause the poet to lose track of the unstated catalyst to his poem which might have set up a larger framework for it, placed a more distant perspective behind the poem, or added a deeper level of meaning.

Some poets feel that t. are as important as keeping one's head on one's shoulders. These poets usually bring their t. through the same series of revisions that their poems undergo. At the other extreme, some poets think of t. as being unnecessary or extraneous to the poem. These poets often use nondescript titles or place the poem in a series of poems that cohere under an overall, general title.

The actual step-by-step process of creating a title is impossible to formulate under general rules, and a formulation would probably be an undesirable undertaking, because creating a title entails the same imaginative and often inexplicable process of conception that writing poetry involves. We do obtain glimpses into the creation of some poems and t. through the commentaries and work sheets left to us by poets, but even these are usually shot full of holes because the poet himself can no more explain the birth of his poem than his best critic could. It is a complex process that takes place at simultaneous levels of consciousness and instantaneous speeds. It involves logic, intuition, and literary insight in varying mixes. Like archeologists, we are left with only the fossilized remnants of a once-living process, and we are bewildered when the poet reports that some t. are simply "given," some are formed by the demands of the poem, some are borrowed from something read or overheard, and some are derived from logical thinking. But what can be seen through the act of critical hindsight is the way in which various t. stand in relation to their poems. We can interpret their meaning(s) and value, and theorize about their conception by understanding the poems.

The first type of title we will consider is both the most complex and perhaps the most aesthetically satisfying construction:

The Layered Title

The layered title is one that contains multiple meanings that are held in potential, as a seed holds a tree in potential, until after the poem is read. The full interpretive value of the title is not released until the reader returns to it with the experience of the poem, and then its RESONANCE, its connotative, denotative, and associational meanings, unfold. Although the poet will almost always allow for some type of first-sight literal GLOSS of the title which doesn't require an understanding of the poem, trying to fully understand a layered title at first glance is like reading the musical notation Bb minor without the experience of hearing the tonal quality of the under- and overtones of the chord itself.

The layers in this type of title may consist of the traditional conventions of anagogical structure—sensual, emotional, intellectual, and spiritual levels (see ANAGOGE). Or the title may combine technical elements of the poem, such as form, theme, subject, metaphorical or symbolic references, and time dimensions. But whatever contents the layered title implies, it always has depth. And although the full interpretation of the title depends upon the poem, the poem does not need the title in order to complete its structural unity. The title simply acts as a kind of capsule version of what the poem has to say. Most layered t. are conceived after the poem has been written, and they represent an attempt to pull together the most salient aspects of the poem. This type of title is particularly well suited to the conventions of modern poetry that stress economy, control, and penetration.

Let's look at a poem by Linda Pastan entitled *A Real Story*. Without having read the poem, we know (1) its name, (2) the implication that we are going to hear something that really happened, and (3) the slightly ironic tension that exists between the words "real" and "story."

> *A Real Story*
> Sucking on hard candy
> to sweeten the taste
> of old age,
> grandpa told us stories
> about chickens,
> city chickens sold
> for Sabbath soup
> but rescued at the end
> by some chicken-loving
> providence.

Now at ninety-five,
sucked down
to nothing himself,
he says he feels
a coldness;
perhaps the coldness David felt
even with Abishag
in his bed
to warm
his chicken-thin bones.

But when we say
you'll soon get well,
grandpa pulls the sheet
over his face,
raising it between us
the way he used to raise
the Yiddish paper
when we said
enough chickens
tell us a real story.

Actually, there are seven different stories being told by the poem. And in a sense, all of them are "real stories," and in another sense the reality of each one of them is debatable. First, let us look at the structure of the time dimensions in the poem. There is (1) the present, in which the poem is being told, (2) the distant past, in which the grandfather told his stories, (3) the near past, in which the grandfather reaches his ninety-fifth birthday, (4) the ancient past of King David and Abishag, and (5) the future, which is represented by life after death. These concentricities of time hold the world of reality (the slaughtered chickens, the sick grandfather, the disbelieving children) and the world of illusion (the "chicken-loving providence," the children telling the grandfather he'll soon be well, and the idea of life after death). The various stories being told by the narrator and characters to one another move smoothly through time and space and occupy so much of the poem that the essential question becomes, not whether the stories are real or not, but why there have to be stories in the first place. Thus Pastan's title not only points to her subject but to the moral theme of her poem.

Now let us look at the layers of stories within the poem. The first and most obvious story being told is the poem itself which recounts the moral interchanges between first and third generations of a family. The second story, chronologically, is the gradual physical weakening of the grandfather who stoically awaits an agnostic death without the possibility of redemption. He is subtly related to the third story of the helpless chickens who are mercilessly sacrificed for Sabbath soup, but mercifully saved in the beyond. A fourth story is that of King David whose robust and royal life ends with the permeating coldness that even the beautiful Abishag can't alter. This ALLUSION is, of course, a conventional STORY-WITHIN-A-STORY device that refers back on the main story being told. A fifth story is what the children tell the grandfather, "you'll soon get well," which echoes the happy ending of the chicken story. The grandfather doesn't believe that he'll get well or that the chickens were saved, and symbolically signifies this by lifting his sheet over his head. The sixth story lies in the

last two lines—"enough chickens [read: stories]/tell us a real story"—
where the children are, in effect, saying that they don't believe the chickens
are really "rescued at the end." And the seventh story is one of innocence,
in which good grandfathers tell stories with happy endings to their good
grandchildren who thus are protected from the world's cruel truths.

Now, when we reread the title, "A Real Story," all the tensions between
illusion and reality, youth and age, spirit and flesh, rise to the surface and
fill out what seems such a simple title. The poem doesn't require its title,
structurally, to be effective, but it is a valuable device for naming the poem
and compressing its ironic story into a single phrase.

The Pun Title
A much simpler version of the layered title is the pun title (see PUN)
which sports a semantic play on words. Again, the contents of the poem
will help interpret the double or triple meanings contained in the title.
Punning has a long history in poetry and has survived the vissicitudes of
changing poetic fashion. Some poets, such as Shakespeare, Pope, and
more recently, Ogden Nash, have raised punning to a complex and
sophisticated level, which delights scholars and critics. On the other hand,
many "serious" contemporary poets disdain the use of the pun as being
too facile and crude a device to interest them. Children who are learning the
malleable possibilities of language revel in the detection of contradictions
and the sometimes humorous double meanings that words contain. They
often store up a series of jokes whose punch lines feature a pun. In the
following poem by David Ignatow, his title is a thematic pun that acts as a
noun (self-identity), an adjective (mood), and a verb (state of being):

Content
I should be content
to look at a mountain
for what it is
and not as a comment
on my life.

The Subject As Title
Sometimes a title will simply announce the subject of a poem in order to
prepare the reader for what is to follow. This type of explicit naming lifts
what is to be talked about out of the complex matrix of the poem so that
the reader can focus more clearly on the subject under discussion. In Louis
Simpson's *Love and Poetry* the title goes beyond the naming of the poem's
subjects by fusing them together as if they were compatible entities. But
the theme of the poem demonstrates how mutually exclusive love and
poetry can be: Poetry is hard, strenuously intellectual work, and love is
natural and easy. So the reader is given not only the name of the poem's
subject, but the antithesis, and the emblems of the characters:

Love and Poetry
My girl the voluptuous creature
was shaving her legs and saying, 'Darling,
if poetry comes not as naturally
as the leaves to a tree
it had better not come at all.'

'Och,' I said, 'and the sorra
be taking your English Johnny!
What, is a poet a thing without brains in its head?
If wishing could do it, I'd compose
poems as grand as physics,
poems founded in botany, psychology, biology,
poems as progressive as the effect
of radiation on a foetus.'

She turned on the switch of the razor
and said, 'When you talk about poetry
it reminds me of a man in long underwear
doing barbell exercises.
His biceps bulge. In the meantime
outside on the gaslit street,
his wife, a voluptuous lady,
elopes with a "swell" who takes her
to Lindy's for oysters,
from there to the Waldorf, and there
on a bed carved like seashells
they move, while the man with the barbells
by gas light is marching
and swinging his arms to the tune of the *Washington Post.*'

I went to the window. It was night,
and the beautiful moon
was stealing away to meet someone.
The bitches! They want to feel wanted,
and everything else is prose.

In his narrative, the writer casts aspersions on the mindlessness and brutishness of the act of love, and in the guise of his female character makes sexual puns on the rigid, "macho" art of poetry. These accusations catch the seemingly straightforward title in a crossfire and create tension between two ostensibly matched activities, love and poetry. Of course, love or the emotional threat of lost love wins out over poetry. But the conflict between the two does not end when the poem ends, for the conflict has, in fact, created Simpson's poem. Like a marriage of opposites, their relationship persists through a kind of complementary dialectic of action-reaction. There are many t. of poems that name their subjects on a one-dimensional level, but Simpson has expanded his to include the THEME, the *characters*, and the STRATEGY of the poem.

Character As Title
   Read the following poem by Stephen Dunn and try to second-guess its title. In this example, Dunn uses his title to specifically locate and define both a character and a system of values. It's a poem about morality:

He is somewhere in our future,
the beggar who gives change.
He is waiting for us perhaps
outside a department store, his pockets
bulging like the stomachs
of starved children: all hope and air.
When we give him a quarter
he'll hand us a note marked
"This is only the beginning, friends."
And we, who have never completed

a single gesture,
will carry that note
for the rest of our lives.

More than likely your tendency would be to entitle the poem after the
beggar. Dunn has chosen to name his poem *Middle Class Prophecy*, a title
that defines the "we" of the poem and sets up an authoritative TONE. In
this contest between the haves and have-nots of society, the beggar plays
upon the guilt-ridden conscience of the middle class by giving them back
change in the form of a note (memorandum, promissory note?) of which
the middle class is incapable of unburdening itself. Although the poem
with its undefined "we" characters could stand without a title, the poem is
clarified and strengthened by its addition.

The Ironic Title

IRONY, which is the tension synthesized by the difference between what
is said and what is meant, focuses one's attention through the voice of
UNDERSTATEMENT. Two or more things are quietly stated in an ironic
expression, as in the case of Wallace Stevens' *Of Mere Being*. He
downplays the magnitude of existence in his surreal and luxurious poem
which vivifies what we normally think of as an emptiness in life. He points
out our blindness to the miraculous state of simply being by setting us up
with limited expectations with his title and then ballooning them with his
gorgeous painting of our inner space.

The Symbol As Title

As Stevens used his golden bird as a symbol for existence or consciousness, Charles Simic's FILL-IN-THE-BLANKS POEM about the everyday activities of the economically oppressed also uses a symbol in its title, *Classic
Ballroom Dances*. He is saying, in effect, that the events that take place on
the seamier side of life have been going on for so long that they have
become ritualized into classical forms, which, in their own way, are as
eloquent and varied as the minuet, the fox trot, and the tango:

> *Classic Ballroom Dances*
> Grandmothers who wring the necks
> Of chickens; old nuns
> With names like Theresa, Marianne,
> Who pull schoolboys by the ear.
>
> The intricate steps of pickpockets
> Working the crowd of curious
> At the scene of an accident; the slow shuffle
> Of the evangelist with a sandwich-board.
>
> The hesitation of the early morning customer
> Peeking through a window-grille
> Of a pawn-shop; the weave of a little kid
> Who is walking to school with eyes closed.
>
> And the ancient lovers, cheek to cheek,
> On the dancefloor of a dim Union Hall
> Where they also hold charity raffles
> On rainy Monday nights in November.

The Outside-Reference Title

Many t. enlarge the range of a poem's message or setting by employing an outside reference that gives an unexpected perspective or larger framework to the poem. J.D. Reed's report of an automobile accident on an urban expressway gains ironic impact and distance with the title *The Weather Is Brought to You.* The title does a lot of work: It implies that tragic human events are only fodder for broadcast commercials; that death and destruction are no longer reported in emotional terms of the real lives involved, but in an objective, statistical manner; and that the "weather," a kind of negative destiny, will inevitably meet up with us as surely as this futuristic "accident":

> *The Weather Is Brought to You*
> It is 64° in Devereaux,
> and a volunteer pumper
> hoses gas from the expressway.
>
> Troopers with the faces of mandrills
> hobnail over crushed metal,
> using big flashlights like pointers
> in a planetarium.
>
> Sprockets dangle in the weeds,
> torn radiators gurgle,
>
> and the dead wait under wool blankets,
> expiring
> like tungsten filament
> in a hissing, broken headlight.

The Visual Title

Sometimes a concrete or visually recognizable title (an IMAGE) says more than words and has a more direct impact on the reader. In Andrei Codrescu's poem, the female narrator speaks of being suicidally drubbed into mental numbness by her desperate financial need and the hatred that others feel for her. Her somnambulant psychic condition is so deep that the poem calls for startling and violent images in order to make her feel something:

> ZZZZZZZZZZZZZ
> i want to touch something sensational
> like the mind of a shark. the white
> electric bulbs of hunger moving
> straight to the teeth.
> and let there be rain that day over new york.
> there is no other way
> i can break away from bad news
> and cheap merchandise.
> (the black woman with a macy's shopping bag
> just killed me
> from across the street.)
> it is comfortable to want
> peace from the mind of a shark.

The Self-Negating Title

Lastly, there are poems that have no t., or are facelessly numbered, or are entitled *Poem.* Charles Bukowski calls attention to the uselessness and

ineffectuality of t. in his poem *What's the Use of a Title?* in which the
narrator speaks in a bitter litany of the fate of the world's innocent and
beautiful people who somehow can't survive their own naiveté. The poem
is a variation on the theme "The Good Die Young":

what's the use of a title?

they don't make it
the beautiful die in flame—
suicide pills, rat poison, rope whatever . . .
they rip their arms off,
throw themselves out of windows,
they pull their eyes from the sockets,
reject love
reject hate
reject, reject,

they don't make it
the beautiful can't endure,
they are the butterflies
they are the doves
they are the sparrows,
they don't make it.

one tall shot of flame
while the old men play checkers in the park
one flame, one good flame
while the old men play checkers in the park
in the sun,

the beautiful are found at the edge of a room
crumpled into spiders and needles and silence
and we can never understand why they
left, they were so
beautiful.

they don't make it,
the beautiful die young
and leave the ugly to their ugly lives.
lovely and brilliant: life and suicide and death
as the old men play checkers in the sun
in the park.

General Categories of Titles

There are five general types of categories of t. that can be stated in
terms of what the title is directed toward. The most common title is one
that in some way *describes the poem itself*, its subject, theme, symbols,
form, etc. Another time-honored title convention is the type that is *reader-
directed*. Still another kind of title ignores the poem and brings in an
outside point of reference to parallel the poem or to place it in a larger
perspective. Another common kind of title that has been handed down
through literature is the *dedicatory* title which is named in honor of
someone or something that may or may not have anything to do with the
body of the poem. And the last type of title is comprised of those poems
that are named to indicate that the title is *of little importance* or that the
poem should remain untitled. Within each of these five categories, there
are variations in form, function, and character, and it is quite common to
find certain titles that fall into two or more of these categories:

(1) TITLES THAT DESCRIBE THE POEM

and show action:

> *Crossing Brooklyn Ferry*—Walt Whitman
> *Stopping by Woods on a Snowy Evening*—Robert Frost

locate the dramatic situation:

> *Our City Is Guarded by Atomic Rockets*—William Stafford
> *My Father in the Night Commanding No*—Louis Simpson

indicate incipient action:

> *Keys in the Car*—Kay Deeter

point out the subject:

> *The Couple Overhead*—William Meredith
> *Church Going*—Philip Larkin

name a theme:

> *Love Calls Us to the Things of This World*—Richard Wilbur
> *The Idea of Order at Key West*—Wallace Stevens

show character:

> *How Beastly the Bourgeois Is*—D.H. Lawrence

show character through dialogue:

> *Sister, That Man Don't Have the Sting of a Horsefly*—Betty
>   Adcock
> *Let's Go, Daddy*—Marvin Bell

ask a rhetorical question:

> *what if a much of a which of a wind*—e.e. cummings [first line]
> *What Are Years?*—Marianne Moore

name the function of a poem:

> *A Pact*—Ezra Pound

indicate a special time or event:

> *Easter, 1916*—W.B. Yeats
> *Ash Wednesday*—T.S. Eliot

indicate the form of a poem:

> *Sestina*—Judith Kroll
> *Sonnet*—Donald Justice

indicate a poetic convention or device:

> *Aubade*—Ezra Pound [meaning "morning song"]

form the framework of an allegory:

> *The Animal That Drank Up Sound*—William Stafford
> *The Breakfast That Came to Dinner*—Russell Edson

explain the catalyst of a poem:

> *My Grandmother's Love Letters*—Hart Crane

pun on an expression:

> *Sea Saw*—Marvin Bell
> *Whoroscope*—Samuel Beckett

indicate the speaker:

> *Maximus, to Himself*—Charles Olson

explain the reason for an action:
> *Because I could not stop for death*—Emily Dickinson [first line]

show irony:
> *Who's Who*—W.H. Auden

exploit a character in literature:
> *Pangloss's Song*—Richard Wilbur [on Voltaire's *Candide*]
> *Gretel in Darkness*—Louise Gluck

create a metaphor for an emotional state: ·
> *Heart's Needle*—W.D.Snodgrass
> *Diving into the Wreck*—Adrienne Rich

show an emotional reaction:
> *Howl*—Allen Ginsberg

use the metaphor for the theme:
> *The Sun Was Trumpet Then*—Daniela Gioseffi

indicate a pattern:
> *Crisscross*—Carl Sandburg
> *Webs*—Carl Sandburg

entreat:
> *Do Not Go Gentle into That Good Night*—Dylan Thomas

use a line or phrase from a poem:
> *No Worst, There Is None. Pitched Past Pitch of Grief*—G.M.
> Hopkins [first line]
> *When I Consider How My Light Is Spent*—John Milton

use a piece of dialogue:
> *Terence, This Is Stupid Stuff*—A.E. Housman
> *You, Andrew Marvell*—Archibald MacLeish

draw a self-portrait:
> *The Heavy Bear Who Goes with Me*—Delmore Schwartz

indicate character via action:
> *I Buy Nothing*—Laura Jensen

name a relationship:
> *Daddy*—Sylvia Plath

indicate an emotional situation:
> *Wanting To Die*—Anne Sexton

pay tribute to a literary influence:
> *Poem after Apollinaire*—Ira Sadoff

indicate a poem's intention or strategy:
> *Conjugation of the Verb, 'To Hope'*—Lou Lipsitz

set up a reader's expectations:
> *The Secret of Poetry*—Jon Anderson
> *Someday Someone Will Tell You This*—Betty Adcock

indicate a transformation in character:
> *Beginning To Say No*—Tess Gallagher

indicate a state of being:
Unwell—Maura Stanton

shows author's tone:
Ah—Greg Kuzma

stands as symbol and subject:
Brooklyn Bridge—Hart Crane
The Wasteland—T.S. Eliot

express variations of a theme or subject:
100 Views of the Charles River—Larry Stark

(2) TITLES THAT ARE READER-ORIENTED

and make a demand or request:
Let Me Enjoy—Thomas Hardy
Ask Me—William Stafford

indicate a greeting:
Good Morning, America—Carl Sandburg

invite:
Come with Me—Robert Bly

instruct the reader to take action:
Take Yourself Back—Diane Wald
Unwind My Riddle—Stephen Crane

directly address the reader:
Dear Reader—James Tate
The Poem You Asked For—Larry Levis

give an ironic didactic instruction:
Provide, Provide—Robert Frost
Lower the Standards: That's My Motto—Karl Shapiro

stipulate a condition for instruction:
If You See This Man—Thomas Lux
Poem for Men Only—Michael Ryan

show an emotional reaction:
To Hell with Your Fertility Cult—Gary Snyder

indicate a warning:
The Penalty for Bigamy Is Two Wives—William Matthews
Poem for Speculative Hipsters—Imamu Amiri Baraka

set up a reader's expectations:
Taking Off My Clothes—Carolyn Forché

(3) TITLES THAT USE OUTSIDE REFERENCES

and indicate the time of composition:
12. 6. 71—Louise Glück

indicate an old expression:
Clothes Maketh the Man—Theodore Weiss
It's Not the Heat So Much As the Humidity—James Tate

quote another piece of literature:
> *To Speak of Woe That Is in Marriage*—Robert Lowell [from Chaucer]

name a famous event or place:
> *Musée des Beaux Arts*—W.H. Auden

indicate conditions under which the poem is composed:
> *Lines Written While Landing at La Guardia*—Ann Darr

indicate time and place:
> *Everything: Eloy, Arizona, 1956*—Ai

(4) TITLES THAT ARE DEDICATORY

> *A Coconut for Katerina*—Sandra McPherson
> *Homage to Rimbaud*—Charles Wright

(to exhort or affirm:)
> *The People, Yes*—Carl Sandburg
> *Rule Britannia!*—James Thomson

(to compliment:)
> *Gee, Marcia You're So Beautiful It's Starting To Rain*—Richard Brautigan

(5) TITLES THAT ARE SELF-EFFACING

> *Untitled*—Alan Dugan
> *Poem*—Frank O'Hara
> *What's the Use of a Title*—Charles Bukowski

See COLOPHON, FORMAT, and TYPOGRAPHICAL ARRANGEMENT. See also *forms* in APPENDIX 1.

tmesis /mē′sis, təmē′sis/ (Greek "a cutting") a rhetorical figure of grammar referring to the separation of the elements of a compound word by the interposition of another word or words, as in "Man shall work *ever*, and a day, *more*." Originally, in Classical prosody, the term referred to the interrupting of a preposition-verb syntactical unit. See HYSTERIOLOGIA and PARENTHESIS. See also *grammatical constructions* in APPENDIX 2.

tone (from Greek "a stretching") an author's identifiable attitude toward his subject matter and/or audience, or the MOOD of a "voiceless" work of literature. Rhetorical structures and devices such as DICTION, argumentation, and IRONY, and poetic devices such as PATHETIC FALLACY, METAPHOR, and IMAGE help to communicate the writer's feelings about his subject. Also various authors' overall tones can be generally described: e.g., Pope's as witty and ironic, T.S. Eliot's as reserved, formal, and serious, and Charles Bukowski's as slangy, rough, and hard-bitten. See AMBIENCE, ATMOSPHERE, SPEAKER, TIMBRE, TONE COLOR, and VOICE.

tone color the emotional texture of sound in a poem achieved through the combination and repetition of vowels, consonants, and sound systems. The American lyric-musician-turned-poet Sidney Lanier (*The Science of English Verse*, 1880) borrowed the term t.c. from music to describe the specific musical qualities of an individual poem. Poets who relied upon the

IMAGE (Imagists, Symbolists, and Surrealists) carried this concept of harmony over to the visual imagination. Other related terms include AESTHETIC SURFACE, ALLITERATION, ASSONANCE, ATONIC, AURAL, BEAST LANGUAGE, BOND DENSITY, CACOPHONY, CONSONANCE, EMOTIVE LANGUAGE, EUPHONY, MOOD, MOTIF, MUSICAL SCANSION, ONOMATOPOEIA, PHONEMICS, POLYPHONIC PROSE, REPETITION, RHYME, SENTENCE SOUNDS, SOUND POEMS, SYNAESTHESIA, and TONE.

topographia (from Greek for "place-writing") a rhetorical *definition by figure of subject and adjunct* (substance and essence) which is subsumed under the general type of imaginative description known as HYPOTYPOSIS. In the case of t., the term refers to the re-creation of once existing places, as Yeats' Byzantium in *Sailing to Byzantium* and Coleridge's Xanadu in *Kubla Khan*. See LANDSCAPE, LOCAL COLOR, MINDSCAPE, TOPOGRAPHICAL POEM, TOPOTHESIA, and TRIGGERING TOWN. See also *figures of subject and adjunct* in APPENDIX 2.

topographical poem a form of rhetorical definition that describes a specific LOCALE. The term was first used by Dr. Johnson to refer to poetry that has as its subject a particular geography: e.g., a tract of land, a city, a village, or even an entire country. The genre was popular in England in the 18th and 19th centuries, and in the modern era, poets such as Sandburg, Betjeman, Dave Smith, Robert Penn Warren, and Richard Hugo (see TRIGGERING TOWN) have used landscape as a catalyst toward meditative, lyrical, or philosophical verse. See also LOCAL COLOR and TOPOTHESIA.

topos: See MOTIF.

topothesia (from Greek for "a proposing of a place") a rhetorical figure of *definition by subject and adjunct* (substance and essence) which is subsumed under a general type of imaginative description known as HYPOTYPOSIS. In the case of t., the term refers to the creation of a fictitious place, such as Camelot of the Arthurian legend. See LANDSCAPE, LOCAL COLOR, MINDSCAPE, TOPOGRAPHIA, TOPOGRAPHICAL POEM, and TRIGGERING TOWN. See also *figures of subject and adjunct* in APPENDIX 2.

totem an IMAGE or ICON associated with a family or tribe.

tragedy (from Greek for "goat-song," perhaps from the ancient ritual in which contests in the writing of tragedies came to be held as part of the ceremonies of the Great Dionysia at Athens, the springtime festival of the death and resurrection of the god Dionysus, patron of fields and vineyards) originally, in ancient Greek literature, a lyric or dramatic piece that contained a sorrowful and dire mood. According to Aristotle's *Poetics*, which was written after the great age of Greek t., it is an imitative device of CATHARSIS in which the audience shares through EMPATHY the emotions and fate of fallen noble figures who—no matter which way they turn—are destined to head toward their destruction. A t., then, is the imitation of an action that is serious, complete in itself, and of magnitude. Watching this action makes the audience experience pity and fear and thus purges it of these feelings.

Although Aristotle's definition is the most influential and widely accepted, it should be noted that the term has been used to apply to many different types of literature. In the Middle Ages, t. was considered to be any genre in which a royal, high-ranking, or especially honorable personage falls toward ill fate because of either inner or outer circumstances. Elizabethan Renaissance theorists used the term to refer to stage works, as did Aristotle, but often playwrights during this period mixed comedy and seriousness in a way that violated Aristotle's dictates. By the 18th century, the term had been expanded to include middle-class characters (see DOMESTIC T.). In modern times, t. includes characters from all levels of society, and has, in fact, often pointed at the values of society itself as the TRAGIC FLAW which brings about the destruction of an individual. See ANTAGONIST, COMEDY, CONFLICT, DRAMATIC STRUCTURE, HARMARTIA, PLOT, REALISM, TRAGICOMEDY, and UNITIES. See also *dramatic terms* in APPENDIX 1.

tragic flaw (see HARMARTIC) the character defect (excessive jealousy, pride, etc.) or the strength which becomes a weakness that leads a once noble figure to destruction. See TRAGEDY. See also *dramatic terms* in APPENDIX 1.

tragic irony: See DRAMATIC IRONY.

tragi-comedy a dramatic form, invented in the RENAISSANCE, that follows the structure and content of TRAGEDY but which contains elements of COMEDY including a final turn in the falling action (see DRAMATIC STRUCTURE) that reverses disaster and leads to a happy outcome for the protagonists. Shakespeare's *The Merchant of Venice* and Corneille's *Le Cid* are two examples of the form. See DEUS EX MACHINA, DÉNOUMENT, and SURPRISE ENDING. See also *dramatic terms* in APPENDIX 1.

transferred epithet the use of a modifying word that usually belongs to one domain of thought or action but which is brought over to another domain. For instance, a common form that uses PATHETIC FALLACY attributes human qualities to inanimate objects: "happy house," "attentive streetlight," etc. See EPITHET.

transformational line ending (see LINE ENDING) an ENJAMBMENT in which the line break causes the reader to understand a word or phrase in more than one way. See JUXTAPOSITION. See also *line endings* in APPENDIX 1.

transition (from Latin for "a going across"; see CINEMATIC TECHNIQUES) any word, line, or passage that contains material that indicates a change from one condition, subject, or action to another. In modern literature, even WHITE SPACE, stanza breaks, dissolving images, and fadeouts act as transitions.

translation (from Latin for "transfer," including a transfer in meaning or language) the rendering of something spoken or written into another language. The Italian proverb *Traduttore, traditore* ("translator, traitor") conveys the long-standing mistrust of t., particularly the t. of poetry. Since poetry depends on SOUND, RHYTHM, and CONNOTATION, all of which are lost in t., how can the t. of a poem communicate the essence of the original? On the other hand, if we consider the many translations of poems that are both notable in themselves and influential in the history of literature—the King James Version of the Bible, the many translations of Homer and Shakespeare, Baudelaire's t. of Poe, to name a few—how can one claim that poetry should not be translated? So the question becomes not whether poetry should be translated, but rather, what particular problems confront the poet-translator? And especially, what should be his or her attitude toward the task so that he or she makes the best choices among the many alternatives in the t. of a specific poem?

Modern translators have taken their cue from Ezra Pound's idea of ADAPTATION, a form of t. that eschews the impulse to transliterate and instead favors the creation of a version that reflects the spirit of the original. In Pound's *ABC of Reading* (1934), he categorizes three main aspects of poetry that reflect problems in t.: PHANOPOEIA, the image content, which is directly transferable to another language; MELOPOEIA, the sound and rhythm, which are lost in t.; and LOGOPOEIA, the logical relationship and arrangement of ideas and associations, which are only saved by paraphrase (see HERESY OF PARAPHRASE). Thus, Pound proposes the practice of adaptation, which would at least produce a good poem in the new language.

In Charles Simic and Mark Strand's *Another Republic: 17 European and South American Writers* (1976), the editors make another set of distinctions germane to t.; they separate those poets whose impulse is toward the mythological from those whose impulse is toward the historical. The former type use *archetypal images* and are primarily concerned with STYLE, that is, *how* something is said, while the latter are primarily concerned with content, with *what* is being said. So the t. of a poem depends on the poet-translator paying attention to the STRATEGY of presentation.

The attempt to reach a satisfying common ground between two languages involves recognizing specific differences in social, psychological, and etymological structures. Northrop Frye speaks of bridging lexical gulfs by building universal symbolic language structures, *ideograms*, by which meaning in its fullest sense can be conveyed. The number "five" carries the same meaning in Spanish (*cinco*), French (*cinque*), and German (*fünf*), but in a broader sense it is difficult to include the cultural associations of the number. For instance, in Christian cultures, the word "three" contains the religious concept of the Trinity, a connotation lost on a person of a non-Christian culture.

John Lyons (*An Introduction to Theoretical Linguistics*, 1969) discusses the recent work devoted to lexical systems in the vocabularies of different languages, with particular reference to such domains as kinship, color, flora and fauna, weights and measures, military ranks, and moral and aesthetic evaluations. His studies confirm the theory that the vocabularies of different languages are nonisomorphic; that is, there are semantic distinctions in one language that do not exist in another language. Moreover, particular domains may be categorized in a totally different way in different languages. These structures not only mark differences in associational values, but extend to how different cultures envision and name the world. The manner in which flora and fauna are grouped may be different in one language from the manner in another language. For example, the Latin word *mus* refers to mice, rats, and other rodents. The French word *singe* refers to apes as well as monkeys.

Even a language structure that is commonly thought of as being universal cannot always be brought into one-to-one correspondence with the words of another language. Lyons points out that color terms are very difficult to translate. The English word "brown" has no exact equivalent in French; it might be translated as *brun*, *marron*, or even *jaune*, according to the particular shade and the kind of noun it modifies. The Hindi word *pilā* is translated into English as "yellow," "orange", or even "brown," though there are other words for shades of brown in Hindi. There is no equivalent to the English word "blue" in Russian; the words *goluboj* and *sinij* (usually translated as "light blue" and "dark blue" respectively) refer to what are in Russian completely distinct colors, not different shades, as their translation into English might suggest. The native speaker of Russian thinks of the two words as referring to different colors, not different shades of the same color, as, say, the English words "crimson" and "scarlet."

The differences in the ways that an American and a Russian, or a Frenchman and a German, perceive colors are slight compared with the differences between a speaker of an Indo-European language and a speaker of a non-Indo-European language. We can analyze color using three variables: *hue* (the reflection of light at different wavelengths), *luminosity* (brightness, the amount of light reflected), and *saturation* (the amount of white diluting the color). Languages differ in the relative weight they give to the three variables in the organization of their color terms. English depends heavily on the *hue*, while Greek and Latin gave more importance to *luminosity*. But, there are languages in which distinctions of color are made along completely different principles. In an essay entitled *Hanunóo Color Categories* (1955), H.D. Conklin has shown that the four main color terms of the Hanunóo (a hunter-gatherer society in the Philippines) are associated with *lightness* (generally corresponding to the light tints of the English colors), *darkness* (corresponding to black, violet, blue, dark green), *wetness* (corresponding to light green, yellow and light brown), and *dryness* (corresponding to maroon, red, orange). The distinction between wetness and dryness is not simply a matter of hue in the Hanunóo language; this fact can be demonstrated in that a shiny, wet, "brown" section of newly cut bamboo is described by the term that is sometimes used for light green. Conklin concludes that color is not a universal concept, and that our perception of color depends on the association of the color with culturally-important factors. For the Hanunóos, an important consideration is whether vegetation is wet (that is, succulent). As the great linguist Sapir has said, "The worlds in which different societies live are distinct worlds, not the same with different labels attached."

Given the fact that our perception of reality is determined, in large part, by the structure of our native language, it is not surprising that poetry is difficult to translate. What is surprising is that it is attempted at all. The translator's attempts depend on two principles: *cultural overlap* and *similar application.*

Cultural overlap refers to the fact that cultures are not co-terminous with languages. Many of the institutions, food, dress, architectural styles, and customs found in France are also found in America. Between any two cultures there will be a certain degree of overlap. We can easily recognize the institution, even though the exact rituals and responsibilties that the term connotes are different in each language.

Similar application refers to the fact that items of different languages can be put into correspondence with one another on the basis of their role in the culture. For example, the relationship between "please" and "thank you" has a certain role in the culture which similar items (e.g., *por favor* and *gracias*) in another language have. Rituals of greeting, friendship, courtship, and dominance have equivalences in every language of the world.

What this discussion means to the poet-translator is that the language of a particular society is an intregal part of its culture, and that in order to build language bridges he or she must use the cultural overlappings and similar applications to create poems that are both true to their originals and true to their new language. Paradoxically, the t. of poetry is impossible *and* absolutely necessary. Furthermore, it has had a tremendous influence on contemporary American poetry. With the example of Pound's translations from Provençal, Chinese, Anglo-Saxon, and Egyptian, as well as the contemporary translations of poets such as W.S. Merwin, Strand, Simic, Richard Wilbur, Richard Howard, Elizabeth Bishop, Robert Lowell, and James Wright, to name only a few, it would be difficult to argue that on balance the new attempts have been fruitless, for new frontiers in FORM, METAPHOR, IMAGERY, DICTION and LOGIC have been discovered. There are critics of this recent trend who claim that its effect on contemporary American poetry has been to dilute the idiomatic quality of the language so that what is produced under the influence of these translations is "translationese," a watered-down version of the American language. But what may, in fact, be happening is that American poetry is finally wresting itself away from the grip of English verse. See IMITATION. See also *meaning* in APPENDIX 1.

Trans-sense Verse a type of ABSTRACT POETRY that concentrates solely on the aural and rhythmical texture of language, as does NONSENSE VERSE. See FUTURISM. See also *diction* in APPENDIX 1.

travesty /trav'-/ (from Latin for "to cross-dress," with the later meaning of "to disguise") any literary work that treats an inherently noble or solemn subject in a comically debasing manner, so that the strategy and TONE contrast with the subject. Cervantes' *Don Quixote* is a t. of the *Medieval romance* (see METRICAL ROMANCE). The form is the opposite of the MOCK EPIC in the sense that the latter presents a frivolous subject in a serious manner. See PARODY and SATIRE. See also *humor* in APPENDIX 1.

triadic stanza (see STANZA and FREE VERSE) a three-line, indented, irregular stanzaic form invented by William Carlos Williams in *Paterson II's The*

Descent. The stanza is based upon Williams' concept of the VARIABLE FOOT, a unit of line measurement that sought to create a loose CADENCE close to the American idiom. In speaking to Professor John C. Thirlwall (*Pictures from Brueghel and Other Poems*, 1962), Williams said:

> The iamb is not the normal measure of American speech. The foot has to be expanded or contracted in terms of actual speech. The key to modern poetry is measure, which must reflect the flux of modern life. You should find a variable measure for the fixed measure; for man and the poet must keep pace with this world.

The ORGANIZING PRINCIPLE for the variable foot and the triadic stanzas is Williams' acute sense of the rhythmical sculpted effect of the line, and many poets have borrowed the form because of the sweep, grace, and delicacy achieved through the gradual accretion of glass-thin sheets of lines. One of the most successful, and risky, uses of the form is David Young's translation of Rilke's *Duino Elegies* (1978). For three poetic movements associated with Williams, see IMAGISM, OBJECTIVISM, and VORTICISM. See also *forms* in APPENDIX 1.

tribrach /trī'brak/ (from Greek for "three short") a Classical Greek FOOT composed of three short syllables in QUANTITATIVE METER, or of three unaccented syllables in accentual-syllabic verse. Generally speaking, the triple foot represents a rhythmical SUBSTITUTION for a duple foot, such as the iamb or the trochee, since in quantitative verse a long syllable is the equivalent of two short syllables ($\smile\smile = \smile\smile\smile$). See METER, PROSODIC SYMBOLS, and SCANSION.

trick ending (also known as "twist ending"; see SURPRISE ENDING) an unanticipated and unprepared-for TURN in a narrative's CLOSURE. The t.e. is usually considered a defect in STRATEGY. See also *closure* in APPENDIX 1.

triggering town a SETTING or LOCALE that acts as a catalyst to the imaginative impulse for creating a poem. According to Richard Hugo, who coined the term, an integral part of his creative process is to visit a town, usually one ruined by poverty or one relatively uninhabited because of climate or inaccessibility, then to take on the MASK of a long-time resident of that town. From this perspective of consciousness (see LOCATION), Hugo finds his VOICE, SUBJECT MATTER, and THEME, and pressured by the weight of the ATMOSPHERE, the creative process begins. This contemporary version of DIVINE AFFLATUS works for Hugo who says in *A Trout in the Milk* (1982), "Decaying shacks, abandoned ranches, desolation, endless spaces, plains, mountains, ghost towns: they're ready-made for my sensibilites." Thus, the t.t. acts as a sort of physical reflection of a state of mind. For further discussion, see *reflection of the setting* under INNER REFLECTIONS.

triggering word (see COMMITTING WORD) a word, phrase, or concept that acts as a catalyst to the imaginative impulse for creating a poem and which is detectable in the work. Much of Richard Hugo's work contains triggering words that work through the logic of association; however, other poets, such as Sylvia Plath, have revised in such a way as to eliminate the associational stepping stones of the triggering words in her final drafts. See TRIGGERING TOWN.

trimeter /trim'-/ (from Greek for "three measures") a line composed of three feet either appearing regularly or as a variation of a two- or four-foot line. Used too regularly, the form tends to be singsongy, reminiscent of NURSERY RHYME and NONSENSE VERSE. See METER. See also *forms* in APPENDIX 1.

triolet /trī'ələt/ (French for "little trio") a French fixed form, invented in the Middle Ages, composed of an OCTAVE that has two recurring rhymes in the pattern ABaAabAB and two recurring REFRAIN lines (1, 2, 4, 7, and 8). It is a simplified form of the 13-line RONDEL. The form was introduced into English by Robert Bridges. The form is uncommon in contemporary poetry although poets such as Sandra McPherson have used it. See BALLADE, CHANT ROYAL, LAI, LIMERICK, RIME COUÉE, RONDEAU, RONDELET, SESTINA, VILLANELLE, and VIRELAY. See also *forms* in APPENDIX 1.

triple meter any poetic measure consisting of three units, such as anapestic, dactylic, tribrachic, molossos, antibachic, amphibrachic, and cretic; or, any poetic measure consisting of three feet, such as a TRIPODY. See DIPODY, METER, SCANSION, and TRISYLLABIC FOOT.

triple rhyme trisyllabic RHYME, as in Byron's *Don Juan*: "land-service/and Jervis," "garrison/Harrison," "paragon/Aragon," "goddesses/bodices," "precocious/atrocious." The device usually has a comic effect. See also MULTIPLE RHYME.

triplet (from Latin for "threefold") any regular or irregular set of three lines, such as the TRIADIC STANZA or a TRISTICH. The specific term for a three-line stanza that contains rhyme is TERCET, as in the form of the TERZA RIMA. Other stanza forms include the COUPLET, DISTICH, MONOSTICH, QUATRAIN, QUINTAIN, OCTASTICH, OCTAVE, PENTASTICH, SEPTET, and SESTET.

tripody /trip'-/ (from Greek for "three-foot") a Greek QUANTITATIVE METER unit composed of three feet. See DIPODY, DUPLE FOOT, METER, SCANSION and TRIPLE METER. See also *forms* in APPENDIX 1.

tristich /tris'tik/ (from Greek for "three lines") any regular or irregular STANZA, STROPHE, or group of three lines. A TERCET is a group of three lines that rhyme. See also other general stanzaic forms under COUPLET, DISTICH, MONOSTICH, OCTASTICH, OCTAVE, OCTET, PENTASTICH, QUATRAIN, QUINTAIN, SEPTET, and SESTET.

trisyllabic foot /tri-, trī-/ any foot of three syllables, such as anapest, dactyl, tribrach, molossos, antibacchus, amphibrach, and cretic. See METER, SCANSION, SUBSTITUTION, TRIPLE METER, and TRIPODY.

trobar clus (from Provençal for "closed writing") a 12th-century Provençal style of gnomic writing that was intended to be obscure and complex. It is the opposite of *trobar clar*, "open writing." See CACOZELIA, PERIERGIA, and SORIASMUS. See also *clichés* in APPENDIX 1.

trochee /trō'kē/ (from Greek for "a running"; also known as "choree" /kō'rē, kərē'/ a disyllabic FOOT composed of a long (stressed) syllable followed by a short (unstressed) syllable, as in the word "running." It is known as a *falling foot*, as opposed to feet such as the IAMB which is a *rising foot* because it ends on an accented or long syllable. The t. is most commonly used as a SUBSTITUTION for the iamb. See METER and SCANSION.

Troilus stanza: See CHAUCER STANZA.

trope /trōp/ (from Greek for "a turning, a turn") a general term for FIGURATIVE LANGUAGE, that is, language whose semantic meaning must be taken in a metaphorical or figurative sense rather than its literal sense. Poetic devices such as METAPHOR, METONYMY, SIMILE, and SYNECDOCHE fall under the category of tropes. But there has been disagreement and debate for hundreds of years over the term. Quintilian classifies tropes as *figures of thought* (distinct from FIGURES OF SPEECH) created by new grammatical or rhetorical usage. Other theorists note the difference between *tropes*, which alter the meaning of a word, and *schemes*, which alter normal word order. And still other theorists, such as Puttenham, classify poetic and rhetorical devices according to what sense (that of the eye, the ear, or the mind) they appeal to. In general usage, most poets and critics use the term to indicate, as Coleridge proposed, any language that aspires toward the state of metaphor. See *figurative expressions* in APPENDIX 1.

troubadour /trōōb'ədôr/ (from Provençal for "to find, to compose [in verse]") a 12th-to-14th-century Provençal poet-minstrel—itinerant or attached to a court—who created songs and verse (CHANSO, ALBA, PASTOURELLE, SIRVENTES, and SESTINA) on the themes of sexual or courtly love. Ezra Pound's adaptations (*Personae*, 1926) renewed interest in these poets, especially the verse of Arnaut Daniel, Bertrans de Born, and Guillaume d'Aquitaine. The troubadours are often confused with the TROUVÈRES, who were contemporaries but who lived in the northern part of France.

trouvère /trōōver'/ (from Old French for "to compose [in verse]") northern French poets of the 11th to the 12th century who worked in the narrative and epic forms of CHANSON DE GESTE, FABLIAUX, and metrical romances. Important among them are Rutebeuf, Jean Bodel, Conan de Béthune, Blonde de Nesle, and Chrétien de Troyes. They wrote at the same time as the troubadours of Provençal. See TROUBADOUR.

true rhyme: See PERFECT RHYME.

truncation (from Latin for "to cut off") the omission of the first or last unstressed syllable in a metrical line of verse. The *terminal t.* is also referred to as CATALEXIS; initial t. is called *acephalexis* (see ACEPHALOUS LINE). When a line is metrically regular, the term ACATALEXIS is used. The addition of syllables is known as ANACRUSIS at the beginning of a line, HYPERCATALEXIS at the end of a line; and the general term for adding extra syllables is HYPERMETRIC. See also BRACHYCATALECTIC.

tumbling verse: See SKELTONIC VERSE.

turn a change in the direction of a poem's ARGUMENT or NARRATION. When the t. occurs near or at the CLOSURE of the poem, it may be a TRICK ENDING or SURPRISE ENDING. See SONNET and VOLTA.

typographical arrangement the FORM and FORMAT of the printed poem; specifically its stichic or strophic (block or stanzaic) shape, the number and length of lines, their indentation or lack thereof, the use of space between words and stanzas, use or lack of PUNCTUATION, kinds of typeface, use of titles, marginalia, epigraphs, and types of line endings. Most modern and contemporary poems have a length of from 20 to 50 lines, a form that some critics have called *magazine verse* because the poem is supposedly prefitted to the exigencies of space in a magazine. For other types of poem shapes, see CARMEN FIGURATUM and CONCRETE POETRY. See also *publishing formats* under *forms* in APPENDIX 1.

U

"ubi sunt" formula /ōō′bē s ŏont′/ (Latin for "where are," plus *formula*) a thematic convention indicating a *where have they gone* motif. The formula originated in Medieval Latin poetry which often opened with *ubi sunt* and which went on to express the theme of loss, transitoriness, and devaluation of culture. The thematic scheme became more fixed and stylized as a REFRAIN or REPETEND in French poetry, as exemplified by D. G. Rossetti's TRANSLATION of François Villon's *Ballade* (*des dames du temps jadis*). A modern example is Edgar Lee Master's *The Hill* (*Spoon River Anthology*, 1915) in which every other stanza opens with "where are." See MOTIF and THEME.

understatement a tonal and stylistic STRATEGY of RESTRAINT, opposite to HYPERBOLE or overstatement, in which something of importance or of a serious nature is deliberately treated with a lesser degree of INTENSITY or AUTHORITY than would usually be appropriate to such a subject. Sometimes u. employs rhetorical devices of contradiction or opposites that lessen the immediate impact of their content—devices such as IRONY, LITOTES, ANTIPHRASIS, PARALIPSIS, EPITROPE, and ANTANOGOGE. At other times, as in the poetry of writers such as T.S. Eliot, Philip Larkin, Louis Simpson, and W.H.Auden, a distinguished and formal TONE sets up a buffer zone of DECORUM and acts as a form of u. See MEIOSIS. See also *diction* in APPENDIX 1.

Unities (from Latin for "oneness, sameness") a set of principles, derived from Aristotle's *Poetics*, that calls for DRAMATIC STRUCTURE to be based upon (1) *unity of action*, one main action "complete, whole, and of a certain magnitude"; (2) *unity of time*, which must "confine itself to a single revolution of the sun, or only slightly exceed this limit"; and (3) *unity of place*, a principle that Italian and French Renaissance critics set down as a natural result of having followed the first two U. The French called these *Des Trois Unitez*. Critics have hotly debated the contention that any shifting of order or deletion of the parts within *The Three Unities* would affect their organic unity, and notable writers have more often than not foregone the restrictions of these rules. Modern examples of plays that follow the U. are Edward Albee's *Who's Afraid of Virginia Woolf*, Tennessee Williams' *A Streetcar Named Desire* and *Cat on a Hot Tin Roof*, and Samuel Becket's *Krapp's Last Tape* and *Waiting For Godot*. See CRITICISM and UNITY. See also *dramatic terms* in Appendix 1.

unity a literary principle and convention of artistic quality in which a harmonic relationship is maintained among the parts of a work so that its overall design and effect represent an organic whole. Plato was one of the first to express (in *Phaedrus*) the relationship in RHETORIC between unities of logic and life. Aristotle's *Poetics* takes up the concept of u. in poetry and drama (see UNITIES). More modern theorists have seen this ORGANIZ- ING PRINCIPLE in terms of thought: The Surrealists spoke of the organizing power and capabilities of the freed subconscious; Freudians saw dream images (see DREAM POETRY) as an organizing tool; Jungian theorists pointed to the universality of archetypes as a creative and interpretive force in civilization's COLLECTIVE UNCONSCIOUS; the NEW CRITICS saw it as the opposite of Western culture's DISSOCIATION OF SENSIBILITY (thought and feeling); and other modern ORGANIC COMPOSITION theorists, from Coleridge to Denise Levertov, see u. as a simultaneity in the creative process between form and content. See CONTROLLING IMAGE, DOMINANT IMPRESSION, DRAMATIC STRUCTURE, FORM, LOGOPOEIA, RHYTHM, STRUC- TURE, and SYMBOLISM.

universality (from Latin for "all taken collectively, the whole world") the quality of a great poem that makes it appeal to all readers of all times. U. is possible because many of the same ideas, values, and emotions exist in many cultures and many eras. Longinus praised writing of quality in saying, "We may regard those words as truly noble and sublime that please all and please always." It has been pointed out that of all qualities that make for u. in literature, the portrayal of human character is the most important, but some critics may argue that the presentation of archetypes that appeal to the COLLECTIVE UNCONSCIOUS may be equally important. See CONCRETE UNIVERSAL, TRANSLATION, UNITIES, and UNITY.

uta: See TANKA.

V

vade mecum /vāʹdē mēʹkəm/ or /väʹdä mäʹk ōōm/ (Latin for "go with me") originally, an article (such as a wallet) that someone regularly carries with him. Out of this concept, the connotation of one's philosophy or values became associated with the term, and finally the phrase came to represent a reference book, such as *The Farmer's Almanac*, a thesaurus, or the Bible, which one might carry with him.

variable foot (see TRIADIC STANZA) a unit of FREE VERSE that can be expanded or contracted in order to create a CADENCE that suits the natural speaking voice. The term and the theories associated with it were invented by W.C. Williams who was interested in creating a PROSODY for American idiomatic speech. See also RHYTHM.

variables those elements of a poem that represent a change from the expected pattern. For instance, the rhythmical devices of SUBSTITUTION, COUNTERPOINT, and SYNCOPATION, which add grace, music, and complexity, depend upon variations from a set design. The concept of variation is as fundamentally important as that of regularity in aspects of verse, and it extends to elements of TONE, MOOD, MELOPOEIA, LOGIC, RHETORIC, FORM and STRUCTURE, IMAGERY, and DICTION. See also AMBIGUITY and RHYTHM.

variable syllable a syllable that may be scanned as being stressed or unstressed according to the dictates of the base or regular meter. See DISTRIBUTED STRESS, METER, PROSODIC SYMBOLS, PROSODY, SCANSION, and SUBSTITUTION.

variorum /varē·ôrʹəm/ (from the Latin phrase *editio cum notis variorum*, for "an edition with notes of *various* commentators or editors") an EDITION of an author's work(s) appended by the interpretations, notes, commentaries, and judgments of other noted writers, scholars, and critics. The *Variorum Edition of the Poems of W.B. Yeats* is a noteworthy example of a compendium that is invaluable because Yeats published many different versions of each poem.

vehicle (from Latin for "to carry") one of the two parts of any METAPHOR. See TENOR AND V.

verbal snapshot a brief description of a character, scene, or event. The term takes its name from that quality of IMAGE captured in a photograph.

verbal texture the combined qualities of DICTION, PHRASING, SENTENCE SOUNDS, SOUND SYSTEM, RHETORIC, and RHYTHM in a poem. The v.t. of Wallace Stevens' *Sunday Morning*, which is elegant, acute, and lush, stands in contrast to that of the PLAIN STYLE prevalent in much contemporary American poetry. See AESTHETIC SURFACE and TEXTURE. See also *diction* in APPENDIX 1.

verbless poetry poetry whose syntax and grammar relies more heavily upon substantive and modifying constructions than on predicative constructions. Thus, v.p. tends to have a more static and introspective quality, as found in Symbolist and Surrealist poetry, then that of, say, "action" poets such as the Futurists, or poets such as G. M. Hopkins and Dylan Thomas. Whether v.p. represents a step toward or away from the post-Romantic dictum that poetry should be modeled on the norms of everyday speech is debatable (see CLASSICAL FALLACY).

verb metaphor (see METAPHOR) a TROPE or *figure of speech* that takes its grammatical form as a verb, and which is generally in an implied or buried form, as in "Jim *high-tailed* it over the fence," which implies the image of an animal such as a deer. Usually, verb metaphors contain more energy than the more static grammatical forms of noun, adjectival, and adverbial metaphors.

verisimilitude /-mil'-/ (from Latin for "true likelihood, true likeness") the quality of presentation that makes for truth or true-to-life resemblance. The source of the concept can be found in Aristotle's MIMETIC THEORY OF ART in which he proposes that art imitate nature, but he is very generous in allowing poets CONVENTION and POETIC LICENSE. Latin theorists, e.g., Cicero, Horace, and Quintilian, allow far less freedom for the poet.

V. is not necessarily based on REALISM; instead, it is achieved by the skillful selection and presentation of details in such a way as to represent the truth. Modern critical theory has been concerned with developing ideas related to v. Wordsworth called for a new DICTION based on the speech of living men, while W.C. Williams' attempt to produce a poetry out of the natural idiom of Americans reflects his desire to write with v. But v. applies not just to diction and usage, but also to CHARACTERIZATION, PLOT, the use of poetic conventions, musical devices such as RHYTHM and REPETITION, and the use of tropes.

Certainly, every poet tries to write in such a manner that he will be believed. This desire influences his choice of form as well as content; indeed, the desire to achieve v. is important in shaping every conscious and unconscious detail in a poem. See ARTIFICIALITY, AUTHORITY, COLLOQUIALISM, CONFESSIONAL POETRY, EMPATHY, IMITATIVE FALLACY, MIMESIS, NATURALISM, PLAIN STYLE, SELECTED DETAILS, SUPERREALISM, SUSPENSION OF DISBELIEF, and TRIGGERING TOWN.

Vers de Société /ver'desôsē-ātā'/ (French for "society verse") LIGHT VERSE that deals in a jesting, witty manner with the values, behavior, and events of upper-class society. The type has been in existence, in and out of fashion, since Greek and Latin antiquity and became very popular in the 17th and 18th centuries in England, as can be seen in the work of Pope. Generally speaking, the genre presents the mannered proprieties, the complexities of sexual liaisons, and fads and fashions of the age. Its style is sophisticated and elegant, often using FIXED FORMS in a vein of SATIRE. See also *light verse* in APPENDIX 1.

verse (from Latin for "to turn" or "a line or row of writing") a LINE in a poem; a STANZA, A REFRAIN, or a section of the Bible; an entire poem based on regular METER; poetry displaying formal, prosodic attributes but lacking penetration and depth; or genres of poetry such as VERS DE SOCIÉTÉ and FREE VERSE. See METER, PROSE, PROSE RHYTHM, and RHYTHM.

verse essay a genre of poetry that provides ARGUMENT, DIALECTIC, and LOGICAL STRUCTURE in order to persuade. Examples include Pope's *Essay on Criticism* and *Essay on Man*, A.E. Housman's *Terence, This Is Stupid Stuff*, Auden's *Musée des Beaux Arts*, W.C. Williams' *Tract*, and many of the philosophical poems of Wallace Stevens. In the term's perjorative sense, as critics and poets such as David Young have pointed out, v.e. refers to discursive, flat, and self-indulgent poems that do not rise to the level of good poetry. See DIDACTIC VERSE.

verse paragraph a section of a poem that functions as an autonomous unit of logic, discourse, or exposition. The unit has found its place in lyric, narrative, didactic, and dramatic poetry in works as diverse as Marvell's *To His Coy Mistress*, Milton's *Paradise Lost*, Wordsworth's *The Prelude*, and Housman's *Terence, This Is Stupid Stuff*. The specific form of the v.p. can be a STANZA, an indented section in a work, or, in the case of the SONNET, the entire work itself. The term's definition places emphasis on the unit of meaning rather than on the structure or form that it takes.

verset /vur'sət/ (from Provençal for "little verse") originally, a verse of inspired, religious origin, such as that of the Bible. Later, the term came to refer to long-lined poetry characterized by fervor and zeal for its subject. In this sense, the apocalyptic works of Allen Ginsberg (*Howl* and *Kaddish*) might be classified as versets. See VISION and VISIONARY POETRY.

versification the act of composing VERSE; the prosodic, formal, and aesthetic features of verse; or a setting to verse of something originally composed in another form. See PROSODY.

vers libre /verlēbr'/: See FREE VERSE.

verso (from the Latin phrase *verso folio*, for "leaf turned") the back of a page in a manuscript or book, the side viewed when the page is turned over. The front side is referred to as the *recto*. See COLOPHON and FORMAT. See also *publishing formats* under *forms* in APPENDIX 1.

view (see CINEMATIC TECHNIQUES) the range of sight, angle of sight, or perspective of consciousness. See POINT OF VIEW. See also *dramatic terms* in APPENDIX 1.

Victorian period the *period of English literature* from 1832 to 1901, named after the reign of Queen Victoria (1837–1901). Generally speaking, the period was one of great progress in science, economics, and social welfare, and, thus, optimistic attitudes concerning the future of Britain were spawned. Literature mirrored the time's burgeoning progress with themes of class struggle and social and moral reform although the age is known for its accent on solemnity, decorum, and rectitude. Major poets include Tennyson, Browning, Arnold, Rossetti, and Hardy. The period is usually characterized in a bifold manner: *early V. p.* (1832–69) and *late V. p.* (1870–1901). It was at this time in literary history that the magazine became an important platform in displaying creative and critical works. See NATURALISM, REALISM, and ROMANTICISM.

villanelle /-nel'/ (from Italian *villanello*, for "rustic"; a form derived from an Italian Renaissance folk-song form) a French fixed form, originally in SYLLABIC METER, usually of a PASTORAL and deceptively simple nature. The form is composed of 19 lines of any length, broken into six stanzas (five tercets and a concluding quatrain which contains two rhymes and two refrain lines: A^1bA^2, abA^1, abA^2, abA^1, abA^2, and abA^1A^2). Two of the most anthologized villanelles are Dylan Thomas' *Do Not Go Gentle into That Good Night* and Theodore Roethke's paradoxical *The Waking*.
     The form has also been used for LIGHT VERSE. One of its major challenges is to make the refrain lines fit gracefully and naturally into the form, and to change their meaning by varying their contexts. See BALLADE, CHANT ROYAL, LAI, LIMERICK, RIME COUÉE, RONDEAU, RONDEL, RONDELET, SESTINA, TRIOLET, TROUBADOUR, TROUVÈRE, and VIRELAY. See also *forms* in APPENDIX 1.

virelay /vir'əlā/ (an alteration of *virly*, a French nonsense dance song composed of refrains; also spelled "virrlai," and also known as "chanson baledée") originally, a 14th-century French lyric verse or song composed of short-lined stanzas turning on two rhymes that interlock with the end-rhyme of the last line of one stanza constituting the main rhyme of the second stanza. The type later became fixed in its syllable count and form and was then composed of nine-line stanzas, rhyming aabaabaab, bbcbbcbbc, ccdccdccd, etc., with alternating four-syllable couplets and one-syllable TAIL LINE, a syllable count identical with the LAI. The form is extremely rare in English. See BALLADE, CHANT ROYAL, LIMERICK, RIME COUÉE, RONDEAU, RONDEL RONDELET, SESTINA, TRIOLET, and VILLANELLE. See also *forms* in APPENDIX 1.

virgule /vur'gyōol/ (from Latin for "small rod or twig") a prosodic symbol used to indicate (1) a CAESURA or PAUSE in a metrical line or, more commonly, (2) a slanted line (/) used to show the division of feet in a line or to mark a LINE ENDING. See FOOT, METER, and SCANSION.

vision a poet's attitude toward life and the world around him; or something seen/felt/thought in an abnormal state of perception, such as a mystical or dream state.
     In the first sense, v. is the sum total of the author's assumptions about the universe; thus, if TONE is the author's attitude toward his specific subject matter and/or audience, and VOICE is the author's attitude toward his own existence, then v. is the author's attitude toward life in general. Poets and critics speak of a poet's v. as it is revealed in his work as a whole: James Wright's nostalgic and romantic v., Sylvia Plath's angry and tragic

v., W.C. Williams' enthusiastic and accepting v., T.S. Eliot's decorous and existential v., and Theodore Roethke's fecund and paradoxical v.

In the second sense of v., the transfiguration of the ordinary into something of a higher and more sublime nature, M.H. Abrams in his study of ROMANTICISM has classified three kinds of "transforming perceptions": (1) that childlike mode which reinstates the magic of the old and familiar, as in D.H. Lawrence's *Piano*; (2) that epiphanic mode (see EPIPHANY) which perceives mystery and profundity in what is ordinary and common, as in Robert Frost's *Stopping by Woods on a Snowy Evening*; and (3) that v. which elevates and makes sublime lowly objects as in Francis Ponge's *The Voice of Things*.

Other uses of the term refer to the genre of the Medieval DREAM ALLEGORY, in which a conventional v. or dream scene is recounted, or of poetry that uses symbolic or archetypal IMAGERY, as in Blake's poetry. In a broader sense, according to Northrop Frye, literature itself is a metaphor for experience created through symbols, and it does not intend to imitate nature (see MIMETIC THEORY OF ART) but aims to project and manifest man's inner states. Poems noted for their unique v. of the world include Yeats' *Sailing to Byzantium,* Blake's *The Marriage of Heaven and Hell,* Arthur Rimbaud's *A Season in Hell* and *Illuminations*, Coleridge's *Kubla Khan,* Eliot's *Four Quartets,* Rilke's *Duino Elegies,* and Hart Crane's *The Bridge.* See ANAGOGOICAL VISION, DREAM POETRY, DREAMSCAPE, INSPIRATION, MYSTICISM, SURREALISM, SYMBOL, SYMBOLISTS, and VISIONARY POETRY.

visionary poetry poetry that recreates a mystical experience by the author or a PERSONA. The speaker usually passes from the ordinary world into a magical or metaphorical world, and the theme of the poem is often the contrast between the world of experience and the world of dream. Poets whose work has been called v.p. include Blake, Rimbaud, Yeats, and Robert Bly. See VISION.

vocalic assonance: See ASSONANCE.

voice in the literal sense, the physical properties of human speech and language; in the metaphorical sense, an author's or speaker's attitude toward him- or herself as represented in a work of literature.

Roman grammarians divided the literal sense of the term into categories of enunciated sound and morphological form, that is, the actual physical sounds of speech created by the vocal chords, and the form of words without regard to their meaning. T. S. Eliot's idea of the *auditory imagination* bridges the literal and metaphorical realms of the term.

The metaphorical sense of the term dates back to Aristotle's *Rhetoric* in which he proposes that an orator establish an ETHOS or CHARACTER that itself functions as a means of persuasion; if the audience perceives him to be a person of intelligence and good will, then they are more inclined to react favorably to his arguments.

Three terms that relate to and overlap with v. are PERSONA (or MASK), TONE, and VISION.

The *persona* of a poem is the first-person narrator, the speaker that we listen to. There are a wide range of speaker identities, from that of an obviously fictional speaker, as in Browning's *My Last Duchess*, to that of the author speaking as himself or herself, as in Anne Sexton's autobiographical poetry (see CONFESSIONAL POETRY). But oftentimes, an audience will be rightly confused as to whether the "I" of the poem is a MASKED PRONOUN or whether it truly represents the author.

An important element upon which v. is built is the concept of *tone*, the author's or speaker's attitude toward his subject matter and/or audience. The tone may be adopted for a specific work, or it may run throughout an author's work. The concept derives primarily from I.A. Richards' *Practical Criticism* in which he points out that the way a person speaks shows his concept of the social level, intelligence, and sensitivity of his audience, as well as his or her personal relationship with them.

The v. ultimately relates to the basic *vision* of a writer, his general attitude toward the world. These two broad attributes of character, voice and vision, are the foundation upon which all other poetic, rhetorical, and logical elements are built. Thus, Wayne C. Booth (*The Rhetoric of Fiction*) prefers to substitute the term *implied author* for v. in order to evoke the sense the reader has of a *whole character*, "an ideal, literary, created version of the real man."

In contemporary poetry, the metaphorical sense of each poet having a distinct v. amounts to a literary principle. In the words of the poet John Haines (*A Field Guide to Contemporary Poetry and Poetics*, 1980):

> It is the voice of the poet, no two alike, that determines the line, rhythm, structure, everything. Once heard, the voice creates the environment of thought and feeling which we come to accept and believe in as an unmistakable mark of the poet's work. The voice refined becomes the poet's style. Unfortunately, the voice is one thing that can't be taught or learned in any school or class, nor can it be counterfeited. It is discovered in the act of living and working, and nourished until it becomes as much a part of the person as an arm or leg.

See also DRAMATIC LYRIC, DRAMATIC MONOLOGUE, AND LOCATION.

volta (Italian for "turn"; also called "volte") originally, an Italian dance, a lively galliard, in which a man turns a woman around and then assists her in making a leap or jump. In poetry, the term signifies the TURN in argument or emotion that occurs between the OCTAVE and SESTET of a SONNET.

Vorticism (from Latin *vortex*, for "whirl, whirlpool" or "peak, top") a movement in the visual arts which Wyndham Lewis in 1914 extended to include poetry. It was one of the more sober reactions to FUTURISM and DADA, and nearly indistinguishable from IMAGISM. V. called for static movement, rather than the Imagists' moving image. V. stood for a nonrepresentational originality of style that was not imitative of nature and which maintained its own identity through the individuality of the artist's imagination. This intellectual, as opposed to instinctual or emotional, approach valued high energy organized into restricted forms. Its ideal was a frozen dynamism, a static image of movement, expressed through the SYMBOL as vehicle for communication. T.E. Hulme was its founder and dogmatist, and Ezra Pound coined the name to depict the confluence of energies that the human imagination is capable of channeling into art.

Turning to attack the excesses of the Futurists, Wyndam Lewis downgraded them as representing "the latest form of Impressionism," and as being imitative because they still relied on "the appearance of the world" for their subject matter. In the short-lived magazine *Blast*, which formalized the Vorticist point of view, Lewis scorned all forms of sentimentality in art and called for artists to attune themselves to the energy of the present. He and Ezra Pound mocked Futurism which romanticized the marvels of the machine age. Eventually, Pound incorporated his Imagist stance into the definition of Vorticism by saying "the primary pigment of poetry is the IMAGE." He pointed to H.D.'s (Hilda Doolittle's) poem *Oread* as the paradigm example of Vorticism because it contains the energetic striking images that typified Vorticist writing:

> *Oread*
> Whirl up sea—
> Whirl up your pointed pines,
> Splash your great pines
> On our rocks.
> Hurl your green over us,
> Cover us with your pools of fir.

vowel (from Latin *vocalis*, for "sounding") a letter of the alphabet representing a sound that is produced without audible friction or stoppage. For a detailed discussion of the relative sound values of the vowels in English, see PITCH. See also BOND DENSITY, melopoeia, phoneme, phonetics, sonics, sound-symbolism, and SOUND SYSTEM.

vowel rhyme the rhyming of vowels in a polysyllabic word ("stalemate") or among different words ("good-looking book"). A more general use of the term is synonymous with ASSONANCE, the rhyming of only stressed vowels in a polysyllabic word or among different words. See RHYME.

W

waka: See TANKA.

weak ending a WRENCHED ACCENT in which the last syllable of a line receives a METRICAL STRESS due to the demands of regular meter even though the syllable would not be stressed in normal speech. See ACCENT and WORD ACCENT. See also *closure* in APPENDIX 1.

weight the combined effect of STRESS and DURATION on a syllable. For instance, in the following three examples, the word "home" contains three different degrees of weight:

heavy	There's no place like *home*.
medium	*Home* is where the heart is.
light	This is a fine *home*coming.

See DISEMIC, METER, PROSODIC SYMBOLS, and SCANSION.

Weltanschauung /velt′onshou·ŏŏng/ (German for "manner of looking at the world") a person's world outlook, that is, his or her concept or philosophy of society, mankind, and existence. The term relates to poetry in the senses of an author's VISION and VOICE. A related word is *Weltansicht* /velt′onzisht/, "world view."

Western ending (also called "closed ending") a poetic CLOSURE that features a strong sense of impact and finality, as opposed to the EASTERN ENDING, which features a softer and more open effect. These types of closure are named after the typical styles of European poetry and Asian poetry. See THEMATIC STRUCTURE. See also *closure* in APPENDIX 1.

white space the blank part of the page on which a poem is printed. W.s. occurs between words, at the ends of lines, between stanzas, and elsewhere in a poem and, in general, is meant to indicate the amount of silence and the speed at which the poem should be read. W.s. may be shaded with a variety of TONE COLOR, semantic value, and thought movement just as line endings may be, according to what the surrounding verbal context evokes. See TYPOGRAPHICAL ARRANGEMENT. See also *forms* in APPENDIX 1.

wildness an element of STYLE featuring an extravagant use of SYNTAX, IMAGERY, TROPE, SONICS, RHYTHM, and/or THEME. In order for w. not be be a defect, there must be a cohesive force at work, such as an ORGANIZING PRINCIPLE or force of RATIOCINATION or ASSOCIATIONAL LOGIC; otherwise, the writing will be arbitrary, wild for the sake of wildness. Some writers who use w. include Tristan Tzara, Arthur Rimbaud, Pablo Neruda, Allen Ginsberg, James Tate, Kenneth Fearing, Gregory Corso, and G. M.

Hopkins, among many others. See FORM, ORGANIC COMPOSITION, and THEMATIC STRUCTURE. See also the opposite of w., CONTROL; also *diction* in APPENDIX 1.

wit originally, knowledge in the sense of mind, the seat of wisdom, but later associated with the functioning of the mind in the sense of general mental acuity and versatility: originality, inspiration, evaluative powers, elocution, ability to amuse, and the capacity for creating impromptu FIGURES OF SPEECH and analogies. During the 19th century, the term IMAGINATION came to mean the capacity to see resemblances between disparate things, and wit came to mean that capacity used in a humorous way. The modern sense of wit emphasizes the manipulation of stock responses, as in Phillip Guedalla's, "History repeats itself. Historians repeat each other." Repartee, a related term, is taken from fencing: It is a contest of wit in which the two opponents try to turn the witticisms of the other to his or her own purposes. Other terms related to wit include COMEDY, EPIGRAM, FANCY, FLYTING, INVECTIVE, IRONY, PARADOX, PARODY, SATIRE, and STICHOMYTHIA. See *humor in* APPENDIX 1.

word accent: See ACCENT.

workshop a formal class of creative writing in a university, or an informal gathering of writers who meet to appreciate, encourage, and criticize finished manuscripts or works in progress. Most workshops are affiliated with academia as part of its regular curricula, or as an ongoing series of short residency sessions in the form of conferences or festivals. Perhaps the oldest model for the w. is the apprenticing of a student to a master artist or craftsman. More modern forms in early and mid-20th-century Europe and America took the form of *magical evenings* in which artists enjoyed the exchange of philosophical, aesthetic, and technical views. The contemporary university w. was instituted at the University of Iowa, under the determined aegis of Paul Engle who later also established there an International Creative Writing Workshop. Currently, there are over 75 creative-writing programs in colleges throughout the country, and almost 2,000 institutions of higher learning that offer this type of loose critical discussion format. The usual courses offered are: *basic workshops*, which focus attention on student writing, the main content of the course; *form* workshops, which concentrate on types and genres of poetry; *craft workshops*, which examine historical and technical achievements in verse; and *revision workshops*, which focus on the polishing and drafting of poems. Although the w. was once viewed skeptically by academics, it is now an integral part of many departments of English and the Fine Arts. What was once the province of the salon, the bohemian loft, the coffeehouse, is now an accepted part of higher learning. See ACADEMIC, REVISION, and SHAPING.

wrenched accent a rhythmical device of POETIC LICENSE in which the demands of METRICAL ACCENT supersede those of ETYMOLOGICAL ACCENT (see accent). This kind of rhythmical distortion is common in LIGHT VERSE, BALLAD and song lyrics. See WEAK ENDING. See also *control* in APPENDIX 1.

writer in the words of William Stafford, "not so much someone who has something to say as [he is] someone who has found a process that will bring about new things he would not have thought of if he had not started to say them."

writer's block the inability, brought about by a lack of confidence, energy, time, or inspiration, of the poet to compose. Some poets, such as James Tate and William Stafford, claim that the way to overcome w.b. is by "lowering your standards" in order to relieve self-imposed limitations. Others, such as Jon Anderson and Donald Justice, claim that not writing can be a creative opportunity in which gains can be made toward establishing new experiences and directions in writing. The phenomenon of w.b. is acknowledged by poets as diverse in time and place as Tennyson, Rilke, and Akhmatova. Pope, writing on "constipated genius" in his *Essay on Criticism*, said, "And strains, from hard-bound brains, eight lines a year." Some contemporary poets claim that w.b. does not exist, and they go on to note that if it does exist, it is more of a contrived, subjective artifact of a writer's psychological tensions than anything of an objective artistic nature. See DEDICATION and INSPIRATION.

Z

zeugma /zo͞og′mə (Greek for "a yoking, a joining") a rhetorical construction of grammar that for the sake of brevity, grace, and ambiguity uses one word to apply to two or more words, as in "Love is the meat and scourge of life." The device has been refined with the use of IRONY and often includes the device of SYLLEPSIS in which the utility word grammatically agrees with only its nearest object and is used in two different senses. Pope's "or stain her honour, or her new brocade" is an example. See DIAZEUGMA, HYPOZEUGMA, MESOZEUGMA, and PROZEUGMA. See also *grammatical constructions that are technically incorrect* in APPENDIX 2.

APPENDIX 1

SELECTED TOPICS

1. ARGUMENTS: STRUCTURES OF ARGUMENTS

centrifugal structure
centripetal-centrifugal structure
centripetal structure
circular structure

deductive-inductive structure
deductive structure
inductive-deductive structure
inductive structure

2. ARGUMENTS: TYPES OF ARGUMENTS

See *figures of argumentation* in APPENDIX 2 (No. 5).

3. CINEMATIC TERMS

angles
associative cut
bird's-eye view
close-up shot
contrast cut
crosscut
deep focus shot
establishing shot
flashback
flashforward
form dissolve

jump cut
juxtaposition
low angle shot
metaphorical dissolve
moving shot
pan
range
straight cut
substitute image
synchronicity
thematic montage

4. CLICHÉS

aphorism
apothegm
archaism
caricature
cliché
colloquialism
convention
dead metaphor
euphemism
given

hack
hackneyed
jargon
Miles Gloriosus
poetaster
stock character
stock response
stock situation
trobar clus

5. CLOSURE

anticlimax
closure
denouement
double ending
Eastern ending
envelope
envoy
epilogue

open ending
poetic closure
resolution
surprise ending
thematic structure
trick ending
weak ending
Western ending

343

6. CONTROL: DEFECTS IN CONTROL

arbitrary figure
archaism
bathos
bombast
bomphiologia
buried theme
cliché
digression
distracting detail
editorial intrusion
hackneyed
Gongorism
metrical filler
mixed message

mood piece
obscurity
overdecoration
overrepetition
overwriting
preciousness
prosy
sentimentalism
slackness
stereotype
strain behind the poem
tautology
wrenched accent

7. CRITICAL FALLACIES

affective fallacy
Classical fallacy
expressive fallacy
imitative fallacy

intentional fallacy
pathetic fallacy
reductive fallacy

8. CRITICISM

absolutist criticism
Aestheticism
analytical criticism
Aristotelian criticism
biographical criticism
Chicago Critics
contextualism
critical feedback
criticism
dissociation of sensibility
explication
expressive criticism
formal (or comparative) criticism
four senses of interpretation
heresy of paraphrase
historical criticism
impressionistic criticism or subjective criticism
judicial criticism
metacriticism

mimetic criticism
moral criticism or ethical criticism
myth criticism
New Criticism
objective criticism
Objective Theory of Art
objectivity vs. subjectivity
Platonic criticism
practical criticism
pragmatic criticism
Pragmatic Theory of Art
relativism in criticism
relativistic criticism
social criticism
Structuralism
technical criticism
textual criticism
theoretical criticism

9. DICTION

abstract terms and concrete terms
abstract poetry
archaism
artificiality
aschematiston
beast language
bomphiologia
cacemphaton
cacozelia
cacozelon

cliché
committing word
connotation
decorum
denotation
dialect
diction
elegant variation
epithet
euphemism

flat statement
hackneyed
homiologia
hyperbole
idiolect
idiom
jargon
kenning
lexical
literal
localism
malapropism
neologism
nonce word
nonsense verse
obligatory word

parelcon
periergia
plain style
poetic diction
poeticism
portmanteau
preciousness
prosy
restraint
soriasmus
Spoonerism
tapinosis
Trans-sense Verse
understatement
verbal texture
wildness

10. DRAMATIC TERMS

ambiance
antagonist
antecendent action
anti-hero
antimasque
antistrophe
atmosphere
catalytic event
catastrophe
catharsis
character
crisis
dénouement
deus ex machina
deuteragonist
dialogue
domestic tragedy
dramatic convention
dramatic dialogue
dramatic irony
dramatic monologue
dramatic situation
dramatic structure
dramatis personae
episodic structure
epode

falling action
flashback
flashforward
hero
in medias res
interior monologue
mask
Miles Gloriosus
obligatory scene
persona
play-within-a-play
plot
protagonist
rising action
round character
scene
setting
soliloquy
stock character
stock situation
subplot
tragedy
tragic flaw
tragicomedy
Unities
view

11. FIGURATIVE EXPRESSIONS (see also *grammatical constructions in* APPENDIX 2)

allegory
ambiguity
amphibolgia
antanaclasis
anthimeria
antiphrasis
antonomasia

apostrophe
auxesis
catachresis
enallage
epitrope
erotema (rhetorical question)
figure of speech

hypallage
hyperbole
irony
litotes
meiosis
metaphor
metonymy
onomatopoeia
oxymoron
paradiastole
paradox

paralipsis
paronomasia
periphrasis
prosopopoeia (personification)
pun
simile
syllepsis
symbol
syncoeciosis
synecdoche
trope

12. FORMS

fixed forms:

alcaics
arte mayor
ballad
ballade
caudate sonnet
chant royal
cinquain
crown of sonnets
curtal-sonnet
dizain
double ballade
haiku
lai
limerick
pantoum

quintilla
rime courée (tail rhyme)
rondeau
rondeau redoublé
rondel
rondelet
roundel
sestina
sonnet
sonnet sequence
tanka
terza rima
triolet
villanelle
virelay

semifixed forms:

amoebean verses
anacreontic poetry
arte mayor
arte menor
barzelleta
caccia
canción
clerihew

correlative verse
cynghanedd
fatras
ghazal
huitain
ode
quatorzain
roundelay

stanzaic forms:

antistrophe
bob and wheel
Burns stanza (six-line stave)
Chaucer stanza (rhyme royal)
closed couplet
common meter
décima
elegiac distich
elegiac stanza
envoy
epode
heroic couplet
heroic stanza

homostrophic
In Memoriam stanza
long meter
monostich
monostrophe
octastich
Omar stanza
open couplet
ottava rima
pentastich
poulter's measure
quatrain
redondilla

Sapphic	strophe
septet	tercet
sestet	terza rima
short couplet	triadic stanza
Spenserian stanza	

line forms:

alcmanic verse	monometer
Alexandrine	monosyllabics
archilochian	octosyllabic verse
blank verse	pentameter
burden	pentapody
Christabel meter	refrain
decasyllabic verse	reciprocus versus
dipody	repetend
echo verse	septenary
fourteeners	tail
hendecasyllabic verse	tetrameter
heptameter	trimeter
hexameter	tripody

irregular forms:

alloestropha	composite verses
astrophic	Cowleyan ode
block poem	epigram
cento	Skeltonic verse

sections of poems:

canto	prelude
epigraph	prologue
invocation	title
interlude	white space

game forms:

abecedarius	fatras
acronym	linked verse
acrostic	mesostich
bouts-rimés	palindrome (sotadies)
Cadavre Exquis	Si ... Quand
cabal	telestich
cross-acrostic	

concrete forms:

altar poem	concrete poetry
carmen figuratum	

structural techniques:

collage	frame story
cut-and-shuffle poem	leitmotif
envelope	montage
episodic structure	pastiche
fill-in-the-blanks poem	sandwich construction

generic and stylistic forms:

apology
aubade
autotelic poetry
ballad
beast epic
beast fable
belles-lettres
bestiary
blason
blues
boasting poem
bucolic
canzo
catalogue verse
chance poetry
chanson de geste
charm
complaint
computer poetry
coronach
cycle
débat
devotional poetry
didactic poetry
dirge
dithyrambic
doggerel
domestic poetry
dream allegory
dream poetry
eclogue
elegy
encomiastic verse
epic
epideictic poetry
epistle
epithalamion
epos
epyllion
eulogy
flyting
found poem
free verse
geste
Goliardic verse
heroic drama
hudibrastic verse
idyll
jeremiad

jingle
juvenalian
lament
light verse
list poem
logaoedic
lyric
madrigal
Marinism
melic poetry
Metaphysical poetry
metrical romance
monody
mood piece
mythopoeia
narrative poem
nature myth
nocturne
nonsense verse
nursery rhyme
occasional verse
ode
paean
palinode
panegyric
pastourelle
personal myth
planh
poetic drama
prose drama
requiem
rhopalic verse
riddle
rock lyric
rune
saga
satiric poetry
sirventes
social myth
sound poems
stichomythia
symbolic narrative
threnody
topographical poem
Trans-sense Verse
Vers de Société
verse essay
verset
visionary poetry

publishing formats:

analects

anthology

broadside
chapbook
chrestomathy
chronicle
dedication
edition
epigram
format
illuminated manuscript

journal
lexicography
limited edition
little magazine
miniature
miscellanies
rubric
typographical arrangement
verso (and recto)

13. HUMOR

beast epic
billingsgate
burlesque
caricature
clerihew
comedy
Dada
doggerel
flyting
hudibrastic verse
invective
irony
jingle
lampoon
light verse

limerick
malapropism
Miles Gloriosus
mycterismus
nonce word
nonsense verse
nursery rhyme
parody
pun
sarcasmus
satire
Spoonerism
travesty
wit

14. IMAGERY

audition colorée
chance imagery
cinematic techniques
controlling image
deep image
distracting details
dream poetry
dreamscape
emblem
epic simile
fixed and free image
form dissolve
icon
image
imagery
Imagism

initiating image
l'image juste
metaphorical dissolve
negative image
obsessive image
opposing image or balancing image
phanopoeia
slant imagery
substitute image
supporting image
symbol
symbolism
Symbolists
synaesthesia
totem
verbal snapshot

15. LIGHT VERSE

abecedarius
acrostic
ballad
belles-lettres
caricature
charm
clerihew
doggerel

flyting
hudibrastic verse
jingle
juvenalian
lampoon
light verse
limerick
nonsense verse

nursery rhyme
occasional verse
parody
riddle

satire
Skeltonic verse
Vers de Société

16. LINE ENDINGS

anticipatory line ending
ascending rhythm
autonomous line
catalexis
emphatic line ending
end-stopped
enjambment
falling rhythm

line ending
line length
lineation
prose poem
shaping
transformational line ending
truncation

17. MELOPOETICS

abstract poetry
acoustic scansion
aesthetic surface
alliteration
alliterative meter
assonance
atonic
aural
beast language
bond density
cacophony
consonance
consonants
decorum
dissonance
euphony
flourish
isochronism
loudness
melic poetry
melopoeia
meter
musical scansion
nonsense verse
onomatopoeia

overdecoration
phoneme
phonetic equivalence
phonetics
phonics
polyphonic prose
resonance
rhyme
rhythm
sentence sounds
sibilants
sigmatism
sonics
sonic structure
sound poems
sound-symbolism
sound system
syncopation
timbre
tone color
Trans-sense Verse
variable
verbal texture
vowels

18. MEANING

abstract poetry
ambiguity
anagogical vision
anagogue
argument
associational logic
buried theme
cognitive meaning
collective unconscious
connotation
critique

denotation
elaboration
emotive meaning
enigma
epiphany
esemplastic
explication
felt thought
figurative language
four meanings of a poem
four senses of interpretation

free association
generative content vs. ornamental content
given
gnomic writing
hermeticism
incremental repetition
intelligence
interpretation
lexical
linguistic associations
literal
literal vision vs. anagogical vision
loading the poem
logic
logic of the metaphor
malapropism
Mimetic Theory of Art
mixed message
multeity

nonsense verse
nuance
objective correlative
originality vs. novelty
overreading
paradox
phoneme
plurisignation
predictability
ratiocination
semantics
semiotics
sentence sounds
suspension of disbelief
syllogism
synchronicity
thematic content
translation
Trans-sense Verse

19. METER

acatelectic
accent
accentual-syllabic verse
accentual verse
acephalous line
acoustic scansion
adonic
aeolic
alcaics
alcmanic verse
Alexandrine
alliterative meter
amphibrach
amphimacer
anacreontic poetry
anacrusis
anapest
Anglo-Saxon Verse
antibacchius
archilochian
arsis and thesis
arte mayor
ascending rhythm
astrophic
bacchic
ballad meter
brachycatalectic
breve
caesura
catalexis
choriamb
Christabel meter
Classical poetics

common meter
contrapuntal
counterpoint
cretic
dactyl
decasyllabic verse
defective foot
dibrach
diiamb
dimeter
dipody
disemic
dispondee
distich
dithyramb
ditrochee
duple foot
duration
elegaic distich
elision
even accent
fixed forms
foot
fourteeners
free verse
French forms
generative metrics
grammatical accent
graphic scansion
hemiepes
hemistich
hendecasyllabic verse
heptameter

heroic couplet
homoeomeral
homostrophic
hovering stress
hypermetric (hypercatalectic)
iamb
ictus
inverted accent
inverted foot
ionic
isochronism
isocolon
light stress
logaoedic
logical stress
macron
meter
metrical accent
metrical filler
metrical pause
metrics
metron
monometer
musical scansion
octameter
octosyllabic verse
Old English versification
overstress
paeon
pentameter
pentapody
polyrhythmic
primary accent
prosodic symbols

prosody
pyrrhic
pythiambic
quantitative meter
quantity
recessive accent
reciprocus versus
resolution
rest
rising foot
rocking rhythm
running rhythm
scansion
short measure or short meter
spondee
sprung rhythm
stich
stress
stress prosody
strong-stress meter
syllabic meter
syllabic-stress meter
syncopation
systole and diastole
syzygy
tribrach
trimeter
triple meter
tripody
trisyllabic foot
trochee
truncation
wrenched accent

20. MNEMONIC DEVICES

form:

abecedarius
acrostic
anagram
homoeomeral
homostrophic
incremental repetition

inner reflections
leitmotif
palindrome
rhopalic verse
structural reflection
typographical arrangement

melopoetics:

alliteration
alliterative meter
assonance
consonance

melopoeia
onomatopoeia
phonetic equivalence

refrain:

bob and wheel
burden
coda

refrain
repetend

rhetoric:

apomnemonysis
catacomesis
contrapuntal

exergasia
metabasis
sorites

rhyme:

amphisbaenic rhyme
analyzed rhyme
apocopated rhyme
backward rhyme
beginning rhyme
bouts-rimés
broken rhyme
chain rhyme
cross-rhyme
crossed rhyme
double rhyme
echo rhyme
end-rhyme
eye-rhyme
full rhyme
headless rhyme

homoeteleuton
identical rhyme
internal rhyme
ironic rhyme
leonine rhyme
light rhyme
linked rhyme
monorhyme
off-rhyme
perfect rhyme
rhyme
rhyme-counterpoint
rhyme scheme
rime riche
synthetic rhyme
triple rhyme

rhythm:

anacrusis
cadence
caesura
counterpoint

isochronism
meter
reciprocus versus

syntax:

balance
chiasmus

polysyndeton

word repetition:

anadiplosis
anaphora
antimetabole
diacope
diaphora
echo verse
epanalepsis
epimone
epistrophe

hypozeuxis
litany
parison
ploce
polyptoton
symploce
tautologia
tautology

21. MOVEMENTS AND SCHOOLS OF POETRY (see also the entry *Periods of English Literature*)

Acmeism
Aestheticism
Beats
Black Mountain School
Cavalier Poets
Chicago Critics
Confessional poetry

contemporary poetry
Continuum poetry
Creationism
Cubism
Dada
Decadence
domestic poetry

experimental poetry
Expressionism
fin de siècle
Fleshly School of Poetry
Found Art
free verse
Fugitives
Futurism
Goliardic verse
Graveyard School
hermeticism
Imagism
Lake Poets
leaping poetry
Minimalism
Minnesinger
Modern Period
Naturalism

Neo-Classicism
New Criticism
New York Poets
Objectivism
Pop Art
Post-Modernists
Pre-Raphaelites
Projective Verse
readymade
Realism
Romanticism
Superrealism
Surrealism
Symbolists
troubadour
trouvère
Vorticism

22. NAMES FOR POETS

bard (pencerdd, bardd teulu, cerddor)
jongleur
minstrel
poet
poetaster
poet laureate

scop
skald
troubadour
trouvère
writer

23. NARRATION

aesthetic distance
antecedent action
associative cut
audience
authority
autologue
carpe diem
catalytic event
character
characterismus
characterization
chronicle
chronographia
cinematic techniques
climax
closure
conflict
control
counterplot
dénouement
description
dialectic
dramatic situation
editorial intrusion
epilogue
epiphany

episodic structure
fable
fabliau
flashback
flashforward
folklore
folk tale
foreshadowing
frame story
hyperbole
idiom
immediacy
in medias res
initiating action
initiating image
interior monologue
interlude
landscape
leitmotif
location
metrical romance
mixed message
mnemonic devices
monolgue
mood
motif

multeity
myth
mythopoeia
narration
narrative hook
narrator agent
narrative poem
obligatory word
obligatory scene
obsessive image
omniscient point of view
open field composition
organizing principles
pathetic fallacy
persona
phrasing
plain style
plot
plurisignation
point of view
prose poem
psychic distance
purple patch
resolution
rising action
round character
saga
selected detail
setting
speaker
stance
stock character
stock situation
story-within-a-story

strain behind the poem
stream-of-consciousness
style
subplot
sub-theme
supporting details
surprise ending
suspension of disbelief
symbolic action
symbolic narrative
synchronicity
tale
tension
texture
thematic content
thematic montage
thematic structure
theme
tone
tone color
topographical poem
tragic irony
transition
trick ending
triggering town
"ubi sunt" formula
understatement
Unities
universality
verisimilitude
view
vision
voice
weak ending

24. PROSE FORMS

allegory
beast epic
beast fable
belles-lettres
criticism
exemplum
fable
fabliau
folklore
folk tale

legend
myth
parable
polyphonic prose
proem
propagandistic literature
prose
prose poem
satire
verse paragraph

25. RHYTHM (FREE VERSE)

accent
balance
cadence
contemporary poetry

counterpoint
conversational rhythm
density
dialectic

duration
enjambment
falling rhythm
felt time
flat statement
flourish
generational rhythm
ground rhythm
idiom
incantation
inversion
leap
lineation
logaoedic
logopoeia
moves

pause
parallelism
phrasing
plain style
Post-Modernists
proprioception
prose rhythm
repetition
rhythm
rising rhythm
sentence sounds
syncopation
variable foot
variables
voice

26. STYLISTIC ELEMENTS

abstract terms and concrete terms
aesthetic distance
antithesis
artificiality
authority
balance
bathos
bombast
contrast
decorum
decadence
density
diction
distance and involvement
earned
elaboration
emblem
emotive thrust
emphasis
ethos
euphony
fancy and imagination
figurative language
felt thought
flourish
focus
hackneyed
hyperbole
idiolect
imitation
irony
leaping poetry
localism
location

logic
melopoetics
metaphorical objectivity
nuance
obscurity
obsessive image
O.R.E.
originality vs. novelty
overdecoration
overrepetition
overwriting
pathos
phrasing
point of view
preciousness
predictability
regionalism
risk
sentimentality
slackness
stereotype
strategy
style
texture
thematic structure
tone
tone color
travesty
understatement
unity
vision
voice
wildness
wit

APPENDIX 2

RHETORICAL, POETICAL, AND LOGICAL DEVICES

1. GRAMMATICAL CONTSTRUCTIONS

rhetorical figures that work through a reorganization of normal word order (hyperbaton):

anastrophe
epergesis
hypallage
hysteriologia
hysteron proteron

inversion
metathesis
parenthesis
substitution
tmesis

grammatical constructions that are technically incorrect but have become traditional devices:

anacoluthon
brachylogia
crasis
diazeugma
elision
ellipsis (eclipsis)
epizeuxis
hypozeugma
hypozeuxis
juxtaposition
masked pronoun or false pronoun

mesozeugma
paragoge
prozeugma
scesis onomaton
syllaba anceps
syllepsis
synalepha
syncope
syzygy
zeugma

grammatical devices of rhythm and balance:

antithesis
asyndeton
brachylogia
chiasmus
epanalepsis
flourish
homeoteleuton
irmus

isocolon
juxtaposition
metabasis
metrical pause
parallelism
parison
perissologia
polysyndeton

grammatical figures of exchange:

anthimeria
enallage

hendiadys

2. DEVICES OF POETIC LICENSE

acyron
amphibologia

amphigory
amphilogia

357

aschematiston
barbarism
bombast
bomphiologia
cacemphaton
cacophony
cacosyntheton
cacozelia
cacozelon
ellipsis
euphuism
Gongorism
homiologia
malapropism
Matinism
metathesis

nonce word
onomatopoeia
parelcon
periergia
perissologia
pleonasm
portmanteau
pun
solecism
soriasmus
Spoonerism
syllepsis
synaesthesia
tapinosis
tautologia

3. FIGURES OF REPETITION

alliteration
anadiplosis
anaphora
antanaclasis
antimetabole
climax
diacope
diaphora
elaboration
elegant variation
epanalepsis
epergesis

epistrophe
hypozeuxis
juxtaposition
otiose
overrepetition
ploce
polyptoton
repetend
symploce
tautology

4. LOGICAL AND FIGURATIVE EXPRESSIONS

types of testimony:

apodixis
apomnemonysis
apothegm
asphalia
chria
diatyposis
epicrisis
euche
euphemismus

eustaphia
imprecation
jeremiad
martyria
ominatio
orcos
paradiorthosis
paraenesis
paroemia

figures of definition:

antanagoge
asteismus
horismus
juxtaposition

peristasis
systrophe
taxis

figures of division:

diaeresis
enigma

enumeration
epanodos

epiphonema	proposito
eutrepismus	restrictio
inter se pugnantia	synathroesmus
prolepsis	synecdoche

figures of subject and adjunct (substance and essence):

antonomasia	periphrasis
characterismus	peristasis
chronographia	personification
dialogismus	pragmatographia
encomium	prosographia
epithet	prosopopoeia
ethopoeia	syncrisis
hypotyposis	taxis
metonymy	typographia
mimesis	topothesia

contraries and contradictories:

antanagoge	irony
antiphrasis	litotes
antithesis	oxymoron
enantiosis	paradox
epitrope	paralipsis
equivoque	syncoeciosis
inter se pugnantia	syncrisis

figures of similarity and dissimilarity:

allegory	metaphor
catachresis	onomatopoeia
fable	parable
homoeosis	paradigma
icon	symbol

figures comparing greater, lesser, or equal things:

auxesis	hyperbole
catacomesis	meiosis
charientismus	paradiastole
dirimens copulatio	paradiegesis
emphasis	parecbasis
epanorthosis	synonymia
exergasia	

figures of cause and effect, antecendent and consequent:

antisagoge	hypothetical proposition
efficient cause	material cause
final cause	metalepsis
formal cause	

figures of notation (sound association) and conjugation (form association):

antanaclasis	noema
asteismus	paronmasia
distinction	schematismus
enigma	

5. FIGURES OF ARGUMENTATION

amphibologia	efficient cause
amplification	epilogus
anacoenosis	enthymeme
analogy	epimone
anthypophora	equivocation
antirrhesis	juxtaposition
aphorismus	metastasis
apodioxis	paradiegesis
apophasis	pareuresis
apoplanesis	paromologia
aporia	procatalepsis
auxesis	proecthesis
commoratio	prosapodosis
concessio	protrope
dialectic	pysma
dialysis	rhetorical question
diasyrmus	sorites
dicaeologia	syllogismus
dilemma	thesis

6. FIGURES OF PATHOS (FEELING OR EMOTION) AND ETHOS (ETHICS OR CHARACTER)

pathopoeia (emotion):

anamnesis	erotema
apocarteresis	erotesis
aposiopesis	eulogy
apostrophe	exuscitatio
ara	medela
bathos	mempsis
bdelygmia	mycterismus
billingsgate	optatio
cataplexis	paeanismus
deesis	paramythia
ecphonesis	sarcasmus
epiphonema	threnos
epiplexus	

figures of ethos (character):

comprobation	onedismus
epitrope	parrhesia
eucharista	proclees
euphemism	syngnome

APPENDIX 3

SELECTED TOPICAL BIBLIOGRAPHY

1. GENERAL REFERENCE

Abrams, M. H. *A Glossary of Literary Terms*. Third edition. New York: Holt, Rinehart, Winston, 1971.

Beckson, Karl, and Arthur Ganz. *A Reader's Guide to Literary Terms: A Dictionary*. Second edition. New York: Dell Publishing Co., 1962.

Bullock, Alan and Oliver Stallybrass, eds. *The Harper Dictionary of Modern Thought*. New York: Harper and Row, 1977.

Deutsch, Babette. *Poetry Handbook*: *A Dictionary of Terms*. Second edition. New York: Harper and Row, 1977.

Evans, G. Blakemore, et. al. eds. *The Riverside Shakespeare*. Boston: Houghton Mifflin, 1974.

Hart, James D. *The Oxford Companion to American Literature*. Fourth edition. New York: Oxford University Press, 1968.

Harvey, Sir Paul. *The Oxford Companion to English Literature*. Fourth edition. London: Oxford University Press, 1967.

Murray, James A. H., et. al. es. *The Oxford English Dictionary: A New English Dictionary on Historical Principles*. London: Oxford University Press, 1961.

The Oxford Dictionary of Quotations. Second Edition. London: Oxford University. Press, 1966.

Preminger, Alex, ed. *The Princeton Encyclopedia of Poetry and Poetics*. Enlarged edition. Princeton: Princeton University Press, 1965.

Shaw, Harry. *Concise Dictionary of Literary Terms*. New York: McGraw-Hill, 1976.

Thrall, William Flint, Addison Hibbard, and C. Hugh Holman, eds. *A Handbook to Literature*. Revised edition. New York: The Odyssey Press, 1962.

2. METER, RHYTHM, AND PROSODY

Dale, Amy Marjorie. *The Lyric Meters of Greek Drama*. Second edition. London: Cambridge University Press, 1968.

Fussell, Paul. *Poetic Meter and Poetic Form*. Revised edition. New York: Random House, 1979.

Gross, Harvey. *Sound and Form in Modern Poetry: A Study in Prosody from Thomas Hardy to Robert Lowell*. Ann Arbor, Michigan: The University of Michigan Press, 1964.

Harding, D. W. *Words into Rhythm: English Speech Rhythm in Verse and Prose*. Cambridge: Cambridge University Press, 1976.

Shapiro, Karl, and Robert Beum. *A Prosody Handbook*. New York: Harper and Row, 1965.

3. RHETORIC

Baker, Sheridan. *The Complete Stylist and Handbook*. New York: Thomas Y. Crowell Co., 1976.

Burke, Kenneth. *A Grammar of Motives*. New York: Prentice Hall, 1945.

Corbett, Edward P. J. *Classical Rhetoric for the Modern Student*. New York: Oxford University Press, 1971.

Joseph, Sister Miriam. *Rhetoric in Shakespeare's Time: Literary Theory of Renaissance Europe*. New York: Harcourt Brace & World, 1962.

Murphy, James J. *Rhetoric in the Middle Ages: A History of Rhetorical Theory from St. Augustine to the Renaissance*. Berkeley: University of California Press, 1974.

Puttenham, George. *The Arte of English Poesie*. Edited by Edward Arber. London: Alex Murray & Son, 1869.
Richards, I. A. *The Philosophy of Rhetoric*. New York: Oxford University Press, 1936.

4. THEORETICAL CRITICISM

Bloom, Harold. *The Anxiety of Influence: A Theory of Poetry*. New York: Oxford University Press, 1975.
Brooks, Cleanth. *The Well Wrought Urn*. New York: Harcourt Brace & Co., 1947.
Empson, William. *Seven Types of Ambiguity*. New York: New Directions, 1947.
Frye, Northrop. *Anatomy of Criticism*. Princeton: Princeton University Press, 1973.
Richards, I. A., ed. *The Portable Coleridge*. New York: Viking Press, 1950.
Richards, I. A., ed. *Principles of Literary Criticism*. New York: Harcourt Brace and Co., 1948.
Wellek, René, and Warren Austin. *Theory of Literature*. New York: Harcourt Brace and Co., 1949.

5. PRACTICAL CRITICISM

Dickey, James. *Babel to Byzantium: Poets and Poetry Now*. New York: Farrar, Straus and Giroux, 1968.
Howard, Richard. *Alone with America: Studies in the Art of Poetry in the United States since World War II*. New York: Atheneum, 1969.
Jarrell, Randall. *Poetry and the Age*. New York: Noonday Press, 1953.
Muir, Kenneth, and S. Schoenbaum, eds. *A New Companion to Shakespeare Studies*. Cambridge: Cambridge University Press, 1971.
Murdy, Louise Baughan. *Sound and Sense in Dylan Thomas's Poetry*. The Hague, Paris: Moulton & Co., 1966.
Packard, William, ed., *The Craft of Poetry: Interviews from the New York Quarterly*. Garden City, New York: Doubleday & Co., 1974.
Perloff, Marjorie. *Frank O'Hara: Poet Among Painters*. New York: George Braziller, 1977.
Pinsky, Robert. *The Situation of Poetry: Contemporary Poetry and Its Traditions*. Princeton: Princeton University Press, 1977.
Pound, Ezra. *The ABC of Reading*. New York: New Directions Publishing Co., 1960.
Richards, I. A. *Practical Criticism*. New York: Harcourt Brace and Co., 1929.
Rosenthal, M. L. *The Modern Poets: A Critical Introduction*. New York: Oxford University Press, 1962.
Shapiro, David. *John Ashbery: An Introduction to the Poetry*. New York: Columbia University Press, 1979.
Stitt, Peter. "John Berryman: the Dispossessed Poet." *The Ohio Review*. (A special section on John Berryman) Winter 1974, p. 67.

6. ANTHOLOGIES

Allen, Donald M., ed. *The New American Poetry: 1945–1960*. New York: Grove Press, 1960.
Allison, Alexander, et. al. eds. *The Norton Anthology of Poetry*. Revised edition. New York: W. W. Norton & Co., 1975.
Bain, Carl E., et. al. eds. *The Norton Introduction to Literature*. Second edition. New York: W. W. Norton and Co., 1977.
Benedikt, Michael, ed. *The Prose Poem: An International Anthology*. A Laurel Edition. New York: Dell Publishing Co., 1976.
Berg, Stephen, and Robert Mezey, eds. *The New Naked Poetry*. Indianapolis: Bobbs-Merrill Co., 1977.
Birch, Cyril, ed. *Anthology of Chinese Literature: from Early Times to the Fourteenth Century*. New York: Grove Press, 1965.
Bly, Robert, trans. *Friends You Drank Some Darkness: Three Swedish Poets – Martinson, Ekëlog, and Transtromer*. Boston: Beacon Press, 1975.
Carroll, Paul. *The Poem in its Skin*. Chicage: Follett, 1968.

Carruth, Hayden, ed. *The Voice That is Great Within Us.* New York: Bantam Books, 1970.
Engle, Paul, and Warren Carrier, eds. *Reading Modern Poetry.* Revised edition. Glenview, Illicrois: Scott, Foresman and Co., 1968.
Gardner, Helen, ed. *The New Oxford Book of English Verse: 1250–1950.* New York: Oxford University Prkess, 1972.
Halpern, Daniel, ed. *The American Poetry Anthology.* New York: Avon Books, 1975.
Heyen, Wiliam, ed. *American Poets in 1976.* Indianapolis: Bobbs-Merrill, 1975.
Kreuzer, James R. *Elements of Poetry.* Toronto: The Macmillan Co., 1955.
Lucié-Smith, Edward, ed. *Primer of Experimental Poetry: 1870–1922.* New York: Bobbs-Merrill, 1971.
Meltzer, David. ed. *The San Francisco Poets.* New York: Ballantine Books, 1971.
Nims, John Frederich. *The Harper Anthology of Poetry.* New York: Harper and Row, 1981.
Poulin, A., Jr., ed. *Contemporary American Poetry.* Boston: Houghton Mifflin Co., 1975.
Rothenberg, Jerome, and George Quasha, eds. *America: A Prophecy.* New York: Vintage Books, 1974.
Schreiber, Ron, ed. *31 New American Poets.* New York: Hill and Wang, 1969.
Simic, Charles and Mark Strand, eds. *Another Republic: 17 European and South American Writers.* New York: Ecco Press, 1976.
Wand, David Hsin-fu, ed. *Asian-American Heritage: an Anthology of Prose and Poetry.* New York: Washington Square Press, 1974.
Weissbort, Daniel, ed. *Post-War Russian Poetry.* Middlesex, England: Penguin, 1974.
Williams, Miller, ed. *Contemporary Poetry in America.* New York: Random House, 1973.

7. Textbooks

Ciardi, John, and Miller Williams. *How Does a Poem Mean?* Second edition. Boston: Houghton Mifflin Co., 1975.
Beacham, Walton. *The Meaning of Poetry: A Guide to Explication.* Boston: Allyn and Bacon, 1974.
Hall, Donald. *To Read Poetry.* New York: Holt, Rinehart and Winston, 1983.
Nims, John F. *Western Wind: An Introduction to Poetry.* New York: Random House, 1974.
Perrine, Laurence. *Sound and Sense.* Sixth edition. New York: Harcourt Brace Jovanovich, 1982.
Scott, Wilburs. *Skills of the Poet.* New York: Harper and Row, 1977.
Skelton, robin. *The Poet's Calling.* New York: Barnes and Noble, and Harper and Row, 1975.
Turner, Alberta, ed. *50 Contemporary Poets: The Creative Process.* New York: David McKay Co., 1977.
Wallace, Robert. *Writing Poems.* Boston: Little, Brown and Co., 1982.

8. Myth and Mysticism

Beyer, Stephan. *The Cult of Tara: Magic and Ritual in Tibet.* Berkeley: University of California Press, 1973.
Brockington, A. Allen. *Mysticism and Poetry.* Port Washington, New York: Kennikat, 1934.
Campbell, Joseph. *The Hero With a Thousand Faces.* Princeton: Princeton University Press, Bollingen Series, Vol. xviii, 1968.
Cowley, Malcolm, ed. *Walt Whitman's Leaves of Grass: His Original Edition.* New York: Penguin, 1976.
Jung, Carl G. *Memories, Dreams, Reflections.* New York: Random House, 1965.
Jung, Carl G. *Man and His Symbols.* New York: Dell, 1968.
Kirk, G. S. *Myth: Its Meaning and Functions in Ancient and Other Cultures.* Berkeley: University of California Press, 1970.
Kroll, Una. *The Healing Potential of Transcendental Meditation.* Atlanta: The John Knox Press, 1974.
Larsen, Stephen. *The Shaman's Doorway.* New York: Harper & Row, 1976.
Sebok, Thomas A., ed. *Myth: A Symposium.* Bloomington: Indiana University Press, 1968.

9. THE OTHER ARTS

Battock, Gregory, ed. *Super Realism: A Critical Anthology.* New York: E. P. Dutton & Co., 1975.

Cheney, Sheldon. *Expressionism in Art.* Revised edition. New York: Liveright Publishing Corp., 1958.

Dick, Bernard F. *Anatomy of Film.* New York: St. Martins Press, 1978.

Dudley, Louise, et. al. *The Humanities.* Sixth edition. New York: McGraw Hill, 1978.

Earp, T. W. *The Modern Movement in Painting.* Edited by C. G. Holme. New York: The Studio Publications, 1935.

Hunter, Sam. *Modern American Painting and Sculpture.* New York: Dell Publishing Co., 1969.

Matthews, J. H. *An Introduction to Surrealism.* University Park, Pennsylvauia: The Pennsylvania State University Press, 1965.

McCurdy, Charles, ed. *Modern Art: A Pictorial Anthology.* New York: Random House, 1974.

Rothschild, Edward F. *The Meaning of Unintelligibility in Modern Art.* Chicago: University of Chicago Press, 1934.

Upjohn, Everard M. *History of World Art.* New York: Oxford University Press, 1958.

10. PERSONAL ESSAYS

Barry, Elaine. *Robert Frost on Writing.* New Brunswick: Rutgers University Press, 1973.

Bell, Marvin. "Homage to the Runner." *The American Poetry Review.* Vol. 4, No. 4.

Cox, Hyde, and Edward C. Lathem, eds. *Selected Prose of Robert Frost.* New York: Holt, Rinehart and Winston, 1966.

Fuller, R. Buckminster, with Jeroure B. Agel. *I Seem To Be a Verb.* New York: Bantam Books, 1970.

Hall, Donald. *To Keep Moving: Essays 1959–1969.* Geneva, New York: Hobart and William Smith Press, 1980.

Hugo, Richard. *The Triggering Town: Lectures and Essays on Poetry and Writing.* New York: W. W. Norton, 1979.

Kunitz, Stanley, *A Kind of Order, A Kind of Folly: Essays and Conversations.* Boston: Little, Brown and Co., 1975.

Mills, Ralph J., Jr. *On The Poet and His Craft: Selected Prose of Theodore Roethke.* Seattle: University of Washington Press, 1974.

O'Connor, Flannery. *Mystery and Manners: Occasional Prose.* Edited by Robert and Sally Fitzgerald. New York: Strauss & Giroux, 1969.

Paz, Octavio, *Alternating Current.* New York: Viking Press, 1973.

Stafford, William. *Writing the Australian Crawl.* Ann Arbor: University of Michigan Press, 1978.

Williams, William Carlos. "How to Write." Edited by James Laughlin. *New Directions in Prose and Poetry.* New York: New Directions.

11. SCIENCE

Bronowski, Jacob. *The Ascent of Man.* Boston: Little, Brown and Co., 1973.

Ornstein, Robert E. *Psychology of Consciousness.* New York: Penguin, 1975.

Phillips, John L., Jr. *The Origins of Intellect: Piaget's Theory.* San Francisco: W. H. Freeman and Co., 1969.

Sagan, Carl. *The Dragons of Eden.* New York: Random House, 1977.

12. METAPHOR AND FIGURATIVE LANGUAGE

Brooke-Rose, Christine. *A Grammar of Metaphor.* London: Secker and Werburg, 1965.

Dickey, James. *Metaphor as Pure Adventure.* Speech given at Library of Congress, Washingston, D.C., 1968.

Ricoeur, Paul, *The Rule of Metaphor.* Toronto: University of Toronto Press, 1977.

13. FORM AND STRUCTURE

Cannon, Harold C., trans. *Ovid's Heroides*. New York: E. P. Dutton, 1971.
Empson, William. *Some Versions of Pastoral*. New York: New Directions, 1960.
Friedrich, Hugo. *The Structure of Modern Poetry*. Evanston, Illinois: Northwestern University Press, 1974.
Hubet, Renee R. "Characteristics of an Undefinable Genre: The Surrealist Prose Poem." *Symposium*. 22, Spring 1978, pp. 25–34.
Turco, Lewis. *The Book of Forms: A Handbook of Poetics*. New York: E. P. Dutton, 1968.
Wayman, Alex. *The Buddhist Tantras*. New York: Samuel Weser, 1973.
    See also II. METER, RHYTHM, and PROSODY.

14. LINGUISTICS

Baker, Janet MacIver. *A New Time-Domain Analysis of Human Speech and other Complex Wave Forms*. Pittsburgh: Carnegie-Mellon University and Pittsburgh University Press, 1975.
Kaiser, L., ed. *Manual of Phonetics*. Amsterdam: North-Holland Publication Co., 1957.
Lyons, ohn. *Introduction to Theoretical Linguistics*. Cambridge: Cambridge University Press, 1969.
Malmberg, Bertil, ed. *Manual of Phonetics*. New York: American Elsevier Publishing Co., 1974.
Pyles, Thomas. *The Origins and Development of the English Language*. New York: Harcourt Brace Jovanovich, 1971.

15. THE CREATIVE PROCESS

Allen, Don Cameron, ed. *Four Poets on Poetry*. Baltimore: Johns Hopkins Press, 1967.
Gibbons, Reginald. *The Poet's Work: 29 Masters of 20th Century Poetry on the Origins and Practice of their Art*. Boston: Houghton Mifflin, 1979.
Maritain, Jacques. *Creative Intuition in Art and Poetry*.New York: Noonday Press, 1955.
Mills, Ralph J., Jr. *Creation's Very Self*. Fort Worth: Texas Christian University Press, 1969.
Rieser, Max. *An Analysis of Poetic Thinking*. Translated by Herbert Schueller. Detroit: Wayne State University Press, 1969.
Stillinger, Jack, ed. *Selected Poems and Prefaces by William Wordsworth*. Riverside Edition Boston: Houghton Mifflin Co., 1965.
Turner, Alberta, ed. *Poets Teaching: The Creative Process*. New York: Longman, 1980.

16. LITERARY HISTORY

Abrams, M. H. *The Mirror and the Lamp: Romantic Theory and the Critical Tradition*. New York: Oxford University Press, 1974.
Benedikt, Michael, ed. *The Poetry of Surrealism: an Anthology*. Boston: Little, Brown and Co., 1975.
Bowra, C. M. *The Creative Experiment*. New York: Grove Press, 1948.
Fitzgibbon, Constantine. *The Life of Dylan Thomas*. Boston: Atlantic-Little Brown, 1965.
Gummere, Francis. *The Beginnings of Poetry*. London: Macmillan Co., 1901.
Pratt, William, ed. *The Imagist Poem*. New York: E. P. Dutton, 1963.
Ross, Robert H. *The Georgian Revolt 1910–1922: Rise and Fall of a Poetic Ideal*. Carbondale, Illinois: Southern Illinois University Press, 1965.
Symons, Arthur. *The Symbolist Movement in Literature*. New York: E. P. Dutton, 1958.
Waley, Arthur. *The Book of Songs*. New York: Grove Press, 1937.

17. POETICS

Allen, Donald M., and Warren Tallman, eds. *The Poetics of the New American Poetry*. New York: Grove Press, 1973.
Bly, Robert. *Leaping Poetry: An Idea With Poems And Translations*. Boston: Beacon Press, 1975.

Friebert, Stuart, and David Young, eds. *A Field Guide to Contemporary Poetry and Poetics*. New York: Longman, 1980.

MacIntyre, C. F. *Rilke: Selected Poems*. Berkeley: University of California Press, 1940.

Scully, James, ed. *Modern Poetics*. New York: McGraw-Hill, 1965.

Shapiro, Karl, ed. *Prose Keys to Modern Poetry*. New York: Harper and Row, 1962.